Public Relations Writing: A Rhetorical Approach

Michael L. Kent
Gaylord College of JMC, University of Oklahoma

Allyn & Bacon
Boston Columbus Indianapolis New York San Francisco Upper Saddle River
Amsterdam Cape Town Dubai London Madrid Milan Munich Paris Montreal Toronto
Delhi Mexico City São Paulo Sydney Hong Kong Seoul Singapore Taipei Tokyo

Editor in Chief: Karon Bowers
Acquisitions Editor: Jeanne Zalesky
Editorial Assistant: Stephanie Chaisson
Senior Managing Editor: Linda Mihatov Behrens
Associate Managing Editor: Bayani Mendoza de Leon
Manufacturing Buyer: Mary Ann Gloriande
Marketing Manager: Wendy Gordon
Art Director/Cover Designer: Nancy Wells
Editorial Production and Composition Service: Chitra Ganesan, PreMediaGlobal
Cover Image: Simon Brown/Getty Images/Digital Vision
Text Font: Palatino

Library of Congress Cataloging-in-Publication Data

Kent, Michael L.
A rhetorical approach to public relations writing / Michael L. Kent.
p. cm.
Includes bibliographical references and index.
ISBN-13: 978-0-205-59544-0 (alk. paper)
ISBN-10: 0-205-59544-8 (alk. paper)
1. Public relations—United States. 2. Public relations—United States—Authorship. I. Title.
HM1221.K48 2010
659.2—dc22

2010010381

Allyn & Bacon
is an imprint of

www.pearsonhighered.com

2 3 4 5 6 7 8 9 10—EB—13 12 11

ISBN-13: 978-0-205-59544-0
ISBN-10: 0-205-59544-8

BRIEF CONTENTS

CONTENTS

PREFACE

There are some who still fondly imagine that knowledge, casting the clear light of awareness, inspires and contains goodness within itself.

—DORA RUSSELL, *The Religion of the Machine Age*

When I began writing this book several years ago, there were no twitters, blogs were something that hardly anyone understood, and there was some question as to whether "social media" would actually catch on. Ten years ago, my lecture notes included a list of sample "media channels" with the following:

- Television, Radio, Newspaper, Magazine
- Circulars
- Direct Mail
- Point-of-Purchase Displays
- Outdoor Posters, Transit Posters
- Public Service Announcements
- Advertisements
- Movie Trailers
- Pamphlets and Booklets
- Speeches
- Computers (E-mail, WWW, Internet, Electronic Bulletin Boards, etc.)

Notice that "computers" are the last thing on the list, and included "electronic bulletin boards" and e-mail. Now, a similar list would probably have new technology at the top, and include social networking, analytical software, online surveys, RSS, and a host of other electronic "media channels."

The profession of public relations is changing, as are all communication-based professions, including advertising, broadcasting, journalism, marketing, and even professional writing. If I asked you what factor is the most important in this transformation, I suspect you could guess: new technology and the Internet. Print and broadcast journalism have seen huge downturns in their fortunes. Media companies struggle to develop business models that appeal to people with access to thousands of free media sources via the Internet and who lead increasingly fast-paced lives.

The conclusion that some professionals reach is that "teaching students how to use new technology is very important." This is true. But this conclusion misses the major part of the equation: Although technology has changed how we conduct public relations, effective writing and research skills are still at the heart of effective public relations and message design.

"May you live in interesting times" was originally meant as a curse: may your life be in turmoil, may you have no rest. Unfortunately, we all live in interesting times now. Every year brings a new communication revolution, a new technology, a new alteration of how we have lived our lives for decades. Thus, my time as a teacher is wasted trying to teach you how to use every—and the latest—communication technology. What will serve you in 10 or 20 years is not whether you understand how to use Twitter to communicate with clients, but whether you know how to write effectively in any medium, whether it employs micro content, spoken words, plain text, or hypertext, and whether you understand the rhetorical principles that underlie effective communication and persuasion.

At the heart of every communication technology is "communication." Understanding the psychology of human nature and the psychology of persuasion is something that we have been working on for more than 2,000 years. What matters in any organization to public interaction is effective communication.

In 5 or 10 years, perhaps even in 2, there will probably be no twittering. If the predictions are true, in 5 to 10 years, 90 percent of all electronic communication will take place on handheld devices. People will not visit Web sites for their information: they will use their holographic cell phones with voice recognition to send messages. The *concept* of micro content ("tweets") is likely to still be around—indeed, the bullet list and the executive summary were the micro content of the last century—but the actual implementation will likely be very different. The mistake is in thinking that as a public relations professional you need to understand every new technology—or worse, that all you need to do is memorize how to write a few dozen professional documents, like news releases, feature stories, or fact sheets. Understanding rhetoric and how effective communication works translates into the ability to adapt your message to any audience, and to figure out which messages and media are the best for reaching your key publics.

Effective communication and persuasion skills are features that cross all technologies: print, broadcast, electronic, and face-to-face. A "public relations writing" class should be about effective writing and communication, not about tweeting, blogging, or social networking. The social media technologies are just tools or options for communicating with stakeholders, just as brochures and news releases are tools. Although the communication tools and media used to reach organizational stakeholders play a role in public relations, understanding how to construct compelling messages still trumps technological expertise. Most employers are confident that you can learn about blogging or the latest software on the job; they are less confident that you can learn how to write well if you come with no communication and rhetorical skills.

Public Relations Writing: A Rhetorical Approach does cover new technology. Given the omnipresence of technology in the communication professions, every good introductory public relations book should. However, *this text* spends more time teaching you about the process of rhetoric, persuasion, and effective communication. In particular, the text spends time on communication and persuasion theory; how to conduct effective research both traditionally and using new technology; how to write compelling public relations messages; how to adapt messages to different media and audiences; and issues relating to international public relations, dialogue, and speech writing. Throughout the text, I try to tie together principles of rhetorical and communication theory and build on previous concepts raised throughout the book. Hopefully, by the end of the semester, you will be able to write compelling messages of any kind—print, broadcast, written, or electronic—or have the skills to teach yourself how to create compelling messages.

Michael L. Kent

ACKNOWLEDGMENT

Over the years, I have read many acknowledgements. I started reading acknowledgements, prefaces, and forwards when I started reading books with words. Sometimes acknowledgements are informative, but most of the time, the author simply thanks a long list of people. As it turns out, a project like this requires a lot of sacrifice on the part of others as well as a lot of feedback from fellow professionals.

The greatest contribution to this project comes from my family and friends: Maureen, Ingrida, Ishmael, Zeba, Horatio, and Helen. One does not realize how important being able to work is when you should be doing other things, like mowing the lawn, trimming the hedges, or finishing that dining room table that you have been promising for four years. Because people were "supportive," I was actually able to finish this project after three years of work.

Equally important, however, is the contribution made by the dozen anonymous reviewers who gave me feedback on earlier drafts of the book. I appreciated the one out of four reviewers who actually liked the initial draft of the book, but it was the other three who were ambivalent about the book or hated it that really made me consider how to make the book better. The reviewers are the people who should be thanked for the book's current organization and for reminding me that a book about "rhetorical approaches to public relations" needed more rhetoric. Originally I placed everything together: a chapter on theory, a chapter on persuasion, one big monster chapter on written documents, etc. After virtually all of the reviewers asked, "Where is the rhetoric?" and "How could I teach using this book?," I realized that the segmented approach actually obscured the book's focus. After several months of rewriting, reorganizing, and adding new sections, I believe the book is better. As authors say in letters to journal editors, "I think the peer review process has made this stronger."

Finally, I would like to thank my editor and her assistants for their organizational skills and support—in particular, Jeanne Zalesky, Megan Lentz, Chitra Ganesan, and David A. Ferman. Obviously, there are a number of behind the scenes—people I have never met—who also deserve a shout-out: typesetters, artists, proofreaders. In particular, I would like to acknowledge the editors and proofreaders. I spent one long winter in Jersey driving the turnpike so that I could proofread high school textbooks 12 hours per day. It is a thankless job—but essential—so I thank you.

Chapter 1

Introduction to Public Relations Writing

Perhaps the obvious questions to begin this book with are, "What is rhetoric?" and "What does rhetoric have to do with public relations writing?" The best answer to the first question might be to consider some of the descriptions of rhetoric that go back more than 2,500 years. Over the course of more than two millennia, rhetoric has been defined by hundreds of people. Some of the earliest descriptions of rhetoric involve an emphasis on persuasion, such as Aristotle's definition: "Rhetoric is the faculty [or art] of discovering, in a given situation, all the available means of persuasion." Bryant said something similar in 1953 when he wrote that rhetoric is "the process of adjusting ideas to people and people to ideas" (p. 407).

Another notable feature of rhetoric has been an emphasis on the ethicality and morality of rhetorical messages. In 2500 BCE Plato wrote: "Rhetoric is speech to please the gods." Five hundred years later, Cicero wrote that rhetoric was "That which links wisdom and eloquence for the enhancement of the state." Two thousand years later, in 1960, Richard Weaver argued that rhetoric was "The truth, plus its artful presentation." For thousands of years, longer than any civilization has existed, philosophers, politicians, priests, professors, and professional communicators have all agreed that effective communication, or rhetoric, should be truthful, honest, inspiring, and compelling. Being an ethical communicator and being a skilled communicator go hand-in-hand.

Rhetoric, or language used artfully, is socially constructed, and constructs society. In other words, our words help construct the world we live in. Many children are told: "Sticks and stones may break your bones but words will never hurt you." We all know *that* is not true. Who among us does not remember something hurtful that was said to us as children? Indeed, most of us have *said* something intended to hurt someone else.

Rhetoric is used to convince people to go to war and to make peace. Rhetoric is used to entertain as well as to deliberate about important social issues. Rhetoric is used to sell nearly every product in the world, as well as to teach people how to be better citizens. Rhetoric forms the basis of the public relations profession. When we use language, either written or spoken, including images and other persuasive tools, we are using rhetoric—the life-blood of every public relations professional.

Some cynics argue that public relations is about deception, or "spinning the truth." However, the key word from a rhetorical and public relations standpoint is "truth." Ethical public relations professionals do not lie. The most skilled professionals act as "organizational counselors," advising managers and leaders how to ethically engage publics. More importantly, public relations professionals are not journalists or marketers. The job of public relations professionals is not to report on organizational events, as a journalist might, or to identify new customer/clients for an organization as a marketer might, but to *build relationships* with stakeholders, stakeseekers, and relevant publics.

TABLE 1.1 Definition of Rhetoric

Isocrates: "Rhetoric is an art based on theory, model, practice, natural ability [or talent], and anima [or passion]." —*Against the Sophists*

Plato: "Rhetoric is speech to please the gods."—The *Phaedrus*

Aristotle: "Rhetoric is the faculty [or art] of discovering, in a given situation, all the available means of persuasion." —*The Rhetoric* [Lane Cooper Trans.]

Cicero: "That which links wisdom and eloquence for the enhancement of the state."—*De Inventione*

Quintilian: "A good man skilled in speaking."—*Institutio Oratoria*

Erasmus: "Speech which creates peace on earth."—*De Copia*

Bryant: "The process of adjusting ideas to people and people to ideas." Alternatively, "the rationale of formative and suasory discourse both spoken and written."—"Rhetoric its function and its scope," *Quarterly Journal of Speech*, *39*, p. 407.

Burke, Kenneth: "The process of creating the screens through which we view reality."—Kenneth Burke, *International Encyclopedia of the Social Science*, pp. 445–452.

Weaver: "The truth, plus its artful presentation" [dialectic plus delivery].—*The Ethics of Rhetoric*, pp. 55–57 (c. 1960).

Hart: "Rhetoric is about the art of using language to help people to narrow their choices among specifiable, if not specified, policy options."—*Modern Rhetorical Criticism*, p. 4.

Perelman and Olbrechts-Tyteca: "The use of language in the probabilistic realm of argumentation to gain adherence to a thesis."—*The Realm of Rhetoric.*

Fisher: [Rhetoric is exemplified by the fact that] "man is in his actions and practices, as well as in his fictions, essentially a storytelling animal."—"Narration as a Human Communication, Paradigm: ..." Communication Monographs, p. 1

Brummett, Barry: "Rhetorical theories are like fishing lures: they are discarded only if they never seem useful. That a lure fails to hook this bass today is not really a test of it. Rhetorical theories are like vampires: you need see one in action only once to believe in what it can do, and it is nearly impossible to kill."—Rhetorical theory as heuristic and moral, *Communication Education*, *3*, pp. 97–107.

Although public relations professionals sometimes *assist* in generating publicity, public relations professionals also create and distribute information to numerous internal and external publics, conduct risk and crisis management, and conduct research. Public relations professionals are, above all, professional communicators who ethically represent organizations and publics.

RHETORIC DEFINED

Rhetoric, broadly speaking, is the study of how language is used effectively. The term rhetoric is a technical term and means different things to different people. To the average citizen, rhetoric often means empty or bombastic speech. Thus, newscasters will frequently say things like "President Obama's rhetoric worries many conservatives ...," or "Why is the rhetoric of Barack Obama so compelling?" In this informal sense, rhetoric means essentially "talk," or "speech." To an English teacher, rhetoric might refer to the study of a particular author's language: "Hemingway's rhetoric fails as persuasion ..." However, to a professional communicator, rhetoric is more closely aligned with persuasion, ethics, and skillful language use.

Much of the research on rhetoric in communication has focused on how language can be used more effectively and on how to inform and persuade, two tasks that public relations professionals do on a daily basis. Over the last 15 years, many public relations professionals have recognized the obvious link between rhetoric and public relations, and have recognized how much effective communication in any realm is based on rhetorical principles (Bostdorff, 1992; Cheney & Dionisopoulos, 1989; Condit & Condit, 1992; Dionisopoulos & Goldzwig, 1992; Heath, 1992, 1997; Ihlen, 2002; Pearson, 1992; Toth & Heath, 1992).

In light of the relationship between rhetoric, rhetorical theory, communication theory, and effective public relations, I have made understanding rhetoric's role in public relations one of the central features of this text. Throughout *A Rhetorical*

Approach to Public Relations Writing, I describe how to use rhetorical principles more effectively and provide examples of how public relations professionals can use rhetorical principles and communication theory to be more-effective writers and communicators. One of the first issues to understand is the role that writing plays in public relations.

Even when you are creating the same types of documents, such as news releases, fact sheets, or backgrounders, the choices that you will make in terms of language, imagery, and structure will vary. A brochure for band camp is not the same as a brochure for graduate school. Both documents may look the same in terms of their external appearance; however, both will use different vocabulary and imagery and focus on different kinds of content issues.

As you will discover in this text, public relations professionals need to produce dozens of different types of written messages. In spite of the television stereotypes of public relations professionals simply holding news conferences and sending out news releases, many public relations professionals spend the majority of their time on internal public relations messages such as newsletters and employee training, while other professionals might spend much of their time meeting with lawmakers (lobbying) or planning events. The diversity of roles played by public relations professionals is great. According to Cutlip, Center, and Broom (1994; cf., also www.ccny.cuny.edu/prsurvey/finding_o.html), only about one in four public relations practitioners work in public relations agencies.

- 40 percent work in business and commercial corporations in internal and external communications departments
- 27 percent work in public relations firms
- 14 percent work in associations, foundations, and educational institutions
- 8 percent work in health care
- 6 percent work in federal, state, and local government
- 5 percent work in charitable, religious and other nonprofit organizations (p. 31)

Thus, to prepare yourself for a career in public relations, you need to learn how to communicate in a variety of contexts and learn how to create diverse and compelling messages that are effective with multiple audiences and very different stakeholders and stakeseekers.

UNDERSTANDING HOW THEORY INFORMS PRACTICE

Communication and public relations theories have been used to help understand the practice of public relations for more than 50 years. In fact, one of the pioneers of public relations, Edward Bernays, was the nephew of Sigmund Freud and the first professional to use social psychological theories in public relations. Sadly, many communication professionals believe that understanding "theory" is a waste of time. "We work in the real world!" many argue, suggesting "theory has no place in the real world." Some teachers will actually say, "We place less emphasis on theory and more on practical skills at my school!"

In most fields, however, including aeronautics, astrophysics, biology, communication, computer science, criminal justice, engineering, geology, medicine, political science, sociology, space exploration, psychology, substance abuse counseling, or dozens of other areas, the idea that theory and practice might not go hand-in-hand is considered absurd. We catch terrorists by using mathematical and computer models based on theories; we build bridges and buildings using theoretical models of the weather and the physical environment; the police and FBI catch serial killers and other criminals using psychological theories and profiles of criminals. Why would a public relations professional not do the same thing?

Every high school graduate is already familiar with dozens of theories about the natural world, psychology, and the sciences, and they take that knowledge for granted. Each of you knows, for example, that "what goes up must come down" (physics), that a fulcrum and lever, or pulley, can be used to lift a heavy load (engineering), that some people are "compulsive" or "overly meticulous" (psychology), or that if we wrap the belt on our bathrobe around itself twice before we pull it tight the belt is less likely to slip (friction). We give almost no thought to any of these theories until we have to fix a flat tire on our rider mower, or until we are trying to understand why our roommate gets so annoyed at us for not cleaning up our side of the room.

Just as engineers need to understand a number of theories to properly design and build products, buildings, bridges, and automobiles, public relations and communication professionals need to understand how to motivate individuals and publics. You will come away from *A Rhetorical Approach to Public Relations Writing* with a better understanding of human motivation and how several theories of

TABLE 1.2 Typical Public Relations Activities

- Write a news release, backgrounder, fact sheet, pitch letter, flier, pamphlet, bulletin, or brochure.
- Write an op-ed article, letter to the editor, feature story, or issue advertisement.
- Write material for an annual report.
- Write a public service announcement or a film script.
- Write or deliver a speech.
- Write a White Paper (position/research paper).
- Write a research paper for a professional conference.
- Buy space for an issues advertisement in a newspapers and magazine.
- Buy advertising to support a new corporate initiative.
- Conduct environmental scanning: read local/national newspapers and industry periodicals, visit chat rooms, watch the local/national news and news programs.
- Commission research, articles, or reports.
- Choose the graphics and color scheme for an organizational logo.
- Conduct lobbying on behalf of your organization.
- Coordinate/organize/host a special event, news conference, exhibit, open house, or annual stockholder meeting.
- Create or design a poster, billboard, transit sign, advertisement, point-of-purchase display, or direct mail package.
- Develop educational materials for public schools.
- Develop, design, or select advertising specialties: pens, magnet, tote bags, coffee mugs, coasters, stress balls, etc.
- Develop or design a Web site, chat room, or electronic information site.
- Edit/Proofread documents: news release, annual report, brochure, magazine article, position paper, speech, advertisement, etc.
- Implement and manage communication initiatives for employees—e.g., a telephone hot line, a bulletin board system, a company newspaper or newsletter, a quarterly video update, etc.
- Meet with city/state/national politician: congressperson, governor, senator, etc.
- Meet with community, city, state or federal leaders, or officials: mayor, school board member, city council member, police chief, ombudsperson, CDC official, etc.
- Meet with a journalist to discuss story ideas.
- Meet with a government bureaucrat, local/state inspector, etc.
- Meet with a spokesperson of a special interest group.
- Negotiate with individuals, organizations, publics, activists, etc.
- Organize or staff a speakers bureau.
- Organize a workshop, professional conference, or news conference.
- Pitch story ideas to a reporter or editor.
- Prepare slides, take photographs, or commission an illustration or artwork.
- Prepare and advise a witness who will give testimony to government committee.
- Prepare and advise an executive who is to be interviewed on a local news network, cable television, or sixty minutes ("Mike Wallace is here to see you sir ...").
- Represent your organization on a radio or television talk show.
- Send (mail, e-mail, fax, courier) news releases, pitch letters, invitations, etc.
- Sponsor book, magazine, or television advertising or editorials.
- Testify before Congress or at a public hearing.
- Testify before a citizens advisory panel or committee.

Based loosely on Ron Pearson's Unpublished Doctoral Dissertation, *A Theory of Public Relations Ethics* (1989), Ohio University.

communication and public relations can help you create more effective, informative, and persuasive messages.

The theories described throughout the text are not trivial concepts useful only to professors, and should eventually be no more "abstract" for communication professionals than an understanding of radiation is to a nuclear scientist or spices are to a chef. Once you begin to understand the basic communication theories, your messages will be easier to construct and your arguments more compelling.

Throughout the text, I will describe an assortment of rhetorical theories as well as communication-related theories from political science, sociology, intercultural communication, interpersonal communication, organizational communication, and a number of other fields. The emphasis will usually be on writing; however, skilled communicators also understand features of content, delivery, style, aesthetics, audience, and occasion. Essentially, there is more to effective writing than just sitting down in front of a computer.

RHETORIC IS TIMELESS

In some branches of science, such as astronomy, medicine, and physics, professionals need to constantly stay up-to-date on the latest findings in order to understand how a recent discovery might inform one's research. Although certain areas of knowledge like mathematics and statistics underlie most scientific research, to understand social phenomenon requires an up-to-date understanding of recent research and findings in that area. Communication, what public relations professionals do when they write and speak, is similar. To be an effective communicator requires an understanding of communication research, theory, and practice.

To understand a specific group of stakeholders requires up-to-date cultural and social knowledge as well as an understanding of the principles of effective language, or rhetoric, that support our messages. Rhetoric is informed by thousands of years of theory, as well as by recent rhetorical and communication theories. For example, persuasive messages still need to be delivered by trusted and compelling sources (ethos), include reasonable or consistent messages (logos), and integrate other compelling features like emotional anecdotes and imagery (pathos). Aristotle introduced the concepts of ethos, pathos, and logos 2,500 years ago. Similarly, modern concepts like identification (making people feel that you understand them and share their experiences) and archetypal metaphors (powerful, evocative references to unchanging social and cultural experiences) are also useful for creating compelling messages. Identification and archetypal metaphors will be discussed later in the text but can be found in all types of documents. Consider the use of archetypal metaphors *emphasis* in the first minute of Barack Obama's inaugural address in January 2009:

> Forty-four Americans have now taken the presidential oath.
>
> The words have been spoken during *rising tides* of prosperity and the *still waters* of peace. Yet, every so often the oath is taken amidst *gathering clouds and raging storms*. At these moments, America has carried on not simply because of the skill or vision of those in high office, but because *We the People* have remained faithful to the ideals of our forbears, and true to our founding documents.

Or from this *Wall Street Journal* editorial from November 2008: "Because of GM's deep commitment to its employees, dealers and communities, the company has been restructuring itself without the *storm and drama* some pundits mistake for actual progress" (online.wsj.com/article/SB122705733362939557.html). Or from this news release released by the nonprofit social cause organization FridayLight: "Amid the destruction and horror of the recent tragedies in Mumbai, FridayLight.org initiated a worldwide campaign to transform the *darkness into light*" (December 3, 2009, PRNewswire.com). Or even from this 2008 annual report from the American Foundation for Suicide Prevention: "Another key element of the plan is AFSP's investment in a nationwide network of local chapters ... [to] raise funds and awareness through the *Out of the Darkness* Community Walks ..." (www.afsp.org/?fuseaction=home.download&folder_file_id=706329c2-cf1c-2465-1f32ac0255fdbb8f). As will be explained throughout this text, rhetorical tactics are part of all effective communication and are not just part of presidential speeches or great literary works.

WHAT IF ARISTOTLE HAD BEEN BORN 2,500 YEARS LATER?

Although Edward Bernays is credited with bringing social psychology and theory to public relations, the idea of using science, theory, and practical experience to inform everyday situations is not new. All great artists, philosophers, and scientists have drawn upon what came before. Aristotle was no different, Galileo was no different, Bernays was no different, and you should be no different.

Aristotle had what amounted to a college education of his day. In ancient Greece, higher education was conducted by philosophers, rhetoricians, and Sophists,[1] and included training in math, philosophy, astronomy, music, and other areas. Essentially, what we call a "liberal arts" education has been around for thousands of years. As Mackey (1882) explained more than two hundred years ago,

> In the seventh century, and for a long time afterwards, the circle of instruction to which all the learning of the most eminent schools and most distinguished philosophers was confined, was limited to what were then called the liberal arts and sciences, and consisted of two branches, the trivium and the quadrivium.... The trivium included grammar, rhetoric, and logic; the quadrivium comprehended arithmetic, geometry, music, and astronomy. (ch. XXVI, ¶ 22)

Great public relations professionals like Edward Bernays, Ivy Lee, and Arthur Page, recognized the value of other branches of knowledge for increasing the effectiveness of organization to public communication. By understanding what motivates someone, and what s/he believes, we are able to better target that person with compelling messages. Similarly, by understanding rhetoric, we can craft better messages that will be compelling to all audiences.

In answer to the question I posed above, "What if Aristotle had been born 2,500 years later?," the answer is that he would use "all the available means of persuasion" at his disposal, just as you should. If your personal career path includes an interest in politics, you should take some political science classes. If your interests include health care, take some courses in health communication. As a public relations professional, understanding rhetoric, communication, theories of motivation and psychology, and other theories will make you a more skilled, successful, communicator.

WHY IS WRITING SO IMPORTANT IN PUBLIC RELATIONS?

Although this is a public relations writing book rather than an introduction to public relations textbook, reviewing some of the key public relations terms is a good way to be reminded about why writing is important to *all* public relations professionals. Additionally, since not every textbook covers public relations in the same way, a review of key public relations terms makes sense.

Although the list in Table 1.3 is alphabetical, one of the most important roles played by public relations professionals is the role of **boundary spanner.** Boundary spanning has to do with the relationship between an organization and its internal and external publics. Because public relations professionals communicate with so many individuals and groups, they do a lot of writing and need to adapt their messages to diverse publics.

A second point worth noting is how many key public relations concepts are encapsulated in the **RACE** (research, analysis, communication, evaluation) acronym. Public relations messages are guided by "research" (deliberate, factual), guided by situational and occasion "analysis" (ethical, environmental scanning), guided by written and spoken "communication" (campaigns, programs, information subsidy), and guided by "evaluative" research (performance, two-way communication).

Many public relations writing texts treat writing as a skill or a knack, rather than as a rhetorical process that is informed by research and theory. Indeed, a dozen reviewers of this book complained "I do not have time to teach students all this ..." or, "It would be good for students to understand rhetorical theory but because of the way that I teach the course, I don't have the time ..." When you consider how much time you spend writing as a public relations professional, and how important writing is to achieving organizational goals, the importance of understanding how to analyze audiences and situations, conduct research, and employ rhetoric becomes obvious. You do not have the time to *ignore* rhetoric.

UNDERSTANDING GOALS, OBJECTIVE, STRATEGIES, AND TACTICS

If you have ever tried baking, you would know that it requires very precise measurements: 2 cups flour, 1½ cups milk, 1 egg, 1 tablespoon oil, ¼ teaspoon salt, etc. By contrast, cooking (making soup, stew, burritos, or even a salad) is very different. If you add an extra cup of peas to split pea soup, or extra radishes to a salad, the recipe will still likely yield a great soup or salad. By contrast, adding an extra half-cup of flower to a brownie mix is likely to ruin the dessert. When we talk about writing, we often speak of the "the writing

TABLE 1.3 Key Public Relations Concepts

Boundary-spanners: Professionals who work with individuals and publics from different divisions, organizations, states, or nations. Public Relations practitioners work with both internal and external groups at all levels of the organization and require skills at communicating similar messages to multiple publics, and bridging relational and cultural gaps among organizational stakeholders.

Campaign: Episodic informational or persuasive efforts targeted to specific groups or publics. E.g., "Advertising (or marketing) campaigns," "informational campaigns," etc. Campaigns are product, event, or circumstance driven and can last anywhere from a week to a year or more depending upon the timing of key activities availability of resources, and the goals of the campaign.

Deliberate: All communication should be deliberate: intentional, purposeful, informed by research and past experience. Public relations activities are extensive and time consuming. Professionals only write news releases or creates materials because some research or past experience suggests that s/he will be successful. Public Relations is not a based on guesswork but should be based on research and theory.

Dominant Coalition: The key decision makers in an organization (not necessarily your boss). The dominant coalition are the people who actually make the decisions either because of their status, knowledge, influence, or experience. Skilled leaders often seek input from people at all levels of an organization, successful practitioners need to learn who the people in the dominant coalition are and make an effort to build relationships and communicate with as many of those individuals as possible.

Environmental Scanning: A form of informal, ongoing research involving monitoring print, broadcast, and electronic media sources for your organization or client, Environmental scanning is essential to monitoring and tracking public sentiment, stakeholder beliefs, organizational reputation and status, and environmental risks.

Ethical: Public Relations professionals always serve the public good and act in the best interest of society as they enact organizational goals. As suggested below under "organizational counsellor," while public relations professionals technically "work" for organizations and clients, they serve the best interests of their clients by doing what is right. Review the PRSA Code of Ethics for details.

Factual: Public Relations deals with facts not omissions, half-truths, deception, or false fronts. Contrary to media stereotypes, professionals never lie or "spin" facts to suit organizational purposes. Although public relations professionals are not journals and their jobs are not to report on organizational mistakes or misdeeds, by calling for accurate organizational and public communication at all levels of the organizational hierarchy, public relations professionals are able to build stronger, more ethical organizations.

Information Subsidy (Gandy, 1982): The symbiotic relationship that exists between organizations and the media. i.e., the media need content and organizations need coverage of issues. By fostering relationships with local and national journalists, public relations professionals are better able to serve organizational interests and achieve strategic goals.

Management Function: The best public relations is integrated into the organization's mission and goals. Although many public relations professionals do not have access to members of the dominant coalition, whenever possible public relations professionals should work to play a role in the managerial process and counsel organizational leaders.

Performance: Public Relations is a results based activity. If you cannot produce results you are pretty much out of a job. Part of the process of results based performance is being able to measure your success and engage in informed decision making. Use the public relations RACE model (Research, Analysis, Communication, Evaluation) to guide your activities and draw upon sound research and theory whenever possible.

Organizational Counsellors: The principle that public relations professionals should provide advice to organizational leaders about how to act in the organization's best interest. Being an organizational counsellor requires being well informed about all aspects of an organizations business or professional activities and being able to support advice to organizational leaders by reference to facts and data. Counsellors do not express their "opinions" so much as frame the facts of a situation in a clear and compelling fashion. Often, public relations professionals need to tell organizational leaders that they are wrong. Thus, strong interpersonal communication skills are essential.

Planned/Systematic: Organizational activities are organized, research based, and produced according to a plan. Again, as RACE suggests, all communication should be guided by research in the beginning and be evaluated by research at the end.

Program: Ongoing informational efforts often targeted to internal publics. E.g., "Employee Benefits," "Professional Development," etc. All *ongoing* organizational and professional activities including things like "speakers bureaus" are considered programs.

(continued)

TABLE 1.3 *Continued*

Public Interest: All organizations have multiple stakeholders and interested publics. A public relations professional must always work to serve the interest of *all* stakeholders and publics, rather than the narrow interests of a expedient individual or group (like one's manager or employer). The public interest is not just the interest of your employer. Your obligations as a public relations counsellor go beyond the narrow or short term interests of a single public.

Relationship: The negotiation and maintenance of relationships with multiple publics is key to the success of all communication professionals. Although many people are not comfortable "schmoozing," having diverse and strong relationships with professionals both outside and inside of one's organization is essential to success.

Reputation: Public Relations practitioners are only as good as their reputations. Successful professionals need to be wary of engaging in unethical actions that might sully their personal or organizational reputations. Fostering and maintaining a solid reputation is not a matter or pride. A professional who is believed to be unethical, or unreliable, reflects poorly on the organizations and clients s/he represents. Professionals with strong reputations and larger networks of colleagues and friends are ultimately better able to serve their clients.

Research/Evaluate: Effective public relations relies upon sound data and critical assessment: research and (evaluation). Remember the RACE acronym.

Service-oriented: Public Relations professionals are concerned with the good of organizational clients and stakeholders and not personal reward, fame, or "gettin' your props." The mistake that many people make is in thinking that when a public relations professional ends up on the evening news after a crisis and does a wonderful job with the news conference, s/he is a skilled practitioner. To the contrary, although some crises are unavoidable, the best public relations professionals never end up in front of the camera in the first place. The best crises are identified and avoided by hard work and planning rather than dealt with after they occur.

Stakeholders and Stakeseekers: Groups and individuals who have a vested interest in the outcome of an event or activity, or who have a vested interest in the activities of groups, individuals, organizations, causes, and social activities are considered stakeholders. Similarly, stakeseekers (such as activists, lobbyists, job seekers, etc.) work to have a say in the activities of organizations and groups. Public relations professionals deal with a variety of stakeholders and stakeseekers and balance the needs of their organization's interests and goals against the needs of multiple (often competing) publics' beliefs, attitudes, values, desires, and goals.

The Strength of Weak Ties (Granovetter, 1973): Professionals who have more relational ties have more access to unique and diverse information and are more successful professionally. Those closest to you have access to the same information; those not so close have access to different information. The importance of maintaining both strong and weak (or informal) relationships with multiple publics cannot be overstated.

Two-Way Communication: The process of give and take, sending and receiving information that characterizes symmetrical relationships, and relationships build on trust and dialogue. Two-way communication involves soliciting feedback from others, actually listening to what others have to say, and acting on the feedback. Many organizations, especially on the internet, take the importance of two-way communication for granted, making it difficult for stakeholders and stakeseekers to reach organizational representatives and often ignoring the feedback obtained from online visitors. Two-way communication is a hallmark of all relational communication and essential to effective public relations.

process." Public relations writing is a process (like making soup) rather than a recipe (like baking a cake). Because communication is so complex, influenced by past experience, the nature of the relationship, the type of person or organization engaging in the communication, the timing of the message, the frequency of the message, and the imagery used, we can safely say that there is no single right way to craft a written message. As you will learn throughout this text, there are "rules" and "conventions," but, in reality, since public relations is a results-oriented profession, professionals often have to adapt their messages to meet the needs of diverse stakeholders and stakeseekers.

The best writing has been carefully crafted, meticulously edited, and written so that the intended audience finds the message compelling. Science fiction books are targeted to specific ages just as public relations messages are targeted to specific stakeholders and written to be compelling for different media outlets.

As you progress through the courses in the public relations sequence at your school, you will probably take a "Public Relations Management" or

"Public Relations Campaigns" course. One of the most common frameworks for how to structure a public relations campaign is called management by objective or MBO. **Management by objective** is a 12-step framework for organizing an informational or persuasive campaign.

Although a book on writing is not the place to go into detail about each part of the MBO process, having an understanding of why you write—to achieve organizational goals—should make you a more skilled writer. At the heart of the MBO process are four things: goals, objectives, strategies, and tactics.

As indicated in Table 1.4, **Goals** refer to desired end states. What you want to accomplish with your messages. **Objectives** refer to the behaviors, attitudes, or knowledge of individuals or groups we need to influence or change in order to accomplish our goals. In order to get someone to do something,

TABLE 1.4 Goals, Objectives, Strategies, Tactics

Goals: Broad, general statements of the desired end-state or outcome. Programs and campaigns may have one big goal or several more modest goals. Goals are usually written as follows:

"To promote positive media coverage of our event."

"To provide customer service of the 'highest quality.'"

"To create a safe workplace for our employees."

"To position ourselves as a leader in healthcare."

"To cut the accident rate among workers."

"To raise our score on the five-point 'Customer Satisfaction' rating scale."

Objectives: What we need to do to accomplish our goals. Objectives involve influencing or changing the behaviors, knowledge, or attitude of stakeholders/stakeseekers. Objectives are particular to each public, measurable, and meet specific time constraints.

Objectives need to be measurable, refer to a specific public/action, and achievable by a specific date/time frame.

Measuring objectives requires pretest (benchmark) data and post-test data.

Quantifiable objectives are preferable to qualitative objectives.

Types of Objectives

Behavioral Objectives try to modify how people act or behave. Behavioral objectives represent the behaviors that are necessary to make the goals happen. Often several behaviors are necessary to accomplish each goal.

Attitudinal Objectives try to modify how people feel or what people believe about something or someone.

Knowledge Objectives try to modify what people know about something or someone.

Behavioral objectives should be written as specific, quantifiable, behaviors with specific timeframes for achievement: "to (verb) X (public) to do Y (behavior) by Z (date)." E.g.:

"To receive comments from 500 customers by the end of the fiscal year."

"To provide information (via our Web site) to 5,000 registered voters by March."

"To convince 500 employees to attend a payroll workshops by November."

"To persuade three media representatives to take a plant tour by March."

"To review 250 applications from undergraduate students by November."

Objectives Example: If your goal is "To create a safe workplace for our employees," several behaviors will be needed to make this happen and might include:

"To encouraging all employees to regularly wear their safety equipment (goggles, earplugs, gloves, etc.) by December";

"To encouraging all employees to report unsafe work conditions as soon they are noticed"; and

(continued)

TABLE 1.4 *Continued*

"To encouraging 20% of all employees to attend a 'safety seminar' each quarter."

Strategies: Used to Encourage Behaviors: The informative/persuasive techniques used to encourage the desired behaviors. How you get publics to do what you want them to do. Strategies are also targeted to specific behavioral objective and publics. What works with one public will not necessarily work with another.

In practice, the strategies that we can use to get people to do what we want them to do are limitless and include: fear, repetition, ego, money or rewards, information, persuasion, entertainment, environmental changes, modeling, celebrities, face-to-face meetings, images, etc.

Strategies Example: Using our goal of "To create a safe workplace for our employees," and one of our behavioral objectives (behaviors), "Encouraging all employees to report unsafe work conditions as soon they are noticed," there are many strategies we could use to get employees to report unsafe conditions:

Information: Post safety signs saying, "Be safe! Report all unsafe conditions!"

Ego: Employees who report unsafe conditions get merit badges, their pictures posted on a bulletin board, a shout-out in the employee newsletter.

Economic: Reporting an unsafe condition earns employees 50 bucks!

Images/Fear: Post signs depicting accidents and encouraging employees to report unsafe conditions.

Diffusion/Repetition: Relate stories about unsafe conditions in newsletters and employee correspondence.

Tactics: The activities we undertake to fulfill the strategies. The things we do. For every strategy you will utilize one or more tactics. Tactics can be face-to-face interactions, speeches, group meetings, and written documents: news releases, brochures, speeches, invitations, media kits, etc. Sometimes the line between strategies and tactics is blurred. Holding meetings can be used to inform organizational members (a strategy) and may also serve as a tactic (the speech given at the meeting).

Tactics Example: Using our goal of "To create a safe workplace for our employees," our behavioral objective of, "Encouraging all employees to report unsafe work conditions as soon they are noticed," and our strategy of "offering an economic incentive (or reward) for reporting unsafe conditions," we need to make employees aware of the reward program so that they start looking for unsafe conditions. Tactics include:

Print: Posters/signs around the plant about the new program; a story in the employee newsletter about the upcoming "incentive program"; create a brochure explaining how the program works to be used in a "point-of-purchase display"; include a copy of the reporting form in employees' pay envelopes, etc.

Spoken: Mentioning the program at the next plant meeting and providing instructions for how to properly report an unsafe condition and claim the reward; mentioning the program during a news conference, interview, or other appropriate public event.

Electronic: Writing a story about the new program for the employee intranet.

Media: Write a news release about the new program and submit it to local newspapers; create a fact sheet about the program for media or informational kits.

---

s/he has to first become aware of the fact that there is a choice to be made. **Strategies** refer to the informative or persuasive techniques used to encourage the audience objectives.

Objectives are individual or public specific and refer to the techniques used to enact our objectives. What we want for one audience is often slightly different than what we want for another audience because each audience has varying levels of knowledge, information, and experience. For example, in order to get people to stop smoking, professionals have tried fear appeals ("Each cigarette takes seven minutes off your life"), economic appeals ("If you stop smoking, you can save $1,500 per year!"), guilt ("You want to be there for your kids don't you?"), and many other strategies. Some strategies work better than others, but strategies should be selected because they best fit the target audience. Strategies are informed by communication, persuasion, and rhetorical theories, such as those illustrated throughout this text.

Finally, we come to the heart of the Goals/Objectives/Strategies/Tactics cluster: **Tactics:** the things that we write, say, or create to achieve our objectives and strategies. Tactics include every written or spoken document described in this book, as well as any not covered. At the heart of MBO, and at the heart of public relations, is writing. Writing is important because public relations would not be possible without it.

WHY PUBLIC RELATIONS PROFESSIONALS SHOULD CARE ABOUT WRITING

On the first day of class, public relations writing professors often explain to students that they will probably have to take a writing test when they go in for their first public relations job interview. (Sample writing exams can be found in Appendix A.) What many employment exams want to evaluate are basic language skills (understanding the difference between "too," "two," and "to," or "its" and "it's") as well as the applicant's ability to write effectively and on deadline.

If you look at the list of "typical public relations activities" (Table 1.1) you will note that a substantial portion of a professional's time involves writing: brochures, e-mails, fact sheets, newsletters, news releases, letters, memos, all of the things that you will learn about in this text. Simply put, public relations is a writing-intensive profession. On any given day, a public relations professional might be called upon to prepare a memo, write a news release, provide copy for a brochure, update an organization's Web site, or pitch story ideas to a reporter. Writing is the lifeblood of public relations.

One of the first theories to help explain the writing process and the role of rhetorical theory is Everett Rogers' diffusion of innovations theory. Professional communicators need to take into account multiple stakeholders and publics, and create messages to appeal to individuals and groups with diverse levels of knowledge, interests, opinions, and needs.

USING THEORY TO REACH KEY PUBLICS: DIFFUSION OF INNOVATIONS (DI)

Assuming that writing is enough to achieve every organizational or campaign goal is a mistake. Although writing is part of all long-term efforts to inform or persuade others, as you know from your own educational experiences, acquiring knowledge and being persuaded to act on new ideas is a process that takes time. Indeed, as the MBO model described in Figure 1.1 suggests, multiple tactics are always employed. Public relations professionals send out many news releases because they are quick and easy. However, in most cases, one tactic alone is not enough to accomplish sophisticated goals that include attitude change and altered behaviors. Ultimately, *many* tactics are needed: this concept is what the Diffusion of Innovations Model explains.

Diffusion of innovations is the process by which innovations are diffused through society. An innovation refers to any new idea, process, object, product, or service. Thus, a new way of tying fishing flies that makes them more durable would be an innovation in the fly-fishing world. A new search engine that anticipates users' preferences would be a technological innovation. A holographic cellular telephone would be a communication innovation. A new procedure for teaching students math would be an educational innovation. A new children's toy that helps them learn social skills would be a pedagogical innovation. Innovations include completely new objects and processes (wearable computers), ideas (global warming caused by toasters), processes (no-till farming), as well as derivations on previous technologies and processes (cell-phone jewelry, the clock radio).

Everything that is new requires time to diffuse through society. Nothing happens overnight. Product releases, book and movie promotions, new software, all require months of publicity and sustained promotion in order to make people aware of the product, event, or activity.

The DI model represents a means of understanding how innovations move through a population. Diffusion is about how to increase the speed at which an innovation is accepted, as well as the features of how the process works. As Rogers explains: diffusion of innovations refers to the "process by which an innovation is communicated through certain channels, over time, among the members of a social system" (1995, p. 5).

Rogers has refined the DI model over the years. In his early work, Rogers viewed diffusion as a linear process. However, later research found that people "personalize" innovations and use them in different ways than originally planned by an innovation's creators (called unintended consequences). As informational and promotional campaigns progress through time, unique adoption trends can be incorporated into future messages.

The law of unintended consequences creates all sorts of positive and negative applications for innovations. Diffusion decisions are not as simple as "accepting" or "rejecting" an innovation. Rather, in diffusion theory the rate of adoption follows an

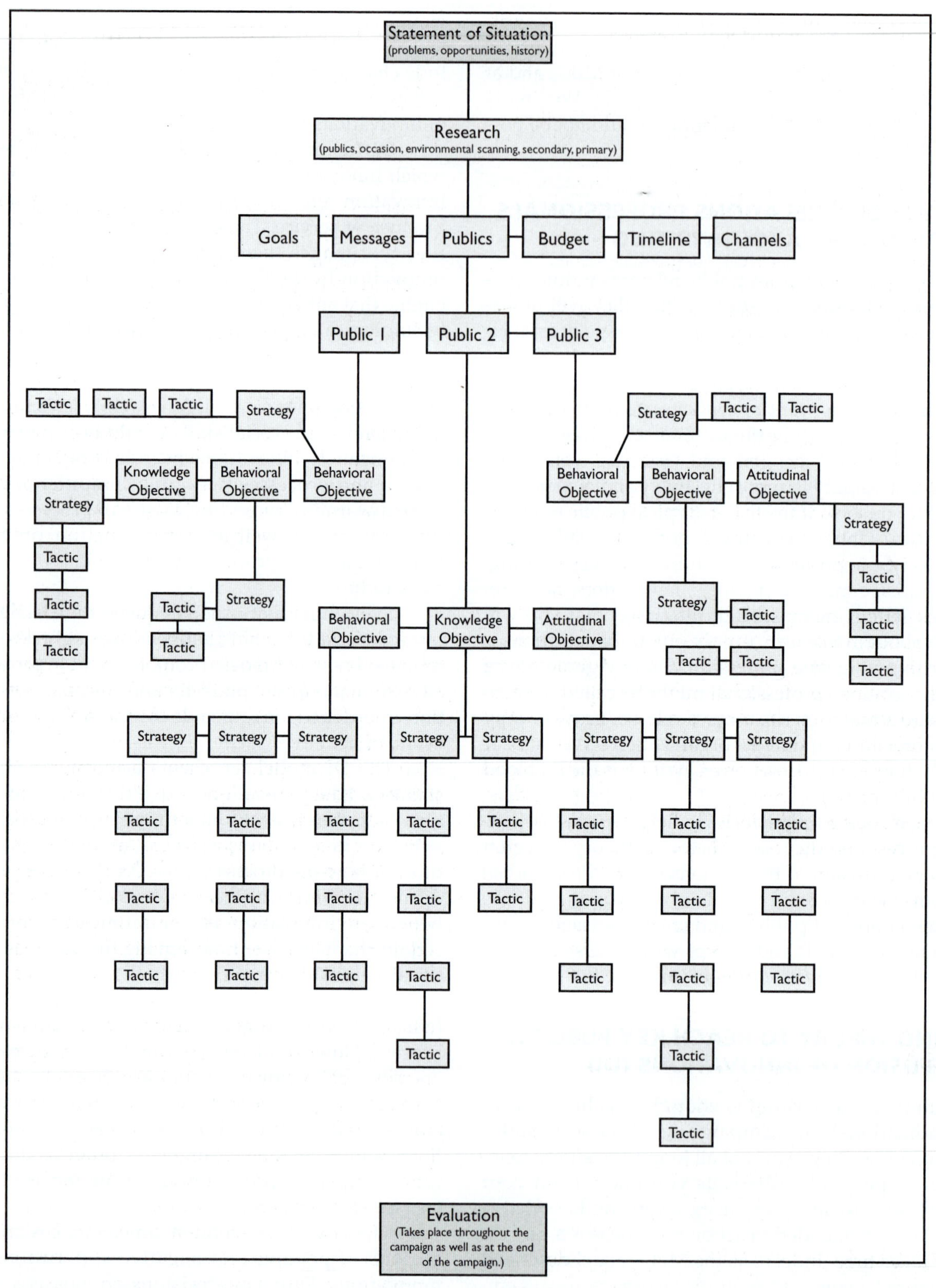

FIGURE 1.1 Steps in the MBO process and MBO Flowchart.

Steps in the MBO Process with Examples

1. **Situation:** A new university graduate program needs to increase attendance to avoid being cancelled.
2. **Research:** Who are the potential students?. What attracted the current students? What local competition exists? What resources can the program bring?
3. **Key Publics:** Potential students: local professionals, current undergraduates, professional staff already working in the school. Media: local media who write about education issues. Current graduate students who work in local media, etc.
4. **Goals:** To increase enrollment in the program. To increase the prestige of the department.
5. **Behavioral Objectives (several per public needed):** "To convince 10 undergraduates to pursue graduate education in the program by next fall," etc.
6. **Strategies:** Appeal to the students' pragmatism by informing them that students with graduate educations earn more over their lifetimes (Maslow); inform the students about other undergraduates who went on for graduate degrees and now have better jobs (social learning theory), etc.
7. **Tactics:** Create a new Web site for students talking about graduate education. Create posters to put around the campus and the department talking about graduate opportunities. Direct mailing. Pitching story ideas to media, etc.
8. **Messages:** "Times are hard—stay in school" "Graduate education makes you more employable"; etc.
9. **Channels:** Web site (electronic), written messages (posters), print (direct mailing), interpersonal contact.
10. **Timeframe (create Gantt charts, etc.):** 6–12 months. Web site and posters during third month; interpersonal contact during sixth month; direct mailing before application deadline; etc.
11. **Budget: Printed materials:** 100 posters—$500; brochures—$300; Web site redesign—$1,000; etc.
12. **Evaluation:** Assess how many undergraduates apply; evaluate level of awareness of program; etc.

FIGURE 1.1 Continued

S-shaped curve, starting gradually at the bottom end of the S, and building to an almost flat plateau at the top (Figure 1.2). Diffusion of any innovation initially occurs slowly and then, at some point, begins to accelerate. "Innovations that are perceived by individuals as possessing greater relative advantage, compatibility, and the like, have a more rapid rate of adoption" (1995, p. 23). Thus, over time, if an innovation is considered by members of a social system to be useful, it will be adopted.

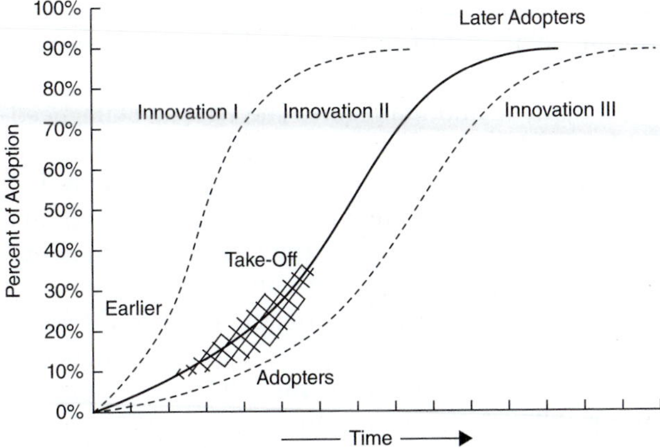

FIGURE 1.2 Roger's diffusion curve.
Source: Reprinted with the permission of The Free Press, a Division of Simon & Schuster, Inc., from Diffusion of Innovations, Fourth Edition by Everett M. Rogers. Copyright © 1962, 1971, 1983 by the Free Press. All rights reserved.

Individuals are classified into one of five adopter categories on the basis on their innovativeness: (1) *Innovators* represent the first 2.5 percent of the people in a system to adopt an innovation. Venturesomeness, or trying new things, is almost an obsession with innovators. (2) *Early adopters* represent the next 13.5 percent of the people in a system to adopt an innovation. (3) The *early majority* represents the next 34 percent of the people in a system to adopt an innovation. The early majority adopts new ideas just before the average person. By the early majority phase, half of all *potential adopters* (50 percent) are using an innovation. (4) The *late majority* represents the next 34 percent of the people in a system to adopt. The late majority adopts new ideas just *after* the average person. They are more patient and cautious. Finally, (5) *laggards* represent the last 16 percent of the people in a system to adopt an innovation. Laggards often look to the past and resist adopting innovations either because *they are new* (quasi-Luddites), or because they *do not* see how a particular innovation is an advantage or makes their life better.

In their defense, laggards are often well-established professionals who are not driven by status reasons to adopt an innovation, or have assistants who implement an innovation on their behalf. Many laggards are often more *critical* of new, "unproven" innovations rather than afraid of them.

According to Rogers, five attributes of innovations serve as predictors of whether individuals or groups will adopt an innovation and can be used to increase the speed at which an innovation is adopted:

1. *Relative Advantage:* People view an innovation as meeting a cost benefit criteria. The benefit brought by an innovation must be greater than the resources used to secure that innovation.
2. *Compatibility:* The more an innovation works with existing technology, beliefs, and structures, the more likely it will be adopted.
3. *Complexity:* Innovations that are easy to master, or seem easy, will diffuse faster.
4. *Trialability:* People like to be able to try something with little risk. People prefer to embrace innovations that can be discarded immediately if the adopters are not satisfied with the outcome.
5. *Observability:* Actually seeing an innovation in action encourages people to adopt the innovation.

For public relations professionals, several aspects of the DI model are important to understand. First, professionals need to understand the importance of utilizing the adoption features when creating messages. Adoption features can be demonstrated rhetorically. For example, relative advantage is frequently illustrated through "features and benefits" language in advertisements, on packaging, and in instructions. Compatibility and complexity can also be "explained." However, attributes of innovations that require trialability and observability call for samples, demonstrations, visual aids, public events, and "money-back guarantees" in order to speed adoption.

Second, when introducing innovations, you must understand that adoption of any innovation is a process that takes time and goes through stages. Frequently opinion leaders (journalists, critics, reviewers, CEOs, celebrities, educators) and current customers who use an organization's other products and services are offered free trials or asked to "beta test" a product or service for several months. Although many professionals refuse free offers on ethical grounds, some are still willing to "test" or "review" products, services, and ideas for organizations. Innovations are not adopted overnight, even in the case of free innovations like upgrades and patches. Organizations that introduce "innovations" and "improvements" also need to continue to service products that have been replaced by upgrades, often for years.

Third, any time individuals and publics are asked to alter the way that they have historically done things there will be resistance and an adoption lag. Adoptions, even of beneficial innovations, require an investment of time and mental energy by the adoptees. In most cases, unsophisticated tactics like blog posts and e-mail messages ("visit our Web site for a free trial ...") will not dramatically speed the adoption of complex or unfamiliar practices. Even when publics are forced to make changes like requiring all employees of an organization to upgrade to a new computer system, resistance will occur. In cases of necessary or mandatory adoption, quick, unilateral, unexpected, and forced adoption may be best. However, in other cases (like the introduction of digital television), a lengthy phase-in period may be necessary.

Although there is no rule on innovation adoptions that works in every case, practitioners need to be sensitive to environmental, organizational, and public constraints and plan accordingly. Thus, the diffusion process is a rhetorical process that includes research, audience adaptation, and messages crafted to appeal to individuals and groups with differing levels of knowledge and interest.

WHERE DOES PUBLIC RELATIONS FIT INTO THE BIG PICTURE?

As you probably learned in your introduction to public relations class, public relations professionals serve many masters (see Table 1.2). In some situations, public relations professionals work closely with marketing and advertising departments (called marketing communications or MARCOM) and help promote an organization's products and services to external publics and stakeholders. In other situations, public relations professionals work on "internal" public relations and craft messages for employees, shareholders, and managers. The writing skills needed by public relations practitioners are as diverse as the types of public relations practiced (see Table 1.5). A public relations professional might end up working for a small plastics manufacturing company, a medium-sized organic food co-op, a college or university, a government agency, a politician, a nonprofit social cause organization, a hospital, a sports franchise, a fashion designer, an entertainment/promotion firm, or a public relations consulting agency. What public relations professionals will ultimately need to know down the road is less certain than their need to know how to write well in a variety of contexts.

The practice of public relations is different in nearly every organization. As mentioned earlier, only

TABLE 1.5 Types of Public Relations

Types of Public Relations
Celebrity/Personal Promotion
Community Relations
Consumer Relations
Corporate Communications
Corporate Publicity
Crisis Management
Employee Relations/Internal Communication
Entertainment/Theatre Production
Health Communication
International Public Relations
Investor Relations
Issues Management
Media Relations
Media/Broadcast Training
Music/Concert Publicity
Political Public Relations
Public Affairs and Government Relations
Strategic Consultancy

about one in four public relations practitioners work in public relations agencies. The types of roles and activities in which professionals participate is largely determined by the type of organization for which one works, and the way in which the organization has practiced public relations in the past.

Many public relations professionals start their careers as "technicians," responsible for producing content, conducting research, and honing their writing skills. The **technician** is an entry-level position and includes titles like "assistant communications director," or "assistant account executive." More advanced professionals are often employed as **managers** or "experts" to solve problems. In many cases, senior managers and **account executives** (an agency title for those who handle one or several client accounts) are brought in from agencies on an ad hoc basis to solve internal communication problems that a local communication professional cannot deal with because of his/her proximity to the organization.

Experienced communication and public relations professionals understand management issues (budgeting, strategic planning, crisis management, scheduling, conflict, interviewing) and function as boundary spanners between their organization and various stakeholders/stakeseekers. Skilled managers keep their ears to the ground by constant environmental scanning, listen, and gather and share information with top management. The most skilled professionals are problem solvers who are able to work with top management as part of the overall organizational management team. **Senior professionals** have titles like "director of internal (or external) communication," "senior account manager," or "partner."

As public relations professionals become more skilled and respected organizational professionals, they participate more in strategic planning, issues management, lobbying, and public communication. A number of public relations activities are commonly practiced depending upon the type of organization in which someone works, and the structural/environmental issues facing the organization. Common activities include:

- **Publicity:** Attracting attention and supplying information about a specific organizational event, activity, or attribute (Heath & Coombs, 2006, p. 10).
- **Promotion:** Sustained publicity over several days, weeks, months, or years intended to supply individuals and publics with information and maintain interest and attention about an event or activity (op. cit.).
- **Press Agentry:** Creating newsworthy stories and events to attract the media (Cutlip, Center, & Broom, 2000, p. 14). Press agentry also includes event planning.
- **Public Affairs:** A governmental title that refers to the practices of public relations since the 1913 Gillett Amendment that stipulated that the executive branch could not use public funds to defeat legislation. Public Affairs refers to efforts to build and maintain government and community relations in order to influence public policy (op. cit)[2]
- **Issues Management:** Involves activities like lobbying, organizational activism, strategic research, and strategic planning. According to Heath, "The management of organizational and community resources through the public policy process to advance organizational interests and rights by striking a mutual balance with those of stakeholders" (2006, p. 79).
- **Lobbying:** Efforts to build relationships with politicians and government officials in an effort to influence legislation, regulation, public policy, political agendas, and government contacts (Heath, 2005, p. 492).

- **Investor Relations:** Efforts to build relationships with shareholders and members of the financial community to maximize market value.
- **Fundraising:** Efforts conducted by communication professionals at colleges and universities (Cutlip, Center, & Broom, 2000, p. 23).
- **Development:** Similar to investor relations but by nonprofit organizations, colleges, and universities to build and maintain relationships with donors and members in order to secure financial and volunteer support (op. cit).
- **Crisis and Risk Communication:** Communication efforts both to identify possible threats to organizations and create strategic plans to deal with them (these include health, safety, and security issues), as well as strategic plans for dealing with organizational misdeeds, accidents, and catastrophes (indiscretions by CEOs, plane crashes, takeover threats, layoffs) (see, Heath 2005).
- **Apologia:** A huge area of research in public relations for many years. Apologia refers to public apologies and strategies for dealing with how to admit wrongdoing, acknowledge fault, avoid blame, move on after crises, etc. Apologia is a sophisticated practice discussed in more detail in Chapter 11.

MAINTAINING ORGANIZATIONAL IMAGE AND UNDERSTANDING THE SITUATIONAL NATURE OF PUBLIC COMMUNICATION

Thinking of public relations professionals as "spin doctors" or "image managers" is a mistake. All people make decisions about the world based on their past experiences and individual mental images. In order to create effective organization to public messages, public relations professionals need to understand how situations and occasions influence the decisions that we make.

More than 30 years ago, Kenneth Boulding, an economist, wrote a description of a mental image as a means of explaining how individual and group "images" (beliefs, values, experiences) influence our perceptions of the world. As Boulding explains:

> AS I SIT AT MY DESK, I know where I am. I see before me a window; beyond that some trees; beyond that the red roofs of the campus of Stanford University; beyond them the trees and the roof tops which mark the town of Palo Alto; beyond them the bare golden hills of the Hamilton Range. I know, however, more than I see. Behind me, although I am not looking in that direction, I know there is a window, and beyond that the little campus of the Center for the Advanced Study in the Behavioral Sciences; beyond that the Coast Range; beyond that the Pacific Ocean .... I know, furthermore, that if I go far enough I will come back to where I am now. In other words, I have a picture of the earth as round. I visualize it as a globe .... I know, furthermore, that I am a husband and a father, that there are people who will respond to me affectionately and to whom I will respond in like manner .... Finally, I am located in the midst of a world of subtle intimations and emotions. I am sometimes elated, sometimes a little depressed, sometimes happy, sometimes sad .... What I have been talking about is knowledge. Knowledge, perhaps, is not a good word for this. Perhaps one would rather say my Image of the world. Knowledge has an implication of validity, of truth. What I am talking about is what I believe to be true; my subjective knowledge. It is this Image that largely governs my behavior (1977, pp. 3–6, Boulding's emphasis)

What Boulding describes is the fact that the messages we create, whether written or spoken, are always grounded in lived experiences. People believe what they believe because of the world in which they live: the neighborhood, the city, the state or nation, one's family and friends, their education. Understanding the situational nature of communication is one of the key features involved in rhetoric. A single, unchanged, organizational message cannot be used for every stakeholder or stakeseeker. Messages need to be adapted so that they have the most impact and appeal, and move diverse audiences. Situational theories of communication have been one of the most influential models for public relations and provide an excellent way of thinking about how to reach key publics.

SITUATIONAL MODELS OF PUBLICS

Situational models help explain how situational factors impact communication success. There are at least three "situational models" of publics in public relations: Dewey and Blumer's, Bitzer's, and Grunig and Hunt's. The first, original treatment of publics can be ascribed to Dewey (1927) and Blumer (1946). Dewey and Blumer suggested that publics[3] have three characteristics:

1. *Publics are faced with similar problems or opportunities* (environmental, social, political, economic, etc.).
2. *Publics recognize and are willing to discuss their problems or opportunities.*
3. *Publics actively organize themselves better to deal with their problems or opportunities.* (One of the signs that an actual "public" exists rather than just a bunch of unhappy students, senior citizens, or teamsters is that people have come together to try and deal with a situation.) This third aspect of a public is often the point at which activist groups become viable social action groups.

Dewey and Blumer's formulation of publics in the situational model also assumes that three things must happen before a group of *individuals* come together as a *group* to deal with a problem:

1. *They must recognize that a problem exists.* ("Something needs to be done about ....")
2. *They must see the problem as being relevant to their lives.* ("If we don't do something about the pollution in the river ....")
3. *They must feel that they can do something about the problem.* ("If we put pressure on the legislature and get the media involved we can force the factory to clean up its operation ....")

Typically, unless all three of the criteria are met, a public will not take any action. Dewey and Blumer's description of publics can help practitioners understand what is necessary to move a public to take action on your behalf or what is necessary to help foster the growth of grassroots efforts.

The second situational theory of publics that is relevant in public relations is Bitzer's (1968) theory of the "rhetorical situation." Bitzer's theory of situation has to do with problems or "exigencies" that emerge and compel organizations to respond. According to Bitzer, "Rhetorical situations are the result of the merging of persons, events, objects, relations, and the ruling exigence" (p. 5). As Bitzer explains, rhetoric is situational,

> (1) rhetorical discourse comes into existence as a response to a situation, in the same sense that an answer comes into existence in response to a question, or a solution in response to a problem; (2) a speech is given *rhetorical* significance by the situation, just as a unit of discourse is given significance *as* answer or *as* solution by the question or problem; (3) a rhetorical situation must exist as a necessary condition of rhetorical discourse, just as a question must exist as a necessary precondition of an answer; (4) many questions go unanswered and many problems remain unsolved; similarly, many rhetorical situations mature and decay without giving birth to rhetorical utterance; (5) a situation is rhetorical insofar as it needs and invites discourse capable of participating with situation and thereby altering its reality; (6) discourse is rhetorical insofar as it functions (or seeks to function) as a fitting response to a situation which needs and invites it. (7) Finally, the situation controls the rhetorical response in the same sense that the question controls the answer and the problem controls the solution. (pp. 5–6, Bitzer's emphasis)

Essentially, Bitzer argues that individuals and organizations have an obligation to respond to important social situations, crises, and national events, in an effort to improve the situation. According to Bitzer, a rhetorical situation (the context in which speakers or writers create rhetorical discourse) comprises three elements:

1. *Exigence*—"an imperfection marked by urgency; a defect, an obstacle, something waiting to be done, a thing which is other than it should be" (p. 6). "Further, an exigence which can be modified only by means other than discourse is not rhetorical" (pp. 6–7).
2. *Audience*—according to Bitzer, audience includes only those people who can be persuaded, and who have the capacity to effect the change that is desired (pp. 7–8). Like Dewey and Blumer, Bitzer means only people who *will* or *can* do something, not *everyone* in an organization, community, or region.
3. *Constraints*—constraints refer to factors beyond a rhetor's control (like an audience's beliefs, attitudes, values, documents, facts, traditions, images, interests, motives, etc.), as well as the

> character and style of the communicator, the logic of the arguments, the type of situation involved, who the people are who are involved, what the time-frame is, etc. (p. 8).

Bitzer argues that communicators also have an *obligation* to speak on matters of importance (pp. 9–10), and that every rhetorical situation necessarily calls for, and contains, a fitting, or proper, response (p. 10). Bitzer also argues that rhetorical situations should be real as opposed to fictive or contrived (p. 11). In other words, creating pseudo-events (publicity stunts) just to have something to say is unethical (cf., Kent, Harrison, & Taylor, 2006).

Bitzer's theory of publics suggests that public relations professionals, as organizational spokespeople and as community leaders, have an ethical and moral obligation to speak on matters of social consequence. Since we help shape reality with the words that we use and messages that we create, we should be willing to write or speak on matters of public interest. Organizations have an obligation to be good citizens and help make the world a better place when exigencies arise.

The third and more recent situational theory of publics is the Grunig and Hunt (1984; cf., also, Grunig 1989) situational model of publics (SMP). Grunig and Hunt's SMP adds little to Bitzer's formulation of situations as inviting responses by individuals and organizations; however, the Grunig and Hunt SMP does add some interesting strategies to describe and understand the behavior of publics described by Dewey and Blumer. Grunig and Hunt argue that publics may be understood by segmenting them in terms of their knowledge or interest in problems, issues, and situations that impact their personal and professional lives. Thus, Grunig and Hunt suggest that there are four types of publics:

1. *Nonpublics,* or individuals and groups who have essentially no social, economic, political, ideological, philosophical, or geographic ties to a problem or issue.
2. *Latent publics,* or individuals and groups who have the potential to *become* publics because of their connection to an issue but either do not know about an issue of relevance, or the issue has not risen far enough above the din of other information in their lives for groups to form an opinion or for individuals to care.
3. *Aware public,* or individuals and groups who are aware of an issue of relevance to their personal, professional, or political lives but who do not care enough about the issue to become involved, or do not have the time or desire to became more active.
4. *Active publics* are the people who attend rallies, donate money to a cause, appear on television getting carried away by riot police, attend shareholder meetings and ask annoying questions, participate in publicizing an issue or seek to influence lawmakers, etc.

At any particular moment, every person in the world falls into one of these four categories on hundreds of issues. For example, I was living in an old, unrenovated apartment building in Latvia on a Fulbright scholarship when I wrote this chapter. At the time, I had no awareness of most local issues (curbing of pets, homeowner taxes, access to public transportation, etc.). Similarly, given the age of my building, the possibility existed that it had lead paint, or old pipes with lead solder. But I did not know about that, nor did I care, because I filtered my water with a carbon filter and had heard nothing about any danger from colleagues. If a problem did exist, I was a latent public because I was not concerned enough to look into it, nor had it become a public issue of concern.

In terms of issues that I was "aware of," the embassy briefed me on the dangers from criminals in certain parts of the city and told me to pay attention to my surroundings. Having traveled extensively, I already knew that. Every large city in the world has criminals, including New York, Chicago, San Francisco, Dallas, Paris, Rome. Had a colleague become concerned about crime and come to talk with me about the problem, I would probably have told him/her that I was unaware of any specific crime problems. I was *aware* of the issue but not *active*. Finally, there are issues that I am actively involved in. On some of those issues, I satisfy myself by contributing to activist groups and organizations that lobby on my behalf, and on other issues, I write letters and encourage others (students, colleagues, friends, family, etc.) to take specific action. On many issues (organic farming, not shopping at Wal-Mart, buying American), I am an active member of various publics.

From a public relations standpoint, understanding publics in terms of their level of interest and motivation in issues is very useful. Organizations frequently try to motivate (or move) individuals and groups to take specific actions. For example, union leaders make recommendations to members about which political candidate to vote for. Representatives of the Fulbright program send e-mail messages to all of the current and former Fulbrighters to tell us when important legislation is before Congress or is being decided by legislators in our state. Many Fulbrighters are unaware of pending legislation until the e-mail arrives, and then they may be motivated to respond with a letter. Other members are *aware* but decide to do nothing. Finally, many Fulbrighters who are actively following issues attend rallies and send e-mail to people, working to motivate others to take action and make *unaware* individuals *aware* of important issues.

Understanding the situational model is important. Individuals and groups *are* motivated to take action when individuals and organizations that they respect contact them, or when they become aware of issues raised in the broadcast and print media. Organizations do play a role in this process by informing individuals and publics about issues and creating persuasive messages designed to move people from *latent* to *aware* or, depending upon the organization's needs, from *active* back to *aware*.

Each of the SMP ideas interrelate and inform the others. Dewey and Blumer give insight into what it takes for publics to form. Bitzer provides insight into what situations warrant an organization's intervention in the public policy arena, and Grunig and Hunt take the model a bit farther by elaborating on various types of publics and how the stage an individual is in informs his/her action.

WHAT IF I AM NOT A SKILLED WRITER?

Writing is a skill that must be honed. No one is born a great writer; but great writers must write. Although this may sound circular, the fact is that to become great at anything requires a lot of practice. Whether you are playing the piano, the latest version of *Grand Theft Auto*, snowboarding in Aspen, racing cars in North Carolina, gourmet cooking, or designing clothes or Web pages, being able to do something well requires practice. The same is true of public relations writing. If you want to become a proficient, or great, writer you need to develop a "habit of writing" (Quintilian, 1979, X.iii.2–10 f).

Public relations professionals need to understand the mass media in order to write effectively. When you finish this chapter, walk over to your student union (or wherever your school's newspaper office is located) and introduce yourself to the editor of the student newspaper and the manager of the student radio station (if you have one). Do this in person, not by telephone or e-mail, so you can hone your interpersonal skills while you are at it. If you do not have a newspaper or radio station on campus, find out if your department or college has a Lambda Pi Eta (LPH), or Public Relations Student Society of America (PRSSA) chapter, or publishes a departmental newsletter. If none of these options exist, you should start your own departmental newsletter, or PRSSA/LPH chapter. Additionally, you should start writing letters to your friends and relatives, write letters of praise to your favorite authors, professors, and restaurants, or begin a blog.[4] The point is, you should start writing *more*, and in new and challenging ways—especially on deadline. Writing a few essays for classes each semester is not sufficient to prepare you for the dynamic writing skills needed in public relations. Similarly, sending e-mail messages that are only a few lines long is not very useful either. Many great writers are also voracious letter writers who correspond with friends and colleagues, writing multipage letters every day.

The fact that many of the best public relations professionals began their careers as journalists is not an accident. Writing skills are essential and journalism (print or broadcasting) is one area where students can hone their skills, contribute to their community, receive feedback on their writing, and gain more confidence. One of the universal complaints of public relations managers for many years has been that "students don't know how to write." But asking who is to blame for poor writing skills misses the point. Whether overworked high school teachers, grade inflation, modern writing strategies that emphasize "finding your voice" rather than understanding grammar, or the Internet and video games are to blame is irrelevant. Graduates who can write well are more employable than those with weaker writing skills. Writing is essential.

HOW CAN I BEGIN TO IMPROVE MY WRITING TODAY?

Two of the best ways to improve your writing skills are to write more and to imitate what other writers do (not their words, but their style). As T.S. Eliot is credited with saying: "Good writers borrow, great writers steal." What Eliot was referring to was imitating the style, structure, allusions, and rhetorical tricks used by "great writers." Eliot was not referring to *plagiarism*, or copying the words or ideas of others and trying to pass them off as your own, but of mimicking the style of great writers, of learning from the masters by writing as they write.

Along with writing *more,* you should also begin *reading* more. Develop a habit of reading a national newspaper (like the *Wall Street Journal*) and a local newspaper every day. Consider reading a weekly news magazine like the *Economist* as well (you should be able to find the *Economist* and local/national newspapers in your school library or student union). If you prefer, you can read on line using RSS.[5]

Reading is valuable for three reasons: First, as you read news periodicals you can begin to pay more attention to how professionals actually craft the message that you yourself will create one day. Begin to pay attention to how news writers structure their ideas, what they highlight, and how they structure their language. Second, within a month, you will become a more informed citizen and better able to understand complicated political and world events. Within a year, you will be able to hold your own in a conversation with almost anyone. Third, as a professional, you will engage in environmental scanning on an almost daily basis. In every organization, public relations practitioners need to keep apprised of local and national events. In many cases, understanding *international* events is also necessary. Many professionals begin their day by scanning three to five national newspapers for relevant organizational issues as they drink their morning coffee. You need to develop your own routines or "habits" of reading and writing. Take advantage of every writing opportunity available to you and try to become proficient in as many different styles of writing as you can.

CONCLUSION

This chapter has covered a lot of ground in an effort to get you thinking rhetorically about the practice of public relations writing. Throughout this text you should try to think about public relations writing as a collection of rhetorical strategies designed to facilitate effective communication rather than a bunch of technical skills, such as how to change a tire. As you progress through this text you will discover that many public relations documents (news releases, business letters, memos, and even research papers) follow a very regimented and relatively simplistic set of rules. Making a news release *look* like a news release is really the easy part of writing an effective news release. The harder part of writing a news release, the part that is rhetorical, is learning how to target specific stakeholders. Knowing when *PRNewswire* is preferable to the *Wall Street Journal,* knowing how to draw upon the most appropriate vocabulary to reach your intended audience, knowing how to time your release to achieve optimal success, and knowing when a news release is not going to be as useful as an appearance on the local talk radio station requires rhetorical skill. Writing "five paragraphs with some quotes" (the basic news release model) is like making toast: if you set the toaster correctly, you get toast. But it takes creativity and passion to bake the bread that you toasted. Rhetoric involves understanding the entire process of communication, rather than just a few writing techniques.

ACTIVITIES

1. Create a list of the types of writing that you feel most comfortable with and the kinds of writing that you need more practice with. Identify five ways in which you will work to develop skills in each writing style. Be specific. What courses will you take or could you take? What writing activities might you become involved in (student newspaper or radio, underground newspaper or magazine, starting a blog, writing letters, etc.)? What professional authors' writing style do you find to be the most compelling? If you cannot name any professional writers, what will you do about that?
2. You recently were asked to join Student Media Incorporated (SMI), the board that oversees your campus radio station and newspaper, as a student representative. SMI wants to increase student awareness of the campus radio station. One of its goals is to "significantly increase student listenership of the station by the end of the academic year." (1) Identify three key publics who might be able to help accomplish that goal and explain why each might be able to help. (2) For each public, identify two objectives, three strategies for each objective, and three tactics for each strategy from Table 1.2. (3) Which public is likely to be the most important for increasing student awareness and listenership, and why?
3. Pick three of the definitions of rhetoric from Table 1.2 and explain how each definition fits in with concepts and principles discussed in your introduction to public relations course. Be specific, cite specific page numbers, and include quotations from your introductory textbook.

4. Using the following public relations concepts (Table 1.3): "boundary spanners," "dominant coalition," "organizational counselors," "service oriented," and "two-way communication," identify the people in your department or university who enact these roles. Do not guess, or write something like "the department head, because that's his job ..." Based on your experience in the organization, list which professors are part of the decision-making structure (dominant coalition), and which members of the organizations are most likely to give you valuable "counsel" (not who your advisor is), etc.

5. Identify five (nontrivial) issues (exigencies) that have attracted some debate or discussion on your campus (tuition, parking, a disturbed student, etc.). Note: This does not have to be a campus-wide issue, this could be departmental, or a student senate or student club issue. Next, using the situational model of public relations (in particular, Bitzer), identify the audiences and constraints for each exigence (issue). How do the constraints limit the range of potential solutions to the problem, and what kind of rhetoric is called for based on the exigencies that you identified?

NOTES

1. Sophists were traveling teachers, sort of the communication consultants of their day.
2. As Turney explains, the Gillette amendment is "often described as a ban on government public relations, but that's not what it started out to be. It doesn't prohibit government public relations; it simply said, 'Appropriated funds may not be used to pay a publicity expert unless specifically appropriated for that purpose'" (www.nku.edu/~turney/prclass/govt.htm). Instead of "public relations," governmental communication professionals often have titles like "public information officer," "public information specialist," "public affairs manager," "public affairs officers," "publication specialists," "communication specialists," "community facilitators," "community relations coordinators," "constituent liaisons," and "client relations managers" (op. cit.)
3. Note: Publics are to be contrasted with the mass, or "heap," which is a concept in media, politics, and sociology. In public relations, professionals are rarely interested in "mass publics," meaning all of the citizens in a city, state, or nation. More commonly, in political public relations or issues management, professionals are interested in "the voters likely to support us," or "the undecided voters," rather than "everyone in the community."
4. The important issue is both to write a lot, and to write in many different ways. Blogging is only one type of writing and a type of writing that many professional public relations professionals will not do a lot of. Try to open yourself to as many different types of writing as you can.
5. In Chapter 8, I explain how RSS (Really Simple Syndication) can give you inexpensive access to thousands of news sources.

Chapter 2

The Role of Rhetoric in Communication

For generations, children have been enthralled by Dr. Seuss' stories about Horton, The Grinch, and the Whos in Whoville, not because of anything special about the story content—children love stories about trains, dogs, cats, and mice also—but because of the rhetorical features of the story: assonance, consonance, repetition, cadence, rhythm, and rhyme. Not every children's book is written like Seuss.' However, all children's books tend to draw upon similar rhetorical strategies prized by children and appropriate to the age group in question.

As explained in Chapter 1, rhetoric refers to artful, eloquent, and compelling writing or speaking. Examples of rhetoric include both written and spoken messages: Lincoln's address at Gettysburg, Martin Luther King Junior's "I Have a Dream" speech, Barbara Jordan's 1976 Democratic National Convention keynote address, *The Federalist Papers*, the U.S. Declaration of Independence, an issue advertisement by Shell Oil in the *Wall Street Journal*, a letter to the editor by an organizational spokesperson, a news release, a backgrounder about an organizational leader. Rhetoric is not only used by great speechwriters and politicians, rhetoric is used every day in conversations, in pitch letters sent to reporters and editors, in messages on organizational Web sites, and in persuasive messages, both print and broadcast. Using language well involves understanding an assortment of rhetorical tools: metaphors, cadence, persuasion, logical fallacies, organization, and structure; however, more importantly, understanding rhetoric means understanding ethical communication.

OVERVIEW OF THE RHETORICAL TRADITION

As explained in Chapter 1, rhetoric goes back thousands of years and has been studied by philosophers, priests, poets, propagandists, and professors. The modern age of rhetorical studies began in the 1920s by Herbert Wichelns (1925) with studies of speeches. For the next 50 years, rhetoric was almost exclusively confined to the study of speeches and was generally thought of as the study of persuasion (cf., Black, 1970, 1978; Perelman & Olbrechts-Tyteca, 1968). In a legendary book from the early 70s edited by Lloyd Bitzer and Edwin Black (1971), *The Prospect of Rhetoric: Report of the National Development Project* (also known as the Wingspread Conference), Johnstone wrote: "Rhetoric has two faces, persuasion and argument" (p. 85).

As we moved into the '70s, scholars began to take up issues raised from the Wingspread Conference and talk about the "ideological turn," a dramatic shift in how scholars were talking about rhetoric and criticism (cf., Black, 1970; Rosenfield, 1971; Wander, 1984; Wander & Jenkins, 1972). The ideological shift in rhetoric involved recognizing that rhetoric was not just about the study of great speeches or rhetorical techniques. All language and communication are rhetorical, from accounting ledgers and annual reports to news releases and workplace chit-chat.

Rhetorical theorists began to move away from evaluations of "great speeches"—what was called Neo-Aristotelian or "great man" criticism (cf. Wichelns, 1958)—toward more ideological and eventually postmodern techniques of analysis (Sproule, 1987, 1988, 1989). By the time Wander wrote his groundbreaking essay, "The Third Persona: An Ideological Turn in Rhetorical Criticism" (1984), most critics had already embraced the basic tenants of ideological criticism and the need for more dynamic, robust, and inclusive rhetorical methods (cf., Nelson, Megill, & McCloskey, 1987; Simon 1990).

Something similar to the ideological turn has been taking place in public relations for about 10 years. "A rhetorical turn" has been steadily working its way into the texts in the field (cf., Botan & Hazleton, 2006; Heath & Coombs, 2006; Treadwell & Treadwell, 2000; etc.) as well as into a lot of the research being conducted by scholars from the U.S. and abroad (cf., Botan & Taylor, 2005; Courtright & Smudde, 2007; Ihlen, 2002, 2005; Kent & Taylor, 1998, 2000; Taylor, 2000). Worth noting is the emphasis that has been given to relational approaches to public relations that include dialogic theory, interpersonal theory, intercultural theory, and a number of other rhetorical/critical approaches to examining and making sense of the practice of public relations.

When we talk about using rhetoric to construct messages there are three ways of thinking about it. *The first way of describing rhetoric* includes the classic theories of rhetoric like those advanced by Aristotle. (Later in the text we will talk about Aristotle's "Canon or Rhetoric," ethos, pathos, and logos, and syllogisms and enthymemes). The classic rhetorical principles still have as much value today as they did thousands of years ago. *The second way of describing rhetoric* is by reference to the many rhetorical techniques (metaphors, ideographs, value premises, and logical fallacies). Many rhetorical techniques, like the research on metaphors, come from work conducted in the last century, particularly in the '80s and '90s. *The third way of describing rhetoric* is to talk about rhetorical "theories" that can be used to create more compelling messages and shared values. Narrative theory, symbolic convergence theory, genre theory, and apologia are rhetorical theories that can help you create more compelling messages.

Because rhetoric focused on the study of persuasion for almost 2,000 years, most of the rhetorical concepts and theories you will learn about focus on persuasion. Since so much of a public relations professional's work involves crafting compelling persuasive messages, the rhetorical techniques and theories that you learn about throughout the text should have a lot of obvious applications. As rhetoric and public relations have become more sophisticated over the last 50 years, public relations professionals have become savvier about understanding persuasion, motivation, and rhetorical concepts.

CONSTRUCTING MEANING: SITUATIONAL PUBLICS AND "MANAGING ISSUES"

Before discussing some of the persuasive rhetorical tools that you can use, you should first understand how meaning is constructed and why various messages are created. Individuals and organizations construct messages because of situational constraints and social conventions (Bitzer, 1968). We communicate and respond to issues because we have to. When you are introduced to another person you will often strike up a conversation; when you get into trouble, you apologize; when you want someone to do a favor for you, you ask "nicely"; when someone does not understand something, you explain it; when you receive a gift, you thank the gift giver, and so on. Such responses to what other people do and say arise because situations are rhetorical and call for particular responses.

Organizations function in the same way. The social, political, and economic environments in which organizations operate create demands on organizations to communicate, and to create rhetoric to satisfy public concerns. As explained in Chapter 1, messages are created because something or someone in the environment creates a problem (an *exigence*) that can only be solved by communicating about it with others (*audiences*). What organizations can and cannot say, however, is always governed by *constraints*: your budget, how much time you have, the level of knowledge of the audience, the audience's level of involvement, current or previous media coverage, and, most importantly, your skills as a communicator.

Well-crafted prose, or "rhetoric," does not happen by accident. When you hear a persuasive speech given by a politician, or read a compelling argument made by a CEO in a newspaper's letter to the editor, you are often hearing or reading the work of a public relations professional. Skilled communicators craft memorable and effective messages by understanding language and how to use it well.

These days, much of the writing that public relations professionals produce ends up online. Online content poses a bit of dilemma for situational models of communication because virtually all of the situational approaches to public relations are passive, assuming reactive models of communication. The situational models assume that communication professionals simply wait for problems to happen and then create responses, are unprepared for problems and are then forced to respond, or, as in the case of the Grunig and Hunt (1984) situational model, "problems" are already known or recognized (something has already happened) and public relations professionals simply craft responses and work to shape the behavior and beliefs of audiences.

Although one of the basic premises of online communication is to be able to proactively get out ahead of issues and shape the beliefs, responses, and actions of stakeholders and key publics (cf., Kent & Taylor, 1998, 2002), much of our communication is still reactive since important public issues persist for decades. To move beyond a reactive approach to public relations requires a proactive emphasis on managing issues rather than reacting or responding.

As early as the late 70s, issues management (a branch of public relations management) described how it was better to be proactive rather than reactive (Crable & Vibbert, 1985; Jones & Chases, 1979). As Heath (1990) explains:

> "Issue(s) management isn't quite public relations. Neither is it government relations, nor public affairs, nor lobbying, nor crisis management, nor futurism, nor strategic planning. It embraces all of these disciplines, and maybe a few more"... This observation highlights the diverse staff functions and perspectives unique to issues management. It emphasizes the tactics and values necessary to assist organizations of various kinds, but especially businesses, in their efforts to adjust to and influence public policy. Following this reasoning, one of the best definitions was provided in the report by the Public Relations Society of America Special Committee on Terminology (1987). That report defined issues management as the "systematic identification and action regarding public policy matters of concern to an organization" (p. 9). Issues management involves communicating, issue monitoring, achieving responsibility, and strategic planning. (p. 30; cf. also, Heath, 1996; Jaques, 2007).

What the situational models tell us, (as well as issues management), is that the importance of well-crafted, rhetorical, public relations content should not be ignored. As public relations professionals, you are not just writing a news release or a blog entry, you are positioning your organization or client within a wider world of issues, publics, and constraints. For now, the place to begin is to learn about some of the basic, language-based, rhetorical strategies.

As is true of all rhetoric, there are no "rules," no absolutes. No metaphor is inherently better than any other, and no individual crisis response tactic or figure of speech is better than another. What matters are the situation, audience, and constraints, as Bitzer suggests, and the kind of image or message that your organization is looking to convey.

ETHICAL PRINCIPLES AND CODES OF ETHICAL CONDUCT

One of the criticisms of all academic textbooks is that they place ethics at the end of the book. Because this is a textbook that emphasizes rhetoric, and because ethics plays such a prominent role in rhetoric and public relations, ethical issues are incorporated throughout the text. Probably the most important ethical framework for public relations professionals to be aware of are the various ethical codes developed by national and international professional associations. In the United States, the Public Relations Society of America's (PRSA) code of professional conduct is probably the most well known (see Table 2.1 for a summary of the code).

Hopefully, you learned about the PRSA code of conduct in your introduction to public relations course or are familiar with the code because you are a member of the Public Relations Student Society of America. The code's articles include a number of important issues for writers (in particular, Articles 4, 5, and 9).

Articles 4 and 5 are titled "Accuracy and Truth in Communications" and "Never Make False or Misleading Statements." Telling the truth and being accurate is not done simply because people think telling the truth is good, but because when a professional shares inaccurate information or deceives others, s/he risks damaging the organization's reputation. In the case of inaccurate financial statements, you also risk being sued or jailed for your actions. That effective public relations is premised on accuracy and truth, and that there is a code of ethical conduct suggesting as much, further

TABLE 2.1 The Public Relations Society of America (PRSA) Code of Ethics

Article 1: Always serve the public interest.
Article 2: Act with honesty and integrity.
Article 3: Deal fairly with publics—past, present, and future.
Article 4: Accuracy and truth in communications.
Article 5: No false or misleading statements.
Article 6: No corrupting channels of communication or government.
Article 7: Identify clients publicly.
Article 8: Never use front groups.
Article 9: Never guarantee results (placement).
Article 10: Never represent competing interests.
Article 11: Never be in conflict with clients' interests.
Article 12: Never accept gifts.
Article 13: Safeguard the privacy or past, present, and future clients.
Article 14: Never damage the professional reputation of another public relations practitioner.
Article 15: Report the unethical actions of other practitioners.
Article 16: You are obligated to testify against others.
Article 17: Sever relations with clients who go against this code.

reinforce the fact that the stereotype of public relations professionals as "spin doctors" is just not true.

Article 9, "Never Guarantee Results" refers to public relations professionals guaranteeing organizations or clients that they will "place X number of news releases each month" or "get X number of stories written about the organization each quarter." This clause often stirs a lot of discussion among midlevel public relations professionals, who ask: "What's wrong with guaranteeing that I will place five news releases per month? I have been working in industry X for a long time and I could easily place that many news releases ...." The problem here, addressed by this clause, is that as organizational representatives, your job is to do your best to represent your organization, clients, and stakeholders, and not to "make your quota" (a personal objective). As a service-oriented profession, public relations professionals, even new technicians whose only job is to write, have an obligation to serve the client's interests at all times.

Never guarantee to do anything, even if you think you could, if it means that you might be required to act in your own interest rather than the client's. When messages are sent out just to fill a quota, there will be a tendency to send organizational content to media sources and clients who "might" have an interest, rather than those who "do." Always place your clients and stakeholders first.

GOING BEYOND CODES OF ETHICS

Applying rhetorical principles to public relations goes beyond mere codes. The ethical professional behaves ethically not because s/he is compelled to but because ethical behavior is the right thing to do. Often, politicians, managers, and organizational leaders choose courses of action that are on dubious moral/ethical grounds. One major problem with acting ethically is that not everyone agrees on what is ethical. Consider the actions of President George W. Bush following the September 11, 2001, attacks on the World Trade Center: the passage of Patriot Act USA legislation allowing no-warrant wire tapping, formation of the Department of Homeland Security, extensive internal spying on U.S. citizens suspected of terrorism, the creation of the Guantánamo detention center, repeated torture of detainees. George Bush, Dick Cheney, Condoleezza Rice, and many others from the Bush White House all insist that their actions were justified. Many Americans did not agree. On a less dramatic scale, consider the decision of the former chairwoman of Hewlett Packard, Patricia Dunn, to bug her boardroom and spy on her board of directors. Although everyone believes what Dunn did was wrong, millions of Americans still believe that Bush's more serious actions were warranted. From an ethical standpoint, there is no way of *proving* whether President Bush and Vice President Cheney were right or wrong; however, in general, ethical decision making can be improved by avoiding something called "Groupthink."

Janis, Groupthink

As communication experts and "organizational counselors," the job of public relations professionals includes ensuring that the best decisions are made. One of the major reasons behind poor decision making is "Groupthink."

The theory of Groupthink was developed in the '70s by Irving Janis (1982) to help explain how small groups of experts and professionals could make bad decisions. Groupthink has been applied to Kennedy's "Bay of Pigs" disaster, the Nazi regime, and dozens of other important and consequential decisions. Groupthink explains why highly cohesive groups—whether experts or novices—make bad decisions. The essence of groupthink has to do with the fact that highly cohesive groups are often closed-minded and fail to ask enough questions. Groupthink is a rhetorical process in that it assumes that no one can know everything, and that questioning ideas leads to better ideas and decisions.

SYMPTOMS OF GROUPTHINK

Type I: Overestimations of the group—its power and morality

1. An illusion of invulnerability, shared by most or all the members, which creates excessive optimism and encourages taking extreme risks.
2. An unquestioned belief in the group's inherent morality, inclining members to ignore the ethical or moral consequences of their decisions.

Type II: Closed-mindedness

1. Collective efforts to rationalize in order to discount warnings or other information that might lead the members to reconsider their assumptions before they recommit themselves to their past policy decisions.
2. Stereotyped views of enemy leaders as too evil to warrant genuine attempts to negotiate, or as too weak and stupid to counter whatever risky attempts are made to defeat their purposes.

Type III: Pressures toward uniformity

1. Self-censorship of deviations from the apparent group consensus, reflecting each member's inclination to minimize to himself the importance of his doubts and counterarguments.
2. A shared illusion of unanimity concerning judgments conforming to the majority view (party resulting from self-censorship of deviations, augmented by the false assumption that silence means consent).
3. Direct pressure on any member who expresses strong arguments against any of the group's stereotypes, illusions, or commitments, making clear that this type of dissent is contrary to what is expected of all loyal members.
4. The emergence of self-appointed mindguards—members who protect the group from adverse information that might shatter their shared complacency about the effectiveness and morality of their decisions.

Antecedent conditions (can be ascertained ahead of time to indicate the potential for faulty decision making)

1. Insulation of the policy-making group.
2. A lack of a tradition of impartial leadership.
3. A lack of norms requiring methodical procedures for dealing with decision-making tasks.

Symptoms of defective decision making

1. Incomplete survey of alternatives.
2. Incomplete survey of objectives.
3. Failure to examine risks of preferred choice.
4. Failure to reappraise initially rejected alternatives.
5. Poor information search.
6. Selective bias in processing information at hand.
7. Failure to work out contingency plans.

Ruling out groupthink

1. Who made the policy decisions? Was it essentially the leader alone or did group members participate to a significant degree? If the members participated, were they in a cohesive group?
2. To what extent was the policy a result of defective decision-making procedures on the part of those who were responsible?
3. Can symptoms of groupthink be discerned in the group's deliberations? (Do the prime symptoms pervade the planning discussions?)

4. Were the conditions that foster the groupthink syndrome present? (Janis, 1982, chapter 8)

As organizational counselors, one of the ways that public relations professionals help ensure ethical decision making is by serving as a "central negative" in small group theory, or the person who questions all decisions. As groupthink proves, questioning decisions is difficult; leaders do not like to be asked to justify their actions and other group members usually do not want to force leaders to justify them, either.

As communication professionals, you should know that being argumentative (what the "central negative" often does) is sometimes not the best strategy. Rather, what you want to do is make it your responsibility to ensure that decisions are properly vetted, that outside experts are consulted, and that a range of possible solutions are considered when making decisions. One of the best ways to achieve a thorough decision-making structure is to work to reform the organizational decision-making procedures over time. Every decision cannot be questioned, or else organizational morale would suffer and decision making would slow to a crawl. However, by creating organizational structures for the process, better decisions can be made.

Classic Ethical Models: Letting Your Decisions Be Guided by What Is Right

Perhaps the most difficult thing that a young public relations professional has to learn is how to speak the truth to power. Doing what your boss wants is easy. Convincing your boss that what s/he wants to do is a bad idea is a lot harder. One of the key things that you need to do as a professional is to decide what right and wrong are (cf., Bowen, 2004). Study after study of public relations professionals often arrive at the conclusion that public relations professionals believe in "situational ethics." However, situational ethics do not mean that someone believes that "everything is cool." Rather, situationalists believe that situational factors have to be taken into account when making decisions. Such a position is entirely consistent with rhetorical theory as well as a number of other theories, including deontology, communitarianism, utilitarianism, and dialogue (see Table 2.2).

Often, people think of ethics in absolutist terms: "good and bad," "right and wrong." Few things are as difficult to figure out as how to decide right from wrong. For example, virtually every student agrees, "Cheating is wrong." And yet, research by educational associations like the American Association of University Professors (AAUP), the United Federation

TABLE 2.2 Ethical Positions

Absolutist: Apply universal, constant, standards that remain unchanged regardless of situations. Examples include equity, "fairness," freedom of choice, the Golden Rule, innocent until proven guilty, justice for all, professionalism, the Ten Commandments, etc. Absolutists have often formed their opinions before crises happen. Many ethical positions are absolutist, such as utilitarianism, which holds the greatest good for the greatest number regardless of the consequences.

Categorical imperative: Your actions should be universally applicable: treat people as ends, and not means to ends. The categorical imperative is not about doing what people like; rather, it is about doing what is "right." We do not litter because if everyone littered, we would have a dirty and unsanitary world. We do not speed because if everyone sped the roads would be unsafe. The categorical imperative is about personal restraint for the good of society. It cannot be used to arrive at the assumption that "one should not look at pornography because if everyone looked at pornography ..." because there is no universally agreed upon social conduct in such matters; however, on issues such as pedophilia, child/wife/animal abuse, etc., the categorical imperative would apply.

Communitarianism: The "Communitarian movement ... is an environmental movement dedicated to the betterment of our moral, social, and political environment ... Communitarians are dedicated to working with their fellow citizens to bring about the changes in values, habits, and public policies that will allow us to do for society what the environmental movement seeks to do for nature: to safeguard and enhance our lives" (Etzioni, 1993, pp. 2–3). Communitarianism refers to the "rejection of the liberal notion of an isolated self with rights, interests, values, and ends independent of social context" (Weiss, 1993, p. 125 f), and instead suggests that people have duties and responsibilities as citizens. Communitarianism is similar to deontology, dialogue, and feminism.

Deontology, or duty: Acting on a set of beliefs about right and wrong no matter what the consequences are. Deontologists are usually unwilling to compromise (satisfice), and often ignore situational factors when making decisions.

(continued)

TABLE 2.2 ***Continued***

Dialogue: A dialogic perspective focuses on the attitudes toward others held by the participants in a communication exchange. People should be treated with respect and not as "others." "Unconditional positive regard for others" is often used to describe the perspective. You believe that everyone involved in an issue is important, and has a unique perspective that should be valued. Note: As a participant in dialogue, you have your own perspective, but you have an obligation to advocate for it in moderation and not at the expense of others.

"Golden Mean"; "satisficing"; compromise between interested parties. You believe in making everyone a little happy. Or, alternatively, not making everyone too unhappy.

Reciprocity, also called the "Golden Rule": A philosophy for leading one's life that suggests that if you personally would not like something done to you, then you cannot impose that fate on others. Examples illustrating the ubiquity of the Golden Rule include:

Hindu: This is the sum of duty; do naught unto others which if done to thee would cause thee pain.

Zoroastrian: That nature alone is good which refrains from doing unto another whatsoever is not good for itself.

Taoist: Regard your neighbor's gain as your own gain, and your neighbor's loss as your own loss.

Buddhist: Hurt not others in ways that you would find hurtful.

Confucian: Do not unto others what you would not have them do unto you.

Jain: In happiness and suffering, in joy and grief, we should regard all creatures as we regard our own self.

Jewish: Whatever thou hatest thyself, that do not to another.

Christian: All things whatsoever ye would that men should do to you, do ye even so to them.

Islamic: No one of you is a believer until he desires for his brother that which he desires for himself.

Sikh: As thou deemest thyself, so deem others.

(NB: Wikipedia has a useful summary of some of the positions of reciprocity and the Golden Rule, but a Web search with quotation marks will locate 1.5 million pages in this en.wikipedia.org/wiki/Ethic_of_reciprocity).

Situational: Holds that the current circumstances or situation should be used as a basis for making choices about right and wrong. True situational ethics downplay other factors influencing our decision making, such as religion, cultural values, the audience, and often rationalize "right and wrong" as what is "good or bad" for the individual(s) involved at a particular time—consider Enron, Bill Gates, Martha Stewart, etc., all of whom knew that what they were doing was wrong, but still did it, making up mental justification (cognitive dissonance) as they went along.

Utilitarianism: The greatest good for the greatest number. You strive to do what is best for most people. This does not mean *everyone*, but rather, the *greatest number* of people. You must not make decisions based on what you want. You must try to decide what is best for everyone. Major critiques of utilitarianism include, "Who decides what is best?" "What is the time frame involved, months, years, decades?" "How do you calculate what is the greatest good?"

of Teachers (UFT), the American Federation of Teachers (AFT), and the National Education Association (NEA), suggest that more than half (50 to 80 percent) of all students cheat during their college careers, with rates on plagiarized material in class essays exceeding 50 percent (www.aaup.org/AAUP/pubsres/academe/2002/JF/Feat/mcca.htm).

The salient ethical issue is not what is "right," which is often easy to identify, but how to act on what is right. In the professional workplace, both subtle and overt ethical issues arise including moral issues: favoritism, discrimination, sexual harassment; and legal and financial issues: being asked to write a false news release, being asked to delay the reporting of bad news, ignoring reports of product flaws/risks, etc. Often, individual public relations professionals do not have the ability to rectify ethical lapses on their own. The ethical codes mentioned in Table 2.2 describe an assortment of "absolutist" positions: acting on duty (deontology), acting for the greatest good (utilitarianism), and valuing all stakeholders/stakeseekers (dialogue); however, what they do not tell you is how to enact the principles. The golden rule and the categorical imperative sound easy: "Do unto others ...." However, what do you do when others are not doing unto you?

Ultimately there are no easy answers. What can be taken as a universal truth is that ethical issues need to be resolved through communication. Learning how to ask questions in rhetorically sensitive ways, to use communication to facilitate dialogue or discussion, to use communication to bring issues to light, and to use rhetoric interpersonally to resolve issues are skills that take years to hone. Do not think of ethics as an afterthought. Try to learn to integrate ethics into every message that you create and every conversation in which you engage. The dialogic approach to public relations ethics (see Chapter 10) says you should have "unconditional positive regard for the other," a difficult but obtainable standard.

ETHICS AND AUDIENCE ADAPTATION

As Peter Parker's (Spiderman) Uncle Ben told him, "With great power comes great responsibility." The same is true of rhetoric. Skilled communicators can both enlighten and deceive. Twenty-five hundred years ago, the philosopher Socrates was said to argue that rhetoric was a "knack" like "cookery," and that the sole purpose of rhetoric was to flatter the audience. Plato portrays Socrates' sentiments in the *Gorgias*:

> SOCRATES: In my opinion then, Gorgias, the whole of which rhetoric is a part is not an art at all, but the habit of a bold and ready wit, which knows how to manage mankind: this habit I sum up under the word "flattery"; and it appears to me to have many other parts, one of which is cookery, which may seem to be an art, but, as I maintain, is only an experience or routine and not an art. (Plato, 1999a, ¶249).

In many ways Socrates was correct: a lot of what passes as public relations today is just flattery. At the 2009 International Communication Association conference in Chicago, on a panel devoted to exploring reputational issues involved in international public relations, one division officer argued that the name of public relations departments should be changed to "publicity," to be consistent with what many public relations professionals do.

Socrates' real concern, as in public relations, was with the truth and welfare of society. To many, suggesting that public relations should serve the public interest may sound strange, but the fact remains that rhetoric constructs and is constructed by society. We help create the world that others live in.

Our understanding of the world is socially constructed, and public relations writers play a role in constructing the visions of society that we see depicted in the news and by organizations. As organizational counselors, our role is often to act as the conscience of organizations. Additionally, practitioners themselves must occasionally persuade managers and stakeholders that their actions might reflect poorly on the organization as well as violate the social contract, public trust, and goodwill that are held by organizations.

Later in Plato's text, Socrates concludes that it is better to suffer injustice than to cause it. Most professionals are in agreement with Plato and Socrates on this point. The many ethical codes that exist in public relations attest to the role of the public relations practitioner as a bulwark against injustice and unethical behavior. You will play a very important role as an organizational counselor. And, although all citizens *should* question what they read and see (Postman & Weingartner, 1969), most people are too busy living their lives to question anything. As representatives of both organizations and the public good, you have an obligation to uphold the standards of ethical conduct that guide the practice of public relations.

As mentioned previously, public relations is about audience adaptation. In the *Gorgias*, Socrates objects to rhetoric being used for base or opportunistic purposes, but not to rhetoric itself, which is a powerful tool. Indeed, Socrates eventually acknowledges that rhetoric plays an important role in public life.

As an organizational representative, you will be expected to communicate with an assortment of publics. What you say to them should not be pandering or "mere cookery" but thoughtful, honest, and compelling. Organizations that lie to the public risk damaging their reputations and losing public trust. The essence of all good persuasion is self-persuasion by the audience. Ultimately, people can only be convinced by what *they* trust and *they believe* to be credible. Thus, when creating messages, you must always remember for whom you write: the public. You may work for an organization but you write for your employer's publics. Different publics have different expectations for organizations, and internal publics have different expectations than external publics, or the media.

Internal audiences have a different level of knowledge and trust in the organization than external audiences typically have. Additionally, the tactics that can be used with internal and external audiences differ. Even with very large organizations, the possibility exists to meet with organizational members face-to-face and communicate more intimately, or dialogically.

A similar situation exists with the media. Although the media, like an internal public, can be communicated with directly and more intimately, the media serve their own interests and publics, often mass publics. When constructing messages for the media you will need to remember that you are not creating messages for the media representatives themselves, the men or women with whom you might have a relationship, but for the *media's publics*, or the individuals whom they represent and whom you are trying to reach.

The media's relationship with their publics is not the same as your relationship with them, because the media's role is different. You will have no success taking a paternalistic stance with the media and lecturing them about what is best for *their* publics. Ultimately, you must understand that the media are a public unto themselves and have tremendous power over your ability to reach your own external publics. Relationships with the media must be nurtured, and you need to develop a solid understanding of what the media do and how they see the world if you hope to be successful with them.

As I emphasized Chapter 1, your messages must be carefully crafted to reach publics on their own level. Your vocabulary should match the vocabulary used by the public you are trying to reach. Your messages must be placed in locations or in media sources where the intended audience will encounter them. Your arguments must draw upon the heroes, villains, icons, and images that target publics identify with.

If, for example, "Made in USA" happens to be a point of pride for your organization and your intended public, mention it whenever you can. However, do not use rhetoric and cultural icons to deceive publics. Placing an American flag on a product to make people think that the product was "Made in America" is unethical If your product is made in China, or even Germany, do not try to trick your customers or clients. As the PRSA code of ethics suggests, do not corrupt the channels of information.

Consider for example the Cuisinart company. Cuisinart advertises itself on its packages as "An American Company" in big letters with an American flag. Unfortunately, Cuisinart's products are manufactured in China. The "An American Company" tagline is added not because some people said "Cuisinart? Is that some foreign company?" but because the company knows that many Americans prefer to buy U.S. products. Socrates held that communicators should not sacrifice their own values, deceptively pretending to hold an audience's beliefs, just to pander to the audience. Professional communicators need to find symbols that resonate with the intended public and that also do not conflict with your organization's own values. Ultimately, individuals are persuaded by what moves *them* and not by what moves *you*. As an organizational communicator, you must constantly monitor the environment, conduct research, and work to understand your publics and audiences. Burke provides an excellent explanation of what it means to adapt to an audience:

> It is not hard to imagine that if a grasshopper could speak he would be much more readily interested in what you had to tell him about "Birds That Eat Grasshoppers" than a more scholarly and better presented talk on "Mating Habits of the Australian Auk." The factor of *interest* play a large part in the business of communication ... A philosopher, if he has a toothache, is more likely to be interested in dentistry than in mathematical symbolism .... The dullest sentences exchanged between young lovers or between employee and employer, may be vibrant, whereas the results of many years' effort and engrossment may seem insipid. We interest a man by dealing with his interests. (1984, p. 37, Burke's emphasis).

For public relations professionals, as professional communicators, rhetoric should be a tool for constructing compelling and moving messages, not a tool of deception. Effective professionals are *more able* to reach their target audiences with their messages, and should be *less likely* to try and deceive stakeholders and stakeseekers.

WRITING VALUE STATEMENTS

Since so much of this chapter has focused on using language rhetorically, and integrating ethics into everyday public relations practices, instructions for how to create mission and vision statements only make sense here. Most major corporations, educational institutions, health-care organizations, and many smaller and midsized organizations are guided by mission and vision statements, or in some cases "credos" or ethics statements. Mission and value statements are intended to guide organizational members and help them make ethical decisions that will benefit the organization. Many organizations actually post their mission and value statements (sometimes called credos) in prominent public locations to remind organizational members about core organizational values, and to encourage people to make the right decisions. The Rotary Club's famous "Four-Way Test," placed on signs, pens, and organizational documents, is one example of this practice:

1. Is it the TRUTH?
2. Is it FAIR to all concerned?
3. Will it build GOODWILL and BETTER FRIENDSHIPS?
4. Will it be BENEFICIAL to all concerned? (www.rotary.org/en/aboutus/rotaryinternational/GuidingPrinciples/Pages/ridefault.aspx)

Mission Statements

Writing mission and vision statements is one of the more challenging forms of public relations writing. A **mission statement** refers to descriptive statements about what an organization does or tries to do, its unique purpose. As Heath & Coombs explain, "mission statements should translate into objectives" that can be "empirically assessed" (2006, p. 153). Mission statements are usually developed early in an organization's existence, or early in the planning stage of program or services-based activities. Mission statements are reviewed once every 10 years or so. A review of mission statements is followed by a review of the long-term objectives of the organization (the vision statement).

Mission statements vary from lengthy, prose-rich descriptions of an organization's objectives to bullet statements alluding to certain features of an organization's objectives. Consider the mission statement of PETA, which describes what the organization does rather than what it believes in:

> People for the Ethical Treatment of Animals (PETA), with more than 2 million members and supporters, is the largest animal rights organization in the world.
>
> PETA focuses its attention on the four areas in which the largest numbers of animals suffer the most intensely for the longest periods of time: on factory farms, in laboratories, in the clothing trade, and in the entertainment industry. We also work on a variety of other issues, including the cruel killing of beavers, birds and other "pests," and the abuse of backyard dogs.
>
> PETA works through public education, cruelty investigations, research, animal rescue, legislation, special events, celebrity involvement, and protest campaigns. (www.peta.org/about)

Similar to PETA, consider the mission statement of the First Marine Expeditionary force, which also describes what it does:

> When directed, I MEF deploys and is employed as a Marine Air Ground Task Force (MAGTF) in support of Combatant Commander (COCOM) requirements for contingency response or Major Theater War; with appropriate augmentation, serves as the core element of a Joint Task Force (JTF); prepares and deploys combat ready MAGTF's to support COCOM presence and crisis response; and supports service and COCOM initiatives as required. (www.imef.usmc.mil/missionstatement.asp)

By contrast, consider the mission statement of Billboard Magazine, which is written more like promotional advertising copy rather than a set of objectives:

> In print and online, through face-to-face events and licensing partnerships, **Billboard** entertains and informs, drives markets, influences decisions, platforms debate, builds community and captures the emotional power of music and entertainment for professionals and fans alike.
>
> **Billboard** is the first name to trust in timely news, expert analysis, trends and proprietary charts for the global music, video and digital entertainment business.
>
> **Billboard's** expert journalists, analysts and event producers around the globe investigate the business of today with an eye towards tomorrow.

> **Billboard's** proprietary charts provide the ultimate measure of success in music, radio, touring, video, digital and mobile commerce.
>
> **When you go to market in music, video, digital entertainment and media, think Billboard first.** (www.billboard.com/images/pdf/content06.pdf, Billboard's emphasis)

Consider the mission statements of Edelman Public Relations, filled with buzz words and jargon, and Maverick Public Relations, that reads like it was actually written by someone from advertising.

> EDELMAN
>
> To provide public relations counsel and strategic communications services that enable our clients to build strong relationships and to influence attitudes and behaviors in a complex world.
>
> We undertake our mission through convergence by integrating specialist knowledge of practices and industries, local market understanding, proprietary methodology and breakthrough creativity.
>
> We are dedicated to building long-term, rewarding partnerships that add value to our clients and our people.
>
> Our clients are leaders in their fields who are initiating change and seeking new solutions. (www.edelman.com/about_us/mission)
>
> MAVERICK
>
> MAVERICK is an award-winning group of PR professionals with a long and successful track record in the communications business. Our talented, passionate team blends the art and strategy of public relations to create and execute highly creative campaigns.
>
> We currently work with a diverse client base from those in packaged goods to esoteric technology. We've launched hundreds of products, developed brand eminence programs and helped our clients spread their news. **In short, we move products, we build brands we develop, enhance and reinforce corporate reputations.** Our clients rely on MAVERICK to help cut through the media clutter and sharpen their image. Harnessing fresh thinking and extensive media relationships across North America, MAVERICK's seasoned communications professionals create campaigns and strategies that matter to prospective customers, media and key stakeholders.
>
> At the end of the day, sustaining the strength of our clients [sic] reputation is our reward. That's only part of the MAVERICK difference.
>
> If you are looking to partner with a PR firm fully committed to driving your business and communications objectives look no further. Call us or make an appointment to visit our offices and meet our people. We're sure once inside the MAVERICK walls you'll know we're a distinctly different kind of agency. (2009, www.maverickpr.com, login required, Maverick's emphasis)

Finally, consider Villanova University's 659-word mission statement which resembles mission statements of other educational institutions:

> Villanova University is an independent coeducational institute of higher learning founded by the Augustinian Order of the Roman Catholic Church. The University is a community of persons of diverse professional, academic, and personal interests who in a spirit of collegiality cooperate to achieve their common goals and objectives in the transmission, the pursuit, and the discovery of knowledge. This community serves society by developing and sustaining an academic environment in which the potentialities of its members may be realized. Villanova is committed to those same high goals and standards of academic integrity and excellence as well as personal and corporate achievement that characterize all worthy institutions of higher learning.... (consortium.villanova.edu/mstatements/villanova_mission.html)

Mission statements set the tone of an organization, establish its character, and define the parameters of its activities. As you can see from the examples above, mission statements may be long, philosophical commentaries on the nature of the organization, or may consist of one or two key paragraphs describing what the organization does. Many mission statements are preceded or followed by longer descriptive statements elaborating on the mission.

Boilerplate Statements

Because mission and descriptive statements are sometimes long, uninteresting, and sophisticated, organizations often write an "identifying statement" (a boilerplate paragraph) to be used in external communication and to accompany organizational documents. Boilerplate paragraphs are found at the bottom of every news release, integrated into fact sheets and annual reports, and placed on home pages.

Boilerplate statements are typically about a paragraph long—60 to 100 words—and are written to be long-lasting. Rather than writing, "Company X employs 2,341 people ..." you would write: "Company X has more than 2,000 employees ...." Boilerplate paragraphs often mention when an organization was founded and where the organization's headquarters is located, as well as making reference to the size of the organization in terms of locations and revenue. As you will see from the examples below, boilerplate paragraphs very widely.

> **COVANCE**
>
> Covance, with headquarters in Princeton, New Jersey, is one of the world's largest and most comprehensive drug development services companies, with annual revenues greater than $1.7 billion, global operations in more than 25 countries, and more than 9,600 employees worldwide. Information on Covance's products and services, recent press releases, and SEC filings can be obtained through its web site at www.covance.com (media.corporate-ir.net/media_files/irol/10/105891/2008Covance_annualreport.pdf).
>
> **MONTCLAIR STATE UNIVERSITY**
>
> The Communication Studies Department offers a professional degree with emphasis on research, writing, oral presentation, and visual communication. Communication Studies allows students to apply communication concepts to almost any area of interest offering great flexibility and practical training. Communication Studies graduates typically secure jobs in public relations, marketing, advertising, human resource management, sales, organizational communication, the broadcast media, and a variety of other communication related careers (news releases, MSU, M. L. Kent, 2004).
>
> **APPLE COMPUTERS**
>
> Apple ignited the personal computer revolution in the 1970s with the Apple II and reinvented the personal computer in the 1980s with the Macintosh. Today, Apple continues to lead the industry in innovation with its award-winning computers, OS X operating system and iLife and professional applications. Apple is also spearheading the digital media revolution with its iPod portable music and video players and iTunes online store, and has entered the mobile phone market with its revolutionary iPhone. (June 8, 2009, PRNewswire.com)
>
> **FANDANGO**
>
> One of the Web's top movie and entertainment destinations, Fandango sells tickets to more than 16,000 screens. Fandango entertains and informs consumers with reviews, commentary and trailers, and offers the ability to quickly select a film, plan where and when to see it, and conveniently buy tickets in advance. Fandango is available at www.fandango.com, 1-800-FANDANGO and via your wireless mobile device at mobile.fandango.com. Fandango is a unit of Comcast Interactive Media. (June 8, 2009, PRNewswire.com)

Writing a compelling boilerplate paragraph takes a lot of time. Consider Apple's paragraph and the emphasis on the Apple II, and iLife, rather than introducing the first mouse-based computer interface, the iPhone, or its ultra lightweight and wafer-thin laptop computers. Thousands of samples of boilerplate paragraphs can be found on the PRNewswire.com Web site.

Vision Statements

A **vision statement** is a statement about how an organization will accomplish its mission—what guides the mission statement (Heath & Coombs, 2006, p. 153). Vision statements include statements of where an organization wants to be at predetermined times in the future and may include specific time frames or may be more general.

Not every organization writes both mission and vision statements. Many organizations roll both statements into one "goal statement," or call their mission and vision statement by different names. No matter how the statements are used, vision statements are about the future and how the organization hopes to get there. Vision statements are similar to "strategies" (Chapter 1). For example, Milwaukee Public Television "educates, informs, entertains, and stimulates" and "encourages people," Harley-Davidson "fulfills dreams" and provides "extraordinary customer experiences," while the Marines remain "highly responsive" and "innovative in mindset." By contrast, such **puffery** (exaggerated or unsupported claims, superlatives) is not found in boilerplate statements or in most mission statements. Consider the following vision statements for ideas about how to write them:

> **MILWAUKEE PUBLIC TELEVISION**
>
> Milwaukee Public Television educates, informs, entertains, and stimulates the imagination of adults and children alike. We make the best use of noncommercial media and related services to enhance the quality of life in our community by encouraging people to consider issues and explore ideas, and by inspiring a continued sense of wonderment. MPTV Friends promotes and generates community support for MPTV (www.mptv.org/insidemptv/visionstatement.php).
>
> **HARLEY-DAVIDSON INC.**
>
> Harley-Davidson, Inc. is a global leader in fulfilling dreams and providing extraordinary customer experiences through mutually beneficial relationships with our stakeholders. (www.harleydavidson.com/wcm/Content/Pages/Student_Center/student_center.jsp?locale=en_US# vision)
>
> **UNITED STATES MARINE CORP.**
>
> The Marine Corps of 2025 will fight and win our Nation's battles with multicapable MAGTFs, either from the sea or in sustained operations ashore. Our unique role as the Nation's force in readiness, along with our values, enduring ethos, and core competencies, will ensure we remain highly responsive to the needs of combatant commanders in an uncertain environment and against irregular threats. Our future Corps will be increasingly reliant on naval deployment, preventative in approach, leaner in equipment, versatile in capabilities, and innovative in mindset. In an evolving and complex world, we will excel as the Nation's expeditionary "force of choice." (www. marines.mil/units/hqmc/cmc/Documents/MCVS2025%2030%20June.pdf)

MEMO WRITING

Although mission and vision statements are written very rarely, memos are one of the most common forms of internal communication documents. I could discuss memos almost anywhere in this book since they are so common, but I am describing them here early on so that you can get some practice writing memos. Occasionally, "memos" are written for external stakeholders and publics but generally, memos are written for one's colleagues. The memo is a standard business document that you will both write and receive in great abundance.

Memos have a very distinctive look and are very different than business letters (Chapter 6). To begin with, memos often have the word "Memo" in big letters at the top. Since memos are "internal" documents, the formal address found on business letters is unnecessary. Memo headers usually include four lines: the date, "To: … ," "From: … ," and "Re: …" (regarding).

Memos are sometimes (but not always) more conversational than a business letter, and often use organizational slang and technojargon since they are intended for internal audiences familiar with insider terminology. Both memos and business letters should be written "professionally." Do not use colloquial language, contractions, or acronyms/abbreviations just because they are easier to type. Since memos are often short, take the time to be clear.

Memos are single-spaced documents and follow most of the rules for how to structure business letters. Major differences include:

- Memos *often* include numbered or bulleted lists to make important content stand out and easier to locate in the future.
- Since memos are internal documents, the sender and receiver are already acquainted, or at least know of each other. Thus, memos are not signed, nor do they end with a "sincerely" and a name and title at the bottom. Instead,

initial a memo at the top, to the right of your name to indicate that you have proofread the memo and agree with its content.
- Because of time constraints, memos are often not edited by others. With many memos you do not have the luxury of a proofread by a colleague; thus, you must proofread and edit them very carefully yourself.

Never assume that a memo will remain "internal," and never write anything in a memo that you would not like to see admitted into evidence in a court of law. Memos have a bad habit off getting saved by people when they know that they are involved in questionable or unethical activities. Better yet, never let anything illegal or unethical happen at your organization by monitoring managerial activities and serving as an organizational counselor (see Tables 2.3 and 2.4)

FIGURES OF SPEECH

Up to now, the focus of this chapter has been on ethical issues and the way that professional communicators make decisions. After ethical issues concerning *whether* to communicate and *how* to communicate most effectively have been decided, come issues of how to convey our messages to diverse publics, of language use.

Historically, skilled communicators have quoted memorable passages from movies, books, and television commercials to create compelling messages. Indeed, many of the early philosophers, religious leaders, and politicians, such as Aristotle, St. Augustine, Caesar, and Cicero, were trained in the use of rhetoric, which is why they were able to create such enduring messages. Today, speakers are more likely to quote Arnold Schwarzenegger, Bill Gates, Donald Trump, Oprah Winfrey, or a Wendy's commercial, because of his or her (or the company's) notoriety, but the rhetorical technique is still the same: to build credibility (*ethos*), to foster identification, and to invoke the words of well-known people with cultural references that audiences will recognize.

As mentioned in Chapter 1, T.S. Eliot wrote: "Good writers borrow, great writers steal." The reason that classic texts, music, and movies are so useful to writers is not because they are divinely inspired, but because the authors used something that everyone knew well. One hundred years ago in the United States, passages from the Bible were as well known as the latest catchphrase from television are today. Before television and radio, people read books and poetry and attended public lectures and political events for entertainment (Postman, 1984). Now, Americans have access to *more information* than ever before: cable television, satellite radio, the Internet, but the publics' storehouse of *shared* knowledge is considerably smaller. Being able to draw upon the words of someone well known or respected by an audience allows a communicator to make a more intimate connection with the audience.

One of the ways that professional writers and speakers (or rhetoricians) create memorable messages is by drawing upon figures of speech. A figure of speech is simply a rhetorical (or language) strategy. There are dozens of figures of speech; I will only cover a few here. Work to familiarize yourself with a few figures of speech at a time and begin introducing them into your writing to create more compelling messages (see Table 2.5).

Asyndeton

Asyndeton is the omission of a conjunction. Caesar's famous line, "I came, I saw, I conquered" (*Veni, vidi, vici* in Latin), is an example of asyndeton (and also alliteration). Although Caesar's statement is not linguistically correct in English, the missing conjunction serves to express his actions more forcefully, more rapidly. One of the most eloquent and famous uses of asyndeton was by John F. Kennedy in his famous inaugural message: "We shall pay any price, bear any burden, meet any hardships, support any friend, oppose any foe to assure the survival and the success of liberty." Although your high school literature teacher might have objected to Kennedy's missing "and" before the last clause, when used in a speech, asyndeton is compelling.

Asyndeton can also be used in feature writing, manuals, brochures, and an assortment of other documents. Indeed, I use asyndeton throughout the book; watch for it as you read. When used well, asyndeton does not draw attention to itself but increases a message's flow and helps with cadence. Although asyndeton is not useful everywhere, such as news releases, where sentences are short and lists uncommon, asyndeton would be perfect in historical or biographical documents, reports, or feature stories in newsletters.

Metaphor

Metaphors are part of our everyday language. When you say, "my dogs are barking" to refer to your sore feet, or "today has been a nightmare" to talk about a bad day, you are using a metaphor. Metaphor is a tool for perspective or comparison and helps structure the way that we think about the world (Held, 1987; Kent, 2001b; Lakoff & Johnson, 1980; Reddy, 1979). The purpose of a metaphor is twofold: metaphors are pleasant, evocative, and eloquent. Metaphors also serve to simplify complicated issues and concepts. Metaphors use words and concepts that people already know to help explain other words, concepts, and relationships that may not be so well known. In a metaphor, a word or phrase that ordinarily designates one thing is used to describe something else, thus making an implicit comparison, as in "a sea of troubles." Metaphors can be woven into extended analogies or used as short comparative tools. Many of the aphorisms that we were taught as children are also metaphors: "Strike while the iron is hot," "Even a blind pig finds an acorn sometimes," "If this works out we'll be settin' in tall cotton," etc. (for excellent discussions of metaphors, see Burke, 1969a, pp. 503–517, 1973b, 293–304; Lakoff & Johnson, 1980; Ortony, 1979; White, 1973, pp. 31–38).

The most well-known metaphor these days might be the World Wide Web. The name "Web" was coined in the early days of the Internet and was intended to help describe how the system functioned to link computers together into a "web." However, "the Web" now qualifies as a "dead metaphor" because the phrase has become so commonplace that its original meaning has been lost, much like "table leg" and "armchair" have lost their original, metaphorical, meanings.

Well-crafted and fresh metaphors can serve a very useful purpose, especially when trying to

TABLE 2.3 Sample Memos

Office of the Senior Vice President and Provost
The University of Oklahoma
Norman Campus

MEMORANDUM

TO: Deans, Directors, and Chairs

FROM: Nancy L. Mergler, Senior Vice President and Provost

DATE: October 30, 2008

SUBJECT: Conflicts of Financial Interest Report Form

As in previous years, most faculty and certain staff members in Provost areas are asked to complete and return a conflict-of-interest report form. Please forward this message to all faculty and to appropriate staff in your unit, and be prepared to provide paper copies of the report form, instructions, and examples for anyone who is unable to access or print them.

SUMMARY OF POLICIES. The Norman Campus Conflict of Financial Interest Policy presumes that personal financial interests should not influence the performance of University duties, but recognizes that many interests presenting a potential conflict are permissible if disclosed and properly managed. The policy requires that certain financial interests should be disclosed if they would reasonably appear related to the exercise of University duties. Other University policies and state ethics rules also define permissible relations between University duties and other activities and commitments. Further information on these policies is available on the Provost's webpage.

WHO SHOULD FILE WITHIN THE PROVOST'S AREA. Generally, faculty and staff who make spending decisions, direct sponsored research, supervise employees, or teach students should be aware of the need to report conflicts of financial interest. Any faculty or staff member with an actual conflict must report it whenever it occurs. Whether or not there is any conflict to report, an annual disclosure form should be filed by the following faculty and staff in Provost areas:

- full-time (1.0 FTE) professor, associate, assistant appointed with tenured, tenure-track, and renewable term
- full-time (1.0 FTE) research professors, associate professors, and assistant professors
- full-time (1.0 FTE) research scientists, senior research scientists, research associates, and senior research associates
- full-time (1.0 FTE) staff members in academic units whose annual salary exceeds $60,000 and other staff that are engaged in outside employment or supplementary employment.

INSTRUCTIONS FOR FILING. The annual conflict report form may be downloaded from the Provost's webpage for conflicts of financial interest and related policies, available at http://www.ou.edu/provost/pronew/content/conflicts.html. The site also contains instructions and examples of interests that should be reported.

DEADLINE: Forms should be completed, signed, and submitted directly to the Provost no later than November 21, 2008.

Please contact Breea Bacon at Redact or use (111)222-3333 (405)325-3224 if you have any questions regarding this form.

TABLE 2.3 ***Continued***

UNIVERSITY OF OKLAHOMA
2008–2009 CONFLICTS POLICY REPORT FORM

Name (please print or type) ______________________

Department (please print or type) ______________________

THE INFORMATION YOU PROVIDE IS CONFIDENTIAL AND WILL BE USED ONLY AS REQUIRED TO REPORT AND MANAGE CONFLICTS OF INTEREST. RETURN THIS FORM DIRECTLY TO THE PROVOST. INSTRUCTIONS FOR COMPLETING THIS FORM ARE AVAILABLE ON THE PROVOSTWEBSITE CLICK HERE

1. Do you have an interest in an entity or activity that ...
   a. Does business with the University in an area in which you make spending decisions?
      Yes No
   b. Profits from the sale of course material (coursepacks, software, etc.) or other goods or services to students whom you teach or evaluate?
      Yes No
   c. Employs University faculty, staff, or students whom you directly supervise or evaluate both in that employment and at the University?
      Yes No
   d. Sponsors a project at the University over which you have any degree of control?
      Yes No
   e. Profits from research you do at the University?
      Yes No
   f. Competes with the University for project funding?
      Yes No
   g. Uses University-owned intellectual property, or University equipment or facilities?
      Yes No
2. Other than those covered in Question 1, do you have an interest in any entity or activity that could reasonably appear to affect, or be affected by, the exercise of your University responsibilities?
   Yes No
3. Do you have any interests reported in questions 1 or 2 that are not already subject to a conflict management plan? (Leave blank if no interests reported)
   All interests are subject to an existing conflict management plan.
   At least one interest is not subject to an existing conflict management plan.

If you had no interests to report, or if the interests reported are already subject to a conflict management plan, skip Questions 4 and 5, sign below, and return this form to the Provost. Otherwise, please complete Questions 4 and 5 before signing. *A "Yes" answer to Questions 1 or 2 does not mean that a conflict exists, but you may be asked to provide further information about the activity.*

4. Continuing on a separate sheet if necessary, please describe ...
   a. The nature of the entity or activity (type and name of business, etc.)
   b. Your relation to the entity or activity (including your position or title, if any)
   c. The *nature* of your interest (ownership, salary, equity interest, etc.) and its *extent* (full ownership, salary in excess of $10,000, etc.):
   d. The nature of the potential conflict
5. Does the interest or your related University responsibility involve receipt of federal funding?
   Yes No

I have read and understood the Norman Campus Conflicts of Financial Interest Policy and declare that I have used all reasonable diligence in preparing this disclosure statement, which to the best of my knowledge is true, accurate, and complete. I understand that under the Policy I have a responsibility to update the above information throughout the coming year if my circumstances change.

______________________ Signature

______________________ Date

TABLE 2.4 Memo Template

Monday, September 17, 2001

Memo

To: Class Members

From: Michael L. Kent

Re: Memo Writing

Most students have never been asked do any business writing. Indeed, most students never write any "professional" documents until they start writing their résumé's and cover letters for jobs. This memo will briefly explain the structure, tone, and format of a typical memo. After reading this memo you should have a fairly good idea of both how a memo might look, and how to structure its content. The first issue to consider here is how a memo should look.

Memos look different than business letters, as this sample document illustrates. Although it is not necessary to put the big "Memo" at the top of a memo, that is often what is done. Also, since memos are "internal" documents, the formal address found on business letters is unnecessary. Memo headers usually include the "date," "To: ..." "From: ...," and "Re: ..." (regarding) lines. Microsoft Word has an assortment of memo templates. Simply go to: "File," "New," and the "Memo" tab and select a memo format (or go to "File" and "Project Gallery" depending upon the version of Word you are using). The next issue has to do with tone.

The differences between a memo and a business letter are few, but the tone of a memo may be slightly more conversational than a business letter—although both are written "professionally." This means that you do *not* use slang, colloquial language, etc., nor do you use technojargon, contractions, or unnecessary abbreviations. Finally, memos are formatted differently.

Memos are formatted differently than business letters. Memos are single-spaced documents and follow most of the rules for how to structure business letters. Major differences include:

1. Memos often include numbered or bulleted lists.
2. Memos are not signed; instead, initial a memo next to your name at the top.
3. Memos are often not edited by others. With many memos, you often do not have the luxury of a proofread by a colleague; thus, you must proofread and edit them carefully yourself.

For class assignments, you should do the following:

- When you turn in your "memo," include both a "final draft" that looks exactly like the real final draft *should* look (single-spaced, no widows/orphans, etc.), and also include an "editable" draft that is double-spaced so that it can be edited/corrected.
- Have as many people as possible proofread your memo for you.

inform someone or explain something that is unfamiliar. A metaphor often draws upon an object, person, or idea, in order to suggest a comparison or analogy. Often the two concepts or things are unlike; for example, "evening of life" to describe old age. Metaphors also shape how we see the world.

A well-crafted metaphor clarifies or distills an assortment of ideas into a readily understood concept or idea rather than drawing attention to itself. Churchill's famous "Iron Curtain" speech is an excellent example: "From Stettin in the Baltic to Trieste in the Adriatic, an iron curtain has descended across the continent." For the Baltic nations bordering Russia, the "iron curtain" was not *just* a metaphor; the iron curtain described their daily life.

Recently, while teaching in Latvia, I visited the "Barricade Museum" in Old Town Riga. The museum had a map of the Baltic region on the wall, but the map was behind a steel barricade (like a chain-link fence). As I was moving my head from side to side, up and down, trying to see the map and thinking to myself, "Why is this map behind this stupid grating?" one of my Latvian students explained to me, "Here is Latvia behind an iron curtain ..." Instantly life in communist Latvia came into focus and I suddenly understood what Churchill's metaphor *really*

TABLE 2.5 Figures of Speech

Accumulatio (ac-cu-mu-lat′-ee-oe) Argument by accumulation. We did all we could; nothing more could be done; everything that could be done was tried.

Anadiplosis (an′-a-di-plo′-sis) Repetition of an end at the next beginning: "When I give, I give myself."

Anaphora (a-naph′-o-ra) Repetition of beginnings: "Mad world! Mad leaders! Mad country!"

Antithesis (an-tith′-e-sis) Repetition by negation: "An organization should be remembered for its good deeds not its mistakes."

Aporia (a′-poe-ree-a) Talking about not being able to talk about something: "We have some initiatives, you'll see."

Asyndeton (a-syn-de-ton) The omission of a conjunction: "I came, 1 saw, 1 conquered."

Asterismos (as-ter-is′-mos) Addition of a word to emphasize what follows: "Indeed, understanding rhetoric is important."

Auxesis (aux-ee'-sis) Arrangement in ascending importance: "One must study to know, know to understand, understand to judge."

Diarope (di-ac'-o-pee) Repetition with only a word or two between: "Improvements, wonderful, inexpensive, improvements."

Ellipsis (el-lip′-sis) Omission: "Everyone's president is nobody's."

Enthymene (en′-the-meen) Omission of a logically implied clause or sentence in a syllogism: "All men are mortal. Socrates is Dead!"

Epanalepsis (ep′-an-a-lep′-sis) Repetition of the beginning at the end: "Hard work is not really that hard."

Epanorthosis (ep′-a-nor-thoe-sis) Addition by correction: "The hour to do something is approaching, no it is at hand."

Epistrophe (e-pis′-tro-phee) Repetition of ends: "We fought for this company because we love this company, believe in this company, and want to save this company."

Hypallage (hy-pal′-la-gee) Reversal, which seems to change the sense: "The lights of the city" becomes "City of lights."

Hysteron-proteron (hys′-te-ron prot′-e-ron) Reversal of temporal order: "Let us solve the problems of today, by taking up the issues of tomorrow."

Metaplasmus (met′-a-plas′-mus) Effective misspelling. For example Burke's "definition of [Wo]man."

Metonymy (me-ton′-y-mee) (from the Greek meta, change, and onyma, a name) is the designation of an object by one of its accompaniments, in other words, it is a figure by which the name of one object is put for another when the two are so related that the mention of one readily suggests the other. Thus when we say of a drinker—"He loves the bottle" we do not mean that he loves the glass receptacle, but the liquor that it contains. Metonymy, has, three subdivisions: (1) when an effect is put for cause or vice versa: as "Gray hairs should be respected" or "He writes a fine hand." (2) when the sign is put for the thing signified: "The pen is mightier than the sword." (3) When the container is put for the thing contained: "The House was called to order" (How to Speak and Write Correctly, "Project Guttenberg," www.gutenberg.org/wiki/Main_Page).

Polysyndeton (pol′-y-syn′-de-ton) Addition of conjunctions: "Many nations have participated as partners in peace: the English, and the Australians, and the Rumanians, and the nation of Tuval."

Praeteritio (pret-e-rit′-ee-oe) The inclusion of something by pretending to omit it: "Who am I to question the wisdom of our leaders?" or "I would not think to question the motives of those who disagree with me."

Synecdoche (syn-ek-do-kee) Substitution of a part for a whole or a whole for the part. "The most common form of this figure is that in which a part is used for the whole; as, 'I have twenty head of cattle,' 'One of his hands was assassinated,' meaning one of his men. 'Twenty sail came into the harbor,' meaning twenty ships" (op cit., How to Speak and Write Correctly).

meant to someone who lived in the region. As someone who was raised in the United States, I always found the metaphor overly dramatic. But as I saw several of my Latvian students weeping in the museum over their recent "freedom," the metaphor gained new meaning, as it probably had years ago when Churchill first said it. See Photo 2.1.

The ability to shape reality is the power of the metaphor. When used well, a single metaphor can clarify a universe of ideas. Metaphors are powerful

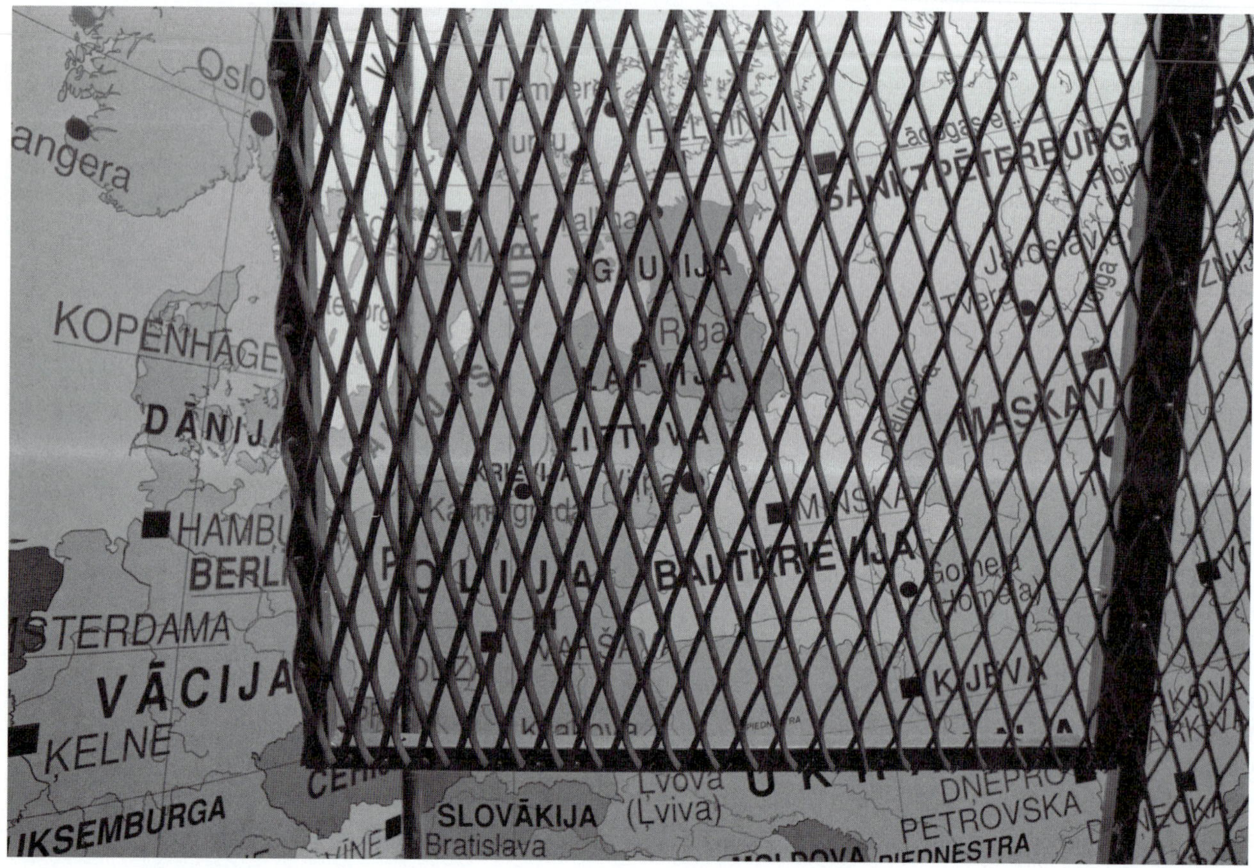

PHOTO 2.1 Map from Barricade Museum

tools and often used by organizations to define their position. For example, "pro-life" and "pro-choice" were adopted to describe an assortment of beliefs that include social, political, religious, and moral components. A carefully chosen metaphor can be powerful.

Metonymy

Metonymy is a technique of reduction or substitution. Metonmy is used to convey the intangible in terms of the tangible, to speak of "the heart" rather than "emotions." Metonymy is also used to convey more abstract concepts: "the pen is mightier than the sword," "a man of the cloth," etc. Metonymy, like metaphor, is used all the time in our everyday speech, often out of habit. We hear reports "from a senior White House spokesperson," or call our favorite sports team "Ducks" or "Boilermakers," or describe a co-worker as "the heart of the firm." In some types of public relations writing, like news releases, metonymy is almost never used. However, in other types of writing, like Web sites, pitch letters, and backgrounders, metonymy plays a prominent role.

Because rhetoric is situational, not every figure of speech is appropriate in every situation. The Dale Carnegie "start every speech with a joke" approach misses the complexity of communication. No single style is appropriate for all situations. The types of messages you create in public relations are as varied as the audience and situations for which you create the messages. Metonymy can add flair and creativity, and is a staple in many types of public relations writing, such as fashion, entertainment, and sports writing.

In sports public relations, for example, writers and announcers are famous for their use of metonymy: "Cinderella kid," "Charlie Hustle," "the Refrigerator," "the Underdogs," etc. In news writing, where precise, accurate language using proper names and exact dates is appropriate, metonymy often leads to puffery. Skilled writers need to have versatility and be able to adapt to different audiences and rhetorical constraints. Some situations call for eloquence and some call for accuracy.

Anaphora

Anaphora involves a repetitive use of the same word or phrase at the beginning of a series of phrases, clauses, or lines. Once again, Churchill provides an apt example with his use of "we shall":

> We shall not flag or fail. We shall go on to the end. We shall fight in France, we shall fight on the seas and oceans, we shall fight with growing confidence and growing strength in the air, we shall defend our island, whatever the cost may be, we shall fight on the beaches, we shall fight on the landing grounds, we shall fight in the fields and in the streets, we shall fight in the hills. We shall never surrender.

A more modest use of Anaphora is found in the next paragraph, where I use "being able to" repeatedly.

Rhetorical tactics can also be combined as Churchill does in his "we shall" speech, where anaphora (with the repeated words) and asyndeton (with the omitted conjunction) are both used. As you develop more writing skill, you will become comfortable drawing upon figures of speech and other rhetorical tactics and your writing will become more distinctive and compelling. Being an effective writer means being able to adapt to your audience, being able to use language that your audience understands, being able to use examples that your audience understands, and being able to sound like you are comfortable speaking your audience's language. Rhetoric is not pandering. But rhetoric requires audience adaptation to be effective. Metaphors only work if your audience knows what you are referring to; your arguments still need to be logically sound to be effective.

Many of you still might think that figures of speech are just rhetorical window dressing (a metaphor), but the truth is, figures of speech are found everywhere. Are you more likely to find figures of speech and compelling language used in presidential speeches? Yes. Speeches are some of the most rhetorical forms of communication. If you examine the transcript of President Barack Obama's speech (Table 2.6), you can find many figures of speech and nearly every rhetorical technique in just the first five minutes of the speech. However, rhetoric, and figures of speech, are used by all professionals. Consider the examples from news releases, annual reports, and other documents below (see Table 2.6):

TABLE 2.6 Obama's Inaugural Address, with Analysis

Published: Jan. 20, 2009 at 12:47 PM

WASHINGTON, Jan. 20 (UPI)—The following is the text of President Barack Obama's inaugural address delivered Tuesday on the National Mall in Washington:

OBAMA: Thank you. Thank you.

CROWD: Obama! Obama! Obama! Obama!

OBAMA: My fellow citizens: I stand here today humbled by the task before us, grateful for the trust you have bestowed, mindful of the sacrifices borne by our ancestors.

I thank President Bush for his service to our nation as well as the generosity and cooperation he has shown throughout this transition.

Forty-four Americans have now taken the presidential oath.

The words have been spoken during rising tides of prosperity and the still waters of peace. Yet, every so often the oath is taken amidst gathering clouds and raging storms. At these moments, America has carried on not simply because of the skill or vision of those in high office, but because We the People have remained faithful to the ideals of our forbears, and true to our founding documents.

So it has been. So it must be with this generation of Americans.

That we are in the midst of crisis is now well understood. Our nation is at war against a far-reaching network of violence and hatred. Our economy is badly weakened, a consequence of greed and irresponsibility on the part of some but also our collective failure to make hard choices and prepare the nation for a new age.

Homes have been lost, jobs shed, businesses shuttered. Our health care is too costly, our schools fail too many, and each day brings further evidence that the ways we use energy strengthen our adversaries and threaten our planet.

(continued)

TABLE 2.6 *Continued*

These are the indicators of crisis, subject to data and statistics. Less measurable, but no less profound, is a sapping of confidence across our land; a nagging fear that America's decline is inevitable, that the next generation must lower its sights.

Today I say to you that the challenges we face are real, they are serious and they are many. They will not be met easily or in a short span of time. But know this, America: They will be met.

On this day, we gather because we have chosen hope over fear, unity of purpose over conflict and discord.

On this day, we come to proclaim an end to the petty grievances and false promises, the recriminations and worn-out dogmas that for far too long have strangled our politics.

We remain a young nation, but in the words of Scripture, the time has come to set aside childish things. The time has come to reaffirm our enduring spirit; to choose our better history; to carry forward that precious gift, that noble idea, passed on from generation to generation: the God-given promise that all are equal, all are free, and all deserve a chance to pursue their full measure of happiness.

In reaffirming the greatness of our nation, we understand that greatness is never a given. It must be earned. Our journey has never been one of shortcuts or settling for less.

It has not been the path for the faint-hearted, for those who prefer leisure over work, or seek only the pleasures of riches and fame.

Rather, it has been the risk-takers, the doers, the makers of things—some celebrated, but more often men and women obscure in their labor—who have carried us up the long, rugged path towards prosperity and freedom.

For us, they packed up their few worldly possessions and traveled across oceans in search of a new life. For us, they toiled in sweatshops and settled the West, endured the lash of the whip and plowed the hard earth.

For us, they fought and died in places Concord and Gettysburg; Normandy and Khe Sanh...

Rhetorical Concepts in Parentheses

OBAMA: My fellow citizens: I stand here today humbled by the task before us, grateful for the trust you have bestowed, mindful of the sacrifices borne by our ancestors [*Ethos*].

I thank President Bush for his service to our nation as well as the generosity and cooperation he has shown throughout this transition [*Ethos, identification by sympathy*].

Forty-four Americans have now taken the presidential oath [*ad verecundiam*].

The words have been spoken during rising tides of prosperity and the still waters of peace [archetypal metaphors]. Yet, every so often the oath is taken amidst gathering clouds and raging storms [archetypal metaphors]. At these moments, America has carried on not simply because of the skill or vision of those in high office, but because We the People [Synecdoche] have remained faithful to the ideals of our forbears, and true to our founding documents [pathos, American values].

So it has been. So it must be [*Epanalepsis, Asyndeton, Hysteron-proteron*] with this generation of Americans.

That we are in the midst of crisis [*Ideograph*] is now well understood. Our nation is at war [*Ideograph*] against a far-reaching network of violence and hatred. Our economy is badly weakened, a consequence of greed and irresponsibility on the part of some [*Pathos*] but also our collective failure to make hard choices and prepare the nation for a new age [*Logos*].

Homes have been lost, jobs shed, businesses shuttered [*Asyndeton*]. Our health care is too costly, our schools fail too many [*Epanalepsis*], and each day brings further evidence that the ways we use energy strengthen our adversaries and threaten our planet [*analogy*].

We find metonymy in a quotation from a news release written by the Corn Refiners Association: "Consumers could be in for a jolt [metonymy, allusion to caffeine] when they realize that there is no scientific basis to suggest that coffee cake made with sugar is 'healthier' than one made with high fructose corn syrup" (June 3, 2009, PRNewswire).

The National Hot Dog and Sausage Council writes: "We want to give Americans one more week to don their creative hats [metaphor], fire up their cameras [metaphor] and send in a new version of this age-old song" (June 5, 2009, PRNewswire).

ProQuest, writing on behalf of Historically Black Colleges and Universities (HBCU) writes: "We are indeed [asterismos, formal tone] grateful to ProQuest for this remarkable gift that will serve our institutions as an important research tool for scholars seeking to learn the rich heritage of African-Americans, worldwide" (March 20, 2009, PRNewswire).

In *The Complete Idiot's Guide to Handwriting Analysis*, Lowe (1999) uses a very common (mis)spelling technique when she writes: "Clothes Make the (Wo)Man" (p. 368) [metaplasmus]. Handy (2007), does the same thing in the title to her master's thesis at the University of Waikato, "A Real (Wo)man's Beer: Gendered Spaces of Beer Drinking in New Zealand" (adt.waikato.ac.nz/uploads/approved/adt-uow20070222.122853/public/02whole.pdf).

In the 2008 annual report for Yum! Brands (Taco Bell, Pizza Hut, KFC, A&W, Long John Silver's) we see many figures of speech being used through the report including:

> A COMPANY WITH A HUGE HEART [metonymy]
> This means truly caring about others. This means opening doors and providing great career paths that allow people to work their way up from the bottom to the top. That also means [anaphora, accumulatio] using our talent, time and imagination to save lives and improve our environment.

Figures of speech are common in all types of writing: annual reports, news releases, feature stories, fact sheets, research reports. Indeed, all but the most straightforward technical writing, such as instruction manuals or news release news-content, can benefit. Notice also how often figures of speech appear in the quotations of news releases. If you visit PRNeswire.com and read some news releases, you will see that many quoted paragraphs in news releases use figures of speech to construct more compelling statements. In journalism, actual quotations cannot be altered without permission. However, since public relations practitioners probably write all news release content, quotations in news releases attributed to organizational members should take advantage of the opportunity to craft compelling prose.

© Darby Conley/Dist. By United Feature Syndicate, Inc.

CONCLUSION

One of the fundamental aspects of rhetoric is appreciating how much difference timing makes, and the subtleties of language. As you will learn in subsequent chapters, rhetoric also informs how we organize our messages and how we convince people to see the world in a certain way. Chapter 2 is designed to get you thinking about the complexities of rhetoric and how much rhetoric informs the practice of public relations. Ethics and rhetoric go hand-in-hand, just as ethics and public relations and rhetoric and public relations go hand-in-hand.

The stakeholders with whom we communicate, the language choices that we make, and the messages that we create shape how other people think about our organizations and clients. More importantly, our beliefs (ethical and moral), and our actions (counselor, information provider), shape how we practice public relations.

ACTIVITIES

1. Write a one-page memo, in memo style, explaining your future professional goals. Where do you see yourself in seven years? How will you achieve these goals? Be specific. Describe what skills you will need to hone (desktop publishing, new technology skills, an internship with a local sports franchise, etc.). The tone of the memo should be as if you were explaining to your professor where you wanted to be so that s/he might make changes to future public relations classes.
2. Interview two people, not students, about the professional risks involved in using Facebook, MySpace, etc. Write a one-and-a-half to two-page memo (follow the memo template above) for your fellow students explaining the risks. Read a few newspaper or magazine articles on the subject before you begin writing.
3. Select three of the figures of speech from Table 2.5 (besides those discussed above) and integrate them into a brief historical narrative (two to three paragraphs) about your department, college, or school suitable for use on a Web site. Do not spend time looking up facts for this activity. Since your goal is to get some practice using the figures of speech, not to write an historically accurate document, go ahead and make up a bunch of names, dates, and events (but be realistic), and then begin telling the story. Be sure to label each figure of speech [like this, in brackets], so they can be easily identified.
4. Select one of the fictive student clubs below and write a mission, vision, and boilerplate statement for them. Obviously, you will need to make up some facts for this assignment; however, before you begin, spend a few minutes researching the organization that you selected or were assigned and make an effort to create realistic, compelling documents. Organizations: (1) Cribbage Club, (2) Fantasy War Gaming Club, (3) Students for Freedom (Underground Magazine), (4) Public Speaking Club, (5) Photoshop Club, (6) Society for Creative Anachronism, (7) Karaoke Club, (8) Student Vintners Club, (9) Motorcycle Club, (10) Inventors Club, (11) Curling Club, (12) Noodling (as in "Okie Noodling") Club, (13) The Left-Handed Albino Student Union, (14) Bruce Springsteen (or Bruce McCulloch) fan club, (15) Creative Writing Club.
5. One clause of the Public Relations Society of America says to "Never damage the professional reputation of another public relations practitioner," while another clause says to "Report the unethical actions of other practitioners." In practice, how is it possible to both turn someone in without damaging his or her reputation? Briefly explain your reasoning and describe which ethical principles might inform your decision making.
6. Using the list of ethical positions from Table 2.2 as a guide, identify which positions come closest to your own ethical framework. Which of the approaches do you believe are the best or most useful and which do you see as not as useful? Explain. Finally, spend a few minutes describing your own ethical values and how you see the world. Are people basically good or bad? Should we live in harmony with nature or control it? How should we treat or interact with other people (friends, family, strangers, etc.)? Note: Although most religions are based on ethical principles, ethics are not contingent on religious principles. Belief about the afterlife, reincarnation, devils and angels, ghosts, etc., are not relevant to ethical belief systems. Although religion plays a prominent role in many people's lives, I am not asking what your religion is; I am asking about how you see the social world, about good and bad, and how you see your role in society and the professional world. Be specific. Talk about any professional issues that help explain your position: CEO salaries, employee absenteeism, whatever helps.

7. The Communitarians believe that we have a responsibility to our community and our society rather than simply to ourselves and our families. Communitarians are not communists or collectivists; they believe people can own property, and deserve privacy rights. However, they also believe that people should take responsibility for their actions rather than trying to blame others or evade responsibility when accidents or mistakes happen. If a ballplayer who uses steroids is caught and s/he is *really* sorry, that player should admit his or her mistake rather than trying to evade responsibility. A CEO who makes 1,000 times as much as a floor manager should not greedily look for more money, etc. Is Communitarianism a viable organizational framework? Explain, give examples, and talk about how a public relations professional might integrate such ethical principles into an actual organizational environment.

Chapter 3

The Importance of Editing and Proofreading

A few years back I saw an invoice for a news release prepared for a research firm in Princeton, New Jersey. The invoice included billing for time spent on the telephone conducting research, an initial draft prepared by an assistant account executive, editing and corrections by an account executive, additional editing by the account manager, and final editing by the assistant account executive before the news release was sent to the organization for approval. The price: $750. Besides the obvious fact that the organization paid a lot of money for someone else to write a news release, something any entry-level public relations professional should already be able to do, this example illustrates the process that all professional writing should go through before being sent to the media. Writing is a process, and *nothing* can be *perfect* in only one draft: not an e-mail message, not a news release, and certainly not lengthy documents like annual reports, newsletters, campaign proposals, Web content, or research reports.

THE IMPORTANCE OF MULTIPLE DRAFTS: PROOFREADING, EDITING, AND REWRITING

Writing, rewriting, and editing are at the heart of all successful public relations. Few things are more embarrassing than creating a 50-foot-high sign with a spelling or grammar error, or presenting a client with a proposal with their name spelled three different ways—all wrong! The best writing has gone through multiple drafts and, ideally, multiple editors.

One issue not appreciated by many students is the amount of work that goes into creating professional documents. Public relations professionals have to take an incipient idea (often from someone else) to a finished product, making decisions along the way as to how the document should look (paper, typography, color, binding), what will be the best format for the target audience (booklet, brochure, Web page, direct mail, PDF), and what is actually possible given the project's budget and time frame. Moreover, a public relations professional usually has to do the majority of the writing, editing, and proofreading him/herself.

Although having multiple people write and edit documents like news releases, fact sheets, and other professional documents, still takes place in public relations agencies and firms, what is more common is that documents are created by individual practitioners and brought as near to final-draft quality as possible. The lone practitioner in a small consulting firm, hospital, nonprofit organization, university, or activist organization does not have the luxury of handing his/her work off to someone else to edit. So how does someone achieve perfection? You guessed it: write, proofread, edit, rewrite, proofread, edit, etc., until the document is perfect.

Editing *any* document requires several drafts. Nowadays, the initial draft of most documents is almost always typed directly into the computer. Few people actually write out their work longhand anymore. Although for complex or creative documents, writers still use outlines and thumbnails to brainstorm ideas. After the first or second onscreen draft, documents should be *printed* and edited on paper. Looking at a hard copy is generally the best way to catch formatting problems, subtle changes in typefaces, and spacing problems. Additionally, editing on paper often makes it easier to catch grammatical errors, flow problems, unclear transitions, and an assortment of other problems. Few professionals do final draft work from beginning to end solely on the computer screen.

One of the biggest mistakes of the computer age has been the erroneous assumption that people no longer need to know how to write or spell well because computers all have built-in grammar and spelling checkers. Do not presume that you can just run your spell checker or grammar checker and everything will be perfect. Grammar checkers only catch mistakes that they understand—and usually errors that you already know how to fix. You still need to know how to change passive voice to active voice yourself, or how to lower a Flesch-Kincaid reading score (discussed in Chapter 9). Additionally, a grammar checker will tell you to change "public relations is" to "public relations are" because it does not know any better. Indeed, your spell checker does not know the difference between "*pubic* relations" and "*public* relations."[1] Only a human can catch such errors.

Employers are looking for people who know how to write, edit, and proofread well, people who know the difference between "its" and "it's" or "because" and "since." When you go in for your first job interviews, you will very likely be given a writing and/or spelling test (see sample employment tests at the end of this chapter). As I suggested in Chapters 1 and 2, writing is a public relations professional's bread and butter. Be sure to take some of my suggestions to heart and actively work on your own writing.

As a professional, you never want to create a proposal for a client that contains misspellings (e.g., "to" instead of "too," "their" instead of "there" or "they're"), unsupported claims, misspelled names, or reads like a class essay. Learning how to write well begins by knowing the rules of Associated Press style and the rules of the source(s) you are writing for.

WRITING TIPS: ACTIVE vs. PASSIVE VOICE, SPLIT INFINITIVES, AND OTHER PROBLEMS

Professional writing is characterized by active sentences and tight prose. If you can say something in 5 words instead of 10, you should. The secret to tight prose is careful editing and clear referents. One of the biggest areas where almost everyone can improve their writing is using active versus passive voice. **Active voice** involves the subject of the sentence, taking the action: "Tamara attended the event." **Passive Voice** involves the subject of the sentence being acted upon: "The event was attended by Sarabdeep."[2] Active voice tends to be less wordy, easier to read, and clearer.

As the Writing Center at the University of North Carolina, Chapel Hill explains,

> Once you know what to look for, passive constructions are easy to spot. Look for a form of "to be" (is, are, am , was, were, has been, have been, had been, will be, will have been, being) followed by a past participle. (The past participle is a form of the verb that typically, but not always, ends in "-ed." (www.unc.edu/depts/wcweb/handouts/passivevoice.html)

Visit the UNC Web site, mentioned above, for a detailed explanation of passive voice.

Consider the examples below from earlier drafts of this book:

> Most organizations are providing few opportunities for stakeholders ...
>
> Few organizations provide opportunities for stakeholders ...
>
> There is not just one model for how strong relationships are fostered ...
>
> Many models exist for fostering strong relationships ...
>
> A lot of the writing that public relations professionals once conducted is now intended to be placed online.
>
> Much of the writing public relations professionals conduct will now be placed online.
>
> The meager supply of oil that has been untapped in places like ...
>
> The meager supply of untapped oil remains in places like ...

An issue similar to passive voice is learning to tighten or edit your prose so that you say something as clearly and concisely as possible. Like active voice, shorter sentences are easier to read. Saying something in fewer words is usually a sign of good writing and editing.

Essentially, there is an enthymeme that gets invoked ...

Essentially, an enthymeme is invoked ...

However, the fact that an organization ...

However, because an organization ...

In spite of the fact that these issues are highly charged ...

Although these issues are highly charged ...

Current estimates by professionals in the oil business are that we have already ...

Estimates by professionals in the oil business suggest we have already ...

... progress often requires hard work on the part of change agents willing to take risks and acting in ways designed to reap short-term rewards but lead to long-term benefits.

... progress requires hard work on the part of change agents willing to take risks and work toward long-term benefits rather than short-term rewards.

... the U.S. is the only First World nation that does not have a national healthcare plan ...

... the U.S. is the only First World nation without a national healthcare plan ...

SPLIT INFINITIVES refer to infinitive verbs ("To verb") being separated or "split." The classic example is *Star Trek's* famous "To boldly go where no man has gone before." The infinitive verb is "to go." The phrase, some argue, should be "To go boldly ..." I say "some argue" because English teachers have been arguing about splitting infinitives for 200 years. In general, avoid splitting infinities except where you clearly want to violate the rule (in headings or titles). You will find that most of the time, when you do not split the infinitive the sentence reads better. Additionally, and more importantly, since many people have been taught to *always* avoid split infinitives, any writing that makes something stand out as wrong to some people should be avoided. See Table 3.1, for other grammatical suggestions.

TABLE 3.1 Writing Suggestions

- No contractions—ever.
- Never start a sentence with "it" ("It stands to reason ..." "It will be shown ..."), "there" ("There are many reasons for the policy ..." "There has been an increase ..."), etc. Write actively. What "it" refers to is usually not self-evident. Revise the sentence and make a proper reference to the thing/phenomenon in question.
- Except in long paragraphs with multiple references to the same thing, use only proper names. Avoid vague use of pronouns and referents:

  Not "This idea ..." but "The idea of culture ...";

  Not "It has ..." "It will ..." "It may ..." but "Korea has ..." "Korea will ..." "Korea may ...";

  Not "The country ..." but "Korea ...";

  Not "he said ..." or "she said ..." but "Smith said ..." or "Karen said ..."
- Work to be less wordy. Do not say "I am going to ...," "I will work to ...," "I will endeavor to ...," etc. Instead say, "I will ..."
- A dash is not a hyphen. Note the difference: hyphens connect one-word-to-another; hyphens are not used to set up clauses, like a colon, or to set up parenthetical insertions—like an em (M—) dash. Hyphens are not used between numbers like "pp. 18–25" like an en (N–) dash.
- Email (email) is always spelled with a hyphen. Email (or email) is a misspelled Cajun name.
- Web site (Web page, Web development, etc.) is always two words and is always spelled with a capital W.
- Years get no apostrophe: "the 1990s were good years ..." not "the 1990's were good years ..."
- All quotation marks are double quotes except for quotes within quotes.
- Punctuation goes inside of "quotes." See the sample essay pages.
- Number manuscript pages, research papers, feature stories, etc., after the title page at the top. Use a "running header" (or slug) with a page number.

TABLE 3.1 *Continued*

- Use 1" margins all around (Left, Right, Top, and Bottom).
- Use the same font, style, and size for everything in the essay (first letter to last), including block quotes, footnotes, endnotes, bibliography, etc. Everything!
- Do not use bigger fonts or "creative" fonts on the title page.
- Be sure you have 25–27 lines per page, double-spaced.
- Do not submit papers with fonts that are not listed on my syllabus. Fonts that are too big look unprofessional, and fonts that are too small are hard to read. I do not care if you like the font or can easily read the font, what matters is that I can. Using a 10-point font instead of a 12-point font will almost never change the length of the assignment.
- Do not use san serif fonts like Ariel or Helvetica—they are hard to read when used for body text.
- If you want to justify both margins because you like the look, then you must turn on auto hyphenation (tools/hyphenation in Microsoft Word). If you do not hyphenate when you justify both margins you will wind up with uneven gaps between words. Not using hyphenation looks amateurish and unprofessional.
- Never use contractions in academic or professional writing.
- Avoid widows/orphans, which are a few words or lines left at the top or bottom of pages.
- "World Wide Web" is a proper name; it is always three words, all capitalized. "Web site," "Web page," "Web master," etc. are all two words with "Web" capitalized.

WHAT IS A STYLEBOOK, AND WHY SHOULD I CARE?

Hopefully, by now you already know about the Associated Press Stylebook or the "AP guide." The *Encyclopedia of Public Relations* defines a stylebook as:

> A … handbook, or manual, used by professionals, academicians, and students, that contains rules/guidelines for how to produce publishable manuscripts. For example, the Associated Press' "Stylebook" … provides guidelines on the use of words/phrases, punctuation, copyrighted material, captioning photographs, writing newspaper copy for sports and business, and an assortment of other publishing rules.
>
> Many professions use manuals of style, including the print and broadcast industries, publishing, law, and psychology. Stylebooks provide structure to publications providing continuity of writing style and consistent usage of words, grammar, and citations.
>
> In professional public relations contexts, the Associated Press' *Stylebook* … is perhaps the most valuable text for a practitioner interested in correctly applying the conventions of print publishing. The bulk of the stylebook consists of hundreds of "definitions" of commonly used words/phrases and how the Associated Press uses the words in publications. (Kent, 2005b, p. 826).

Table 3.2 contains a list of many of the essential terms you should know as public relations professionals. The reason that understanding AP style is so important is because, as suggested in Chapter 1, journalists do not work for you. When you submit a news release or a feature story to a journalist, you are essentially saying: "I think this might be of interest to your readers. Please consider publishing this on their behalf." You are telling the editor that you believe your news release will interest their readers, that your submission is *newsworthy*, as the name "news release" implies. In order to increase the chances an editor will use your submission, and to make using your work easier and more attractive, you need to create documents that are as close to AP style as possible.

If you recall the information subsidy from Chapter 1 (key terms table), Gandy (1982) suggests that the media need us as much as we need them. Public relations professionals provide journalists with news content so journalists do not have to gather all of the information for a story themselves, making their job easier and cheaper. Unfortunately, given the abundance of organizational sources willing to provide content to the news media, public relations professionals still need journalists more than journalists need them.

TABLE 3.2 List of AP Terms

abbreviations	governor	possessives
academic degrees	government bodies	pre
accept/except	high-tech	principal/principle
affect/effect	historical periods	quotations
a.m./p.m.	holidays	race
B.A., M.A., Ph.D.	hometown	release times
because, since	home page	R.S.V.P.
brand names	in/into	seasons
call letters	initials	semi
capitalization	its/it's	sentences
co-	lay/laid/lie	should/would
compliment/complement	legislative titles	south
composition titles	long-term	state names
congress	majority/plurality	telephone numbers
corps	man/humanity	that, which
county	Medicare/Medicaid	their, there, they're
couple	mid-	time element
courtesy titles	months	time zones
dangling modifiers	Mr., Mrs., Ms.	titles
dates	music	to, two, too
datelines	newspaper names	TV/television
distances	large numbers	verbs
Dr./doctor	part-time	Website and Webpage, etc.
dollars	party affiliation	weekend
either/neither	people/peoples/person/ persons	Western Hemisphere
editor	Ph.D./Professor	who, whom
e-mail	phenomenon/phenomena	World Wide Web
family names	plurals	years
fewer/less	polls	
fractions		
fund raising/fund-raising/ fund raiser		

Many novice public relations professionals unknowingly submit news releases that contain non-Roman formatting, such as underlining, bolding, and italicizing. Pick up a student newspaper or a local newspaper later today and look at the kind of text used in the news sections. There are two typefaces: plain text and headlines, no bolding, no italics, no underlining. If you want your organizational documents to be used by the media, you have to make the editor's job easier. If an editor has to spend his/her time fixing your formatting or AP mistakes in order to use your news release, there is a good chance the editor will select another news release. Moreover, as you develop relationships with professionals in the media, ask the reporters and editors of the publications most important to your organization how *they* want your news releases formatted: Do they prefer "full block" or modified full-block formatting? Do they prefer paper or electronic copies of news releases (or both)?

Similarly, returning to the list of AP terms (Table 3.1), an understanding of basic AP style is essential. Times, dates, money, book titles (or "composition titles"), etc., need to be used correctly. Editors will not spend their valuable time fixing news releases or other free content filled with AP errors. The list in Table 3.1 represents some of the most common terms that a public relations writer should be familiar with. You are expected to know AP style well (which differs from broadcast writing style and APA style), know to use only Roman (plain) formatting in AP documents, and to know what each editor expects in terms of delivery (FAX, e-mail, hard copies, etc.).[3]

On the most basic level, you should know that there are rules for how dates, times, book titles, movie titles, etc., are written and know to check your AP guide when writing a news release or other Associated Press document. After six months on the job, you will discover that you still use your AP guide a lot. After a year, you probably will discover that you use your stylebook less often because you have memorized the basics, but you will still use it.

AMERICAN PSYCHOLOGICAL ASSOCIATION (APA) STYLE GUIDE

Just as the AP *Stylebook* is the bible for U.S. public relations practitioners, the *Publication Manual of the American Psychological Association (6th edition)* (APA guide) is the Bible if you are writing research papers. APA would also be the guide you used if you were writing a white paper for an organization or client. Research based work that includes "references," like your papers in college, should be written using APA style. Similarly, although *most* public relations professionals do not write research papers for professional conferences, *many* do. At some point, as you become more experienced, you may want to write a research paper for one of the many professional associations like the Public Relations Society of America (PRSA), the International Association of Business Communicators (IABC), or the International Communication Association (ICA). APA will be the style guide that you use.

BASIC APA STYLE

- Everything in the document (everything!) gets double-spaced. Did I mention *everything*?
- All documents have one-inch margins (L/R/T/B).
- Use the same font, style, and size for everything in the essay (first letter to last)—do not use bigger fonts or "creative" fonts on the title page. You many use underlining, italicizing, etc., as necessary; however, never use more than one font or change the font size.
- Use standard *serif* fonts: Bernhard Modern, Bookman, Caslon, Garamond, New Century Schoolbook, or Palatino.
- Before you begin writing, turn on "Widow and Orphan Control" (found in Microsoft Word in the "Format/Paragraph" menu, under the "Line and Page Breaks" tab).
- Do not activate auto-hyphenation (do not hyphenate words at the ends of lines).
- Left justify everything except for headings.
- After page 1, number all pages in the upper right-hand corner.
- Set a half-inch header and footer.

Become Familiar With the Following Sections of the *APA Guide* [6th Edition]

Agreement	78–79
Anthropomorphism	69
Article/Report structure	23
Citing sources	174–192
Electronic sources	203–204, 214–215
Headings	62
Multiple authors	18–19
Numbers	111–114
Order of manuscript pages	241–243
Punctuation	87–96
Quotes	170–174
Referencing examples	193–224
Running head	239
Sample paper	41–59
Table check list	150
Tables	128–150
Unbiased language	70–77
Verbs	77f

In-Text Citation in APA Style

- When citing authors in the text of documents, include the following information in the first cite (author, year of publication, and page number or numbers): "The changes to the profession have resulted in … (Botan, 1999, pp. 1–5)." If you use the author's name as part of your sentence, you only need to give the date and page number(s): "According to Botan (1999), the changes to the profession … (pp. 5–9)."

- For page number abbreviations, use "p." for "page" or "pp." for "pages": "According to Ferguson … (2001, p. 5)," or "According to Marken … (2000, pp. 5–10)."
- On subsequent references to the same author (*provided that no other author has been cited in between*), you do not have to mention the author's name or the year of publication again in your citation, indicating page number(s) only: "According to Botan (1999), 'the average article is 17 pages long' (p. 12). One of the things that many authors do not understand, however 'is that those 17 pages have been edited 17 times' (p. 17)."
- Use an ampersand (&) before the last name of authors listed in multiauthor works when writing their names in parenthetical cites and in the bibliography: "Citation is important (Coombs & Heath, 2004, p. 25)."
- *Do not* use an ampersand when you use the authors' names as part of your sentence: "According to Hearit and Smith … (1999, p. 87)."
- *Do not* include first names or initials when mentioning or citing authors except when multiple authors with the same family name could lead to confusion. In general, one of the ways of maintaining gender anonymity is by only using last names. Occasionally, such as in historical discussions, the names of famous scholars are given in full. In general, use only last names.
- When referencing what one source said about another source, (e.g., in a book chapter, the author you are reading quotes someone else or refers to an article by someone else), cite the author of the text you are reading the citation from, *not* the author to which your source refers. For example, "After reviewing the text, we see that Taylor's claim is reasonable (Kent, 1999, p. 5)." The only way you would cite "Taylor" in this example is if you actually went and got Taylor's book, read it, and then cited Taylor directly. If you did that, you would not be writing the sentence using a quotation from Kent.
- Authors are listed in books, articles, etc., in the order in which they made a contribution (i.e., who did more work), *not* alphabetically. Thus, when you refer to a source by name in the text, a cite, or the bibliography, the authors' names are listed in the order in which they appear on the cover of the book or article. For example, in an article by White, Cockett, and Green, you would not reorder the names to be alphabetical. In the bibliography, the entry will be "White, W., Cockett, L., & Green, K … ."

  Multiple citations in text are listed alphabetically and then chronologically. For example: "Web sites have proven to be unreliable (Toth, 1999, 2001; Turcilo, 2000; Webb, 2001, 2005)." In the bibliography, citations are also listed alphabetically and then chronologically:

  Tufte, E. R. (1990). *Envisioning information*. Cheshire Connecticut: Graphics Press LLC.

  Tufte, E. R. (1997). *Visual explanations: Images and quantities, evidence and narrative*. Cheshire Connecticut: Graphics Press LLC.

  Tufte, E. R. (2001). *The visual display of quantitative information (Second Edition)*. Cheshire Connecticut: Graphics Press LLC.

  Tufte, E. R. (2006). *Beautiful evidence*. Cheshire Connecticut: Graphics Press LLC.
- When referencing sources in your bibliography, carefully note the form they should take from the examples above and below.
  - Do not spell out the author's(s') first or middle names. Use initials with spaces. Note: AP and APA style differ on the use of initials. When initials are used in AP style—and they should be avoided—they *are not* separated by a space (R.L. Kent). When initials are used in APA style—and they are always used in bibliographies—they *are* separated by a space (Kent, R. L.).
  - Do not capitalize the first letter of every word in the title of a book or article.
  - Do not include a URL address as part of your bibliographic citation unless you are citing an online-only source, or a PDF that you know can be accessed by anyone. If you accessed the file as a PDF from a university library database, not accessible to everyone for free, you cite the document as if you had the actual journal in front of you). If you have a "full-text" copy, but not an "exact" copy, then indicate that in brackets:

    McGee, M. C. (1980). The "Ideograph": A link between rhetoric and ideology. *The Quarterly Journal of Speech, 66*, 1–16 ["full text" not "exact" copy].
- When you do not have an "exact" copy (like an HTML version that has all of the information run into one big document), cite paragraphs instead of page numbers in your essay. For example, "According to Kent … (1999, ¶ 10)."

- Quote marks are never used in a bibliography unless the book or article actually includes quotation marks as part of the title.
- Always include complete information about the author, source, and publisher.

Sample APA Citations

WEB SITE *The rule for Web sites is to include enough information for the reader to go back and find the document cited. If you can cite an exact Web page, cite it. However, Web pages are often taken down or moved. The preferred method is to do what is illustrated with Clinton below. The brackets <> allow you to properly punctuate the sentence without placing commas or periods in the URL. If a "permalink" is available, use that. A permalink is a "permanent link" that is designed not to be moved or taken down.*

Clinton, W. (1999, January 19). *State of the Union Address.* Office of the Press Secretary. Text available at <www.Whitehouse.gov>.

Note: This shorter home page address is preferred to a lengthy citation for the actual speech, since URL addresses change frequently but archived files like speeches typically remain on a site indefinitely. The White House Web site has been reorganized by each president since Clinton. The only reliable method of citing a speech there is simply to give the subject or title and date and point the reader to the home page.

Madden, M. (2006). *Internet penetration and impact.* PEW Internet & American Life Project www.pewinternet.org/pdfs/PIP_Internet_Impact.pdf.

Journal article (single author) (Note: Italics are used for the journal title and volume, but not for the issue).

Kent, M. L. (1985). The future of the Internet in Public Relations. *Critical Studies in Public Relations, 18*(3), 1–15.

Journal article (two or more authors) (Note: Italics are used for the journal title and volume only. When a journal numbers each issue of a journal from 1–x, then you must include an issue number (like the Kent 1985 example above). However, when each issue in a volume starts where the previous issue left off (vol. 1, pp. 1–97; vol. 2, pp. 98–195, vol. 3, pp. 196–291, etc.), all you need to include is the volume in your citation.)

Kahneman, D. & Tversky, A. (1982). The psychology of preferences. *Scientific American, 246,* 160–173.

Book (Note: Italics are used on the book title only). Only the first letter of the book title, and first letter after subtitles are capitalized.

Postman, N. (1993). *Technopoly: The surrender of culture to technology.* New York: Vintage Books.

Book (second edition) Laing, R. D. (1969). *Self and others (2nd edition).* New York: Pantheon Books.

Magazine (Note: Italics are used on the magazine title only).

Postman, N., & Paglia, C. (1991, March). Dinner conversation: She wants her TV! He wants his book! *Harper's Magazine,* 44–55.

You should be aware that the APA guide has a lengthy section describing how to cite dozens of different kinds of sources, including research papers, government reports, dissertation and theses, interviews, audio recordings. Be sure to consult the APA guide when you cite any unfamiliar document type.

UNDERSTANDING AND USING PROOFREADER MARKS

Proofreading is an essential part of *all* writing. No professional writing ever takes place without several proofreads. Proofreading takes place informally, on a computer screen, as well as formally, on paper. Proofreading is also a part of the writing process that needs to be conducted several times. With the possible exception of a very short message, like a one-paragraph e-mail message, all writing that will be posted to a Web site, distributed to the media, broadcast, or committed to paper, needs to be proofread and edited several times, preferably on paper, in order to ensure accuracy and quality.

Proofreader marks are a universal set of symbols used for editing professional writing (see Figure 3.1). The symbols are standardized so the corrections of one person who uses the marks can be understood and interpreted by someone else.

Proofreading is best done with a colored pen or pencil so the corrections stand out from the text. The reason your professors so often edit your papers with red pens is not because it looks like blood, but because red ink is high contrast and easy to see.

In practice, there are two types of proofreading: informal and formal. Informal proofreading is the basic proofreading that takes place in the early stages of any work. When you write an essay for class, an early draft of a news release, the text for a newsletter, or a report for a client, and then print it and proofread it for errors, you typically use informal proofreading. When you have reached the final stages of a document and are working with a publisher, you usually have to use formal proofreading techniques because single spaced documents often do not leave enough room for editing.

Informal Proofreading

INFORMAL PROOFREADING is more common and is what you do whenever you mark up your own work or the work of colleagues. Informal proofreading can only be done when there is adequate space, such as with draft documents. With single-spaced documents and documents with small text or tight spacing, formal proofreading is necessary. Formal and informal proofreading still use the same proofreader marks; however, when you edit a draft for yourself or for a colleague, you make the editing marks in the text itself (see Figure 3.1).

The proofreading conducted in the early stages of writing is much more comprehensive. Often, when editing a manuscript for the first time, you make major revisions, crossing out entire sections and inserting new content. Early proofreading and editing includes:

- Tightening your prose by replacing three words with one, five words with two, etc.
- Replacing vague references ("it," "her," "the event," "the organization") with proper nouns and references to a person's name, the proper name of the event or place, etc.
- Deleting double words and extra spaces.
- Removing double or triple spaces after punctuation. Note: You should insert one space *only* after all periods in both AP and APA style. Draft manuscripts including professional writing (short stories, novels, plays, movie scripts) and scholarly research (articles, books, chapters) often use two spaces after periods for ease of reading (APA, 6th edition, p. 88).
- Correcting contractions.
- Checking to see that possessives and apostrophes are placed correctly.
- Checking to see that hyphenation is correct.
- Correcting misspellings, poor word choice, incorrect synonyms selected hastily from the spell checker, and so on.
- Correcting alignment and spacing errors, checking to see that paragraphs are justified correctly, making sure margins are the proper size, marking incorrect type sizes or style changes, etc.
- Making sure hyphens (-), en dashes (–), and em dashes (—), are used correctly.

Basically, proofreading for everything!

As suggested above, all writing involves multiple drafts. Because of their clarity and consistency, proofreader marks are an effective way to mark up a document and will save you a lot of time and effort figuring out where to insert corrections and comments and what deletions or changes are recommended when editing.

Formal Proofreading

FORMAL PROOFREADING involves editing a document twice: once in the text itself, near the error or item being corrected, and once in the margin to the left or right of the correction (so you can be sure that the typesetter understands your in-text correction). As mentioned above, documents with small text and close leading like brochures or newsletter copy can only be edited formally because of the tight space. As you practice using proofreader marks correctly, occasionally try using the formal method so you learn how to do both formal and informal proofing correctly.

Final draft documents are usually being edited for the last time and you are usually only correcting minor errors. Most printers will charge you a new setup fee if a document requires major changes or new typesetting, so you want to be sure to catch substantive errors during the early phases of editing. At the final draft stage, you usually cannot make major insertions or deletions without paying more money, and you need to be aware of whether your changes will cause paragraphs or pages to break differently, or cause other problems. Most of the time, proofreading and editing are done to improve your work and not simply to find mistakes—although finding mistakes is always part of proofreading.[4]

Although I suggested that proofreader marks are "universal," they do vary slightly from publisher to publisher. The basic dozen marks (inserting, deleting, changing cases, transposing text, etc.) are more or less the same, but slight differences do exist. Be flexible. Most large organizations (and virtually all publishers) have their own "house style" and their writing rules and proofreader marks vary slightly. In the professional world, you do what your employer wants you to do. If your organization writes all memos in Garamond with Arial Black for headings, *so do you*. If the organization uses a slightly different set of proofreader marks, *so do you*.

Informal proofreading

Proofreadermarks are an efficient way of editing documents and and making them stronger and more compelling. As suggested above, in the early stages of writing, proofreading is used simply to correct errors, such as you see here. However, on documents that are more advanced, proof reading is made 2 improve the prose, add rhetorical features andgenerally make messages more com pelling.

In hte early stages of writing, getting the ideas on the page is perhaps the most IMPORTANT part of creating a message.

however, once basics the of graMMar and sentence structure have been resolved, organization, and rhetorical structure (cadence, flow, metaphor, etc.) Become more important When editing documents at any stage of writing, proofreader marks make editing and corrections easier. When using proofreader marks, there are often several ways to do the SAME things, such as "align on margin" or "m o ve right."

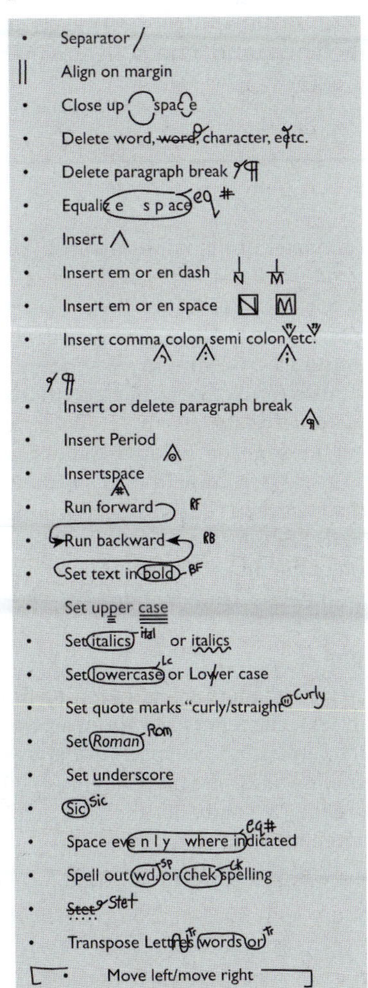

Separator
Align on margin
Close up space
Delete word, word, character, etc.
Delete paragraph break
Equalize space
Insert
Insert em or en dash
Insert em or en space
Insert comma, colon, semi colon, etc.
Insert or delete paragraph break
Insert Period
Insertspace
Run forward
Run backward
Set text in bold
Set upper case
Set italics or italics
Set lowercase or Lower case
Set quote marks "curly/straight"
Set Roman
Set underscore
Sic
Space evenly where indicated
Spell out wd or chek spelling
Stet
Transpose Letters words or
Move left/move right

Formal Proofreading

proofreader marks are are an efficient way of editing documents and and makking them stronger and more compelling. As suggested above, in the early stages of writing, proof reading are used simply to correct errors, such as you see here.However, as documents that are more advanced proofreading is made to improve the prose, add rhetorical features and generally make messages more compelling..

In the early stages of writing, getting the ideas on the pg. is perhaps the most important part of creating a message However once the basics of gramar an sentence structure have been resolved, organization, and rhetorical structure (cadence, flow, metaphor, etc.) become more important. When editing documents at any stage of writing, proofreading marks make editing nad corrections easier. When using Proofreader marks, there are often several ways 2 do the same things...

FIGURE 3.1 Sample of Informal & Formal Proofreading.

CONCLUSION

Learning to follow various style manuals and learning how to edit and proofread properly are just part of being a professional. You will need a lot of practice in order to learn how to make your writing more active and learning how to write lean, compelling, prose. You spent 12 years in grade school and high school learning how to make your writing appropriate for college students and professors. Although becoming a skilled public relations writer will not take you 12 years, you will need a lot of practice.

You will need at least 5 to 10 hours of editing practice to get the hang of how to use proofreader marks effectively. The sooner you start using the marks, the sooner you will be able to understand what your public relations professors are writing on your class papers when they hand them back to you. You will need even longer to learn the rules of AP and APA style. If you start looking up words in your *Stylebook* now, and start learning about proper citations as you go along, the learning curve will be less steep. By the end of this class you should have a firm grasp on AP style; by the time you graduate you should be able to use edit and use proofreader marks well. Editing and proofreading are fundamental skills.

Consider the internship request I received recently from Rex, a local public relations agency. Under the list of "Qualifications" were seven things. Number one was "having completed at least a year of public relations coursework." Number two was "Proficiency in AP Style." The skills outlined in this chapter are not trivial or optional. If you want to practice public relations for a living some day, you need to learn them. Even if you do not intend to work in public relations when you gradate, proofreading and editing skills are important in any writing profession. Start practicing and you will have the skills down before you know it.

ACTIVITIES

1. Download 10 public relations articles from your library's databases. Print off the titles pages (only), type up citations to the articles using APA style, attach the title pages to the bibliography, and submit.
2. Consult your AP *Stylebook* and read the sections on punctuation. When would parentheses be preferable to a dash? When is an en (N) dash used rather than an em (M) dash or a hyphen? What is the difference between each of the bracket types ({ [< >] })? Be able to discuss all of the standard punctuation marks in class.
3. Consult your *AP Stylebook* and read the sections on "Business" and "Sports Writing." Prepare a one-page memo (in memo form) summarizing the key issues you need to understand and be prepared to discuss the content, or be quizzed on the content, in class.
4. Print a new copy of one of your class essays or public relations documents from last semester (at least six pages long) and edit the document(s) using proofreader marks from the back of your *AP Stylebook* (or Figure 3.1). Concentrate on correcting formatting, spelling, and grammar mistakes as well as making the document better: i.e., tightening the prose; using one word for three; clarifying vague reference like "she," "he," "they," "it,"; adding some rhetorical techniques like those from Chapter 2, etc. Use "formal" proofreading techniques when you edit the document(s).

Look up at least a dozen of the AP terms from Figure 3.1. For each term, *indicate all relevant (general) rules and be sure to provide an example(s)* of the term's proper usage. Negative examples (e.g., "do not do *this* ...") may help clarify usage in some circumstances. Be sure to give examples of each term if two or more terms are indicated (to, too, two, etc.). Use public relations–related examples, *not* a "letter to your mom," e-mail message, or dialogue to illustrate terms (avoid "Bill said ..." or "According to ..."). *Be sure to use each word in a complete sentence—do not simply rewrite a term with one or two words and consider it sufficient.* Some terms require illustration of the thing the term refers to and not the term itself—like "dateline" and "holiday."

Sample Answer: am/pm

a.m. and p.m. are used to refer to morning and evening time elements. When used in text, the letters are all lower case, have a period after each letter, and no space in-between letters. Do not include trailing zeros in time references (:00). A space is inserted before the "a." and after the "m." Avoid redundant use like "3 a.m. in the morning."

Correct: The open house will run from 8 a.m. until 5 p.m.

Incorrect: The open house will start at 2:00 p.m. in the afternoon.

NOTES

1. To see how often this mistake is made in real life, go to any search engine like Google and type in "pubic relations" (with quotation marks) and you will find the mistake in thousands of documents. There were more than a million pages the last time I checked.
2. Note: You can set up your grammar checker to catch passive voice, and it will flag such errors as you write. (In Microsoft Word: Preferences/Spelling and Grammar/Grammar/settings.)
3. If you look at some sample news releases, you will see that many professionals do not follow AP style rules, using italics, underlining, and bolding. If you are writing a "news release" for your organization's Web site, non-Roman formatting is fine; you are not really writing a "news release" because you are not releasing it to the news media. But when you distribute a news release via PR Newswire (www.PRNewswire.com) or to an actual reporter or editor, be sure to follow AP style.
4. Knowing how to proofread can be a valuable skill for students looking for part-time work. Assuming that you live near a publishing center (Chicago, New York City, New Jersey, California, Connecticut, etc.), publishers are always looking for people who know how to use proofreader marks. Usually you will work through a temp agency. The work often consists of reading an original manuscript written in APA style (i.e., double-spaced, etc.) and comparing the original document to typeset, single-spaced drafts, using a publication guide. Mistakes like changing foot or inch marks to typographer quotes, checking the spacing around text boxes, etc., are corrected using formal proofreading techniques. Compensation ranges from $10-25 an hour and employers are often flexible about work schedules.

Chapter 4

What Difference Does It Make How It Looks?

Visual rhetoric is a part of all messages, whether spoken or written. Amateurish-looking brochures, fact sheets, Web pages, or signs practically ensure that a message will not be taken seriously. The emphasis on the visual is relatively new but has already become engrained in people's thinking. Twenty years ago, before the Internet and desktop publishing software, no one expected every professional publication to use images or have professional typefaces. For more than a hundred years (since 1868) the only typeface you might have had was Courier, or ITC American. For decades, most typos were simply corrected with correcting tape or whiteout, and corrections typed on top of the error. No one saw a problem with this because no real option existed except retyping the entire page.

The computer changed everything. With modern desktop publishing and Internet access, has come the expectation of perfection. You can now own the same software that professional publishers use. Many schools, like my own, offer students access to stock photography. As communication professionals, you will literally have all of the resources at your disposal that professional designers do (except for the degree in graphic arts). Even if you are not asked to create professional documents yourself (and most of you will), you need to understand a number of design principles in order to think visually and work with publishers. This chapter covers the basic principles of effective design as well as several types of written documents that are expected to be professional looking.

THE MEDIUM IS THE MESSAGE

Media critic Marshall McLuhan (1999/1964) is famous for saying "the medium is the message." What McLuhan meant was that the method used to distribute a message has as much meaning as the message itself. Choosing to break up with your boyfriend or girlfriend by letter (or UPS), is a different experience than breaking up face to face. Similarly, television creates different expectations for audiences about messages than print or radio.

Currently, online newspapers are struggling with the question of how to present news content in the Internet age. Historically, newspaper stories were written by journalistic "experts" (reporters and editors) that audiences trusted. However, in online environments, what happens to a reporter's "authority" when readers are allowed to post comments and openly disagree with the opinions of others?

Older generations of journalists and newspaper readers are uncomfortable with the notion of everyday people commenting on stories, but younger readers of online news who have grown up with Facebook and MySpace are very comfortable with collectively produced news and *expect* to be able to post comments and read what others have to say. The "message" of the classic newspaper, McLuhan might have suggested, is "conservativeness," "trustworthiness," and "professionalism," while the message of the online newspaper is "equality," "dialogue," and "openness."

What McLuhan said is true of all media. The medium *is* the message. For a public relations professional to create an effective feature story, the audience for the story must be understood. The story needs to be rhetorical, fit the source, and satisfy the expectations of the audience. You need to answer questions like "What do readers already know and expect?" and "What have previous stories been like?," before you can start writing. Messages must conform to the expectations of the medium for people to pay attention.

What is also important to understand is that not all print messages are the same. As Lupton (2004) points out, readers of Web content have different expectations than book readers (p. 74), just as each kind of media (print, electronic, broadcast) has content and stylistic features, print messages also have aesthetic features.

Aesthetics refers to the study of beauty or features that make something pleasant and appealing. The kinds of documents that professionals are responsible for producing vary widely and include electronic content placed on an organization's Web site, print materials produced for a public information campaign, and research reports used by decision makers. People naturally respond more favorably to messages that "appear" more credible, or have "ethos," to things that are attractive.

This chapter will introduce you to some basic design skills that will make your public relations documents more professional looking and more compelling. Understanding how to create more professional documents requires an understanding of everything from basic graphic design principles to an understanding of typography, paper, white space, and binding.

UNDERSTANDING BASIC DESIGN PRINCIPLES

Not all documents are the same. What is effective on a printed page, where a reader can take in everything at once, is not likely to work as well on a computer monitor with a different resolution and page orientation. Public relations professionals design for interest, legibility, informativeness, persuasiveness, readability, and success. Public relations is a results-oriented profession.

When you are in the planning and development stages of any document or design project, you must address questions like:

- How will the finished product be used?
- Will brochures have three, or four, panels?
- Should brochures be folded like an accordion, folded inward on both sides, or map-folded?
- Who will visit our Web site and why?
- What speed Internet connection will users to our site use?
- Will a newsletter be read only once by a recipient and then thrown away, or is the newsletter intended to have a longer shelf life, filed for future reference, left on a coffee table in a waiting room, or passed along to colleagues?

Questions about document use and audience needs influence the type of materials to use when designing or printing documents, as well as how documents should be structured. One of the first design principles to understand is the use of space.

SPACE

Learning to use space effectively takes a bit of practice. For many years in high school and college, you were conditioned to think in terms of creating "essays" and "class papers": double-spaced, numbered pages, centered headings, left-justified margins, one font for everything, etc. Then, in a publication class, or a class like this, your professor comes to you and says: "Okay, except for the spell checking part, throw everything you learned out the window. You are designing finished products now, no more double-spacing between lines, no more double spacing after periods, no more 12-point Times New Roman," etc.

Thinking in terms of the eye rather than your APA stylebook is not an easy transition. Creating brochures, annual reports, posters, signs, newsletters, and Web pages is a creative act both in terms of the writing and in terms of the design. You should also start collecting samples of appealing, creative, and effective documents (a swipe file)[1] and look at documents in terms of how they are designed. Every professional uses models to inform his or her own work. One of the first questions asked of musicians, artists, actors, and other creative professionals in interviews is, "Who were your influences?" All professionals receive inspiration from others. You should too.

One of the fundamental design skills is to understand how to effectively use both negative and positive space, including "white space," and how to *balance* negative and positive space. Negative and positive space are two sides of the same coin. **Positive space** refers to the parts of an image or document designed to be read or attended to. **Negative space**

Public Relations Quarterly

VOLUME 50 NUMBER 4 WINTER 2005

CELEBRATING 50 YEARS OF PUBLICATION

Bernays Cup Winner: Genevieve Sadler-Trainor
Page 7

1 In and About this Issue
2 Letter to the Editor
13 Online Public Relations
G.A. Andy Marken
16 Superstar PR
Ronald N. Levy
23 Segmenting Publics
Linda P. Morton

3 An Adventure in Publishing: The First Five Years (written in 1961)
Howard Penn Hudson

10 The Sago Mine Disaster: A Crisis in Crisis Communications
Edward J. Lordan

19 Too Hot to Handle: Competency Constrains Character in the Chi-Chi's Green Onion Crisis
Shari R. Veil, Min Liu, Sheri L. Erickson, Timothy L. Sellnow

25 Mistakes Made in Companies' Press Releases
Edd Applegate

31 The Brave New World of Public Relations: A look back
E.W. Brody

35 Conducting Better Research: Google Scholar and the Future of Search Technology
Michael L. Kent

41 Good Writing is Good Public Relations
Hal D. Steward

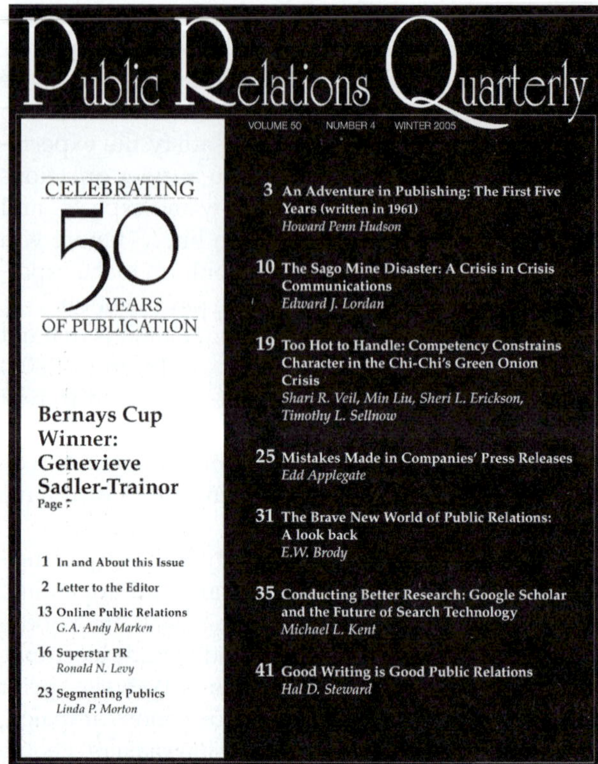

Public Relations Quarterly

VOLUME 50 NUMBER 4 WINTER 2005

CELEBRATING 50 YEARS OF PUBLICATION

Bernays Cup Winner: Genevieve Sadler-Trainor
Page 7

1 In and About this Issue
2 Letter to the Editor
13 Online Public Relations
G.A. Andy Marken
16 Superstar PR
Ronald N. Levy
23 Segmenting Publics
Linda P. Morton

3 An Adventure in Publishing: The First Five Years (written in 1961)
Howard Penn Hudson

10 The Sago Mine Disaster: A Crisis in Crisis Communications
Edward J. Lordan

19 Too Hot to Handle: Competency Constrains Character in the Chi-Chi's Green Onion Crisis
Shari R. Veil, Min Liu, Sheri L. Erickson, Timothy L. Sellnow

25 Mistakes Made in Companies' Press Releases
Edd Applegate

31 The Brave New World of Public Relations: A look back
E.W. Brody

35 Conducting Better Research: Google Scholar and the Future of Search Technology
Michael L. Kent

41 Good Writing is Good Public Relations
Hal D. Steward

FIGURE 4.1 Examples of positive and negative space.
Source: Photo courtesy of Elaine F. Newman Hudson, Editor, *Public Relations Quarterly*.

refers to those parts of an image or document in the background that work to make the positive elements more prominent. See Figure 4.1 for an example.

In both examples, the positive space is the text; everything else, white or black, is the "negative space." Positive space refers to the textual and graphic content in the foreground meant to stand out. Often, negative space is referred to as "white space," even though the empty space can be any color. Negative and positive space balance images and pages. In this photo from Venice, for example (Photo 4.1), the positive space is the Doge's Palace, the bridge overlooking the Bridge of Sighs, and the shops extending into the distance; the negative space is the cloudless sky and the flagstones reflecting the morning sunlight. For excellent treatments of negative and positive space, consider Fulks (www.apogeephoto.com/mag1-3/mag1-3mf1.shtml), and Stevens (www.signmuseum.com/bio/stevens2.php).

Both positive and negative space have visual "weight," or substance, and influence how the eye travels along a page, which design elements will be most prominent, and whether a document is appealing to look at and easy to use. Westerners read from left to right and top to bottom so pages are designed to encourage the eye to travel in a clockwise direction around a page, arriving at attention-getting design elements (headlines, pull-quotes, graphics) in logical ways.

Additionally, design elements usually are organized so that the entire page (white space, typography, shapes, lines, symbols, graphics) achieves "balance," or harmony, encouraging a reader to focus on a headline, an image, or a text box, rather than a blank space at the bottom of a page.

Balance

Balance deals with having similar amounts of negative and positive space on a page, as well as with how space is assigned or weighted on a page. Consider the sample layouts in Figure 4.2. In each case, the layouts draw upon different amounts of white space to create balance. In the upper left layout, a wider column of white is used to balance out the thinner (but heavier) column of gray. In the case

PHOTO 4.1 Venice, Doge's Palace, near St. Mark's Square and the Bridge of Sighs, Grand Canal.

of the upper right layout, the two lighter columns of text balance the shaded box on the top third of the page. Both designs involve different kinds of balance and utilize positive and negative space differently. Balance, like many other design elements, is something you eventually develop an eye for and something you can improve with a bit of practice. What is often easier to see is when a layout *lacks balance*, drawing attention to one element in the layout at the expense of the intended message.

One of the ways to judge balance and space is to hold a document up in front of you at arm's length and squint your eyes. If the elements on the page appear in harmony, without one part of the page standing out, you have balance. If something stands out because of its color, visual weight, or placement, you may need to make some changes in order to achieve balance. A more difficult concept to understand is symmetrical versus asymmetrical design, which goes hand-in-hand with balance.

Symmetrical/Asymmetrical Design

Symmetrical refers to balance along the horizontal or vertical planes. An all-centered layout is symmetrical because if you fold a page in half along the vertical plane, the document appears the same on both sides. The lower right example in Figure 4.2 is symmetrical: the columns on the left and right are divided evenly along the vertical middle of the page, and the headline and horizontal paragraph serve to divide the page in two down the horizontal middle. The document has balance and symmetry.

By contrast, the upper and lower left documents in Figure 4.2 are asymmetrical. **Asymmetrical** layouts lack "balance" in the formal sense of a balance beam (suggesting two equal parts). Asymmetrical layouts are more interesting to look at and often convey a sense of modernism and creativity. Moreover, asymmetrical layouts tend to attract more attention. Like the stereotypical "FREE BEER!" signs often

Public Relations Quarterly

VOLUME 50 NUMBER 4 WINTER 2005

CELEBRATING 50 YEARS OF PUBLICATION

Bernays Cup Winner: Genevieve Sadler-Trainor
Page 7

1 In and About this Issue
2 Letter to the Editor
13 Online Public Relations — *G.A. Andy Marken*
16 Superstar PR — *Ronald N. Levy*
23 Segmenting Publics — *Linda P. Morton*

3 An Adventure in Publishing: The First Five Years (written in 1961) — *Howard Penn Hudson*
10 The Sago Mine Disaster: A Crisis in Crisis Communications — *Edward J. Lordan*
19 Too Hot to Handle: Competency Constrains Character in the Chi-Chi's Green Onion Crisis — *Shari R. Veil, Min Liu, Sheri L. Erickson, Timothy L. Sellnow*
25 Mistakes Made in Companies' Press Releases — *Edd Applegate*
31 The Brave New World of Public Relations: A look back — *E.W. Brody*
35 Conducting Better Research: Google Scholar and the Future of Search Technology — *Michael L. Kent*
41 Good Writing is Good Public Relations — *Hal D. Steward*

Communication Teacher

NCA — Published by the National Communication Association
Previously published as Speech Communication Teacher

Ideas & strategies for the classroom
www.natcom.org/pubs/ct/ct.htm

Vol. 17 No. 3 — Spring 2003

Touchstone Award

Production, Performance, and Portfolios: A Final Project for Diverse Learning Styles

Objective: To complete a final course project that incorporates kinesthetic, auditory, and visual learning styles.
Course: Intercultural

Diversity has become an important component in many communication courses. Nowhere is that component more apparent than in the intercultural communication course. Although instructors may focus on the incorporation, understanding, and appreciation of diversity in course content, diversity often is not reflected in the assessment of the material taught in this course. Because students have multiple learning styles (Manner, 2001; Park, 2000), the purpose of this activity is to help instructors incorporate diversity into their assessment of intercultural communication course material. The three options provided in this activity incorporate three learning styles: kinesthetic, auditory, and visual. *Kinesthetic learners* learn best through experience. *Auditory learners* learn best through hearing (e.g., listening to lectures). *Visual learners* learn best through seeing (e.g., reading textbooks).

The Activity

This activity provides students with the opportunity to use the medium of communication with which they are most comfortable when completing a final project for the intercultural communication course. Simultaneously, this activity provides the instructor with the tools to assess students' understanding of the course material. Listed below are the options for the final project. When incorporating this activity into a 16 week semester, students must select their final course project option by Week 6. Project presentations occur during Weeks 14-16.

Option 1: Video Documentary. For this option, students create a 20-30 minute video documentary on some aspect of intercultural communication. Students can conduct on-the-spot interviews with people about an intercultural communication issue or they can tell a story about an intercultural communication issue through video scenes. Students should be informed that this assignment is not a video of a performance, but a video of a story created from scenes and events they will videotape. Students should be encouraged to incorporate their own voice into the video as narrator (i.e., clearly explaining to the audience the particular intercultural communication issues that were videotaped). The video should be presented in a fairly professional manner. Although students are not expected to produce a PBS quality video, there should be evidence of editing rather than simply turning the camera on and off. (Students are expected to use basic editing by hooking two VCRs together and recording segments from the roughly shot tape onto a second tape.) Students should be sure that (1) the video tells a story, (2) the story is easy for the audience to follow, and (3) the story is no longer than 15 minutes. Once the video is completed, students write a 4 page paper relating the issues addressed in the video. Students are required to have three references for this paper. (Only one reference can be the course textbook and only one reference can be obtained from the Internet.) This final project option engages all three learning styles: kinesthetic

IN THIS ISSUE

Maximizing Media Relations: A Web Site Checklist

By Michael L. Kent and Maureen Taylor

Most organizations believe that a Web site is an important part of their corporate communication efforts. Web sites, for better or worse, are the windows through which organizations are viewed. Every day journalists visit organizational Web sites for specific reasons — gathering information for news stories, confirming rumors, to write features, etc. Unfortunately, many journalists leave dissatisfied with what they find. It does not have to be this way.

The purpose of this article is to provide public relations practitioners with a checklist to evaluate the strengths and weaknesses of their Web sites as a media relations tool. This diagnostic tool will help practitioners assess the effectiveness of their Web site for meeting media needs. Before we explain what makes an effective media relations site, pull up your Web browser and go to any site other than your organization's. Once there, open the preferences menu on your browser and delete the cache of stored images and list of visited links (on *Microsoft Explorer:* edit/preferences/Web browser/advanced/history/"clear history" and edit/preferences/Web browser/advanced/cache/"empty now"; on *Netscape:* edit/preferences/advanced/cache/"clear disk cache now" and edit/preferences/navigator/history/"expire now." *Note:* this procedure will not affect anything but how fast Web pages load the first time you visit and whether previously visited links are highlighted).

Michael L. Kent

Once you have made these changes in your preferences, you are ready to go back to your organization's Web site. Be sure to pay attention to how many seconds it takes the page to load when you are visiting your site "for the first time." Once your site loads, place a check in each of the check boxes from the list below if the item is present on your organization's home page or within one "obvious" (or easy to locate) click.

Now that you have completed the checklist, score it according to the following scale: 0-10: poor media site; 11-15: a good start on media relations but a long way to go; 16-25: A useful site for meeting the needs of the media; 26-30: Great job! You are maximizing your media relations potential. Since most organizations are not in the 26-30 range, let's look at each category on the checklist in more detail. The remainder of this article is dedicated to explaining how you can maximize your media relations on the Web. The first item is "attracting media."

Attracting Media

How do you get the media to visit your Web site? Adding your organization's Web address on company publications is a good start. News releases, ad-

14 — Public Relations Quarterly

Critical Studies in Media Communication
Vol. 18, No. 3, September 2001, pp. 359–375

Managerial Rhetoric as the Metaphor for the World Wide Web

Michael L. Kent

—This article explains how metaphors influence how we experience events, and how the Web, viewed through a different metaphor or lens, currently appears a little less valuable as a tool of education or democracy. Although the Web constitutes a new communication milieu, possessing the potential to revolutionize communication in the next millennium, its rhetoric is currently one of consumerism and capitalism–economic not political ideologies pertain. This article conducts a metaphorical analysis of the World Wide Web positing that the Web might be understood best through a managerial metaphor rather than the current spatial/relational metaphor. Using Sproule's 1988 categories of managerial rhetoric, this article critiques contemporary Web practices in an effort to better understand the Web and its communicative potential.

As Postman suggests in *Conscientious Objections,* "To have an answer without knowing the question, without understanding that you might have been given a different answer if the question had been posed differently, may be more than meaningless; it may be exceedingly dangerous" (1988, p. 26). Nevertheless, this is exactly what is taking place with the World Wide Web (WWW). Dozens of articles have been written predicting what is likely to happen with Webbed communication–the direction the Web will take, how important the Web will become, who's lives will be influenced by the Web, and who should pay attention to it (cf., Bettig, 1997; Campbell, 1995; Gunkel & Gunkel, 1997; Gustafson & Thomsen, 1996; Hansen, 1998; Harper, 1996; Marken, 1998). Indeed, given the volume of scholarship currently talking *about* the WWW, the implication seems to be that its impact is already understood.

Skepticism and criticism of new technologies in mass communication and computer science is not new (cf., Badgikian, 1990; Burnham, 1984; Postman, 1984, 1988, 1991, 1993; Schiller, 1989; Stoll, 1995). Unfortunately, critiques of new technologies often seem to come too late, taking the form of "laments for simpler times." This article explores the rhetorical characteristics of the WWW advancing a new metaphor for understanding the Web and a critical examination of the Web's rhetoric.

The Web is often touted as a panacea for many of our modern social ills

Michael Kent is an Assistant Professor and the Director of Graduate Studies, in the Department of Speech Communication, Montclair State University. Kent conducts research on Webbed communication and dialogic Public Relations. Thank you to Maureen Taylor, Rutgers University, and three anonymous reviewers for their invaluable comments. Telephone (973) 655-5130. E-mail: kentm@mail.montclair.edu.

Copyright 2001, National Communication Association

FIGURE 4.2 Four journal covers illustrating white space and balance.
(top left) © National Communication Association. (top right) © Taylor and Francis Group, UK. (bottom left) Photo courtesy of Elaine F. Newman Hudson, Editor, *Public Relations Quarterly.* (bottom right) Kent, M. L., (2008). Critical analysis of blogging in public relations. Public Relations review 34(1), 32–40, © Elsevier Inc.

found on college campuses followed by, in smaller letters, "Free Beer! is great, but what is better is voting for ..." As much as you *know* there will be no "free beer," *not* reading such messages is difficult. The headline copy attracts your attention. Asymmetrical design works similarly by piquing readers' interest in documents and making them *want* to read messages.

The trick to creating a compelling asymmetrical layout is to understand that you need to combine principles of balance, space, typography (discussed in Chapter 12), creativity, and a willingness to experiment with several possible layouts in order to achieve just the right effect for the audience and occasion. One of the ways we develop creative designs is to use "thumbnails."

Thumbnails and Mockups

Thumbnails are scaled-down copies of larger documents, like those in Figures 4.3 and 4.4. **Mockups** refer to either rough sketched draft copies of design ideas, or working documents taped, stapled, or glued together in order to determine if a document layout works properly. Many organizations, especially small ones, do not have printers capable of double-sided output. Professionals either have to send pages through the printer a second time, or tape both sides of draft documents together to see if documents are formatted properly and if all pages are printing properly.

Professionals use thumbnails and mockups for every project. Virtually no one sits down with a blank computer monitor and just designs a document from

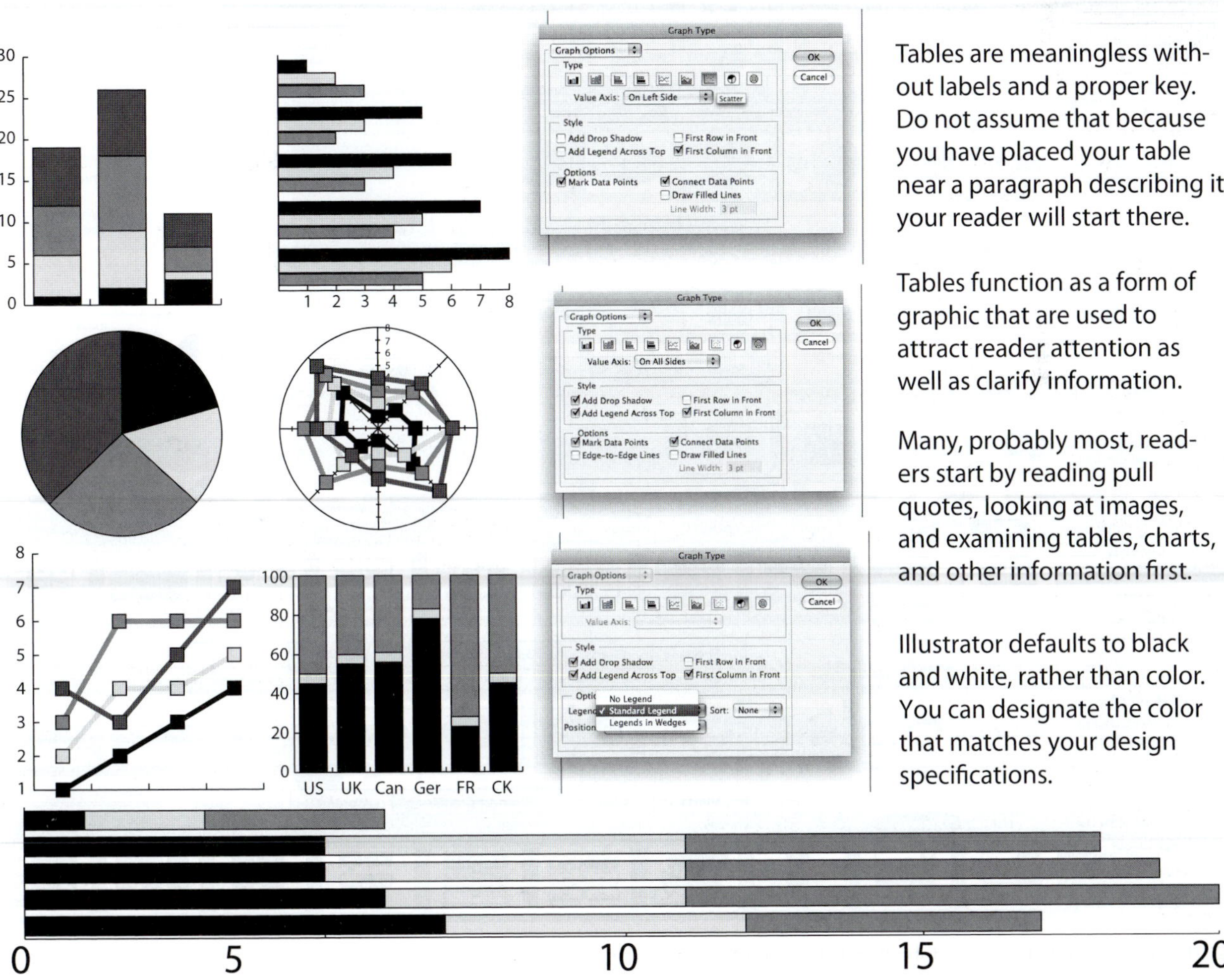

Graph Type
Graph Options
OK
Cancel
Tables are meaningless without labels and a proper key. Do not assume that because you have placed your table near a paragraph describing it, your reader will start there.
Tables function as a form of graphic that are used to attract reader attention as well as clarify information.
Many, probably most, readers start by reading pull quotes, looking at images, and examining tables, charts, and other information first.
Illustrator defaults to black and white, rather than color. You can designate the color that matches your design specifications.
US
UK
Can
Ger
FR
CK
0
5
10
15
20

FIGURE 4.3 Samples of Charts and Graphs.

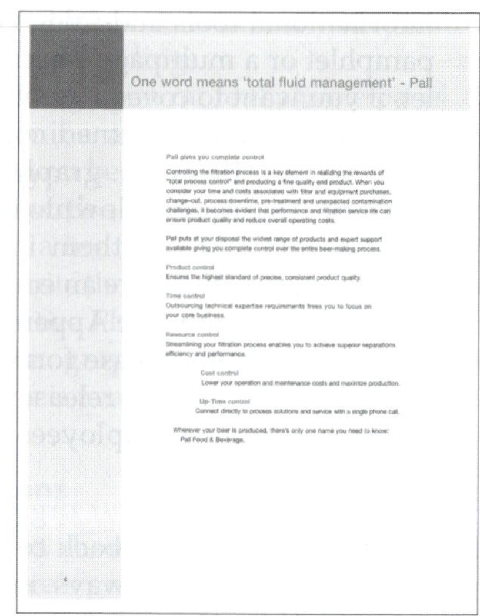

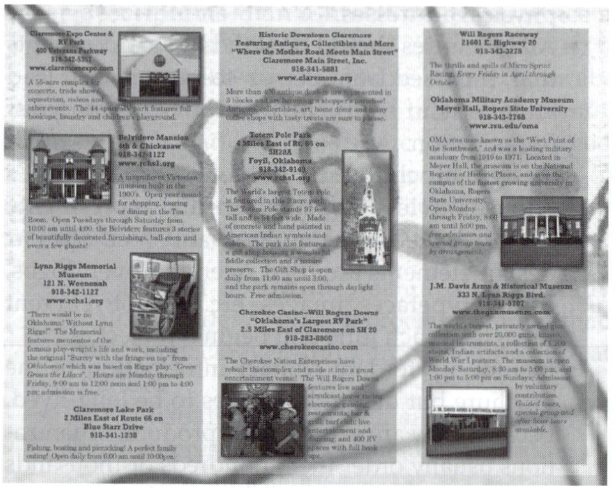

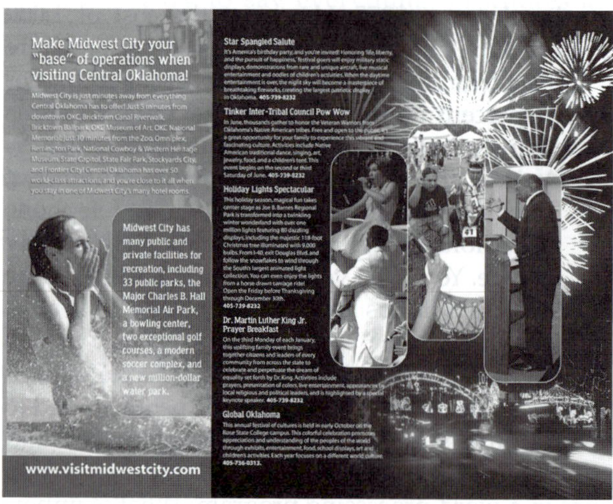

FIGURE 4.5 Sample Brochures.
Source: © Claremore Convention & Visitors Bureau.

organization's position on political, social, or strategic decisions.

Although pamphlets and leaflets usually do not have "covers," pamphlets are often produced by folding an 8.5" × 11" page in half along the vertical, resulting in a 5.5" × 8.5" "booklet" with four panels. Several pages are often combined to produce multipage booklets with cover information printed on the front and back of the outside page.

Pamphlets are often created for special events, although they might also be used to transmit persuasive messages to key publics or stakeholders, or distributed at public events or in media kits. Since the range of possible uses for pamphlets is so varied, there is no single rule for how to write one. The tone of pamphlets depends upon the purpose of the document: internal versus external, informational versus persuasive, etc. Pamphlets often include images, diagrams, and bulleted lists, but having all textual content is also common.

OBTAINING STOCK PHOTOGRAPHY AND GRAPHICS

Many people have never given much thought to the role of photography in design. Photographs and images are everywhere: in magazines, newspapers, brochures, annual reports, on billboards, posters, signs, transit stations, moving vehicles (buses, trains, delivery vehicles, semis), and on television and the Internet. Photographs are an integral part of design. Because of the importance of the image as a persuasive and informative tool, communication professionals need to understand some basic photographic issues.

Hiring a Photographer

Photography is expensive. The cost of hiring a professional photographer for one day can easily run $1,500 just for the photographer. Additional fees for expenses include lighting assistants, models, props, travel expenses, costumes, hair stylists, etc.

In the past, photographers charged fees for film, processing, preparing proof sheets, etc. Now, with digital photography, such fees have been eliminated, but photographers still have to charge per-photo fees for "processing" (color correction, data formatting, etc.). Anyone who has worked with digital pictures knows the process is time-consuming. Additionally, understanding the contract and agreeing on ownership and use rights of the photographs *before* you hire a photographer is important.

Large organizations can afford to hire professional photographers. Organizations that regularly release new products each year, like automakers, have ongoing agreements with professional photography firms. Where photography becomes more of a problem is with small and medium-sized organizations that cannot afford to hire professional photographers every time they need to take employee photographs or create advertisements or brochures.

Use Stock Images

One solution for obtaining images without having to pay the high fees associated with a photographer is to purchase them *à la carte* from a stock image/photography provider (e.g., <pro.Corbis.com>, <www.DreamsTime.com>, <www.GettyImages.com>, <www.JupiterImages.com>, <www.QueerStock.com>), or to buy royalty-free CDs of relevant images: dogs, cats, medicine, houses, athletes, weather, Halloween, Christmas, Hanukah, roads, etc.

Stock photography providers grant three basic types of rights for use of their images. They offer *project specific rights*, which means the images may be used in a specific project (books, corporate annual reports, advertisements, Web sites, etc.); *limited rights*, which means the images may only be reproduced a set number of times (e.g., 5,000, 10,000, 25,000 copies, etc.); and *unrestricted rights*, which means an organization may use images however it wishes. Images are also "licensed" for use based on the distribution size (limited visibility like catalogs versus larger visibility like magazines or billboards), Web use (home page use versus secondary page, half-screen versus full-screen), and specialty uses like T-shirts, coffee mugs, etc. Additional licensing fees are charged when images are used for multiple projects.

An alternative to paying licensing fees for images each time you use them is to purchase a CD of stock photography that allows for unrestricted use of the images. However, the images from stock photography CDs are not the most sought-after images. More desirable images can be sold individually for more money.

Take Photographs Yourself

Because of the cost of professional photography, many public relations professionals learn basic photography skills so they can take their own photographs of organizational members, products, events, etc. If you take the pictures yourself, always be sure to obtain media releases from all of the people who appear in the photographs you want to use. Obtaining signed releases will save you from getting in trouble down the road. Indeed, photo releases should be obtained whenever *any* photo is used. Obtaining releases is part of doing business and should not be seen as a chore. See Appendix B for sample photo release forms.

Also important is avoiding controversial subject matter in the photographs you take, like those taken at social events, openings, fundraisers, etc., where people are drinking, smoking, or engaging in other activities that might make them look unprofessional. Because people *do* smoke and drink and sometimes fraternize at social events, take a lot of pictures, since many of them will be unusable.

Use Copyrighted Images Only with Permission

Perhaps the most important issue to remember is that you cannot indiscriminately use photographs that you do not own the rights to. You *cannot* use photographs for professional purposes that were obtained from the World Wide Web, even in internal company presentations. The U.S. copyright law gives copyright protection to anyone who takes a picture or writes anything, even if the individual or organization does not file for protection (see Chapter 13). Thus, assume all images—even those found on social networking sites—are copyrighted. If you want to send a funny picture of a cat you downloaded from TheDailyKitten.com to your mother you can, but you cannot use copyrighted or downloaded images for organizational or promotional documents (even documents not available publicly or only produced for a few employees in house), unless you obtain permission or pay licensing fees (Casarez, 1997).

EDITING IMAGES

Besides learning how to use a digital camera, public relations professionals should also learn some basic digital photo editing skills like cropping and scaling photos, color corrections, and photo retouching. Magazines like *Photoshop User* feature beginning, intermediate, and advanced tutorials on photo editing and manipulation.

With a program like Adobe Photoshop and a few hours of training, anyone with moderate computer skills can learn how to correct color, remove wrinkles and lines, whiten teeth, and insert/remove people from images. To give an example, imagine an employee has resigned (or worse, died) and she or he appears in an organizational photograph you want to use in an upcoming newsletter. Depending upon where the person appears in the photograph (front row, middle, back), s/he can be easily cropped out, replaced with a potted plant or another person, or removed from the image, enabling its use.

Scaling

Pictures are often larger than the layout area and may need to be **scaled** down (decreased) to fit. Avoid scaling pictures up; enlarging photographs causes a loss in resolution and may render the picture unsuitable for professional purposes. As online printer PrintForLess.Com (www.printingforless.com/resolution.html) explains, "Resolution and size (dimensions) are inversely proportional to each other. So, if you enlarge an image, you lower its resolution. If you reduce an image, you increase its resolution."

Images intended for Web use should be saved as JPGs using an RGB (red, green, blue) color scheme, while images intended for printing should be converted to "CYMK" (cyan, magenta, yellow, black four-color processing, like an ink-jet printer) and saved at a resolution of at least 300 dpi at the final print size. You should take digital photographs at the highest resolution setting your camera allows, since photographs can always be reduced, but enlarging photographs may pose a problem. Desktop publishing programs like InDesign allow pictures to be "scaled to fit" designated spaces so very accurate sizing is possible.

Cropping

Cropping involves altering a picture/image so only the part of the image that is desired is retained. If you take an actual paper photograph and cut parts of it off, you have cropped the image. Electronically cropping a picture involves either one of two procedures. *One,* the picture can be permanently cropped by selecting the part of the picture that you want to keep and deleting the rest. Or *two,* desktop publishing programs have a "crop" feature that masks the content of the picture you want hidden but does not actually *delete* the masked content. This sort of cropping allows you to easily reposition the photograph in its frame or to change the area of emphasis in the photograph without permanently altering the photograph.

Exposure, Sharpening, Color Corrections

When you take your own photos, you need to learn how to adjust your images to get the most out of them. Virtually every professional image has been corrected in some way: contrast, exposure, saturation, sharpening, temperature, softening skin tones, removing blemishes, etc. For professional purposes, a format called RAW or digital negative (DNG) is used that allows photographs to be adjusted just like real photographers used to do in the darkroom. Very few photographs, even those taken by professional photographers, are perfect as taken. If you have access to a folder full of stock photography, you can often see the corrections that have been made to many of the images by using a photo program like Adobe Bridge.[2]

Programs like Bridge and Adobe Lightroom allow you to conduct an assortment of basic to sophisticated photo corrections (see Photos 4.5 and 4.6, Adobe Bridge, Camera Raw Editing Window). Learning how to edit photographs is quite easy. Online tutorials like Lynda.com offer A/V training in dozens of programs for about $25 per month. Dozens of books are available, such the Peachpit Press series of texts on Photoshop, Illustrator, and other programs.

Many basic and advanced corrections can be done in the Camera Raw window in Bridge allowing poor-quality images to be improved, and high-quality images to be made better. Dozens of more advanced settings are also available in the Camera Raw Window or in Adobe Lightroom. With absolutely no training, basic corrections to exposure, saturation, contrast, and temperature can be made in almost any graphics program, whether on a PC or a Mac. With careful cropping and conservative photo corrections, even a mediocre picture can be improved dramatically.

Integrating Images Effectively

Photographs can add an element of interest and creativity to an otherwise dull document, but they should not be used just to take up space. Your readers will figure out very quickly that your documents lack content. Although headshots and group photos of people posing are common in employee newsletters and other internal documents, the best photographs show some sort of action. A picture of the CEO holding big scissors to a ribbon is more interesting and dramatic than a picture of him or her posing in front of the cut ribbon. A shot of someone breaking a

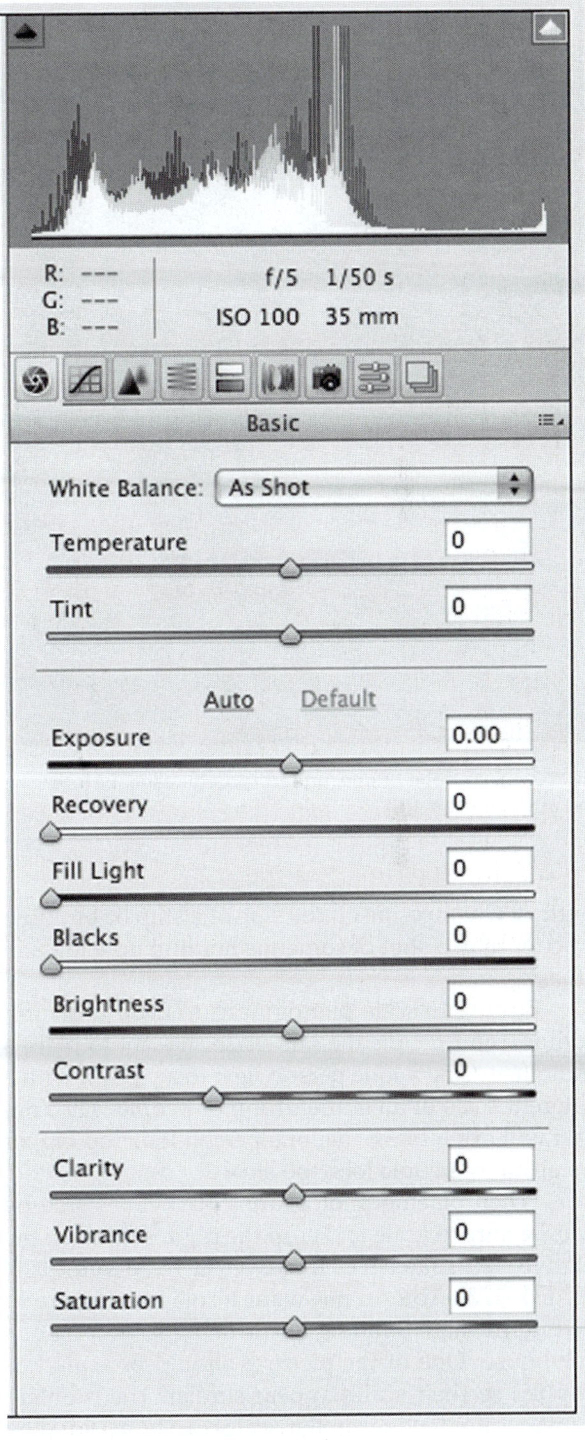

PHOTO 4.5 Adobe Bridge, Camera Raw Editing Window.
Source: © 2009, Adobe Systems Incorporated.

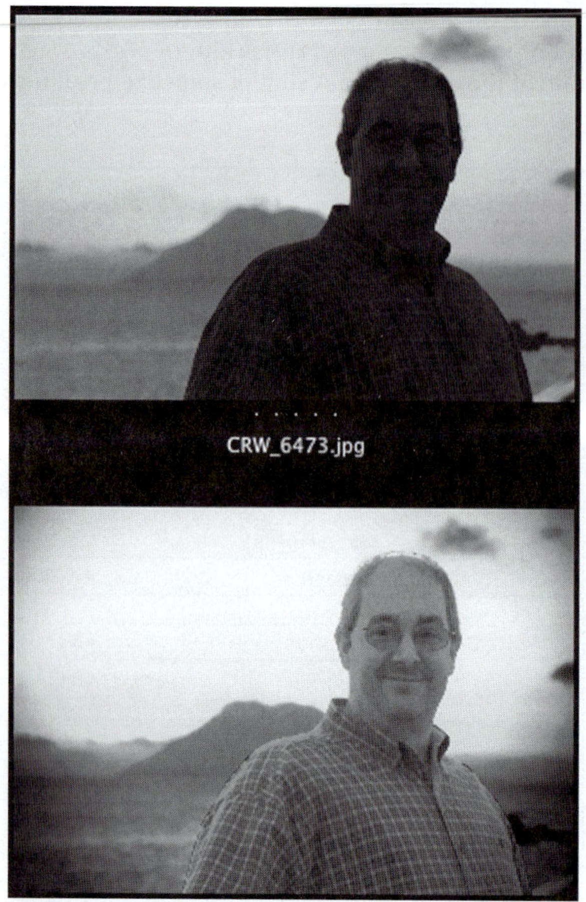

PHOTO 4.6 Adobe Bridge, underexposed image, before and after adjustment.

bottle of Champagne on the side of a ship or building is better than a shot of someone holding up a glass in a toast.

Be sure to scale photographs to keep horizons, skylines, and people the same size. Try not to place a photo featuring a lone person next to a picture with a different scale of an entire group of people. The contrast will often make the lone person look too big, or the group of people look too small.

When placing photographs of skylines side by side, be sure to scale and crop the photos to make the relative sizes match (cf., Treadwell & Treadwell, 2000, pp. 171–173). You do not want to place a picture of the Empire State Building next to a bigger picture of a row house. One of the pictures should be scaled or cropped so their scales appear similar. The problem of images not having similar scales can be avoided by not positioning photographs next to each other on the page.

Finally, pictures are typically scaled to reflect their relative importance in a layout. You have undoubtedly noticed that most daily newspapers feature large photographs to accompany their front page stories whenever possible. The most important photograph on the page is usually the biggest photograph. Learn to scale and manipulate photographs properly by examining how professional publications use images so you can maximize their value in documents.

INFORMATIONAL GRAPHICS

Informational graphics (infographics for short)[3] are used to both clarify messages in speeches and provide additional information in print documents. Infographics are often part of annual reports, fact sheets, feature stories, news conferences, speeches, and professional presentations. In general, messages that draw upon multiple channels of information (spoken, written, images, etc.) are easier to comprehend and tend to be more memorable. Incorporating visual aids into spoken presentations has been standard for decades, just as using stock photography, graphs, charts, and other sources of information has become standard for print documents.

Informational graphics (infographics) are essentially visual aids. Visual aids serve two general purposes: they clarify information and they provide a second or third channel of information (symbolic, graphic, textual). Research on nonverbal communication suggests that when people are presented with conflicting messages, they tend to believe the nonverbal channel. As Treadwell and Treadwell explain "we receive approximately 11 percent of our acquired knowledge through hearing and 83 percent through seeing" (2000, p. 457). Similarly, combining visual information with spoken, or textual, information can increase long-term recall fivefold (p. 457).

The problem with many informational graphics, however, is that often the person creating the graphic just types some numbers into a program like Excel, and tells the computer to spit out a bar graph or pie chart with little regard for color contrast, number of colors used, table labels, the amount of information contained in a single graphic, or the clarity of the information as a stand-alone graphic. Another problem has to do with simply taking someone else's informational graphic and importing it into your own work with little regard for the fact that someone else's graphic was created to illustrate *their* point, not *yours*.

The best informational graphics do more than simply illustrate what you can say with words. Straightforward, "off the shelf" graphics are perfectly fine for a Slideware presentation given on short notice. However, for use in fact sheets, newsletters, brochures, Web sites, and other purposes, specially designed informational graphics can attract attention, increase readability, and help clarify information (the real purpose of an infographic).

One of the finest examples of excellent information design is the informational graphic of Napoleon's march to Moscow by Charles Joseph Minard (Figure 4.6). Minrad graphically depicts the size of the army as it entered Russia in 1812 and the size of the army as it departed. Additionally, the graphic indicates the temperature during the campaign, the distance traveled, geographic obstacles like rivers, as well as graphically illustrating the route taken by the troops on their campaign. With no additional information than this one graphic and a paragraph of information, a casual observer could vividly describe the entire campaign.

Critics of Tufte, who reintroduced Minard's graphic a number of years ago in his books on information design (1990, 1997, 2001, 2003, 2006) have complained that Minard's graphics are not self-evidently easy to read and require reading the text that accompanies the graphic. This is true. However, should difficult and complicated issues be reduced to "simplistic" data under the assumption that readers or listeners are too lazy to read a paragraph? Tufte (2003) was invited by NASA to examine the decision making behind the Challenger shuttle explosion (1986), and concluded that the reason the space shuttle crashed was because "simplistic" data was used to evaluate the risks. The poorly designed informational graphic (actually, a bullet list), led decision makers to underestimate the risks involved in a launch. Most professional decisions are not life-and-death decisions, but many are in fields like engineering, pharmaceuticals, chemistry, medicine. The assumption made by Tufte, and other information design professionals, is that to make sophisticated decisions, like war, launching a space shuttle, assessing risks involved in terrorism or disease, or even minor decisions like which consultant to use, requires sophisticated graphics. Pie charts and

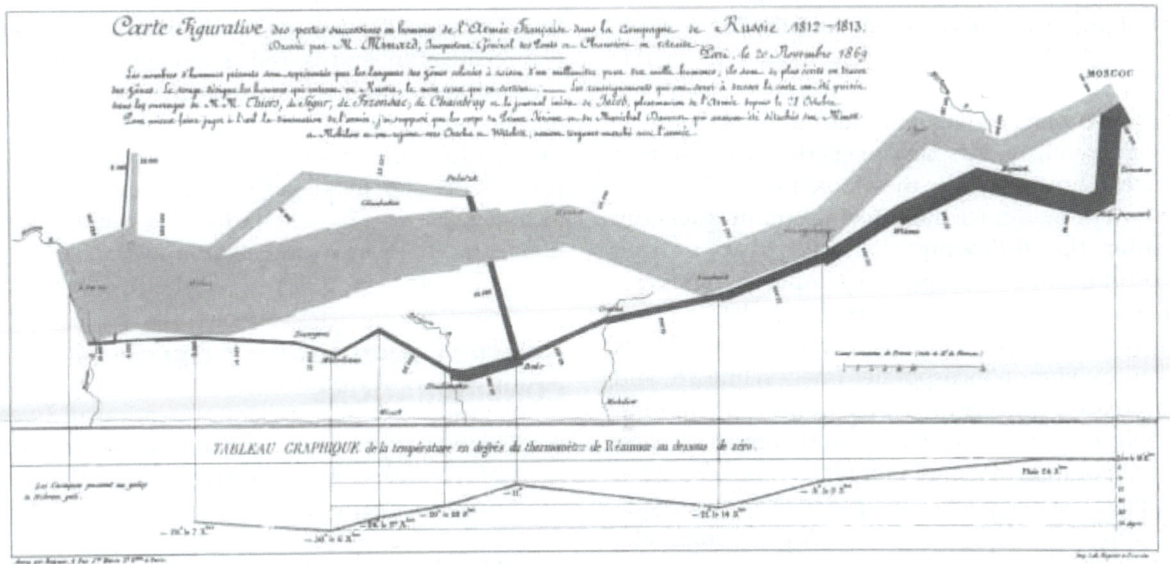

This map drawn by Charles Joseph Minard portrays the losses suffered by Napoleon's army in the Russian campaign of 1812. Beginning at the left on the Polish-Russian border near the Niemen, the thick band shows the size of the army (442,000 men) as it invaded Russia. The width of the band indicates the size of the army at each position. In September, the army reached Moscow with 100,000 men. The path of Napoleon's retreat from Moscow in the bitterly cold winter is depicted by the dark lower band, which is tied to temperature and time scales. The remains of the Grande Armée struggled out of Russia with 10,000 men. Minard's graphic tells a rich, coherent story with its multivariate data, far more enlightening than just a single number bouncing along over time. Six variables are plotted: the size of the army, its location on a two-dimensional surface, direction of the army's movement, and temperature on various dates during the retreat from Moscow. It may well be the best statistical graphic ever drawn.

FIGURE 4.6 Minard, Napoleon's March.

Source: Reprinted by permission, Edward R. Tuffe, *The Visual Display of Quantitative Information*, Graphics Press LLC, 1983, 2001.

bar graphs could have been used by Minard to plot the temperature and indicate the casualties in his graphic, but the *relationship* between these variables would have been less obvious. Tufte envisions infographics as decision-making tools rather than as mere support tools like PowerPoint slides in a speech to the board of directors.

In most modern infographics made using Slideware like PowerPoint, each bit of data (temperature, death tolls, routes) has to be plotted on separate graphs[4] and usually with no effort made to integrate the information and show how a variety of factors contribute to a particular outcome (in Napoleon's case, the geography, the distance, and the weather).[5] Since infographics often stand alone as part of creative documents, they should be clear and concise—simple but not simplistic.

The most common types of professional graphics include pie charts (circular, pull-apart, three-dimensional, etc.), graphs (line, plot, or scatter, horizontal/vertical), and bar graphs (side by side, stacked, three dimensional). See Figure 4.3.

There are of course nearly limitless variations of these basic types, and as with so many areas of public relations writing, you should begin to pay more attention to informational graphics and start collecting effective examples in your swipe file. Often, infographics place more emphasis on making the table or pie chart look "pretty" than on the information the chart is supposed to convey. Three-dimensional pie charts with exaggerated perspectives and a dozen colors, or difficult to interpret, overly spiky bar charts, are often used because of how dramatic they look, rather than how well how they depict the information in question. Consider the following distorted graphs from Microsoft *Excel*, as well as more simple graphics created using Adobe *Illustrator* (see Figure 4.4).

Another form of informational graphic that is also quite common incorporates images, line art, and other creative features in order to attract attention and help explain relationships and complex ideas. This type of informational graphic is similar to what you might see in a science magazine or in a newspaper like *USA Today*. The more creative informational graphics are often used both to explain complicated phenomenon and attract the attention of readers (readability). See Figure 4.7 A–D for excellent informational graphics originally published in several national newspapers by graphic artists Philip Loubere and Megan Jaegerman.

The best informational graphics are created on an ad hoc basis, rather than adopted from someone else's book, Web site, article, etc. As students, you have probably used data and graphics from other sources (books, magazines, the Internet). However, creating original photographs, artwork, and informational graphics is mandatory in the professional world where there are no charts or tables already prepared depicting your own organization. As Tufte (2001) explains: "Graphical excellence is the well designed presentation of interesting data—a matter of *substance*, of *statistics*, and of *design*. ... And graphical excellence requires telling the truth about the data" (p. 51, Tufte's emphasis). Statistical tables are best created using software like Adobe's *Illustrator*, which allows you to create scalable graphics and control line weight, color, typography, placement of labels, etc. Tables can also be created in *Photoshop* and *InDesign*, but require more work. Programs like Microsoft *Excel* can also be used to create tables, however, avoid adding noisy backgrounds, three-dimensional and perspective effects, or creating graphics that exaggerate effects such as spiky peaks on bar graphs. See Figure 4.4, above, for what to avoid.

There are several suggestions for designing the more creative and specialized types of informational graphics, like Minard, Loubere, or Jaegerman's, and the samples above. Always remember that informational graphics are designed both to clarify information (especially numbers) as well as serving rhetorical ends, increasing credibility and attracting readers or audience members who might not be inherently interested in the topic (Elaboration Likelihood Model). When used for decision making, try to represent relationships as accurately as possible and create useful informational graphics that are more than "eye candy."

GENERAL INFOGRAPHIC DELIVERY CONSIDERATIONS

- Newspapers and similar media: Provide black-and-white photographs, high-quality printed graphics, or attached files (at least 150–180 dpi).
- Magazines: Provide color photographs, 35 mm slides, or attached files (at least 300 dpi).
- Television: Provide 35 mm, color, slides, digital images (at least 72 dpi), and high-quality video (not cell phone footage).

All print and broadcast media are increasingly willing to use high-resolution graphics delivered via CD-ROM or the Internet.

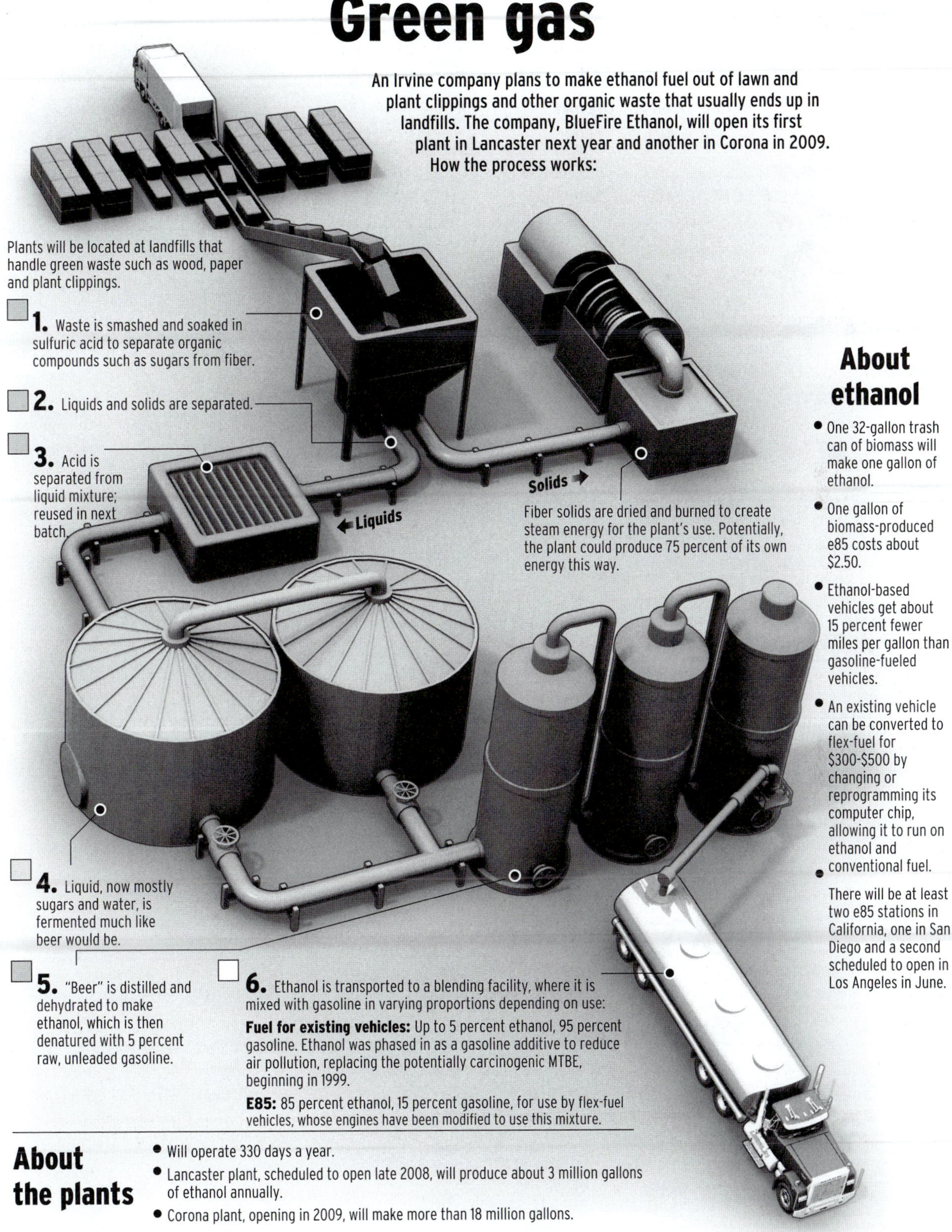

Green gas
An Irvine company plans to make ethanol fuel out of lawn and plant clippings and other organic waste that usually ends up in landfills. The company, BlueFire Ethanol, will open its first plant in Lancaster next year and another in Corona in 2009. How the process works:
Plants will be located at landfills that handle green waste such as wood, paper and plant clippings.
1. Waste is smashed and soaked in sulfuric acid to separate organic compounds such as sugars from fiber.
2. Liquids and solids are separated.
3. Acid is separated from liquid mixture; reused in next batch.
Liquids
Solids
Fiber solids are dried and burned to create steam energy for the plant's use. Potentially, the plant could produce 75 percent of its own energy this way.
About ethanol
• One 32-gallon trash can of biomass will make one gallon of ethanol.
• One gallon of biomass-produced e85 costs about $2.50.
• Ethanol-based vehicles get about 15 percent fewer miles per gallon than gasoline-fueled vehicles.
• An existing vehicle can be converted to flex-fuel for $300-$500 by changing or reprogramming its computer chip, allowing it to run on ethanol and conventional fuel.
• There will be at least two e85 stations in California, one in San Diego and a second scheduled to open in Los Angeles in June.
4. Liquid, now mostly sugars and water, is fermented much like beer would be.
5. "Beer" is distilled and dehydrated to make ethanol, which is then denatured with 5 percent raw, unleaded gasoline.
6. Ethanol is transported to a blending facility, where it is mixed with gasoline in varying proportions depending on use:
Fuel for existing vehicles: Up to 5 percent ethanol, 95 percent gasoline. Ethanol was phased in as a gasoline additive to reduce air pollution, replacing the potentially carcinogenic MTBE, beginning in 1999.
E85: 85 percent ethanol, 15 percent gasoline, for use by flex-fuel vehicles, whose engines have been modified to use this mixture.
About the plants
• Will operate 330 days a year.
• Lancaster plant, scheduled to open late 2008, will produce about 3 million gallons of ethanol annually.
• Corona plant, opening in 2009, will make more than 18 million gallons.
Source: BlueFire Ethanol Inc.
Reporting by Chantal Lamers, graphic by Phil Loubere / The Register

FIGURE 4.7 Infographics: edit the Ethanol graphic: Image by Philip Loubere.
Source: Philip Loubere ©1992 The New York Times.

The Cost of That Dog in the Window

Here are estimated costs of caring for a pet dog. Lifetime figures are based on an average life span of 11 years. Totals do not include purchase price, which ranges from no cost to $5,000.

	INITIAL	ANNUAL	LIFETIME
Food, treats	—	$400	$4,400
Veterinarian visits, licenses	$150*	290*	3,340*
Training	50–100	50–200	600–2,300
Grooming supplies	130	100	1,230
Leashes, collars, toys	100	100	1,200
Flea and pest treatment	—	80	880
TOTAL	**$430–480**	**$1,020–1,170**	**$11,650–13,350**

Source: American Kennel Club

*Medical costs could be substantially higher in cases of serious illness or injury.

Megan Jaegerman/The New York Times

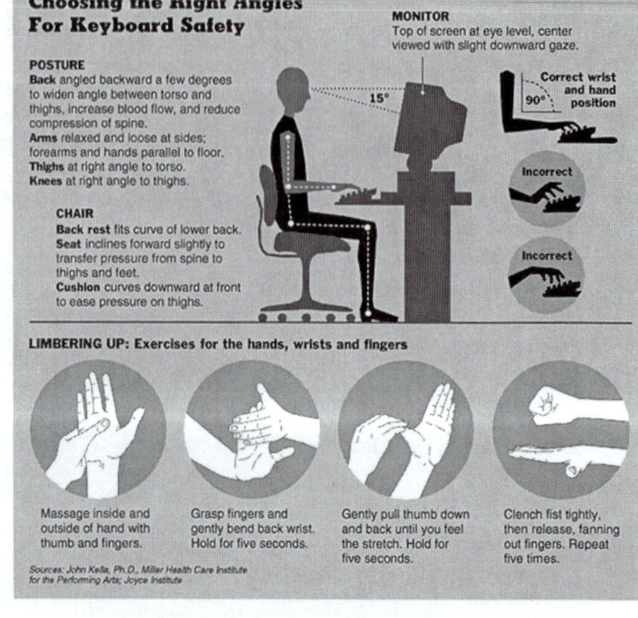

Price Tag: Mowing the Lawn

Estimated costs and recommended uses of lawn-cutting equipment. Maintenance expenses vary by climate and use. Prices are averages and may vary by region.

	CUTTING WIDTH	LAWN SIZE	COST
Reel mower Nonmotorized push mower with three to five steel blades. Provides clean, high-quality scissor cut. Blades require sharpening each season.	14 - 16 inches	1/8 acre or less	**$100**
Electric (plug in or battery powered) Plug-in mower operates on standard 110-volt current, using 100-foot extension cord. Best for small property with few hills or trees. Battery-powered model uses 12-volt battery and requires recharging after approximately one hour of use.	16 - 18 inches	1/8 acre or less	**$200**
Gas-powered rotary motor Three- to five-horsepower motor operates on regular gasoline. Available in self-propelled and push models. Requires annual change of oil, filter and spark plug.	18 - 22 inches	1/2 acre or less	**$250**
Riding mower Eight- to 12-horsepower motor; wide cutting swath is suited to larger lawns. Annual maintenance required for tires, belts and other small parts.	30 - 38 inches	1 acre	**$1,500**
Lawn tractor Twelve- to 18-horsepower motor; suited to large property. Attachments can be added for clearing brush, tilling soil. Annual tuneup is recommended.	30 - 38 inches	2 acres or more	**$1,800**
Sheep Nonmotorized; consume grass as well as brush and weeds. Three to five sheep recommended per acre for larger property, or one sheep per 1/5 to 1/3 acre for small yards. Low summer maintenance; winter feeding requirement is approximately 1/2-ton of hay ($40 to $50) per sheep.		1/5 to 1/3 acre per sheep	**$65**

Sources: Outdoor Power Equipment Institute, Jersey Power Equipment Company, Doug Hogue of the Cornell University Animal Science Department

Megan Jaegerman/The New York Times

FIGURE 4.7 (continued).
Source: Megan Jaegerman. ©1992 The New York Times.

Infographics Should Combine the Following Elements in Creative Ways

- **Typesetting:** Stick to one font or font family unless a client or house style dictates otherwise (do not allow your type to become the content; type should help clarify your message, not be your message. Type should blend, in not stand out).
- **Graphics:** (figures, pictures, drawings, symbols, etc.). In effective informational graphics, the relative sizes of objects used to represent something should be drawn to scale. An informational graphic about inflation affecting manufacturing costs should portray images in proportion to each other. If costs have risen by 25 percent over the previous year, then the image of the dollar should be only 25 percent larger than the one before, not 1.25 percent larger in each direction, which illustrates an almost 150 percent increase. For example, to double the volume of a 4" × 4" image, you would scale it by a little over 1.6" in each direction (5.65 × 5.65 = 31.9). If you scale the object six inches in each direction, as many informational graphics do, you are actually illustrating a 225 percent increase. When illustrating percent of change, exaggerating the change *visually* leads to an inaccurate picture of reality and increases the chance of overestimating the consequences or the benefits. Creating interesting and creative graphics using images is common in newsletters, on Web sites, and in brochures, but be careful how you represent the data.

100%

125%%

156.25%

100%

FIGURE 4.8 Illustration of increases in relative size.
Source: (c) Don Mason/CORBIS

- **Graphic use:** Be sure to give some thought to how the graphic will be used. Business and communication professionals do not expect dancing cupcakes or walking cars when they are looking for straightforward "facts." Infographics that look like they were designed to attract the attention of schoolchildren are not appropriate for most occasions. Professionals want to be able to quickly identify relationships, trends, and key points. Simple, high-contrast, uncomplicated, utilitarian infographics are best when reporting financial information, stock information, and budgets to professionals.
- **Comparison/contrast:** Comparisons and analogies are at the heart of the best informational graphics. When reporting trends, be sure to provide baseline data, current data, and change over time.
- **High contrast:** Many novices create tables with so much visual noise (multiple colors, unnecessary grid lines, watermarked backgrounds), that the data cannot be easily interpreted or understood. Keep your graphics simple, leave off all extraneous information, and be sure that everything is clearly labeled.
- **Design principles:** Use the fundamental design principles: space, balance, symmetry, and others, to facilitate understanding.
- **Use symbols:** Symbols aid in quick comprehension (icons, figures, line drawings, stylized punctuation).
- **Use color:** Color attracts attention and clarifies content, but be careful not to distract the audience. Do not use too many colors. Pie charts with so many slices that each slice cannot be identified are useless. Instead, use a stacked bar chart, a table of numbers, or some other form of data representation that allows for changes and comparisons to be seen.
- **Appropriateness of the design:** Different mediums and industries have different expectations. Annual reports prepared to meet SEC regulations never include anything more than simple,

black-and-white, high-contrast tables and charts. A full-color annual report intended for stockholders, potential investors, the media, will include photography, illustrations, feature stories, editorials, and often presents some of the data in a more interesting and visually appealing fashion.

UNDERSTANDING PHYSICAL DESIGN CHARACTERISTICS

Up to now, I have focused on content and stylistic design features. Now we turn to the actual physical properties of documents, including paper, color, special effects (finishes, die cuts, etc.), and binding. Since paper represents one of the biggest costs in a project, we begin there.

Paper

Few things in the design process evoke more passion than paper. Paper has a sensual quality that most people identify with immediately. A résumé, book, or brochure printed on high-quality paper stands out and can make a message appear more important.

Paper is, or should be, one of your major considerations when designing documents. Paper "can represent 35–55 percent of the final cost of the printed job" (Bruno, 1997, p. 182). There are also hundreds of kinds of paper, including recycled paper, paper made with virgin wood pulp, regular copy paper, ornate, textured, linen paper, papers with metallic finishes, papers with matte or glossy finishes, book paper, and card or cover stock. Indeed, this list does not even begin to account for all of the types of paper available. Each style of paper usually comes in several colors and weights and has specific properties (resistance to tearing, opacity, transparency, water resistance, brightness, smoothness, gloss, refractiveness, etc.) (cf., Bruno, 1997, pp. 182–190).

Most paper companies provide free samples of their products. A good way to develop a range of paper samples is to subscribe to one of the graphic design magazines (like *How*) and, using the business reply card in every issue, check all of the boxes for samples from paper companies listed on the card. Additionally, graphic design magazines themselves usually contain excellent advertisements for paper you can remove and keep in your swipe file. At some point you should also spend a few hours at a large paper store and familiarize yourself with an assortment of papers (see International Paper's *The Pocket Pal* for descriptions of dozens of papers; Bruno, 2000).

Begin to pay more attention to how paper is used when you examine written documents so you can answer questions like: When are heavier paper stocks used? When are coatings and special effects like die cuts (discussed below) appropriate? How much do particular papers cost? What sort of effects can be achieved with different types of paper?

The type of paper you use can have a powerful effect on an audience's perception of the message or the organization. Oftentimes, as with business cards and other documents intended to be handled (brochures, resumes, etc.), the extra expense of cotton bond, linen, or laid paper, cardstock, film, vinyl, etc., more than pays for itself in terms of the attention the document receives.

Color

After paper, and perhaps images, color is usually the next biggest expense. Typically, we distinguish between "spot" colors and "process" colors. **Spot colors** are single colors (there are thousands) created by mixing together inks of several hues, much like a paint or hardware store does when you buy custom tinted paint for your home or apartment.

Because of the importance of matching spot color exactly (e.g., Campbell's, Nike, Marlboro, and Coca-Cola red, AT&T blue, etc.), ink producers are required to submit samples for testing to the major ink companies in order to ensure accuracy. Some of the most well-known color companies are Focoltone (a Singaporean company), Pantone (an American company), and Toyo (a Japanese company). When paying a professional printer to produce a document containing only a few colors (typically fewer than four, including black) most documents can be produced less expensively using spot colors of differing hues. However, when a project requires more than a few colors, the economics of publishing typically call for four or six-color "process" printing.

Process color is what is used in offset printing and ink-jet printers, where millions of colors can be produced by combining four (or sometimes six or more) basic colors: cyan, yellow, magenta, and black (CYMK for short). Process printing tends to be more expensive both because more colors are used and because the technology requires more precision to obtain perfect color fidelity.

Print costs vary dramatically depending upon how much of the page is actually covered with ink

(10–60 percent) and how many copies are made. In general, for small run color copies (200–500 pages) with modest ink/toner levels (10 percent page coverage), in house printing is fairly economical. The break-even point for an inexpensive printer can be reached after only a few thousand copies. However, organizations with printing needs requiring more ink or toner coverage (50–60 percent) may need to make 20,000 or more copies in order to break even on the purchase of a printer. Hewlett-Packard provides a comparison of printing costs using its ink-jet and laser printers and how many jobs would be required to break even on the purchase of a color printer for use in-house (www.hp.com/sbso/productivity/color/print_cost_calc.html).

In general, the three things to consider when incorporating color into documents are:

1. The more colors used, the more the project will cost.
2. In professional printing, spot color is usually less expensive than process color.
3. The amount of ink used on the page increases the cost of the project.

Thus, full-page bleeds (printing to the very edge of the page), using background color or images on an entire page, and the intensity of colors (value and saturation), can dramatically influence price.

Folds, Perforations, Finishes and Coatings

As we progress through the cost hierarchy of document design we come to the miscellaneous issues of folds, perforations, finishes, and coatings. Brochures, for example, need to be folded one to three times or more, depending upon the design of the document. In some cases documents are accordion folded a dozen times (maps, instructional materials, etc.). Typically, folds are an added design expense to be considered in the planning stage and involve a setup fee of $15–$20 per fold. Thus, the more documents printed, the lower the cost per fold.

Often, when documents are not needed immediately or when a cadre of volunteers or interns exists (such as in political public relations), the expense of document folding can be avoided by "letting the interns do it." In general, however, (especially with large runs) folding adds little to the overall per-item cost of a project. Consult your intended printer during the design phase to make decisions about folding expenses.

Perforations, like folds, will add nominally to the cost of a project. Usually, since only a single page or a few pages require perforation, the cost for perforations might be a few cents per perforation (depending upon how many pages are printed and how elaborate the perforations are). In the case of a workbook where *all* of the pages might need to be perforated, the cost for perforation will be higher than if only a few pages are perforated, but pre-perforated paper is also available quite inexpensively. Again, consult your intended printer during the design phase to make decisions about perforations.

Many papers come with finishes: glossy, matte, metallic, antique, vellum, smooth, etc.; however, there are also an assortment of finishes applied to documents after they are printed in order to improve their appearance or durability. Coatings include aqueous, lacquer, laminate, and Ultraviolet (UV), and can be applied in different finishes, including gloss, dull, and satin. The features of coatings vary. Laminate coatings, for example, are used on book covers, menus, and other documents that receive a lot of abuse and/or, the occasional liquid or spill. UV coatings and varnishes can be used to protect documents from fingerprints and physical abuse and also can be spot applied to achieve special effects (shiny lettering, "glass," "liquids"). Aqueous coatings are more environmentally friendly (because they are water-based), and provide excellent protection against physical abuse, scuffs, fingerprints, liquids; however, aqueous coatings cannot be spot applied and are about twice as costly as varnish.

Although some finishes and coatings can be applied after printing, applying coatings during the initial print run is usually the most economical choice. According to Waxman, "You cannot print ... glue, or foil stamp over coatings, so you need to leave an uncoated window if you want to do any of these (coatings should be the final finishing step on a printed piece)" (www.printindustry.com/newsletter_18.htm). Since aqueous coatings can only be applied at the end, you need to design accordingly.

SPECIAL EFFECTS: DIE CUTS, EMBOSSING, FOIL STAMPING Everyone has seen greeting cards, magazines, and children's books with cut-out sections in various shapes: hearts on Valentine's Day cards, windows on magazines so something from the next page can be seen, pop-up pictures or graphics, etc. These special effects are **die cuts**. Die cuts can be applied to virtually any project and, as with everything else, add to the price of a project. Die cuts are used regularly to add a feeling of uniqueness to a document.

Embossing (or debossing) also adds flair and uniqueness as well as adding a textural feature to documents. Shapes, designs, words, images, and logos can all be embossed.

Another special effect is the use of **foil stamping**. With this technique, a metallic foil is affixed to specific parts of a document using heat. The metallic effect achieved through foil stamping is often used on logos and small portions of text, sometimes with 18k gold leaf, and can give a document a special, expensive look. Foil stamping can also be combined with embossing/debossing.

One thing to keep in mind with all of the special effects is that they are expensive and used in small quantities. If special effects were inexpensive, they would be used more often. Special effects also need to mesh with the image the organization is trying to convey as well as be appropriate for the occasion. Costly documents might appear out of place in materials for a small nonprofit organization or might be unremarkable when created by a large, profitable, corporation. Conversely, a small nonprofit may want to convey an image of professionalism and class by embossing or foil-finishing invitations for its annual fundraising event. Appropriateness can only be evaluated on a case-by-case basis, depending upon the audience and the rhetorical situation, as well as the funds available for an event.

Binding

Whether binding is necessary depends upon the nature of the project. A multipage, professional document like an annual report typically calls for a professional glue binding. Similarly, a training manual or informational booklet might call for saddle stitching or a comb binding. The type of binding needed is typically an issue incorporated into planning decisions.

There are several basic types of binding options:

- *Edition binding:* Your basic hardcover book. Pages are sewn together and glued, and then covers are permanently attached. Edition binding can be used on documents of almost any size from 10 pages to 1,000 pages or more.
- *Perfect binding or glue binding:* Your typical paperback. Pages are glued together along the spine and held together with a cardstock or stiff cover. Glue binding can be used for almost any size document from 1/8"–4".
- *Spiral/coil binding:* Your basic spiral notebook. Involves a metal or plastic wire passed through a series of small holes drilled along the binding edge of the pages to hold the document together; wires can be single or double strands and sometimes "hook" the pages rather than being inserted as a continuous coil. Spiral/coil binding can be used from about ¼" to 1½".
- *Comb binding:* Similar to wire binding except a circular, plastic "comb" is inserted through small rectangular cuts or holes made along the binding edge. Combs can range in size from about ¼"–2".
- *Saddle/side stitching:* What is used to bind many commercial magazines or booklets and involves using two or three staples along the spine, or a "saddle" of pages that have been folded in the middle. Side stitching is similar, except pages do not have to be folded because two or three staples are placed along the binding edge of the pages. Saddle and side stitching are very versatile and can be used effectively with 2–150 pages. Note, with saddle stitching, as the number of pages increase beyond about 75 pages, there is a tendency of the document to tear away from the cover or to lose pages from the back or front as documents are handled.
- *Corner Stapling:* Used with 2–100 pages. Industrial staplers are often needed if 30 or more pages are stapled.
- *Clipping:* Clips are useful for binding from about 5–300 pages, and they are reversible—i.e., documents may be taken apart if pages need to be removed or inserted. Clip binding runs the gamut from standard metal or plastic binder clips to hard, book-like covers that can be opened up and clipped to document pages. Additionally, several forms of folders have mechanical clips that grasp and hold pages as well as plastic strips that can be levered or slipped down the edge of pages.
- *Ring/wire binders:* Your basic "three-ring binders." Binders hold pages together after they have been punched or drilled along the binding edge. They have hard or soft covers of cardstock, plastic, or vinyl and can range in size from ½" to 3–5". Ring binding uses from 1–20 or more rings, although 3 is the most common. Other forms of ring or wire binders include mechanical apparatus affixed along the edge of plastic or cardstock covers used to hold from 1–100 pages. Medical charts, legal briefs, and

student papers often utilize this sort of binding, which is versatile, reversible, and reusable for different purposes. Ring/wire binders are often combined with transparent plastic page protectors that make the insertion of new pages easy and serve to protect pages.

The type of binding selected depends on the purpose for which the document is designed. Documents intended as reference books like the *AP Stylebook* are often wire or comb-bound so they lay flat and are easy to use. Conversely, student reports placed into three-ring-binders and page protectors are difficult to comment on or "grade." Similarly, reports or proposals may also be permanently bound with glue or combs, or placed in plastic page protectors. Ultimately, the type of binding selected depends upon one's budget and the end use of the materials.

Binding Margins: When designing documents to be bound, the designer needs to take into account "binding margins," or the width of the binding space when setting the margins. In order to obtain 1" margins on a single-sided document intended to be comb-bound, an extra ¼"–⅜" needs to be added to the binding (left) margin so the document will have the same size margin on both sides after the document is bound. When double-sided pages are bound, the binding edges of pages need to alternate. All desktop publishing programs have automatic settings for binding margins.

FACT SHEETS

Fact sheets are some of the more creative professional documents and integrate text, photographs, and graphics. As discussed previously with backgrounders, what constitutes a fact sheet varies widely. Fact sheets are used to provide supporting information. They are often created on short notice to respond to crises, requests for information, or special events. Fact sheets are also created to provide supporting material about products or services in media kits, at community events, and on the Internet.

Fact sheets are often more creative than backgrounders, utilizing graphics, dingbats, and artwork. Typically, fact sheets have the words "Fact Sheet" printed in big letters across the top and include bulleted lists in a "Q&A," "FAQs," or "Key Facts" format. Occasionally, depending upon the audience, fact sheets rely heavily on text.

In some cases, fact sheets are nothing more than straightforward lists of information: parts lists, menu items, news features, etc. However, in other cases, fact sheets are used to put a new or interesting twist on everyday information. For example, a boutique winemaker who produces 5 million bottles of wine a year might, with a little math, discover that if 5 million bottles were placed end-to-end, they would stretch from New York City to Niagara Falls and back again.

SAMPLE "FACTS" Sample facts like these might be used on a fact sheet:

- If all of the candles sold annually in the U.S. were stacked end to end, they would reach to the moon and back three times.
- The Castle of Wittemburgh burned 35,750 pounds of wax per year for 900 years, nearly one pound of wax for every resident of Denmark, Greece, Hungary, Ireland, and Switzerland.
- The U.S. produced 782 million gallons of wine in 2006. This means that the average American adult each drank about 3.9 gallons of wine every year, or a bottle every month.
- If all the bottles of wine produced each year in the U.S. were stacked end-to-end, they would circle the Earth 22.8 times.
- The FDA has determined that the consumption of one or two glasses of wine each day reduces the chance of a heart attack by 20 percent.
- The average *Fortune* 500 executive reads three books a year, watches fewer than 50 hours of television per year, and encourages his/her children to major in business or marketing.
- Students who play chess score 20 percent higher on the SAT—regardless of their economic background.
- Seventy percent of all college students report having plagiarized at least once in their college careers. Plagiarism is up from 25 percent in 1970, and 5 percent in 1960.

  If every high school and college student caught cheating in the U.S. each year were fined $1,000, the national deficit could be erased in two years.

Fact Sheets Suggestions

Fact sheets are used to provide background information in everything from news conferences and media kits to crisis situations (where they are produced with only a few hours of preparation). The fact sheet is a staple of campaigns and programs and can be used for dozens of purposes.

- Fact sheets should always include complete organizational information (logos, contact information, etc.). Assume that they might be passed on.
- Fact sheets should be written as final draft documents (single-spaced, spell checked, etc.).
- Fact sheets should have visual appeal. Utilize graphics, dingbats, and artwork when appropriate.
- Fact sheets are often written with short sentences and include bulleted lists.

Fact sheets often make an effort to make the "information" interesting by employing metaphors, comparison/contrast, simile, etc.

Media/Informational Kits

Media and informational kits represent the height of information and design, integrating many different types of text-based and visual images into a coherent whole. Media and informational kits vary so widely that there is really no one standard type. They are regularly prepared for the media, investors, and for marketing purposes (customers, clients). Media and informational kits are expensive to produce and typically have a short shelf life so they are almost always prepared in small quantities for special events (promotions, store openings, trade shows, product expos, etc.).

An *investor kit* typically looks just like a media kit from the outside unless special binders or folders have been created that have "investor kit" printed on the front. Investor kits typically contain annual reports, stock and financial information, backgrounders on organizational members, reprints of favorable news stories, etc. The intent is not to persuade a reporter to write a story, but to convince a potential investor that your organization is one of quality and worth risking money on.

Advertising kits are often prepared by media outlets (newspapers, magazines, and broadcasters, as well as advertising agencies/firms) for potential advertisers and are similar to investor kits in that they are intended to be compelling persuasive documents. Advertising kits typically contain information about rates and advertising contracts (how much for a transit sign of x size for n duration), samples of their advertising placement (pictures of buses or billboards with signs, etc.), as well as demographic information about the target audiences reached. An investor or advertising kit is very easy to distinguish from a media or special event kit.

A typical *media kit* consists of a stylized folder (often a standard, two-pocket, cardstock folder that has been printed with the organization's logo and/or a specialized logo designed for an event or activity. Folders imprinted with an organization's logo are often ordered in bulk (to save on costs) and used in various capacities for several years (investor, media, recruiting, etc.).

These days, many organizations create electronic media kits that are distributed via CDs or DVDs or accessed through an organization's home page. Printed media kits are still quite common. However, for organizations with limited resources, the online media kit can make more content available and is often used to supplement a modest, printed media kit. Most media professionals still prefer a printed media kit to an electronic kit. Many print-based media kits are very impressive, with custom folders, color photographs, and print specialties (magnets, bookmarks, tote-bags). Online media kits force journalists to go looking for your information, rather than having the information presented to them.

Media kits are filled with information that supports a particular event or purpose:

- Contact information for organizational members: business cards, fact sheets with contact information, etc.
- Information for a journalist or editor to write a feature story about your organization, organizational members, events, products, services, or whatever the kit was prepared for. Typically a media or special event kit will contain several relevant news releases of varying length—shorter versions for newspaper and television and lengthier versions for magazines and other periodicals.
- Background information on the organization and its members (fact sheets, organizational and member backgrounders, news clipping reprints, etc.), enabling a journalist who is new to an organization, news region, beat, or profession, to tell your story well.

QUESTIONS TO ASK OF A MEDIA KIT YOU ARE PREPARING

- Has the information been organized "rhetorically?" (Has it been placed into the folder in the best way, are there items that seem out of place or do not belong?) Try to put yourself into the

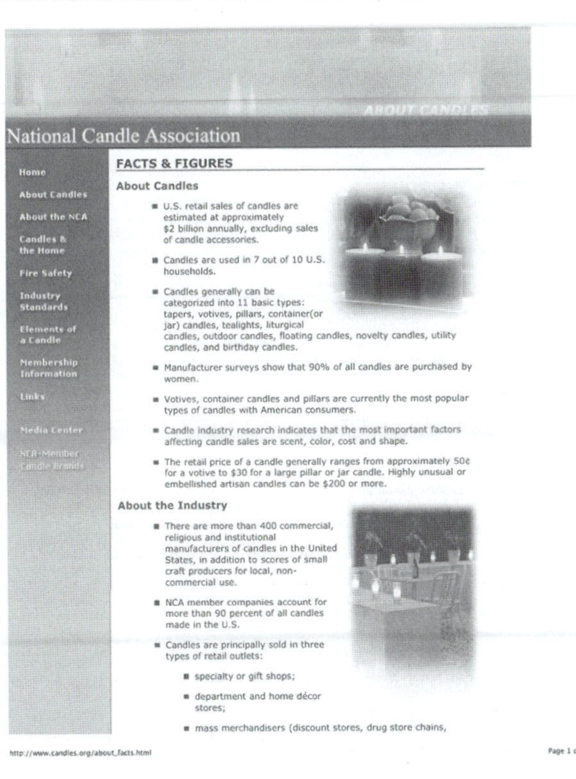

ABOUT CANDLES

National Candle Association

Home
About Candles
About the NCA
Candles & the Home
Fire Safety
Industry Standards
Elements of a Candle
Membership Information
Links
Media Center
NCA-Member Candle Brands

FACTS & FIGURES

About Candles

- U.S. retail sales of candles are estimated at approximately $2 billion annually, excluding sales of candle accessories.
- Candles are used in 7 out of 10 U.S. households.
- Candles generally can be categorized into 11 basic types: tapers, votives, pillars, container(or jar) candles, tealights, liturgical candles, outdoor candles, floating candles, novelty candles, utility candles, and birthday candles.
- Manufacturer surveys show that 90% of all candles are purchased by women.
- Votives, container candles and pillars are currently the most popular types of candles with American consumers.
- Candle industry research indicates that the most important factors affecting candle sales are scent, color, cost and shape.
- The retail price of a candle generally ranges from approximately 50¢ for a votive to $30 for a large pillar or jar candle. Highly unusual or embellished artisan candles can be $200 or more.

About the Industry

- There are more than 400 commercial, religious and institutional manufacturers of candles in the United States, in addition to scores of small craft producers for local, non-commercial use.
- NCA member companies account for more than 90 percent of all candles made in the U.S.
- Candles are principally sold in three types of retail outlets:
  - specialty or gift shops;
  - department and home décor stores;
  - mass merchandisers (discount stores, drug store chains,

http://www.candles.org/about_facts.html Page 1 of 2

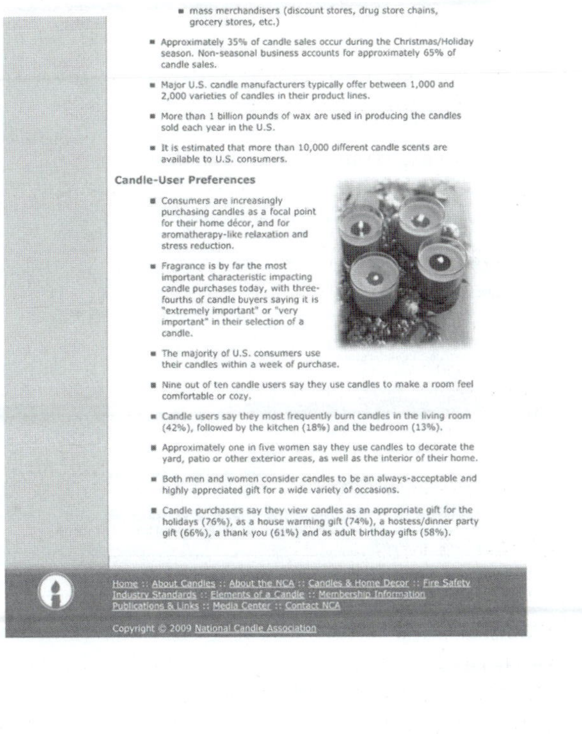

- mass merchandisers (discount stores, drug store chains, grocery stores, etc.)
- Approximately 35% of candle sales occur during the Christmas/Holiday season. Non-seasonal business accounts for approximately 65% of candle sales.
- Major U.S. candle manufacturers typically offer between 1,000 and 2,000 varieties of candles in their product lines.
- More than 1 billion pounds of wax are used in producing the candles sold each year in the U.S.
- It is estimated that more than 10,000 different candle scents are available to U.S. consumers.

Candle-User Preferences

- Consumers are increasingly purchasing candles as a focal point for their home décor, and for aromatherapy-like relaxation and stress reduction.
- Fragrance is by far the most important characteristic impacting candle purchases today, with three-fourths of candle buyers saying it is "extremely important" or "very important" in their selection of a candle.
- The majority of U.S. consumers use their candles within a week of purchase.
- Nine out of ten candle users say they use candles to make a room feel comfortable or cozy.
- Candle users say they most frequently burn candles in the living room (42%), followed by the kitchen (18%) and the bedroom (13%).
- Approximately one in five women say they use candles to decorate the yard, patio or other exterior areas, as well as the interior of their home.
- Both men and women consider candles to be an always-acceptable and highly appreciated gift for a wide variety of occasions.
- Candle purchasers say they view candles as an appropriate gift for the holidays (76%), as a house warming gift (74%), a hostess/dinner party gift (66%), a thank you (61%) and as adult birthday gifts (58%).

Home :: About Candles :: About the NCA :: Candles & Home Decor :: Fire Safety
Industry Standards :: Elements of a Candle :: Membership Information
Publications & Links :: Media Center :: Contact NCA

Copyright © 2009 National Candle Association

http://www.candles.org/about_facts.html Page 2 of 2

SEVERE ACUTE RESPIRATORY SYNDROME

Fact Sheet: Basic Information about SARS

SARS
Severe acute respiratory syndrome (SARS) is a viral respiratory illness caused by a coronavirus, called SARS-associated coronavirus (SARS-CoV). SARS was first reported in Asia in February 2003. Over the next few months, the illness spread to more than two dozen countries in North America, South America, Europe, and Asia before the SARS global outbreak of 2003 was contained. This fact sheet gives basic information about the illness and what CDC has done to control SARS in the United States. To find out more about SARS, go to www.cdc.gov/sars/ and www.who.int/csr/sars/en/.

The SARS outbreak of 2003
According to the World Health Organization (WHO), a total of 8,098 people worldwide became sick with SARS during the 2003 outbreak. Of these, 774 died. In the United States, only eight people had laboratory evidence of SARS-CoV infection. All of these people had traveled to other parts of the world with SARS. SARS did not spread more widely in the community in the United States. For an update on SARS cases in the United States and worldwide as of December 2003, see www.cdc.gov/mmwr/preview/mmwrhtml/mm5249a2.htm.

Symptoms of SARS
In general, SARS begins with a high fever (temperature greater than 100.4°F [>38.0°C]). Other symptoms may include headache, an overall feeling of discomfort, and body aches. Some people also have mild respiratory symptoms at the outset. About 10 percent to 20 percent of patients have diarrhea. After 2 to 7 days, SARS patients may develop a dry cough. Most patients develop pneumonia.

How SARS spreads
The main way that SARS seems to spread is by close person-to-person contact. The virus that causes SARS is thought to be transmitted most readily by respiratory droplets (droplet spread) produced when an infected person coughs or sneezes. Droplet spread can happen when droplets from the cough or sneeze of an infected person are propelled a short distance (generally up to 3 feet) through the air and deposited on the mucous membranes of the mouth, nose, or eyes of persons who are nearby. The virus also can spread when a person touches a surface or object contaminated with infectious droplets and then touches his or her mouth, nose, or eye(s). In addition, it is possible that the SARS virus might spread more broadly through the air (airborne spread) or by other ways that are not now known.

What does "close contact" mean?
In the context of SARS, close contact means having cared for or lived with someone with SARS or having direct contact with respiratory secretions or body fluids of a patient with SARS. Examples of close contact include kissing or hugging, sharing eating or drinking utensils, talking to someone within 3 feet, and touching someone directly. Close contact does not include activities like walking by a person or briefly sitting across a waiting room or office.

CDC's response to SARS during the 2003 outbreak
CDC worked closely with WHO and other partners in a global effort to address the SARS outbreak of 2003. For its part, CDC took the following actions:

- Activated its Emergency Operations Center to provide round-the-clock coordination and response.
- Committed more than 800 medical experts and support staff to work on the SARS response.

January 13, 2004 Page 1 of 2

DEPARTMENT OF HEALTH AND HUMAN SERVICES
CENTERS FOR DISEASE CONTROL AND PREVENTION
SAFER • HEALTHIER • PEOPLE™

Basic Information about SARS
(continued from previous page)

- Deployed medical officers, epidemiologists, and other specialists to assist with on-site investigations around the world.
- Provided assistance to state and local health departments in investigating possible cases of SARS in the United States.
- Conducted extensive laboratory testing of clinical specimens from SARS patients to identify the cause of the disease.
- Initiated a system for distributing health alert notices to travelers who may have been exposed to cases of SARS.

What CDC is doing now
CDC continues to work with other federal agencies, state and local health departments, and healthcare organizations to plan for rapid recognition and response if person-to-person transmission of SARS-CoV recurs. CDC has developed recommendations and guidelines to help public health and healthcare officials plan for and respond quickly to the reappearance of SARS in a healthcare facility or community. These are available in the document *Public Health Guidance for Community-Level Preparedness and Response to Severe Acute Respiratory Syndrome (SARS)* at: www.cdc.gov/ncidod/sars/guidance/index.htm. CDC provides the latest information on SARS on the SARS website: www.cdc.gov/sars/.

For more information, visit www.cdc.gov/ncidod/sars or call the CDC public response hotline at (888) 246-2675 (English), (888) 246-2857 (Español), or (866) 874-2646 (TTY)

January 13, 2004 Page 2 of 2

DEPARTMENT OF HEALTH AND HUMAN SERVICES
CENTERS FOR DISEASE CONTROL AND PREVENTION
SAFER • HEALTHIER • PEOPLE™

FIGURE 4.9 Sample Fact Sheets.

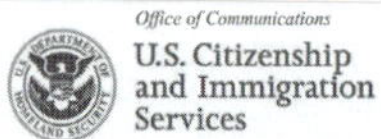

Office of Communications

U.S. Citizenship and Immigration Services

Fact Sheet

Updated:
January 28, 2008

NATURALIZATION THROUGH MILITARY SERVICE

Members and certain veterans of the U.S. Armed Forces are eligible to apply for United States citizenship under special provisions of the *Immigration and Nationality Act (INA)*. In addition, U.S. Citizenship and Immigration Services (USCIS) has streamlined the application and naturalization process for military personnel serving on active-duty or recently discharged. Generally, qualifying service is in one of the following branches: Army, Navy, Air Force, Marine Corps, Coast Guard, certain reserve components of the National Guard and the Selected Reserve of the Ready Reserve.

Qualifications

A member of the U.S. Armed Forces must meet certain requirements and qualifications to become a citizen of the United States. This includes demonstrating:

- Good moral character;
- Knowledge of the English language;
- Knowledge of U.S. government and history (civics); and
- Attachment to the United States by taking an *Oath of Allegiance* to the *U.S. Constitution.*

Qualified members of the U.S. Armed Forces are exempt from other naturalization requirements, including residency and physical presence in the United States. These exceptions are listed in Sections 328 and 329 of the INA.

All aspects of the naturalization process, including applications, interviews and ceremonies are available overseas to members of the U.S. Armed Forces.

An individual who obtains U.S. citizenship through his or her military service and separates from the military under "other than honorable conditions" before completing five years of honorable service may have his or her citizenship revoked.

Service in Wartime

All immigrants who have served honorably on active duty in the U.S. Armed Forces or as a member of the Selected Ready Reserve on or after September 11, 2001 are eligible to file for immediate citizenship under the special wartime provisions in Section 329 of the INA. This section also covers veterans of designated past wars and conflicts.

Service in Peacetime

Section 328 of the INA applies to all members of the U.S. Armed Forces or those already discharged from service. An individual may qualify for naturalization if he or she has:

- Served honorably for at least one year.
- Obtained lawful permanent resident status.
- Filed an application while still in the service or within six months of separation.

How to Apply

Every military installation has a designated point-of-contact to assist with filing the military naturalization application packet. Once complete, the package is sent to the USCIS Nebraska Service Center for expedited processing. That package will include:

- Application for Naturalization (USCIS Form N-400) (Members of the military are not charged a fee to file the Form N-400.)
- Request for Certification of Military or Naval Service (USCIS Form N-426)
- Biographic Information (USCIS Form G-325B)

Posthumous Benefits

Section 329A of the INA provides for grants of posthumous citizenship to certain members of the U.S. Armed Forces. Other provisions of law extend benefits to surviving spouses, children, and parents. A member of the U.S. Armed Forces who served honorably during a designated period of hostilities and dies as a result of injury or disease incurred in, or aggravated by, that service (including death in combat) may receive posthumous citizenship.

- The service member's next of kin, the Secretary of Defense, or the Secretary's designee in USCIS must make this request for posthumous citizenship within two years of the service member's death.
- Under section 319(d) of the INA, a spouse, child, or parent of a U.S. citizen, who dies while serving honorably in active-duty status in the U.S. Armed Forces, can file for naturalization if the family member meets naturalization requirements other than residency and physical presence.
- For other immigration purposes, a surviving spouse (unless he or she remarries), child, or parent of a member of the U.S. Armed Forces who served honorably on active duty and died as a result of combat, and was a citizen at the time of death (including a posthumous grant of citizenship) is considered an immediate relative for two years after the service members dies and may file a petition for classification as an immediate relative during such period. A surviving parent may file a petition even if the deceased service member had not reached age 21.

Statistics

- USCIS has naturalized more than 36,920 members of the U.S. Armed Forces since the beginning of the War on Terror. (September 2001)
- In October 2004, USCIS hosted the first overseas military naturalization ceremony since the Korean War. During this time and since, USCIS has naturalized more than 4,735 Soldiers, Sailors, Airmen and Marines during ceremonies in Afghanistan, Djibouti, Germany, Greece, Iceland, Iraq, Italy, Japan, Kenya, Kosovo, Kuwait, South Korea, Spain, the United Kingdom and in the Pacific aboard the USS Kitty Hawk.
- USCIS has granted posthumous citizenship to 109 members of the U.S. Armed Forces stemming from the War on Terror.
- Historically, the U.S. government has conducted overseas military naturalization ceremonies during times of war. During World War II, 20,011 service members were naturalized overseas. During the Korean War, 7,756 service members were naturalized overseas. Although authorized, no overseas military naturalization ceremonies were held during the Vietnam War.

– USCIS –

USCIS Military Help Line: 1-877-CIS-4MIL (1-877-247-4645) www.uscis.gov/military

United States Department of Labor

Bureau of Labor Statistics **Washington, D.C. 20212**

FOR TECHNICAL INFORMATION:
Stephen B. Reed (202) 691-7000
CPI QUICKLINE: (202) 691-6994
FOR CURRENT AND HISTORICAL
INFORMATION: (202) 691-5200
MEDIA CONTACT: (202) 691-5902
INTERNET ADDRESS: http://www.bls.gov/cpi/

USDL-09-0171
TRANSMISSION OF
MATERIAL IN THIS
RELEASE IS EMBARGOED
UNTIL 8:30 A.M. (EST)
Friday, February 20, 2009

CONSUMER PRICE INDEX: JANUARY 2009

The Consumer Price Index for All Urban Consumers (CPI-U) increased 0.4 percent in January, before seasonal adjustment, the Bureau of Labor Statistics of the U.S. Department of Labor reported today. The January level of 211.143 (1982-84=100) was virtually unchanged from January 2008.

The Consumer Price Index for Urban Wage Earners and Clerical Workers (CPI-W) increased 0.4 percent in January, prior to seasonal adjustment. The January level of 205.700 (1982-84=100) was 0.5 percent lower than in January 2008.

The Chained Consumer Price Index for All Urban Consumers (C-CPI-U) increased 0.5 percent in January on a not seasonally adjusted basis. The January level of 121.208 (December 1999=100) was 0.5 percent lower than in January 2008. Please note that the indexes for the post-2007 period are subject to revision.

CPI for All Urban Consumers (CPI-U)

On a seasonally adjusted basis, the CPI-U increased 0.3 percent in January after declining in each of the three previous months. The energy index climbed 1.7 percent in January, its first increase in six months, but it was still 31.4 percent below its July 2008 peak level. Within energy, the gasoline index rose 6.0 percent in January after a 19.3 percent decline in December. However, some energy components continued to decline; the fuel oil index fell 3.7 percent in January and the index for natural gas declined 3.6 percent. The food index, which rose sharply during the summer and moderated through the fall, increased 0.1 percent in January after being virtually unchanged in December. The food index has risen 5.3 percent over the past year. The (cont.)

Table A. Percent changes in CPI for All Urban Consumers (CPI-U)

Expenditure Category	Seasonally adjusted								Un-adjusted 12-mos. ended Jan. 2009
	Changes from preceding month							Compound annual rate 3-mos. ended Jan. 2009	
	July 2008	Aug. 2008	Sep. 2008	Oct. 2008	Nov. 2008	Dec. 2008	Jan. 2009		
All items	0.7	0.0	0.0	-0.8	-1.7	-0.8	0.3	-8.4	0.0
Food and beverages	.9	.6	.5	.4	.2	.1	.1	1.4	5.2
Housing	.6	.0	-.1	.0	-.1	.0	.0	-.3	2.2
Apparel	1.0	.4	-.3	-.7	.1	-.6	.3	-.9	-.9
Transportation	1.4	-.9	-.1	-4.8	-9.7	-5.0	1.3	-43.0	-12.6
Medical care	.1	.2	.3	.2	.2	.3	.4	3.9	2.6
Recreation	.3	.4	.2	.2	.0	-.2	.0	-.5	1.6
Education and communication	.5	.2	.1	.2	.2	.3	.3	3.3	3.6
Other goods and services	.4	.2	.2	.3	.0	.0	.3	1.5	3.3
Special indexes:									
Energy	3.5	-2.0	-1.0	-7.8	-16.9	-9.3	1.7	-65.4	-20.4
Food	.9	.6	.5	.4	.2	.0	.1	1.1	5.3
All items less food and energy	.3	.2	.1	.0	.1	.0	.2	.9	1.7

food at home index declined 0.1 percent in January as the fruits and vegetables index continued to fall. The index for all items less food and energy rose 0.2 percent in January after being virtually unchanged in December. Contributing to the increase were larger advances in the indexes for rent and owners equivalent rent and upturns in the indexes for new vehicles and apparel.

The food and beverages index increased 0.1 percent in January, the same increase as in December. A 0.3 percent increase in the index for food away from home and a 0.2 percent rise in the alcoholic beverages index more than offset a 0.1 percent decline in the food at home index. The food at home index has risen 5.7 percent over the past year. Within food at home, the indexes for four of the six major grocery store food groups declined in January. The index for fruits and vegetables fell 1.3 percent, its fifth consecutive monthly decline. The index for fresh fruits fell 2.2 percent and the fresh vegetables index declined 1.6 percent. The dairy and related products index, down 1.1 percent in December, fell 0.6 percent in January, with the milk index declining 1.4 percent. Also declining in January were the indexes for meats, poultry, fish and eggs and for nonalcoholic beverages, each down 0.1 percent. The index for cereals and bakery products was virtually unchanged in January, but was still up 11.3 percent over the last year. The index for other food at home rose 0.6 percent in January, the only major grocery store food group index to increase for the month.

The housing index was virtually unchanged in January for the second straight month. However the shelter index, virtually unchanged in December, rose 0.2 percent in January. Over the last 12 months, the housing index has risen 2.2 percent and the index for shelter was up 1.8 percent. Within shelter, the indexes for rent and owners' equivalent rent both rose 0.3 percent in January after rising 0.2 percent and 0.1 percent, respectively, in December. The index for lodging away from home fell 1.1 percent in January and has declined 4.7 percent over the past 12 months. The household energy index fell 0.9 percent in January, its sixth consecutive monthly decline. Within household energy, the electricity index rose 0.2 percent, but the indexes for fuel oil and natural gas both declined. Despite the recent declines, the household energy index was up 4.9 percent over the past 12 months. The index for household furnishings and operations turned down in January, declining 0.1 percent after increasing 0.1 percent in December.

The transportation index rose for the first time since July, increasing 1.3 percent in January. The index has declined 12.6 percent over the past 12 months. The index for motor fuel, which had been declining in recent months, rose 5.3 percent in January. However, the motor fuel index is still 48.1 percent below its peak in July. The index for new and used motor vehicles increased in January after posting 12 straight declines, rising 0.2 percent. The index for new vehicles rose 0.3 percent in January but has declined 2.6 percent over the past year. The index for public transportation continued to decline, falling 1.8 percent in January. The airline fare index fell 2.1 percent in January and was down 0.9 percent compared to a year ago.

After declining 0.6 percent in December, the apparel index turned up in January, rising 0.3 percent. The index for men's and boys' apparel rose 1.6 percent and the index for women's and girls' apparel rose 0.2 percent. (On a not seasonally adjusted basis, the apparel index declined 2.0 percent in January and was down 0.9 percent over the last 12 months.)

The medical care index climbed 0.4 percent in January following a 0.2 percent increase in November and a 0.3 percent advance in December. The index for medical care commodities rose 0.4 percent, with the prescription drugs index rising 0.5 percent. The medical care services index rose 0.5 percent in January. Within this group, the index for physicians' services rose 0.2 percent and the hospital and related services index increased 0.8 percent.

The index for recreation, down 0.2 percent in December, was virtually unchanged in January. The indexes for photography, toys, admissions, and for pets, pet products and services all rose in January. These increases offset declines in the indexes for video and audio and for sporting goods. The recreation index is up 1.6 percent over the past 12 months.

The education and communication index increased 0.3 percent in January and was up 3.6 percent over the past year. The education index, which rose 0.5 percent in December, advanced 0.3 percent in January. The index for communication climbed 0.2 percent for the second straight month. Within communication, the telephone services index rose 0.2 percent and the index for information technology, hardware and services increased 0.1 percent.

FIGURE 4.9 (Continued).

Revised seasonally adjusted changes

Over-the-month percent changes in the U.S. City Average Consumer Price Index for All Urban Consumers (CPI-U) for All Items and for All Items less food and energy, seasonally adjusted, using former and recalculated seasonal factors for 2008.

All Items

2008	Former	Recalculated	Difference
January	.4	.4	.0
February	.0	.2	.2
March	.3	.4	.1
April	.2	.2	.0
May	.6	.5	-.1
June	1.1	.9	-.2
July	.8	.7	-.1
August	-.1	.0	.1
September	0	.0	.0
October	-1.0	-.8	.2
November	-1.7	-1.7	.0
December	-.7	-.8	-.1

All Items less food and energy

2008	Former	Recalculated	Difference
January	.3	.3	.0
February	.0	.1	.1
March	.2	.2	.0
April	.1	.1	.0
May	.2	.2	.0
June	.3	.3	.0
July	.3	.3	.0
August	.2	.2	.0
September	.1	.1	.0
October	-.1	.0	.1
November	.0	.1	.1
December	.0	.0	.0

C-CPI-U Index Revisions

In accordance with the previously-announced schedule, the Bureau of Labor Statistics is revising the 2007 and 2008 values of the Chained Consumer Price Index for All Urban Consumers (C-CPI-U), effective with the release of January 2009 data.

The C-CPI-U was introduced with release of July data on August 16, 2002. The index in its final form employs a Tornqvist formula and utilizes expenditure data in adjacent time periods in order to reflect the effect of any substitution that consumers make across item categories in response to changes in relative prices. The C-CPI-U was designed to be a closer approximation to a "cost-of-living" index than the CPI-U and CPI-W. The use of expenditure data for both a base period and a current period distinguishes the C-CPI-U from the other CPI measures, which use only a single expenditure base period to compute price change over time.

Because the current expenditure data required for the calculation of the C-CPI-U are available only with a time lag, the index is issued first in preliminary form, using the latest available expenditure data at the time of publication, and is subject to two subsequent revisions. The preliminary values for each month of the preceding two years are revised annually with release of the January index. Expenditure data for the year 2007 are now available, and the C-CPI-U indexes for that year are now in final form. The initial indexes for 2008 are now revised interim indexes. The C-CPI-U U.S. All Items index values for 2007 and 2008 as originally published and revised are shown below.

For more information on the C-CPI-U, write to:

Bureau of Labor Statistics
Division of Consumer Prices and Price Indexes
2 Massachusetts Ave. NE, Room 3130
Washington, DC 20212

Or contact Rob Cage either by telephone at (202) 691-6959 or by electronic mail at Cage.Rob@bls.gov

U.S. City Average C-CPI-U All Items

2007	Interim	Final
January	117.310	117.330
February	117.897	117.877
March	118.978	118.913
April	119.712	119.666
May	120.290	120.292
June	120.478	120.439
July	120.384	120.377
August	120.198	120.288
September	120.538	120.638
October	120.823	120.885
November	121.443	121.481
December	121.322	121.295
Annual average	119.948	119.957
2008	**Initial**	**Interim**
January	121.895	121.868
February	122.251	122.224
March	123.204	123.177
April	123.845	123.817
May	124.645	124.617
June	125.582	125.554
July	126.116	126.088
August	125.843	125.815
September	125.774	125.746
October	124.784	124.757
November	122.284	122.257
December	120.661	120.634
Annual average	n.a.	123.880

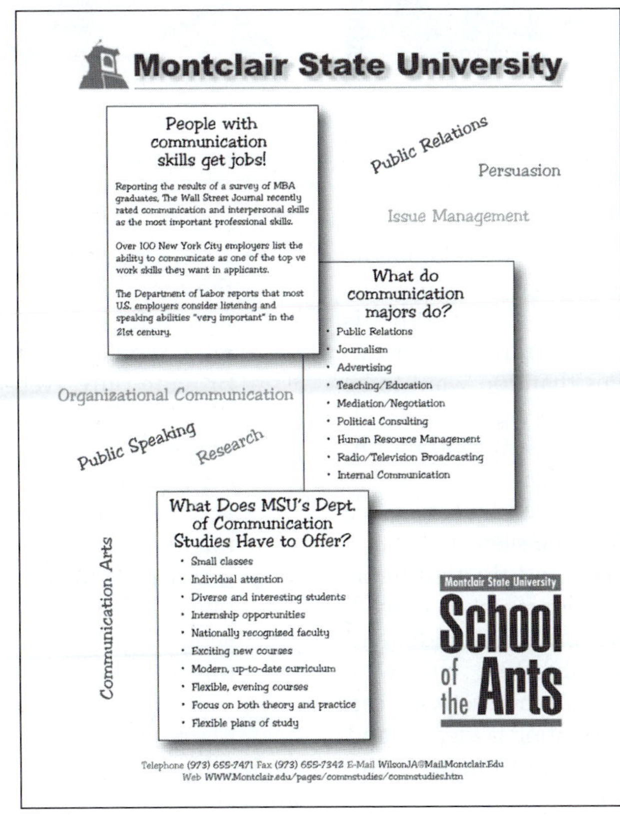

FIGURE 4.9 (Continued)

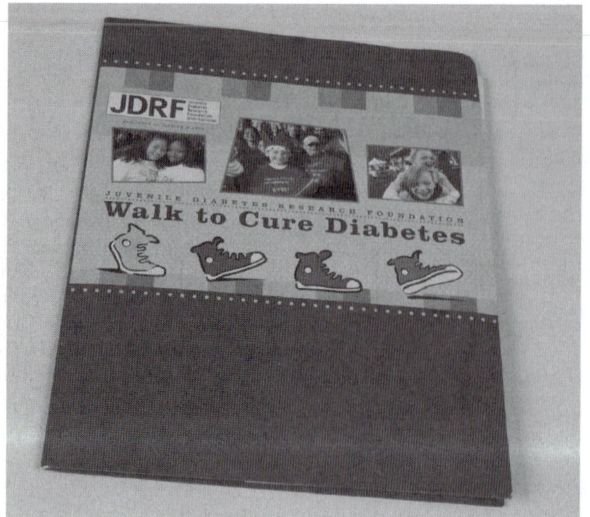

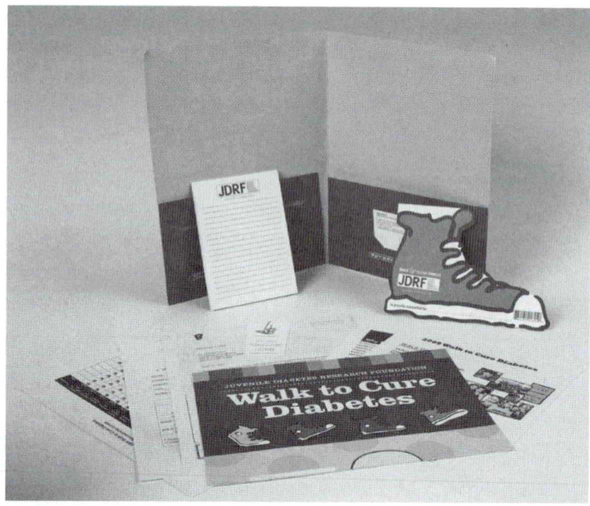

PHOTO 4.7 Sample Media Kits. Media and informational kits like JDRF's are very common. Mega kits like GM's product information guides are less common and can have great impact. *Source:* Photos © 2009 Joy Payne & Matt Fager.

shoes of the person who is receiving the media kit. What is the first thing that s/he will see when opening the folder or package? What is the best order in which to arrange the documents? Position the items that you want to be seen first on the top left and right sides, followed by the items that are less important underneath the top pages. Content that is inside on the right is usually examined first, so place the items that you want to be seen first there. Once a folder is fully open and the first items have been perused, the order is not as crucial. Recipients will take things out of the folder and put them back in randomly. Ring, coil, wire binders, and other fixed binding methods can help control how the information is viewed and keep everything in order but can make using the documents more difficult.

- Is the physical design of the kit appropriate for the organization it represents? Should a small nonprofit organization prepare $300 media kits? Should a billion-dollar-a-year corporation provide only Web-based or electronic media kits on CDs or DVDs? The rhetorical choices made should fit the nature of the individual organization.
- Is the kit compelling? What information/documents would be useful to include? Have you included professionally reprinted media clippings, black-and-white and color photographs, slides, a CD of high-resolution jpg files, or feature stories?

Many media kits are put together on short notice from organizational documents that have already been prepared (brochures, fact sheets, backgrounders, booklets, Q&As, etc.). Special event kits obviously require a lot of advance planning and can be quite costly ($100 or more per kit) depending upon whether the kit requires original photography, stylized dividers/inserts, or specialty items (pens, rulers, coffee mugs, etc.).

Typical Media Kit Items

- Custom binding (spiral, wire, comb, perfect, etc.) in a specialized folder is used on many media kits to give them a more professional look.
- Business cards and contact information sheets with organizational member's names, telephone numbers, e-mail address, etc.
- General organizational information and documents about the organization and its key members, and specific information about particular events. Typical documents include brochures, fliers, annual reports, news releases, media advisories (short, two-paragraph, news releases used for television), fact sheets, professional article reprints, etc. Remember, you cannot just make your own copies of journal articles, and newspaper and magazine stories. Making your own copies of documents is a violation of copyright law and makes the organization look unprofessional. Order actual, professional reprints from publishers (all publications sell reprints) or use original copies of the news source.
- Color photographs or slides and black-and-white photographs have been media kit staples for decades. However, videos/DVDs, CDs with high-resolution pictures and graphics, and Web pages with links to high-resolution graphics have become increasingly common and are less costly than printing up batches of color or black-and-white photographs.
- Specialty items with organizational logos and design elements are frequently included in media kits (bookmarks, magnets, pens, calculators, stickers, posters, toys, etc.).

CONCLUSION

It will take you some time to master the dozens of techniques, concepts, and design principles discussed in this chapter. As with so many of the other concepts mentioned in this book (rhetoric, persuasion, etc.), you need to practice. Begin looking more closely at how documents of all kinds are designed—transit signs, brochures, textbooks, point-of-purchase displays—and expand your swipe file. Also, start looking for training seminars, short courses, or design classes to take so you can hone many of the design skills mentioned throughout this chapter.

Consider attending one of Edward Tufte's courses (www.edwardtufte.com/tufte/courses) or reading some of his books (1990, 1997, 2001, 2006). Tufte is an internationally recognized expert on information design and has consulted with NASA and other organizations about how to use information effectively in decision making and informational communication.

Public relations professionals, especially those who work for smaller organizations where they are responsible for "everything," are increasingly expected to understand design issues and how to format documents to increase their visual appeal. Aesthetics go hand-in-hand with content. Great content that looks "boring," will often get skipped by people who do not have to read it, just as boring content dressed up with special effects and graphics is a waste of time. Design and content go hand-in-hand when creating organizational documents, just as "content and delivery" in public speaking are two sides of the same coin. With time and practice, you will master all of these concepts and begin to integrate them into your work.

ACTIVITIES

1. Take a fact sheet or brochure from your instructor or a document you download from the Internet and redesign it so you have two symmetrical and two asymmetrical versions of the document. Using a paper and pencil, create thumbnails of your designs. Which version is the best? Is the original still better or is one of your redesigns better? Explain using concepts from this chapter.
2. Visit a stock photography Web site and locate an image you believe most closely matches these words: angry, elated, honored, frantic, satisfied, successful, terrified, unhappy, victorious. Try to find as close a fit as you can. Keep in mind that "angry and livid" and "heartbroken and sad" might be synonyms but they do not really imply the same thing. Stock photography Web sites are

searched by key word, just like Internet search engines. The word "angry" will return hundreds of hits (or thousands, depending upon the site searched). "Angry boy," "angry storm," or "angry dog" will narrow your search. However, just because someone else has labeled an image as depicting "anger" does not mean that the image is appropriate to use. Exercise judgment and be able to support your choices. Do not select images with words in them already.

3. Using five images obtained from a stock photography Web site, crop each photograph twice to change the emphasis in the picture. Be creative: do not just crop the image into a headshot. Try to use the image in an entirely new way. Write a photo caption for each image that is consistent with what it portrays after your editing.

4. Using only your own magazines, books, documents, etc., locate as many examples as you can of "special effects" and bring them to class. Be prepared to explain whether the special effect was worth the expense, and why. Is there another technique that could have been used or a better way the same feeling or mood might have evoked the same feeling or mood?

5. Redesign the cover of your favorite magazine to have 10 different symmetrical and asymmetrical designs. Use a quarter of a blank page to thumbnail five different designs for each. In a separate, typed document, explain what images you would use, what the areas of emphasis would be (i.e., where will the eye be drawn and why). Be sure to create detailed thumbnails. Do not create boxes with big Xs for graphics and squiggly lines for type, but sketches of images and actual letters/words.

6. Fold full-size pieces of legal (8.5" × 14") and letter-sized (8.5" × 11") paper to create a brochure. Label each panel. Then, using another piece of paper, sketch (thumbnail) an asymmetrical brochure for a class that you are taking. Be sure to indicate what images might be used, what colors, and what typefaces. Do not use any boxed text in your design.

NOTES

1. A swipe file is a folder or box where you keep samples of effective documents and messages for ideas and inspiration. Whenever you run across an interesting document, whether junk mail, a brochure at a truck stop, an annual report, a magazine advertisement, or a feature story layout, make a copy of the document, or mark the page and throw the entire document into your file/box so that you can go back for ideas and inspiration when you are designing your own documents.
2. Most photographers remove this information from their photos to protect their techniques. However, depending upon the photographer, everything from camera data, to Camera Raw edits will still be accessible in the image.
3. As mentioned in the research chapter, the word infographics is used to talk about both "informational graphics" (graphics designed to clarify information) and informational data about what a person reads or listens to. The words are usually clear from the context, much like *too* means both "also" and "a lot."
4. The resolution of information projected by a data projector or on a computer monitor is only 72 dpi, while the resolution of a professionally printed page can be as high as 10,000 dpi (600–1,800 with personal printers). Thus, a page-sized table of statistics used in a slideshow either needs to be broken up into a number of separate graphics, or requires the audience to be given printed copies of the graphic so that they can follow along as the presenter points out and explains features of the graphic.
5. For excellent discussions on information design, and for information about his seminars and books, visit Edward Tufte's Web site (www.edwardtufte.com/tufte). Be sure to review the "Ask ET" discussion.

Chapter 5

Writing for Print, Broadcast, and the Web

By now you undoubtedly understand that the way you write in terms of style, content, tone, and vocabulary, will vary depending upon your audience. How you write also varies depending upon the medium your message uses (print, broadcast, Web). Traditionally, print media (newspapers, magazines, newsletters) were seen as ideal places for sophisticated and nuanced arguments while broadcast media were better suited for simple messages. The Internet has changed everything. Although the Internet offers organizations and professionals a place to say whatever they want to say, and in great detail, most organizations have not taken advantage of the opportunities the Internet offers (Kent, 2008; Kent & Taylor, 2002). Ironically, every printed document or speech that an organization creates could easily be integrated into an organizational Web site and stakeholders and stakeseekers could be allowed to interface with organizational members and build stronger organization–public relationships.

In this chapter, I will highlight some of the major stylistic and content differences among the various media used in public relations and try to give you a sense of how to adapt to different media outlets. In many cases, what dictates the media used by organizations is whether the organization retains control over the message. When a news release is sent to an editor, the editor can decide whether to publish the release in its entirety or whether the release will be rewritten, perhaps placing a different spin on the organization's message. When a news release is posted to an organizational Web site, or posted for a fee to a media service like PRNewswire, an organization retains more control over its actual message but sacrifices the reach possible through print and broadcast channels. However, releases that are posted to organizational Web sites and wire services only get seen by people who go looking for them.

CONTROLLED VERSUS UNCONTROLLED MEDIA

One of the fundamental issues in public relations writing deals with how much control you have over your messages. For example, news releases and feature stories (those actually sent off to the media as opposed to posted on organizational Web sites) are *uncontrolled*, since you have no control over what happens to such documents after they are placed in the hands of the media. Content posted on sites like PRNewswire (which charges a fee) is somewhere in the middle, since such sites are primarily used by the news media and industry professionals but allow organizations to get their word out. Advertisements, brochures, annual reports, and organizational Web sites, are *controlled* media because organizations have complete control over their content, placement, and distribution.

"Controlled" and "uncontrolled" are somewhat flexible terms. For example, a letter to the editor might be printed exactly as written or may receive some editing for length. However, letters to the editor are also not published when they are off topic or intended as free advertising. Similarly, a news release posted to an organizational Web site is a controlled document, while a news release sent to a newspaper is uncontrolled.

boards glued end-to-end would circle around the globe, etc. (see fact sheets below).

- A backgrounder should be a self-contained organizational document created using the organization's house style, typefaces, logos, etc., and should contain complete contact information (e-mail, telephone, URL) serving as stand-alone documents. Note: usage varies. Internal "employee backgrounders" are often just typed up on a word processor and placed into a file, while backgrounders intended as part of an investor kit are printed in full color on glossy paper.

Backgrounder Styles

- Address three to five points that might be covered in a 5–10-minute speech introducing your organization to the local chamber of commerce (an FAQ approach).
- Employ the 5Ws and H structure (who, what when, where, why, how). This is useful for information about a new product, service, factory, company initiative, etc.
- Employ a Q&A (question and answer) or FAQ (frequently asked questions) format. Indeed, Q&As *are* a form of backgrounder.
- Employ an acronym—"T-R-U-S-T," "O-P-E-N," "F-U-T-U-R-E," "M-O-M," whatever fits.

Organizational Backgrounders

Backgrounders on organizational members typically take one of three forms: the data sheet, the straight chronological, or the narrative.

- When writing a "data sheet" backgrounder, you typically include the date of hire, position within the company, educational qualifications, civic activities and memberships, family information as appropriate to the type of organization (husband/wife/partner, kids, pets, etc.).
- A chronological backgrounder is like an organizational resume, and may include information about employee accomplishments, projects s/he has worked on, positions held within the organization, previous positions held, etc.
- When writing a narrative backgrounder, you might include personal quotes, references to sources of inspiration, favorite books, movies, television programs, quotations from people who have inspired the person in question, and sometimes, personal information: hobbies, favorite foods, pets, etc. Be sure to provide enough information for a journalist to be able to create a brief personal profile.

Typical backgrounders are about 250–500 words, include pictures of organizational members being profiled, diagrams, illustrations, etc., and often have the word "Backgrounder" in big letters at the top of the page. There is no rule about how a backgrounder should look. In general, a backgrounder is a final draft document, so it is single-spaced, and from 1 to 10 pages (or more) in length. Some backgrounders (especially historical backgrounders) primarily consist of text-based prose, while others incorporate graphics, dingbats, bulleted lists, professional graphic design, etc.

INTERNAL COMMUNICATION

One of the most important issues for public relations managers to understand is Burke's (1973a) notion of Identification by Unawareness. As discussed in Chapter 8, identification by unawareness refers to the kind of implicit identification people feel as a result of being part of an organization, group, cause, or activity, and the implicit otherness/enmity people feel toward those who are part of groups, causes, or activities, that compete with our organizations and views (pp. 263–275). When employees believe they are being treated fairly, public relations managers can expect loyalty and employee support because of their identification with their employer, branch, group, etc. Managers and employers who do not treat employees fairly, who do not acknowledge employee value, or who exhibit a lack of trust in employees will have reduced levels of trust, and employee identification in return.

A wide range of public relations and organizational communication research supports the not-surprising conclusion that treating employees well has tangible organizational benefits. Research going back decades on dialogic communication (Pearson, 1989; Kent & Taylor, 2002), industrial psychology (Franke & Kaul, 1978), interpersonal communication (Buber, 1970, 1985), psychology (Haley, 1969, pp. 119–146; Laing, 1969), and social and family psychology (Rogers, 1994; Watzlawick, Beavin, & Jackson, 1967), all support the notion that individual acknowledgment and recognition leads to increased satisfaction, more productivity, and what Burke describes as identification by unawareness (a powerful form of identification).

Keeping employees in the dark about organizational activities and future plans leads to speculations and rumors. Ignoring employees and failing to acknowledge important individual and social events (birthdays, births, deaths, marriages, patents, promotions, relationships, scientific discoveries, etc.) leads to lower levels of satisfaction and trust. Finally, employees who do not identify with organizational goals and objectives see no reason to be loyal (Kent, 1995). If for no other reason than employees are expensive to recruit and train, organizations and public relations practitioners have a vested interest in developing healthy, positive, and stable work environments involving trust and compassion rather than secrecy and apathy (cf., Anderson, Cissna, & Arnett, 1994; Kent & Taylor, 1998, 2002).

The importance of keeping employees informed and knowledgeable about organizational issues cannot be overstated and has value both in times of crisis and in times of tranquility. In times of crises, whether acute (a plane crash, a train derailment, an explosion, a CEO being indicted) or chronic (multiple quarters of losses, a persistent increase in the price of raw materials, widespread employee dissatisfaction), employees want to know what is happening. Are employee jobs at risk? Might there be layoffs? Will there be criminal/legal implications? Questions about the future naturally arise in such times of crisis and organizations that provide employees with answers to their questions, rather than allowing employees to speculate and seek information through informal channels like employee gossip, or worse, by listening to the media, will enjoy greater employee loyalty and trust. One means of structuring internal communication is through a dialogic workplace (discussed in detail in Chapter 10), where employee feedback is solicited and valued by organizational leaders.

Internal Communication Structures

Internal publics are relatively easy to reach and to communicate with. A number of tried-and-true communication mechanisms have already been developed. One of the easiest ways of reaching employees is through memos/messages sent via intraorganizational mail, inserted into quarterly newsletters, or placed into pay envelopes. (However, sending printed messages stuffed into pay envelopes has become less useful as more employees use direct deposit). Employee messages can also be posted on bulletin boards or signs as employees enter their work sites, or distributed personally by managers.

A plethora of electronic tactics can also be used to keep employees informed, engaged, and feeling as if they are part of organizational activities: employee blogs, e-mail messages, postings on Internet and intranets, Facebook and Twitter postings, calendars of events that can be posted or distributed, Flicker albums can be created around organizational events, etc. More traditional communication tactics include direct mailings to employees; broadcast messages on organizational telephones; face-to-face tactics, like employee meetings and town halls; announcements at union meetings; etc. Whatever the written or spoken tactic used, a consideration of which tactics are most effective with each audience should drive your choice of communication medium.

E-mail, for example, is not a very efficient communication tool for people who have to read a lot of e-mail every day. Because of the volume, messages are often only skimmed when they arrive and attention is often placed on crisis issues (damage control) rather than mundane activities. An informational e-mail (even if important) is easy to overlook or ignore, especially if an organization sends out a lot of e-mail messages. For organizations that *do not* use e-mail often, electronic messages can be very effective. Similarly, organizations that regularly stuff employee pay envelopes or mailboxes with a lot of "junk" will discover that most messages wind up in the trashcan next to where paychecks are distributed and many people do not even read them. Thus, each communication tactic has its strengths and limitations. Sometimes, a sign posted next to the timeclock or coffeemaker or in the break room or elevator is the best choice.

The communication tactics that work best depend upon the organizational culture and employer–employee communication dynamics. Some organizations code paycheck inserts using colored paper, posting a colored paper key near to where employees pick up their paychecks so employees know what to pay special attention to. Similarly, a direct mailing to employees' homes can have great impact, especially if such tactics are uncommon. Although expensive, a direct mailing with a well-crafted cover letter can have a huge impact.

Ultimately, organizations that communicate regularly and honestly with employees will be seen as more caring and trustworthy. Because of identification, employees who feel valued are also less likely to abuse the organization–employee relationship, steal supplies, quit without notice, or to try to take advantage of supervisors.

KNOWLEDGE NETWORKS

One excellent internal communication tool is a **knowledge network**, sometimes called a wiki (en.wikipedia.org/wiki/Wiki) or a **"collaborative network."** The idea for collaborative knowledge networks goes back more than 20 years. A collaborative network allows users to come together and share "knowledge," or information. Like Wikipedia, for example, where anonymous people can make encyclopedia entries and create "knowledge" databases that can be accessed and shared by others, knowledge networks allow organizations to create information repositories that other members of the organization can access remotely, with descriptions of how organizational problems and issues can be resolved.

Collaborative networks used within organizations are usually not anonymous like Wikipedia is, and therefore provide more credible information. Additionally, since the person who came up with the solution to the organizational problem in the first place is a colleague, who can be easily consulted for details or elaboration and his or her own insight, knowing whom to contact for help is easy. Moreover, your own insight or approach to solving the problem can be added to the original posting (like Wikipedia), thereby making the solution more robust.

Knowledge networks are easy to implement and the Wiki software (en.wikipedia.org/wiki/Wiki_software) is easy to use. Knowledge networks are built over time and evolve organically. Once a knowledge network is in place, organizational members have access to organizational "wisdom" that few organizations bother to retain. Knowledge networks are an excellent internal communication tool and also work to foster identification, loyalty, and trust.

NEWSLETTERS

One of the most common internal communication tools is the employee newsletter. There are tens of thousands of employee newsletters nationwide and many large and complex organizations have dozens of newsletters. These days, in order to save money on printing costs, and because of the convenience, many newsletters are distributed electronically as PDFs or as html content. Many organizations also produce *both* print and electronic versions of their newsletters, often encouraging members to subscribe to the electronic version, or using the electronic version as an additional tool of awareness.

Newsletters can be a lot of fun to produce, given that they are often intended for internal audiences and are often less formal than other types of organizational documents. All types of organizations—from small nonprofits to large megacorporations and everything in between—produce newsletters. Tens of thousands of organizations produce newsletters each month in the U.S. Professional associations produce monthly or quarterly newsletters, and distributing newsletters as PDF files can save on printing and postage costs.

The tone of a newsletter varies depending upon what purpose it serves. A newsletter intended for outsiders as an "informational" document may contain a statement by the president or CEO, regular updates by department heads or organizational leaders commenting on organizational issues, and special sections dealing with relevant issues to the target publics. The tone of external newsletters is often (but not always) formal. However, an internal newsletter intended as a morale booster and to keep members informed usually has a less formal tone and may include employee information and personal announcements, profiles of employee activities, and organizational announcements. See Figure 5.5 for samples.

Vol. 44, No. 3

NCA Spectra

March 2008

Promoting the study, criticism, research, teaching, and application of the principles of communication

New Journal of International and Intercultural Communication Launches

Thomas Nakayama, Editor, *Journal of International and Intercultural Communication*

Journal of International and Intercultural Communication

See "New Journal" on page 28

2nd VP Candidate Statements page 8

Committee on Committees Call page 18

2 Spectra March 2008

The Measure of an Association

Roger Smitter
NCA Executive Director

Spectra

About NCA

Got a story idea?

Correspondence

NCA Executive Committee

www.natcom.org Spectra 3

An Impoverished Professoriate and the Future of Tenure

Arthur P. Bochner
NCA President

See "The Future of Tenure" on page 4

8 Spectra March 2008

Candidate Statement: Sherwyn P. Morreale

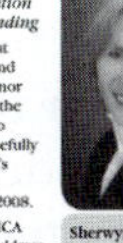

Sherwyn P. Morreale
Candidate

See "Sherwyn P. Morreale" on page 10

FIGURE 5.5 Sample of Newsletters
Source: National Communication Association, www.natcom.org

www.natcom.org Spectra 15

NCA Honor Societies Prepare to Induct New Student Members

Sara Baker, Student Organizations Coordinator

2006 Sigma Chi Eta National Secretary David Preston (Pi chapter, Gainesville State College) reads the name of the new inductees while National President Megan Hill (Pi chapter, Gainesville State College) presents the new student members with their honor cords.

Common ingredients to an induction ceremony include:

1.) Welcome and officer/special guest introductions made by the faculty adviser.

2.) Honor society overview given by the chapter president.

3.) Lighting of the candles, articulation of purpose, and outlining of membership requirements presented by the current chapter officers.

4.) Chapter president announces each new inductee and the faculty adviser presents him or her with their membership materials.

Traditionally the month of April serves as the primary time for Lambda Pi Eta and Sigma Chi Eta chapters to recognize and induct its newest members. Lambda Pi Eta annually inducts over 6,000 new members in the course of the year, while Sigma Chi Eta members are steadily increasing as the honor society continues to establish and develop chapters. An induction ceremony is the perfect time to involve communication department faculty, staff, and administration in this celebration of honor.

An induction ceremony can be a stand alone event or combined with another chapter or departmental activity. Events that could be held in conjunction with the ceremony include:

1.) Banquet/Dinner - Examples: West Virginia Wesleyan College, Missouri State University, Stephen F. Austin University, University of Wisconsin - LaCrosse, San Diego State University.

2.) Movie Night - Salem College hosted a screening of "Good Night and Good Luck" after its induction ceremony.

3.) Departmental Awards Ceremony - Examples: University of Wisconsin - Parkside, Rider University, Central Michigan University, Northern Kentucky University, Ohio Northern University, George Mason University.

4.) Guest Speaker - Examples: University of Wyoming and Vanguard University of Southern California.

Lambda Pi Eta chapters can place induction orders online at www.awardconcepts.net/nca and will use its Greek name to access the site. Orders can be placed for membership certificates and pins, honor cords, and merchandise and paid for using a check or credit card. Credit cards payments will be processed for fulfillment as soon as the order is placed. Check payments should be mailed to the national office and will be authorized for fulfillment once the payment has been received. Chapters should place spring induction orders by March 30 of each year to guarantee delivery by the May graduation festivities. Due to the volume or orders placed during March & April, chapters should expect a four week turn around time on its order once payment has been received and should plan ceremonies accordingly. Replacement certificates can also be processed online.

Sigma Chi Eta chapters can download induction orders forms off the SCH website under the section labeled "Induct Students" and should mail this form with a check or credit card payment to the national office. In the busy months of March & April, SCH chapters should also adhere to the four week fulfillment schedule and plan ceremonies accordingly.

Questions regarding all aspects of the induction and graduation ordering process should be directed to Anissa Dickerson at adickerson@natcom.org or 202-464-2622. The mailing address of the national office is: National Communication Association, 1765 N St., NW, Washington, DC 20036

www.natcom.org Spectra 21

News & Notes

News and Notes contains information about NCA members and the communication discipline. It typically includes convention and conference dates and locations; calls for papers and programs, recently published books within the discipline, articles on the subject of communication published in other disciplines, and information regarding awards, grants, appointments, and promotions. Copy may be edited to conform to Spectra style and space requirements. Calls must be limited to 1,350 characters. To submit an item for News & Notes, visit www.natcom.org/newsandnotes1.

Convention and Conference Calendar

Kentucky Conference on Health Communication, April 17-19, 2008. Crowne Plaze, Lexington, Kentucky **Nancy Harrington.** *nancy.harrington@uky.edu* 859-257-3622, comm.uky.edu/kchc.

Appointments

University of Miami School of Communication, **Joseph Treaster,** Knight Chair in Cross-Cultural Communication and **Rich Beckman,** Knight Chair in Visual Journalism.

UIC Department of Communication, **Sharon Meraz,** Assistant Professor.

Awards

Kevin Barnhurst, UIC Department of Communication, was named a Fellow of the Reilly Center for Media & Public Affairs, at the Manship School of Mass Communication. He also delivered a lecture Jan. 28 and participated in research meetings and roundtables during a three-day fellowship at Louisiana State University, Baton Rouge.

Michael Pfau, University of Oklahoma, and **Michel Haigh,** Pennsylvania State University were winners of two top faculty paper awards: one from the Mass Communication Division of ICA (for the paper "The Influence of Television News Depictions of the Images of War"), and the other from the Mass Communication and Society Division of AEJMC (for the paper "Don't Tread on my Blog: A Study of Military Web Logs").

Will Anderson, Central Michigan University, has been awarded tenure within the College of Communication and Fine Arts.

Olga Idriss Davis, Arizona State University, Co-PI, with PI and Center Director, **Flavio F. Marsiglia,** received a $7,178,038 grant from the National Center on Minority Health and Health Disparities to establish the Southwest Interdisciplinary Research Center (SIRC) as a National Institutes of Health Center of Excellence. It will explore complex factors influencing minority health and health disparities among racial and ethnic minorities in the Southwest. Other Co-PIs from ASU include: Eddie Brown, Felipe Castro, Mary Gillmore, and Stephen Kulis.

Grants

Ted Zorn, University of Waikato, received a grant for NZ $43,519 from the BRCSS (Building Research Capacity in the Social Sciences) Foundation to study the current and potential impacts of Web 2.0 applications on New Zealand Not-for-Profit organizations. Alison Henderson of Waikato University is collaborating on the research.

Kate Willink, University of Denver, has received a grant from the University of Denver's Center for Community Engagement and Service Learning for work with El Centro Humanitario in Aurora.

Michael Hecht, Penn State University, and colleagues Michelle-Miller-Day, and John Graham of Penn State and Janice Krieger of Ohio State were awarded a 5-year, $3,272,367 grant from the National Institute on Drug Abuse (NIH) for their project, "Adaptation Processes in School-Based Substance Abuse Prevention". The grant continues the Drug Resistance Strategies Project's work on adolescent drug prevention by examining how their federally-recognized keepin' it REAL curriculum is adapted when used by rural middle schools in PA and OH.

William Kinsella, North Carolina State University, has received a $3,000 Interdisciplinary Studies Curriculum Initiative Grant from the College of Humanities and Social Sciences, to develop a course titled "Communication and Nuclear Technologies: Rhetoric, Culture, and Public Discourse."

Janet Rice McCoy, Morehead State University, was awarded $4,000 from the Center for Regional Engagement at her institution for "Engaging the Region through Public Relation Writing: Exploring Partnerships with Non-profit and Educational Organizations." The project will survey current public relations practices at area non-profits then provide training to staff and volunteers. Public relations students will also be matched with agencies to meet their self-identified public relations needs.

Of Interest

University of Miami School of Communication announced the appointment of two internationally renowned journalists to prestigious Knight Chairs in Journalism endowed by the John S. and James L. Knight Foundation. With the appointments, the University of Miami becomes the 21st institution in the nation to have Knight Chairs. Joseph Treaster will join the journalism faculty as the Knight Chair in Cross-Cultural Communication and Rich Beckman will join the Visual Journalism Faculty as the Knight Chair in Visual Journalism.

On Leave

Laura Ellingson, Spring 2008, Fall 2008, *Santa Clara University*, Sabbatical leave

Bernadette Calafell, Spring 2008, *University of Denver*, Sabbatical Leave

See "News and Notes" on page 23

Newsletters are published as often as once a month, but quarterly or biannual newsletters are also common. Be aware that a newsletter is very labor intensive and takes a lot of time to produce. Increasing the frequency of a newsletter later is easier than having to explain a decrease. Begin with a modest publication schedule of perhaps two to four times a year and adjust as needed.

Newsletters often consist of several stock sections followed by one to three feature stories. Newsletter sections can include upcoming events, opinion and editorials, employee letters, promotions, employee information/announcements, personal events (birthdays, weddings, marriages), job listings, research findings, etc.

Always remember to check your facts before publishing any personal information, even about issues of fact like weddings. Some people do not like to share information about their personal lives at work. Occasionally employees will submit bogus announcements as jokes. An announcement about a birth might be embarrassing to an unmarried woman (whether the event is true or not). Never publish personal information or pictures without confirming the

CAMPUS CONNECTIONS

May 2009

SERVING THE FACULTY AND STAFF OF THE UNIVERSITY OF OKLAHOMA

Four Outstanding Individuals to Receive Honorary Degrees at Commencement

McCullough

Hamm

Helmerich

Perkins

Three outstanding individuals will join OU Commencement speaker David McCullough, two-time Pulitzer Prize-winning historian and author, in being awarded honorary degrees at OU's 2009 Commencement Ceremony, scheduled for 7 p.m. Friday, May 15, at The Gaylord Family – Oklahoma Memorial Stadium.

In addition to McCullough, the following will be awarded honorary degrees:

- **Harold Hamm** of Enid, founder, CEO and chairman of the board of Continental Resources Inc. and founding donor of the Oklahoma Diabetes Center
- **Walter H. Helmerich III** of Tulsa, chairman of Helmerich & Payne Inc., civic leader and philanthropist
- and **Edward Joseph Perkins** of Washington, D.C., former U.S. ambassador to the United Nations, Liberia, South Africa and Australia and former director of the OU International Programs Center.

Please refer to the story in the April issue of Campus Connections for information on David McCullough.

Hamm rose from humble beginnings in Oklahoma as the 13th child of sharecroppers to being named to *Forbes Magazine*'s list of the 400 most successful Americans and serving as founder, CEO and chairman of the board of Continental Resources Inc., a successful oil and natural gas exploration company and a leader in applied technology.

A good student with a strong work ethic, by the age of 17, he was married and had graduated from Enid High School. At the age of 21, Hamm purchased a bob tail tank truck to start his own oilfield service company, Hamm-Phillips, in Ringwood. The next year, he incorporated Shelly Dean Oil Co., which later became Continental Resources Inc. Hamm also serves as chairman of the boards of Hiland Holdings and Hiland Partners. Today, Hamm companies operate in 12 states, employing hundreds of people. He is past chairman of the Oklahoma Independent Petroleum Association and served as a founding board member of the Oklahoma Energy Resources Board.

With a passion for the health, education and welfare of people, Hamm and his wife, Sue Ann, were the founding donors who made possible the creation of a world-class Diabetes Center for Oklahoma.

In 2007, Hamm was honored with the Ernst & Young Master Entrepreneur of the Year Award and the national Ernst & Young Entrepreneur of the Year Award in the Chemical, Energy and Mining Category for his accomplishments in the oil industry over the past 40 years.

Hamm also played a pivotal role in bringing increased access to public higher education to Enid-area students, is a longtime donor to scholarships, served as campaign chair of the $2.5 million project to renovate the YMCA in Enid and is a major benefactor of the YMCA. He also has been recognized by the Enid Chamber of Commerce as Businessman and Citizen of the Year.

A Tulsa native and a member of a pioneer Oklahoma family, **Helmerich** is chairman of Helmerich & Payne Inc., one of the major land and offshore platform drilling contractors in the world.

Helmerich earned his bachelor's degree in English in 1948 from OU and his master of business administration degree from Harvard in 1950, with the goal of becoming a teacher. He joined Helmerich & Payne Inc. of Tulsa in 1950, becoming president in 1960, chairman and CEO in 1987, and chairman of the board in 1989.

Helmerich's other business and corporate affiliations include serving as director emeritus of Atwood Oceanics Inc., trustee of the Northwestern Mutual Life Insurance Co., and director of Bank One, Oklahoma, N.A., Caterpillar Inc. and Whitman Corp.

Helmerich comes from a family with a long tradition of devotion to civic, educational, health care and cultural affairs in their home community of Tulsa as well as throughout the state and nation. Together with his wife, Peggy – who was known as Peggy Dow during her acting years in

(continued on page 2)

FIGURE 5.5 (Continued)

(continued from page 1)

Hollywood prior to the couple's marriage in 1951 – he is active in the Philbrook Museum of Art, for which he currently serves as a director, the Salvation Army and the Retina Research Foundation. For 17 years, he served on the Tulsa Parks and Recreation Board. Also for 17 years, he was a trustee of the Gilcrease Museum. Helmerich served on the board of the Young Presidents' Organization for eight years as well.

Helmerich is the sole trustee of The Helmerich Foundation, created in 1956. Through the foundation, the couple has generously supported several Hillcrest HealthCare System projects, including the Helmerich Center – a same-day surgery and conference facility. In 1985, they established the Peggy V. Helmerich Distinguished Author Award that recognizes nationally known authors and brings them to the state to speak.

The Helmerich family and The Helmerich Foundation have been exceptionally generous to OU, supporting the academic, cultural and athletics programs of the university. He has helped endow gardens at OU, and founded an endowment and chair for the library and an endowment for the Drama School in his wife's honor. He was also a leading donor to the restoration of Boyd House and to the OU North Tulsa Medical Clinic. Helmerich served as a member of OU's Reach for Excellence Campaign Committee and is a founder of the President's Associates program.

A career diplomat whose distinguished foreign service career included ambassadorships to the United Nations, Liberia, South Africa and Australia, **Perkins** retired from OU in June 2007 after 11 years of service as the William J. Crowe Chair in Geopolitics in the School of International and Area Studies and executive director of the International Programs Center. From 2006 to 2007, he also served as senior vice provost for International Programs.

Perkins has published numerous articles on foreign policy and served as co-author of the OU Press book, *Mr. Ambassador: Warrior for Peace* (2006).

Perkins served as representative to the Commonwealth of Australia from 1993 until 1996, retiring that same year with the rank of Career Minister in the U.S. Foreign Service. From his initial appointment as chief of personnel at the Army and Air Force Exchange in Taipei, Taiwan, in 1958, he went on to serve in a number of positions around the world, including director of the Department of State's Office of West African Affairs; ambassador to Liberia and the Republic of South Africa; and Director General of the Foreign Service and director of personnel in the Department of State. In 1992 he was appointed as U.S. ambassador to the United Nations and U.S. representative in the United Nations' Security Council, where he served from 1992-1993, until taking up his post in Australia.

Born in Sterlington, La., and raised in Portland, Ore., Perkins earned his bachelor's degree from the University of Maryland and his master's and doctor of public administration degrees from the University of Southern California.

During his Foreign Service career, Ambassador Perkins received numerous awards, including the Presidential Distinguished and Meritorious Service Awards; Department of State's Distinguished Honor and Superior Honor Award; and Una Chapman Cox Foundation Award for Distinguished Foreign Service Work. In On Sept. 10, 2001, he received the Director General's Cup, awarded by the Department of State.

Commencement to Feature David McCullough, Photo Highlights of Graduating Class and Music

The pageantry and pomp of herald trumpets and the Kiowa Black Leggings Society as well as the Bagpipes and Drums of the Highlanders will usher in OU's 2009 Commencement ceremony, to be held at 7 p.m. Friday, May 15, at The Gaylord Family – Oklahoma Memorial Stadium.

Two-time Pulitzer Prize-winning historian and author David McCullough, who has been widely acclaimed as a "master of the art of narrative history" and "a matchless writer," is OU's 2009 Commencement speaker.

The processional of the president's platform party, faculty and graduates to the stadium will begin at 7 p.m. Friday along the Brooks Mall area, located north of the stadium. During the pre-Commencement concert, beginning at 6:15 p.m., family and friends of graduates can view a presentation on SoonerVision of photos of OU's graduating class taken for the Sooner yearbook.

Music will be provided by the OU Chorus and Wind Ensemble. International flags representing OU's international students will be displayed during the ceremony.

The Commencement ceremony will feature the official conferring of degrees by OU President David L. Boren. During Commencement, OU expects to confer about 2,690 bachelor's degrees, 853 master's degrees, 97 doctoral degrees and 568 professional degrees. The ceremony will be capped off with a gigantic fireworks display as a salute to the Class of 2009.

Stadium gates will open at 5:30 p.m. and guests are asked to enter the stadium through gates one, five, six, seven and 11 and 12. Gate nine is reserved as the Special Services entrance, for guests with limited mobility or disabilities. To obtain Special Services parking and seating passes, please contact the Graduation Office at 325-0841.

Parking will be available at Lloyd Noble Center, and free shuttle service will run continuously from 5 to 11 p.m. for those attending Commencement. To arrange disability accommodations involving the shuttle, call the CART/Metro Transit office at 325-CART (2278).

Further information on Commencement and a complete schedule of college convocations are posted to the university's Commencement Web site at www.ou.edu/commencement.

For additional information on Commencement, and for accommodations on the basis of disability at the stadium, please contact the Graduation Office at 325-0841 or visit ou.edu/commencement.

2

Dr. Jesus Medina Recognized as Otis Sullivant Award Winner

Joining Dr. Jesus Medina (second from left), professor and chairman of the Department of Otorhinolaryngology at the OU Health Sciences Center, at a recent ceremony honoring him as the 2009 recipient of the Otis Sullivant Award for Perceptivity at OU are (from left) Robert "Bob" Ross, president and CEO of the Ethics and Excellence in Journalism and Inasmuch foundations; William "Bill" Ross, chairman of the board of the Ethics and Excellence in Journalism and Inasmuch foundations; and OU President David L. Boren. (Photo by Rhonda L. Patterson)

Nationally noted ear, nose and throat cancer treatment specialist Dr. Jesus Medina has been named the 2009 recipient of the $20,000 Otis Sullivant Award for Perceptivity at OU.

Patients travel from many states to take advantage of the revolutionary treatments pioneered by Dr. Medina, professor and chairman of the Department of Otorhinolaryngology, and his team. Through his efforts, the department has become widely known for its proficiency in treating mouth and throat cancers and advanced cancers of the face and neck.

The Ethics and Excellence in Journalism Foundation and the selection committee, which is composed of faculty and staff members, students and alumni, makes the selection.

"Dr. Medina is not only a leader and creative pioneer in his field of medicine," said OU First Lady Molly Shi Boren. "He is known for his care and concern for his patients and as a master teacher of medical students."

"Each year we are proud to present the Otis Sullivant Award for Perceptivity to an individual whose keen insight benefits the community," said Bob Ross, director of the Ethics and Excellence in Journalism Foundation. "This year's recipient, Dr. Medina, embodies the spirit of the award."

The late Edith Kinney Gaylord of Oklahoma City established the $500,000 Sullivant Prize endowment shortly before her death in January 2001. The award honors the late longtime Oklahoma journalist Otis Sullivant, who covered Oklahoma and national political news for several decades and was known for his ability to analyze and accurately predict political trends. Edith Kinney Gaylord was a longtime supporter of many OU programs and a pioneering journalist. She was the first woman reporter to join the New York bureau of the Associated Press, and was the second president and one of the founders of the Women's National Press Club in Washington, D.C.

The award is presented to a faculty or staff member at OU who exhibits "keen perceptivity." The agreement establishing the prize also states that a person "who manifests intuitiveness, instant comprehension, empathy, is observant and interprets from experience" should be selected. The benefit to society and the broader community, which comes from the insight of the recipient, also is considered.

Dr. Medina, a native of Peru, came to Oklahoma City in 1984 from the University of Texas M.D. Anderson Cancer Center in Houston to develop a head and neck cancer surgery program at the OU College of Medicine. He became chairman of the Department of Otorhinolaryngology in 1991 and currently holds the Paul and Ruth Jonas Chair in Cancer Treatment and Research.

In the past few years, Dr. Medina was elected president of the American Head and Neck Society, the largest scientific organization of head and neck surgeons in the world; selected as a director — and subsequently president — of the American Board of Otolaryngology; and named as one of 12 members of the Residency Review Committee of the Accreditation Council for Graduate Medical Education, the group that oversees otorhinolaryngology training programs nationwide.

In 2006, Dr. Medina delivered the prestigious Hayes Martin keynote address to the American Head and Neck Society. Next year, he will deliver the Jatin Shah keynote address at the World Congress of the International Federation of Head and Neck Societies in Seoul, South Korea, and is one of eight clinicians from around the world invited to participate in the "World Tour" of lectures organized by IFNOS. The tour will take this group of experts to 10 countries around the world during October 2010.

In 2008, he was presented an award of distinction in recognition of his medical service to the OU College of Medicine during the college's Silver Anniversary Evening of Excellence gala.

4

HEALTH SCIENCES CENTER NEWS

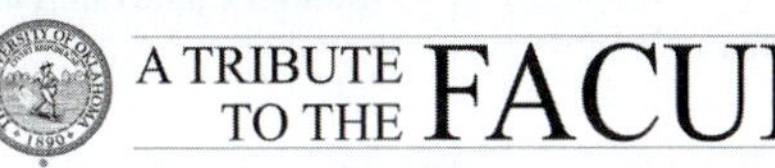

CONGRATULATIONS! to the following University of Oklahoma faculty members who were honored April 27 at a faculty awards ceremony at the Health Sciences Center.

PRESIDENTIAL PROFESSORSHIPS
Darrin Akins, Department of Microbiology and Immunology, College of Medicine
President's Associates Presidential Professor

Laura Ann Beebe, Department of Biostatistics and Epidemiology, College of Public Health
President's Associates Presidential Professor

Thomas Hennebry, Department of Medicine, College of Medicine
Robert Glenn Rapp Foundation Presidential Professor

Dean Myers, Department of Obstetrics and Gynecology, College of Medicine
President's Associates Presidential Professor

Muna Naash, Department of Cell Biology, College of Medicine
Edith Kinney Gaylord Presidential Professor

GEORGE LYNN CROSS RESEARCH PROFESSORSHIP
Joan Walker, Department of Obstetrics and Gynecology, College of Medicine

DAVID ROSS BOYD PROFESSORSHIP
Mary Zoe Baker, Department of Medicine, College of Medicine

REGENTS' PROFESSORSHIP
Robert McCaffree, Department of Medicine, College of Medicine

REGENTS' AWARD FOR SUPERIOR RESEARCH AND CREATIVE ACTIVITY
Chinthalapally Rao, Department of Medicine, College of Medicine

REGENTS' AWARDS FOR SUPERIOR TEACHING
Gary L. Loving, College of Nursing

David M. Thompson, Department of Biostatistics and Epidemiology, College of Public Health

REGENTS' AWARD FOR SUPERIOR PROFESSIONAL AND UNIVERSITY SERVICE AND PUBLIC OUTREACH
S. Terence Dunn, Department of Pathology, College of Medicine

PROVOST'S RESEARCH AWARD FOR SENIOR FACULTY
Shrikant Anant, Department of Mediciney, College of Medicine

PROVOST'S RESEARCH AWARD FOR JUNIOR FACULTY
Xin Zhang, Department of Medicine, College of Medicine

FACULTY GOVERNANCE AWARD
Kevin Haney, Developmental Dentistry, College of Dentistry

PATENTS
Paul L. DeAngelis, Department of Biochemistry and Molecular Biology, College of Medicine
Wei-Qun Ding, Department of Pathology, College of Medicine
Richard F. Harty, Department of Medicine, College of Medicine
William H. Hildebrand, Department of Microbiology and Immunology, College of Medicine
Hsueh-Kung Lin, Department of Urology, College of Medicine
Bradley P. Kropp, Department of Urology, College of Medicine
James F. McGinnis, Department of Opthalmology, College of Medicine
Anne Pereira, Department of Pathology, College of Medicine
Paul Weigel, Department of Biochemistry and Molecular Biology, College of Medicine

10

FIGURE 5.5 (Continued)
Source: Campus Connections: University of Oklahoma.

Volume 23, Number 7 · THE Teaching PROFESSOR · August/September 2009

Teaching Strategies That Help Students Learn

By Sara J. Coffman, Purdue University, Indiana - coffmasj@purdue.edu

What skills do you wish your students had prior to taking your course? Reading comprehension, time management, listening, note-taking, critical thinking, test-taking? Let's face it, most students could benefit from taking a course in learning how to learn. But who wants to take a *study skills* class?

My solution: sneak study skills into your class along with the content.

Course structure:

1. Select a textbook that has learning aids (study guides, online materials, and/or audiotapes) and encourage your students to use them. Point out features in the book that students can use to help them study and review text material.
2. Craft your syllabus carefully. By setting the right tone, you can motivate students. For example, here's an "encouraging" excerpt from an English syllabus:

"I realize that some students are shy and consequently do not participate much in class even though they are prepared. It would be unfair if they suffered on their grades because of this. Therefore, class participation can only help students and will never hurt them. But I do wish to emphasize that you should feel free to express your views in class, that your ideas will always be treated with respect, and that I will do everything I possibly can to create a class environment in which you will be comfortable participating in discussions."

3. Design clear, meaningful assignments that enable students to accomplish course objectives.
4. Space the workload out evenly throughout the semester.
5. If students don't master an assignment the first time, give them constructive feedback, and the chance to redo it. You may not want to do this for every assignment, but doing it for one early in the course "sets the bar" and encourages them to do quality work.

The first week:

1. If your class is small, set up interviews with students individually or in pairs to find out why they're taking the course and what they want to get out of it. Not only will you learn about who's in the class, but you'll increase students' commitment to work hard and communicate with you. If the class is large, use email to collect information about students and to establish connections.
2. Talk to students about how to study for your course. Give them a list of study techniques recommended by students who've taken the course and earned A's.
3. Early in the course, have students use their textbooks in class. By using class time, you acknowledge the book's value. If you can't afford class time, have students do a homework assignment that they can't complete without using the book.
4. Offer students time management suggestions. How much time should they be spending on the course? Talk about how daily study keeps the information fresh and helps avoid cramming. Show how longer assignments can be broken into small pieces.

Techniques for teaching:

1. Start class with something that gets their attention and then quickly review what was covered in the previous class.
2. Show students "tricks of the trade," or how you learned the material. Talk aloud when you solve a problem. Show students what you do when you get stuck.
3. Provide a partial outline and have your students fill in the missing material during the lecture.
4. Leave five minutes at the end of each class for students to check their notes with those of their neighbor, review major ideas, and indicate what they thought was important and why.

Testing tips:

1. Assign heterogeneous study groups prior to the first exam, have them exchange contact information, and require a one-hour study session outside of class. Help them be more productive by providing a study guide and/or sample test questions they can submit for bonus points.

PAGE 8 ➧

In This Issue

A MAGNA PUBLICATION

For subscription information, contact:
Customer Service: 800-433-0499
E-mail: custserv@magnapubs.com
Website: www.magnapubs.com

Submissions to *The Teaching Professor* are welcome. When submitting, please keep these guidelines in mind:

- We are interested in a wide range of teaching-learning topics.
- We are interested in innovative strategies, techniques, and approaches that facilitate learning and in reflective analyses of educational issues of concern.
- Write with the understanding that your audience includes faculty in a wide variety of disciplines and in a number of different institutional settings; i.e., what you describe must be relevant to a significant proportion of our audience.
- Write directly to the audience, remembering that this is a newsLETTER.
- Keep the article short; generally between 2 and 3 double-spaced pages.
- If you'd like some initial feedback on a topic you're considering, you're welcome to share it electronically with the editor.

The Teaching Professor (ISSN 0892-2209) is published 10 times per year by Magna Publications Inc., 2718 Dryden Drive, Madison, WI 53704. Phone 800-433-0499 or 608-246-3590. Email: custserv@ magnapubs.com. Fax: 608-246-3597. Website: www.magnapubs.com. One-year subscription: $89 (Multiple print subscriptions and Group Online Subscriptions are available.) POSTMASTER: Send change of address to *The Teaching Professor*, 2718 Dryden Drive, Madison, WI 53704.

To order back issues ($20 each) or for more information about multiple print subscription discounts and Group Online Subscriptions, call Customer Service at 800-433-0499.

Do Students Really Know Their Academic Strengths?

By Brian A. Vander Schee, Aurora University, IL - bvanders@aurora.edu

Students focus on grades far more so than faculty would like. This is particularly true when students do not receive the grades they believe they deserve. They think that some assignments disadvantage them. I wondered how students would respond if they were given the opportunity to select the weight distribution for graded course components. The assignments would be preset, clearly described in the course syllabus and students would complete each one, but they could select the percentage of their grade accounted for by each assignment.

I took this approach in two sections of the Capstone: Strategic Management course. Students were given a grading agreement on the first day of class that asked them to select one of the designated percentage weights for each assignment that I would use in calculating their final course grade. I would now recommend letting the students have until the second week of class to finalize their decisions. They need time to get acquainted with the course and find out about their assignments in other courses. The four graded components in the course included: (1) case preparation and class participation (10 percent, 15 percent, or 20 percent); (2) individual written case analyses (30 percent, 35 percent, 40 percent, 45 percent, 50 percent, 55 percent, or 60 percent); (3) group case presentation (10 percent, 15 percent, or 20 percent); and (4) business strategy game (15 percent, 20 percent, 25 percent, 30 percent, or 35 percent). Once submitted, students were not permitted to make any changes to their designated distribution.

Students submitted a written rationale explaining how they decided on their particular distribution. Most said they chose the assignments they thought maximized their strengths as learners (53.8 percent) or they decreased the value of assignments that required skills they considered weaknesses (30.8 percent). I solicited feedback about this approach at the end of the course and most students were satisfied with the process. They perceived that they had more control over their final grade which motivated them to engage in the learning process.

If students really knew their academic strengths, their final grades would be higher than when I set the assignment percentages. However, the actual manipulation of the percentages did not determine how well students performed in the class. There was no significant difference in average final grades when students selected the assignment weights and when I set the weightings as I had done in the previous year.

In general, higher-achieving students rated the experience more positively than did the lower-achieving students. It may be that higher-achieving students have a better sense of their academic strengths. It is also possible that their locus of control is more internal, which contributes positively to learning. This research was conducted with graduating seniors, which probably influenced the outcome. Seniors have had more time in college to assess their academic performance in terms of knowing which assignments work well for them. First- and second-year students, even high achieving ones, may not be able to handle this approach as well.

Other research documents that students often expect grades much higher than they ultimately earn. This is particularly true of low-achieving students who may be less motivated when the teacher sets the grade weights. Giving students more control over grading at the outset by allowing them to select the percentage value of each assignment may increase their motivation. Doing so does not jeopardize how well they do in the course, or at least it didn't in my course.

Why Don't My Students Think I'm Groovy?

By Christy Price, Dalton State College, GA cprice@daltonstate.edu

Ask veteran teachers if students have changed, and they typically respond with a resounding, "YES!" My interest in this new breed of students was piqued when I began to notice unrealistically high expectations of success among my students combined with an astonishingly low level of effort on their part.

The gap that existed between students' levels of effort and their expectation of success was only one of many Generation Y or Millennial issues thwarting my efforts to change the world through molding young minds, so I did what any other self-respecting teacher of psychology would do. After expressing my negative emotions through interpretive dance, I went to the literature and I conducted a qualitative analysis of narratives provided by more than 100 Millennial learners. Their perceptions in four areas were enlightening—they transformed my teaching.

Al Gore has his Inconvenient Truth, and I have mine—whether we like it or not, the Millennial learner is the new generation of student that we must influence, inspire, and serve.

Professors familiar with millennial student culture versus those who were not

1. **Techno-savvy:** Millennials view a professor's ability to effectively utilize technology as an indicator of connectedness to their culture. One student wrote in frustration, "My professor is not up to date with technology. He is still confused about how to work the VCR!"

2. **Currently relevant:** Use of "real," "relevant," and "current" examples was one of the most obvious themes apparent among professors perceived as connected to millennial culture. As one commented, "Old shows like Taxi are not practical references that the average college student can relate to."

3. **Minimally lecturing:** Of all the themes students touched on in this category, I was most surprised to see Millennials view our teaching methods as an indicator of our connection to their culture. Respondents thought professors who involved them in class with a variety of methods (not just lecture) as more connected to millennial culture.

4. **Seriously humorous:** Surprisingly, Millennials associated tone of voice with being connected to their culture. Instructors perceived as "boring" or "monotone" were seen as lacking connection to Millennial culture. Connected professors used "humor" and were "fun."

5. **Relaxed and relatable:** Respondents perceived professors who "listened," "related," and "talked to students about their lives" as connected to Millennial culture, as opposed to those solely focused on course content. As one respondent lamented about her biology professor, "… he doesn't really talk about anything that we are interested in … he only talks about strictly class stuff and he won't go off onto anything else … he doesn't seem like he is into anything but scientific things." Imagine that, a biology professor who wants to talk about science!

Millennials also identified professors they perceived as "down to earth," "informal," "relaxed," and "flexible" as being connected to the culture; while those described as "uptight," "strict," "intimidating," or "condescending" were perceived as not connected to Millennial culture. Respondents relayed numerous examples of what they viewed as rigid course policies and harsh reactions used by professors perceived as not connected with their culture.

Millennials' ideal professor

Perhaps not surprising, but what these students basically want is for us to be decent individuals who are responsive to them! We should give them credit for not expecting us all to have chili peppers at ratemyprofessors.com. Further analysis of responses reveals something intriguing missing from their lists. They seem to care more about who we are and how we interact with them than they care about what we know. This doesn't mean that knowledge of subject and pedagogical expertise are insignificant, but perhaps they are simply a minimal qualification expected of us. Painfully obvious is how highly Millennial learners value positive interactions with their professors.

Millennials' ideal learning environment

The most consistent theme present in the analysis of responses to the ideal learning environment was Millennials' preference for a variety of teaching methods, as opposed to a "lecture only" format. I did note that these Millennial students did not attack the lecture method altogether, only when it was the teacher's only method.

Millennials' ideal assessments and assignments

When asked to describe their ideal assessments or assignments, several respondents left this particular section blank, perhaps suggesting the ideal assessment would be no assessment at all. The responses I did receive suggest that Millennials prefer a variety of assessments given regularly throughout the semester, as opposed to just having a mid-term and final. They also expressed a preference for "experiential" and "relevant" assessments. Finally, Millennials want their assignments "graded." The idea that time, effort, or contribution merit extrinsic rewards is in keeping with the "everyone gets a trophy" culture in which Millennials were raised. This became very personally apparent to me a year ago when my own five-year-old informed me he would "give me a sticker" if I helped him clean his room.

PAGE 8 ➧

Three Things to Do with Cell Phones (Besides Confiscate Them)

By Karen Eifler, University of Portland eifler@up.edu

My class had just finished covering three chalkboards with a rather dazzling array of concept clusters, illustrations, and links among disparate ideas. Clearly, a lot of learning had been generated. As I picked up the eraser to clear the board, I mentioned it was too bad that Chelsea and Eric (who were absent) had missed this vibrant discussion. "Well if you promise not to bust me, Dr. E, I could take a picture of all this and send it to them," offered Claire. She pointed at the laminated sign in the front of the room that said in huge font, complete with helpful picture, NO CELL PHONES ALLOWED IN CLASS.

Now, I am just as annoyed as the next person by the rude, thoughtless use of cell phones in public and have no patience with the thought of students using them to talk or text during my class. But Claire's comment reminded me that most cell phones today are powerful little handheld computers and, like any tool, I could put them to use to facilitate and enhance several aspects of the teaching and learning I want to happen in my classroom. That was a new insight for me. It motivated me to start using cells phone in class rather than just being offended by them. Let me share three simple ways they've helped my students and me in recent months:

1) **Archive content from the chalk or white board by taking a picture of it, as in the vignette referenced above.** Sure, interactive Smart Boards offer the same option, but for those of us who do not teach in rooms equipped with those, the cell phone camera is a fine low-tech option. Sometimes classes yield tremendous spontaneous insights that we may want to draw upon later. Claire sent the pictures to her classmates who missed class, and although I do not advocate making it easier on students who are absent, neither do I want them to miss out on crucial content. Claire also sent me the picture, and I have drawn upon this use of the cell phone frequently ever since, as now I have an artifact of teaching and learning and very often an image to use as a springboard into a new class session. We have also used the cell phone cameras to capture 3-D structures and role-plays that have come up in class to which we know we will want to refer later without necessarily saving the original items. The real coup was using my own cell phone camera to document the board notes from a freewheeling faculty meeting that would have otherwise vanished. My most antitechnology colleagues were pleasantly taken aback.

2) **Time small group activities using the built-in clock functions.** In any group of three or four students, at least one (if not all) will have a cell phone. When we break out for intimate discussions or application tasks, I have the phone holders synchronize times and timers, and then let the groups do their work. This frees them from having to keep glancing at the room clock and keeps them more focused on the task. I have also experimented with all students using timers set on "vibrate" to monitor timed reading and individual in-class exercises and am pleased with the sense of calm this elicits, quite different from the tenser "countdown" atmosphere we have when I am the sole timekeeper.

3) **Google it.** There are times when what's happening in class veers in an unanticipated direction and we need a fact I simply do not have at my disposal, nor does anyone in class. If it's true that "all of us are smarter than one of us," then literally bringing in the world via the Internet capacities of my students' cell phones makes us collectively brilliant. We can do a quick search to find the missing details, and then move on. For readers concerned that the students might keep cyber-wandering once the fact is retrieved, I can report that having several students on the same hunt moves the process along, and once we have our answer, a swift application of the patented, expectant "teacher look" usually brings them back in. It has also been instructive to probe and push and ponder when diligent students come up with differing facts. These are great teachable moments that help me underscore why their research must not begin and end with Wikipedia—and the evidence is right there in their hands.

The list above is hardly exhaustive, but perhaps it can help us begin to refocus the cell-phones-in-class conversation. New technologies require us to harness our wisdom and imagination. They also challenge us to think differently about what we do and why. Based on what's happened in my classroom I now propose that there are pedagogically defensible alternatives to silencing cell phones in our classrooms.

FIGURE 5.5 (Continued)
Source: The Teaching Professor.

authenticity of an announcement and obtaining a photo release.

Always keep in mind what the goal or purpose of your publication is, and avoid the temptation to stray. Feature stories are occasionally solicited or accepted from organizational members or business professionals but more often you will be writing stories or editing stories yourself. Never permit profanity or other unprofessional language in a newsletter, no matter what the tone is, and never refer to or draw attention to sex, gender, race, ethnicity, or other irrelevant workplace issues. Unless a feature story specifically discusses a new "women-friendly policy," or "ethnic tensions in," avoid mentioning the sex, race, gender, or other physical or cultural feature of employees. Such references are irrelevant and inappropriate for professional documents.

Newsletters are created using desktop publishing software like Adobe InDesign or QuarkXPress and by applying basic design principles. Consider the following important technical and design issues: *First,* since newsletters are typically created using two or three columns per page, your must bring your type size down to 8 to 10 points. Generally, newsletters resemble newspaper pages, with two or three column spreads, large headlines and subheads, and graphic images. If you use an 11- or 12-point font, your newsletter will look amateurish. A good rule of thumb is to have about 8 to 10 words per line. Note, also, that when you are using smaller type sizes, you often need to add a bit more than the default leading (1.25-spaced rather than single-spaced) between lines to increase readability.

Second, the best newsletters, magazine, booklets, etc., have harmonious design elements that are carried throughout the entire document. Typically, newsletters (or any substantive document) use only a few fonts (or one font family) for everything except for advertisements and feature story headlines. Occasionally, newsletters and magazines also have unique artistic layouts for the splash page of individual stories, but everything else follows the newsletter's default style and design. More commonly, however, a newsletter will use a single font family like Caslon, Gill Sans, or Sabon for everything. Additionally, newsletters sometimes adopt a dingbat (a symbol) to indicate that the end of a story has been reached, or to indicate section breaks or transitions.

Third, as explained in Chapter 4, consistent spacing is perhaps the most important design technique that you can employ. *Consistent* spacing among graphics, body text, headlines, pull quotes, etc., is more important than *how much* space is used. Every story should have exactly the same space before and after it, every quote should have the same design and spacing, every box should have the same runaround and inset space, every photo should have the same captioning font, everything needs to be meticulously spaced and replicated from page to page.

The greatest challenge in designing a newsletter is deciding how it will look and developing a template that allows you to create multiple editions of the newsletter, all with the same look. If possible, consider hiring a professional graphic designer to create the newsletter design elements and style and templates for you to use in future editions of the newsletter.

If you develop the entire newsletter yourself, you must learn how to create style sheets (see Chapters 4 and 12 on aesthetics and software for details). Style sheets are used to create consistent formatting that, once applied to characters, paragraphs, symbols, textboxes, etc., can be globally changed or updated, saving a lot of time and reducing the chances that you will make a mistake when formatting each edition. Style sheets can be created in virtually every professional business application (Microsoft Word, InDesign, QuarkXPress, etc.) and are indispensable whenever you are creating lengthy documents with various levels of headings and textual or design styles.

VIDEO SCRIPTS

Another common internal communication tactic is the training video. Organizations create video packages for an assortment of purposes. Many organizations have training videos that employees watch in order to learn about the organization, equipment, or multi-step processes. Also common are informational videos offered as CD/DVDs to customers, clients, investors, and the media. Many organizations create videos for marketing purposes. For example, Procter & Gamble created informational videos about the safety of Olestra, when they first introduced the fat substitute in the mid-'90s. Around the same time, Miejers, a Michigan-based retail chain, distributed free videos about store openings to members of the local community by regular mail.[1]

Video scripts are written for informational videos, training videos, infomercials, and many other video applications. I cannot teach you how to write a video script in a few pages. In order to prepare a video script you have to have some idea about camera angles, video and lighting effects, acting, how to write compelling dialogue, etc.

Typically, scriptwriting is taught as an entire course (or several courses) in broadcast journalism programs. You can also purchase a book on scriptwriting and learn how to do it, but you should not consider writing a script until you have some idea about what you are doing. Producing a professional quality video is not likely to be possible without a lot of training in how to use a video camera, how to shoot the video, how to edit the footage once you have it, and how to assemble it into a coherent package using one of the many digital video-editing programs.

Unless you have a real interest in script writing, shooting video, editing, etc., and have taken a few courses on these topics or read a number of books, you will need to hire a professional videographer, scriptwriter, actors, etc. Producing a professional video for training, informational, or marketing, can cost from $15,000–100,000, depending upon the quality and production values sought, the length of the video, and whether professional actors are needed. A series of training videos with, say, John Cleese, will double or triple the cost of a project, while a local acting student might save $50,000. John Cleese, of course, will help sell a lot more copies of the video than a local actor if you plan on selling the video to clients, libraries, or universities.

EXTERNAL COMMUNICATION ISSUES

As always, effective communication is contingent upon understanding your target audience. Additionally, you need to be aware that the communication needs of publics vary widely. Media choices and message tactics are not equal. A social networking site may be an excellent way to reach college students but is not as likely to be as effective with the students' parents or older alumni. Ultimately, *what* you communicate (content, tone, style) and *how* you communicate (channel, frequency, distribution) will vary depending upon the public involved. What should not vary, however, is your commitment to public relations ethics, dialogic communication, and meeting the informational needs of your publics. Organizations are better served by meeting the informational needs of stakeholders and stakeseekers rather than keeping secrets from the media or employees.

If the media, a customer or client, a fellow professional, a professional association, or even a high school student contacts a public relations professional, s/he should do his or her best to respond with honesty and integrity. In many cases (especially with the media) people who ask questions already know (or think they know) the answer to their questions. Stonewalling and deception only breed a lack of trust, defiance, and a desire to find the truth some other way.

As the old adage says, "it only takes 17 muscles to smile but it takes 43 muscles to frown" (which is actually not true, but the sentiment is sound), organizations that tell the truth get to spend more time on message and less time on damage control. Do not make the mistake of trying to use communication to deceive people or to silence debate. Organizational communication is at its best when professionals respond to publics with honesty and respect.

One of the best examples of the value of organizations being honest is the McDonald's "McLibel" case. McDonald's historically has sued activists and outspoken critics rather than trying to meet with them about their concerns. In the widely publicized "McLibel" case (www.mcspotlight.org/case/index.html), McDonald's sued two unemployed British activists for distributing leaflets about McDonald's on the streets of London (www.mcspotlight.org/case/factsheet.html).

Many issues were raised in the libel suit but in the end, after several years of bad publicity and the posting of the original leaflet (that actually contained factual information) on the Internet—which led to millions of people seeing it instead of a few hundred people on the streets of London—a judge eventually ruled that McDonald's actually did

> "exploit children" with their advertising, produce "misleading" advertising, are "culpably responsible" for cruelty to animals, are "antipathetic" to unionisation and pay their workers low wages. But Helen and Dave [the activists] failed to prove all the points and so the Judge ruled that they HAD libelled McDonald's and should pay 60,000 pounds damages. They refused and McDonald's knew better than to pursue it. In March 1999 the Court of Appeal made further rulings that it was fair comment to say that McDonald's

> employees worldwide "do badly in terms of pay and conditions", [sic] and true that "if one eats enough McDonald's food, one's diet may well become high in fat etc., with the very real risk of heart disease." … As a result of the court case, the Anti-McDonald's campaign mushroomed, the press coverage increased exponentially. (www.mcspotlight.org/case/index.html)

Had McDonald's met with the activist and actually considered their claims (a dialogic approach), which were essentially true,[2] McDonald's would have been years ahead of its competition in terms of offering more nutritious food, recyclable packaging, employee satisfaction, and a host of other issues that the "Golden Arches" has only recently begun to embrace. McDonald's is still reeling over the harsh criticism from the 2004 movie *Super Size Me*, and the film of Eric Schlosser's (2002) best-selling book, *Fast Food Nation*.[3] McDonald's really should take a page from the alcohol industry and reform now before the law forces it to.

WRITING FOR PRINT

For public relations professionals to be successful they need to understand the strengths and weakness of the various print and broadcast media. In general, the first issue to consider when writing for print sources is who is the audience? According to The Project for Excellence in Journalism (www.journalism.org), an initiative by journalists to clarify and raise the standards of American journalism, the Pew Research Center "found that 52 percent of college graduates reported reading a newspaper 'yesterday,' compared with 41 percent of high school graduates and 24 percent of people without a high school degree" (www.stateofthemedia.org/2004/narrative_newspapers_intro.asp). Additionally, although the audience for all print sources tends to be the more educated citizens, only about half (50–60 percent) of the adult population in the U.S. between the ages of 35–54 report reading a daily newspaper (ibid). Independent reports of readership suggest Americans have one of the lowest levels of global newspaper readership, at around 25 percent of the adult population.

The newspaper data are also suggestive because not only is newspaper readership related to age and education, but newspapers are rapidly becoming a poor choice for reaching specific portions of the population. Only about 38–43 percent of the population between the ages of 18–34 report reading newspapers each week (op. cit., www.stateofthenewsmedia.org …).

A better choice for targeting individuals and publics are the outlets that cater to particular groups. When you consider that there are about 8–11,000 subscription-based magazines, 4,000 business-to-business magazines, and 10,000 member and industry publications, your chances of reaching a more specific audience through a tailored news source (magazine, newsletter, listserv, blog) are much higher and more precise then if you rely upon newspapers.

WRITING FOR NEWSPAPERS

Given the wide demographic and educational level of newspaper readers, the level of the prose crafted for newspapers needs to be low, typically ninth or tenth grade reading level. In order to write prose appropriate for the average newspaper reader, you need to write in short, uncomplicated sentences using simple vocabulary free of technojargon and sophisticated words.

One way to measure the complexity of your sentences is by checking the **reading ease score**. Two of the most common measures of **readability** are the "Flesch Reading Ease" formula and the "Flesch-Kincaid Grade Level Score." Readability scores are fairly easy to calculate and measure sentence length and number of syllables. The higher the Flesch Reading Ease score (a number from 0 to 100), the easier the text is to read. This paragraph scores a 60.5, and is written at the ninth grade level.

Readability Statistics	
Words	86
Characters	411
Paragraphs	1
Sentences	5
Sentences per Paragraph	5.0
Words per Sentence	17.2
Characters per Word	4.6
Passive Sentences	20%
Flesch Reading Ease	60.5
Flesch-Kincaid Grade Level	9.0

FIGURE 5.6 Flesch reading score table.

No one calculates Flesch scores by hand anymore since word processing programs and Web sites do it automatically. For example, if you are using Microsoft Word, simply go to "Spelling and Grammar" and check your document. Be sure the program options are set to "show readability statistics" (you can set the options in the spelling and grammar window). After the spelling and grammar check are complete, a box will appear displaying readability data. With a bit of practice, after your document is checked, you can simplify your prose and increase the readability of your documents.

Whatever type of message you are creating (but especially in newspaper and broadcast writing), work to write active, tight, uncomplicated prose. For example, rather than writing: "It is not uncommon to find students who download music on college campuses" you might say: "Students often download music with their school account." or "College students are increasingly downloading music" Six words instead of 13, positive phrasing ("Students often ..." or "College students ...") instead of a double negative ("not uncommon"), and a clear referent to the subject ("Students") rather than a vague reference to "It," (cf., Burke, 1966, pp. 359–379.

When writing for print sources with clear demographics, target the educational level and technical knowledge of your audience. Thus, if you are submitting a letter to the editor of the local newspaper, your writing style should be easy to follow, straightforward, and lean. However, if you were writing a commentary or white paper for an organizational Web site, or responding to a blog in some specialized area, your writing style should mesh with the reader/member style. You always want to have clean, tight, prose; however, your vocabulary and the sophistication of your arguments can be higher with experts and more educated audiences.

FEATURE WRITING

Features are a staple of newspaper content. Because of the information subsidy and the many cutbacks in journalism nationwide, newspapers are always looking for free content. There is some disagreement over whether public relations professionals should bother writing unsolicited "feature stories." Some practitioners argue that they are never printed while others argue that they are sometimes accepted if tailored and localized properly. Whether unsolicited stories are used or not, practitioners do write feature stories as accompaniments to special advertising sections and issue advertisements. Feature stories are also common in newsletters, magazines, and on Web sites.

The rules for Associated Press style apply to feature stories intended for newspapers. Follow AP style for dates, composition titles, etc. Follow AP formatting for the appearance as well: wide margins (at least 1.5." left and right), no textual effects like bolding, italics, or underlining (they are not allowed in newspaper copy so make your message clear without them), double-space everything to leave ample room for editing the copy, and include photographs and caption suggestions.

When writing feature content intended for newsletters or the Web, you have complete control over the formatting and layout. Web and newsletter content should be accompanied by photographs, pull quotes, and drop caps. Web content should also link to related information on your organization's Web site and be written in a fashion consistent with your organization's image.

In terms of length, feature stories vary widely. Occasionally, lengthy feature stories are serialized and appear over several weeks or months in different issues of a newspaper or magazine. In other cases, like feature stories in soft news sections (sports, fashion, cooking, education, gardening, religion), the length can very from a few hundred words to several thousand.

In general, your best chance of placing a feature story is to understand the conventions of the source, the needs of the editor for whom you are writing, and to carefully tailor and localize your prose so that the tone, examples, and style, matches that of past feature stories printed in the source you are submitting your story to. Remember, to be successful, the feature story needs to serve the needs of the newspapers readers rather than your own needs. Editors do not run feature stories to provide organizations with free advertising, but feature stories can be a great way for stakeseekers and interested publics to learn about your organization.

At the heart of every good feature story is a compelling "event." Many people find feature stories that focus on the human element, characters, and experiences, more compelling than mere "how to" articles. Draw upon narrative structure when you tell your story (i.e., have a beginning, middle, and end), include vivid and interesting examples and have character development, use comparisons and analogies, and use concrete and familiar imagery. Tell a story! People identify more closely with things that they know well, so use local, and familiar illustrations to explain unfamiliar activities and events.

As suggested in Chapter 1, your best opportunity for becoming skilled at feature story writing is to take advantage of the opportunity to write for your student newspaper or other local media outlet. Additionally, if your public relations program does not include a course on journalistic writing, you should consider taking one somewhere else. A better understanding of how to write compelling feature stories will also come to you as you *read* more feature stories. Begin paying more attention to the news. Subscribe to a couple of national newspapers like the *New York Times*, the *Wall Street Journal*, the *Washington Post*, or read them in your school library every day. Also, subscribe to a reputable international news magazine like the *Economist*. Begin to pay more attention to how journalists write so that you can effectively mimic the style.

WRITING FOR BROADCAST

The big difference between print writing and broadcast writing is, of course, the spoken word. Because newspapers are *read*, they can present more sophisticated arguments and minute details. However, broadcast writing calls for entirely different writing skills. For example, when people are listening to the radio during "drive time" (a large segment of the radio audience), listener attention is on more than one activity: driving, of course, but also, increasingly, talking on cellular telephones, text messaging, eating, drinking coffee, shaving, applying makeup, reading or listening to a GPS system, etc. In general, most people do not drive while they are reading the morning newspaper nor are they likely to be shaving or putting on makeup. Reading is a fundamentally different activity than listening (cf., Postman, 1984; Postman & Paglia, 1991).

Broadcast messages, both radio and television, often rely upon a series of musical or audible cues (increased volume, sound effects, etc.) to alert listeners to their favorite programs. Commercials, Public Service Announcements (PSAs), and news segments both on radio and on television, often begin with a "headline," music, or sound effects, in order to alert the listener and allow him/her to divert some mental attention to the story.

Broadcast news sources, especially radio, are also far more segmented than the newspaper. Just get in your car and start surfing through the stations. You will find alternative, classic rock, college, country, oldies, top-40, metal, public broadcasting, reggae, rap, religious, talk, and many others.

According to the U.S. Census Bureau (www.census.gov), there are currently more than 25,000 cities and towns in the U.S. and, according to Bagdikian (2000), fewer than 1,500 daily newspapers published nationwide (p. liv). Only 1 in 16 towns has its own newspaper, or more than a few choices. Moreover, of the industrialized countries, the U.S. has the lowest per capita newspaper consumption: 287 readers per 1,000 citizens versus 572/1,000 in Sweden (p. 203). Even small markets have more than a dozen radio stations (www.publishers-edge.com/index_files/Paper_vs_Radio.htm), and those stations will typically consist of more finely segmented demographics than any newspaper in the country.

Broadcast writing (and writing broadcast dialogue) needs to mesh with the style of radio, which calls for short, punchy, simple, prose, is appealing to the ear, and meshes with the format of the station. If your message is appropriate for listeners of the Diane Rhem Show, or Brian Lehrer (both "liberal" public broadcasting programs), your message will probably not be suitable for a more conservative station. Similarly, if you are interested in reaching men and women ages 35–45, an '80s station or a mainstream rock station might be a better choice than a statewide or national newspaper.

Although there are more broadcast radio stations than television stations nation wide, with the exception of people who listen to satellite radio, or people who tune into Internet radio, most people in the U.S. probably have more television choices via cable or satellite than radio choices. Television also allows for more segmentation of publics than newspapers (although newspapers have dozens of sections intended to appeal to specific audiences), thereby allowing more targeted messages. However, television is also the most expensive (for advertising) of the public media and offers few opportunities to express detailed or substantive organizational positions. Network television provides no outlet for a local businessperson or politician to be heard. Each medium has its strengths and limitations. What your ultimate communicative goal is, and the key public sought for your message, are what matter most when writing for the broadcast and print media.

MEDIA TRAINING

One of the situations where you might be called upon to craft some of your most compelling and memorable messages is when you are preparing responses to questions by journalists or preparing an organizational spokesperson for a talk show. As professionals, you need to think in terms of quotable messages, or "sound bites," if you want to maximize the chance an organization or client's message will be repeated and used by broadcast journalists. Additionally, whenever organizational representatives appear on radio or television they need to be taught to "stay on message" and to repeat key words and phrases throughout their answers to questions.

Similarly, if you are preparing a manager for an appearance on *CNN, Crossfire, Diane Rehm, Lou Dobbs, The Colbert Report*, *The News Hour,* or *60 Minutes*, you need to understand what kind of talk takes place on each program, what to expect from the moderator, and how to prepare effective answers to questions. In all cases (radio or television), comments should be direct, quotable, and compelling. Writing possible questions and practicing answers to an assortment of questions is common. With each round of practice, answers can be refined and the potential interviewee will become more comfortable with talking about the ideas/issues.

VIDEO NEWS RELEASE (VNRS)

VNRs are a common broadcast tactic for larger organizations with abundant financial resources. A video news release is not like a standard news release. A VNR typically consists of what is called B-roll (or video) footage of an event, along with separate voiceover (VO) audio footage that tells the story (like what you might hear accompanying an actual news story). A VNR package also includes a printed copy of the text that is being read on the audio footage, as well as a complete package with the voice and video synced, that could, hypothetically, be aired exactly as you have produced it.

The premise of a VNR is that a news outlet has the choice of using the full package, produced to look exactly like a story might on CNN, NBC, CBS, or MSNBC, of creating its own story based on the video and audio B-roll, or, just using the video and telling the story with local talent (network anchors). Most VNRs are edited by the stations that use them, often using the B-Roll and script and local talent to tailor the story for local viewers.

As suggested above, producing video of any kind is expensive. As with a training video, a VNR can cost $5,000–100,000 to produce depending upon whether it includes a complete package with celebrity talent, or whether you just submit video footage with a script. Whatever you do, consult a video professional before trying to prepare a VNR.

NEWS CONFERENCE

The news conference is perhaps the most common broadcast tactic for public relations professionals because of its relatively low cost. A news conference is a public event held by individuals and organizations where the media (print, broadcast, online, etc.) are invited to come and ask questions of organizational spokespeople. Typically, a news conference involves a scripted opening statement by a representative of the individual or organization who called the news conference, followed by an opportunity for the media to ask questions, and concluding with a brief, scripted, concluding statement (See Table 5.1).

News conferences are used to announce timely organizational information and to respond to crises. News conferences are often the quickest way to get information out to competing news sources at the same time. For this reason, news conferences are used in crisis situations or when an organization wants to control the flow of information to the media. News conferences must be "newsworthy" or no one will come—never use them to grandstand. If the media *does* attend your news conference and the information has been hyped or oversold, the reporters who attend will remember you and your organization as having wasted their time and not come again.

Answering Questions for the Media

1. When you respond to questions, paraphrase the question before you begin. Paraphrasing questions helps audience members who may not have heard the question (often the case when news conferences are broadcast and the audience members were not given a microphone for their questions), helps speakers provide clear responses, and allows speakers to limit their response to the issue(s) *they* want to address.
2. If your topic is controversial, take questions one at a time and then move on to someone else. Avoid getting into a debate or argument with

TABLE 5.1 News Conference Checklist

- ☐ News conferences are usually held in the morning and early in the week.
- ☐ Begin with a brief, scripted, opening statement, then open the floor to comments.
- ☐ End with a brief, scripted, concluding statement.
- ☐ Never speak "off the record" to anyone in the media. "Off the record" only exists on television or when someone has a well-established relationship with a journalist.
- ☐ Never lie. You represent an organization. Lying is a violation of the PRSA code of ethics as well as the trust that individuals and public hold in organizations.
- ☐ Never say "No comment." Real life is not an episode of *Law & Order*. People assume that "no comment" means that the organization is hiding something. More importantly, why hold a news conference if you do not have anything to say? The news conference is a tool to get your message out. You plan and schedule the event. Do not hold a news conference if it you have nothing to say.
- ☐ Anticipate and prepare for difficult questions or questions likely to be asked.
- ☐ You will be subjected to intense scrutiny—be prepared, be polished, and do not get defensive.
- ☐ Never give impromptu answers. Be sure that you have prepared and rehearsed answers to as many foreseeable questions as possible. Do not be tricked into "speculating."
- ☐ Always use your prepared manuscript for the opening and closing statements and only speak about what you are sure about.
- ☐ Rehearse answering sample questions. Practice until you can give sound-bite answers (15–30 seconds).
- ☐ When answering questions, you should appear helpful and positive. Do not get defensive or resentful of journalists' questions. You need them and they need you (the information subsidy).
- ☐ Practice monitoring your nonverbals (videotape yourself practicing). You do not want to appear angry, insincere, or evasive.
- ☐ Do not stonewall or refuse to answer questions. Why hold the news conference if you do not want to use it to control the issue or discussion?
- ☐ Make copies of news conference materials available to all attendees.
- ☐ News conferences and public statements may be used for both offensive and defensive purposes (cf., Nixon's Checkers speech and Clinton's "I did not have sexual relations with that woman . . .").
- ☐ Invite everyone who might be interested. Every news outlet will not attend but they should be given the opportunity.
- ☐ Decide on the best time to hold the event to allow for both print and broadcast media sources to report the event and prepare a story.
- ☐ Always be sensitive to print and television deadlines; do not ignore print sources that might be interested in covering the story by holding the news conference too late in the day.
- ☐ Select an appropriate date and time to make your announcement or respond to the issue. Be aware of competing events, ceremonies, holidays, governmental or political scandals or crises, or other important events (a Martian landing, etc.).
- ☐ Select a convenient location. Major cities all have media centers set up for conducting news conferences.
- ☐ Secure the location well in advance—be sure to have enough chairs, leave the center aisle and front clear for photographers, reserve a room with electrical outlets, wireless access, etc., in which can journalists work.
- ☐ Arrange a secure place for broadcast reporters to store equipment.
- ☐ Be sure to provide wireless computer access (if possible), paper and pencils, water pitchers and glasses, etc.
- ☐ Issue invitations well in advance (six to eight weeks or a month if possible for product announcements; a week or more for investigations; a few days if possible for crises events).
- ☐ News conference invitations should indicate the purpose of the news conference, the names of organizational spokespeople, why the event has significant news value (this is an argument, not a claim; briefly explain what will be shared that the media care about), and the date, time, and location of the event.
- ☐ Distribute a news release about the upcoming news conference with the invitation.

Stylistic Devices

- Timeliness: holiday, "annual"
- Rarity: "first time," "never before seen"
- Local angle, proximity, relevance to community
- Human interest
- Humorous dialogue
- Instructive dialogue
- Monologue
- Celebrity monologue
- Prominence: "the VIP effect"
- Creative devices: jingles, raps, and original music

Visualization Strategies

1. Character voices: imitated celebrities, actual people, stereotypes (like the "dumb guy," "the sports fanatic," "the know-it-all")
2. Music
3. Sound effects (SFX)
4. Cue words in the copy: "What are you doing with that *Purdue sweatshirt*, Roger?"
5. Repetition
6. Exaggeration
7. Jingles
8. Foreshadowing/forewarning
9. Humor

Reasons That Stations Reject PSAs

1. The message is not compelling.
2. The PSA is not relevant to the local community.
3. The tone of the PSA is not consistent with the station's format.
4. The format of the PSA is not up to the technical standards of the station.
5. The spot lacks a "public service" angle.

PSAs are very common and regularly used by for-profit and nonprofit organizations of all sizes (cf., 4-h.org/b/Assets/BrandNetwork/Radio%20PSA%20Tips.pdf). The Weatherization Assistance Program offers additional samples and practical suggestions (www.waptac.com/sp.asp?mc=public_guides_psas):

1. Listen first! Target specific radio stations, television programs, and print outlets, according to your desired audience.
2. Check with the radio/television stations to see what lengths of PSA would work for the broadcast. Most stations broadcast PSAs early in the morning or very late in the evening. Ask the station's public service director to consider placing your PSA in an available day or prime-time spot.
3. Always send a letter on your organization's letterhead asking for the PSA to be run. (Remember to include why the service to the community is important, and that you are a nonprofit organization).
4. Put a desired start and end date for the PSA. If there is no limit, just label it TFN—"Till Further Notice."
5. Be absolutely sure you give enough lead-time in getting the material to the station. Send the information about three to four weeks before you want the spot to start airing. If possible, visit the station to hand-deliver your PSA and meet the public service director.
6. Follow up with a phone call, a fax, or an e-mail to make sure that your material arrived.
7. For radio PSAs: Time your copy with a stopwatch. Read it aloud to see how it sounds. Write 12 seconds of script for a 15-second spot, and 27 seconds for a 30-second spot. This allows for the variation in the announcer's speech pattern and will assure that all your information gets read.

WRITING FOR THE INTERNET

Writing for the Internet is arguably the most challenging activity for public relations professionals. Besides the fact that there are an assortment of theories about what Internet content should consist of (Kent, 2001b; Kent, Harrison, & Taylor, 2006); and besides the fact that the anonymity of the Internet makes it difficult to gather reliable information about publics; and besides the fact that public relations professionals often do not have control over the content, design, and goals of their organization or client's Web site; and besides a dozen more reason I could list, writing for the Internet is difficult. Moreover, professionals have been writing for print and broadcast sources for decades, but the Internet is much younger, changes rapidly, and can reach tens of millions of people very quickly. There is not one style appropriate for all online venues. In spite of the difficulties, there are some basic suggestions for "webbed" public relations writing.

First, as with all public relations writing you need to understand your audience. If you are considering contributing to a blog, listserv, newsgroup, or other online commentary to "correct a mistake," or "provide background information," be sure you have spent some time understanding what the reader's expectations are and how they treat such commentary lest you wind up being attacked as a "hack" or "corporate apologist."

Second, when you are creating content for an organization or client's Web site, whether you are writing a news release or creating copy for the home page makes a big difference. Documents like news releases should take the proper form and tone so the media might actually use them when they visit your Web site. Keep your prose straightforward, uncomplicated, and newsworthy, but, at the same time, take advantage of the ability to incorporate images, hyperlinks, pull quotes, and other hypermedia.

Third, take into account some basic Web writing suggestions:

1. Keep content designed to be read on the computer screen short. Most people will not read lengthy documents on their computer screen. Short concise paragraphs are preferred to more detailed paragraphs. Since space constraints are irrelevant on the Web, you can provide information that is more detailed to visitors who want more content via links to PDFs and other documents or Web pages.

2. Remember that "Web" is a metaphor (Kent, 2001b; Kent, Harrison, & Taylor, 2006). "Web site," "Web page," "Web master," these phrases were borrowed from other situations and media as a means of describing the Internet. The Web is not passive in the way that newspapers and television are and people use the Internet very differently than they do other media. How you create content should be driven by rhetorical forces: how your audience will use the information that you produce, what the audience needs to know, where your audience enters your Web site from, etc. Consider Chapter 8 on analytics for more details.

3. As with business letters, news releases, and pitch letters, include only one idea per paragraph and create uncomplicated, easy-to-follow content. Again, because reading a lot of text on computer screens tires the eyes, many readers just scan for content of interest. Do not force readers to wade through lengthy introductions to find out your point; suspense is not an effective tool in electronic writing. Cut to the chase.

4. Use headings, bullets, pull quotes, graphics, and hyperlinks as design elements to allow readers to quickly navigate through your documents. Because the logic of the Internet is "pull" rather than "push," visitors come to organizational Web sites looking for information to meet *their* needs. Understand and acknowledge why people are there and design the content accordingly. Do not try to force visitors to your site to read your blog posting or CEO editorials. Be sure to design pages with clear navigational cues, tables of contents, and site search boxes so that visitors can interact with your organization on their own terms.

5. Make your writing interesting. Most Web sites are visited by people who share similar interests. Visitors to organizational Web sites are typically not there for fun. Visitors to a flooring company are generally interested in flooring. The same is true for a doctor, a plastic manufacturer, a car dealer, or an auction site. As the Kinks say, "Give the people what they want." Thus, assume you are communicating with a sympathetic audience who has arrived on your site for information or answers to specific questions, or to purchase a product or service from you. Do your best to incorporate anecdotes, illustrations, analogies, and narrative. Be professional, but be conversational.

Try to write more intimately than you might when creating a business letter or memo, but not like you are sending an e-mail message to a friend or your mother. Depending upon the type of company, some levity might be in order, such as this e-mail message from a lumber company:

> Good news, Paul, our highly trained and skilled team of 50 employees has—with great care and attention—selected, packaged and shipped your order (#123456) on this beautiful day, 9/9/2010.
>
> We had a lively celebration afterwards and the whole party marched down the street where the entire city of Phoenix came out, waved "Bon Voyage!" to your package, and patted the UPS driver on the back.
>
> Local TV stations sent in cameras and reporters who asked, "What does Paul intend to make with this?" We offered no comment so we wouldn't spoil your surprise. We do hope to see pictures of what you make so we can have another city-wide celebration.
>
> I hope you had a wonderful time shopping at Woodworkers Source.
>
> With other types of organizations, order confirmation messages might be more reserved. What is important to understand is that the Internet affords you the most intimate access to stakeholders short of a face-to-face meeting. When you create online content, consider who might be reading your messages and write accordingly.

DARK SITES

Dark sites refer to Web sites that are prepared ahead of time and kept in reserve to be posted after a crisis, or in response to an important organizational issue. Essentially, a dark site is an organizational Web site that has just not been put up yet. Like any Web site, dark sites contain an assortment of written content and organizational messages. Depending on the depth or size of the site (tens of pages to hundreds of pages), dark sites can take months to prepare and require all of the work debugging and testing that a standard Web site requires. Dark sites begin by adapting or repurposing existing organizational materials to suit the intended need and then create new content specifically related to the anticipated situation.

Learning to **repurpose** your work in a variety of ways is essential. For example, the boilerplate text from the end of a news release might be incorporated into a Web site or might have originated in an annual report. Speeches given by organizational spokespeople can be converted to podcasts and uploaded to organizational home pages. Infographics created for annual reports can be reused in newsletters. Artwork commissioned to commemorate an historic event can be used in organizational documents. Historical background information written for a Web site can be used to produce a brochure or as part of a special event bulletin. Since so much of public relations takes place under time constraints, learning to repurpose your previous work is essential.

Using the basic organizational Web site design (logos, colors, typography, æsthetics), dark sites incorporate new content intended to address specific (anticipated) issues. For example, say an organization develops a crisis plan to deal with a potential problem—a natural disaster, an accident. As part of that plan, Web materials are developed for the media and external organizational publics, including informational documents, fact sheets, and lists of contact information. Once the information has been prepared and the Web site designed and tested, dark sites can be activated on a moment's notice, allowing an organization to appear super responsive, proactive, and prepared to deal with the issue. Dark sites are developed to deal with potential crises, anticipated public issues, the release of new products, and a host of other issues.

NEWS RELEASES

News releases are one of the most common types of public relations documents. They are used by diverse organizations of all sizes, in all parts of the country and world. A typical news release is about 5 to 10 paragraphs long and has a very standard look. Lengthier news releases of 5 to 10 pages are also written for newsmagazines and other sources that are likely to write lengthier feature stories or include more story details than a newspaper might. News releases intended for newspapers or wire services tend to be five to six paragraphs long; they have become standardized because of services like PRNewswire, which charges $635 for a 400-word news release plus $170 for each additional 100 words (PRNewswire.com).[4]

News releases are written to announce almost any newsworthy activity or event. Since news releases essentially represent free advertising for organizations, they must be "newsworthy" and draw upon accepted "hard news" determinants (timeliness, human interest, community development or outreach, grants, gifts, donations, sponsorships, awards, new services, economic issues, sports, fashion, weather). News releases about softer news issues (opinion, editorial) are unlikely to be published.

Just because your organization wants a news release published about its titanium widget does not mean that the topic is newsworthy. News releases should have the same tone as hard news content and are written using the inverted pyramid. When using the inverted pyramid, the most important content is placed at the top of the news release and the least important content appears at the bottom. The inverted pyramid structure allows an editor to simply cut paragraphs from the bottom up until space constraints are met. See Figure 5.8.

Several news releases are included here, but you can find thousands of examples on the PRNewswire Web site. PRNewswire as an excellent resource for distribution of news releases. PRNewswire charges fees for distributing news releases based on the desired reach of the news releases, its length, and other variables.

Typical News Release Structure

In general, there is no single way to write an effective news release. Several articles have been published over the last 20 years in publications like *The PR Strategist, Public Relations Quarterly, Public Relations Tactics,* and other PRSA and IABC publications each suggesting how to write the best news release. There is no *one* correct way to write a news release, but the basics include the following:

- *An interesting and informative headline* that is *not sensational,* and not written like an actual

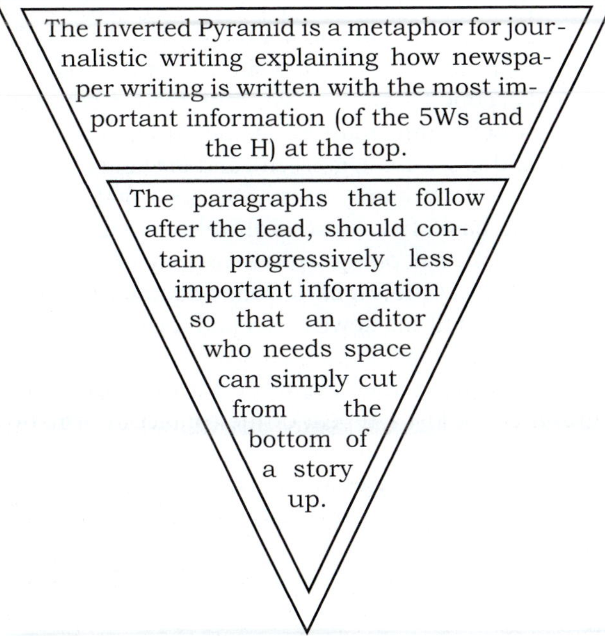

The Inverted Pyramid is a metaphor for journalistic writing explaining how newspaper writing is written with the most important information (of the 5Ws and the H) at the top.
The paragraphs that follow after the lead, should contain progressively less important information so that an editor who needs space can simply cut from the bottom of a story up.

FIGURE 5.8 Inverted Pyramid Graphic.

newspaper headline. Think journal article title here (informative) rather than newspaper headline (attention getter). Actual headlines are written by editors and depend on space constraints, the length of the story, the orientation of the story in the news source (wide vs. narrow), judgments of newsworthiness, etc. Since you never know how a news release will be used, you cannot write the actual headline. Do not try; you are not the editor. Instead, write an informative headline that reveals the topic and piques the journalist's interest. A news release headline should get attention and interest, reveal the subject, and be written clearly.

- *Paragraph one (the "lead"):* Follow the headline with basic "news-related" information. Do not introduce another topic that is not alluded to in the headline. Although you cannot write the headline, the lead paragraph is often published verbatim, so write the paragraph for the readers rather than the editor. The lead should contain everything essential in the body of the news release. Remember the *inverted pyramid*: editors cut from the bottom up, so news releases should include the most essential information near the top of the release. Like a speech, an introduction should get the interest and attention of the reader, preview the main point, reveal the thesis or claim, establish the newsworthiness of your topic, and establish your organization's credibility, if necessary. *Do not* try to include every detail about what will happen, or who, where, when, why. Instead, focus on having a useful and compelling introduction.
- *Paragraph two:* Additional information about the event like basic history or background of an event, information about the event itself (where it will be held, how long it will last, etc.). Stick to elaborating on the lead in paragraph two. Never introduce a second issue into a news release. If you have more than one newsworthy issue, write a news release for each one.
- *Paragraph three:* Quotations. Never use hyperbole, slang, or contractions in your writing. However, since people *speak* in contractions and slang, in a quotation, someone who attended an event last year can say whatever they want (Dude! It was awsome!). Since news releases are written in a "hard news" style, you (the organization) cannot say things in your own voice like "this year's carnival is going to be the best ever!" In journalism, exaggerated claims and matters of opinion are called "puffery." Since quotations are not "news," you can say whatever you want. Thus, use quotations to your advantage. Do not write, "According to Jane Doe, V.P. of public relations …" Who cares what the V.P. of public relations Jane Doe has to say? Jane Doe is biased. Speaking well of the organization and its products and services is her job. Instead, secure a quotation from someone who has local appeal (a mayor, a business person, a celebrity), credibility with the target audience (a professor, a CEO, an attendee), or has an "expert" connection (a research scientist, a governmental spokesperson, etc.).

The best quotes come from local community members, politicians, well-known CEOs, not the "communications director," whose job it is to say nice things. Additionally, use quotations to their fullest. Quotations are not something to be wasted. In a quote, you can say things that you (the organization) cannot say in the release.

Quotes are often written by public relations professionals for other organizational members (with their approval). Speaking for other people is what public relations professionals do. In journalism, writing quotations for others will find you quickly out of a job. However, as the voice of the organization, you speak for many people, and you often have to write speeches or create presentations for others. You of course cannot write quotes for people who are unrelated to the organization. Furthermore, quotes by organizational members should never be "fabricated": they should always be as close to the actual words that your colleague might speak as possible. However, writing quotes for clients or your organization is part of the job. What you should *never* do is to make up fictitious quotations and attribute them to "a recent participant," or attribute quotations to organizational members without their permission.

- *Paragraph four:* The boilerplate paragraph (see Chapter 2). A boilerplate paragraph is a stock paragraph or statement that rarely changes. Boilerplates are like mission statements. A boilerplate paragraph gives background or history about the organization itself (when it was founded, how many people it employs, where it operates, what it believes—mission/principles). Boilerplate paragraphs should be written so that they do not have to be constantly changed or checked. The organization employs "more than 300 employees" rather than "326 employees." Typically, a well-written boilerplate paragraph can be used in many places (on Web sites, in annual reports) and is not rewritten or revised for every news release or document.
- *Paragraph five* (or the *last paragraph,* if you write a longer news release): "For more information. …" A paragraph that includes information about who should be contacted with questions—include full name, title, telephone, fax, and e-mail. Do not try to be creative here. Write: "For more information about (whatever the news release was about), contact …" (and give a person's full name and title). Do not add anything extra. Not: "For more information about the new XZC Fingerprint Eraser, *or to find out about our exciting line of personal protection products. …*" Remember, the news release is not a free organizational advertisement or plug; you are reporting (or should be reporting) on a newsworthy event. If you are trying to use a news release as a free advertisement, you will have little success getting it published. Be sure to include complete information for the contact person. Do not make your reader go looking for the information. Do not write: "For more information, visit our Web site …" or "… join our Facebook page." Give your reader complete contact information (name, title, telephone, address, e-mail, fax, cell), and *then* the URL.
- For lengthier news releases that exceed the basic five paragraph release, simply add additional paragraphs two and three (background/quotes, background/quotes) as necessary to fit the news outlet and the event.

Take note, the "for more information" paragraph is not just a repeat of the contact information from the top of the first page of the news release. As a public relations representative for an organization or client, *your* name is very likely to be at the top of the news release as the contact person for a reporter or editor. Occasionally, you are *also* the contact person for the event or product announced in the news release. However, the "for more information" paragraph is intended for *the reader of the newspaper,* not the editor. Ideally, this paragraph will be published verbatim so that interested individuals can know whom to contact for more information. Thus, the contact information from the top of a news release is often not the same as the information in the last paragraph. See Figures 5.9–5.11.

News Release Formatting

Every organization has a slightly different way of formatting their news releases. Ultimately, house style dictates how your news release will look. However, many organizations do not realize that news releases should be formatted to meet the needs of journalists, and mistakenly use italics, bolding, or reduced spacing in order to make releases look more like final draft documents. Proper news releases are *intended* to be edited, so they are double-spaced, printed only in plain text (since there is no bolding or italics in news copy), and follow AP style. Here are the formatting basics:

- Use 8.5" × 11" white paper (unless in Europe, and then use A4).
- Identify yourself in the upper-left corner. Include the name and title of the contact person for the *reporter or editor* (not the readers), address, telephone and cellular phone numbers, fax numbers, e-mail address, URLs, etc. Additionally, be sure that your telephone

News Release Checklist

Name: ____________________ **Assignment:** ____________________ **Date:** __________

Overall Release Format

- ❑ 8.5" by 11" white paper.
- ❑ Wide margins—at least 1.5."
- ❑ Double-space the entire release except for the address information and header—double, double space between the release's paragraphs.
- ❑ Identify yourself in the upper left corner—include: contact person's name, title, company name, postal address, telephone, fax, e-mail.
- ❑ "For Immediate Release" line—or embargo date (only when absolutely necessary).
- ❑ Headline: **CENTERED, BOLD AND CAPITALIZED**. Neither write a catchy, newspaper-like headline nor a boring academic paragraph. Write an "informative" headline.
- ❑ Leave about two inches between the bottom of "for immediate release" and the top of the release's first paragraph for editing—center the headline in this area.
- ❑ Never break a paragraph across pages—start the paragraph on a new page if you have to.
- ❑ Include "More" at the bottom of all pages that continue to another page.
- ❑ Include a "slug" and page number, on all pages after the first (identifying info., top, right).
- ❑ Include a "boiler-plate" (informational) paragraph about the organization—2nd till last paragraph. The boiler-plate paragraph is about the organization sending the release not the Public relations firm writing it.
- ❑ Include a "for more information, contact..." paragraph—last paragraph.
- ❑ Place hash marks (###), centered, at the end of the document on a separate line.

Content

- ❑ Dateline (location and date, no year, in parentheses)—capitalize the city and state.
- ❑ Your news release has a news angle (state it briefly):____________________
- ❑ Compelling/interesting summary lead using some (not all) of the five W's and H.
- ❑ The introduction should get interest/attention, reveal the topic, establish the newsworthiness, and reinforce your organization's credibility, if necessary.
- ❑ Make the release concise—you are reporting a newsworthy event not writing an editorial.
- ❑ Use short, active, sentences. If you need a comma, then the sentence is probably too long.
- ❑ Include supporting quotes that add information to your news angle.
- ❑ Localize and tailor the release, quote well-known, credible, sources not the Pub. Rel. director
- ❑ Be sure the release is free of cliches, technojargon, and unfamiliar terminology.
- ❑ Check the Associated Press Stylebook for proper usage: numbers, times, abbreviations, etc.
- ❑ Be sure that every fact is checked—be sure names are correct, check grammar/spelling.
- ❑ Review your organizations policy on disclosure.
- ❑ Write according to the inverted pyramid.
- ❑ The topic in the news release is localized and tailored for this media outlet.
- ❑ Someone else has read the final release before you give it to the instructor or mail it off. Final drafts are expected to be ready to be put in the envelope and mailed to the media.

Miscellaneous

- ❑ Lead and following paragraphs are short and kept to three–five sentences.
- ❑ Each paragraph follows-up on the news angle mentioned in the headline and the lead.
- ❑ If you have quotes, then start the paragraphs with them, then provide attribution.
- ❑ Never use "which" (this is often a run-on).
- ❑ Avoid vague pronoun use: "he, she, it, they, their." Be specific. Always use proper names.
- ❑ Avoid starting sentences with a dependent clause. "Because of the number of people interested in the event, . . ." Instead: "The event is attracting a lot of attention. . . ."
- ❑ Periods, commas, etc. go inside of quotes—as illustrated throughout this handout.
- ❑ Avoid "ing" verbs like the plague. Not: "Big Widget Corp. is planning to..." Instead: "Big Widget Corp. will . . ."
- ❑ Watch slang—got to, would of, could of, should of, etc.
- ❑ Can you say this more concisely?

FIGURE 5.9 News release checklist.

News Release Evaluation Checklist

- ❑ **Did not meet the requirements** (on time, long enough, etc.) ________________

  ____

- ❑ Did not **use all plain/Roman (Rom) text** throughout.
- ❑ Did not **use a single font size/style throughout** the document (with the exception of logo, if applicable). Note: the font should also be a serif font.
- ❑ Did not **have a clear headline** or attempted to write an actual headline.
- ❑ Did not **double-space everything** (with the exception of logo, if applicable).
- ❑ Did not **have "wide" margins** (1.5" left and right, 1" top and bottom) for easy editing.
- ❑ Did not **keep paragraphs together,** i.e., broke paragraphs across pages.
- ❑ Did not have a **"For Immediate Release,"** "**More**," "**Slug**" "Hashmarks" **(###).**
- ❑ Did not **include complete contact information at the end of the release** that included an e-mail address, telephone, fax, cell, and URL (if applicable).
- ❑ Did not **include complete contact information at the beginning.**
- ❑ Did not **use proper names/referents.** Do not use "he," "she," "it," "they," "the event," "the organization," etc.
- ❑ Did not **spell check the release.** You would get fired if this were a real job.
- ❑ Did not **check spacing after periods,** period placement, comma, and quote mark placement, watch spacing between words and after periods, etc.
- ❑ Did not **proof read carefully.** Do not misspell names, the word "Web site," etc. Do not write "Phone" (use "Telephone"), use composition titles, etc.
- ❑ Did not **follow AP style** for dates, times, money, telephone numbers, proper names or composition titles, etc.

Note, a standard news release has a headline and five paragraphs:

1. A Lead paragraph that follows directly from the headline;
2. An elaboration paragraph that adds to paragraph 1;
3. A quote paragraph that is more than a sentence long (about 3–6 sen.) and is interesting.
4. A "boilerplate paragraph that provides information about the organization.
5. A "for more information" paragraph that includes complete contact information (sometimes repeated verbatim from page 1).

Additional follow up paragraph are also written (elaboration/quote, elaboration/quote, etc.)and placed in-between paragraph 3 (the quote paragraph) and the boilerplate.

FIGURE 5.10 News release evaluation sheet.

Office of Communications

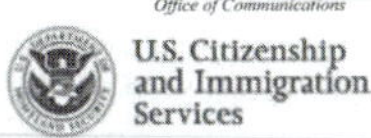

May 29, 2007
(Revised, May 30, 2007)

Press Release

USCIS Sets Final Fee Schedule to Build an Immigration Service for the 21st Century

Public comments prompt reduction in fees for some families applying for adjustment of status, expands fee waiver and exemption eligibility, permits one free extension of approved orphan petitions

WASHINGTON— Following a comprehensive review of more than 3,900 public comments, U.S. Citizenship and Immigration Services (USCIS) announced today a final fee structure that includes benefits for some families with children and also expands the availability of fee waivers and exemptions.

The rule, scheduled to be published in tomorrow's *Federal Register*, sets fees for the processing of immigration benefit applications and petitions and includes some substantive revisions from the proposal published in February of this year while providing necessary funding for the agency to continue strengthening the security and integrity of the immigration system, improving customer service, and modernizing business operations for the 21st century.

"We proposed our new fee structure with the expectation of ongoing discussions with the public on this important issue," said USCIS Director Emilio Gonzalez. "The volume and value of the comments we received has provided an opportunity to fine-tune our final fee structure that we believe is both fair to our customers and vital to our Nation as we continue to build a secure and efficient national immigration service."

Key revisions in the final rule include a 25 percent reduction to the proposed filing fee for Form I-485 (Adjustment of Status to Permanent Resident) for children younger than 14 years old, translating to a $360 decrease from what was proposed for a family of two adults and two children filing together. The rule will also allow a one-time free extension of approved orphan petitions for prospective adoptive parents, and expands the availability of fee waivers for some adjustment of status cases that arise from asylum or other humanitarian categories, and certain juvenile immigrants. USCIS will also exempt "Special Immigrant – Juveniles" from the $375 filing fee for Form I-360 (Petition for Amerasian, Widow(er), or Special Immigrant). Finally, USCIS will be able to waive the $80 biometric fee, in addition to the application/petition fee, on an individual basis.

The final rule retains the fee exemption for T visas (Victims of Human Trafficking) and self-petitioners seeking immigrant classification under the Violence Against Women Act (VAWA) for humanitarian reasons, as well as an exemption for all refugee and asylum applicants. The final rule also allows USCIS to waive the filing fee for U.S. citizens seeking immigrant status for their alien spouses (K-3 visas) and will continue to waive fees for members of the U.S. Armed Forces applying for naturalization.

USCIS expects that the revenue from the new fee structure will lead to a 20 percent reduction in average application processing times by the end of fiscal year 2009, and will cut processing times by the end of fiscal year 2008 for four key application types: the I-90 (Renew / Replace Permanent Resident Card), I-140 (Immigration Petition for Alien Worker), the I-485, and the N-400 (Naturalization). These four application types represent one-third of all applications filed.

The new fee structure is effective on July 30, 2007, and is posted at www.uscis.gov. Applications or petitions postmarked or otherwise filed on or after that date must include the new fee. More information on the final rule is available in the accompanying Questions and Answers document and a chart explaining the fee schedule for applications and petitions.

– USCIS –

BOSTON

AnnBeha Architects

Contacts:

FOR IMMEDIATE RELEASE

MUSEUM OF FINE ARTS, BOSTON, SELECTS ANN BEHA ARCHITECTS TO UNDERTAKE MASTER PROGRAM PLAN FOR THE MFA, PROMPTED BY RECENT ACQUISITION OF FORSYTH INSTITUTE BUILDING

The Forsyth Institute building at 140 The Fenway,
Photo Credit: Peter Vanderwarker

BOSTON, MA (November 13, 2008)—The Museum of Fine Arts, Boston (MFA), has commissioned Ann Beha Architects (ABA) of Boston to develop a Master Program Plan for its campus, including The Forsyth Institute property that the MFA purchased in September 2007. The Forsyth Institute's historic Beaux Arts building, located at 140 The Fenway adjacent to the MFA building's east side, extends the Museum's landmark campus along Boston's historic Fenway. ABA's Master Program Plan will examine the MFA's current and projected space needs and analyze how the Museum's facilities could accommodate them. The effort will include a comprehensive assessment of the Forsyth property, and will explore how to integrate it programmatically as well as physically into the MFA.

"The purchase of the Forsyth building provides an opportunity to reassess the MFA's entire campus and determine the best ways to use our real estate to achieve our strategic goals," said Malcolm Rogers, Ann and Graham Gund Director of the Museum of Fine Arts, Boston. "ABA's experience in adapting historic buildings, coupled with the firm's understanding of Boston and its communities, will serve the Museum well as we look toward successfully incorporating the Forsyth property into the MFA's environs."

—more—

MFA Boston, Ann Beha Architects, Press Release, p. 2

Completed in 1914, The Forsyth Institute comprises approximately 115,000 square feet on 1.6 acres of land bordering Forsyth Way and the Fenway. It overlooks the Back Bay Fens portion of Frederick Law Olmsted's Emerald Necklace, as do the Museum and the School of the Museum of Fine Arts. The newly expanded MFA campus represents the largest frontage along the Fens. ABA will address the relationship between the Fens and the Forsyth property, recognizing the importance of the landscape to the Fenway neighborhood. The Master Program Plan will incorporate information gathered from meetings with Museum staff, Trustees, and community leaders, and will include sustainable design principles. The MFA has also hired Smith + St. John Inc., a Boston-area development and project management services group, to serve as owner's representative in managing this effort.

"This project joins heritage with future vision. These significant buildings, with their extensive frontage on the historic Fens, reflect the Museum's identity and reach," said Ann Beha, Principal of ABA. "Our job is to find the most creative path for the Museum as it expands its remarkable campus."

Based in Boston, and practicing nationally and internationally, Ann Beha Architects (www.annbeha.com) was founded in 1980. The firm is engaged in both contemporary design and in the preservation and adaptive use of landmark buildings. Representative projects include Master Plans for the Huntington Library, Art Collections and Botanical Gardens in San Marino, CA; the Hillwood Museum and Gardens in Washington, DC; and Old North Church in Boston. Recent building projects include the New Britain Museum of American Art in Connecticut, the Mary Baker Eddy Library for the Betterment of Humanity in Boston, the Currier Museum of Art in New Hampshire, and the Portland Art Museum in Oregon, as well as projects at Boston's Symphony Hall and the Tanglewood Music Center. ABA also served as the Preservation Architect for adaptive re-use of the historic Charles Street Jail, which is now Boston's Liberty Hotel. ABA's projects have been honored by the American Institute of Architects, the Boston Society of Architects, the National Trust for Historic Preservation, the Boston Preservation Alliance, and the Victorian Society in America.

—more—

MFA Boston, Ann Beha Architects, Press Release, p. 3

The Museum of Fine Arts, Boston (www.mfa.org), is recognized for the quality and scope of its encyclopedic collection, which includes an estimated 450,000 objects. The MFA opened the doors of its red brick and terra-cotta building in Copley Square on July 4, 1876. Over time, the rapid growth of the collection made a new location necessary and the Museum hired architect Guy Lowell to develop a master plan for a grand, classical museum. In 1909, the MFA moved to its present Beaux-Arts-designed granite structure on Huntington Avenue. Throughout the century, the Museum continued to expand with major additions, such as its Evans Wing (designed by Lowell) in 1915, and its West Wing (designed by I.M. Pei) in 1981. In 1999, the MFA commissioned the architectural firm, Foster + Partners (London), to develop a Master Site Plan that would reflect the strong north/south axis of Lowell's original design while addressing the MFA's growing collection as well as the visitor experience. The Building Project features the construction of an American Wing and the glass-enclosed Ruth and Carl J. Shapiro Family Courtyard. Other highlights include the Linde Family Wing for contemporary art (previously named the West Wing), as well as additional galleries, educational spaces, conservation facilities, and enhanced visitor amenities. (The Building Project is expected to be completed in late 2010.)

For additional information or to request digital photography, please contact Kelly Gifford (MFA) at 617.369.3540 or kgifford@mfa.org; or Katelyn Cotter (ABA) at 617.226.1672 or kcotter@annbeha.com.

###

FIGURE 5.11 Sample news releases.

A. JAMES CLARK
SCHOOL OF ENGINEERING

News Release

FOR IMMEDIATE RELEASE
June 25, 2007

CONTACT: Melissa Corley
(301) 405-6501; mcorley@umd.edu
OR
Ted Knight
(301) 405-3596; teknight@umd.edu

New Era of "Desktop Supercomputing" Made Possible with Parallel Processing Power on a Single Chip
Public Asked to Help Name New Technology

COLLEGE PARK, Md.—A prototype of what may be the next generation of personal computers has been developed by researchers in the University of Maryland's A. James Clark School of Engineering. Capable of computing speeds 100 times faster than current desktops, the technology is based on parallel processing on a single chip.

Parallel processing is an approach that allows the computer to perform many different tasks simultaneously, a sharp contrast to the serial approach employed by conventional desktop computers. The prototype developed by Uzi Vishkin and his Clark School colleagues uses a circuit board about the size of a license plate on which they have mounted 64 parallel processors. To control those processors, they have developed the crucial parallel computer organization that allows the processors to work together and make programming practical and simple for software developers.

Parallel processing on a massive scale, based on interconnecting numerous chips, has been used for years to create supercomputers. However, its application to desktop systems has been a challenge because of severe programming complexities. The Clark School team found a way to use single chip parallel processing technology to change that.

Vishkin, a professor in the Clark School's electrical and computer engineering department and the university's Institute for Advanced Computer Studies, explained the advantage of parallel processing like this:

"Suppose you hire one person to clean your home, and it takes five hours, or 300 minutes, for the person to perform each task, one after the other," Vishkin said. "That's analogous to the current serial processing method. Now imagine that you have 100 cleaning people who can work on your home at the same time! That's the parallel processing method.

-more-

Supercomputer 2

"The 'software' challenge is: Can you manage all the different tasks and workers so that the job is completed in 3 minutes instead of 300?" Vishkin continued. "Our algorithms make that feasible for general-purpose computing tasks for the first time."

Vishkin and his team are now demonstrating their technology, which in future devices could include 1,000 processors on a chip the size of a finger nail, to government and industry groups. To show how easy it is to program, Vishkin is also providing access to the prototype to students at Montgomery Blair High School in Montgomery County, Md.

Desktop Supercomputing to Revitalize the Computer Industry

For years, the personal computer industry achieved advancements in computer clock speed, the fundamental rate at which a computer performs operations, thanks to innovations in chip fabrication technologies and miniaturization. Moore's Law—which dictates that the number of transistors on integrated circuits in computers will double every 18 to 24 months—was coupled with a corresponding improvement in clock speed.

But no advancements in clock speed have been achieved since 2004. From an early stage, Vishkin foresaw that Moore's Law would ultimately fail to help improve clock speed due to physical limitations. This has guided his perseverance over his professional career in seeking to improve computer productivity by distributing the load among multiple processors, accomplishing computer tasks in parallel.

In 1979, Vishkin, a pioneer in parallel computing, began his work on developing a theory of parallel algorithms that relied on a mathematical model of a parallel computer, since, at that time, no viable parallel prototype existed. By 1997, advances in technology enabled him to begin building a prototype desktop device to test his theory; he and his team completed the device in December 2006.

The prototype device's physical hardware attributes are strikingly ordinary—standard computer components executing at 75 MHz. It is the device's parallel architecture, ease of programming and processing performance relative to other computers with the same clock speed that get people's attention.

"Based on the very positive reactions of my graduate students this spring," Vishkin stated, "I knew that it was time to take the technology public."

Earlier this month, Vishkin and his Ph.D. student, Xingzhi Wen, published a paper about his newly-built parallel processing technology for the Association for Computing Machinery (ACM) Symposium on Parallelism in Algorithms and Architectures, and showcased it at a major computing conference, the ACM International Conference on Supercomputing (ICS) in Seattle.

At the ICS event, Vishkin allowed conference participants to connect to the device remotely and run programs on it in a full-day tutorial session he conducted, offering colleagues and student participants the opportunity to experience the prototype technology firsthand.

Supercomputer 3

"The single-chip supercomputer prototype built by Prof. Uzi Vishkin's group uses rich algorithmic theory to address the practical problem of building an easy-to-program multicore computer," said Charles E. Leiserson, professor of computer science and engineering at MIT. "Vishkin's chip unites the theory of yesterday with the reality of today."

Vishkin also participated in a panel discussion at a special invitation-only Microsoft Workshop on Many-Core Computing on June 20-21 in Seattle, Wash. In August, Vishkin will present a keynote address at the Workshop on Highly Parallel Processing on a Chip in Rennes, France, held in conjunction with the 13th Euro-Par, an international European conference on parallel and distributed computing.

"This system represents a significant improvement in generality and flexibility for parallel computer systems because of its unique abilities," said Burton Smith, technical fellow for advanced strategies and policy at Microsoft. "It will be able to exploit a wider spectrum of parallel algorithms than today's microprocessors can, and this in turn will help bring general purpose parallel computing closer to reality."

Vishkin has filed several patents on his parallel processing technology since 1997. Funded by the National Science Foundation and the Department of Defense, his research has also received significant interest from the computer industry, which he believes his technology will revitalize.

"The manufacturers have done an excellent job over the years of increasing a single processor's clock speed through clever miniaturization strategies and new materials," he noted. "But they have now reached the limits of this approach. It is time for a practical alternative that will allow a new wave of innovation and growth—and that's what we have created with our parallel computing technology."

In addition to Xingzhi Wen, Vishkin's research teams includes students Aydin Balkan, George Caragea, Mike Detwiler, Tom Dubois, Mike Horak, Fuat Keceli, Mary Kiemb and Alex Tzannes, as well as electrical and computer engineering professors Rajeev Barua and Gang Qu.

Naming Contest

To increase awareness of his new technology, Vishkin is inviting the public to propose names for it. The name should reflect the features and bold aspirations of the new machine and its parallel computing capabilities, Vishkin said.

The winner will receive a $500 cash prize and be credited with the naming of the innovative technology. Visitors can submit their ideas online at the Clark School of Engineering website, www.eng.umd.edu. The deadline for submissions is September 15, 2007.

Supercomputer 4

NOTE TO EDITORS:
High-res photos and a glossary of terms are available online:
http://www.eng.umd.edu/media/pressreleases/pr062607_supercomputer.html

Additional Information on Vishkin's Parallel Computing Research
For Prof. Vishkin's paper and presentation:
http://www.umiacs.umd.edu/users/vishkin/XMT/spaa07paper.pdf
http://www.umiacs.umd.edu/users/vishkin/XMT/spaa07talk.pdf

For more information on Prof. Vishkin's research, visit:
http://www.ece.umd.edu/research/spotlight/comp_eng/vishkin/
http://www.umiacs.umd.edu/~vishkin/TUTORIAL/tutorial6-07/

About the A. James Clark School of Engineering

The Clark School of Engineering, situated on the rolling, 1,500-acre University of Maryland campus in College Park, Md., is one of the premier engineering schools in the U.S.

Academically, the School offers 13 graduate programs and 12 undergraduate programs, including two degree programs tailored for working professionals and one certification program. The Clark School's graduate programs are collectively the fastest rising in the nation in *U.S. News & World Report's* annual rating of graduate programs.

The Clark School of Engineering is home to one of the most vibrant compilations of research activities in the country. With major emphasis in key areas such as communications and networking, systems engineering, rotorcraft technology, optoelectronics, transportation systems and space engineering, as well as electronic packaging and smart small systems and materials, the Clark School is leading the way toward the next generations of engineering technology.

Visit the Clark School homepage here: http://www.eng.umd.edu/

###

FIGURE 5.11 (Continued)

FOR IMMEDIATE RELEASE

CONTACT: Lisa MacDonald
Marketing Supervisor
949.855.8822 x.3345
949.855.3045 fax

DOGCHANNEL.COM ANNOUNCES ITS NEW VIRTUAL DOG SHOW

THE INTERNET'S HOTTEST WEBSITE FOR DOG LOVERS TO AWARD PRIZES TO WINNING DOGS ACROSS 12 EXCITING CATEGORIES

IRVINE, CA, April 5, 2007 – DogChannel.com, the premier doggie destination on the Internet, is announcing its first-ever "Virtual Dog Show," where visitors can enter their dogs to be judged online by the site's other users. Users can enter their dogs to compete in 12 exciting categories:

• Longest Tongue • Best Smile • Biggest Feet • Longest Hair • Biggest Ears
• Best Coat • Prettiest Hairless Dog • Most Colorful • Best Eyes
• Best "Feed Me" Look • Best Owner Look Alike • Most Stylish Dog

Entries will be accepted from April 1st through June 30th, 2007.

The first-place winner will receive a Vari Kennel Ultra portable kennel and sheepskin liner from Petmate. The second-place winner will receive a Nap of Luxury designer pet bed from Petmate. The third-place winner will win Petmate's new Stainless Style Fresh Flow purifying pet fountain.

To participate, simply log on to DogChannel.com and click on the "Virtual Dog Show" link.

Also appearing exclusively on DogChannel in April:

- New Living with Dogs Section – Includes tips on traveling with dogs to dog-friendly destinations, incorporating dogs into family activities, and maintaining dog-friendly homes and yards.
- New sections on grooming, flea & tick prevention, obesity, housetraining, and senior dog issues have been added. A new "Dog Style" section informs about the latest canine fashion trends.
- Updated Dog Activities Area – Features dog sports, the latest dog show news and great ideas for exercising with dogs. Upcoming canine competitions and local dog events are profiled.

About DogChannel.com
DogChannel.com is the Internet's premier website dedicated to all things dog. Everything related to the dog owning experience can be found here, from information on feeding and grooming to details on every breed of canine under the sun. In addition to quality editorial features written by dog experts, DogChannel features Club Dog, an interactive dog club and message board where users earn points for dog-related rewards. DogChannel also allows users to create Web pages for their dogs for other users to view. With thousands of page views daily, DogChannel is the hottest canine website on the Internet.

About BowTie, Inc.
BowTie, Inc., is the leader in special interest pet magazines, trade magazines, books and websites dedicated to pet-loving consumers, pet-supply retailers, veterinarians, breeders, and pet professionals worldwide. Divisions of BowTie, Inc., include BowTie Magazines, BowTie Press, BowTie News, Thoroughbred Times Company, Global Distribution Services and AnimalNetwork.com.

FIGURE 5.11 (Continued)

numbers are for human beings and not machines. The goal is to be reached by reporters and editors and not to avoid them.
- Near the top of the release, write "For Immediate Release" or "Embargo until …" a specified date. Only use "Embargo until …" when absolutely necessary. Only embargo recurring or banal news items; do not embargo genuinely newsworthy events that you do not want leaked. Embargoing has no legal status and will not prevent a news organization from using breaking or newsworthy public interest content.
- Leave ample space (about 1.5" inches) above the headline for editing.
- Use wide margins (1.5" left and right) and double-space all of the text except for your address and contact information at the top.
- Never break paragraphs from one page to the next: break the entire paragraph to the next page to keep the content together. If a paragraph is longer than one page, it is too long.
- Place an identifying "slug" (a running header) and page number on the top of each page after the first page and write "p. 2 of 3," "p. 3 of 3," etc., so that if pages get separated, the editor knows what is missing.

Delivery of News Releases

- A 2008 survey by Bulldog Reporter found that 75 percent of journalists preferred to receive news release through e-mail (www.bulldogreporter.com). Learn what each of your target media prefers and deliver the release that way. Do not assume that e-mail is okay; one in four still prefer other channels.
- If postal mail is preferred, send news releases by first-class mail in a 9" × 12" envelope to a specific individual, not to the "business editor." Again, consult a media directory for the correct name or consult your media list.
- Know the deadlines of all of the journalists you are trying to reach and submit news releases accordingly. Consult Bacon's (us.cision.com) or Burrelles*Luce* (www.burrellesluce.com) media

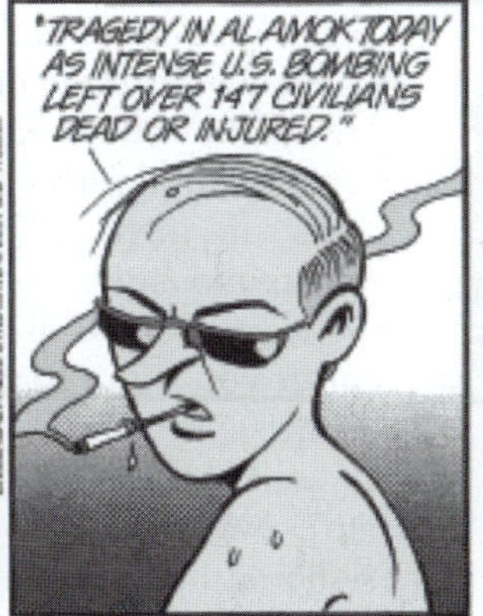

Source: Doonesbury Cartoon, News releases.

guides to determine deadlines or ask reporters/editors how much lead time they require for news releases. A news release should not be sent out at the same time to every source. If you send a news release too early to a source that requires a long lead time, your release will not be used. Similarly, if you send your release too late to a newspaper that requires a short lead time, then your release will be ignored.
- Only send a news release to a news sources that might have a clear interest in the news event. Do not use the shotgun approach and flood all media outlets with your releases. In the long term, such lazy public relations practices will sour sources to your organization and damage your professional reputation.
- Localize and tailor the release for every news outlet. Be sure the news angle is clear from your release's headline and is relevant for each outlet.

News Release Suggestions

- Effective leads (the first paragraph of a news release) use some but not all of the five W's and H.
- Be concise: Get your news angle across quickly.
- Avoid clichés, technojargon, and unfamiliar terminology.
- Check every fact twice (like Santa Claus). Make sure names are correct. Double check grammar/spelling.
- Shorter is better than longer. News outlets and editors can call for more information but may not be inclined to edit ten pages down to two.
- Know your organization's policy about disclosure before you send out a news release, and be sure to obtain approval before distributing a release.
- Check the AP Guide when in doubt about numbers, times, and abbreviations.
- Use short active sentences. If you need to use one or more commas, the sentence may be too long for news release writing.
- Think of the format of a news release as the beginning, middle, and end of a story. Each release tells only one particular story.
- Supporting quotes help humanize the news release. Make sure that the quote relates to the news angle.
- Have someone read the final release before you give it to your instructor or mail it to a journalist. Final drafts are those that are ready to be put in an envelope and mailed to the media. In other words, make your news releases "flawless."

News Release Writing Tips

- Keep your lead to two–three sentences.
- Keep paragraphs short, three or four sentences each.
- Start quotation paragraphs with the quote and attribute the source afterward: "Dogs are becoming a problem in Springfield ..." said Detective Mike Sobeski. ...
- Never use "which" (which is often a run-on and may result in overly long sentences). "Many of the stray dogs have been getting into dumpsters, which has been causing a problem for the kids in the neighborhood, who ..." Break long, multiclause sentences into two or more sentences. "Many of the stray dogs have been getting into dumpsters. Children in the neighborhood have had problems getting home after packs of dogs ..."
- Avoid he, she, it, they, their. Be specific. Not "She said," "They said," "It has been shown," but "Smith said," The government official said," etc.
- Use clear referents. Never start a sentence with "it." In fact, try to avoid the word "it" entirely. Instead of "It has been shown" or "It will be a difficult year for ...," say "The research indicates ..." and "The year ahead will be difficult for ..."
- Who/whom refers to people or animals with names; that/which refers to people and animals without names, and inanimate objects. Review the rules in your AP guide.
- Avoid starting sentences with a dependent clause. Not, "If it were not for the Republicans, we would not be in this mess." But, "Many have blamed the Republicans for the current economic situation."
- Periods go *inside* of quotations, as illustrated throughout this text.
- Avoid "ing" verbs. Not "Speaking on condition of anonymity. ..." Rather, "The source spoke anonymously."
- Always ask, "Can I say this more concisely?" after you think that you have already made it concise.
- Avoid slang: "got" (received), "got to" (have to), "would of" (would have), "should of" (should have), "could of" (could have), "disrespected" ("spoke discourteously," or "treated disrespectfully"), etc.

More Writing Tips

1. Avoid alliteration. A news release is not meant to be eloquent, just interesting relevant, and clear.
2. Keep your vocabulary simple. Avoid 25¢ words.
3. Never use five words to say what you can in three, or one. Not, "Indeed, it has been shown that …" but "Experience teaches …"
4. Avoid abbreviations except for the few authorized in the AP guide.
5. Do not use contractions or ampersands (&) except in proper names like J&J (Johnson & Johnson).
6. Parenthetical remarks (however relevant) are unnecessary. People do not speak in parentheses. When someone is being quoted, do not add (parenthetical) remarks. Instead, rewrite the quote to be clear without the parentheses.
7. Avoid split infinitives. Not "to boldly go" (to modifies go), but "to go boldly" ("to go" is the infinitive).
8. Never write in generalities and be as specific as possible. Not "people believe" but "Many members believe" (or "most"). Not "everyone knows" but "our clients know" or "a majority of Texans believe …"
9. Avoid hyperbole and puffery.
10. Work to eliminate passive voice. Use your grammar checker to flag the use of passive voice until you start getting more comfortable avoiding passive voice and learn to write more actively.
11. Never use profanity, technojargon, colloquialisms, clichés, or purple prose.
12. Do not write one-word sentences or one-sentence paragraphs.

HISTORIES

Another common internal and external writing activity are historical documents. Histories vary widely, from documents that are only a few paragraphs long and posted on an organization's home page or Web site, to actual books written by organizations for their members. Although there is some debate among historians about how historiography (the study of how to write history) should inform history, you do not have to concern yourself with theory. About the only two rules that you should adhere to are these: First, the story should be compelling. A good history has characters, structure, drama, and plot (good vs. evil, a protagonist/antagonist). You will find the most compelling models in biographies rather than textbooks. Read a half a dozen biographies and you should get a feel for the tone of history writing.

Second, be sure that you have had a conversation about the kind of history that you are writing with your supervisor and colleagues. Most organizations do not expect to read (nor want) a completely "objective" account of their organization and its leaders. Be sure that you understand the depth, candor, and intent of the historical narrative that you are writing before you put in a lot of time on interviews and research.

Finally, understand that histories are not easy to write. Indeed, writing a compelling historical document is no job for a novice. All historical documents, even very short ones, require archival research, interviews, research into the time period being described, and an understanding of how people thought of the world and the historical institutions and figures described. A good history is more than a propaganda document: histories are meant to enlighten and educate. Approach a history or biography with the respect that it deserves.

Historical Research

Basic historical writing, creating brief organizational histories for Web sites newsletters, etc., is very common. However, on occasion, organizations actually want to write historical books for internal audiences like shareholders, employees, and managers.

Writing an organizational history book or manual is not easy and not something that can be done well in one's spare time. Very often, professional writers are hired to write (or ghost write) organizational biographies. To write a reliable historical text requires that authors have access to accurate, copious, and candid information. Histories that are written while people are still alive call for in-depth personal interviews—indeed, a "biography" on an organizational founder will require hundreds of hours' worth of interviews: dozens with the individual him or herself, assuming that she or he is still alive, and access to the person's notes, diaries, or other personal and professionals documents.

Historical texts written about deceased founders or leaders require examination of family documents, interviews with living relatives, archival research to gather newspaper articles, obtain supporting references and economic and social information, and efforts to uncover relevant facts like the rate of organizational growth, shinning moments and tragic defeats, economic ups and downs, important products and discoveries, etc.

Anyone who attempts to write a historical text for the first time is advised to read several books on historiography (how to write history) first, as well as read a number of biographical, autobiographical, and historical texts. There are several approaches to writing histories in terms of the persona taken, the time period (or scope) to be examined, and the tone of the writing.

Answer these questions before you begin writing: Will passages of the text be autobiographical, drawing upon the actual words of the founder? Whose voice(s) will be privileged, the founders, the media, current and former employees, the CEO? Will we hear from the leader or founder's spouse and children, colleagues, rivals, mentors? Will the history be candid, including failures and mistakes, or is the text intended as a corporate myth that glosses over blemishes and errors? What will you do if you discover that something damaging or unlawful has taken place?

As with many of your other research activities, spend some time learning how to conduct historical research. You need to understand how to gather the archival information you will need as well as how to organize and interpret the voluminous data that you will gather. Writing a historical text can be a great challenge. Most professionals never have the chance to create such important documents. Additionally, a well-written history will be of interest to the general public, scholars, reporters, libraries, and other professionals in your field.

Q&AS (QUESTIONS AND ANSWERS) AND FAQS (FREQUENTLY ASKED QUESTIONS)

Question and answer (Q&A) and frequently asked questions (FAQs) documents have been around for some time. Originally (before the Internet), the Q&A format was used in informational documents (in media kits, brochures, fact sheets), and is still used from time to time. Q&As abound on the Internet and can be found on everything from small nonprofit organizations' Web sites to multinational corporations and governmental sites.

The essence of the Q&A is quite simple, and, as the name implies, FAQs are created to help individuals locate answers to common, technical, or organizational questions without having to ask an organizational representative.

Each of you has undoubtedly encountered this ubiquitous informational tool, so you are aware that some Q&As anticipate questions better than others. The best Q&As either anticipate likely questions (when created for the first time), or consist of answers to questions that are frequently asked. A good technique for creating Q&As is to save a list of questions and answers for a few weeks (or months, depending upon how often questions are asked/answered), and then use those as the basis for your Q&A document. For an online Q&A, if you have the expertise, or if a professional firm handles your Web site, consider using Web analytic software to track which questions are most frequently clicked on and moving these to the top of the list.

Q&As are prepared for an assortment of purposes: they can be about the organization itself, products or services, billing procedures, organizations' ethical activities. The list is endless. Basically, you should consider creating a Q&A anytime you have an issue or area that generates a lot of the same questions. For example, colleges and universities frequently have Q&As about "how to apply," "campus life," graduate school," "financial aid," or any other area of campus life about which students or potential students are likely to ask questions.

For an online Q&A, include a way for visitors to write with questions not on your list; in print, include an e-mail, telephone, URL, etc. Always remember that Q&As are a work in progress. For large organizations that receive a lot of the same questions, having Q&As is essential and can save a lot of person-hours answering the same questions.

FAQs About Q&As

Q. Are there any length restrictions when creating Q&As?

A. No, there are no length restrictions when you create online Q&As; however, when you are creating a brochure, for example, your Q&As need to be carefully edited to make the most of your space.

Q. How long should my answers be?

A. Your answer should be just long enough to answer the question. If, given the nature of your organization and corporate culture, giving "thorough" answers to questions is more common, just be sure that you structure answers with the most important information near the top so that people in a hurry can stop reading when they have found the answer to their question.

Q. What should the tone of a Q&A be?

A. The tone should be "helpful." You should never engage in sarcasm or suggest that the question asked is "silly," etc. You are here to help. For complicated topics, consider adding links for "more information." Be sure that links open in new windows or frames, so that visitors do not have trouble finding the way back to your site.

Q. What if there are so many "commonly asked questions" on our Web site and we end up with 300 of them?

A. There really is no limit to the number of Q&As that you might have. However, if your list is long, or very thorough, consider adding a search box to the top of the list, alphabetizing the list, or creating a table of contents to make it easier for visitors to locate answers to their individual questions. Also, consider listing only the *questions*, and placing the answers in separate files (or at the bottom) and allowing the visitor to click on the question for the answer.

MORE WEBBED PUBLIC RELATIONS

Whether to produce content for the World Wide Web has become a nonissue. You will. Virtually every for-profit organization has a Web site, as do millions of organizations globally. Nearly every nonprofit organization and religious group, and all educational institutions, hospitals, political parties and candidates, and regulatory organizations have Web sites.

As I alluded to earlier, the Web is a "pull" rather than a "push" medium. Push and pull are advertising terms. Traditional advertising "pushes" products and services to individuals and publics via advertisements, direct marketing, or telephone calls. "Pull" is when stakeholders come to an organization looking for information, products, or services themselves. When you call a carpet cleaner to inquire about its services, that is pull; when you see an advertisement for a carpet cleaner in the newspaper, the telephone book, or the back of a truck, that is push.

Except in very limited ways (popup advertisements, advertisements on search sites), most of the traffic on the Internet is pull. People go looking for products, services, information, rather than being enticed or driven there through advertisements (sponsored advertisements on Google and Yahoo are an exception). Thus, Web sites need to be designed to appeal to the needs of publics who come looking for information, products, and services, rather than having been pushed to visit through an advertisement.

Effective public relations writing includes a consideration of content, style, and audience adaptation. "Readability," the ability of a printed page to attract attention (White, 2002, p. 7), and "legibility" the adequacy of a message to be deciphered (p. 9), or read, go hand in hand. If a person thinks your home page is cluttered and hard to read, s/he will likely not invest as much time as s/he might if the page were easier to navigate. Consider Google's home page versus Yahoo's.

Additionally, when you work with content for a long time, noticing the details becomes more difficult. A cluttered and difficult-to-navigate Web page stops looking cluttered and hard to navigate the more time you spend on it. Always conduct readership studies on Web sites with disinterested parties, and nontechnological experts. Consider testing Web interfaces with older, less tech-savvy users (I call it the "Grandmother Test"). Additionally, be sure to monitor how organizational Web pages are navigated using Web analytics (see Chapter 8) and encourage visitors to your organization's Web site to provide suggestions for improving the site.

When writing for the Internet, keep in mind that visitors have many choices. Thus, a Web site needs to be easy to navigate, interesting, compelling, and provide substantive information. Your organizational Web site is unlikely to be the electronic equivalent of "the last service station for 150 miles." With the exception of internal stakeholders, or media representatives pursuing a story, Web visitors have many choices. You must design Web content accordingly.

Take an active role in shaping both the look of your organization's Web site and its content. Avoid what Flanders calls "mystery meat" navigation (www.WebSitesThatSuck.com). People do not like to waste time trying to figure out where to click to access your information or randomly rolling around the page looking for instructions to pop up.

Always go with a traditional navigation scheme with links at the left or top of the screen. Always include a search box on large, complicated Web sites. Include a link to a site map to make it easier for visitors to understand the layout of the site and find information. Counsel Web designers to avoid special effects. No one except for the designer appreciates them. Think about how irritating you find Web sites that are hard to navigate, require logins to see the content, force you to enter through a lengthy splash screen *every time you visit,* or require graphics or scripts to load before you can access any information.

Make sure menu labels and body text appear in legible font sizes on *every browser*, and that your site content actually works with *all* Web browsers. Do not allow Web sites to be created that work only with Microsoft's browser. Be sure your Web page is compatible with *all* of the mainstream Web browsers (especially FireFox, which is the number two browser in the world, and Safari, which is number three and used by most Macintosh users). Very few organizations have visitors who use *only* Microsoft's browser (cf., Flanders & Peters, 2002, pp. 68–70), and, in many industries/professions, the number of Macintosh users exceeds 25–50 percent. One-quarter to one-half of your potential visitors is too many people to ignore simply because it is "easier" for your Web designers to create a PC-only interface. If your Web master cannot design your Web content to work effectively on any platform, you need to hire a new Web firm.

WEB PAGE DESIGN PRINCIPLES

Web pages are horizontal spaces. Home pages are where organizational images and "brands" are first proffered. The home page sets the tone for many visitors to an organization's Web site. If the home page is difficult to navigate, the entire Web site is likely to be. Many Web sites are designed to make the Web master look cool, or to impress clients who often have limited training in communication, rather than with the end user in mind.[5]

The splash page of a Web site is essentially the same as a book or magazine cover. More often than not, people select books and magazines *because of* their covers. People *do* judge books by their cover just as people judge Web sites by their home page. Thus, presenting an interesting, compelling, and easy-to-navigate home page (and Web site) is an essential ethos or character-building tool. Similarly, Web sites that allow visitors to choose between "basic" (slower) sites and "supercharged" (fast) sites with more graphics and special effects, to select among different language choices, or to choose an RSS (text-based) feed rather than a graphic interface are giving Web site visitors what *they* want, rather than forcing them to adapt to the Web designer who already "knows where everything is."

Part of creating a compelling Web site, many argue, is to cut down on the amount of clicking visitors have to do to find what they want. Research suggests people do not mind scrolling, but most information on Web sites should be accessible within three clicks.

As the elaboration likelihood theory suggests (Chapter 6), individuals and publics can be described by their level of knowledge about something or level of interest. In light of this, Web content should be dynamic and appeal to people at all stages of the information and interest hierarchy. Creating dynamic Internet content is easy. Graphics, hyperlinks, color, and textual special effects require no more effort to create online than they do in InDesign or QuarkXPress. The principles of effective design are the same online and in print. Headlines, graphics, pull quotes, bulleted or numbered lists, and hyperlinks can be easily incorporated into page content, making messages more compelling and easier to read.

In terms of an actual writing style, think "public speaking" or broadcast writing more than print or newspaper content. Visitors to Web sites are often in a hurry and want to find their information quickly. Detailed content can be placed behind links, just as video and audio content can be added to make the experience of interacting with your site more dynamic and compelling.

As mentioned already, site speed is always an issue. Even when users have very fast connections, no one wants to watch your splash screen with its "please wait" message, followed by a slide show and scrolling text or a flash video and monotonous soundtrack (cf., www.stuhrling.com/splash.cfm). Put yourself in the shoes of the visitors to your site.

The last issue in creating effective Web content is to remember that the Internet allows you to offer everything: speeches, movies, graphics/illustrations, and print content. Do not let your experience with the many "bad" Web sites out there cloud your judgment when it comes to creating an excellent site. Interactivity and dialogue are one of the hallmarks of compelling Web content. Indeed, every generation of the Internet just brings us closer to the ideal communication state: face-to-face. Fifty years ago, green letters on a black background was all that existed in terms of electronic communication, and few people had access to e-mail outside of their own organization (e.g., BITNET). Today, organizations are using avatars (videogame or cartoon-like characters) to help answer customer questions, video interfaces that allow visitors and organizational members to communicate in "face-to-face" settings, as well as including video and audio components to their Web sites with speeches, short films, 365° virtual tours, etc.

The important message in this chapter is that the best means of communicating with your stakeholders is to use what *they prefer* in terms of print/broadcast messages. Your ultimate goal in creating message content is to effectively communicate with stakeholders and stakeseekers. Not every person wants to use the Internet to communicate with organizational members—many prefer just to pick up the telephone and make a call. Indeed, as you will discover when you take your first professional job, much more, and in a shorter period, can often be accomplished by picking up the telephone or walking down the hall than by sending out e-mail messages.

E-mail is a good way to *avoid* talking to someone (just like you might screen out an unwanted caller on your cellular telephone), but hardly the most efficient or compelling means of communicating with others when you have something important or relevant to say (cf., Daft & Lengel, 1986; Daft, Lengel, & Trevino, 1987). Current research suggests e-mail actually reduces efficiency (www.csmonitor.com/2007/1017/p16s01-stct.html). Some organizational efficiency consultants have begun pushing for "no e-mail Fridays" and reduced reliance on new technologies like PDAs and Blackberries (ibid).

Given the many advances in electronic communication, as professional communicators in the 21st century, your task will be to sort out what is easy and what works best. Just because a technology is new does not mean it is better. A great example is digital radio and television broadcasts. With a digital receiver, you either get the signal or you do not—digital signals do not come in well when there is interference. With an analog tuner, small adjustments to the "dial" will often yield a suitable signal (albeit with some static), but the broadcast can still be received. In a storm, digital broadcasts (via dish and antenna) are often useless, while analog signals still come in. Not every technology works with every public in the same way. As communication professionals, understanding how print, broadcast, electronic, and interpersonal communication works will allow you to create more compelling and effective messages.

CONCLUSION

As this chapter explains, the type of written messages you create will depend upon whether you are trying to reach internal or external audiences, how much time you have to prepare responses, and the intended goal of your message. Reaching internal public is easier than reaching external publics, but when messages for external publics or the media need to be distributed, you cannot send an e-mail to everyone or expect them to find the information in your Facebook page. More importantly, to create successful messages, you must understand the differences between the print and broadcast media, as well as how to best reach potential stakeholders and publics.

Much of this chapter has been pragmatic descriptions of the media and an assortment of written tactics. Never forget your rhetorical skills. As organizational spokespeople, your messages still should draw upon rhetorical theories and principles and take into account the specific features of your target audiences and the narrative and situational demands of messages. Over time, you will come to understand the local and national media, develop relationships with professionals in the media and other organizations, and be able to better reach your target publics.

ACTIVITIES

1. Write a realistic entry for a departmental "knowledge network." Describe a solution to a problem that you believe many students confront and talk about how to deal with the problem. This should be a substantive issue related broadly to your department and not "If you get a parking ticket here is what you do" or "If you have to take a class with professor X. ..." Write at least one page, double-spaced, and include half-a-dozen key words useful for indexing your entry.
2. Write a 200-word feature story about your public relations writing class that is suitable for publication in a departmental newsletter. Submit a double-spaced "manuscript" rather than an actual newsletter layout.
3. Create a five-question Q&A or FAQ related specifically to your department. Pick the big five. Try to anticipate what your fellow students need to know and write accordingly.
4. Using students as a potential internal public, identify, and rank order (1 is most important, 10 is least important), 10 possible ways of reaching students with relevant internal messages (about your department, college, or university). Be able to explain the strength of

each message outlet, which are likely to be the fastest, which are likely to be the most influential at getting your fellow student to take some action, and how much each venue is likely to cost if used.

5. Find an article about an organizational scandal or crisis in a national newspaper. Based on the facts presented in the article, write a one-minute opening statement and one-minute closing statement for a news conference. Also, write a dozen possible questions that the media might ask you (put yourself in their shoes and try to anticipate what you need to be prepared for). List the questions from most to least likely.
6. Create a one-page, 150-word backgrounder about yourself that includes a headshot (a photograph) of *you* only (not a crowd, action, or group photo). Scale/crop the photograph to take up no more than about 3" × 3" and write the text to focus on your professional career (your major, minor, internships, etc.) rather than personal information. Be sure to include *complete* contact information (name, title, telephone, e-mail, cell phone number). Design your backgrounder to resemble one of the samples from the text.
7. Based on the following scenarios: (1), your organization begins to offer domestic partner benefits, or (2), your organization had a 7 percent increase in profits over last year), write three different news release headlines and three accompanying leads for each scenario. Each headline/lead should take a different angle on the story (three angles per scenario). Remember, do not write a sensational, "newspaper" headline (review the news release rules), and be sure that your lead follows exactly from the headline and is interesting and compelling.
8. Download a news release from PRNewswire or directly from an organizational Web site. Based on the content from the news release, (1) write a broadcast version of the story suitable for discussing on a radio talk show like *Talk of the Nation* or *Science Friday*, or a local talk show. Create a brief script with talking points highlighting key issues. Then (2), write a one paragraph version of the news release for use on an organizational home page under "Company News: ..." or "For the Media ..." In each message, your goal is to capture the tone of the media you are writing for. For radio, be conversational, tell the "story," use some repetition. For the Web, make the story interesting but brief. Summarize everything in a few hundred words. Be conversational. Include a headline and sub headline, etc.
9. Spend a few hours listening to the local radio stations in your community. Identify all of them by call letters and locations on the dial (i.e., 103.9 KUAC FM) and answer the following questions: What is the station format? Based on the types of advertisements, music, stories, and news, identify the target audiences. Does the station have an ideological bias (Republican vs. Democrat, religious, apolitical)? What kind of music or entertainment does the station offer? What are the advertisements like (shouting, intimate conversation, professional tone)?
10. Visit the Web sites of your local radio stations. What services do they provide? Are there streaming audio links or content? Is the network schedule or calendar available on the site? What advertising information is available? Are there talk show venues that a local person might be able to visit or secure an invitation to? Based on the information provided, what are the stations' demographic profiles?

NOTES

1. In one campaign in the mid-90s, Meijer gave customers $10 off of their first purchase if they returned the videos (then on VHS tapes), enabling Meijer to reuse the videos for future openings and also to track customers.
2. Since the McLibel case was a libel suit, the court did not actually find McDonald's had been defamed, only that the two unemployed activists whom McDonald's sued could not prove *their* claims were true. Under English Common Law, the person being accused of defamation must prove their claims are true. The activist were able to prove a few of their claims—but they had to defend themselves against a team of corporate lawyers. The activists were fined £60,000, which was later reduced to £20,000. The case is still pending an appeal, although experts agree that the activists' claims were true.
3. McDonald's decision to sue in the McLibel case—which cost them more in terms of real dollars in lost sales and legal fees spent defending themselves, as well as a loss to its reputation—was a mistake. Your job as public relations professionals is to encourage organizations to come clean and not be deceptive and exploitative. When the real costs in reputation, sales, legal fees, and regulatory fees are added up, the idea of corporations ignoring their critics or abusing activists with lawsuits *because they can* should be seen as a price not worth paying.

   Your job is to advocate for all publics that the organization serves and not just the ones with the deepest pockets (i.e., the shareholders). Just because shareholders cannot *today* see the impact an organization might have on their own grandchildren in 20 years, does not mean public relations professionals should abdicate their responsibility to all organizational publics.

4. PRNewswire has decided not to publish its rates anymore so costs may vary.
5. Nearly 20 years ago I ran a computer lab—I had lobbied to take it over after I grew frustrated with how the server was organized. The lab manager at the time buried programs inside vaguely named folders; only a few people (including the lab manager and me) who had looked through *every* folder knew where all of the software applications were located. One day, in frustration, after explaining to the hundredth person where the word processing program was located, I confronted the lab manager and suggested he place all of the programs together in a folder called "applications" or "programs," and he replied, with great sincerity and naiveté, "But I know where everything is."

    The notion that "this looks good to me," or "I know where everything is," misses the point. People do not all see the world in the same way. Vision is one excellent example. Currently, using small san serif type is quite popular among Web designers. Unfortunately, those of us who do not see well find such trendy Web sites "frustrating" rather than "cool."

Chapter 6

Creating Persuasive Messages

Effective persuasion is central to public relations. Indeed, persuasion is a feature of most "informational" communication and organization–public messages. According to Bryant (1953), persuasion is "the process of adjusting ideas to people and people to ideas" (p. 407). Persuasion includes efforts to sell products and services, efforts to convince stakeholders to trust and support organizational initiatives, efforts to convince legislators to pass favorable regulations, and efforts to exert interpersonal and group influence in order to achieve one's goals. As professional communicators, public relations professionals participate in campaign planning and strategic decision making and must be able to craft compelling and effective messages. As organizational counselors, public relations professionals also must advise supervisors and clients to take a course of action that they might not want to take. Thus, public relations professionals need to understand public, group, and interpersonal persuasion.

Systematic efforts to persuade individuals and groups go back at least 2,500 years. Although we can be sure that people used persuasion before that, the earliest writing on the subject date back to philosophers like Isocrates, Socrates, Plato, and Aristotle.

Religious groups like the early Catholic Church in the first century CE used persuasive tactics to secure new converts (Pagels, 1988, 1989, 1995). Legislators in Roman politics saw persuasion as integral to good government and to secure support for policies. And modern leaders have used persuasion to inflame citizens and incite nationalist tendencies (Taylor & Kent, 2000).

Individuals, groups, and organizations from all walks of life have studied persuasion. Persuasion is regularly used by politicians, lawmakers, the U.S. military, philosophers, psychologists, rhetoricians, religious groups, collection agencies, university administrators looking to control students, university health departments seeking to discourage drinking on campus, and grade school teachers interested in more orderly classrooms (cf., Aristotle, 1991; Kotler & Zaltman, 1971; Multhauf, Willower, & Licata, 1978; Perelman & Olbrechts-Tyteca, 1968; Wittig, 1976).

The ability to shape or control the actions of others is an incredible skill. Some scholars have placed persuasion along a continuum from mere agreement to radical self-persuasion (Black, 1978, pp. 133 ff). On the one hand, getting someone to simply acknowledge a point and nod his/her head in agreement is relatively easy. Little risk is involved in mere agreement. However, actually moving people to take action takes a lot more work, more sophisticated arguments, and more time.

Persuasion is also an integral part of all marketing and advertising. The average American watches more than four hours of television per day (www.tvturnoff.org/images/facts&figs/factsheets/FactsFigs.pdf) and sees more than 50,000 television commercials per year (Postman, 1984). By the time the average American teenager enters college, s/he has seen more than a million television commercials! Given that a single 30-second beer advertisement can cost more than $500,000 to produce (www.aap.org/advocacy/hobbs398.htm), advertisers would not spend that kind of money if persuasion did not work. Fifty years of research into media effects has shown conclusively that television is a powerful motivator and persuasion *does* work (cf., Entman, 1989; Iyengar & Kinder, 1987; Kellner, 1990; Wartella, 1984) .

In order to help you understand how rhetorical theory and communication theory inform public relations and the construction of persuasive messages, this chapter will cover many of the basic persuasive concepts, like ethos, pathos, logos, syllogisms and enthymemes, and cover more sophisticated persuasive concepts, like identification, symbolism, and ideology.

This chapter begins with a discussion of the theory of reasoned action to help illustrate how much of people's decision-making processes take place outside of the rational world of logic and reason. The theory of reasoned action tells us that people often take actions because of how they may look in others' eyes. Knowing that actions are often not "reasoned" should help you appreciate how the many classic and contemporary rhetorical concepts work to achieve success.

THEORY OF REASONED ACTION (TRA)

Fishbein and Azjen (Azjen & Fishbein, 1980; Fishbein & Azjen, 1975) explain that behavior is not predicted by beliefs, as many people think. People who profess the same beliefs often do not act in the same way. For example, a majority of Americans profess religious faith, a central tenant of virtually every faith being not to kill, and yet, millions of Americans support the death penalty and war, and more than 17,000 people are murdered every year in the United States. Examples of people not consistently acting on their beliefs or doing what they say others should do are easy to find. Plagiarism is an example close to home for most students. Virtually everyone agrees that cheating is bad, and yet more than half of all students occasionally plagiarize work from the Internet.

The **theory of reasoned action** tells us that individual behavior is better predicted by the *ability* to behave, but only when the behavior is under a person's control and perceived to be socially desirable. Behaviors are most predictable when people have a positive opinion of a behavior ("It's cool," "The chicks will dig this," "If I get straight As I'll get into Harvard") and believe that other people, whose opinions are important (peers, friends, role models, parents), also have positive opinions of the behavior. In other words, behavior is largely the result of conforming to perceived social norms rather than acting on moral and ethical beliefs. The desire to conform comes from our positive view of behaviors ("people will think that I'm nice") and by other people's attitudes toward the behavior.

From a public relations standpoint, you need to understand two things: *First,* peer pressure exerts tremendous power over individuals (especially the young) to conform. Take the now infamous Nancy Reagan "Just say no" antidrug campaign from the 80s. Here we have a classic communication paradox in action (cf., Watzlawick, Beavin, & Jackson, 1967). What do teenagers do when someone they like, respect, or want to build a relationship with asks them to "get high?" If they say no, as Reagan advocated, they run the risk of damaging a current or potential relationship; if they say "yes". ... Let's just say that the campaign did not encourage a lot of teens to say "no."

The campaign failed because the premise of the campaign was based on a stereotypical (Hollywood) model of drug "pushers," rather than a more realistic portrayal of friends and peers making the offer. Saying "yes" worked to build interpersonal relationships and trust, saying "no" meant you were not "cool," could not be "trusted," and did not to get hang out with people you liked or wanted to know better. In other words, saying "yes" (the "bad" choice) offered only positive results, while saying "no" (the "good" choice), resulted in negative consequences. Although there *are* drug pushers, they are not the people whom the suburban high school students Nancy Reagan was targeting needed protection from.

The second issue to understand is that in many cases, rules/laws are necessary to enforce certain types of behavior. Student loans are one of the best examples of the TRA in action. Everyone agrees that people should pay back money that they borrow, and many people argue that if it were not for financial aid (student loans) many students would never be able to go to school. But the U.S. government wisely excluded student loan debt from bankruptcy laws, understanding the TRA and the fact that the first thing that most college graduates would do when they graduated from college with \$50,000–\$100,000 in student loan debt would be to file bankruptcy—a socially acceptable means of dealing with out-of-control financial burdens. The urge to "do what is right" (beliefs and values) is easily trumped by the recognition that a potentially more appealing social commodity—money—could be retained.

A third and final issue to understand is that people often make decisions based on the consequences of their actions and the perceptions of others rather than on their own beliefs. "If I lost 20 pounds I would be more attractive" is more likely to go through a young person's head than "If I lost 20 pounds I might live five years longer," which is really a better reason in the long run, but not as likely to move a young person to action.

Many messages that public relations professionals craft are intended to get people to take specific actions (organ donation, breast and prostate screenings, volunteering, donating money). By understanding the TRA and how/why people take actions, your chances of successfully influencing a target public are increased.

UNDERSTANDING THE CLASSIC RHETORICAL CONCEPTS

As suggested in earlier chapters, the study of rhetoric as a tool for effective public communication is quite ancient. The Greeks and Romans understood rhetoric going back to the fifth century BCE, as did the authors of the books of the Bible in the first century CE. Throughout the past two millennium, many philosophers, historians, and scholars studied rhetorical concepts; the list of influential figures is long. However, for a number of reasons, notably wars and the crusades, many of the ancient rhetorical texts were destroyed and rhetoric nearly disappeared. Had the Turks not preserved many of the ancient rhetorical texts, like Aristotle's *Rhetoric*, the texts would have perished.

Beginning in the early part of the 20th century, U.S. scholars in departments of English, Linguistics, and Communication began to translate and study the ancient rhetorical texts and departments of Communication and Rhetoric were eventually established in all major U.S. colleges and universities. The study of rhetoric (from a communication angle) flourished in state universities across the nation but never took hold in elite private schools like Harvard, Princeton, or Yale. Thus, the best departments of rhetoric historically have been in large midwestern universities.

The study of communication and rhetoric has also been relatively uncommon throughout Europe. In the 1960s, two European legal scholars, Chaim Perelman and Lucy Olbrechts-Tyteca, published an influential text called *The New Rhetoric: A Treatise on Argumentation*, where they described a model of rhetoric suited to courts of law. Since then, rhetoric has come to be understood to have value in an assortment of academic and professional settings.

For more than 30 years, scholars have been looking at public relations activities from a rhetorical standpoint. A number of excellent books and articles have been written summarizing the influence of rhetoric on public relations (cf., Heath 1990, 1992), and now there are very few public relations professors or professionals who would not acknowledge the importance of rhetorical concepts and activities, such as apologia, crisis, issues management, dialogue, and other areas. In particular, the study of new technology in public relations has been heavily influenced by rhetorical concepts and many professionals in advertising and marketing are also beginning to see the merit of key rhetorical concepts like "relationship building" and "identification."

The remainder of this chapter will cover basic and advanced rhetorical strategies as they relate to persuasion, as well as relevant communication theories. Persuasion is a fundamental skill for public relations professionals given that so much of our time is spent communicating with various stakeholders and key publics. Knowing how to shape people's beliefs and influence their values and attitudes is a powerful skill.

Ethos, Pathos, and Logos

Ethos, *pathos*, and *logos* are rhetorical concepts that go back to ancient Greece and Rome. ***Ethos***, or credibility, refers to "competence, integrity, and good will." Essentially, when a person is trustworthy and seems (or has proven to be) honest, they have *ethos*. Most professionals and leaders are assumed to be competent and trustworthy until they have acted otherwise. Thus, not surprisingly, honest organizations and professionals who behave professionally have more ethos than organizations or individuals known for deception. For example, consumers trust Johnson & Johnson because of its ethical handling of the Tylenol tampering incident in the '80s, while Big Tobacco is usually viewed less favorably because of its continued insistence that cigarettes are not addictive (cf., LeBow, July 30, 1997, *Talk of the Nation*, 26:50, www.npr.org/templates/story/story.php?storyId=1010758).

Pathos refers to the use of emotion in messages. Pathos includes both speakers who appear emotional (choking back tears at a funeral) as well as using emotional appeals in one's message: "Fifty years ago, three brave pioneers. ..." Mario Cuomo's 1984 democratic national convention keynote address is an excellent example of the use of *pathos*. For example, when Cuomo describes how:

> The Republicans believe that the wagon train will not make it to the frontier unless some of the old, some of the young, some of the weak are left behind by the side of the trail. ... We Democrats believe in something else. We Democrats believe that we can make it all the way with the whole family intact (www.americanrhetoric.com/top100speechesall.html).

Cuomo draws upon the emotional premises of family, faith, and perseverance to construct a very moving message.

Logos is generally understood to mean "logical argument," or use of logic and reason in persuasive messages. Appeals to facts, figures, "experts," the use of **inductive** reasoning (reasoning from specific instances to a general conclusion) and **deductive** reasoning (reasoning from a general rule to specific instances), and the use of syllogisms and enthymemes (discussed below) are examples of logos.

Aristotle argued that when you are trying to persuade someone, you should use "all of the available means of persuasion in a given instance" (1991, 1355b, 25). For Aristotle, all of the available means of persuasion were *ethos, pathos,* and *logos*. As a general rule, Aristotle's claim is sound; however, Burke provides a more apt description when he explains that persuaders should use "all that is there to use" (1973a, pp. 263–275). Not every individual or organization has a strong reputation. Not every persuader is skilled with emotional appeals. Nevertheless, as rhetoricians, you must learn to use "all that is there." Additionally, as you learned about rhetorical situations in Chapter 1, all situations and types of writing have constraints. In news releases, the writing is supposed to sound like "hard news"; however, news release quotes often invoke emotion and use hyperbole, making the most of the opportunity to say what cannot be said in the other parts of the news release.

On the most basic level, communicators should dress appropriately in each situation, create written documents that conform to expected standards and *look* professional, and demonstrate through their arguments that they have "done their homework" and are well informed on issues. Additionally, the best persuaders use *facts* rather than propagandistic strategies like name-calling, glittering generalities, or hyperbole, and explain to listeners or readers how they will be affected by organizational goals and actions.[1]

To lose *ethos,* all that a communicator has to do is appear unprepared, ill informed, uncaring, unsympathetic, or neglect to structure one's arguments compellingly for the *audience*. Thus, proper audience analysis and research are the first steps to effective persuasion.

Although many of the great persuasive examples are of speeches (where the ancient Greeks originally envisioned rhetoric being used), ethos, pathos, and logos apply equally to all types of written documents. Indeed, Web sites are an excellent example. Web sites that appear amateurish (ethos) will reflect negatively on the organization, no matter how qualified the organization and its members might be. Similarly, virtually every print or electronic document (from brochures and annual reports to Web pages and electronic media kits) produced by organizations will use emotional images (pathos) as a means of increasing readership and demonstrating sincerity (ethos). Finally, the enthymematic logic of the image, discussed below, allows images to be used to make powerful arguments (logos) without the aid of actual verbal or textual arguments.

The Syllogism and the Enthymeme

The syllogism and the enthymeme are fundamental types of logical arguments that are used in writing and speaking, and symbolically. A **syllogism** has three parts: a major premise that must be all encompassing, a minor premise that must follow from the major premise, and a conclusion that usually takes the form of "therefore ..." and follows logically from the major and minor premise. One well-known syllogism, stated two different ways, is:

Major Premise: All men are mortal.

Minor Premise: Socrates was a man.

Conclusion: Therefore, Socrates was mortal.

Or

Major Premise: All men are mortal.

Minor Premise: Socrates is dead.

Conclusion: Therefore, Socrates was a man.

The strength of the syllogism is that when constructed properly, syllogisms necessarily lead the audience to the conclusion that you want the audience to reach. The problem with the syllogism, however, is that in most situations outside of a philosophy or debate class, persuaders rarely say: "My major premise is … ." Instead, a persuader might make an argument like: "Every major airline has had accidents … we haven't had one … we can be trusted." When properly constructed, the syllogism creates a nearly airtight argument that can only be overcome by either proving that one of the premises is flawed, that a different conclusion should follow, or that one of the premises should be rejected.

One of the ways that we get around the possibility of someone attacking our arguments is with the **enthymeme.** The enthymeme is a form of syllogism that involves leaving out the major premise, the minor premise, or the conclusion, and constructing your argument in such a way that the audience mentally fills in the missing premise or conclusion. For example, consider the "All men are mortal" syllogism. With an enthymeme, a speaker can dramatically declare: "Socrates is dead!" and the audience, assuming that they know something about Socrates, will mentally fill in the missing premises themselves.

Another strength of the enthymeme is how it can be combined with images in newsletters, brochures, print advertisements, and television commercials, creating "arguments" that are both obvious and difficult to argue with or refute. Consider the advertisement from the Australian Red Cross in Figure 6.1.

Three words in the headline say it all. And yet, if I asked you what the advertisement means, the premise of the argument, I am sure that every one of you could construct a syllogism to explain it.

> *Major Premise:* Donating money is important but it's not blood.
>
> *Minor Premise:* Without blood, injured people die.
>
> *Conclusion:* Therefore, money can't replace blood.

Or, more to the point:

> *Major Premise:* People need blood to live.
>
> *Minor Premise:* The Red Cross gives blood.
>
> *Conclusion:* Therefore, giving blood saves lives (or, "The Red Cross saves lives").

The strength of enthymematic advertisements is that there is no single correct interpretation. Everyone fills in the missing information in his or her own way. All interpretations are equally valid and all interpretations are personal. When enthymemes are constructed properly, everyone arrives at the same conclusion, but the individual mental paths used to reach the conclusion are as different as each person who sees or hears the message. The strength of the enthymeme is

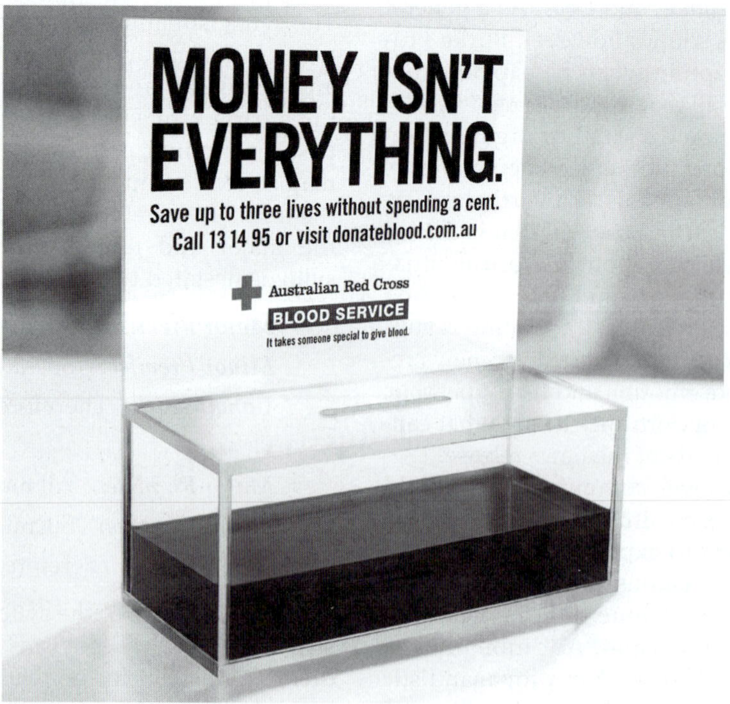

FIGURE 6.1 Australian Red Cross.

self-persuasion. The audience of an enthymeme is not told *what* to think, as they are with a syllogism, but almost everyone arrives at the same conclusion without an overt argument ever being advanced. Of course, enthymemes do not *require* images to work. Aristotle had no database of stock photography. Enthymemes can be used in annual reports, feature stories, memos, speeches, anywhere that the audience has the knowledge needed to complete a message. Since enthymemes are not based on fully formed logical arguments, constructing counter arguments is more difficult.

The only weakness with the enthymeme is that it only works when the audience knows something about the subject matter. For example, if you were to construct an enthymeme intended for an audience of retirees or business executives using an example from *Family Guy* or *The Vampire Diaries,* programs with younger demographics, your audience may not understand your point since they do not share the same cultural knowledge.

Another main feature of persuasion is that persuasion is a long-term process that involves exposure to multiple messages. Almost no one is convinced to become a vegetarian after hearing a five-minute speech on the subject in his or her public speaking class. No one goes out and buys a pizza after watching one Papa John's commercial. But 100 pizza commercials viewed over several weeks, or dozens of messages about the ethics of eating meat delivered by a roommate over an entire semester, can have a profound impact. The long-term process of persuasion and the impact that people's beliefs and attitudes have is reflected in the elaboration likelihood model.

ELABORATION-LIKELIHOOD MODEL (ELM)

The research on the **elaboration likelihood model** is extensive and has been primarily carried out by two researchers: Petty and Cacioppo (1981, 1984, 1986a, 1986b; cf., also, Stephenson, Benoit, & Tschida, 2001). Basically, what the elaboration likelihood model tells professionals is that audiences do not process messages equally. People with high involvement in an issue pay more attention than people with low involvement.

In other words, although source credibility is important, when a person has high involvement or interest in an issue (a person who is thinking of buying a new computer sees a computer advertisement, a person who has cancer sees a report about a new cancer study), the issue itself and the quality of the information and arguments are more important factors in determining attitude change and persuasion than the source or spokesperson of the message (Tan, 1985, pp. 141–143). People with high involvement want *more* information while people with low involvement in the issue will pay more attention to a funny message (a talking dog or gerbil) or an appealing spokesperson than to the information itself.

Since persuasion and long-term attitude change occur more often when people both focus on messages and elaborate on messages while thinking about them (the enthymeme), the individuals who are more likely to engage in message elaboration are those who already know something about an issue. Knowledgeable individuals want *more details*. People who are not familiar with products, services, arguments, or ideas are more attracted to cosmetic issues. In other words, we talk ourselves into "needing" or wanting many things (a new car, a cellular telephone, a cashmere sweater, a software upgrade) once we start to imagine what it would be like to have them.

Publics can be described or targeted by the degree to which they are likely to elaborate on the messages they receive. For example, placing a detailed advertisement for a new cordless drill in a home and garden magazine (a magazine read by a variety of individuals in terms of age, sex, profession, and interests) will likely result in the advertisement being ignored by most. An advertisement for garden equipment would make more sense. Conversely, were a cordless drill advertisement placed in a carpentry magazine (read by hobbyists and people with an interest in power tools), the advertisement would likely be of more interest to the target audience.

The nature of persuasion described by the ELM, where messages are targeted to key publics and only relevant information shared with each public, is the reason why news releases, feature stories, and other types of written documents are not sent to *every* newspaper but only to newspapers that care about what you have to say.

Ultimately, the ELM suggests that practitioners need to take into account their various publics and level of knowledge/involvement when preparing messages. In many cases, several versions of a key message need to be prepared with varying levels of content and sophistication in order to meet the needs and attention of various publics. People in the early stages of issue recognition—"I wonder if I need a new computer?"—are not prepared to process sophisticated messages and understand product details, while people at the later stages of elaboration—"I need an *Apple* computer"—want to know more.

UNDERSTANDING PUBLICS: FEATURES OF SOURCES, MESSAGES, AND RECEIVERS OF PERSUASION

Knowing something about how people process information (ELM and TRA), and understanding that arguments and persuasive messages should draw upon multiple levels of meaning (ethos, pathos, and logos) is important. However, you should also understand that message types, a communicator's status, and the characteristics of audiences also affect the success of persuasive messages.

A lot of persuasion hinges upon people actually remembering what you said. Additionally, sometimes what is important is who makes a claim rather than what the claim actually is. In order to be a successful persuader you should understand the basic constraints associated with message sources, message receivers, and the message structures.

The research summarized in Table 6.1 highlights many of the key issues, but a few points are worth emphasizing:

1. *Having a strong argument is more important than source credibility*, however, strong arguments coupled with credibility or expertise are even better.

TABLE 6.1 Features of Persuasion

Sources and Audiences

- Self-persuasion (internalization) by the audience seems to be the most permanent source of persuasion, followed by identification and compliance.
- Source credibility may not matter if the messages themselves present reasonable arguments.
- Credibility of a source does not affect message recall.
- High-credibility sources do not need as much support to be persuasive as low-credibility sources.
- Credibility has a greater impact than attractiveness.
- Messages from high-credibility sources are evaluated more favorably.
- Biased sources are less likely to be believed if they are perceived to be experts.
- Expertise adds more to persuasive impact than trustworthiness, and we are more likely to be influenced by experts than by peers.
- Powerful, attractive, biased sources can be more effective than unbiased sources in reinforcing opinions.
- Attractive sources are more effective than unattractive ones, but source credibility has more impact.
- Both attractive and unattractive sources are more effective when they advocate unexpected positions.
- Liking, similarity, familiarity, and physical attractiveness are positively related to opinion change.
- High-credibility sources, when the messages are remembered, produce more immediate opinion change than low-credibility sources.
- Information [recall] from low-credibility sources does not persist over time.
- Both attention to, and retention of, messages is higher if the message was not expected from the source.
- Sources offering rewards are more effective than sources who threaten punishments.
- Mild threats may be internalized and may lead to compliance over time, while strong threats often stimulate defiance.
- Threats can be more effective than promises of rewards when message recipients are given a choice regarding how to comply.
- A source that threatens one of several punishments for noncompliance may be as persuasive as one that promises rewards.
- People do not necessarily avoid disconfirming messages. When messages offer rewards, for example, the audience will attend to them.
- Perception is subjective. Even when information is not adequate, receivers often focus on their immediate needs or desires, mental state, etc., and use information to address current issues.
- Accurate and favorable perceptions of a message can be facilitated by establishing early bonding with the target public, by using familiar objects and categories, and by using message cues that the public can easily recognize.
- There is no evidence of selective retention of information based on the receivers' attitudes and values.

TABLE 6.1 *Continued*

- Publics tend to disregard supportive messages that are easy to refute, and nonsupportive messages that are difficult to refute.
- Most mental and personality traits of receivers have diametrically opposed effects on message reception and yielding. Intelligence, for instance, facilitates reception but inhibits yielding.
- Adjusting messages to minimize differences between the source and extreme receivers facilitates greater acceptance.

Messages

- Messages with explicit conclusions are more effective than messages with implicit conclusions.
- Receivers will often miss the point if conclusions are not explicit.
- Good news presented first then bad news increases acceptance of a message when a message contains both good and bad news.
- Information at the beginning and end of messages is recalled better than information in the middle.
- Two-sided messages (telling the other side and refuting it) are advisable if the recipient is educated, is likely to hear the other side anyway, is familiar with the issue, is opposed to the side being advocated, and is likely to be exposed to the other side of the issue.
- One-sided messages work well when the audience is less educated, not likely to be exposed to the other side, not familiar with the issue, and when the topic is uncontroversial.
- High-fear appeals can be more effective than low-fear appeals when receivers have low chronic anxiety or don't see themselves as vulnerable, and when the recommendations are specific, clear, and easy to follow.
- Generally, there is no difference in the persuasive impact of emotional versus rational appeals.
- Increased comprehension of a message increases agreement.
- Learning increases with message repetition, but repetition can eventually cause an increase in counter argumentation and a decrease in favorable thoughts.
- Repeated exposure to a message can increase agreement, but too much exposure can lead to boredom and reduce agreement. A period of nonexposure can overcome effects of overexposure. Overexposure is better than no exposure.
- Generally, comparative and noncomparative ads are equally effective, but comparative ads are more effective on television, when used with new or novel products, when market share is small, or when the desired public does not have established preferences.
- If there is little supporting evidence for a message, source credibility is more important.
- Communicators are evaluated more favorably to the extent that their messages have the following qualities: listenability or readability, human interest, vocabulary diversity, and realism.

Media

- Live or videotaped messages are more effective in changing attitudes, followed by oral (audiotaped) messages. People are more critical of written messages.
- Television involves its audience more than does radio, which is more involving than print.
- Written messages—especially complex ones—are more easily learned and remembered than either videotaped or audiotaped messages.
- When the message is simple, videotapes are more effective than written presentations.
- When a message is complex, or recipients will only be exposed to the message one time, print is more easily learned and remembered.
- Trustworthy sources are more effective in changing attitudes when they use television rather than print or radio media. Untrustworthy sources are more effective when using print or radio.

Tan, A. S. (1986). *Mass Communication Theories and Research*, 2nd ed. New York: Macmillan Publishing, pp. 141–143, 164–165, 176–177, 204–205.

2. *"Attractiveness" means both physical attractiveness as well as social attractiveness:* liking, familiarity, status, wealth, etc. Donald Trump may not be a looker, but his wealth makes people listen to what he has to say.
3. *Promising a reward for taking an action is a more useful tactic than making threats.* However, messages that contain several threats of punishment for noncompliance, or threatening messages that allow recipients to choose how to comply, can be more successful than rewards. In other words, "If you drink our tasty shake, you'll lose weight ..." is good. However, "If you do not take action now, you have a future of ... to look forward to" may be better. Both of these persuasive strategies are sometimes combined, as will be described in Monroe's Motivated Sequence later in the text.
4. *Emotional appeals and appeals to reason are essentially equal,* however, as suggested by Aristotle and Burke, the best persuaders draw upon credibility, emotion, and logic so their arguments appeal to everyone. Since different strategies move different people, the best persuasive appeals draw upon multiple persuasion techniques.
5. *When you have both good news and bad news to report, always remember: good news first and then bad news.* Never give your audience a choice.
6. *Educated audiences are suspicious of persuaders who present one-sided arguments.* The best approach with educated, or informed, audiences is to present both sides, refute the other side, and then reinforce your own position.
7. *It is easier to explain things to educated audiences than to less educated audiences* (informing). However, getting educated audiences to take a desired action (yielding) is more difficult.
8. *Less educated audiences are more likely to yield (take an action) to "good reasons"* but are less able to *understand* difficult concepts (informing).
9. *Messages with explicit conclusions are always better,* since some people will miss the point if you do not make it explicit.

MODERN RHETORICAL CONCEPTS

Although many of the classic rhetorical concepts like ethos, pathos, and logos might sound somewhat familiar, given that they are often talked about in philosophy and public speaking classes, the more modern rhetorical concepts like "archetypal metaphors" and Burke's "psychology of form" are probably less familiar. The next section will describe modern rhetorical concepts and talk about how they fit into public relations writing.

Home Style and the Presentation of Self

Besides being a term we use to describe pancakes, "home style" actually describes how communicators adapt to regional and geographic differences. Essentially, home style is a form of ethos or audience adaptation. As Fenno (1978) describes it:

> [M]embers of Congress go home to present themselves as a person and to win the accolade: "he's a good man," "she's a good woman." With Goffman, they know there is a "promissory character" to their presentation. And their object is to present themselves as a person in such a way that the inferences drawn by those watching will be supportive. The representatives' word for these supportive inferences is *trust*. (p. 55)

As public relations professionals you need to understand the importance of the presentation of self (Goffman, 1959). More importantly, you need to appreciate how your "self" is also an extension of your organization. Many years ago, a colleague who was working as a campaign manager and I were going out for a drink. On the way into one of the most respectable bars in the city, my colleague took off his campaign button. I commented that I did not think anyone in the bar would be less likely to support his candidate because they saw him having a beer, and he reminded me that "that may be true, but I represent the *candidate* and not *myself* when I wear this button."

Fenno and Goffman both suggest that as professionals, we are expected to fit in with the crowd (the everyday people) in certain situations, especially events like organizational picnics and community events. However, we also have an obligation as organizational representatives to be sure that the organization fits into its community and is viewed by citizens as being "a good community member." Part of being a good community member has to do with how we look and how we act. And how we look and act is an extension of our organization's image.

For Goffman and Fenno, home style, and the presentation of self, are concepts that have meaning in face-to-face settings. However, just because Goffman was not a public relations professional does not mean that we should ignore his insights. Ethos and the presentation of self are enacted in every document the organization creates, in every e-mail message you send, and in every Web page. Research shows that organizational Web sites that *appear* more user-friendly and *appear* to care more about stakeholders, tend to actually *be* more user friendly, and create more effective communication interfaces on their Web sites (Kent, Taylor, & White, 2003; McAllister & Kent, 2009). The presentation of self and enacting a home style or "audience adaptation" is part of all effective professional communication. As organizational representatives, you will want to monitor internal and external communication (environmental scanning) and make an effort to counsel colleagues and organizational leaders on how to maintain an appropriate tone and enact a positive image for organizations and clients.

Archetypal Metaphors

Although I discussed metaphors in Chapter 2, I never raised the concept of **archetypal metaphors.** According to Osborn, "Archetypal metaphors represent basic, unchanging, patterns of experience" (1967, p. 116). Categories of archetypal metaphor include *light and dark metaphors* (sun/moon, day/night, high/low, the seasons) (Osborn, 1967), *metaphors of the sea* (turbulence/optimism, separation/freedom, stability—the "ship of state") (Osborn, 1977), and *premillennial and postmillennial apocalyptic metaphors* (we are on the brink, the end is near, now is the time to get saved, things will get worse before they get better) (Brummett, 1984, 1991).

Essentially any universal or unchanging experience, situation, or character type might be called archetypal. Thus, fire and ice or hot and cold are archetypes, but heat and cool are not. There are also archetypal narrative characters that can be used in messages: the miser, the saint, the bully. Archetypes are symbolic rather than merely descriptive. "Meanness" is not an archetype but "evil" and "villain" are. According to Osborn (1967), features of archetypal metaphors are grounded in universal human experience like life and death. Archetypal metaphors come already linked to prominent features of human experience and therefore are powerful persuasive tools. Archetypal metaphors are memorable and draw on important situations (pp. 116–117).

Archetypal metaphors allow persuaders to draw upon their strong positive and negative associations with survival and development. Light–dark metaphors also express intense value judgments and often elicit significant value responses form an audience (p. 117). According to Osborn,

> Light-dark metaphor combinations carry still another important implication which students of rhetoric appear to have neglected. There are occasions when speakers find it expedient to express an attitude of inevitability or determination about the state of present affairs or the shape of the future. Change not simply *should have occurred* or *should occur* but *had to* or *will* occur. (1967, pp. 117–118, Osborn's emphasis)

Speakers and writers can use the strong and universal associations that are attached to archetypal metaphors to create images and associations in an audience's mind that might not be possible using other metaphors. Messages like issue advertisements placed in newspapers often refer to "turbulent times," "the sun coming up" and technology "lighting the way." Another prominent use of archetypal metaphors is to use archetypal imagery in print and electronic documents. Images expressing light and dark are common, as are images of the sea, space, and the desert. Images are used to create specific moods and to invoke primordial feelings in readers. More importantly, given the visual nature of our society, professional communicators need to think in terms of images when they are creating printed documents. Given the increasing importance of the Internet for communicating with stakeholders and publics, archetypal metaphors and images can be used in historical documents, online editorials, reports, white papers, blogs, fact sheets, letters, and other documents.

The "Psychology of Information" and the "Psychology of Form"

The psychology of information and the psychology of form (Burke, 1968/1931) might have been saved for the chapter on aesthetics because it explains how form is often more important than content. For Burke, the "psychology" he refers to is the psychology of the audience, or how people can be encouraged to respond.

As Burke explains, **form** "is the creation of an appetite in the mind of the auditor (listener), and the adequate satisfying of that appetite." If, in a message, the persuader says something, let us say, about a meeting, writes in such a way that we desire to observe that meeting, and then, if he places the meeting before us—that is form (p. 31).

In contrast to form, the **psychology of information** has to do with *content* rather than style. The "whodunnit?" detective genre (*Law and Order, Columbo, Poirot*) is a good example of the psychology of information. Once we know who the murderer is, unless we forget, the story will never be as exciting as it was the first time. Although people often enjoy watching a movie or reading a book over and over because of the skill or art of the author, director, cinematographer, or musician, the "information" can never be taken back. Indeed, all of the things that allow us to enjoy a book, movie, or song almost infinitely have to do with form and not content.

The example Burke uses to drive home the power of form is music. You have undoubtedly observed how your parents are still listening to the same songs they listened to 25 years ago, before many of you were even born. The phenomenon of the "oldies" has been around for more than 60 years, since radio discovered they could get people to listen by playing old music (cf., Levinson, 1997; McLuhan, 1999/1964). You will probably be listening to the "oldies" on the "nineties" or "two thousands" station in 20 years, too.

The point of the psychology of form is to understand that rhetoric and persuasion are about satisfying desire and fulfilling expectations. Effective persuasion identifies needs that the audience does not know it wants filled. The psychology of information, which is essentially the satisfaction of learning something new, appeals to some people, but not as many as the psychology of form, Burke argues.

Form ties in with many of the rhetorical tactics we have already discussed. When an audience mentally finishes an argument (an enthymeme), that is the psychology of form; when an audience feels the tension created by a skillful juxtaposition of words (figures of speech), or a skillful use of repetition, timing, or cadence, that is form. The best persuasive messages are more than information—they are also form. Being able to enact compelling form is the reason behind maintaining a swipe file.[2] By preserving examples of messages that utilize effective form, you can incorporate the ideas into your own work, much like rock musicians have borrowed riffs from classical music, jazz, and blues artists for 70 years.

The Tyranny of the Definition

As rhetoricians have known for a long time, the power to define something is immense. *The person who controls the definition controls the debate.* Public relations professionals working in the 21st century need to understand that one of the primary ways in which people get their information now is from the Internet (Fallows, 2004). With three-quarters of all U.S. citizens having Internet access (Lenhart, et al., 2003; Madden, 2006), people use it for everything from buying theatre tickets and booking flights to checking the weather.

Not surprisingly, journalists have been using the Internet for some time to verify facts, obtain background information for stories, locate sources, and yes, even obtain information to write stories when organizational representatives are not available (Middleberg & Ross, 1999a, 1999b, 2000a, 2000b, 2002; Wright, 2001). More importantly, recent research indicates journalists actually use what is provided to them verbatim in news releases as the basis for quotations in stories or to provide background in stories (Caldiero, Taylor, & Ungureanu, 2009).

Two issues are important about definitions. First, once a definition has been advanced, anyone who disagrees with the organization's position has to expend its scarce resources, time, and money arguing about *your* definition rather than advancing their own positions and policies. Thus, when you are in a position where you have a chance to shape debate, it is to your benefit to offer *your* definitions and key terms first.

Second, since the media have begun to interface with organizations via their Web sites and online sources, organizations must take advantage of the opportunity to provide their own content and present the organization's position on issues to the media. Few politicians or organizations have unrestricted access to the media. However, using Web sites to highlight organizational positions on policy and substantive issues—even if only with news releases—can give an organization an edge when issues begin to be discussed by the mainstream media. Take advantage of opportunities to advance your own definitions whenever you can by producing news releases, fact sheets, policy papers, and "dark sites."

Casuistic Stretching

Casuistry refers to overly subtle or meticulous reasoning typically used by critics and lawyers. As Burke (1961) explains, **casuistic stretching** is the practice of "introducing new principles while theoretically remaining faithful to old principles" (p. 229). In other words, casuistic stretching is a rhetorical device used to incorporate, broaden, or constrict an already accepted definition or policy (p. 229).

One of the best examples of casuistic stretching was President Reagan's efforts in the '80s to justify cuts to a number of social programs in the nation's "social safety net," and was seen as untouchable by most politicians. Reagan argued that he would maintain a "social safety net for the *truly needy*," but that "*reform was needed*." As Zarefsky, Miller-Tutzauer, and Tutzauer (1984) explain,

> Reagan did not specify who *were* the "truly needy" or what characteristics distinguished true from only apparent need. This omission might have been a wise move, since those with a vested interest in any program would perceive that program as addressed to true need. Thinking it therefore immune from cuts, its supporters might be less inclined to attack the general strategy of cuts, so long as the ox to be gored belonged to someone else. (p. 114, authors' emphasis)

By modifying the concepts of a "social safety net" and the concept of citizens who are "truly needy" to a "safety net for the truly needy," Reagan was able to substantially decrease funding for the nation's social support programs. By stretching the definition of needy, Reagan was able to define the terms of the debate and how the media would cover the issue.

Definitional stretching can be used effectively but requires strategic and thoughtful language choices. If terminology is stretched too far, persuaders are open to attack for their "new proposal." Part of successful definitional stretching comes from having an intimate understanding of the subject matter in question and part of successful definitional stretching comes from knowing your target audiences and stakeholders well. The idea of thorough audience analysis is central to both rhetoric and public relations.

Understanding when casuistic stretching is being used is also essential. As noted above, if definitions are not challenged when they are introduced, they become more difficult to attack down the road as the concepts become entrenched. An essential feature of successful persuasion is being able to recognize when an opponent is advancing new definitions or trying to stretch long-accepted premises.

LOGICAL FALLACIES

Another essential skill for public relations writers is to understand how to construct sound arguments, avoid flaws in reasoning, and recognize when others are making flawed arguments. To do all of this, you need to understand **logical fallacies**. For an argument to be sound, ideas and **premises** (the assumptions upon which an argument rests) have to be linked together logically. Often, arguments are flawed because a rhetorician (speaker/writer) draws an erroneous conclusion. You might remember, for example, being asked by your parents, "If all your friends jumped off a building, would you jump off too?" after you said something like, "But everyone else has a *Zena Warrior Princess* lunch pail!" Actually, what your parents were referring to is a logical fallacy known as the "argumentum ad populum," or the appeal to the people (see Table 6.2 for a list of common logical fallacies).

Doing what everyone else does, or doing what someone says should be done because "everyone is

TABLE 6.2 Logical Fallacies

Argumentum ad antiquitam: Asserting that something is right or good simply because it is old: "That's the way it's always been done" or "Our forefathers believed. …"
Argumentum ad baculum: An argument that uses threats of force to cause the acceptance of the conclusion. Ad baculum arguments also include threats of fear: "Do this or you'll go to Hell!" "If we don't monitor the telephone calls of Americans the terrorists win."
Argumentum ad crumenam: Believing that money is a criterion of goodness. Believing that those with more money are more likely to be smart or correct: "As smart as Bill Gates is, we should make him president."
Argumentum ad hominem: An argument that attacks a speaker personally rather than the speaker's arguments. There are two basic types of ad hominem arguments: (1) abusive: "Only a communist would believe that"; and (2) circumstantial: "Since my opponent has never served in the armed forces he would not understand."
Argumentum ad ignorantium: Arguing that something is true because it has not been shown to be false, or that something is false because it has not been shown to be true: "Since no one has ever reached the summit of Mount Invincible, it must be impossible to climb." Ad ignorantium arguments are also known as "appeals to ignorance."

(continued)

TABLE 6.2 ***Continued***

Argumentum ad lazarum: Arguments suggesting that because someone is poor, s/he is better or more virtuous than someone who is wealthy: "Edith Smith should know what the city's homeless people need since she lives in one of its homeless shelters ..."

Argumentum ad misericordiam: An argument that uses pity to convince the audience to take action: "For only pennies a day, you can send a child to school and feed his family ..."

Argumentum ad nauseum: An argument that assumes that if something is said enough times it must be true. Most propaganda works this way.

Argumentum ad novitam: Arguing that something is better simply because it is newer, or newer than something else ("New and Improved!"). Or that something is better because it is bigger, faster, etc.

Argumentum ad numeram: An argument that asserts that the more people who support or believe in something, the more likely a proposition is to be true. The ad numeram fallacy equates mass support with correctness: "Nine out of ten Americans believe ..."

Argumentum ad populum: Arguments appealing to the beliefs of the multitude (i.e., the "people"). Rhetors deal with the passions of audience members rather than with salient issues. This fallacy is also known as "Appeal to Tradition": "The citizens of Springfield believe that a marriage is. ..." Ad populum arguments occur in propaganda, demagoguery, and advertising.

Argumentum ad verecundiam: An argument in which an authority (or expert) is invoked on matters outside his/her field of authority. Ad verecundiam fallacies also invoke rules and laws as reasons for maintaining the status quo. "My pastor says that the new building codes are unfair."

Bandwagon: An argument that suggests that because other people are already doing something we should as well. An appeal to the people. In advertising, products claim to be the "Number #1 acne cream" or "The most popular brand of headache medicine," etc., but such claims have nothing to do with a product's effectiveness.

Begging the question (circular reasoning): Arguments that assume, as one of the premises, the very conclusion that is to being argued. (A is true because A is true.) There are two types of circular reasoning: (1) calling for a decision on an issue that has not been sufficiently proven: "that begs the question. ..."; and (2) using the very issue being argued to prove one's point: A is true, because B is true; and B is true because C is true; and C is true because A is true: "Since students only get grades for working hard, students who work hard will get better grades."

Bifurcation: Also referred to as the "black and white" fallacy. Bifurcated arguments characterize situations as having only two alternatives: "You are with us or against us," or "You are either for immigration or against America."

Converting a conditional: Arguments that assume that if one thing leads to another (if A, then B), the reverse is also true (if B, then A): "Just as increased economic stability leads to increased immigration, increased immigration leads to greater economic stability."

Cum hoc ergo propter hoc: An argument in which two events which occur simultaneously are assumed to be causally related: "Nearly everyone who had died has eaten pickles, therefore, pickles are unhealthy."

Division: An argument that assumes that various parts have a property solely because the whole has that same property: "All Muslims are terrorists."

Equivocation: Equivocal means (1) of uncertain significance, undetermined; and (2) having different meanings that are equally possible. Equivocation is a fallacy of ambiguity where an expression is used equivocally in one premise and in a different sense in another premise, or the conclusion: The president argued, "we need a safety net for the *needy* ..." and later argued, "We need a safety net for the *truly needy*." The opposite of equivocation is "univocation," in which a word always carries the same meaning through different contexts.

False analogy: An analogy is a comparison of two like things or events for which a comparison can be made. A false analogy involves comparing two things that are not similar ("apples and oranges"). Note: In a false analogy, the two things may be similar in superficial ways (both fruit), but not with respect to what is being argued.

Gambler's fallacy, or the "hot hand" fallacy: An argument that implies that something is likely to happen "because it is due" or "overdue" or is likely to continue because of a streak. This fallacy involves willfully ignoring or not understanding statistics. "Streaks" do not change the probability of an event happening. Because someone tosses a coin 10 times and receives the same result (all heads or all tails), does not change the probability that the next toss still only has a 50/50 chance of occurring.

TABLE 6.2 *Continued*

Interrogation: An argument where the question asked presupposes something that the answerer wishes to deny and would accept if s/he actually answered the question honestly: "I did not have sexual relations with that woman, Miss Lewinsky. ..."

Ignoratio elenchi: An argument that is supposed to prove one proposition but succeeds only in proving a different one. Ignoratio elenchi means "irrelevance" or "ignorance of refutation."

Non causa pro causa: An argument to reject a proposition because of the falsity of some other proposition that seems to be a consequence of the first, but really is not: "I can name 50 people who have smoked their whole life and do not have cancer" (thus cigarettes do not cause cancer). However, that particular individuals do not get cancer does not prove that cigarettes do not cause cancer.

Non-sequitur: An argument in which the conclusion does not follow from the premises. A conclusion drawn from premises that provide no logical connection to it. "I have a 3.8 GPA and I have never received a grade this low before, so the test must have been unfair."

Plurium interrogationum (many questions): A demand for a simple answer to a complex question: "The voters demand to know who is to blame for the housing scandal."

Post hoc, ergo propter hoc: An argument asserting that an earlier event A was caused by a later event B. Because one event precedes another event in time does not mean that the first event is the cause of the second event. This argument is similar to a "hasty generalization." In statistics we learn: "Correlation does not equal causation." Learning that a quarterback was sick after a game was lost does not prove that the game was lost because the quarterback was sick.

Red herring: A fallacy of diversion where irrelevant arguments or information is introduced into a discussion in order to divert people's attention away from the issue under discussion and toward a different conclusion: "Before we address this new policy, we should first talk about how it will be implemented ..."

Reification (to "make real"): Reification involves converting an abstract concept into a concrete thing: "Only someone who does not love freedom would allow this to happen."

Secundum quid ("hasty generalization"): An argument where a proposition is argued without sufficient attention being given to some obvious condition that reduces the proposition's value. Hasty generalizations take evidence from several, possibly unrepresentative, cases to a general rule, generalizing from few to many. Note the relation to statistics: Much of statistics concerns whether or not a sample is representative of a larger population. The larger the sample size, the better the representativeness.

Shifting the burden of proof: The burden of proof is always on the person making the argument. Shifting the burden of proof involves putting the burden of proof on the person who denies or questions the assertion being made. The fallacy assumes that something is true unless proven otherwise: "Since you can offer no valid reason *not* to take the action I propose, we should pass the law."

Slippery slope: An argument in which a series of small steps is claimed to eventually lead to a catastrophic event (A will lead to B, B will lead to C ... X will lead to Y, and Y to Z). Thus, the initial event should not be allowed to happen: "If we do not stop China now, soon we will all be speaking Chinese."

Special pleading: Special pleading typically happens when one party insists upon less strict treatment for the argument s/he is making than would be given to someone else's argument. Special pleading tries to invoke a double standard for the person making the assertion.

Straw man: Arguments where an opponent's position is misrepresented as being weaker than it actually is (a "straw man") so that it can be more easily attacked. The rhetor's own position then is more forcefully advanced. "The antigun lobby would take away your guns and have you live in fear, unable to protect yourself from harm. ..."

Sweeping generalization: An argument where a general rule is applied to a particular situation in which the features of that particular situation render the rule inapplicable: "Birds can normally fly. Earl the Emu is a bird. Therefore Earl can fly." Or, "Politicians normally lie. You are a politician. Therefore you must be a liar."

Tu quoque (two wrongs make a right): A fallacy of consistency and diversion. Two wrongs can never make a right; you cannot right a wrong by applying yet another wrong. Tu quoque often involves a person who has been accused of a crime turning the question of his or her guilt back on the accuser as s/he attempts to defend him or herself (often putting the accuser on the defensive).

doing it" does not make it right, or even a good idea. Unfortunately, because of peer pressure and other social pressures, children (and even adults) often have trouble doing what they think is right. The "logic," or faulty logic, of the argumentum ad populum fallacy is also the basis for a lot of advertisements that try to convince the listener, reader, or viewer that they are out of step, or old-fashioned, for not having the latest holographic cell phone or drinking the latest carbonated malt beverage. Understanding logical fallacies is important both to avoid creating flawed arguments and recognizing when others are making weak or misleading arguments.

The news media regularly reduce complicated issues to sound bites and catchphrases. Two of the most well known instances of this are "the War on Terror" and the "the War on Drugs." In both instances, the "war" is only metaphorical and the phrase was chosen for impact rather than accuracy. Americans are at war with Iraqi insurgents, Taliban leaders, and Columbian drug lords, not with "terror" or "drugs." Public relations professionals who understand that language influences how people talk and think about issues are better prepared to respond to negative publicity and to create more compelling messages and arguments for clients. A political leader or antiwar activist group, for example, cannot just accept the definitions of others and must be able to point out when arguments are flawed and propose alternative ways of interpreting events. Although dozens of logical fallacies can be identified on any given day in the print and broadcast media, four logical fallacies stand out as particularly important to understand: bifurcation, straw man, red herring, and the gambler's fallacy.

Bifurcation

Bifurcation is called the black-and-white fallacy. Basically, whenever a speaker or writer claims that "there are two possibilities," you can be sure that s/he is either trying to mislead you, or does not really understand the complexity of the issues. With the possible exception of "death and taxes," as the expression goes, virtually every issue has more than two sides. Even highly polarized issues like abortion, euthanasia, gun control, war, and gay rights have an assortment of nuanced and highly sophisticated positions. One can be "pro-choice" but still believe that abortion is wrong, just as you can be "pro-life" and not believe that "life begins at conception." Issues, especially social issues, are complicated. Many practitioners represent organizations that have a stake in social and political issues: activist organizations, drug companies, nonprofit organizations, religious organizations, and professional associations, to name but a few. Arguments, attacks, misleading claims, and outright lies will eventually end up being discussed by the media; your job as a public relations professional might become to present the organization's position on an issue or to counsel management about how to effectively respond to the media. Many organizations create "white papers" and "speaker's bureaus" as a means of responding to issues and advancing their own position.

You should also understand that bifurcation is often used intentionally. Recognizing that bifurcation is taking place at all is the first step. Bifurcation is used strategically by organizations for both offensive and defensive purposes. Although reducing complicated issues to polar opposites is considered logically flawed, bifurcated arguments are difficult to refute. As Taylor and Kent (2007) explain:

> Bifurcation … is a third way in which a governmental rhetor might persuade others. Strictly speaking, bifurcation is a logical fallacy in which a persuader outlines an argument in such as way as to suggest that there is only one of two possibilities—typically diametrically opposed options. Undoubtedly everyone has heard the expression "you are either with us or against us." Such a polar argument is the essence of bifurcation. Bifurcation is used every day, consciously and unconsciously, by people from all walks of life. More typically, however, bifurcation is used when an individual is trying to persuade another. A contemporary example of bifurcation can be seen in the way that United States leaders talk about "the war on terror": "If Americans don't do … then the terrorists win." Bifurcation is also closely linked to Kenneth Burke's (1969) notion of identification and is used to rally support and quash dissent. (pp. 132–133)

Understanding that some logical fallacies, like bifurcation, are used intentionally should give you an edge when constructing counterarguments. Once a rhetor (short for "rhetorician," or communicator) recognizes that his/her opponent's arguments rest of a false dichotomy, a successful defense might involve little more than pointing out the flaw and offering an alternative, more compelling position somewhere in the middle. Conversely, large corporations and governments that have powerful public voices and more access to the media will often intentionally simplify issues with bifurcation in order to advance their own positions (Taylor & Kent, 2006).

The only defense for bifurcation in either case is to first understand what is happening, and then to reject, redefine, or reframe the dichotomy in a positive way. One well-known example of bifurcation where reframing was used is the pro-life/pro-choice debate over abortion. In the early to mid-'70s, the pro-life movement was the first group to assign a label to its movement. Implied by pro-life was its opposite, pro-death (the opposite of "life" being "death," not "choice"). For a while, the pro-choice movement had trouble countering the rhetoric of the pro-life movement because of this dichotomy (bifurcation). Eventually pro-"choice" was identified as a means of avoiding the "pro-death" label that some opponents were using and as a means of reframing the debate and redefining the situation to an issue of limited "choice," or "freedom," rather than morality (cf., Hopkins & Reicher, 1997; McCaffrey & Keys, 2000).

Straw Man

The **straw man** fallacy is an error of distortion or misrepresentation. Rhetors who use the straw man fallacy typically misrepresent another's position in order to make an issue more vulnerable to attack. What often happens is that an individual or organization (e.g., an activist group attacking an organization's position, an organization attempting to discredit an activist group, etc.) will intentionally make inaccurate or false claims about another individual or organization's position, simplifying, exaggerating, mischaracterizing, or out and out misrepresenting the opponent's position. The explanation of the other's side (the straw man) is created to be weak and unsupportable, or absurd and unreasonable. Once the opposition's weak (straw) arguments have been presented, the rhetor then offers up his/her own arguments to show why they are better, stronger, and typically, a viable solution to the problem/issue at hand.

The straw man fallacy is arguably one of the most common fallacies you will encounter. All types of individuals and organizations use straw man arguments to (mis)represent the opposition's position/arguments. The crux of the straw man fallacy is distortion or misrepresentation. However, the straw man fallacy is also a fallacy of misdirection, redirection, and evasion because it allows a rhetor to ignore the actual arguments of the opposition and try to refocus attention on one's own arguments rather than actually dealing with the substantive issues at the heart of a debate.

The key to combating the straw man fallacy effectively is a process called redefinition. Rhetors confronted with straw man attacks must acknowledge that their arguments have been mischaracterized, correct any mistakes, and "redefine" the situation, attempting to refocus attention on core issues. What often happens with highly charged issues, however, is that both sides advance straw man arguments and neither side makes an effort to genuinely confront the issue(s) at hand.

Straw man arguments are used effectively when speaking to sympathetic publics ("preaching to the choir"). With partisans, there is no real need to be fair, since the audience already agrees with you. The danger for public relations practitioners, however, is when individuals allow partisanship to cloud sound issue examination. Practitioners need to be aware both of when a straw man argument is being utilized, as well as when their own position is being distorted by opponents. Proper issue analysis must include an objective analysis of the opposition's position(s) if a practitioner hopes to truly understand public sentiment on an issue and act in the best interest of one's organization or client.

Red Herring

The **red herring** fallacy is a technique of diversion. The name itself is a metaphor for what happens when the fallacy occurs—throwing a smelly fish into the middle of the room to divert attention from the issue at hand. Essentially, the fallacy involves irrelevant material being introduced into a discussion or debate. Often, the red herring has absolutely nothing to do with the issue under consideration. Frequently rhetors will introduce a topic that is only tangentially related to the topic at hand as a means of intentionally distracting or stalling discussion, or diverting attention to another issue. The purpose of the red herring is to redirect the audience's attention away from the current issue, situation, or decision, and toward a different one. The red herring fallacy is often seen in small group meetings where a group member will constantly change the subject, tell jokes, and redirect the conversation to topics of his/her own interest rather than dealing with the group's current business.

In practice, the red herring fallacy is used to shift the terms of a debate, to direct attention to a new or tangential issue, or to redefine an issue, arguing that what is "really important" is something different. Contemporary examples of the red herring fallacy can be found in several areas including politics and business.

For example, during the 2004 Kerry/Bush campaign, several political action groups affiliated with the Republican Party accused John Kerry of being unpatriotic because he spoke at an antiwar rally in the '60s, and only pretended to throw his medals away during the event. Kerry was among a group of some of the most decorated war veterans in the U.S. who were called "unpatriotic" during the 2004 presidential election campaign (Frank, 2004).[3]

The goal of the red herring attack was to distract Kerry from the campaign and to focus the public's attention on erroneous issues. If the news media and the nation can so easily be distracted from real issues[4] by false charges, accusations, and innuendo, then an organization's opponent (activist group, competitor) can just as easily focus media attention on the "smelly fish," rather than the real issue.

The red herring fallacy, as with the straw man fallacy, requires rhetors to exert energy and resources both pointing out what is being done (distraction) as well as trying to direct attention back to the key issues and questions. The problem rhetors face with the red herring fallacy and other fallacies of distraction and misrepresentation is that the news media typically have a vested interest in prolonging debate and sensationalizing news content (cf., Kent, Harrison, & Taylor, 2006). Some of the ways that organizations have tried to get around the media's bias for sensationalism have been to take their message directly to interested parties through direct mailings, issue advertisements, Web sites, and public forums.

Be aware that either party can employ the red herring fallacy. Although the tactic is considered a "logical fallacy," the distractions that are caused by misdirection are often intentionally orchestrated. Indeed, all three of the fallacies described here—bifurcation, straw man and Red Herring—are often employed intentionally/strategically by communication professionals, and public relations professionals need to know how to recognize them and respond to them when they are used.

Gambler's Fallacy

The gambler's fallacy, or the "hot hand" fallacy, are essentially fallacies involving a misunderstanding of probabilities and lack of research. The idea of the "hot hand" or the "streak" comes from sports, where many people believe that when someone is "hot" or on a streak, they have a greater chance of success. In reality, odds do not fluctuate based on someone's emotional state, and just because someone wants something to happen does not mean it will. Conversely, just because something bad has been happening for a long time does not mean "you are due" for a change.

We see the essence of the gambler's fallacy written about almost every day in stories about new technology. Because many people (citizens and professionals alike) do not really understand Internet technologies very well, believing that some new activity (Facebook, Twitter, YouTube) will revolutionize the public relations world is easy to believe. Additionally, many arguments rely on incomplete knowledge and anecdotal information: "I have a colleague who moved his entire call center online ..." Before you take action, or advise your colleagues about the best course of action, make sure you have data to back up your position. Because something is popular (bandwagon fallacy) does not make it important. The Hula Hoop was once very hot, but had no impact on the business world. Similarly, Twitter is currently very popular, but there is very little evidence proving that organizations benefit from its use. Be careful of arguments about "new" and "revolutionary" products and business practices (bandwagon, argumentum ad novitam, and gambler's fallacies).

WRITING PERSUASIVE LETTERS

The letter is one persuasive tool that has been used for literally thousands of years. Not every type of business letter is designed for persuasive purposes, but many are (letters of recommendation, application letters, and responses to angry customers). There are dozens of different types of letters: cover letters, letters to the editor, letters of recommendation, letters of transmittal, thank you letters, letters of invitation. In general, business letters all look alike. What varies a great deal, however, is their content. A letter to the editor in support of an organizational campaign or in response to media criticism has a very different tone than an "open letter" published in the newspaper as part of an issues management campaign. Similarly, a letter of recommendation has a very different tone than a letter of invitation, a fundraising letter, or a letter responding to an angry customer.

Business Letter Style

Business letters have both a content dimension and an appearance dimension. In general, business letters rarely exceed two single-spaced pages and are typically one page long.

Business letters are written with the text left justified. You should have a "ragged right" margin (*do not* justify both margins). You *may* hyphenate the document if you prefer the cleaner look, but unless you have large gaps because of long words, hyphenation is unnecessary (you can also hyphenate long words manually). As mentioned above, single-space *everything* in a business letter, except when you are writing a draft that will be edited by a colleague or teacher (Table 6.3).

You may use **bold**, *italic*, underline, and superscript, if appropriate, but use non-Roman (plain text is called "Roman" text) formatting sparingly. Set all margins to one inch. Be sure to use the same font and the same font size throughout the letter. Do not use a font that is smaller than 10 or 11 points.

Use full-block or modified full-block format. Full-block formatting is when you have no tabs at the beginning of paragraphs but you insert an extra space between paragraphs. Modified full block format is like what you were trained to use when writing class essays: half-inch indents at the beginning of all paragraphs with no extra carriage returns after paragraphs. Full-block formatting is often considered more formal than modified-full-block but is appropriate for all occasions.

Keep all paragraphs short—just a few sentences. Limit each paragraph to the discussion/elaboration of a single idea. This makes it easier for the reader to "scan" the letter for relevant content issues. Try to keep business letters to only a few (two to three) paragraphs, and do not write one-sentence paragraphs. Bullets are uncommon in business letters.

Keep letters short—*never* more than one and a half pages. Busy professionals often will not take the time to read a lot of details. Organize information according to its order of importance. Very often professionals do not read letters when they first arrive, but save them for when the information is more relevant—like five minutes before the meeting. Most professionals, however, will read the first paragraph (or first few paragraphs) for the main idea, and then scan the rest of the letter for the general content.

Being "somewhat" conversational in a business letter is acceptable. However, avoid contractions, technojargon, colloquial language, purple prose, clichés, and sounding too academic.

Always proofread! Always spell check! Always fix errors—even minor errors. Never send a letter out with errors. Similarly, never send out a letter with editing marks on it where you corrected your mistakes.

Conclude the letter with an appropriate closing phrase: "Cordially," "Respectfully," "Sincerely," etc. Never conclude with: "Cheers," "Your Obedient and Very Humble Servant," "With a Handshake in Mind," "God Bless," etc.

Finally, be sure to sign the letter. Few things are more disconfirming than to receive a professional letter that a person was "too lazy to even sign." Some professionals actually recommend typing out the recipient's full name in the "Dear ..." line and then crossing it out with a dramatic pen stroke and hand-writing the recipient's first name. The idea of this is that when you are finished, the letter should look like "Mr./Ms. Important Executive, who is very busy and important, cares enough about you as a person to "correct the mistake that the *secretary* made." To be honest, the first time that I saw this I thought that the person was too lazy (or stupid) to correct his mistake. If it takes me a paragraph to explain this, what in the world makes someone think the recipient will understand your intent? Professional communicators should avoid such facile tactics. If you want to appear intimate, actually write a letter with a real pen on some nice stationary and hand-address the envelope. All "thank-you" cards and letters, for example, should be hand-written, signed, and addressed.

Cover Letters

Cover letters are one of the more common types of letters. Cover letters accompany feature stories and other documents for the media; internal documents like research reports, communication analyses, and campaign proposals; and résumés, articles, and RFPs ("request for proposal"). Cover letters are also used to sell yourself, your work, and your services. Cover letters are written when applying for jobs, submitting professional articles, and requesting information from government agencies. In short, cover letters are one of the most frequently written persuasive documents in your writing arsenal.

Writing a compelling cover letter takes time. Indeed, writing any effective business letter takes time. A first draft of a well-written cover letter can take several hours to craft. Your words should be carefully chosen for impact and to avoid redundancy.

WRITING COVER LETTERS

1. Do some research about the organization and the reader or audience before you write your letter. Make sure that you address the issues that the client, organization, or agency cares about. At a minimum, visit the organization's Web site, and talk to current and former employees or members of the organization.

TABLE 6.3 Business Letter Template

If you use letterhead, *your* contact information will not appear below. Include information that is not in the letterhead (e-mail, telephone extension, etc.), under your name and title at the bottom of the letter.

Letterhead

Monday, September 2, 2002

(Optional placement here)

Michael Kent, Graduate Director
Communication Studies
Montclair State University
050 Life Hall
Upper Montclair NJ 07043
Telephone: (973) 655-5130
E-mail: KentM@Mail.Montclair.Edu

Michael Kent, Graduate Director
Speech Communication
Montclair State University
050 Life Hall
Upper Montclair NJ 07043
Telephone (973) 655-5130
E-mail: KentM@Mail.Montclair.Edu

Jane/John Q. Public, Student
Communication
Avenue Upper
Montclair NJ
07043

Dear Ms/Mr. Public,

This letter is intended to discuss the characteristics of a business letter. I cover both formatting and content issues here. Use it as a model. Keep your letters shorter than this one.

It is appropriate to have all text in your business letter left justified. You should have a "ragged right" margin (do not justify both margins). You *may* hyphenate the document. You should also single-space *everything* (except for documents you hand in to be critiqued, which should have the body text double-spaced for editing purposes). You may use **bold**, *italic*, underline, and superscript if appropriate—but use non-Roman formatting sparingly. Set all margins at one inch.

Be sure to use the same font and the same font size throughout the letter. Do not use a font that is smaller than 11-point Helvetica, Garamond, or Times New Roman; or 10-point Bookman, Palatino, New York, or New Century Schoolbook. This letter is written in 10-point Bookman Old Style.

Use full-block or modified full-block format. Full-block format is like this letter: there are no tabs at the beginning of paragraphs, an extra space inserted between paragraphs. Modified full-block format is similar to what you were trained to use when writing class essays: insert a half-inch tab at the beginning of all paragraphs and do not insert extra spaces after paragraphs.

Keep all paragraphs short—a few sentences only, such as illustrated here. Limit each paragraph to discussion/elaboration of a single idea. By limiting each paragraph to a single idea, the letter is easier to "scan" for relevant content issues. Try to keep business letters to only a few (two to three) paragraphs. Do not write one-sentence paragraphs.

Keep the entire letter short—never more than one and a half pages. Busy people do not have time to read a lot of unsolicited information. Also, organize information (such as three story ideas used in a pitch letter) according to order of importance. Very often a busy person will not read the whole letter when it first arrives but save it for when it is more relevant. S/he will read the first paragraph (or first few paragraphs) for the general idea, and then scan the rest of the letter for content. That busy person will then save the letter until it is relevant to them—i.e., before a meeting.

It is okay to be "somewhat" conversational in a business letter. However, avoid technojargon, colloquial language, purple prose, clichés, and sounding too academic.

Always proofread! Always spell check! Always fix errors—even minor errors. Never send a letter out with errors that you know about. And never send out a letter with editing marks on it where you corrected your mistakes.

Cordially, (Respectfully, Sincerely, etc. *Not:* Cheers, Your Humble Servant, etc.)

Michael Kent
Director, Educational Communication

2. Keep cover letters short—three to four paragraphs (under one page in almost all cases).
3. In the first paragraph, concisely explain why you are writing (what position you are applying for, what the report is about, what need your article fills).
4. Sell yourself when applying for jobs, submitting feature stories, soliciting business, or looking for assistance—tell the reader why you are the best person for the job or explain why the story that you are submitting is perfect for the readers. Be specific. Rather than "this story would be perfect for your readers since it deals with …," a better approach is "last Wednesday you published an article about … this articles builds on that by …"
5. Be confident, do not apologize for skills you do not have (or even mention them), and be sure to identify the skills that you do have.
6. Tell the reader why you want to work for his/her organization and what you can do for the organization.
7. Do not be redundant. Drawing the reader's attention to some aspect of your résumé, a report, or an article is appropriate (as is your work with similar organizations, your experience with their type of organization, etc.), but *do not* restate the obvious.
8. Stating what you seek in a position is appropriate; however, do not make "demands" ("I would expect to start as an account executive …"; "I will only be in town for two days, so please respond immediately …") or suggest that you will do "anything" they want, if you want to be considered further.
9. Be sure to include an action step (see Monroe's Motivated Sequence from Chapter 9). "I would love an opportunity to tell you about myself in person. I am available for an interview …"; "I would be happy to come by and discuss these results with you on Wednesday. …"
10. Balance the white space. Add a few extra spaces at the top of the letter, and below, before the signature, so that you do not have a half-inch of white space at the bottom of the page. Do not add extra spaces between the paragraphs of the letter.
11. Thank the reader for his/her time. "As a busy professional I appreciate how valuable your time is and I look forward to your thoughtful consideration of this article"; "Your experience in matters such as this is greatly appreciated. I look forward to your evaluation of my proposal" etc.
12. Always frame your letter around what you can do for *them* rather than what *they* might do for *you*. Cover letters (especially for jobs) are about meeting the recipient's needs, not about what the applicant wants. The employer usually has the power.
13. Write deferentially but not fawningly or facetiously. Showering the recipient with false praise will not be met with alacrity.
14. Sign your letter in ink unless it is being e-mailed. As suggested above, unsigned letters suggest either laziness or ignorance. Forgetting to sign a business letter that you have proofread is nearly impossible. Before you put a letter in an envelope you should always conduct a final quick scan to look for stray printing marks, awkward paragraph breaks, and yes, a signature.
15. Whenever possible, have someone proofread your letters before you mail them.

Apologies and Responses to Angry Letters

Virtually every type of organization (for-profit, nonprofit, healthcare, governmental, political, Internet, educational, retail) occasionally receives an angry letter, or a letter expressing disapproval. Resource dependency theory suggests that organizations that depend more upon their publics for their survival (smaller businesses and donor organizations, for example) need to be more responsive to publics than other types of organizations (Emerson, 1962; Pfeffer & Salancik, 1978; Taylor, Kent, & White, 2001). Most public relations ethicists would say that organizations should respond to *all* publics who have a stake in an organization, even those with limited resources, and the letter is one of the primary means of responding to individual customer, client, or public concerns.

Effective businesses know that unsatisfied customers can cost a company more money in the long run than treating customers with respect and responding to customer concerns. Whatever the situation, knowing how to respond to angry customer or clients effectively is important for all public relations professionals.

Although a single letter from one dissatisfied client/customer might seem inconsequential to a large company, research suggests that for every letter written, hundreds—sometimes thousands, or tens of thousands—of individuals feel the same way. Indeed, a single disgruntled employee who writes a blog or tells a few friends an organizational secret about a product flaw or a health risk can mean millions of

- Get useful letters of recommendation when they are required. Letter writing is an art; do not go to an amateur. If you want to get into a public relations program, get public relations teachers to write you letters. If you are submitting a proposal for a grant project, get a former surgeon general or influential doctor to write you a letter. The best letters come from people who know you well and are familiar with your work.
- University presidents, CEOs, deans, and administrators write notoriously bad letters because they often pass off such tasks to support staff. Even when such professionals do write the letters themselves, they are often too busy to put in the time to write a good letter. For some committee members, just having a letter of recommendation from Carl Botan, Tim Coombs, Robert Heath, James Grunig, Maureen Taylor, Elizabeth Toth, the surgeon general, or the CEO of a major corporation is enough. For other committee members, a letter needs to sound as if that professional actually wrote it. Be sure that you request letters of recommendation from the best people possible and not just from whoever is convenient or important.
- Avoid hyperbole. Review committee members are usually experts in their fields and will not be fooled by flattery or exaggeration.
- Do not write about your dreams ("As a child I knew that I wanted to work with people ..."), or about how much getting a grant or contract will mean to *you*. Assistantships, contracts, fellowships, and grants are always about meeting the needs of the organization, not your own.
- Unless you are applying to a religious institution (and even then, avoid it) do not say "God bless," "Insha Allah," etc. in your application materials. Religious references have no place in professional documents.
- Do not write about yourself in the third person ("Let me tell you about a young man who ..."; "ABC Consulting believes ...").
- Do not use a narrative style ("Once upon a time there was a group of hardworking consultants ...").
- Never, never, never, never, *never,* never ever, have spelling errors or leave proofing marks on your final draft. If I have to explain this, you should not be calling yourself a "professional."

Letters to the Editor

A letter to the editor is fairly common and usually written when an organization wants to respond to a current events issue, such as charges made against the organization or industry, a proposed policy that might impact the organization, or a local hiring initiative. A letter to the editor is sometimes used strategically to announce new policies or strategic positions; however, as a rule, unless the letter is clearly seen as responsive to issues relevant to news content, an announcement-type letter will never be published.

A letter to the editor is meant to be a timely document. If you send it out a month after an issue, it will fall on deaf ears and will not be published. The public attention span is short. To have impact, a letter to the editor needs to be mailed or delivered the next day.

Additionally, a letter to the *editor* needs to be written to the editor. The tone of the letter should be as an actual response to an issue in the paper; letters that are intended to grandstand or garner publicity will not be published.

Also worth noting is that while most organizational letters to the editor are *signed* by executives, CEOs, and other high-ranking organizational figures, the letters are usually written by communication professionals. On more than one occasion, I have had students express surprise when their boss took the letter to the editor that s/he was asked to write, signed their name to it, and sent the letter off to the newspaper. Students often feel used or cheated: "That was my letter and he just wrote his name on it!" Be aware that virtually everything in public relations is attributed to corporate authors. Although your name is often listed as the contact person on a news release, you will never receive any credit for having written it. No one knows the names of the best public relations professionals in the world because they never appear in front of the camera except when they are representing client interests. Your job is to represent the organization. If you want to receive personal credit, run for public office, then you can take credit for what *your* speechwriters do. Legally, anything you write while working for an organization belongs to the organization (review the discussion of copyright in Chapter 13).

SUGGESTIONS FOR A LETTER TO THE EDITOR

- Try to capture the prose style and tone of the person for whom you are writing the letter.
- Know what the length constraints are for letters to the editor in the source you are writing

for and stick to them. Most newspapers limit letters to about 250 words. If the maximum length of a letter to the editor is 250 words, the newspaper will not publish your 1,000-word *magnum opus*. At best, the source will publish excerpts that *it* selects, robbing you of the ability to control the framing of your message (cf., Hallahan, 1999, on framing).

- The tone of the letter should be conversational and intended for the common citizen. Keep your writing to about the tenth-grade level (check your Flesch-Kincaid reading ease score for this). But, as noted above, write your letter to the *editor*. Advertising pitches and marketing letters will be ignored.
- Avoid uncommon or technical words and never use organizational jargon.
- Use several forms of support (analogies, anecdotes, comparisons, illustrations, quotes, testimony) (see speechwriting in Chapter 9), and employ rhetorical techniques to make the letter as compelling as possible.
- Have something new, insightful, or original to say. Merely agreeing with what someone else has already said is not worthy of publication. Letters usually respond to other people's comments, defend the position of an individual or organization that has been attacked, correct errors, or, occasionally, praise the news source for its good sense and coverage of an issue.

CONCLUSION

Understanding persuasion is a skill of great value for a public relations practitioner. However, understanding persuasion fully is not an easy task. As suggested above, persuasion involves more than just a few tricks. Effective persuaders are skilled interpersonal, group, and public communicators. Skilled persuaders are also skilled researchers and understand how to learn about individuals and publics and target messages effectively. A college-level course in persuasion is recommended as well as a course in rhetoric, if one is available to you. Becoming a skilled persuader will lead to great success in your professional careers.

This chapter has not covered *every* aspect of persuasion. A number of other theories and issues will be taken up in later chapters. However, since there are so many features of persuasion, literally thousands of years of research into persuasion in rhetoric, and almost a hundred years of social scientific and rhetorical research from the modern era, I could easily devote an entire book just to persuasion. Persuasion is part of the writing process in dozens of subtle and obvious ways. Always keep in mind who your target audience is and make an effort to "use all that is there to use," as Burke suggests.

ACTIVITIES

1. Using five images provided by your instructor or downloaded from a stock photography Web site, explain what syllogisms and enthymeme might be constructed if the image were used as part of an advertisement, brochure, or newsletter. Be sure to select images without any words in them.
2. Review the editorials and letters to the editor in your school, local, or national newspaper and identify all of the ideographs that you can find. Do, or how do, the ideographs make the argument more compelling? What would happen if nonideographic language were substituted? Take three of the examples that you found and write the message without an ideographic word or phrase. Can you make the message as compelling?
3. Listen to or read three recent speeches by the U.S. president, a congressperson, or a business professional and write down all of the archetypal metaphors that are used. How common are they? Did the archetypal metaphors make the messages stronger? Were they used well? Explain how a substitution of a normal metaphor might have changed the message (see *Vital Speeches of the Day* for speech manuscripts).
4. Pick up a copy of your student newspaper and read the articles on the editorial page. Identify all of the logical fallacies. Given the context of the messages, do you believe that the strategies were used intentionally, as rhetorical tactics, or were the authors unaware that their arguments were based on logical fallacies? How might you refute the claims that were made, and what persuasive strategies might be best?
5. Write (and mail) a 150–200-word letter to the editor of your student or local newspaper on a topic of interest. Be sure to address the letter to the editor, and stick to a topic relevant to the news source.

6. Write (and send) a four-paragraph (one-page) letter of praise or recommendation on behalf of a fellow student or professor. Follow business letter formatting. Try to incorporate several persuasive strategies and make the letter as compelling as possible.
7. Visit the Web site of an organization of interest and locate information regarding its position on a topic of relevance to the organization. How does it use its definition in its materials? If it does not offer any definitions, what sort of definitions might strengthen its Web content?

NOTES

1. A number of unethical persuasive techniques, called "propaganda" strategies, have been in use for about 75 years and include "appeals to authority, bandwagon, fear, glittering generalities, name-calling, plain folks, testimonials, transfer," and "slippery slope."
2. As a reminder, swipe files, mentioned in Chapter 4, are folders or boxes where you keep samples of effective documents and messages for ideas and inspiration. Whenever you run across an interesting document, whether junk mail, a brochure at a truck stop, an annual report, a magazine advertisement, or a feature story layout, make a copy of the document, or mark the page and throw the entire document into your file/box so that you can go back for ideas and inspiration when you are designing your own documents.
3. In a 2008, 60 *Minutes* interview, Oklahoma billionaire T. Boone Pickens admitted that he funded the Kerry attacks and expressed no remorse about the fact that they were not true. Many organizations face attacks by activists, disgruntled employees, and social cause groups that are not based in fact, but are intended to distract stakeholders and decision makers.
4. The truth is that John Kerry had substantial military combat experience, while George W. Bush was, by all accounts, AWOL from the Texas National Guard because he could not pass a drug test.

Chapter 7

The Basics of Public Relations Research

Aristotle suggested that you should use "all of the available means of persuasion"; Burke suggested that you should "use all that is there to use." Even though they wrote 2,500 years apart, both had in mind something similar: audience adaptation. In Aristotle's day, target audiences were much less complicated. Ancient Greece only allowed adult male citizens to vote (no women, no foreigners, no slaves, no children), and only people who could afford not to work could vote, since participating in politics involved hanging around the *polis* (city center) all day listening to speeches. Today, publics are much more complicated in terms of age, gender, race, ethnicity, interests, and reading or viewing habits.

In order to adapt messages to your public you need to understand them. Research is the reasoning behind the R in the RACE formula, research in MBO, and environmental scanning. This chapter consists primarily of an overview of research methods accompanied by discussions of relevant rhetorical concepts and theories. Since every school's public relations program is different, this chapter may come as a "review," or a "preview," depending upon when you are required to take your research methods class. However, because there are so many different types of research, and because public relations professionals need to know how to conduct several types of specialized research (Delphi studies, SWOT analyses, Nominal Group Technique), this chapter should serve as an important frame-setter and help clarify why we need research in public relations writing.

IDEOLOGY, PARADIGM, NARRATIVE, AND IDEOGRAPHIC LANGUAGE

One of the main reasons that public relations professionals conduct research is to understand key publics, including stakeholders, stakeseekers, lawmakers, and media outlets. If you examine the list of research techniques covered in this chapter, almost every one of them is used to learn about characteristics of publics and enable professionals to craft effective messages. We do research so that we can write effectively, create successful and compelling campaigns, and monitor the environment for organizational issues. But more than trying to "understand" key publics, public relations professionals also work to create (or co-create) the world for others. As suggested earlier in the text, rhetoric shapes reality. As Burke explained, rhetoric is "the process of creating the screens through which we view reality."

Given the rhetorical nature of public relations, much of what public relations professionals write is dedicated to shaping what stakeholders and publics know and believe. Your messages are rhetorical, intended to inform, persuade, and move, and also intended to create the stories (narratives) that internal and external stakeholders will find compelling. As part of our shared narratives, each of us has both an individual view of reality—what Boulding described as an *image* in Chapter 1—as well as the shared images of our ideologies and paradigms.

Ideology refers to the body of doctrine, myth, values, and beliefs that guide individuals, groups, institutions, and social classes. On the most basic level, the Democrat and Republican political views are ideologies. However, ideology includes more than mere political parties. Ideology also includes religion, and beliefs about social conventions and relationships (gender, marriage, family). Thus an "ideology" is a collection of beliefs about the social world. Ideologies are often based on normative beliefs about how the world *should* work: "the poor are lazy and if they would only get jobs they would not be poor ..." or "the rich are not like us ..." Ideology consists of social views about the world, and beliefs about the organizations and agents in society who represent our own interests.

A **paradigm,** or worldview, is similar to an ideology except that paradigms are more personal and represent models, assumptions, beliefs, and values that constitute how individuals and groups view reality. Thus, ideologies are frameworks that describe the social world and the actors in it (which groups can be trusted, who runs things), while paradigms describe the world itself for the community that shares them (what counts as "good" and "bad," which individuals can be trusted). Our ideologies and paradigms influence our mental images of the world. If, for example, we believe that the world is a "mean" place, then we are likely to support calls for increased penalties for criminals, few gun restrictions, etc. Conversely, someone who sees the world optimistically might call for *reform* for criminals and stricter gun laws.

Of course, these examples are an oversimplification. The point here is to appreciate how much individuals' and groups' ideologies and paradigms are impacted by messages that they hear in the news media, from organizational spokespeople, in television commercials, and from opinion leaders and lawmakers. As organizational spokespeople, you will play a role in shaping the reality of others. One of the major ways that organizations play a role in constructing the reality of others is through the stories that they tell. Although many people have never given it much thought, we make sense of the world via the stories that we construct in our heads, our beliefs about who the heroes and villains are, and the piece of mind that we derive from various aspects of our social and family lives.

Narrative Theory

Narrative theory goes back to the work of Walter Fisher (1978, 1984, 1985) and attempts to explain how we make sense of the world as actors on the stage of life. As communication professionals, the messages that we create employ narratives or stories.

Consider, for example, the now famous "I'm a Mac. And I'm a PC. ..." commercials that Apple computers has been running. With each commercial, we see the "actors" (Apple and Microsoft) portrayed in very specific ways. Apple clearly is the hero of the narrative (it *is* Apple's narrative) because he is young, likable, somewhat naïve, friendly, helpful, and most importantly, "more reliable." Microsoft's character is clearly the villain. He is older, quirky (portrayed as uptight), aloof, uncaring to the plight of customers, greedy, and most importantly, he is not as safe and reliable. Microsoft, playing off the narrative that Apple paid to create in its advertisements, started its own batch of "I'm a PC" commercials where instead of going head to head with Apple, they construct a narrative of hip, young, likable *customers* who are on a quest for the best computer. In the Microsoft advertisements, Apple computers are always quickly dismissed by the customers as "too expensive," or "not flexible enough" (a straw man approach), who then gleefully walk away with a new "PC" paid for by the benevolent giant Microsoft.

With very little work, we could construct similar narratives to describe the Walt Disney Company, McDonald's, MTV, Verizon, or any number of other organizations. The reason that we are able to easily identify organizational narratives is first, because we are "homo narrens" or storytelling animals (Vasquez, 1993), and second, because organizations have already meticulously crafted their public messages to harmoniously create particular images. Most organizations cast themselves as the "hero," or sometimes the "underdog," because such archetypal characters resonate with people.

Rhetoric is about helping your audience understand how you are like them, and how their interests and your interests mesh (co-creating reality or "identifying" with stakeholders and publics). For Burke, the process of creating a shared reality is a process called "consubstantiality" (1969b, pp. 20–23). Consubstantiality is when individuals and groups feel that they are essentially the same, that they are of one substance or "co-substantial."

Fisher's narrative paradigm describes how professional communicators construct narratives. According to Fisher, compelling narratives require three features: "narrative fidelity," "narrative probability," and "good reasons." **Narrative fidelity** refers to a story's correspondence with reality. Is the story believable? **Narrative probability** refers to a story's internal coherence. Does the story hang together? **Good reasons** refer to the elements in a story that ring true to an individual's lived experience and worldview. In many ways, what Fisher is describing is what we see at the movies or read in a book. A science fiction story might be believable to a 12-year-old (narrative fidelity) but may lack the critical truth elements to be compelling to a physicist (narrative probability). Similarly, a story might be "unbelievable" (talking animals in cartoons) but hold together because of a coherent structure (fairy tales). The last part of Fisher's narrative paradigm, good reasons, is as important as the others. The most effective narratives have coherent structures, believable events, and also resonate with an audience's lived experiences and ideological backgrounds.

As a professional communicator, you need to understand that coherent narratives are not just something for movies and television commercials. The reason that Nike has the image that it does is largely because of advertising. However, the narrative (or story) that Nike chose to construct did not come from thin air. Organizational leaders and managers worked for many years to hone Nike's image. Similarly, the way that we think about any organization is directly related to the story that is constructed.

Because people have different ideological baggage and worldviews, not everyone can be moved by the same story. This does not mean that an organization should alter the narrative that it is trying to construct, but that organizations need to understand that individuals and publics do not all agree on the status of each organizational hero or villain. The hero (Microsoft) in one story might be the villain (Apple) in another.

For example, Rutgers University in New Brunswick, New Jersey, has a reputation among its student body for not caring about its students. The students actually have a name for how they are mistreated: "The Rutgers Screw." Many students have told me how "no one respects Rutgers because they all know that the school just treats us like numbers." On several occasions, I have explained to students, "when you get outside of New Jersey, where people are not familiar with the school, you will discover that Rutgers has a very different reputation. Many people think that Rutgers is a private school, because of the name, and others, even former students, will identify positively with you because they shared the same experience." The external fiction of many organizations is very different than the internal reality.

Learning to appreciate the role of narrative in your writing is crucial. Your task as a public relations professionals is not to create 20 *different* documents every week, but to create 20 harmonious documents that tell the same story and build on the meta narratives of the organizations and clients you represent. One important part of the narrative-building process is appreciating the subtleties of language and how much meaning is contained in seemingly everyday words and phrases.

Ideographs

Ideographs are symbolic words used in arguments. Ideographs are words like "freedom" and "family" and phrases like "support the troops" that have ideological associations and, on the surface, often seem to imply only one thing. Ideographs, like enthymemes, are difficult to argue with. How can someone argue against "family," "democracy," or "freedom?" Who would argue against a goal that includes "defeating the evil doers," or "liberating the people"? Ideographs are used precisely because they close off debate. Professional communicators use ideographs because they force opponents to accept *your* characterization of events.

According to McGee, the ideograph is a link between language and belief. Ideographs are ordinary-language terms that seem simple and concrete, like "family," or "patriot." In reality, ideographs are abstractions (1980, p. 15). Everyone may implicitly accept that "family" is a good thing; however, when family is unpacked—"single parent families," "abusive families," "dysfunctional families," "same-sex partner families"—we realize that family has many meanings and the assumptions about it are not so clear. Ideographs function because of this ambiguity. Everyone believes in families and patriotism, but not everyone believes that all families are the same, or that all patriots are "former soldiers."

By "link" between language and belief, McGee means an enthymematic link such as what is implied, or left out, when concepts like "freedom" and "liberty" or symbols like the U.S. flag are used to construct arguments (cf., Black, 1970; McGee & Martin, 1983; Wander, 1984). As McGee (1980) explains, ideographs have meaning because of people's lived experiences. "Freedom" probably has more meaning to a war veteran than to a high school student; however, both have probably been raised with similar messages about the concept (p. 16). Ideographs also identify and describe characteristic worldviews held by individuals and groups. As McGee explains:

> No one has ever seen an "equality" strutting up the driveway, so, if "equality" exists at all, it has meaning through its

> specific applications. In other words, we establish a meaning for "equality" by using the word as a description of a certain phenomenon; it has meaning only insofar as our description is acceptable, believable. If asked to make a case for "equality," that is to define the term, we are forced to make reference to its history by detailing the situations for which the word has been an appropriate description. (1980, p. 10)

According to McGee, individuals and leaders who speak for the people frequently invoke ideographic language because of its power to characterize (or sum up) a situation as well as the difficulty that ideographs present opponents who do not want to be seen being against "fairness," or "equality." When "supporting the troops" is used to mean "not saying anything bad about them," disagreeing with governmental policies or holding peaceful antiwar protests can be characterized as un-American or antitroop.

Like symbols, ideographs should be used judiciously; they can be used to create very compelling and powerful messages. When faced with ideographic language by one's opponents, typical responses are redefinition (rejecting the opposition's position entirely), or, when possible, forcing the opposition to clarify what s/he actually means by the ideographic term, which can offer an opening to "stretch" an ideograph to suit your own purposes. Another tool for constructing meaning and better understanding stakeholders is Maslow's hierarchy of needs.

MASLOW'S HIERARCHY OF NEEDS

Maslow's hierarchy of needs is a psychological framework used to explain people's innate needs. From a public relations standpoint, understanding what physiological, psychological, or environmental stage a person might be at in his or her life can give great insight into how s/he might respond to particular messages and what types of issues are of interest and value. The hierarchy is depicted as a pyramid, with physiological needs at the bottom and psychological needs at the top (See Figure 7.1).

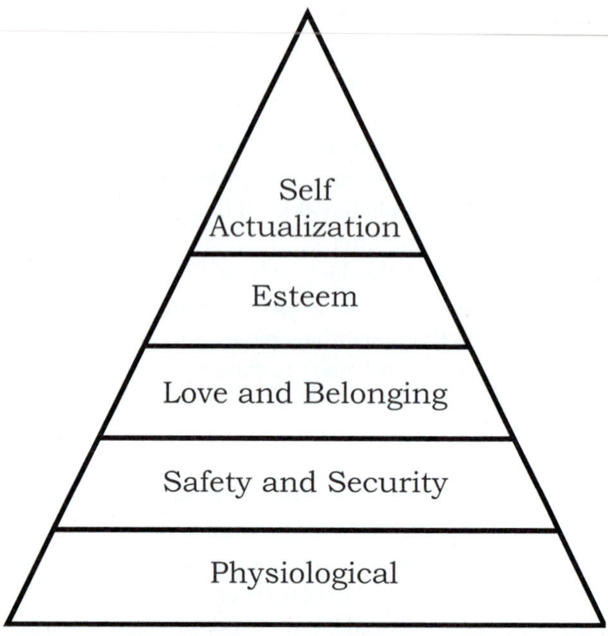

FIGURE 7.1 Maslow's Hierarchy Diagram.

The hierarchy tries to account for what motivates and influences people at different stages of their life. Thus, for a homeless person living on the street, food and water come first, followed by shelter and freedom from harm. A public relations practitioner who is working with an urban aid organization, religious group, or city-based homeless project would likely find it helpful to understand what will "motivate" homeless people by considering where they are on Maslow's hierarchy.

A college student's physiological and safety needs are already met. More typical motivating factors include relational needs (belonging) and all of the issues that go along with that: being perceived as attractive, desirable, confident, keeping up with what is fashionable or cool, and perhaps the esteem needs of getting an education or finding a job.

The problem with a hierarchy, Burke tells us (1966, pp. 15 ff), is that when you are at particular stages, knowing both what you strive for and what you fear is obvious. Those at the top of the hierarchy (or those who think that they are at the top) fear being down. Thus, selling security systems to wealthy, mature (the esteem or self-actualized stage) people is pretty easy. All you have to do is make them afraid of other people and you have a sale. Similarly, selling Yuppies the latest cell phone or prestige auto is also pretty easy, since people at the esteem stage want to be perceived favorably by their peers.

People who are lower on the hierarchy (the "working class," who may never have a rewarding career or aspire to self-actualization), can also be made afraid of falling lower on the hierarchy or motivated to rise higher. Consider how the automobile security system has become standard now (fear), and how advertisers have made nearly everyone feel deserving of indulgences like takeout food, plasma television sets, imported beer, and surround-sound home theatre systems (hope).

As public relations professionals, you do not need to understand Maslow to sell more cellular telephones (the advertising department already knows how to do that), you need to understand Maslow so you can create effective, rewarding, and useful relationships with your publics. You need to understand where stakeholders are in their lives to understand how to communicate with them effectively. Maslow's hierarchy of needs gives communicators insight into motivational appeals as well as fear appeals. The hierarchy can also be useful for understanding how people who are at different life stages see the world.

By this point in your academic career, you probably already know a great deal about research. You may already have taken a research methods class, depending upon the requirements at your school. Although a public relations professional needs to understand an assortment of research techniques, most of the research skills used on an everyday basis in public relations are not very advanced (cf., Lindenman, 2006, www.instituteforpr.org/files/uploads/2006_Planning_Eval.pdf). Informational interviewing, for example, is not a sophisticated skill, but does require practice in order to know how to ask effective questions and useful probing questions.

Public relations professionals, especially those who work for small agencies/firms, must be able to bring themselves up to speed on new areas quickly. For example, say your company wants to bid on a contract to conduct media training in Afghanistan. Organizational members need to be brought up to speed on the military, economic, social, and cultural condition of the region. Additionally, no one in your organization may have experience conducting media training. Thus, in order to effectively bid on the contract, a public relations professional in the agency will need to read articles/books on media training, read government reports about media training efforts in other nations, and perhaps interview some international relations experts. Research should inform everything we plan and write in public relations.

The remainder of this chapter will review most of the fundamental public relations research techniques used by communication professionals. This chapter will also explain the value of each research method to public relations professionals. Hopefully this chapter will be a review for you, but if you have not taken a research methods course yet, this chapter and the next should bring you up to speed in many areas.

PRIMARY AND SECONDARY, QUALITATIVE AND QUANTITATIVE RESEARCH

Primary research, also called original research, is what you find in journal articles and scholarly books rather than in textbooks, newspapers, and magazines and on the World Wide Web.[1] Primary research is conducted to determine the answer to specific questions ("Would the community support a golf course on the site of the botanical garden?" "How many of our customers also use software by our competitors?" "What factors might lure employees to our competitors?" "What words or phrases do our stakeholders find most compelling?"). Any question not already answered somewhere else requires primary research.

Secondary research is essentially research conducted by someone else and organized for the benefit of others. Thus, if you read a newspaper article about Congressman Smith's position on free trade, you are using a secondary source. If you have a meeting with Smith and ask him about trade yourself, you are engaging in primary research. A lot of public relations requires primary research (interviews, telephone calls to verify facts, monitoring blogs and RSS feeds); however, for other information (opinion research, trends, demographic data), secondary research is needed.

Whether you are talking about primary or secondary research, there are two general types of research: quantitative and qualitative. **Quantitative research** has to do with things that can be counted, or "quantified," with tangibles (age, sex, gender, income, number of children, eye color, number of electrons, gravitational forces). In contrast, **qualitative research** is about things that have to be defined or described into existence. Qualitative research deals with qualities, or intangible things: the number of customers who use your product and also believe in environmentally friendly production methods; the types of words or phrases used on Google to search for organizations like yours; the likelihood your organization will be impacted because of a terrorist act, etc. Thus, the *nature* of someone's belief in a higher power is qualitative (it can only be described), but *whether* someone believes in a higher power is quantitative (we can count how many people say they are atheists, agnostics, Buddhists, Catholics, Jews, Latter-Day Saints, Protestants, Muslems, Taoists, Unitarians).

RESEARCH SKILLS FOR PUBLIC RELATIONS

All research begins with an examination of secondary sources (a literature review). Never spend your time reinventing the wheel. If the answer to your question can already be found in an issue of *Public Relations Quarterly*, then do not waste your time or money on interviews or a survey. A thorough literature review should examine all relevant primary sources (journal articles, books, governmental reports, experts, etc.) and secondary sources (newspapers, magazines, blogs, etc.).

One of the mistakes novice practitioners and students make when they are developing their first campaign proposals is to start with surveys (primary research), and an *assumed* target public, rather than examining the secondary research that already exists or conducting targeted interviews with "experts." Surveys seem easy and are often portrayed as a first step: "Let's see what people think...." However, before you can ask what people "think," you have to know what the questions are, and you need to know how to ask the questions. Surveys are rarely a useful starting point, and they are conducted only after you have developed a hypothesis (a belief about something you think is true) to test. Although we see surveys on the nightly news and the Internet every day, television, and Internet surveys are usually conducted symbolically, for entertainment purposes, and to make television viewers and visitors to Web sites feel like their opinions matter (Kent, Harrison, & Taylor, 2006), rather than to allow professionals to learn something of importance.

In reality, gathering reliable survey data is expensive and time-consuming, and can be misleading if the results are not interpreted correctly and informed by secondary research. With the possible exception of information-gathering interviews, which are a fast and generally inexpensive way of learning about the issues in an area, *you always start with secondary research and environmental scanning.* Research techniques like focus groups and surveys come later.

ENVIRONMENTAL SCANNING

Environmental scanning is the practice of scanning the media and social environment (newspapers, television, radio, magazines, e-lists, blogs, newsgroups, social media) for information of value to your organization. Environmental scanning is an ongoing process and not something you only do on Mondays or prior to a campaign or program. Public relations professionals are always on the lookout for stories or information relevant to their industry or organization.

Say you conduct public relations for a home décor company. Your environmental scanning will include reading newspaper and magazines stories about home decorating, reviewing all of the magazines and trade journals in your area of specialization (there are dozens), attending "home expos" and seminars where professionals from across your industry gather, reading books on design, and keeping up on the latest home design trends. You will be expected to know who the major home decorating organizations and professionals are in your city, state, region, nation, and perhaps even internationally. You will also be expected to know about home decorating Web sites, electronic mailing lists from various organizations and vendors, and be familiar with online news and discussion groups about home decorating. In short, you should know everything.

Of course, an understanding of everything is not expected on the first day, especially if you are new to an area. However, within a few weeks or months, your knowledge should have expanded dramatically, and within a year you should be *very* knowledgeable. Every communication professional, from journalists, public information officers, writers, and communications specialists in the military to advertising executives, marketers, politicians, and, of course, public relations professionals, engage in environmental scanning every day.

QUALITATIVE RESEARCH

Qualitative research is research that requires interpretation of the data and facts in order for the information to have meaning. Facts do not speak for themselves. If you learn that 90 percent of all North Americans believe in God (2003, <www.harrisinteractive.com/harris_poll/index.asp?PID=359>; see also, 2006 data, www.harrisinteractive.com/news/allnewsbydate.asp?NewsID=1131) and that 43 percent report weekly attendance to religious services, but that in reality, only about 25 percent of all Americans *actually* attend church (half lie), the facts, or quantitative "statistics," do not explain *why*—only what is happening (cf., www. religioustolerance.org/rel_rate.htm). Only qualitative data (information about people's beliefs, values, and attitudes) can help explain the question of "why." The most common forms of qualitative research are archival research, interviews, and content analyses.

Archival Research

Archival research involves reading, studying, and consulting primary research sources—the same thing you do when you write a class paper. Contrary to popular belief, the Word Wide Web *is not* the place to start archival research, but the *Internet* is, and you need to understand the difference.

The Internet consists of all of the interconnected computers in the world that hold the information you see on the World Wide Web and allow the information to be moved from place to place. The Web is just an interface for accessing the Internet. The relationship is a bit like broadcast television versus cable. The television allows you to see "shows" but the shows are not on the television, they are owned by content providers who essentially lease them to broadcasters. To have access to the best movies, you first have to pay to see them in the theatres, then they might be released on DVDs or online, and then, finally, after months, and in many cases years, movies reach television (cable first, then network). The Internet is similar. Internet research is housed on organizational databases and only the "not very valuable" content is given away for free. If the information were valuable, it would be sold like everything else on the Internet.[2]

Archival research involves what we might call nowadays "real research." You read. You read books, you read journal articles, you read dissertations and theses, you read government documents and reports, and you read magazines and newspapers. Primarily, however, you consult reliable and credible sources.

How much archival research is necessary before you "know enough?" That depends upon how complicated the issue you are researching is. To understand why the Palestinians and Israelis are killing each other is at least a half-dozen books and a dozen articles. To understand blogs is one good journal article and one magazine article. You consult as many sources as it takes to become an "expert," or at least "qualified" to talk about an issue or problem and to solve it.

Depending upon the type of organization that you work for, you may be called upon to conduct a lot of research, perhaps preparing reports on the status of campaigns or organizational programs, or developing white papers outlining your organization's position on social or public policy issues.

Reports

Reports vary a great deal in terms of rhetorical goals (to inform, to persuade, to evaluate, to convey research results, etc.) but in general, reports are similar to what you have written in college. Depending upon the purpose of the report, a report may very from a few pages in memo form to 50 or 1,000 pages with appendices, tables, references, etc. There are three basic types of reports: informal, formal, and research.

The basic "informal" report structure (as in, "get me a progress report on how the campaign is going") consists of an introduction, body, and conclusion. Often reports like this are put into memo form, with bulleted lists and short explanations of issues. As with all memos, you should start with a brief introductory paragraph that explains what the report is about and previews each section. Follow this paragraph with the body content and be sure that each paragraph deals with a separate point/issue (one idea per paragraph). Finally, conclude with a brief summary, making an effort to anticipate and address the questions that the recipient of the report might have ("Are we succeeding?" "Is this money well spent?" "Should we continue?"). Reports are not just summaries but also analyses. Headings and subheadings are expected in reports.

Be sure to introduce bulleted or numbered lists in paragraph form and with complete sentences. Do not just have a heading and a bulleted list. In no way are a bunch of bullet points a report. Take advantage of your introduction and the chance to introduce and frame each section of the report.

For formal reports, the entire document is expanded to include front material, including a cover letter (or letter of transmittal), title page, table of contents (TOC), lists of tables, figures, and diagrams, and an executive summary (see below) or abstract. The body of a formal report typically consists of a standard introduction, body, and conclusion format, with the body divided up into sections or chapters as needed. Finally, the back-end material includes (often in this order) references, appendices, tables, glossary (if appropriate), and notes.

The formal report is typically a more professional document. Such reports are commissioned by organizations in response to changing market trends, evaluations of competition, reports to lawmakers about industries/competition, and for many other reasons. The formal research report is typically more academic looking and more official (more like an essay or a master's thesis than a memo). "Recommendations" are also made at the end of formal reports. The formal research report is often professionally printed and bound with a cardstock cover and glue or staple binding, or placed in a three-ring binder.

Research reports give the results of scientific studies, experiments, stakeholder research, or other formal research questions. The purpose of an organizational research report is to report what was learned and what the implications/consequences are for the organization. In almost no cases are public relations professionals concerned with academic questions such as advances in theory, or lengthy discussions of methodological issues. Rather, research reports focus on what the results of the research mean for the organization, its future progress, and how much the organization might have to spend to deal with the issue.

Research reports often follow a standard academic structure (like what is found in the American Psychological Association's (APA) publication manual (see Chapter 3 on APA style). Research reports often include an abundance of figures and tables designed to clarify the content of the report, and may also include the following sections: executive summary, introduction, background, literature review or previous research, research questions or hypothesis, methodology, results, discussion, recommendations and conclusion, bibliography, appendices, tables, and notes. You will find reading the first hundred pages of the APA guide useful for advice on the proper tone, writing style, and other technical issues. You will also find it helpful to review a number of research reports before you embark on writing one or designing a research project.

The tone of all research reports is formal. Contractions, as always, should be avoided and references and support are expected. Even with informal reports the tone should be formal. This does not mean that you should try to write like a professor does in a journal article (you should not); a style more like that of a book is appropriate in most cases. As with all reports, structure is important. One of the most important parts of the report is making it easy to follow. Be sure to use headings, subheadings, and a table of contents (TOC) when appropriate. Also, be sure that you include an **executive summary** on reports longer than a few pages. See Figure 7.2.

The purpose of the *executive summary* is to provide a concise summary of a proposal/report so that decision-makers and managers have an overview of the project without having to read a lengthy document. Executive summaries are written for individuals who do not have time to read lengthy reports. Executive summaries should be written with complete sentences and in paragraph form. However, some items, like key findings, may be placed in bulleted lists. In most cases, an organizational decision maker who reads a report wants to see answers to the following questions in the executive summary: "What is important?" "Why should we care, what does this have to do with us?" "What should we do?" or "What can be done, if anything?" And, "What will it cost?"

WHITE PAPERS AND POSITION PAPERS

The term "white paper" is used to describe a variety of documents, including "fact sheet"–like documents describing procedures or practices; "technical papers" explaining chemical, biological, mechanical, and other processes; and what might be called "position papers." You will find examples of thousands of documents of all three varieties labeled "white papers" on the Internet. See Figure 7.3.

The type of white paper that I will describe here is the "position paper" variety. The other documents mentioned above are really just various types of fact sheets and technical papers (also a type of fact sheet) that are erroneously called "white papers." Traditionally, a white paper was so-called because it was printed on simple, unadorned white paper and expressed an individual or organization's position on an issue. The best examples of white papers are those produced by politicians outlining their positions on issues.

Like a research report, a white paper contains citations, sources, and support for the claims that are made. However, unlike a research report, which is more like a journal article, the purpose of a white paper, or position paper, is to make an argument. The white paper lays out an organization's position with supporting materials, facts, figures, data, etc. White papers are persuasive, polemical documents. Moreover, white papers are intended for educated audiences. "Joe Six-Pack" is not likely to read a white paper outlining Wal-Mart's position on the importation of Chinese goods.

Given that white papers are primarily read by educated and informed citizens, and given that the research on persuasion suggests that messages sent to educated publics who might hear arguments on both sides of an issue should avoid straw man arguments and name calling, organizational white papers should appear balanced and present both sides of an issue.

A typical argumentative structure is to present your side of the issue, present the opposition's side, refute the opposition's side, and reaffirm your own position. In reality, many organizations present the opposition's side as straw man arguments or present them unfairly. Since primarily educated audiences read white papers, straw man arguments should be avoided.

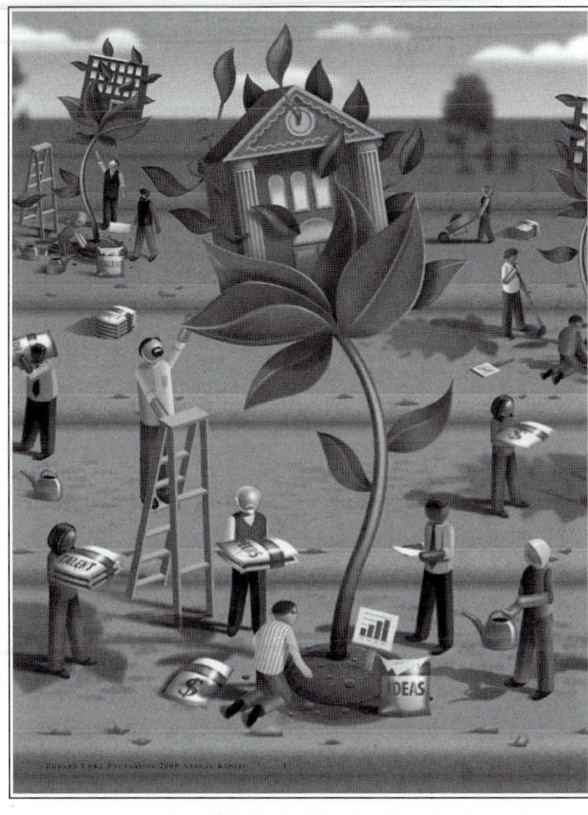

GROWING OPPORTUNITIES

Much like the entrepreneurs we serve, the Edward Lowe Foundation has gone through an evolution. Our mission—to champion the entrepreneurial spirit—has remained constant during the past two decades, but we continue to search for the best way to accomplish that mission and grow opportunities for companies, organizations and communities.

From the beginning, the foundation has been involved in a wide variety of programs, ranging from youth entrepreneurship and mentoring programs for college students to policy conferences and publishing. Although these were all worthwhile programs, we realized that the foundation couldn't be all things to all people.

With that in mind, the foundation has narrowed its focus to second-stage companies, a segment of entrepreneurs we believe to have the greatest positive impact on the U.S. economy. We also embrace the concept of economic gardening, in which communities provide a nurturing environment for their existing businesses as a means to cultivate new jobs.

The foundation now delivers its programs, such as Companies to Watch℠, educational retreats and PeerSpectives® roundtables, through regional entrepreneur support organizations. Working through their existing networks enables us to be more efficient with the foundation's resources and still directly touch entrepreneurs with our programs.

I'm very excited about this direction because it means we can have greater impact and reach more second-stage companies. And that's important because there is surprisingly little support or recognition for this important group.

Granted, many people have ideas for new products and services, but few act on those ideas. In contrast, second-stagers are out in the trenches creating new technology, products and services—and new jobs in the process. They are the engine driving the U.S. economy.

By providing more resources and support for these entrepreneurs, we believe the foundation can be a catalyst for innovation and change to help communities throughout the country become more vibrant places to work and live. In the process, we see many opportunities for growth within our own organization, and Ed would be very pleased with that.

Darlene Lowe

Darlene Lowe
CEO and Chairman

2 | Edward Lowe Foundation 2006 Annual Report

ABOUT THE FOUNDATION

Ed and Darlene Lowe established the Edward Lowe Foundation in 1985. They envisioned an organization that would leverage entrepreneurship as a strategy for economic growth, community development and economically independent individuals.

Today the foundation conducts educational programs and provides information and recognition for second-stage entrepreneurs—companies that have moved beyond the startup phase with the potential and desire to grow. We encourage economic gardening, an entrepreneur-centered strategy providing balance to the traditional approach of business recruitment.

The foundation is also committed to preserving the natural resources and historically significant structures at Big Rock Valley, its 2,600-acre home in southwest Michigan.

The stories and case studies presented in this annual report illustrate how the foundation's educational programs, information and activities are enhancing the capabilities of entrepreneurs, the organizations assisting them, and the communities in which they live.

Edward Lowe Foundation 2006 Annual Report | 3

FIGURE 7.2 Sample Report—PDF of Government Reports.

PEW INTERNET & AMERICAN LIFE PROJECT

Bloggers

A portrait of the internet's new storytellers

July 19, 2006

Amanda Lenhart, Senior Research Specialist

Susannah Fox, Associate Director

PEW INTERNET & AMERICAN LIFE PROJECT 1615 L ST., NW – SUITE 700 WASHINGTON, D.C. 20036

202-419-4500 http://www.pewinternet.org/

Summary of Findings

Blogging is bringing new voices to the online world.

A telephone survey of a nationally-representative sample of bloggers has found that blogging is inspiring a new group of writers and creators to share their voices with the world. Some 54% of bloggers say that they have never published their writing or media creations anywhere else; 44% say they have published elsewhere. While generally youthful, these writers otherwise represent a broad demographic spectrum of people who cite a variety of topics and motives for their blogging.

Eight percent of internet users, or about 12 million American adults, keep a blog. Thirty-nine percent of internet users, or about 57 million American adults, read blogs – a significant increase since the fall of 2005.

Telephone surveys capture a current snapshot of an ever-changing blog universe.

The Pew Internet & American Life Project deployed two strategies to interview bloggers.

First, as part of our standard random-digit dial tracking surveys about internet use among a nationally-representative sample of American adults, we asked respondents if they maintain a blog. Then, we called back these self-identified bloggers between July 2005 and February 2006. Seventy-one percent of those called back completed this second telephone survey, which focused exclusively on blogging. The remaining 29% said they were no longer keeping a blog or were not willing to take another survey, and we eliminated them from the callback interviews. This strategy yielded a relatively small number of respondents (n=233) but allowed us to ask in-depth questions of a nationally-representative sample of bloggers. Numbers cited in this report are based on the callback survey unless specifically noted.

Our second strategy for preparing this report involved fielding additional random-digit surveys between November 2005 and April 2006 to capture an up-to-date estimate of the percentage of internet users who are currently blogging. These large-scale telephone surveys yielded a sample of 7,012 adults, which included 4,753 internet users, 8% of whom are bloggers.

This Pew Internet & American Life Project report is based on the findings of daily tracking surveys on Americans' use of the internet and a special callback survey of bloggers. All numerical data was gathered through telephone interviews conducted by Princeton Survey Research Associates. The tracking surveys were conducted between November-December 2005 and February-April 2006, with a combined sample of 7,012 adults, aged 18 and older. For results based on internet users (n=4,753), one can say with 95% confidence that the error attributable to sampling and other random effects is +/- 3%. For tracking survey results based on bloggers (n=308) the margin of error is +/- 7%. The blogger callback survey was conducted between July 5, 2005, and February 17, 2006, among a sample of 233 bloggers, age 18 and older. The margin of error for this sample is +/- 7%.

Pew Internet & American Life Project, 1615 L St., NW, Suite 700, Washington, DC 20036
202-419-4500 http://www.pewinternet.org

Summary of Findings

While many well-publicized blogs focus on politics, the most popular topic among bloggers is their life and experiences.

The Pew Internet Project blogger survey finds that the American blogosphere is dominated by those who use their blogs as personal journals. Most bloggers do not think of what they do as journalism.

Most bloggers say they cover a lot of different topics, but when asked to choose one main topic, 37% of bloggers cite "my life and experiences" as a primary topic of their blog. Politics and government ran a very distant second with 11% of bloggers citing those issues of public life as the main subject of their blog.

Entertainment-related topics were the next most popular blog-type, with 7% of bloggers, followed by sports (6%), general news and current events (5%), business (5%), technology (4%), religion, spirituality or faith (2%), a specific hobby or a health problem or illness (each comprising 1% of bloggers). Other topics mentioned include opinions, volunteering, education, photography, causes and passions, and organizations.

The blogging population is young, evenly split between women and men, and racially diverse.

The following demographic data comes from two surveys of internet users conducted in November-December 2005 and February-April 2006 (n=7,012).

- The most distinguishing characteristic of bloggers is their youth. More than half (54%) of bloggers are under the age of 30. Like the internet population in general, however, bloggers are evenly divided between men and women, and more than half live in the suburbs. Another third live in urban areas and a scant 13% live in rural regions.
- Another distinguishing characteristic is that bloggers are less likely to be white than the general internet population. Sixty percent of bloggers are white, 11% are African American, 19% are English-speaking Hispanic and 10% identify as some other race. By contrast, 74% of internet users are white, 9% are African American, 11% are English-speaking Hispanic and 6% identify as some other race.

Relatively small groups of bloggers view blogging as a public endeavor.

Despite the public nature of creating a blog, most bloggers view it as a personal pursuit.

- 55% of bloggers blog under a pseudonym, and 46% blog under their own name.
- 84% of bloggers describe their blog as either a "hobby" or just "something I do, but not something I spend a lot of time on."
- 59% of bloggers spend just one or two hours per week tending their blog. One in ten bloggers spend ten or more hours per week on their blog.

Bloggers -ii- Pew Internet & American Life Project

Summary of Findings

- 52% of bloggers say they blog mostly for themselves, not for an audience. About one-third of bloggers (32%) say they blog mostly for their audience.

The main reasons for keeping a blog are creative expression and sharing personal experiences.

The majority of bloggers cite an interest in sharing stories and expressing creativity. Just half say they are trying to influence the way other people think.

More Blog to Share Experiences Than to Earn Money

Please tell me if this is a reason you personally blog, or not:	Major reason	Minor reason	Not a reason
To express yourself creatively	52%	25%	23%
To document your personal experiences or share them with others	50	26	24
To stay in touch with friends and family	37	22	40
To share practical knowledge or skills with others	34	30	35
To motivate other people to action	29	32	38
To entertain people	28	33	39
To store resources or information that is important to you	28	21	52
To influence the way other people think	27	24	49
To network or to meet new people	16	34	50
To make money	7	8	85

Source: Pew Internet & American Life Project Blogger Callback Survey, July 2005-February 2006. N=233. Margin of error is ±7%.

Only one-third of bloggers see blogging as a form of journalism. Yet many check facts and cite original sources.

- 34% of bloggers consider their blog a form of journalism, and 65% of bloggers do not.
- 57% of bloggers include links to original sources either "sometimes" or "often."
- 56% of bloggers spend extra time trying to verify facts they want to include in a post either "sometimes" or "often."

Bloggers -iii- Pew Internet & American Life Project

FIGURE 7.2 (Continued) *Source*: PEW Internet & American Life Project: *Bloggers A portrait of the internet's new storytellers* <www.pewinternet.org/%7E/media//Files/Reports/2006/PIP%20Bloggers%20Report%20July%2019%202006.pdf.pdf>.

108TH CONGRESS 1st Session | COMMITTEE PRINT | COMMITTEE PRINT 108–D

COMPILATION OF SELECTED ACTS WITHIN THE JURISDICTION OF THE COMMITTEE ON ENERGY AND COMMERCE

COMMUNICATIONS LAW

As Amended Through December 31, 2002

INCLUDING

COMMUNICATIONS ACT OF 1934
TELECOMMUNICATIONS ACT OF 1996
COMMUNICATIONS SATELLITE ACT OF 1962
NATIONAL TELECOMMUNICATIONS AND INFORMATION ADMINISTRATION ORGANIZATION ACT
TELEPHONE DISCLOSURE AND DISPUTE RESOLUTION ACT
COMMUNICATIONS ASSISTANCE FOR LAW ENFORCEMENT ACT
ADDITIONAL COMMUNICATIONS STATUTES
SELECTED PROVISIONS FROM THE UNITED STATES CODE

PREPARED FOR THE USE OF THE

COMMITTEE ON ENERGY AND COMMERCE
U.S. HOUSE OF REPRESENTATIVES

APRIL 2003

Table of Contents

COMMUNICATIONS ACT OF 1934

Title I—General Provisions

Title II—Common Carriers

Part I. Common Carrier Regulation

v

TABLE OF CONTENTS

CHILDREN'S ONLINE PRIVACY PROTECTION ACT OF 1998

Title XIII—Children's Online Privacy Protection

TITLE III OF THE BALANCED BUDGET ACT OF 1997

Title III—Communications and Spectrum Allocation Provisions

TELECOMMUNICATIONS ACT OF 1996

Title II—Broadcast Services

Title III—Cable Services

Title IV—Regulatory Reform

Title V—Obscenity and Violence

SUBTITLE B—VIOLENCE

SUBTITLE C—JUDICIAL REVIEW

Title VI—Effect on Other Laws

xi

COMMUNICATIONS ACT OF 1934, AS AMENDED

AN ACT To provide for the regulation of interstate and foreign communication by wire or radio, and for other purposes.

Be it enacted by the Senate and House of Representatives of the United States of America in Congress assembled,

TITLE I—GENERAL PROVISIONS

SEC. 1. [47 U.S.C. 151] PURPOSES OF ACT, CREATION OF FEDERAL COMMUNICATIONS COMMISSION.

For the purpose of regulating interstate and foreign commerce in communication by wire and radio so as to make available, so far as possible, to all the people of the United States, without discrimination on the basis of race, color, religion, national origin, or sex, a rapid, efficient, Nation-wide, and world-wide wire and radio communication service with adequate facilities at reasonable charges, for the purpose of the national defense, for the purpose of promoting safety of life and property through the use of wire and radio communication, and for the purpose of securing a more effective execution of this policy by centralizing authority heretofore granted by law to several agencies and by granting additional authority with respect to interstate and foreign commerce in wire and radio communication, there is hereby created a commission to be known as the "Federal Communications Commission," which shall be constituted as hereinafter provided, and which shall execute and enforce the provisions of this Act.

SEC. 2. [47 U.S.C. 152] APPLICATION OF ACT.

(a) The provisions of this act shall apply to all interstate and foreign communication by wire or radio and all interstate and foreign transmission of energy by radio, which originates and/or is received within the United States, and to all persons engaged within the United States in such communication or such transmission of energy by radio, and to the licensing and regulating of all radio stations as hereinafter provided; but it shall not apply to persons engaged in wire or radio communication or transmission in the Canal Zone, or to wire or radio communication or transmission wholly within the Canal Zone. The provisions of this Act shall apply with respect to cable service, to all persons engaged within the United States in providing such service, and to the facilities of cable operators which relate to such service, as provided in title VI.

(b) Except as provided in sections 223 through 227, inclusive, and section 332, and subject to the provisions of section 301 and title VI, nothing in this Act shall be construed to apply or to give the Commission jurisdiction with respect to (1) charges, classifications, practices, services, facilities, or regulations for or in connection with intrastate communication service by wire or radio of any

3

FIGURE 7.2 (Continued)

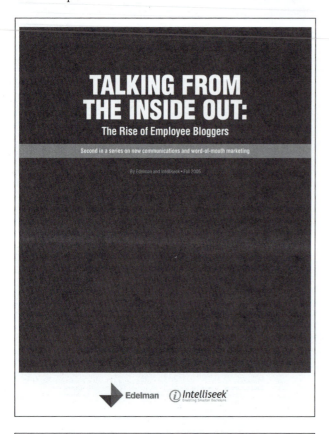

TALKING FROM THE INSIDE OUT:

The Rise of Employee Bloggers

Second in a series on new communications and word-of-mouth marketing

By Edelman and Intelliseek • Fall 2005

Edelman Intelliseek Enabling Smarter Decisions

Table of Contents

The Rise and Effective Management of Employee Bloggers 2

INTRODUCTION

The rise of the blogosphere has the potential to empower employees in ways not unlike the rise of labor unions in the late 19th and early 20th centuries. Although more subtle than those fundamental shifts in the labor-management dynamic, employee bloggers, in many cases, have tipped the balance of influence in their favor to establish levels of credibility that many CEOs can only dream of.

When trying to understand why bloggers have taken the communications reins and seem to be here to stay, one should consider the results of Edelman's 2005 Trust Survey. Edelman found that by a 3-to-1 margin, people are far more likely to trust "average people like me" than to trust authority figures such as CEOs. Employees at all levels have suddenly found themselves in powerful positions to advocate either for or against their companies' products, policies and stances – and have found that people are listening to what they have to say.

Indeed, a 2003 study by McKinsey & Co. found that 67 percent of consumer goods sales are based on word-of-mouth, highlighting the role that a company's employees can play to promote sales or discourage them through online comments. And a 2004 Intelliseek/Forrester study revealed that consumers trust word-of-mouth recommendations far more than they trust traditional marketing/advertising. Word-of-mouth recommendations represent the most trusted form of advertising with the highest impact,[1] suggesting that people would rather hear about real experiences and perspectives than marketing speak.

Employee blogs have helped enhance the reputation of their employers (as in the cases of Microsoft, Sun Microsystems and Stonyfield Farms). Conversely, companies have seen their reputations damaged by high-profile firings of employee bloggers (as in the cases of Google, Delta Air Lines, Waterstone's and Friendster). CEO blogs are growing in frequency[2] as a credible way to reach both internal and external audiences. Blogs are establishing in the online world much of the value that public relations has brought traditionally.

As the potential assets of employee bloggers become apparent, so do the corresponding liabilities. Blogs can influence news, analysts and regulators. Blog information also rises with alarming speed to the top of search engine placements due to sites' frequent updates and concentration of similar keywords. Organizations need to have a well-formed point of view on how employee blogging and CEO blogging fit into their communications mix, and need to put policies or guidelines in place to enable blogging to happen in a more controlled – and ultimately productive – way.

This white paper seeks to explore the phenomenon of employee blogging, how companies are coping with this new form of internal and external communication, and how organizations can harness the power of employee blogging to their benefit. We'll also review blogs that communicators should be interacting with regularly, commonly used terms of the blogosphere and resources for instituting blogging policies, guidelines and platforms.

[1] Forrester Research, Inc. and Intelliseek

[2] Edelman 2005 New Frontiers in Employee Communications Survey

WHY BLOG?

An estimated 34 million blogs will exist by the end of 2005[3], many of them in developed countries where the number of blogs is doubling nearly each year. The Japanese government estimates 3.35 million blogs currently exist in Japan and that the number will double by 2007. France is estimated to have somewhere between 3 to 4 million blogs and Germany has an estimated 200,000 to 300,000 and is growing quickly. This phenomenon is clearly no longer limited to the United States, which was long the leader in blog innovation and growth.

As one might expect, the millions of blogs around the world cover every topic imaginable (and even some unimaginable!). This white paper focuses on the narrow slice of the blogosphere created by employee and CEO bloggers, most of whom are blogging for one or more of these reasons[4]:

- **Become the Expert**
  Position themselves and their company as the thought leader of their industry.
- **Personalize Customer Relationships**
  In a forum where the main objective is not to sell, they'll have a more personal relationship with their customers. Blogs are a fast way to join the customers' discussions, provide tips and insights or receive feedback.
- **Provide Trusted Context When There is News — Good or Bad**
  By having public-facing blogs, a company develops a trusting relationship with its customers. When the company has good news, customers will turn to the bloggers they already trust for interpretation. When there is bad news, nothing can better aid crisis management than already having trusting relationships with customers.
- **Improve Media Relations**
  It's every PR consultant's dream to create a channel where media regularly check what a company has to say, instead of media just being passive – sometimes indifferent – recipients of press releases.

[3] Pew Internet and American Life Project, 2005

[4] CorporateBlogging.Info, 2005 (http://www.corporateblogging.info/basics/why/)

Blogs 101

Weblogs, or blogs for short, are easily published, personal Web sites that serve as sources of commentary, opinion and uncensored, unfiltered sources of information on a variety of topics. Each new entry is called a "post," and posts appear on a blog page in reverse chronological order. Blog posts typically are characterized by numerous links to other pieces of information, including other blogs, news stories, images/photos, commentaries, videos and audio clips. Blogs also have other distinguishing characteristics, including a calendar or archives and a permanent Web address for each post (called a permalink). While primarily a one-way communications channel, many blogs do allow readers to post comments and many blogs expand their reach by being linked to other blogs on related topics. This collective conversation is called the blogosphere and it's one of the fastest growing areas of new content on the Internet. The term Web log was coined in 1997 by Internet writer Jorn Barger, with the shorter term "blog" first appearing in 1999.

For more information on blogs and influence on the media landscape, go to //www.edelman.com/insights to download our first white paper called "Trust 'Media': How Real People Are Finally Being Heard."

FIGURE 7.3 Sample White Papers.

TYPOGRAPHY PRIMER

What's in a Letter

Every serious subject has a language of its own. Typography is no exception. The following diagram shows a few terms used to talk about letterforms. Many more appear in the Glossary of Typographic Terms at the end of this document. These terms let you discuss type like an expert.

Serif and Sans Serif

The serif, or cross-line at the end of a stroke, probably dates from early Rome. Father Edward Catich proposed in his seminal work, *The Origin of the Serif*, that the serif is an artifact of brushing letters onto stone before cutting them. Serif types are useful in text because the serifs help distinguish individual letters and provide continuity for the reader's eye.

Serifs come in many styles. Compare the tapered serifs of Kepler® to the slab serifs of Chaparral® and the wedge serifs of Warnock.™

Kepler Chaparral Warnock

Typefaces without serifs are called sans serif (sans is French for without) designs. The first sans serif type design is credited to William Caslon in England in 1816. Sans serif designs are also sometimes referred to as gothic or grotesque designs.

Myriad® Cronos® Ocean Sans™

x-height

Traditionally, x-height is the height of the lowercase letter x. It affects the feel of a typeface, how many characters fit on a line, and depending on how the type is set, how easily your text can be read. At very small point sizes, a font with a larger x-height is easier to read, everything else being equal. Compare the following examples of Adobe Jenson,™ Utopia,® and Minion,® all at a point size of 10:

You can't really talk about type without talking about x-height. Simply put, x-height is the height of the lowercase letters, excluding the ascenders and descenders. Unlike point size, x-height is not a unit of measurement. Rather, it's a proportional description of the lowercase letters. A typeface with a large x-height simply means the lowercase letters are proportionally large in relation to the ascenders and descenders.

Adobe Jenson 10-point type / 13-point leading (10/13)

You can't really talk about type without talking about x-height. Simply put, x-height is the height of the lower-case letters, excluding the ascenders and descenders. Unlike point size, x-height is not a unit of measurement. Rather, it's a proportional description of the lowercase letters. A typeface with a large x-height simply means the lowercase letters are proportionally large in relation to the ascenders and descenders.

Utopia 10/13

You can't really talk about type without talking about x-height. Simply put, x-height is the height of the lowercase letters, excluding the ascenders and descenders. Unlike point size, x-height is not a unit of measurement. Rather, it's a proportional description of the lowercase letters. A typeface with a large x-height simply means the lowercase letters are proportionally large in relation to the ascenders and descenders.

Minion 10/13

TYPOGRAPHY PRIMER 3 www.adobe.com/type

Word and Letter Spacing

You can also adjust word and letter spacing to improve legibility. Although typefaces are designed with the correct spacing between characters for general use, special situations can result in the type looking crowded or too loose. For example, words printed in all UPPERCASE tend to look too tight because the designer assumed that uppercase and lowercase letters would be mixed. If your application allows you to adjust letter spacing, you should add a small amount of letter space to words printed in all uppercase.

LETTERSPACE LETTERSPACE

Some letter combinations, particularly in words set in capitals, result in awkward spacing unless they are kerned. Kerning is the adjustment of space between pairs of letters. Kerning is especially important at large point sizes. As the characters are enlarged, so is the space between them.

AVOID
AVOID

Task Toolkit 118
Task Toolkit 118

Word spacing, the space between words, should be constant in flush left, flush right, or centered text. However, for justified text, word spacing varies from line to line to keep margins even.

To aid readability, it's important to keep word spacing as consistent as possible—even if it means hyphenating words. Tight word spacing lets you place more text on the page, but can make it difficult to distinguish words from each other. Loose word spacing fills up a page with a small amount of text, but the text becomes harder to read as the words begin to look disconnected.

When you justify a column of type, never allow letterspacing to vary. Each letter is designed with just the amount of space it needs to look right and be most legible. Watch that word spaces don't create awkward gaps or rivers. They are disruptive to comfortable reading. Choose a column width, typeface, and point size that work to enhance readbility.

Uneven word spacing

When you justify a column of type, never allow letter-spacing to vary. Each letter is designed with just the amount of space it needs to look right and be most legible. Watch that word spaces don't create awkward gaps or rivers. They are disruptive to comfortable reading. Choose a column width, typeface, and point size that work to enhance readbility.

More consistent word spacing, better typographic color

TYPOGRAPHY PRIMER 6 www.adobe.com/type

Times Kepler Adobe Jenson Ellington
Chaparral Bembo Utopia ITC Veljovic

While some of the differences between serif text fonts seem almost insignificant when single words are isolated, each of these fonts has a distinct look and feel when applied to extended copy. Some look more (or less) modern, formal, or just better than others in a given situation. Having a wide variety of serif text faces to choose from means that you'll be able to most effectively convey the intended message of any publication or document.

Choosing Fonts for Headlines

You have many more options in style and flavor when choosing fonts for headlines. Headlines are arguably the most important part of a publication—whether or not they're understood at a glance can determine if anything else is read (or looked at), regardless of how easy or hard it is to read the remaining information. Considerations beyond readability—such as the publication's style, content, or other design considerations—will also affect your choice of headline fonts.

Serif versus Sans Serif

There is virtually no difference in the readability of headlines set in serif versus sans serif typefaces (see *Type and Layout* by Colin Wheildon, Strathmoor Press). Other typographic considerations, such as whether or not the headline is set only in capitals versus mixed (upper- and lowercase) will have a more dramatic impact than whether or not your typeface has serifs. Headlines that are set in capitals are significantly harder to read than those of mixed case.

HEADLINES SET IN ALL CAPS ARE SIGNIFICANTLY HARDER TO READ THAN MIXED CASE

Headlines Set in All Caps are Significantly Harder to Read than Mixed Case

Display and Decorative Typefaces

Many display and decorative typefaces are eye-catching and visually pleasing, but can be hard to read. Should they be used in headlines? If you consider readability alone—probably not. But many display and decorative typefaces are very effective at attracting attention—which may be your main goal when you are designing for competitive spaces such as magazine layouts. You must balance readability with the attention-grabbing ability of a display or decorative typeface.

Having a wide variety of display and decorative typefaces to choose from will keep your creative options open and help ensure that you can convey the intended message of the publication.

Calcite™ Pro
Blue Island™
Voluta® Script
Spring™
Shuriken Boy®

TYPOGRAPHY PRIMER 11 www.adobe.com/type

Reversed Text

For print publications, white text on a black background should be used sparingly, and never at small sizes. Similarly, for web projects and video titling jobs, white text on a black background is an effective way to grab attention, and works well when there is a minimum amount of text.

Reversed type

Avoid reversing small type or type with thin strokes or serifs that may fill in. You may want to letterspace bold, condensed faces slightly.

Using Styles

Styles are paragraph descriptors that specify, for example, what font to use and how much to indent. If your design application supports styles, you can build a set to give all your documents a consistent look.

When styles are applied to your documents, you can easily change the entire look of a document just by changing the style definitions.

Keeping It Simple

Good document design is mainly a combination of common sense and keeping things simple. Look at attractive examples of documents that are similar to what you're trying to create. The following list explains some basic rules.

- Long lines of text are hard to read. Generally, a line should have 55 to 60 characters, or 9 to 10 words. Try multiple columns or, if you are stuck with a long line length, increase the leading slightly to make it easier for the eye to move from line to line.
- White space on the page makes your document cleaner-looking and easier to read.
- Use indents and bullets to highlight important points. Use headings and subheadings to help your readers find the information they're interested in.
- Avoid using more than two type families on a page. Generally one serif and one sans serif make a nice mix. Using the sans serif for headlines and the serif for body text is a common and effective formula.
- Use italics or bold to highlight words and phrases, rather than using all uppercase. All uppercase is hard to read.
- Left justification can be easier to read and looks less formal than full justification. Pick the alignment option that matches the tone of your document.
- Graphs, pictures, and charts add interest to your documents and clarify your text. Horizontal and vertical lines can be used sparingly to break up blocks of text.

TYPOGRAPHY PRIMER 13 www.adobe.com/type

Optical Sizes

High-quality typefaces have always had different designs depending on the point size of the text to be set. In the days of metal type, each point size had its own unique design that was specifically tailored for its usage. For example, a typeface to be used at 6 point, such as in a photo caption, would be a bit thicker or denser than a typeface used for a headline set at 72 point. Several of Adobe's OpenType® fonts include four optical size variations: caption, regular, subhead, and display. Called Opticals, these variations have been optimized for use at specific point sizes. Although the exact intended sizes vary by family, the general size ranges include: caption (6–8 point), regular (9–13 point), subhead (14–24 point), and display (25–72 point). Several of Adobe's Multiple Master fonts also include the ability to select an optical size.

Warnock Pro Caption
Warnock Pro Reg (text)
Warnock Pro Subhead
Warnock Pro Display

All fonts shown at 30 point

Getting Your Quotes Right

The neutral quote marks, ' and ", that are accessible from your keyboard are traditionally used to indicate units of measure. True, or directional, quotes, ' ' and " "(sometimes called curly quotes), should be used whenever possible. Some applications automatically apply true quotes by changing the application's preferences.

4'6" = 4 feet, 6 inches
4'6" = 4 minutes, 6 seconds

"Typography is not an independent Art: it is a means to an end, not an end in itself. It must always be subservient to the text which is its 'raison d'être'…"
—HERBERT SPENCER

Using the Experts

Adobe sells a number of expert-set typeface collections. These collections contain many of the less frequently used characters that add a professional look to your documents, including oldstyle figures, small capitals, ornaments, and ligatures. For example, you can use f-ligatures, which eliminate awkward character combinations. Compare the fi, fl, ff, ffi, and ffl ligature combinations in the second line with the individual characters in the first line.

fi fl ff ffi ffl difficult sniffle
ﬁ ﬂ ﬀ ﬃ ﬄ diﬃcult sniﬄe

Adobe's OpenType Pro fonts typically combine these special expert-set characters and the base character set in a single font. With an application that supports OpenType features, such as Adobe InDesign,® substitution of these characters can be automated.

TYPOGRAPHY PRIMER 8 www.adobe.com/type

FIGURE 7.3 (Continued)
Source: Adobe Systems Inc., © 2000: <www.adobe.com/education/pdf/type_primer.pdf>.

White papers are not written in the simplistic (ninth-grade level) prose of newspapers, news releases, and magazine articles. The tone of a white paper is typically academic or professional, intended for readers who know more, or want to know or understand more, about an organization's position on an issue.

White papers are well-referenced documents that contain information that can be easily looked up or verified (never include proprietary information unless you are prepared to make it public), and employ issues of fact, not opinion, to support claims. Although white papers can be written about issues of fact, value, or policy, the arguments made must be supported by facts and reliable information from a variety of sources that the *audience* finds trustworthy and compelling. For example, research by a tobacco company about the health benefits of cigarettes will not be seen as compelling. White papers tend to advance nuanced and sophisticated arguments and explanations and well-defined and articulated positions.

White papers tend to be closer to research reports then anything else that a public relations practitioner might create. Although white papers *are* a sort of research paper, they are intended as "final draft" documents, are usually single-spaced, and often include graphics (tables, figures, illustrations) and design elements (color, dingbats, etc.).

As mentioned above, white papers are polemical. White papers delineate an organization or individual's position. White papers are not moderate or middle-of-the road documents. They are written *because* an individual or organization wants to differentiate him/her/itself from others or clarify a controversial or complicated position.

A white paper gives an organization or individual an opportunity to lay out a course of action, to provide long-lasting and compelling definitions, and to shape the future of debate about an issue. White papers are often used as background documents by lawmakers, the media, and other professionals when making decisions and conducting research. A well-crafted white paper can be worth a lot in terms of how the media defines an issue, or how regulators treat an industry.

White Paper Details

1. White papers should be developed as final draft documents with appropriate design elements (stylized formatting, organizational logo/letterhead, graphics, etc.).
2. White papers should draw upon abundant sources (especially scholarly sources) and a multitude of other sources. Include a minimum of two to three sources per page. Do not rely on nonscholarly sources for anything more than background information, anecdotes, and illustrations. Always backup your claims with sound "research" and logical arguments.
3. White papers should be structured to deal with issues "fairly." A white paper that does nothing but put forth your own corporate/organizational dogma is worth less than the paper it is printed on.

Additional suggestions for writing white papers come from Heath and Coombs, (2006, p. 294):

- Avoid technojargon, acronyms, etc. Write content and use vocabulary that is appropriate to the readership/educational levels of the audience.
- Focus on components of issues (facts, values, policies).
- Present both sides of the issue (especially with educated/informed publics). Present your side, present the opposing side, and then return to your side and explain how it is best.
- Avoid threats and privileging your position.
- Use comparison/contrast to contextualize *your* organization's position vs. *their* position on issues.
- Present information in layers (headings, introductions, overviews/summaries, more detailed information, etc.) and use structural cues (headings, bolded terms, citations, etc.) to make the paper compelling and easy to read.
- Provide "talking points," advance definitions, and structure introductions and conclusions so that issues are easy to discuss and talk about in the way you want.
- Integrate the organization's reputation and expertise into talking points, claims, etc.
- Adopt a tone of fairness and positive regard for others in your statements and content.

INFORMATIONAL INTERVIEWS

Informational meetings over lunch or coffee where you "pick the brain" of a colleague, client, expert, or professor, are a common research tool. Typically, such meetings are informal, and although you might ask questions and take notes, the interviews are not recorded, content is not analyzed, and they are not used as official sources. Informational meetings are designed to help give you focus and give you an idea about where to start.

Formal interviews, however, are a different story. Formal interviews are usually recorded or videotaped and copious notes are taken during the interview. Whenever you intend to conduct formal interviews for research or professional purposes, you should obtain written consent from the interviewee. Consent should be requested in advance of the interview. Consent forms should explain the exact nature of the research, what will be done with the information gathered, and what will be done with transcripts/recordings after the information has been used.

Basic Interview Suggestions

Consider these important issues when planning interviews:

1. Once interviewees have been identified and consent obtained, interviews should be scheduled at the convenience of the interviewee. Unless you are paying people to participate, *you* should work around *their* schedule.
2. Be prepared to safeguard interviewees' personal information by disguising their identities and/or omitting or changing their names if you will be asking about personal issues (health issues, personal habits, sexuality, etc.). Also, be aware that you should protect all personal information and never upload *anything* to an online database or an unencrypted computer.
3. Provide interviewees with copies of the interview questions in advance.
4. Prepare an interview guide. An interview guide is simply a printed list of your questions with space inserted for note-taking and comments. Be sure to include any anticipated follow-up questions, prompts, or alternate questions. *Note:* follow-up questions, prompts, and extra space for writing comments do not belong in the copies provided to interviewees.
5. Before each interview, record (both on tape and in your interview guide) the time, date, location, name, and title of the person/people you are interviewing.
6. Check your equipment before interviews. Make sure batteries are fully charged and all equipment is working (weak batteries can result in a poor recording level).
7. Be courteous and sensitive. Avoid saying things like "I'm interviewing you because you are the most convenient …" Or, "As the secretary, you probably overhear a lot of things …"
8. Begin by explaining the purpose of the interview and how the information will be used. Open your interview with some small talk or background information about the project to set yourself and the interviewee at ease. Try to avoid sounding contrived; do not arrive with "make small talk" written on the top of your interview guide. Many people can read upside down.
9. Inexpensive digital tape recorders allow you to upload interviews to computers and perhaps to use voice recognition software to create transcripts. Again, be sure to encrypt sensitive interview data.

No Matter How Well Prepared You Are, There Will Be Problems

Lack of confidence: Although you may be nervous, especially if talking to someone of authority, remember that most people will be flattered to be interviewed. Being nervous is okay. Most interviewees do not have a lot more experience being interviewed than you have conducting an interview, so they will not be as critical as you think. Experienced professionals will often sense your nervousness and try to put you at ease.

Worrying about being able to think up questions during the interview: You *will* be nervous until you have done a number of interviews. One of the best ways to ensure you have something to ask is to write interview probes into your copy of the interview guide (this also makes taking notes easier). If you still have trouble coming up with questions, as sometimes happens with terse interviewees, do not panic: you can almost always schedule a follow-up interview. By then, you will know what to expect from the interviewee and will have time to develop *new* questions.

Be sure you know as much as you can about your interviewee before you begin. Do your homework. Look at any books, articles, or campaigns your interviewee wrote or created. Visit the person or organization's Web site. Try to get to know the interviewee before you meet for the interview.

Work to understand the big picture: Be sure you understand the issues you are asking the interviewee about thoroughly before scheduling a formal interview. With only rare exceptions, formal interviews are not the place to be trying to learn the basics of an issue. Learn the basics through the Internet, or ask a colleague at another organization (remember the strength of weak ties). Real understanding, requires that you access experts and authoritative texts. Be sure you have a complete interview guide so you can make the most of the interview opportunity. Ask probing and follow-up questions to learn about relationships. Take careful notes (recording devices occasionally fail). Ask for copies of any documents or materials mentioned by the interviewee. Learn from your mistakes.

Taking notes: Interview note taking is not like class note taking. First, in a lecture, you can usually identify and record main points. Identifying key points is not as easy in an informal conversation where someone is talking to you. Second, you need to record supporting material and illustrations—colorful quotes, revealing anecdotes, facts, figures, etc. Recording interviews can help, since you can go back and listen later;[3] however, some individuals are not comfortable with being recorded and will not reveal important information until after the recording device is turned off. In fact, some of the best information comes at the very end, as you are wrapping up and saying your goodbyes.

Keep nonverbals in check: Often, the questions we ask, or our nonverbals, telegraph our feelings about the issue or the interviewee. Always work to appear attentive and interested and provide abundant nonverbal feedback: head nods, smiles, vocalics (ahh, hmm, mmm, uh huh), etc.

Terse and talkative interviewees: Again, here is where an interview guide can help. If an interviewee seems to be rambling to avoid answering a question, try asking the question differently. If the interviewee simply rambles by nature, use the interview schedule to bring him/her back around to the issue at hand. You can write the answers to unanticipated questions, or questions planned for later in the interview, as your interviewee talks, so talkativeness is not really a problem. When asked the first question, some interviewees will talk for 20 minutes, answering a dozen questions along the way. When asked an open-ended question, some interviewees will answer with one word. With both extremes, having a number of prompts and follow-up questions in your interview guide will help.

Other interviewing problems include: *An aversion to asking questions for fear of appearing ignorant; failure to define and clearly state the purpose of the interview; a lack of enthusiasm; failure to listen* (because of nervousness); *lack of preparation; failure to probe*; and *vagueness.* Be sure to ask concrete questions relevant to the interviewee. Do not ask an IT expert, "Where do you think the organization is going over the next ten years?" Unless the interviewee is a senior manager, his or her opinion is not of much value. Instead, you might ask the interviewee "to describe how s/he sees IT fitting in with the organization's long-term technology needs" (cf., Metzler, 1989).

Keep questions short: Limit questions to 15–20 words and use simple language whenever possible. Not "heretofore you have suggested that ..." but "do you believe ..." or "what do you think ...?"

Do not come to the interview with assumptions about what you will find, looking to the interviewee only as a source for verifying what you already believe. Listen to what the interviewee has to say and allow him or her to tell their story.

Do not expect brilliant answers to poorly worded questions. If you cannot articulate your question well, most interviewees will not be able to respond well.

Conducting a professional interview is not like what you see on television. Rarely will you ever be conducting a hostile interview—think Letterman rather than Couric. Most interviews are conducted on amenable terms and designed to obtain valuable information. Do not ask inflammatory questions. If you get out of line with a professional, you will be shown the door.

Questions and Their Uses

The way you ask a question (called a "framing bias") can have a profound impact on the kind of answer you receive (cf., Kahneman & Tversky, 1982). For example, if you ask 100 people, "Would you be willing to fire nuclear weapons if it meant you would *kill* half the people in the U.S.?," fewer people will say yes than if you phrased the question as, "Would you be willing to fire nuclear weapons if it meant you could *save* half the people in the U.S.?" Although the end result is the same, how a question is asked influences how people answer. Questions need to be posed as neutrally as possible and carefully phrased to get at the desired information. In their seminal text on interviewing, Stewart and Cash (1994) describe the many types of interview questions and their uses:

Open-ended questions are easy to answer and allow the interviewee to express his or her feelings. Open-ended questions also allow interviewees to obtain a lot of information. Although asking open-ended questions takes more time (interviewees may focus on irrelevant information and tend to ramble), open-ended questions are the only way to get at difficult concepts and to really understand how someone feels or what s/he believes about something. Sample questions include: "Tell me about what it's like to be a ...?" "What do you know about ...?" "How do you feel about ...?" "What do you think would solve the problem of ...?"

Moderately open questions are more focused and less prone to rambling responses, but still elicit complex and substantive responses from interviewees. Sample questions include: "Tell me about your musical hobbies." "What kind of public relations experiences have you had?" "How do you feel about the PRSA's new ethics policy?"

Closed questions ask for specific information and give you more control over the answers. However, closed questions often elicit too little information, requiring additional follow-up questions. Sample questions include: "How old were you when ...?" "What are three ways you think ...?" "When did you last receive feedback on ...?"

Forced choice questions ask respondents to choose among a number of predetermined alternatives. Most people are probably familiar with this kind of question; it is a staple of public opinion, marketing, and voting behavior research. Sample forced choice questions include: "Which brand of ... do you prefer, A, B, or C?" "Will you be voting for the Republican, Democratic, or independent candidate in the election on Tuesday?" Forced choice questions have several limitations. First, in order to be able to write an effective forced choice question, the interviewer must have a sophisticated grasp of the subject at hand. Forced choice survey and interview questions should not be used to obtain completely new information about a belief, value, attitude, or behavior. Second, forced choice questions, even when an "other" choice is allowed, force interviewees to answer questions in predetermined ways that may mask trends or subtle rationales for behaviors.

Bipolar questions ask respondents to choose between two alternatives. For example, "Do you usually take classes with your friends or without?" "Do you live in a rural or urban area?" Bipolar questions have some of the same limitations as those mentioned above except bipolar questions require an even more refined understanding of an issue and will provide absolutely no insight into alternative possibilities. Ask bipolar questions judiciously.

INTERVIEW STRATEGIES

1. *Opening questions:* Begin interviews with a few easy or "softball" questions designed to put the interviewee at ease and encourage him/her to talk candidly.
2. *Tunneling, funneling, and reverse funneling:* Ask questions that remain at about the same level of specificity and relevance (tunneling) throughout the interview, or question that build on each other from general to specific or specific to general (funneling and reverse funneling).
3. ***If you believe an interviewee has not provided an answer or is hesitant to answer,* try waiting a few seconds**, or use eye contact or nonverbal gestures like a nod, smile, frown, or quizzical look. If necessary, use a "nudging probe" such as: "I see." "Go on." "And then?" "Yes?" "What happened next?" "Uh-huh?"
4. ***Follow-up questions and probes* are designed to elicit more information.** They can take many forms: Passive ("Hmm, I see ..."); responsive ("Really! How interesting ..."); repetition of a phrase that the interviewee has just uttered; silence, followed by some verbal/nonverbal signal for the interviewee to continue; elaboration ("Tell me more about ..."); clarifying ("So, what you're saying is one in five ..."); or diverging or clarifying ("You said ... and yet ..."); segue ("Moving along...").
5. ***Avoid leading, loaded, double-barreled, and double-bind questions*** *unless intended to stimulate an interviewee:* leading questions ("Don't you believe...?"); loaded questions ("Isn't there something criminally wrong when...?"); double-barreled questions ("Do you know how and why the events occurred?") double-bind questions ("Have you stopped helping clients create deceptive Web sites?").

Interviewing is a skill that requires practice. Try to take a course on interviewing if one is available at your school or read one of the many books on interviewing. Do not let the most important interview of your life be the first interview you conduct. Practice first and learn some of the skills involved in the different types of interviews.

CONTENT ANALYSIS AND COMMUNICATION AUDITS

About 10 years ago, a colleague and I wanted to look at the phenomenon of organizational name change. Since several high-profile organizations had changed their name, we were interested to see what we could learn about it for public relations professionals. We started with a literature review on naming, name changes, and branding. We moved to some interviews with professionals about their own experiences conducting name changes; and then proceeded to gather all of the news stories about organizations that had changed their names. We stopped gathering information at about the time that we realized that *thousands* of organizations change their name every year in the United States. The technique that we used to examine the documents was content analysis, a technique suited to examining large amounts of similar data.

Content analysis is a data analysis technique that involves evaluating the language (vocabulary, heroes and villains, persona adopted, changes over time, images created, ideographic language, etc.) used in print, broadcast, and electronic content. Many professionals in large organizations are asked to evaluate their organization's documents, Web site, marketing materials, speeches, and news releases to ensure employees are using consistent vocabulary and messages in their external communication.

There are many content analysis techniques: close readings, cluster analysis, symbolic convergence, q-sorting, etc. (Bormann, 1972, 1977; Bormann, Cragan, & Shields, 1994; Burke, 1973b, Cragen & Shields, 1981). In general, content analyses examine texts (brochures, annual reports, Web content, position papers) in order to understand more about the author of the texts and how publics respond to the messages. For example, you discover your organization is being talked about pejoratively on several blogs. A content analysis might allow you to examine the postings to determine how your organization is being portrayed and what is leading to the negative descriptions of your organization.

Content Analysis Method

Frey, Botan, Friedman, and Kreps (1992) describe the content analysis process very clearly:

> ***Obtain texts/artifacts:*** A census (everything in an area) is preferred, but if a census is not possible, a random sample of messages must be selected. If a random sample is not possible, a nonrandom (but representative) sample is the last choice.
>
> ***Identify the units of analysis before you begin:*** Units of analysis include *physical units* (texts, books, television programs, speeches); *syntactical units* (symbols, words, phrases, metaphors, diagrams, etc.); *referential units* (what the text is about, heroes, villains, etc.); *prepositional units* (positions taken, types of appeals used, logical fallacies, etc.); and *thematic units* (topics like racism, sexism, elitism, etc.).
>
> ***Content categories are generated*** and should meet three criteria: (1) *Mutually exclusive*, or each category can mean only one thing. (2) *Equivalency*, or each category must have the same level of importance. (3) *Exhaustive*, or all of the categories used to evaluate the text(s) in question have been identified.
>
> ***Content categories must be "valid":*** (1) "Face validity" (the weakest kind, but necessary) means the researcher can argue or show that the categories are correct based on "common sense." (2) "Semantic validity" (better) means that when someone familiar with a category (a trained coder) examines the categories and items placed into them, s/he agrees that the categories are accurate. (3) "Criterion-related validity" exists when a coding schema can be shown to relate to a specific outcome. Finally, (4) "construct validity" is when the categories come from theoretical proposition and predictions (pp. 195–197).
>
> Another form of content analysis is a communication audit. Public relations practitioners are more likely to conduct—or assist with—a communication audit then they are to conduct a content analysis.

Communication audits are common public relations activities and revolve around examining organizations' communication (documents, speeches, advertising, Web content, e-mail messages, messages from organizational leaders—blogs, news stories, etc.). One major decision in a communication audit is to decide how deep the audit will go. As Kopec explains in an excellent summary:

> **1.** What is a communication audit? It is a complete analysis of an organization's communications—internal and/or external—designed to "take a picture" of communication needs, policies, practices, [sic] and capabilities, and to uncover necessary data to allow top management to make informed, economical decisions about future objectives of the organization's communication. An audit should also lead to a series of recommendations.
>
> **2.** What is the scope of an audit? The scope of an audit may be as broad and as deep as the size and complexity of the organization demands. The audit can measure the effectiveness of communication programs throughout an entire organization, in a single division or department, or within a specific employee group. It can examine communications on a particular subject or

communications via individual media, it can uncover misunderstandings, information barriers and bottlenecks, as well as opportunities. It can help measure cost effectiveness, evaluate ongoing programs, confirm hunches, clarify questions, and, in some instances, reorient concepts among senior management.

3. What does the communication audit provide? It provides meaningful information to members of management concerned with efficiency, credibility, and economy of their communications policies, practices, and programs. It also provides valuable data for developing or restructuring communications functions, guidelines, and budgets, as well as recommendations for action tailored to an organization's particular situation as uncovered by an analysis of the collected data. (kopecassociates.com/audits.aspx)

A communication audit can be an excellent technique for harmonizing visions when organizations have merged, or when an organization has several operating locations or Web sites that have slightly different missions or management teams.

One of the major issues of a communication audit has to do with the ability of the practitioner to be objective about content that s/he likely created, and about the organization itself, as well as the ability of the professional to gain unfettered access to organizational leaders. Many communication audits involve interviews with senior managers and organizational leaders. Because of power dynamics, getting organizational members—both superiors and subordinates—to be candid and honest can be almost impossible. Thus, external consultants are often hired because of their perceived objectivity and freedom from organizational power dynamics.

In general, a communication audit is a form of content analysis used to gather information about how an organization is perceived by internal and external audiences and to better understand the nature of the communication messages transmitted to an organization's various publics. The International Communication Association (ICA) has a reliable and detailed content analysis procedure that can be used to evaluate an organization's communication.

FOCUS GROUPS

A focus group is a study of a group of professionals or lay people who share a common interest or connection to a problem or question. For example, if a researcher working for a health organization were interested in how stress has affected veterans who served in Afghanistan, s/he might conduct a focus group with former or current soldiers. A videogame manufacturer interested in how people might respond to a new game idea might hold focus groups with teens. An accounting firm interested in how employees are reacting to a new employee benefits program might hold focus groups with members. Or, focus groups with voters might be held to determine how they feel about a new political policy or legal issue.

Focus group interviews typically involve groups of 5 to 7 (but never more than 8 to 10) individuals of the same gender, age, socioeconomic status, and ethnic background.[4] Focus groups can last two to three hours. Because of power, status, sex, age, and ethnic dynamics, the best focus groups are homogeneous. When you mix people in groups you cannot be sure that their comments and reactions are not an outgrowth of the group dynamics (influenced by power, status, or other factors) rather than their genuine opinion.

Additionally, focus groups require a skilled facilitator who can elicit comments from everyone and politely keep in check loquacious group members who might be boisterous or discourteous. The goal of a focus group is not—like a jury—for everyone to agree, but for the researcher to solicit comments from everyone involved and get an accurate understanding about how people represented by the focus group feel.

Since participating in a focus group is something of a burden, requiring several hours of time, focus groups participants are often compensated (modestly) for their participation, provided with transportation, served lunch or snacks (or, with some international groups, given beer and cigarettes), and paid a small stipend.

Focus group interviews are often used in public relations, media studies, politics, and marketing research to generate possible interview or questionnaire questions, to evaluate new programs, and to understand unfamiliar issues. Typically, a focus group consists of the following steps:

- Clearly identify what the purpose of the focus group is and identify specific questions to be asked.
- Identify the target populations and select participants who represent members of all relevant groups.
- As with interviewing, develop an interview guide with plenty of follow-up and probing

questions—and enough questions to get at all of the issues of relevance.

- At the start of each focus group, the researcher makes a statement like:

  Our goal is to learn about … there is no hidden agenda here and you should feel free to talk about whatever you want. Please share all of your thoughts, opinions, hunches, or feelings with us. Please try not to argue with one another or talk over others; everyone will get a chance to express their opinions. The interview will be recorded for the sake of clarity and research purposes and to aid in our remembering what you said. All of your comments will be kept strictly confidential and your comments will be reported anonymously.

- After each question, the moderator gives everyone an opportunity to respond and summarizes what the group said so that everyone agrees that their voice and opinion have been heard.
- Just as you might with an interview, try to sequence questions so those asked early on do not stimulate a lot of disagreement. This will give everyone a chance to get warmed up and feel more comfortable with one another.
- Researchers must be sure to ask the same questions of each group in the same order and in the same way to ensure the results are reliable.
- Since the results of focus groups are often used to make decisions about how to act or about the future, focus group interviews are usually transcribed, and their content analyzed to identify themes, consensus, and points of disagreement.
- After focus group interviews, participants should be thanked and compensated (if applicable).

Note: Forcing employees to participate in focus groups will result in unreliable results.

MESSAGE TESTING: READABILITY, RECALL, TRANSLATION

Message testing for readability, recall, and translation is frequently needed in public relations. For example, with surveys, pilot studies are essential to ensure that questions will be read and interpreted as intended by the researcher. Similarly, when surveys are used cross-culturally, translation and "back translation" (e.g., translating a survey to Chinese and then back to English to ensure the translation is effective) is essential. Additionally, when messages are created for younger audiences, uneducated audiences, or individuals from different ethnic or cultural backgrounds, readability is an important issue, as is translating metaphors and examples into culturally appropriate language.

NOMINAL GROUP TECHNIQUE (NGT)

Nominal Group Technique (NGT) is a research method designed to elicit new information and to achieve consensus (or high agreement) on potential problems and solutions, as well as how to deal with crisis and uncertainty. Many organizations have chronic problems related to their geographic location, type of organization, or historic practices. NGT can be used to brainstorm ideas and generate possible solutions to difficult and protracted problems. In practice, NGT is a form of advanced brainstorming and has been used by universities, the U.S. military, book publishers, and professional organizations of all sizes.

NGT can be used to identify potential problems, or respond to existing problems. The basic steps involved in NGT are as follows:

1. Before the meeting, decide what the best questions to discuss are. Be precise. No double-barreled questions, no yes/no questions, no multipart questions. Carefully formulate a list of possible questions relating to a substantive issue. The more questions you ask, the longer the process will take.
2. Pose all questions in writing to the group and ask group/committee members to evaluate the questions *individually* and in *silence*. All group members should work in silence for 15–30 minutes. You should provide paper and writing implements and ask the group to provide, in writing, what is believed to be the best answer to the questions asked.

   You will probably need to monitor the group members' work and occasionally remind them to work silently and individually. Ask group members before the meeting to turn off their cellular telephones and not to check messages during the meeting. Silence now will lead to more to discussion later.
3. After everyone has finished answering the questions, begin listing their answers/ideas publicly on flip charts and posting the answers around

the room—number the answers as you go. Note: 3M makes large, 2' × 3' pads of "stickum notes" that work well for this, but plain white butcher paper taped to the wall is also fine. A data or overhead projector will not work for NGT: you will have dozens of answers to each question and group members need to be able to see *all* of the responses *at the same time*. You should proceed question by question rather than dealing with all of the questions randomly. Go from person to person and list one idea each. Ask that all ideas be different. Do not discuss the ideas yet; just list them without discussion (quietly).

4. Only after all of the ideas have been placed on butcher paper or flip charts around the room can you begin considering the merits of each idea. Do not collapse or combine ideas at this point. The next step is "voting on top choices." However, before voting, the group leader should consider each idea and solicit elaboration and discussion. If any idea is unclear, the originator of the idea should explain it to the group. Discussion is still individualized and not interactive or a free-for-all at this point.
5. After everyone is clear about the ideas, the group is asked to vote on their top 5–10 choices. Choices can be reverse-weighted for scoring (i.e., rate choices 1–10 and then assign them weights of 10–1), written on separate index cards, and then added up to order the group's choices—the highest points equals the top choice, etc.
6. When the top choices have been identified (finally), the floor is opened for discussion. Discussion can be a free-for-all, participants can be broken up into smaller groups and given time to make reports to the entire body, or items can be discussed one at a time. An assistant should take careful notes at this point and the process can be recorded or videotaped for future use in a formal report or an analysis. Lists should be saved, and may be photographed with a digital camera in order to analyze the information later or to share with participants.

The NGT process often identifies potential problems and solutions not readily apparent to individuals. NGT is an excellent technique for obtaining participation by all members of a group, even normally reticent organizational members. NGT takes a lot of time, so be prepared to spend all day (or half a day) on one problem. Be sure to provide drinks and snacks to participants, and provide short breaks from time to time if you want participants to be at their best.

DELPHI STUDIES

A Delphi study tries to learn about trends and make predictions about the future. The Delphi research technique is used to gather information from experts and professionals with unique, specialized knowledge. For example, an organization that makes desktop publishing software might want to know about upcoming trends that might influence their products and perhaps give them an edge over the competition. Perhaps the greatest strength of the Delphi is the ability to bring together dozens of experts from diverse (but related) areas and have them tackle a single problem or issue. According to McElreath (1997), the steps in conducting a Delphi include:

1. Try to find 30 to 50 panelists. This number is large enough to allow trends in responses to be identified but small enough to allow the researcher to analyze the data and keep track of the respondents. Identify a panel of "experts" or specialists by consulting experts in the field or area of interest and inviting them to participate.
2. Invitations to participate in the study should include an explanation of what is requested of each panel member in terms of time and effort to complete each wave of the Delphi study. Cooperation and participation can be improved if people are told that their peers nominated them and that other experts will be participating. Letters of invitation should be written to highlight what might emerge from the professional collaboration and to emphasize that the participants will have first access to the information after the study. Panelist qualifications are based on their specialized knowledge. Panelists must also be willing to share their ideas throughout the process—i.e., not in competition with each other or likely to withhold important information.
3. Distribute the initial survey instrument (questions). In the past, Delphi studies were conducted through postal mail. Now, however, e-mail, FTP sites, interactive Web sites, and other electronic tools can speed things along. The initial survey instrument might contain open-ended probes or closed-ended questions. Approaches to questions

are often changed as the study progresses and more open-ended answers are needed to understand the phenomenon being explored as the study progresses.

4. As responses are returned, begin analyzing the initial wave of data. Compile the responses to each question with only minor editing of responses to help clarify the meaning and provide consistency. If open-ended questions are used it may be necessary to compile, content analyze, and present the first wave of data with an appropriate theoretical framework, topology, or outline.
5. Distribute the second survey instrument. Panelists are often asked in the second wave to clarify and rank order the responses of other panel members, as in NGT. How much elaboration and justification is needed for rankings is up to the researcher. During the second wave of the study, asking for *additional* ideas, clarifications, and elaborations is appropriate.
6. Analyze the second wave of data. Analysis of the second wave of data will involve subjective decisions about rewording and revising the initial responses. Be sure to include all new ideas and suggestions at this point. The main purpose of the Delphi study is, after all, to generate new ideas. Do not discourage or downplay radical or unorthodox ideas: the radical ideas of today are often the reality of the future.
7. Distribute the third wave of the survey instrument. At this point, panelists are asked to clarify and rank order survey responses to the revised survey items.
8. Analyze the third wave of data. By this stage, the analysis is probably less subjective and judgmental and more quantitative and objective (as much as possible).
9. Repeat the process with additional waves or questions as necessary. Often, by wave three of the Delphi, specific items are selected for more in-depth treatment by the panelists. Panelists may be asked to propose answers to problems that were identified, to offer short-term and long-term solutions, to evaluate goals, and to predict possible outcomes.
10. Once you are satisfied that you have exhausted the research subject or obtained all of the information you can reasonably expect, prepare and distribute a final report to the panel members. One of the motivations for participating in a Delphi panel, particularly for specialists, is to learn first-hand, before others, what the findings are of the Delphi study. Your report should be detailed and include all relevant comments and feedback from the panel participants.
11. Thank the panel members for participating with a personal letter. Additionally, be sure to include all of the names of the panelists on any future reports, articles, evaluation instruments, or studies that come out of the Delphi research (cf., McElreath, 1997, pp. 229–230).

Understand that participation in a Delphi study is a time-consuming and arduous commitment. Never withhold information from panel participants or attempt to steer results in the direction you would like. The Delphi method is worthless if it is manipulated. Trying to mislead a group of professionals who undoubtedly have strong ties among themselves will spell disaster for your research and probably damage your organization's reputation permanently among the experts consulted. A Delphi can reveal groundbreaking trends but requires everyone involved to have access to the data and conclusions.

STRENGTHS, WEAKNESSES, OPPORTUNITIES, THREATS (SWOT)

A SWOT analysis, sometimes called a TOWS analysis, is an analytical tool for focusing attention on key issues faced by individuals and organizations. Like the nominal group technique, a SWOT analysis is a tool for analysis, decision making, and problem solving. SWOT analyses are conducted when organizations are considering moving into new business areas, taking innovative courses of action, or faced with unexpected circumstances. Individuals (rather than groups) usually conduct SWOT analyses and the results are used for making planning decisions.

The best SWOT analyses are backed up by archival research. A SWOT analysis should never be someone's opinion but should be based on supportable and verifiable claims. An effective SWOT analysis can identify issues that need to be given more attention in a campaign, issues likely to cause the most trouble, and issues with the greatest potential for success. See Table 7.1 for a sample SWOT analysis of a communication department as it worked on developing a new master's program.

Having reviewed the key *qualitative* research techniques used in public relations, I will now move to a discussion of quantitative research methods. Quantitative research is a staple of public relations

TABLE 7.1 SWOT Analysis: Terminal Master's Program in Public Relations and Organizational Communication†

Terminal Master's Strengths

Offer a growing and desirable major.

Serve a varied student clientele.

Located centrally (geographically) for students from across the region.

Supported by the administration.

Terminal Master's Weaknesses

Inability to teach all of the proposed graduate courses without at least two hires.

Students will be difficult to attract and retain if courses are offered erratically or not at all.

Difficult to balance "scholarly/professional" demands in a high-bred program.

Terminal Master's Opportunities

Ability to grow the department and increase prestige nationally and internationally.

Ability to attract new applicants from the undergraduate program.

Pique the interest of current undergraduate communication students by allowing them to take up to two cross-listed graduate/undergraduate classes as electives.

Attract students from other master's programs (e.g., business, social work) in the university to take some of our classes as electives.

Attract "continuing education" students from local businesses.

Attract graduates from other programs, such as X (which currently has no master's program in public relations).

Attract undergraduates uninterested in competing in the current economic environment (i.e., when the economy is poor, students stay in school).

Attract students from the surrounding communities.

Attract international students who are more business (less critically) oriented.

Professional master's students can help to solidify relationships with the surrounding business communities through internships and professional networking.

Terminal Master's Threats

Competing programs, such as A, B, C, and D.

Inability to accept new students under the current program, and an inability to recruit new students until course proposals are approved.

Ability to hire qualified faculty to teach classes—especially in public relations—will be impaired if the administration "micromanages" our hiring decisions and we are not allowed to begin the hiring process until January or later.

†: A "terminal" master's program is a master's program that ends with a master's degree and preparation for the business world, rather than preparing someone for a doctoral program. No one is harmed in the process.

because effective and accurate audience analysis is central to communication success.

QUANTITATIVE RESEARCH

Quantitative research focuses on things that can be counted or quantified. The most common types of quantitative research are demographic, psychographic, infographic, geodemographic, survey, and readership or media impressions research.

Demographic Research

You are probably familiar with **demographic research:** age sex, gender, race, ethnicity, educational level, income, marital status, number of children, number of pets, home owner or renter, apartment or house, weight, height, quality of vision, etc. There are hundreds, perhaps thousands, of demographic qualities that may be gathered. As suggested above, demographic data is central to creating effective messages. Understanding what your audience looks like (age, sex, weight, race), where they live (income, socioeconomic status, occupation), etc., is a prerequisite of effective communication.

The U.S. government Web site **FedStats** (www.fedstats.gov) links to demographic data from dozens of government agencies including the Bureau of Labor Statistics, the U.S. Census Bureau, the Department of Defense, the National Science Foundation, and Social Security (www.fedstats.gov/agencies). Additionally, government statistical databases like FedStats list topics alphabetically in hundreds of categories, including food consumption patterns, health information, homelessness, marijuana use, personal wealth, poverty, vital statistics, and women-owned businesses, to name but a few (www.fedstats.gov/cgi-bin/A2Z.cgi). See Figures 7.4 and 7.5.

Other excellent sites to gather statistical, aggregate, and demographic data include the Pew Research Center (pewresearch.org), the Pew Internet & American Life Project (www.pewinternet.org), Nielsen/NetRatings (www.nielsen-online.com), Stanford University's Web Credibility Project (credibility.stanford.edu), and Webcontent.gov (www.firstgov.gov/webcontent/improving/evaluating/audience.shtml).

As pointed out above in the discussion of archival research, demographic and other data is most desirable when you do not have to pay to gather it yourself. Surveys are expensive to administer, correlate, and analyze, as are professional demographers. Obviously, the U.S. Census Bureau will not have individualized data about your organization's customers or employees; however, the Census Bureau does have state, regional, and national data in dozens of categories.

Organizations can gather some demographic data relatively inexpensively through their own organizational Web sites, but such data is always suspect unless skilled online researchers have been employed. The reliability of Web data depends upon how it is gathered: voluntary data, versus data users are forced to provide in order to gain access to a Web site. Reliability also depends on whom the data was gathered from: tech savvy users, new users, professionals in your area. Except for demographic data gathered by survey takers and professionals in person, much (perhaps most) of the demographic data gathered by anonymous surveys, business reply cards, warranty cards, and Web sites is unreliable.

For example, many Web sites force visitors to sign up for "free memberships" in order to obtain access. Very often, memberships are required because an organization wants to obtain some demographic data about Web site visitors. The problem is, many Internet users (myself included) see this as intrusive. If users are not allowed to see what a Web site offers, how can they know if a site is worth providing one's personal information in order to gain access? When I am required to provide demographic data in order to gain access to a Web site, I am a 100+-year-old Hispanic woman born on January 1, 1900, who earns poverty level wages and has a high school education. Many people do the same thing when forced to provide personal information in order to sign into a Web site.

Erroneous responses like mine are actually quite common; some sophisticated organizations anticipate this happening and send back error messages asking you to "please enter your *real* information." Many Internet studies have shown that men frequently pretend to be women in online chat rooms and that women pose as men to avoid being harassed because of the high male-to-female ratio on many sites. Online demographic data is no less subject to falsification. Thus, demographic data must be judiciously gathered and carefully screened for erroneous names, dates, etc.

Psychographic Research

Psychographic research refers to beliefs, attitudes, and values—lifestyle data—rather than to individual characteristics. For example, health choices, diet and exercise choices, preferences in entertainment (music, theatre, sporting events, rock concerts), Internet usage, belief in a higher power, religious and political affiliations, opinions on same-sex marriage, gun control, abortion, drinking and drug use, etc. Understanding an audience's psychographic profile is necessary when you are trying to influence beliefs and behaviors. For example, if you want to convince teenagers to wear their seatbelts, you need to know what the teens not wearing them believe. If you want to convince voters to support a ballot measure to build a halfway house for abused women, you need to know how the voters (especially the intended neighbors) feel about the people who will be living/working there.

FEDSTATS

Celebrating over 10 years of making statistics from more than 100 agencies available to citizens everywhere

Links to statistics

- ★ Topic Links - A To Z - Direct access to statistical data on topics of your choice.
- ★ MapStats - Statistical profiles of States, counties, cities, Congressional Districts, and Federal judicial districts.

Alabama [Submit]

- ★ Statistics By Geography From U.S. Agencies -- International comparisons, national, State, county, and local.
- ★ Statistical Reference Shelf - Published collections of statistics available online including the Statistical Abstract of the United States.
- ★ Search across agency websites.

Links to statistical agencies

- ★ Agencies Listed Alphabetically with descriptions of the statistics they provide and links to their websites, contact information, and key statistics.
- ★ **Agencies by subject** - Select a subject:

Agriculture [Submit]

- ★ Press Releases - The latest news and announcements from individual agencies.
- ★ Kids' Pages on agency websites.
- ★ Data Access Tools - Selected agency online databases.

Additional Links to other statistical sites and general government locator sites.

Federal Statistical Policy - Budget documents, working papers, and Federal Register notices.

Fedstats - www.fedstats.gov/
About Fedstats
Send Your Feedback To Fedstats

Information Quality
Privacy And Accessibility
Home page last updated *March 12, 2007*

Statistical Agencies FEDSTATS

Back To Fedstats Home Page | Topic Links - A To Z | Search

Federal Agencies with Statistical Programs

A B C D E F G H I J K L M N O P Q R S T U V W X Y Z Principal Statistical Agencies

- **Administration For Children And Families** [Dept of Health and Human Services]
- **Administration On Aging** [Dept of Health and Human Services]
- **Agency For Healthcare Research And Quality** [Dept of Health and Human Services]
- **Agency For International Development** [Independent agency]
- **Agency For Toxic Substances And Disease Registry** [Dept of Health and Human Services]
- **Agricultural Research Service** [Dept of Agriculture]
- **Army Corps Of Engineers** [Dept of Defense]
- **Broadcasting Board Of Governors** [Independent agency]
- **Bureau Of Customs And Border Protection** [Dept of Homeland Security]
- **Bureau Of Economic Analysis** [Dept of Commerce]
- **Bureau Of Justice Statistics** [Dept of Justice]
- **Bureau Of Labor Statistics** [Dept of Labor]
- **Bureau Of Prisons** [Dept of Justice]
- **Bureau Of Reclamation** [Dept of Interior]
- **Bureau Of Transportation Statistics** [Research and Innovative Technology Administration, Dept of Transportation]
- **Census Bureau** [Dept of Commerce]
- **Centers For Medicare And Medicaid Services** [Dept of Health and Human Services]
- **Consumer Product Safety Commission** [Independent agency]
- **Defense Manpower Data Center, Statistical Information Analysis Division** [Dept of Defense]
- **Department Of Veterans Affairs** [Cabinet]

FIGURE 7.4 FedStats.Gov.

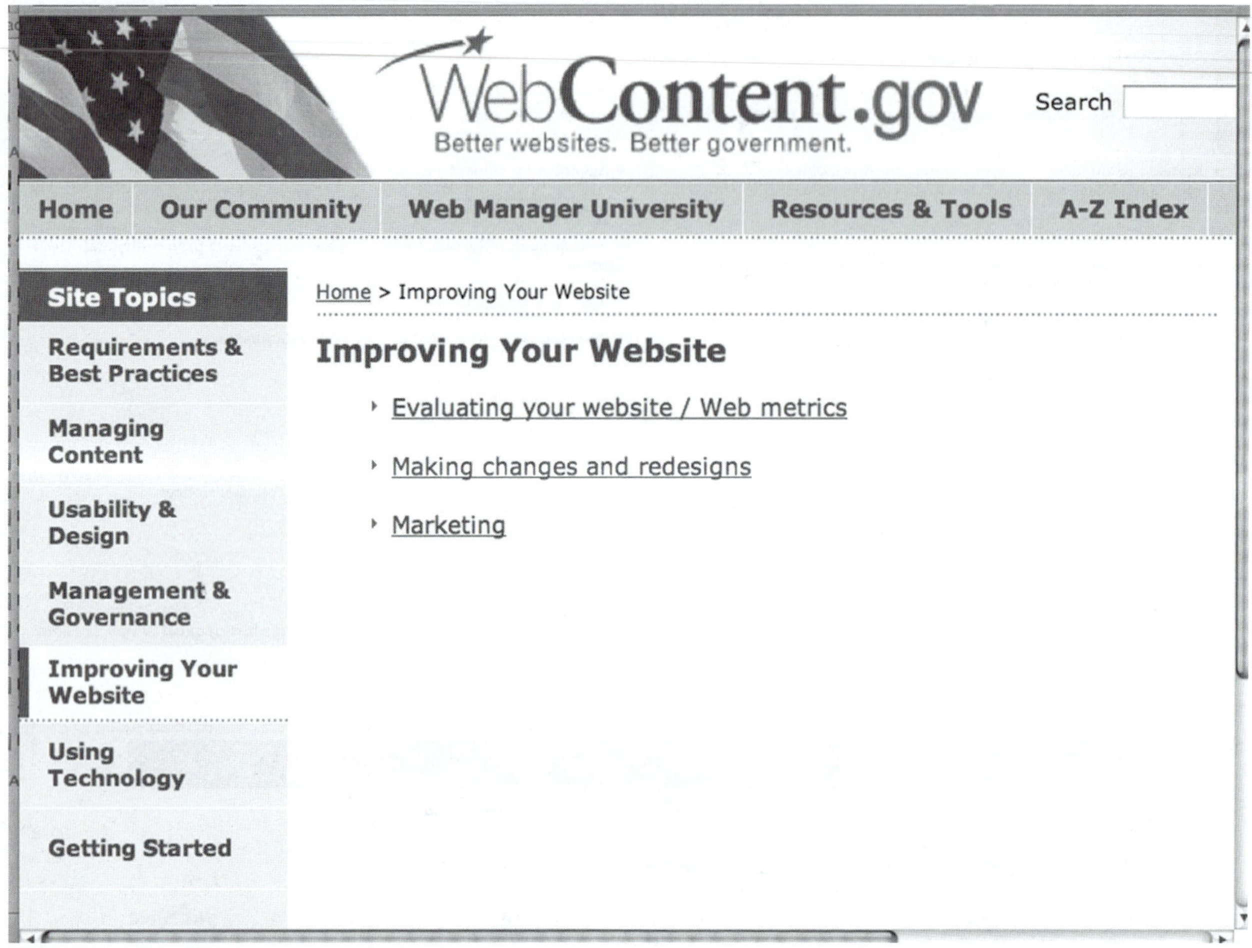

FIGURE 7.5 WebContent.Gov.

In many cases, psychographic data is gathered in the same fashion as demographic data, by counting and doing math. Both demographics and psychographics are used to describe individuals and publics, and both are used to create compelling messages and effectively target individuals and publics. As Aughton explains:

> While the US music industry has successfully sued many thousands of alleged illegal file sharers over the past couple of years it has also stealthily been using file sharing networks to gather valuable information about their customers.
>
> A US company, Big Champagne, regularly prepares reports for labels, detailing the number of p2p users who are sharing a particular artist or song, which music those people are also buying and where they live.
>
> In the first week of August, for example, Arcade Fire songs were being shared by 1.3 per cent [sic] of p2p users, an estimated 200,000 to 300,000 people, the largest proportion of whom live in San Francisco. And 60 per cent [sic] of them also have Coldplay in their collections. For record company marketing executives this kind of information is invaluable, enabling them to target advertising campaigns and push radio stations to play the most popularly shared tracks.

> "You can get a really good psychographic profile of a listener base by just looking at the collections of people who download this or that," said Big Champagne's Eric Garland. "And that becomes tremendously important, because early in the life of a record, labels don't necessarily know who the audience is. They just know they've got something great." (www.pcpro.co.uk/news/77568/music-industry-turns-to-p2p-for-psychographic-data.html)

Psychographic data, like demographic data, needs to be gathered with care. People tend to be even more sensitive about sharing personal information about their musical, reading, religious, and sexual preferences. As the news story above suggests, Big Champagne's data is gathered surreptitiously, since few of the p2p users would probably volunteer such information. Public relations professionals also need to be careful when using psychographic data. As the debate surrounding the USA Patriot Act illustrates, many Americans feel very strongly about their privacy; when organizations intrude on individuals' private lives and activities, people get angry.

When purchasing psychographic or infographic data from marketing or advertising firms, be sure the vendor's data gathering methods are up to the ethical standards of your organization. Similarly, if you decide to purchase mailing, telephone, or e-mail lists of individuals or publics who fit specific demographic or psychographic profiles, be very sure you are complying with federal "do not call regulations" and the most recent legislation on "canned spam" and unsolicited postal mail. Always be sure your message is about "information of value" rather than an attempt to market a product or service. Never use lists of individuals and publics except for the reason provided when your organization obtained the personal information. Additionally, never sell your mailing, telephone, or e-mail lists to anyone else. Just because others do, does not mean you should.

Infographic[5] Research

Infographics, in the sense used here, refers to research about where individuals and groups get their information, including newspapers, magazines, broadcast, cable or satellite radio/television, the Internet, professional publications, books, and interpersonal sources such as friends, family, or colleagues. The importance of infographics comes into play when making decisions about what medium to use in a public relations campaign, and the best way to reach individuals and publics with messages.

Knowing where individuals and groups turn for information can be very valuable. For example, many communication professionals belong to professional associations; monthly or quarterly newsletters are often prime places for announcing employee promotions, grants, jobs, and other information of value to members. Many organizations and groups also use Listservs and e-lists to distribute information to members.

With some publics, including teenagers, children, stay-at-home mothers, the working poor, and others, the question of the appropriate medium is more difficult to answer with certainty. Teenagers, for example, might watch the same two or three television programs or listen to the same two or three radio stations. However, many organizations cannot afford to take out radio or television advertisements in order to reach their key publics. Having detailed information about where particular individuals and groups get their information is vitally important to the success of a campaign.

One of the reasons organizational mailing lists are so valuable (and sacrosanct), and why they are so expensive to rent, is because direct mail is one of the only ways to reach certain individuals and groups. The Internet is of course another valuable tool. However, Internet lists need to be voluntarily joined or opted into to be effective. Legislation regarding unsolicited e-mail precludes the Internet from being used by reputable organizations in the same way that unwanted postal mail is sent. Most people resent all unsolicited spam.

Some of the most viable informational sources are the various electronic channels that allow narrowcasting (or reaching very specific individuals and groups) rather than broadcasting (sending out messages to *everyone*). Narrowcasting is not a new concept but requires public relations professionals to become closer, more intimate, with publics. In terms of electronic sources, public relations professionals need to become familiar with electronic lists, newsgroups, online magazines, blogs, social networking Web sites, and other Web sites of interest. Such data is fluid, changing quickly as tastes and fashions change. According to popular wisdom, the Internet advances in dog years, and many organizations need to stay on top of trends, fashions, and tastes to be successful.

Old school public relations involves maintaining mailing lists with names and contact information for journalists and editors, and periodically updating organizational materials for direct mailing or event distribution. In terms of knowledge about publics, knowing which newspapers or magazines were read by specific publics and where to position advertisements (geographically and demographically) was sufficient for most purposes.

New school public relations, however, requires public relations professionals to have a much more sophisticated understanding of publics. When the only game in town was the local daily newspaper and a few radio stations, creating effective campaigns was easy. Now, everyone from preteens to grandparents obtain a lot of their information online. According to the Pew Internet & American Life Project, 84 percent of teenagers ages 12–17 "surf the Web for fun" (Lenhart, Rainie, Lewis, 2001, p. 6). Lenhart, Rainie, and Lewis also note:

> There are significant differences between how boys and girls use the Internet and how young teens and older teens use the Internet. And, just as in the case of adults, experience with the Internet matters. Those who have more experience use the Internet differently from those who are newcomers to the online world. (p. 6)

Similar issues exist in terms of how older American use the Internet and how minorities, less educated citizens, and college students use the Web (www.pewinternet.org). Ultimately, all organizations need to identify relevant infographics for their own publics.

There are tens of thousands of different organizations, each with different publics, interests, and goals. An assortment of marketing and demographic sources can provide basic demographic and psychographic information, but developing effective infographics is a job for individual public relations organizations and professionals and depends upon each individual organization's goals and interests and the interests of each organization's stakeholders and publics.

Geodemographic Research

Geodemographic data is data that combines information about geography—or location—with demographics or characteristics of individuals and groups. An example of efforts to gather this type of research is when a department store cashier asks you for your zip code. Knowing where the people who buy particular items live gives an organization the ability to target specific regions with messages and advertisements.

As Andreas, a freelance writer from California explains:

> Most marketers are familiar with the basic tenet of geodemographic neighborhood classification systems: People with similar cultural backgrounds, means and perspectives naturally gravitate toward one another—or—[sic] to form relatively homogeneous communities. (It's the old "birds of a feather flock together" phenomenon.) [sic] Once settled in, people naturally emulate their neighbors, adopt similar social values, tastes and expectations and, most important of all, share similar patterns of consumer behavior toward products, services, media and promotions. (www.andreas.com/faq-geodemo3.html)

Organizations of all sizes use geodemographic data to target publics, create more compelling messages, and help organizations know where to devote scarce resources. One excellent example of geodemographic data and how it can provide insight into the beliefs and values of key publics is the maps that were created by Jon Kilpinen, Valparaiso University, to indicate where people of different religious faiths in the U.S. live (see Photo 7.1). Although Kilpinen's data is fairly general (more detailed data would allow for better targeting of publics), a public relations professional who was working on behalf of a political or nonprofit organization concerned with issues like politics, abortion, teen pregnancy, or education, and where support differs by religious faith, would have a good idea of where to seek support or opposition for the organization's issue.

Geodemographic data can also be gathered via Web sites, point of purchase (cash registers), telephones (call centers and sales), aggregated data purchased by organizations, and through marketing and advertising organizations. Geodemographic data, like all of the data discussed above, must be regularly "screened and cleaned" (updated and refined), to maintain its viability and accuracy. Although geodemographic data might have a longer life than other forms of data (neighborhoods, cities, regions do not change overnight, but they can change quickly), immigration, economic trends, and employment opportunities can alter the accuracy of data.[6] When communicating with individuals and publics via direct mail or e-mail, you need to keep your lists updated, as e-mail and postal mail are returned. Many organizations opt for the added expense of first-class mail so their print messages will be forwarded or returned and the organization can maintain a more effective list.

SURVEYS AND QUESTIONNAIRES

Surveys and questionnaires allow professionals to generalize about a population based on their responses to questions (Frey, Botan, Friedman, & Kreps, 1992, p. 6). Surveys and questionnaires are staples of sales and marketing research. Typically, a small number of individuals (the "sample") are surveyed in an attempt to make predictions about an entire population. Surveys of sample populations are appropriate when a **census** (asking everyone) is not possible because of time, money, or logistics. However, a census (the complete group) is *always* preferable to a sample.

As you probably already know, **surveys** and **questionnaires** ask participants to comment on their behaviors, beliefs, values, practices, etc., usually in a self-report instrument. Based on the answers to the questions asked, predictions can be made about possible behaviors, trends, and preferences.

Strengths of the Survey Method

- Surveys are useful for learning how large groups of people think.
- Surveys allow *sampling* of populations rather than asking everyone.
- Surveys are useful for assessing opinions, market trends, and political preferences.
- Surveys are more convenient. Asking a *segment* of a population about their behaviors is easier than going out and observing the actual behavior of members of the group (Frey, et al., 1992, pp. 85–124).

Weaknesses of the Survey Method

- Survey results are always based on probabilities. Surveys are never completely accurate.
- People misremember their actions and behaviors from the past and often exaggerate their importance or actions.
- Individuals all see the world differently and surveys force people to respond to categories you have created. As mentioned earlier in this chapter, to be effective, survey questions can only be written after a researcher already knows a lot about a public.
- Surveys are never suitable as a primary means of data gathering. Secondary research and interviews should first inform all survey construction.
- When intimate, embarrassing, or socially unacceptable behaviors or actions are asked about (like church attendance, mentioned earlier), people will often exaggerate, lie, or try to guess the answer they think the surveyor is looking for and give that answer.
- In intercultural research, some cultures, because of "courtesy biases," simply give the answer they think the surveyor is looking for. Or, worse still, people hired to conduct surveys on your behalf might simply spend the day at a café drinking cappuccinos, smoking cigarettes, and filling out the surveys based on what they believe everyone would say.
- Surveys are poor tools for getting at complex phenomena (interviews are better).
- People lie. As noted above, if people will lie about whether they attended church, they will lie about anything. Survey data has to be carefully screened and interpreted (Frey, et al., 1992, pp. 85–124).

Components of survey research: Selection of respondents

The population: All members of a group who possess specific characteristics, beliefs, etc. When all members of a population are interviewed, the research is called a *census*.
The sample: The segment of a population surveyed in order to learn about the entire population. To generalize, samples must be representative of the population surveyed.

Sampling Frame

The sampling frame is the part of a population that can be reached for study. There are several possible sampling frames: ***simple random samples***, where anyone in the target populations has an equal chance of being selected; ***stratified random sample***, where the population is grouped along some sort of coherent lines (freshman, sophomore, junior, senior, new employees versus experienced employees, etc.) and *then* randomly sampled; and ***nonrandom***

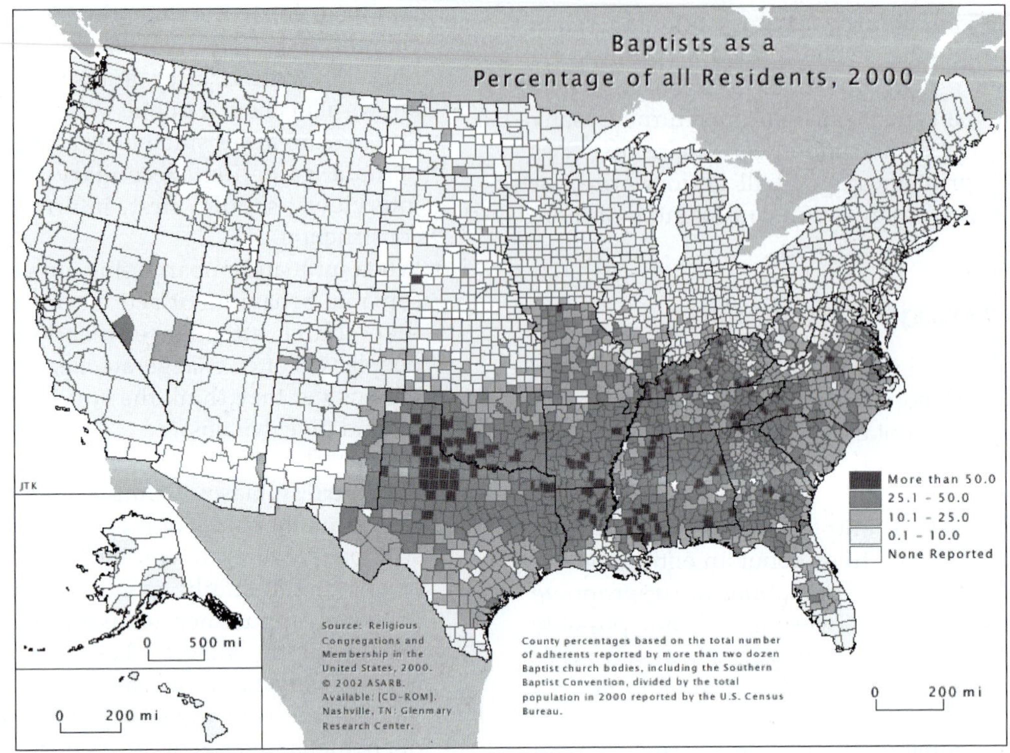

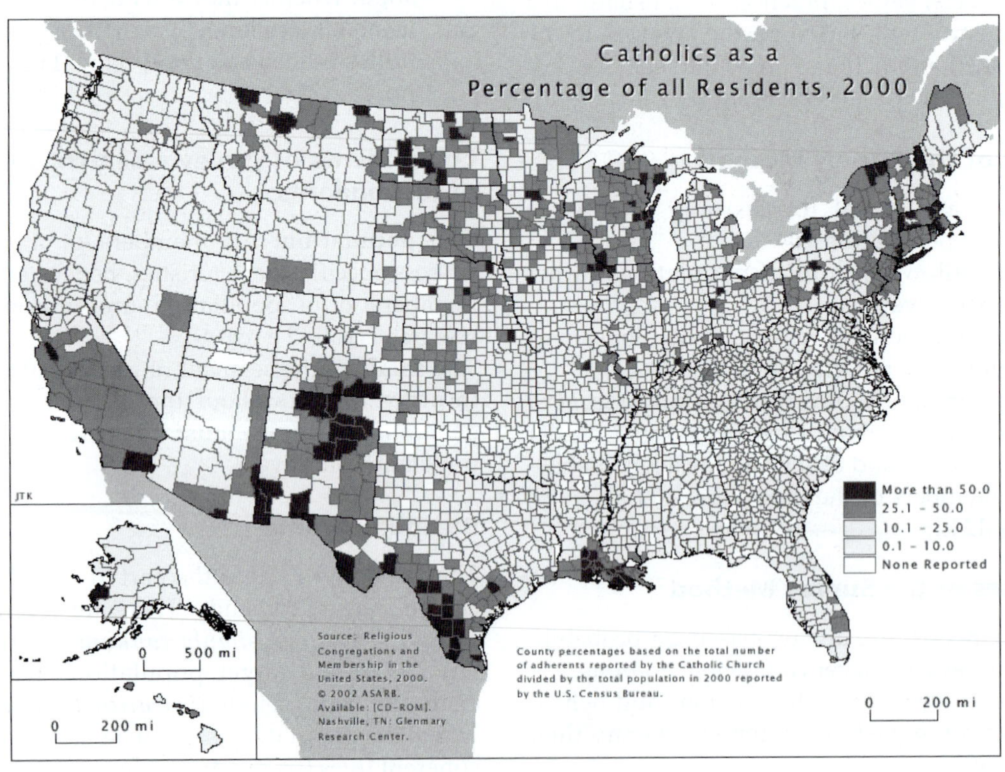

Religious maps.

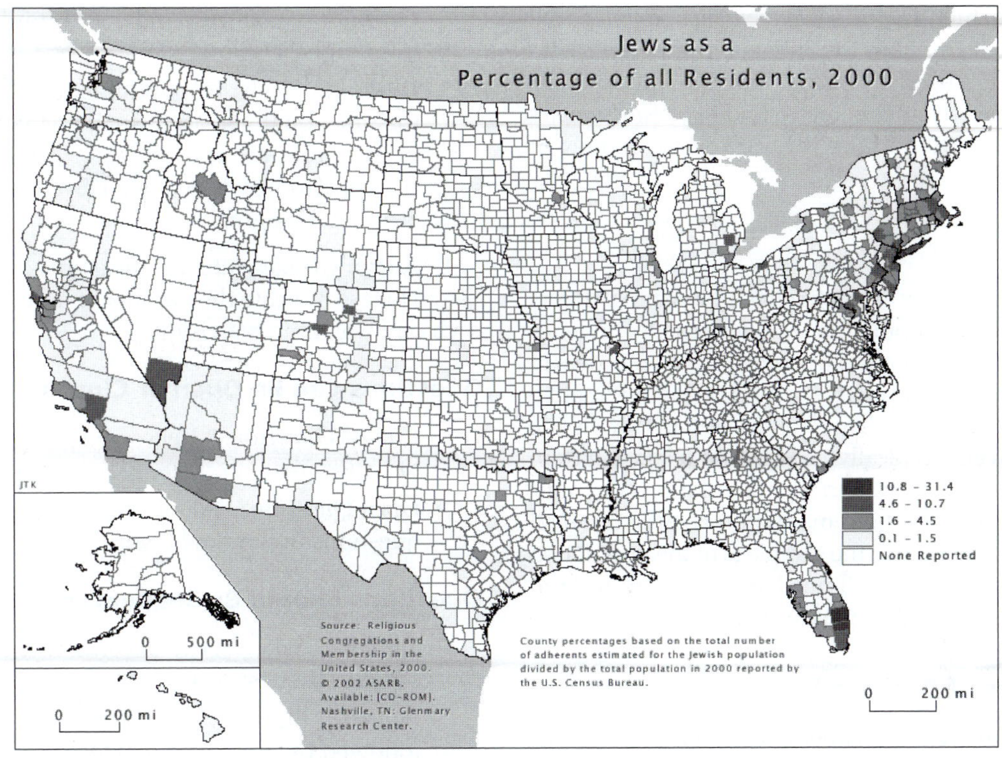

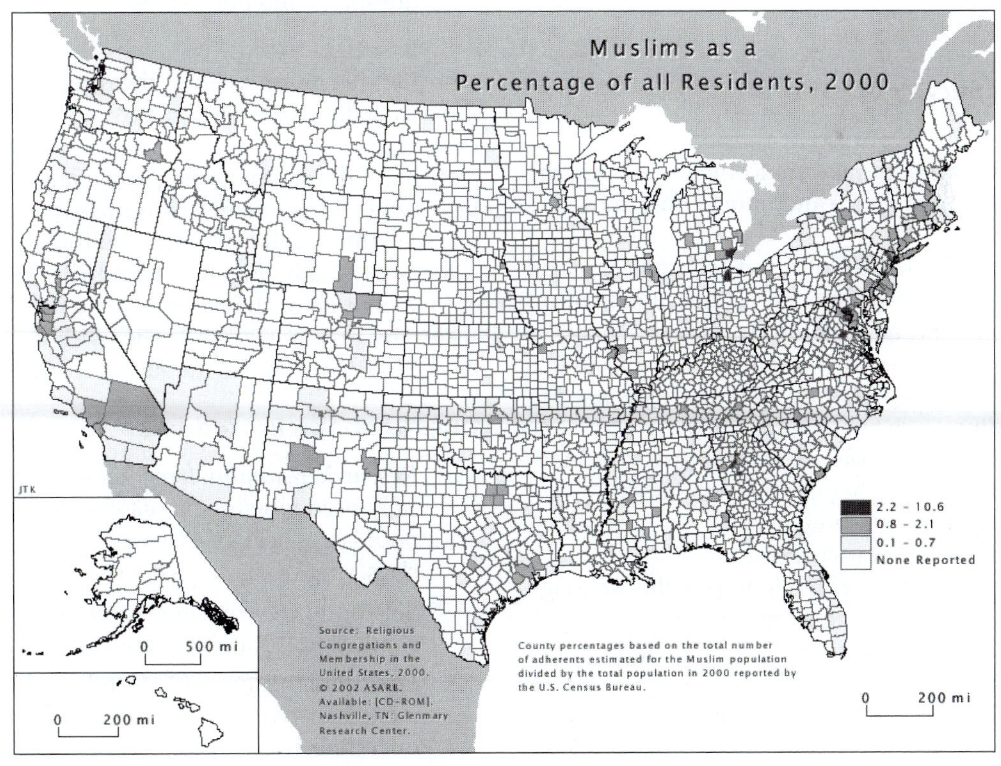

Religious maps. (Continued)
Source: Jon T. Kilpinen.

sampling, which includes *convenience samples* (the people down the hall, the interns, the people who come by the store), *volunteer samples* (people answering advertisements, etc.), and *snowball samples* (asking people who take the survey for names of other people to survey).

Sampling Error

Sampling error is the extent to which the sample differs from the general population. A 95 percent "confidence level" is typically sought. The *"confidence level"* refers to the degree of confidence when generalizing to the larger population. The *"confidence interval"* is the "+/− x percent" typically reported on television or in newspapers with polling data. Calculations of confidence depend upon how many people are surveyed and how representative the sample is of the population being surveyed. You will need statistical training to learn how to calculate confidence intervals.

Techniques of Data Gathering

Questionnaires: Paper-and-pencil or electronic responses to written questions.

Interviewing: Face-to-face responses to spoken questions.

Designing Survey Questions

Questions must be phrased to produce ***reliable*** or consistent answers. If answers to the survey are the same from group to group and time to time, the questions are reliable.

Questions must be phrased to produce ***valid*** responses. If one person interprets a question to mean "my opinion" and another interprets a question to mean "an average person's response" the question is not measuring the same thing. Pilot testing is used to ensure validity.

Avoid *double-barreled questions*: "Are you nervous about giving speeches and writing papers?"

Avoid *leading* questions: "Don't you agree that the current situation was caused by ...?"

Surveys must be written to mirror the language skills and expectations of the target groups. In general, stick to a ninth-grade reading level when designing questions.

Questions can measure responses in one of four ways:

Nominal: Gives a choice between two options, Candidate A or Candidate B.

Ordinal: Asks respondents to rank variables from highest to lowest.

Interval: Asks respondents to rate variables that are equally spaced, such as **Likert,** semantic differential, and scales: "Strongly Agree, Agree, Neither Agree nor Disagree, Disagree, Strongly Disagree."

Ratio: Utilizes interval measures but also uses zero: "Please indicate the number of hours you spend each day watching television."

Questions Can Be Open or Closed

Closed Question: Relies on specific categories or scales: Yes/No, True/False, etc.

Open Question: Allows respondents to answer questions in their own words.

Questions Should Be Sequenced

Tunnel: Asks a series of consistent or similarly organized questions.

Funnel: Starts with broad, open questions, followed by more narrow, closed, questions.

Inverted funnel: Begins with narrow, closed questions, and builds to broader, open questions.

Researchers must be wary of response sets and wording questions so all of the questions run in the same direction, such as "Strongly Agree" to "Strongly Disagree," etc. Many people who do not want to participate in a survey, or who are participating just to win a prize, will give the same answer to every question (all one's, all three's, all five's, etc.). With paper-and-pencil surveys especially, questions need to be asked in different ways. If all of the responses are on one side of a scale, the researcher can know, with a quick visual inspection, to throw out the survey as unreliable.

Questionnaire Procedures

Researcher-administered questionnaires: Typically used when the researcher has access to the population being surveyed, such as students in a class, employees at a work site.

Self-administered questionnaires: Typically conducted through the mail or the Internet.

Longitudinal surveys: Conducted over several months or years to describe respondents' changes over time.

Effective questionnaires are accompanied by clear instructions, and respondents are all asked to respond to the survey under the same conditions, with the same amount of time, etc. Response rates vary. Depending upon the type of survey, the population, etc., the U.S. Office of Management and Budget considers a threshold of 75 percent to be good, but response rates as low as 25 percent are common in some types of research.

In order to be successful with surveys, survey *reminders* and duplicate surveys are often sent to participants driving up the cost and time needed to complete the survey research. Survey researchers also offer *incentives* to increase response rates. Token rewards of $1, donations on behalf of the survey taker to charitable causes, opportunities to win a prize, frequent reminders, telephone calls, copies of reports, and other techniques are all used to coax respondents into participating in the survey.

Be careful when engaging in follow-ups on surveys alleged to be "anonymous." People often become suspicious when they receive an e-mail or letter indicating they have not completed a survey and asking them to do so when survey responses are supposed to be anonymous. Similarly, never *require* survey completion as part of employment related duties. People cannot be compelled (ethically or legally) to provide their personal opinions. Also, avoid the "United Way" technique of "You do not have to give any money but we would like everyone to return the envelope." Many organizations use this approach to increase participation. Besides being coercive and unethical, making people feel forced to comply only breeds resentment and mistrust of the group involved.

The question often arises about whether to conduct a survey, a questionnaire, or an interview. Consider these issues:

1. The education/literacy of the audience influences the decision to use questionnaires. With less educated audiences, there is a risk that they might not understand some of the questions. Additionally, one of the issues the Census Bureau faces when it conducts face-to-face interviews is that many racial and ethnic groups do not trust "officials" (including the police, INS, child welfare, and many others). The education of your audience, accessibility, and likelihood of misunderstanding what you ask are factors to be considered. Moreover, objective research is more likely if the survey researchers look like the survey takers.
2. Questionnaires typically employ closed questions and may be conducted in person, or by telephone, print, or e-mail. Interviews typically employ open-ended questions, although many face-to-face "interviews" are just surveys seeking forced choice answers. The depth of answers you seek should influence which method is selected. Genuine interviews typically allow interviewees to answer in-depth while most survey typically do not allow much space for qualitative answers.
3. Questionnaires (often anonymous) are more appropriate for studying sensitive subjects like sexual behavior.
4. Researcher-administered surveys typically have a higher response rate.
5. Time, cost, and organizational resources all matter. Mail surveys are often the least costly, but waiting for responses can take a long time and follow-up expenses must be calculated into the cost. Telephone interviews are the next most costly (when you consider training, the cost of telephone access, and the cost of paying researchers). Face-to-face surveying is the most expensive (especially if travel is required).

As this lengthy discussion suggests, survey research involves a lot more than just asking a few questions of people, which is the approach many organizations take to survey research. In general, you are advised to hire a professional researcher or contract with an academic researcher rather than attempting to conduct a large-scale survey on your own with no training.

Additionally, I have mentioned nothing about how you will analyze the data once you have gathered it. Will data be input into an Excel spreadsheet or will you use SPSS? Do you know how to conduct proper statistical analysis? Questions about how the data will be analyzed need to be asked *before* you administer the survey, when you are designing it, rather than after the survey is done. If a question is not written properly from the start, it cannot be evaluated properly at the end.

In many cases, simple data is all that is needed, and means and standards deviations are sufficient. However, in other cases more sophisticated data analysis is required. If all you know how to do is input numbers into a spreadsheet and add them up (calculate means, medians, modes, standards deviations) then you probably need to know more, like how to conduct a factor analysis, how to measure significance, etc. Consider taking a few graduate classes in statistical methods before you attempt a broad, comprehensive survey.

EXPERIMENTAL RESEARCH

Experimental research is conducted to test the relationship between some phenomenon and relevant variables. For example, "What would happen if we required reporters to log into our online pressroom?"

In general, public relations professionals are almost never asked to devise experiments or assist with scientific research. With very few exceptions, the communication issues public relations professionals encounter on a day-to-day basis do not require experimental research to address. Archival research is sufficient. Experimental research is not something to consider until you have taken a number of graduate-level research methods classes. The role you might play in terms of conducting experimental research is unlikely to extend beyond contacting qualified researchers.

READERSHIP, MEDIA IMPRESSIONS, AND ADVERTISING EQUIVALENCY

Readership—or placement data—and media impressions have been gathered by organizations for years. Essentially, when a news release that was sent to a newspaper or other source is published, a story is written or broadcast, or an organization is mentioned in print or on the radio, television, or the Internet, there has been a "media impression." A recent survey by the Institute for Public Relations reveals that measurement is valued by most public relations professionals. "The survey found that the tools used by PR professionals includes press clippings—still the favourite—[sic] closely followed by AVEs (advertising value equivalent) and more rigorous tools including internal reviews, benchmarking, and the use of specialist media evaluation tools." (www.instituteforpr.org/release_single/global_communicator_survey).

The problem is that a "media impression" (a story appearing in a publication), does not mean anyone read the story. Moreover, newspaper stories often contain both favorable and unfavorable news, so how can you evaluate story placement? Similar problems exist with calculating "advertising equivalency" (the value of a story if the space the story occupies had been purchased as an advertisement). Since fewer people actually read advertisements, and, since stories are considered "more credible," how can comparisons be made?

For example, the *Chicago Tribune* is read by more than 570,000 people. If a news release is published and receives five column inches of space, we can calculate the number of "media impressions" based on readership numbers, as well as "advertising equivalency" (Smith, 2002, pp. 243–244) by comparing the amount of space a news release received to how much it would cost to place a comparable advertisement. Since news items are considered to have from three to five times the credibility of advertisements (p. 244), their actual value is even greater, some argue.

Much controversy exists regarding calculating media impressions or advertising equivalency. Both Jeffries-Fox (www.instituteforpr.org/ipr_info/internet_audience_measurement) and Macnamara (www.pria.com.au/resources/list/asset_id/153/cid/6/parent/1/t/resources) argue that calculations of advertising equivalency have problems. At the same time, advertising equivalency and media impressions often accompany quarterly media reports and clippings files as a means of supporting the arguments made by public relations professionals about outcomes, or to impress clients with a campaign's "success."

Opponents to calculations of advertising equivalency argue that there is no way to compare advertisements to editorial or news content since both have different constraints (control over timing and placement versus potential front page status and free coverage). Additionally, very few publications actually allow advertising on their front pages (except for online publications), so there really is no advertising equivalent of a "front page story." Both positions have merit. But both beg the question of "For what purpose are media impressions and advertising equivalency used?" If media impressions and advertising equivalency are used as a way of proving productivity or success, then they are being used improperly. However, the fact remains, thousands of organizations (from small nonprofits to multinational corporations) prepare quarterly media reports replete with press clippings and data about advertising equivalency and media impressions. When such data are used as a means of gauging whether there has been *placement* success, or "potential" audience members reached in specific markets, such data seems useful. Additionally, advertising equivalency and media impressions can be very useful for making budgeting arguments and obtaining support for campaign proposals. From a rhetorical standpoint, advertising equivalency and media impressions have a lot of persuasive potential.

Many media research organizations currently offer media tracking and data services. Some of the leading firms include: Cision (formerly Bacon's and Bowden's) (us.cision.com), Burrelle's *Luce* (www.burrellesluce.com), PR Newswire (www.prnewswire.com), and others. Many of these organizations also produce media directories (cf., Bacon's, Burrelle's) that provide complete information about readership, publication deadlines, news release acceptance, editors, etc.

CONCLUSION

As explained above, research is an essential component to understanding issues, stakeholders, and publics. Research informs the writing process, enabling you to construct compelling narratives and effective persuasive messages.

Research is a substantive process involving more than just a "Google search." All public relations practitioners need to be proficient with both qualitative and quantitative research. Quantitative techniques like demographic, psychographic, infographic, and geodemographics, as well as qualitative techniques like communication audits and environmental scanning are staples of public relations practice.

ACTIVITIES

1. Working individually or in groups of two, write 10 interview questions using funneling, reverse funneling, or tunneling. Assume you are interviewing three professors about the possibility of going to graduate school next year. Be sure to address issues like funding opportunities, expectations, options for majors, how to succeed, etc.
2. You work for a nonprofit organization for the uninsured and working poor that is trying to enact national healthcare legislation. What kind of environmental scanning would you do on a weekly basis? Be specific. What newspaper, radio, or television programs should you read, listen to, or watch? What kinds of Web sites should you monitor? Whom should you keep in contact with? What journals might you monitor? How would you locate the answers to these questions? Be specific.
3. You have been asked by a supervisor to find out more about social networking as a possible tool for your organization to use to attract clients and communicate with publics. Identify five people by name and title whom you might interview to learn the basics about this topic. Why are the people you selected good choices?
4. Assuming the situation in question 3 above, write three questions (for each person) that are open-ended, moderately open, closed, forced choice, and bipolar. Which types of questions might be the most useful during these interviews?
5. Working in groups of two or three, visit your school's Web site and conduct a communication audit of the messages and information there. Each member of the group should visit a different departmental Web site, i.e. Communication, Journalism/Mass Communication, Honors Program (if applicable), Graduate School, Political Science, Business, etc. Before visiting each department, decide as a group on the scope of the audit and the unit of analysis. Be sure you all agree on what you will examine before you begin, and create a coding sheet.
6. As a class, use the nominal group technique (NGT) to address an issue of importance at your school—housing, parking, food in the dorms, grading systems, etc. Select a substantive issue from your school's environment and address several questions using NGT. Be conservative: do not pick more than two questions since you will only have a short time in class for a process that might take all day.
7. In groups of two or three, identify 20 experts on one of the following areas who might be suitable to participate in a Delphi study (the future of public relations, new technology in public relations, international public relations, or another area specified by your instructor). Prepare a letter inviting the people you identify to participate in the study. What questions would you ask? Be specific.
8. Visit the FedStats Web site (www.fedstats.gov) to see what information of relevance to your state, region, or industry you can find. What kind of information is available? How up-to-date is the information? Is the information credible/trustworthy? Why or why not?
9. You will be assigned to one of three groups. *Group one* will identify demographic information about your university population; *group two* will identify psychographic information about your student population; and *group three* will identify infographic information. Be sure to consult sources such as your university's Web site, college catalogues, the housing office, FedStats (www.fedstats.gov), MySpace and YouTube, local legislators' Web pages, the local chamber of commerce, local news providers, PR Newswire, journalism or broadcasting departmental Web sites, college radio or newspapers, etc. Be prepared to present your results to the class and explain the significance of your findings.

NOTES

1. Note: a primary "source" is not the same as primary "research." If a communication professional is interested in how a specific news source is describing its organizational activities, the news source itself (newspaper, magazine, Web site, etc.) would be a "primary source."
2. For example, a Google or Wikipedia search may or may not turn up reliable information. How can you know? Wikipedia entries are anonymous; the identity of contributors is not publicly available. Many false and inaccurate Wikipedia entries are made every day (some corrected and some not). If the identity and credentials of contributors are kept secret, how do you know that the entry was not written by a competitor trying to mislead someone, a disgruntled worker, or a vandal making something up (as was the case with Alaska Governor Sara Palin's page after she was picked as John McCain's running mate in 2008). Similarly, Google, because of its "relevance"-based search technology, is *more likely* to take you to a corporate Web site (with an agenda), than a research scientist's article.
3. Professional voice recorders usually have a button you can press to flag important points and make them easier to locate on the tape/data file after the interview.
4. Many textbooks and communication professionals suggest, erroneously, that focus groups might have as many as 15 to 20 people in them. An abundance of research into small group communication suggests this is incorrect. As groups get larger, individuals have a tendency to participate less. Many people are not comfortable in crowds, and many people will nod their heads to things they do not agree with as a sign of politely listening to others (this is especially true of women who tend to provide more nonverbal feedback than men do). Additionally, even when a skilled focus group facilitator solicits the opinion of all focus group participants, 20 people all expressing their opinions on a topic will leave little room for exploring other issues unless a six-hour focus group is planned.
5. The word infographics is used to talk about *both* "informational graphics" or graphics designed to clarify information, as well as the sense used in this chapter to mean informational data about what a person reads or listens to.
6. Consider, for example, what can happen to a community when an organization lays off thousands of workers, such as happened in Michigan on a number of occasions in the auto industry. Entire cities can be completely changed in a few months. In Princeton, New Jersey, off of Route 1, sits Johnson & Johnson's corporate headquarters. Almost across the street from that building are neighborhoods where hundreds of J&J employees and executive families live. Imagine what would happen if J&J laid off a few hundred or thousand of those highly paid workers.

   In November 2008, more than a half-million workers were laid off in the U.S., with several organizations laying off tens of thousands of workers at a time. Organizations need to be aware of what is happening to publics' geodemographically in order to adapt to changing economic and social landscapes.

Chapter 8

Archival Research and Technology

Many college students take the World Wide Web for granted, having lived with it most of their lives. Indeed, many students were *required* to use the Internet, PowerPoint, and several other technologies for class assignments in grade school and high school. As you move through college and begin to prepare for entry into the "real world" you need to unlearn many of the "shortcuts" you learned to take like using pictures you downloaded from the Internet, or using Wikipedia as a research tool, and learn how to obtain reliable, professional, information.

The previous chapter highlighted many of the basic research skills needed by public relations professionals to gather information, create effective messages, and conduct campaign planning. This chapter covers *active* research techniques like using databases and new technologies, and *passive* research techniques (environmental scanning). This chapter also goes further by elaborating on new archival research techniques, online databases, journal databases, and news and legal databases that can be used to gather information about stakeholders and publics and to distribute messages effectively through electronic channels.

Over the last decade, technological advances have transformed how we conduct research. Although journal articles and magazines have been widely available online since the mid-1990s, if the trend continues, soon every book ever written will also be available online—making online research even easier than it is now. Understanding the principles of online research is essential, and keeping up with new technology will be one of your everyday tasks as a public relations professional.

TECHNOLOGY USED FOR CONDUCTING RESEARCH

In many ways, learning to write effectively for the Web will be the most difficult task you have ahead of you as professionals since there are so many issues to understand, including style, tone, persuasion, imagery, graphic design, dialogic communication, and rhetoric. The Web is useful for secondary research using blogs, Listservs, and online databases, as well as for primary research in the form of surveys and online research. The information needed to create effective and compelling messages is often obtained through electronic sources.

Survey Software

Survey research is easier than ever with online survey software. Indeed, the survey has become one of the primary ways in which organizations learn about their publics (Kent, Harrison, & Taylor, 2006). A survey runs the gamut from a business reply card or product registration card to formal data gathered by professional pollsters. Somewhere in the middle of these extremes are online surveys, which are often conducted using the Internet and survey software. Survey software automatically generates the computer code needed for online surveys to look like surveys and to have survey data automatically reported as the survey is taken.

In general, before you use survey software, be sure you understand something about survey methodology and what you want to learn from the individuals or publics surveyed. Many online surveys are poorly written and force respondents to answer *every* question, even if the survey taker has no relevant experience with the subject of the question or is reluctant to answer the question. Consequently, many survey takers simply refuse to complete the survey, which results in unreliable data. Additionally, when respondents are *forced* to answer each question in order to move to the next question, determining how many of the people who completed the survey were telling the truth becomes impossible. The data become useless.

Many survey takers are curious enough about the questions being asked that they will provide answers to every question just so they can see all of the questions (or be eligible for a prize). Be careful when using survey software since the important part of a survey is *what you want to know* and not *whether every survey taker completes every question on the survey.*

CREATING ONLINE SURVEYS

As public relations research tools, online surveys have become commonplace. Surveys are used for marketing purposes, to gather opinions from customers and organizational members, and to determine public sentiment on issues. Online surveys have serious limitations in terms of anonymity and reliability of demographic information. Nevertheless, a number of survey tools have been developed that allow professionals to rapidly and easily gather survey data.

There are hundreds of online survey software companies, and each emphasizes an assortment of features. Two of the most well-known companies are SurveyMonkey and Zoomerang. Be aware that many survey services charge for access to their software, but offer little more than many of the inexpensive survey companies like SurveyMonkey or Zoomerang. Additionally, many "free" survey services will work perfectly for students who want to learn how to conduct online surveys. As the SurveyMonkey Web site explains:

> A basic subscription is totally free and includes all of the basic features of SurveyMonkey. It's a great option for individuals, students, and anyone who doesn't need the advanced features of SurveyMonkey. Unlike other services, there are no annoying banner ads on your surveys. In addition, all of your survey responses remain absolutely private. Please note that basic subscribers are limited to a total of 10 questions and 100 responses per survey.... A professional subscription is only $19.95 USD/month (or only $200 USD/year), and includes up to 1,000 responses per month. If you exceed 1,000 survey responses in any given month, there is an additional charge of $.05 USD per survey response. There are no long-term contracts, and you can cancel at any time. As a professional subscriber, you have access to all of the advanced features of SurveyMonkey. You can create an unlimited number of surveys, with an unlimited number of pages and questions. In addition, all of your surveys are completely unbranded. (techtraining.brevard.k12.fl.us/BETC2007/GipsonSurveyMonkey.pdf)

One of the most robust and flexible online survey packages I have run across is Qualtrics, which claims, "SurveyMonkey and Zoomerang both offer 15 different question types. We provide 88 different question types" (www.qualtrics.com). However, Qualtrics charges a great deal more for access than SurveyMonkey, Zoomerang, or others.

Whatever program you select should be based on your needs, rather than just saving a few dollars. The cost of paper surveys and postage is quite high in comparison to e-surveys, so you already save a lot by paying for an e-survey service. The added information that can be obtained from a more robust survey package could easily offset the cost. By the same token, be sure to shop around. Many of the online survey companies are charging thousands of dollars a year to do what others will do for $200.

Most of the online survey tools make constructing surveys and compiling data very easy. Indeed, there is no reason *not* to gather such data when appropriate from online groups since the tools are easy and inexpensive. SurveyMonkey is something all public relations students should experiment with when conducting class research so they learn how to use online research tools and become comfortable gathering data.[1]

One thing to keep in mind, however, when conducting surveys, or e-surveys, is never to allow organizational lists of stakeholders and publics to be used for marketing purposes. Marketers often do not understand the relationship-building role of public relations and instead want to use surveys to try and sell something to the target audience. Many deceptive marketing surveys are used to obtain answers to marketing questions about customer/client preferences with no real interest in asking people what they want or need. No one is fooled by marketing surveys, and many find the practice insulting. Do not allow your organization's stakeholders and publics to be harassed in this fashion. Even when you have subscriber-only lists for customers who want to receive "messages of interest," do not be tempted to send your subscribers a survey asking them for their "important insight" when you are really just trying to sell them something. Few things will alienate stakeholders (who were proactive enough to contact you and become affiliated with an organization) as much as being sent a *faux* survey. As the Public Relations Society of America (PRSA) code of ethics suggests: Deal fairly with publics—past, present & future; Ensure accuracy and truth in communications; Never transmit false or misleading statements; and Do not corrupt the channels of communication or government. Marketing surveys do all of these things.

Another important issue has to do with the way survey companies charge for surveys. Many of the online survey tools *require* people to "complete every question on the survey" because "only completed surveys" are counted. Forcing survey takers to answer every question is a mistake. In many cases, some people cannot answer ambiguously written questions, or questions that assume there are only a limited number of "forced choice" answers to questions. In such cases, two things can happen: (1) the survey taker will lie (or guess) in order to continue the survey, resulting in unreliable data; or (2) the survey taker will quit taking the survey, again resulting in lopsided data that only represents those who finished the survey and not everyone in the target population.

More importantly, however, on a "real" (face-to-face, telephone, or mailed) survey, when a survey taker refuses to answer a question or admits that s/he "cannot answer the question," the survey designer learns that there might be a bad question, or learns that s/he needs to know *more* before the question can be answered.

If the survey company or software you are using does not allow survey takers to skip questions, or does not encourage them to select "other" or "explain," you should consider using another survey tool/company. If necessary, surveys can also be created manually using HTML software. The only real reason to use survey software is because it makes analysis of the data easier. When small groups are being surveyed or when you have access to a professional who can create an electronic survey in-house, do not hesitate to create your own electronic survey and skip the off-the-shelf vendors.

SOCIAL NETWORKING

Another area becoming important to professionals are social networking sites, like Facebook and MySpace. Most college students understand Facebook and MySpace, so I will not explain them here. In the professional world, the most popular social networking site is LinkedIn (www.linkedin.com). However, since social networking technologies change all of the time, LinkedIn may not even be used by the time this book goes to press. The real point to appreciate here is that social networking has taken hold in many places, and you will undoubtedly be expected to understand it.

One of the reasons that social networking has become so popular in the professional world is because of the ability to connect directly with key publics. As suggested elsewhere, public relations is about creating and maintaining relationships among organizations, stakeholders, and publics. The public relations professional acts as a liaison or "boundary spanner." In order to help create effective relationships and construct compelling organizational narratives, social networking tools can be used to monitor publics and share information. Ultimately, your success at creating mutually beneficial relationships is based on your understanding of your stakeholders and publics and co-creating a shared reality. The coorientational model of communication helps describe how this process works.

COORIENTATIONAL MODEL OF COMMUNICATION (CMC)

Coorientation theory considers how groups see each other and what they believe other groups think about them. In any relationship, people are aware of at least three perspectives: (1) the perception of self (as honest, strategic, powerful, etc.); (2) the perception of the other (as friendly, self-serving, manipulative, elitist, etc.); and (3) metacommunication assumptions, or the assumptions about what the individual or organization thinks the other individual or group thinks about them ("They hate us," "They think we do not care").

Disagreements over definitions of these three perspectives often lead to intractable situations. One group may see itself as the "supermarket to the world" (ADM, the Archer Daniels Midland Company) but an activist group with a different world view and set of experiences may see your organization as "exploiters of the world." Ironically, and the real difficulty with coorientation, both of the perceptions are correct. Individual perceptions of the world cannot ever be proven "wrong." As Mandrik, Fern, and Bao explain:

> Prediction accuracy is considered "an essential measure of the effectiveness of communication between two people"... because as communication increases between two people, logically so should their ability to accurately state each other's views ... Therefore, it is inferred that the better able a daughter is to predict her mother's brand preferences and values, the more communication (direct or indirect) must have taken place and the more likely the daughter is to have been influenced to adopt the mother's consumption orientation or brand preference. (2005, p. 817)

The coorientational model of communication can be used to help organizations understand how individuals and groups external to an organization perceive issues (Chaffee & McLeod, 1968; Mandrik, Fern, & Bao, 2005; Taylor & Kent, 2006). Stable interpersonal relationships (and intergroup relationships) require some accurate level of intersubjectivity or coorientation in order to understand and explain the actions of others. For example, an organization discovers that an activist group has set up an "I hate [your organization]" Web site. Your initial reaction might be to wonder, "Who do these people think they are?" and ignore the group. But, over time, the activist group may attract the attention of the media, or adversely affect your sales or ability to attract new customers. Something needs to be done. Some informal coorientational research might be a first step. Before you decide what to do, you need to understand the group and whether it has a legitimate complaint.

Coorientation encompasses efforts to come to honest and objective perceptions of the other group or organization's views and to try to understand how it thinks about your group or organization and why it believes what it does. There is intersubjectivity when both parties in a communicative exchange share the same views. Intersubjectivity is difficult and often unobtainable depending upon the degree of ideological, economic, or social distance between organizations and publics. A lack of intersubjectivity on the part of individuals is why it is so difficult for people in the U.S. to understand why other nations fear, hate, or mistrust us (Taylor & Kent, 2006, pp. 352–355).

A coorientational position represents a commitment among individuals and groups to try to *understand* the other's definition of reality and events, in spite of whether that definition is shared. For intersubjectivity to be achieved, both parties in an interaction must be willing to see the world differently and accept that the other's view of the world is not necessarily "wrong," only different (Taylor & Kent, 2006, pp. 352–355; cf., Broom, 1977; Springston & Keyton, 2001; Springston, Keyton, Leichty, & Metzher, 1992). The ability to create compelling informative and persuasive messages is contingent on accurate coorientational understanding of target audiences.

Coorientational communication, or efforts to communicate with individuals and groups in such a way as to genuinely understand their beliefs, values, and opinions, is challenging but can be extremely valuable when an organization is dealing with oppositional publics, like activist organizations. Coorientation can be evaluated both internally and externally. For example, organizations are often very interested in understanding how workers view the organization (whether they trust or respect the organization/management) so that organizational climate changes can be made if necessary and employee loyalty and productivity increased.

Coorientation is more than just tolerance, however. From a public relations standpoint, coorientation means that two or more individuals or parties have an awareness of how they are *actually* perceived by others, not just a belief about what they think the other group thinks about them. Coorientation requires individuals and groups to engage each other to learn about how each sees the world and what each individual or group *actually* believes. A coorientational approach is closely tied to the dialogic approach discussed in Chapter 10.

For the U.S. government to take a coorientational approach with other nations, for example, would require U.S. leaders to actually interact with citizens and leaders of other nations. Coorientational understanding among leaders comes not from prearranged, perfunctory ceremonies but from actually trying to engage citizens and leaders in realistic settings and trying to understand why they see the U.S., their own country, and the world the way that they do. On the most basic level, coorientation requires a commitment to understanding, a willingness to listen, and the capacity to change your mind when you discover that you are wrong (Taylor & Kent, 2006, 352–355).

Public relations professionals need to understand that the coorientational approach to communication is vital when an organization is facing oppositional interests or when an organization is trying to forge a relationship with individuals and groups who have different cultural or worldviews. One of the essential features of effective persuasion and coorientational relationship building is Kenneth Burke's concept of identification. Burke's writings on rhetoric and persuasion, via identification, have been among the most influential writings of the last 50 years. Identification has been embraced as a central tenant of self-persuasion and relationship building by advertisers, governmental officials, marketers, legislators, nonprofit organizations, political scientists, public relations professionals, sociologists, psychologists and others.

IDENTIFICATION

The list of contributions that Burke has made to communication is long. Of particular interest to public relations is Burke's insight into persuasion (1969b, 1973a). According to Burke, persuasion is based on a concept called "identification." As the word implies, rhetoric (or persuasion) is about helping your audience understand how you are like them, and how their interests and your interests mesh (Photo 8.1). For Burke, persuasion is built around making your audience feel that you are like them and understand them. Burke used the term **consubstantiality** (1969b, pp. 19–29), or of one substance, mentioned earlier, to describe the process.

According to Burke (1973a pp. 263–275), there are three kinds of identification: by sympathy, antithesis, and unawareness. ***Identification by sympathy*** attempts to make your audience feel positively toward you. Strategies like, "I have been where you are" or "I am working for you to try and make things better," are used to portray the rhetor (persuader) as someone who has the best interests of the audience in mind. ***Identification by antithesis*** attempts to invoke commonalities (called *congregation*) and differences (called *segregation*): common goals, heroes, and lived experiences, common enemies, villains, and differences that make *us* (the audience and the persuader) special, better, different, etc. ***Identification by unawareness*** is in some ways like *ethos*, and refers to the kind of implicit identification that we possess as members of an organization, group, cause or activity, and the implicit enmity that people feel for those who are part of *different* groups, causes, or activities.

PHOTO 8.1 Source: Kenneth Burke, Special Collections Department. The Pennsylvania State University Libraries

The first kind of identification (sympathy) is easy to employ and cultivate. Images used in advertisements, newsletters, posters, and signs are selected to resemble the demographics of the target audience. Speakers will often comment on the occasion as being a "difficult time," or congratulate the audience for "coming out so late." Indeed, any attempt to garner a bit of sympathy from an audience can work in a rhetorician's favor when persuading—"I was a student once, I know how boring textbooks are." Or, when sending an e-mail to someone busy or an organizational superior, we often write "I know how busy you must be right now with…."

The second type of identification (antithesis) involves explicit efforts to establish similarity or difference. Burke argues that every effort to create identification and draw upon similarities is also an effort to show how you are *not like* something. Thus, when a legislator speaks of his/her party, "The Democrats believe …" s/he is also saying "But the Republicans don't …" Essentially, an enthymeme gets invoked whenever identification takes place. A rhetorician might say, "We are not like them …" but at the same time, s/he is also saying "We are like something else…." Both arguments exist at the same time even though a writer or speaker only makes one of them.

Consider President Nixon's famous Checkers speech, where Nixon explains, "that Pat doesn't have a mink coat. But she does have a respectable Republican cloth coat." Nixon was trying to both identify with the average American, who does not have a mink coat, as well as to distance himself (and the average American) from the rich elites who do.

The third form of identification, and the most difficult to use, is identification by unawareness. Sports teams are a great example of identification by unawareness. Most people have never been part of the teams that they root for, or even played the sport, and yet, people from Wisconsin, who are not normally Packers fans (if that is possible), suddenly care a lot about whether the Packers win when they are in the playoffs. Similarly, many Los Angeles Dodgers fans will root for the Los Angeles Angels if they are playing in the World Series against the New York Yankees, even though they are not Angels fans, because the team is from *Los Angeles*.

The more difficult part of identification by unawareness is how to use it to your benefit. Identification by unawareness is very powerful. People identify with their schools, towns, states, countries, companies, and products/brands, often for their entire lives. Equally often, people identify with things that they do not even like because they "survived" (consider the Rutgers University anecdote mentioned in the previous chapter). Take for example the many people who might say that they hate their job, their major, their school. In 20 years those same people might be endowing a scholarship, building a building on campus, or running the company they hated, and fondly remembering their days as an intern in the communications department.

Communicators can never know with certainty what people will identify with; however, effective research and audience analysis will point a rhetorician to the areas that people may not be aware they identify with, but that could be used persuasively. Nationalist rhetoric, for example, which draws upon national loyalty and perceived "slights" (often fabricated) by other people or nations, is used to stir people to action. You may recall the anti-French rhetoric a few years ago because France opposed the Iraqi war. Many U.S. restaurants began calling their fried potatoes "freedom fries" rather than "French fries." Be aware that rhetoric that draws upon deeply held symbolic associations (God, country, the state) can be used to motivate people to do great things but also great harm, and is difficult to combat. Invoke such images with care: using them insincerely can lead to a backlash from people who might feel that their emotions are being toyed with.

Identification and Social Networking

Returning to social networking, professionals are not interested in social networking technologies simply to make friends, as college students might be, but as strategic communication tools that can be enormously powerful for identification, coorientation, and generating shared organizational narratives. Many organizations are trying to mine social networking sites for information about college students' beliefs, attitudes, and values, and the demographics and psychographics of individuals and groups who use Facebook, MySpace, or other social networking sites.

Two issues are of particular importance for professionals:

1. Be aware that what you post on your own pages will not only be read by others but also archived and saved. What you post *today* may still be available to someone 5 or 10 years down the road, even if you delete it or have it locked up. Many job seekers are surprised to learn that employers conduct Google searches of potential employees as well as directing interns and

current employees try to trick job applicants into granting them access to their Facebook or MySpace pages and to those of their friends. If you *do* maintain a social networking presence, be careful about what you post there; it could cost you your next job or damage professional relationships (cf., <www.computerworld.com/action/article.do?command=printArticleBasic&articleId=285324>, <www.computerworld.com/blogs/node/4260>, <www.techdirt.com/articles/20060118/1056224.shtml>).

2. As a professional, you may be asked to mine social networking sites for information about potential employees or recommend the strategy to an employer. Be aware that many online companies now specialize in providing social networking and demographic data culled from millions of people's pages. Your future employer may want to use such information to reach specific publics or to learn about their interests/preferences.

ONLINE NEWS SITES AND ONLINE RESEARCH

Online research is attractive to most people because it seems easy. A student or researcher does not even have to go to the library any more. All you have to do is type a few words into your search engine and *voilà*, what you are looking for pops up like magic. Unfortunately, professional research requires more than a Google search. Valuable information can also be found in blogs, news groups, and the Usenet.

Like social networking sites, blogs and news sites are visited for professional purposes: to gather demographic and psychographic data and for environmental scanning. One of the reasons that blogs and news sites are so important is that people are attracted to areas that interest them.

The research on uses and gratifications (called uses and grats) tells us that people seek out information and entertainment that has relevance to their lives and that they find rewarding or "gratifying" (identification). Thus, we discover that people who have an interest in firearms are likely to visit gun blogs and news sites about gun issues. Similarly, a professional who works in an arts and crafts profession is likely to visit and monitor craft sites. Equally important, however, is that parents who have autistic children visit Web sites and read blogs about autism; people who care about homelessness visit Web sites and read blogs about helping homeless people; people who are interested in technology spend time on technology sites and subscribe to Listservs in their areas of interest.

Professionals who understand uses and grats know that although not everyone who visits a news site or blog is an expert with great interest in the subject, many of those who do visit are experts and professionals. From the standpoint of a professional communicator, blogs and news sites are not just places that may be of "interest," but places where opinion leaders, experts, and fellow colleagues congregate. Community power theories help explain how such relationships can be used for strategic purposes.

COMMUNITY POWER THEORIES (CPT)

Essentially, what **community power theory** tells us is that people turn to networks of family members, friends, and other influential people and groups for advice. CPT also assumes that behavior, attitudes, and opinion change are less likely and more difficult without the aid of a supportive network of family, friends, and social organizations.

Community power theories span a wide range of areas: everything from college students making decisions about which college to attend, a person asking a more knowledgeable friend or colleague for advice on what kind of cellular telephone to purchase, or guidance counselors advising students how to attend college draw upon "community" experts for advice and counsel.

To put the matter more keenly, how might a public relations professional reach any segmented public with a relevant message? Young children, for example, tend not to watch the local network news or read the local newspaper, the number of children-oriented magazines is quite small, and children do not drive themselves around town a lot so they do not pay attention to billboards or signs, so how does a practitioner reach them? Other groups that are difficult to reach include high school students, the homeless, intravenous drug users, runaways, prostitutes, and a host of other individuals and groups that exist on the periphery of society, outside of the media and cultural mainstream.

The answer to how to reach such individuals and groups should be obvious, they are reached through community groups, influential citizens, and professionals. Children are reached through their parents, teachers, school nurses, counselors, doctors, and community groups and organizations. College-bound teenagers are reached through their parents, school counselors, coaches, and teachers. Professionals are reached through editorialists, colleagues, and opinion leaders. Homeless and runaway youths, drug users, and other individuals and groups, who tend not to have e-mail and postal addresses, are reached through shelters, religious groups, and organizations that work to assist such people.

Public relations professionals should be aware that often a peripheral route is the best means of reaching certain individuals and groups and professional communicators need to be prepared to use an assortment of nonstandard strategies when designing campaigns and messages. Influence via the direct route of advertising and the media is often too expensive or not practical. "Community power" is often the only way to reach some individuals and groups with messages of interest or importance. At the heart of community power is the concept of "word of mouth," which is believed to be one of the most persuasive tools for advertising, marketing, and informational communication. Thus, being able to reach mainstream publics directly is one of the most valuable ways to reach peripheral publics. Informing opinion leaders, experts, and community members about issues of importance to family members, friends, and professional colleagues is a well-established persuasion technique.

USING BLOGS IN PUBLIC RELATIONS

The word "blog" refers to a Web log, or an online diary of posts sorted in reverse chronological order. Thus, as many of you probably know, a blog will have the most recent entry at the top followed by older entries. Some blogs also sort the content by subject or title so particular entries may be easily located. The primary feature of an online log (or blog) as opposed to an actual diary is that blogs are public documents. Because blogs are public, they are written to be "entertaining," whereas diary entries are usually less self-consciously written since they are not written as public documents. As Kent (2008) explains:

> There are several types of blogs. The traditional or historic blog is written like a diary entry, or an op–ed page. Bloggers rant about whatever injustice draws their attention on a particular day (Finneran, 2006; Lenhart, 2006, p. 12). Entries tend toward narcissism. By contrast, another type of blog, the "news blog" has emerged. News blogs are essentially clearinghouses of news headlines or abstracts that usually link readers to an actual news story as a means of establishing ethos and credibility.[2] The classic news blog is the Drudge Report (www.DrudgeReport.com) or Drudge Retort (www.drudge.com). Most blogs (90%) also contain threaded dialogue[3] allowing readers to comment on news items and posts (Lenhart, 2006, p. 20). Consequently, many blogs are filled with rants, flames, and irrelevant comments. (p. 33)[4]

Blogs have been around since the late 1990s and, depending upon the interests of the author, typically focus on a single area (politics, technology, etc.). A number of true bloggers have received attention from the media after being fired for posting comments critical of their employers. Several news blogs have also received attention for timely and biting coverage of social and political issues.

Some well-known news blogs that have received attention for breaking important stories ahead of major news outlets or have made news for fighting censorship issues include: *BoingBoing: A Directory of Wonderful Things* (www.boingboing.net), *DrudgeReport* (www.DrudgeReport.com), and *Slashdot: News for Nerds: Stuff That Matters* (slashdot.org). Indeed, there really is no such thing as a "typical" blog. Blogs run the gamut from Web commentary posted by citizens about their everyday lives (true online diaries) to blogs by employees who have an axe to grind. In general, the blog has a place in public relations as a research tool more than a communication tool (cf., Kent, 2008).

Blog Significance

What the blog offers is the power to reach the choir. Blogs are excellent environmental scanning and monitoring tools and are useful for framing messages (Kent, 2008, pp. 34–35). Blogs are read *more* by young, male, well-educated, wealthy, and experienced Internet users. Young, wealthy, educated males are obviously an attractive demographic for many organizations; however, because blogs are currently something Web users seek out (they have not reached mainstream status yet), those who read them are often already members of the "choir."

Blogs offer organizations another route for distributing public relations positions in a controlled fashion. However, blogs also have risks. Because Blogs are written on short notice and in some cases with little organizational oversight, bloggers have to be well-trained, high-ranking, communication professionals capable of making judgments about what can and cannot be said in a blog. Additionally, if organizations are going to allow threaded dialogue to be part of their blogging efforts, blog postings need to be monitored to correct erroneous information and so irrelevant postings are removed (advertisements for other businesses, pornography links, etc.). Never remove substantive responses because you do not like what has been written: such behavior will only undermine the trust in the organization when it gets out on someone else's blog that your organization deletes negative comments. Do not allow threaded dialogue if your organization is concerned about what people might say.

A final point worth noting, and something almost completely ignored in the discussions about blogs, has to do with persuasion. If you refer back to Chapter 6 (Table 6.1, Features of Persuasion), you will remember that messages in print tend to succeed or fail based on the quality of the arguments and writing, rather than who the author might be: "Untrustworthy sources are more effective when using print or radio." In print, "good arguments" are "good arguments" whether they come from a CEO or a dogcatcher. If your organization is planning to blog, be sure the bloggers are well trained and that supervisors clear messages before posting them.

Using Blogs for Research

For professionals who want to keep up with what the "experts" are saying (if we want to call bloggers experts), there are software applications called aggregators that automatically compile data from blogs and other Web sites. Compilers are actually very easy to use and one of the greatest research tools ever developed for monitoring newspapers, Web sites, blogs, and many other communication sources. If you can use e-mail, you can figure out how to use a compiler. Consider the following free aggregators that you can get up and running in about 5 to 10 minutes: NetNewsWire (www.newsgator.com/Individuals/Default.aspx), and NewsLife (www.thinkmac.co.uk/newslife) (Figure 8.1 illustrates a signup window for Google Reader).

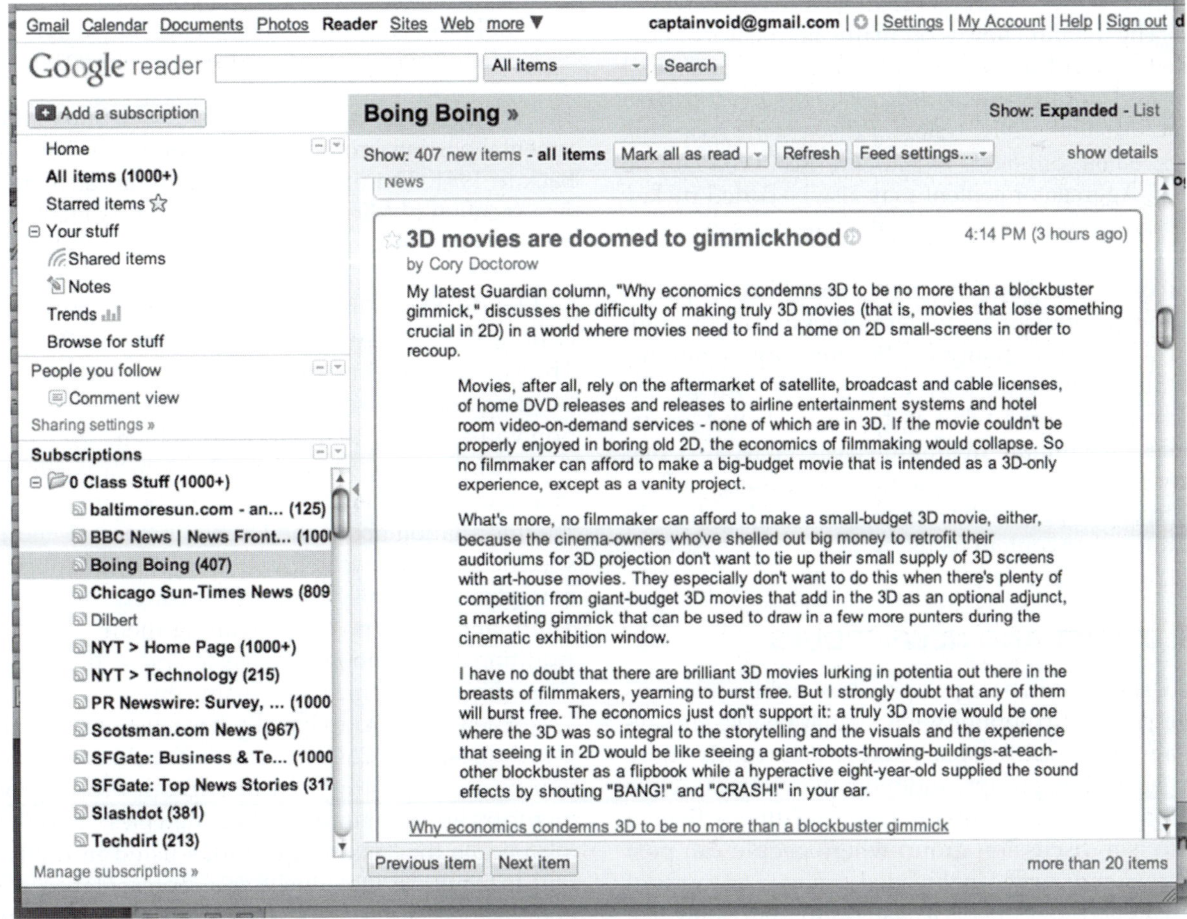

FIGURE 8.1 RSS signup window.
Source: © 2009 Google.

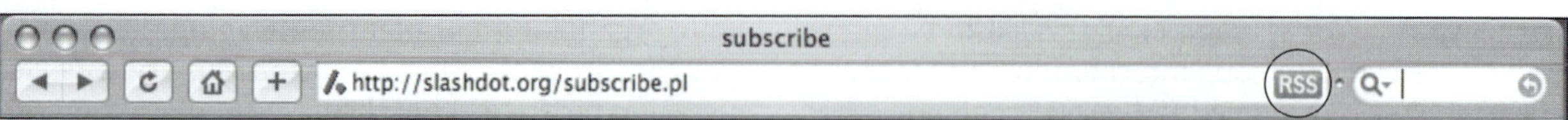

FIGURE 8.2 Browser Toolbar with RSS.
Source: Used with permission from Microsoft.

Aggregators bring in what are called RSS (Really Simple Syndication) feeds. The principle of RSS is a lot like a personalized newspaper that leaves out the sections you never read. RSS uses a programming language called XML (similar to HTML) to convert Web content into an easily shared, text-based format. You probably have visited hundreds of Web sites with RSS feeds and never knew it. For example, next time you are using the Internet, take a look at the address bar, or sometimes the top or bottom of the Web page you are visiting, and you will see a small box with "RSS" or "XML" inside it. How obvious the RSS link is depends on whether you are using the latest browser and which browser you are using (Figure 8.2). Browsers interpret RSS pages differently, just like different Internet browsers interpret HTML in different ways.

The default choices on many aggregators allow users to select from among several dozens to several thousand popular feeds: *BBC, BoingBoing, Christian Science Monitor, CNN, NASA, PRNewswire, New York Times, Salon, Slashdot, Wired. Any* RSS feed can be added. Aggregator content may also be sorted by key words, with some aggregators allowing users to receive only the content that interests them based on preset key words. Using an RSS aggregator will allow public relations professionals to very quickly sort through information from many media sites, organizations, and bloggers, essentially giving professionals the ability to monitor what is being said by various sources on a minute-by-minute basis. Note, also, that many Internet content providers like Google allow you to create personalized news sites and easily add RSS and other content feeds.

THE USENET AND NEWSGROUPS

The Usenet and newsgroups allow public relations professionals to monitor what regular people are saying about organizations. There are currently more than 3.5 million groups, and more than 100,000 active groups (groups.google.com/groups/dir). A Usenet group is a discussion group where people can post messages and engage in threaded dialogue on topics of mutual interest. Usenet is a chat group, something like IRC (Internet Relay Chat) but without simultaneous interaction. Google acquired all of the Usenet archives (some 500 million archived messages dating back to 1981) from Deja News when Google acquired the company in 2001. Google describes the Usenet and what have been called "newsgroups" for more than 20 years (groups.google. com/support):

> Usenet refers to the distributed online bulletin board system begun in 1979 at Duke University. Usenet users can post messages in newsgroups that can be read or contributed to by anyone with access to the Internet and special newsreader software. Over the years, the number of newsgroups has grown to the thousands, hosted all over the world and covering every conceivable topic. (groups.google.com/support/bin/answer.py?answer=46854&topic=9246)

Google provides a very useful timeline of monumental postings from its Web site of the Usenet going back to 1981. The timeline includes items such as the first mention of Microsoft in 1981, the first mention of the emoticon (smiley) in 1982, the first post from an AOL account in 1992, Gene Spafford's final post in 1993, and the first September 11, 2001, posts (www.google.com/googlegroups/archive_announce_20.html). The Usenet timeline might be a good place to start learning about newsgroups and the sort of information you are likely to find posted in them.

Additionally, if you intend to join or participate in a newsgroup as part of your job, be sure you read the information about the Usenet in general and the specific groups to which you may post. Members of newsgroups are suspicious of "outsiders" who join a group and never post to it (calling them "lurkers"). Additionally, members who ask too many direct questions also make some users suspicious.

Each newsgroup usually has a list of frequently asked questions (FAQs) that you should read before you consider posting to a newsgroup. Newsgroup members are often intolerant of "newbies," and flaming people for "asking questions listed in the FAQ file" is common. Obviously, as a representative of an organization, you do not want to be accused of lurking, flaming, or harassing group members. Similarly, be sure to learn the conventions of online dialogue. ALL CAPITAL LETTERS is considered "shouting" and people do not like it. Be sure that if you are going to use all capital letters you do it for a good reason (For example, to set your comments apart from another message). There are many other typographic conventions you should understand; you should join a few newsgroups and familiarize yourself with the various rules before joining on behalf of an organization. Watch the episode of *The West Wing* where Josh Limon tries to correct a newsgroup posting for a better understanding of how some newsgroups function (season 2, "The U.S. Poet Laureate").

When posting to any electronic source on behalf of an organization, including newsgroups, blogs, and Listservs, always identify yourself (either as part of the message introduction or in your address line) whether you are asking questions, posting corrections, or offering explanations. Never try to pass yourself off as a "random citizen." As a public relations representative you are not just anyone, you represent the organization.

Many blogs will actually examine metadata from messages and track down the source of suspicious messages when they are too supportive of organizations or when a message poster seems too knowledgeable. Many managers and communication professionals erroneously think anonymous postings cannot be tracked back to their source. They can, and anonymous posters are regularly outed by list moderators for being deceptive. Failed attempts to pass yourself off as a "random member" always make the organization that posted the message look desperate or ignorant. Public relations professionals are organizational representatives and they should never lie about who they are, disguise their identity, or try to "subvert the channels of communication" (a violation of the Public Relations Society of America's Code of Professional Ethics).

Like blogs, newsgroups can be useful for taking the temperature of regular people with a big enough interest in a subject to want to talk about it with other people. In many cases, Usenet groups are filled with fanatics—like the people who spend their time discussing the latest episode of *CSI* (for which there are a few dozen newsgroups), or a controversial *Babylon 5* episode from 1995. Obviously, you should not place too much stock in what a few dozen people committed to a cause, issue, or product say; however, you should also be aware that for each fanatic there are hundreds, perhaps thousands of people who feel similarly (albeit less passionately). Blogs, RSS, listservs, and newsgroups are excellent tools for monitoring what individuals and publics are saying and for keeping up-to-date in specialized areas.

USING SEARCH ENGINES AND EFFECTIVE SEARCH TECHNIQUES

Most people believe they know how to search the Web effectively. Indeed, many professionals and students think that all there is to conducting a Web search is to open up Google and type in a few words. Research by Middleberg and Ross (1999a, 1999b, 2000b), and a more recent study in *Editor & Publisher*, confirm that journalists use the Internet a lot (www.editorandpublisher.com, March 27, 2008, "Survey Finds Journalists Are Working More—and Working More Online"), which is probably not surprising. What *is* surprising is how poor the search skills of journalists actually are.

Most journalists complain that when they conduct a search they get "too many results." The problem with this complaint is that the more sites a search engine indexes, the higher the chances are you will find what we are looking for. More results are good not bad; the trick is to know how to sort the results. But how is someone supposed to sort through 43 million pages of "junk?" If you follow the suggestions on the list that follows, I can guarantee that even the most seasoned searcher will discover an improvement in their search success.

Ten Tips for Searching the Web

1. *Search for words in quotation marks*, called "phrase searches." Enclosing words in quotation marks tells the search engine that you want to look for an exact combination of words. Use quotation marks whenever feasible, especially when searching for names. A search for "Michael L. Kent" *without* quotation marks yields 2,640,000 Web pages. A search for "Michael L. Kent" *with* quotation marks yields 2,550 Web pages. Quite a difference.
2. *The more key words used the better*—sometimes a dozen or more. Begin searches with a few of the most important words. If you wind up with millions of hits (and you will), and your answer is not at the top of the list, simply add another word or two and resubmit the search. After you have half-a-dozen words, you will usually be approaching a reasonable number of results. Consider the following search: Michael: 641,000,000, add Kent: 15,000,000, add *Public Relations*: 654,000, add *Communication*: 109,000, add *Dialogue*: 8,700, add *Ph.D.*: 4,320. If you

integrated quotation marks, as noted above, far fewer words would be needed. If you use phrase searching (quotation marks) *first*, and then start adding keywords, you will have much greater success. For example, a search for ("Michael L. Kent" "Public Relations") yields 83 hits. If you add *Dialogue* ("Michael L. Kent" "Public Relations" *dialogue*) you get 40 hits, all relevant.

3. *Do not waste your time searching through large lists of hits.* If what you are searching for is not at the top of the list, add another key word and try again.
4. *Use search engines that support Boolean logic.* Boolean logic is the use of logic terms (AND, OR, NOT) to construct search phrases. Typically search engines are not case sensitive, however, in the case of Boolean logic, they are. Four logical terms are accepted by the majority of search engines, but be aware, not all search engines use logic the same way or accept all of the terms. Be sure to read the advanced searching instructions on the search engine you use most often. Google, for example places an automatic AND between all words, so you never need to type AND (cf., Kent, 2000, 2001a).
5. Use AND between words ("Public Relations" AND Crisis) to search for results for *both* terms (narrower). Use OR between words ("Public Relations" OR Crisis) to search for *either* result from terms (wider). Use NOT between words ("Public Relations" NOT Crisis) to *exclude* results. Use an asterisk (*) to conduct a wildcard search, to replace unknown parts of words, prefixes, or suffixes. "Communi*" for example, to search for a suffix, will return hits for "community, communication, communicative." Using "*pound" will return results for "impound, compound, Ezra Pound, English Pound, dog pound," etc. For example, if you did not remember a name completely, you might search for "*spinner" with as many other key words as you could remember to find "PageSpinner" (an HTML editor). With many search engines, +/− symbols are interchangeable with AND or NOT. Note: when using symbols instead of words, insert a space before the symbol, but no space before the word (e.g., Dogs +Cats –Garfield).
6. *The order of the words affects your results.* Order your search terms with the most important terms first and try reordering your words if you get too many hits. For example, "Michael L. Kent Public Relations Dialogue" (without quotation marks) yields 19,300 results, but, "Public Relations Dialogue Michael L. Kent" yields only 17,900. Same words, big difference in results.
7. *Very common words,* like "computer" (found on 4,460,000,000 pages) *are much less useful* when trying to narrow down information.
8. *Rare or unusual words like "defenestrate"* (found on only 130,000 pages) *are easier to find.* If you have an *uncommon* word you can couple with a *common* word, you can narrow your search tremendously. Thus: "defenestrate Bush," with quotation marks, yields only 20 pages.
9. *Search engines free of graphics and advertisements are better.* Clean search sites like Google, Dogpile, and Mamma are best when your connection is slow.
10. If you get an error message telling you that a "page no longer exists" when you are using Google, try using the "cached" feature in Google (just below the result link). This will show you an older, saved copy of the page.
11. *Miscellaneous:* Typing "Define:Word" (no quotation marks needed, no space needed) into most search engines will give you a definition. Typing a package tracking number (UPS, FedEx, etc.) into Google will bring you straight to your personal tracking page. Google will also calculate math: For example, typing "sqrt(25)" or "cube root (27)" will return accurate results.

Improving your search technique will make conducting online research much easier. The tips described here are organized from most important to least important. Using only tips 1 through 4 will usually narrow any search down to a few dozen results. Once you use these search tips for a few searches, you will never go back to your old habits. The search techniques outlined here work for most electronic databases, but not all. Whenever you are having trouble finding what you are looking for, take a minute to read the search instructions for the databases or search engine you are using and you will have more success. Many databases have idiosyncratic rules. Google, for example, does not support "OR," and requires a hyphen for NOT.

GOOGLE SCHOLAR

Google Scholar (www.scholar.google.com) is one of the least-known features of the popular search engine. As the name implies, Google Scholar searches for scholarly articles, books, and documents, including dissertation and theses, government documents, journal articles, and more. Google has been able to create a massive database of scholarly sources by signing agreements with most of the major book and journal publishers. According to Kent (2005c):

> [A] multi-publisher system [is] being tested by a consortium of 35 academic publishers and including more than 1,000 scholarly journals, and Google.... Google Scholar also draws upon scholarly material gleaned from other sources especially the Web. Currently, Google and ... publishers in the CrossRef consortium, ... have given Google permission to index their databases. (p. 35)

Google Scholar works like every other search engine in terms of search logic. However, because Google Scholar returns search results for articles, books, dissertation/theses, and other scholarly works *only*, users need to have access to the scholarly databases where journal articles are housed in order to make the most of the search engine.

Obtaining access to scholarly databases is not a problem for most college students. However, for public relations professionals who are no longer in school and do not have access to the many databases students take for granted, obtaining articles is more difficult. Google Scholar searches typically return results for PDF files. However, when a PDF link is followed, users are usually taken to a publisher's Web site for the journal or book that is sought. Without a professional affiliation with a university or college, (some larger companies do pay for access privileges), articles need to be purchased separately. The cost for a single article runs $20–30. Many professionals subscribe to important journals in their fields to gain free electronic access to specific journals; however, when conducting research, the idea of subscribing to *every* journal is unrealistic, as is purchasing every article à la carte.

Lack of access for practitioners is one of the main drawbacks to conducting online research. Some of the professional associations, like the PRSA, have experimented with access to EBSCO for members, but currently the PRSA does not provide access. Some states and professional organizations, however, have negotiated statewide contracts (New York State's PRSA, for example). Individual subscriptions are very expensive. Thus, unless a researcher is affiliated with a university with substantial access to scholarly databases, Google, Yahoo, Google Scholar, and all of the other search engines available for free on the Internet are of limited value. Fortunately, for most college students, access is not a problem. After you graduate, however, being able to access scholarly databases will become a problem (cf., Kent, 2005c for options).

Many authors of scholarly articles post copies of their articles on their home pages. When you cannot obtain an article from one of the online databases, be sure to conduct a quick search for an author's home page to see if the article is posted there, before you consider paying for an article. Google Scholar search results also have a "Web Search" link at the bottom of them that searches the Web for articles (Figure 8.3).

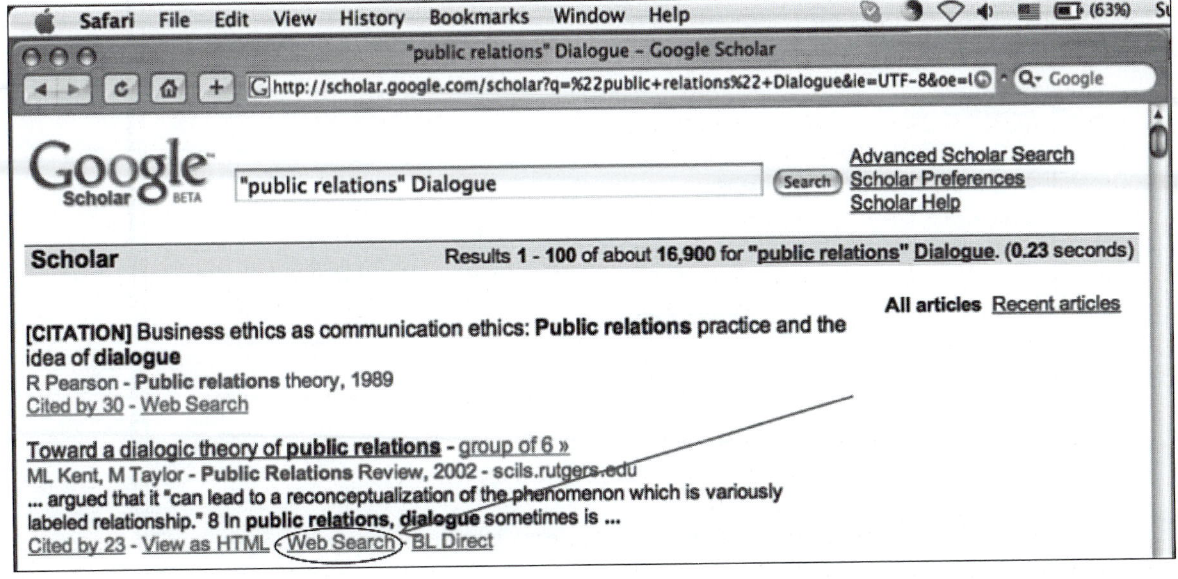

FIGURE 8.3 Google Search Results.
Source: © 2009 Google.

Many authors also post earlier (conference paper) versions of articles and PDFs on their home pages. If all of the Google Scholar options fail, try running a search on the regular Google database for a conference paper with a title based on the article title. Most authors do not change the names of their articles from the conference paper's title when they publish their work.

If everything else fails and you simply cannot find the article anywhere, most libraries provide access through "Interlibrary Loan" (ILL) where articles and books can be borrowed (usually for free) from libraries in the ILL consortium. ILL often takes a few days or a week, so fill out the forms quickly (online when possible). As a final resort, you can always try contacting an author directly and requesting a copy of the manuscript via e-mail or fax. With obscure journals, many professors are happy to fax you a copy of the article for scholarly or professional purposes.

Google Scholar is a great resource because it gives students and professionals the ability to search virtually every scholarly database all in one place. Google will also link researchers to older, obscure books and articles that might be easily overlooked. Google Scholar (and the regular Google search engine) rank articles by "relevance." Books and articles considered to be the most central come up at the top of the list. Google Scholar also provides bibliometric data about articles indicating how many times an article has been cited. Often, you can find related work by looking at the list of people who have cited an article or book.

LEXIS/NEXIS

Lexis and Nexis are research goldmines. In common parlance, the databases are usually called "Lexis/Nexis." However, a lawyer might say "I searched Lexis for case law on Smith ...," or a journalist might say "I searched Nexis to see if the story had been picked up yet by the wire...."

Lexis/Nexis is a combination of several databases, including business, legal research, medical, news, biographical information, country profiles, polls and surveys, quotations, state profiles, and a world almanac. Lexis/Nexis also contains information on members of Congress, legislative histories, bills and laws, business regulations, environmental information (journals, commentary, codes, and regulations), a government periodicals index, and statistical databases with thousands of statistical data sets on every topic imaginable.

Lexis, the legal database, provides access to an impressive array of legal information including: legal news, law reviews, legal cases, Supreme Court cases, federal and state case law, the federal code, federal regulations, state regulations, tax law, Canadian, E.U., and other foreign law, patent research, law firms, and law schools (see Figure 8.4).

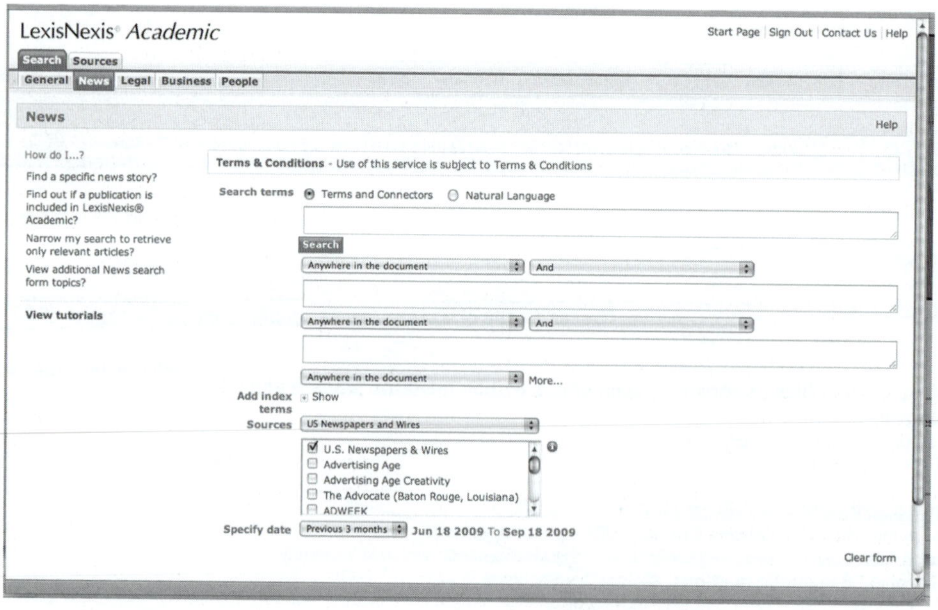

FIGURE 8.4 Lexis.

Source: © 2009 LexisNexis, a division of Reed Elsevier Inc. All Rights Reserved. LexisNexis and the Knowledge Burst logo are registered trademarks of Reed Elsevier Properties Inc. and are used with the permission of LexisNexis.

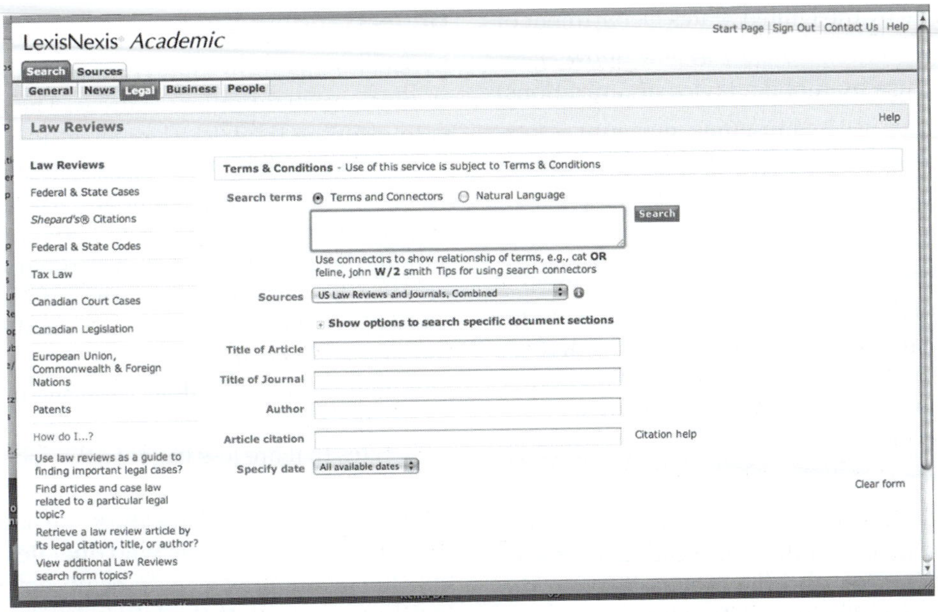

FIGURE 8.5 Two Nexis screen shots.
Source: © 2009 LexisNexis, a division of Reed Elsevier Inc. All Rights Reserved. LexisNexis and the Knowledge Burst logo are registered trademarks of Reed Elsevier Properties Inc. and are used with the permission of LexisNexis.

Nexis, the news database, provides access to daily news, U.S. news, world news, news wires, news transcripts, arts and sports news, non-English news, business news, legal news, and university news. The medical databases provide access to medical news, medical journals, and medical abstracts (see Figure 8.5).

As a research tool, especially for environmental scanning and monitoring, Lexis/Nexis is a tremendous resource. The ability to search through thousands of regional, state, national, and international newspapers makes Nexis invaluable, especially when conducting content analysis and communication audits. The value of each database obviously varies depending upon the industry or profession an individual works in, but their potential should be obvious.

Spend some time familiarizing yourself with what each database has to offer. Consult Lexis/Nexis when you are conducting research for classes to discover what Lexis/Nexis can do. Learn what databases Lexis/Nexis offers in terms of primary and secondary research. After you use the Lexis/Nexis databases a few times, you will wonder how you ever got along without them.

EVALUATING WEB SITE VALIDITY AND RELIABILITY

When you use Web sites for informational purposes, you need to be sure you are dealing with credible, accurate, and reliable sources. As I have previously suggested you should *never* go to the WWW for "research" except to verify simple facts, dates, spellings, definitions, etc. The Web contains a lot of inaccurate information. However, the Web is also seductively *easy* to use. Thus, you need to learn how to distinguish reliable from unreliable sources and learn the difference between a Web site and a database of scholarly articles.

Understanding ICANN

Web site addresses are controlled by an organization named ICANN, the Internet Corporation for Assigned Names and Numbers. ICANN is a California nonprofit corporation created to oversee the Internet on behalf of the U.S. government. The most common top-level domain name designations include the following:

.biz (for business use)

.com (for use by for profit companies)

.coop (for use by business cooperatives)

.edu (for use by educational institutions, primarily in the U.S.)

.gov (for use by the U.S. federal government)

.info (for use by informational Web sites; also available to the general public)

.int (for use by international treaty organizations, the UN, and related groups)

.mil (for use by the United States Department of Defense and its subsidiary organizations)

.mobi (for use by mobile device organizations)

.museum (for use by museums, museum associations, and individual members of the museum profession)

.name (for use by individuals)

.net (for use by anyone, including businesses)

.org (one of the original top-level domains, established in January 1985; originally intended for use by organizations that did not meet other requirements, but now available to anyone)

.pro (available to professionals: athletes, doctors, lawyers, etc.)

.tv (the Internet country code for the island nation of Tuvalu; anyone in the world can register a .tv domain for a fee, and the income goes to the government and people of Tuvalu)

Early in 2010, ICANN decided to allow foreign language domain names, opening the door to Arabic, Chinese, and Russian (Cyrillic) domains that will only be accessible to people who understand the language and have special keyboards.

Understanding URLs

In general, there are a few commonly used techniques to find out about online sources. The first technique is to examine the URL (Universal Resource Locator) to see if the source is affiliated with a college or university (.edu), the government (.gov), or a nonprofit organization (.org). When you see a .com, .gov, or .edu designation as part of the primary Web address, you can be somewhat sure the information posted comes from a group not trying to make a profit from the site—i.e., the organization is not trying to sell you anything (besides ideology)—so the information can be trusted a bit more.

Sites that are less trustworthy include .biz, .com, .name, .net, and .tv, and you need to pay more careful attention to who operates those sites. In general, the easiest way to determine who operates a site, its parent site, or home page is to begin deleting blocks of text from the end of the URL address. For example, while doing some research for this book, I followed a link in a news story to this page, ocw.mit.edu/OcwWeb/Global/AboutOCW/media-access.htmv[5] (see Figure 8.6).

The first thing you should note is that the page is "clean." There are no advertisement, no popups, etc.

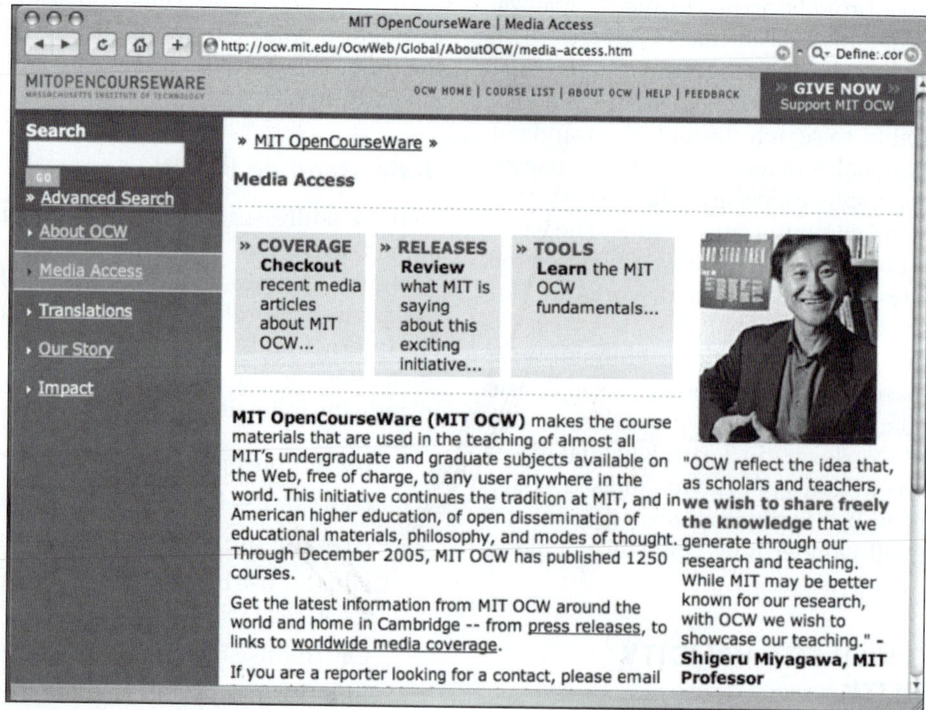

FIGURE 8.6 MIT OpenCourseWare.
Source: MIT OpenCourseWare.

The page was advertisement-free because, as you can see from the URL, this is an educational site (ocw.mit.edu). Finding Web pages that are free of advertisements, even .com or .biz sites, is a good sign because it usually means that the organization has a worthwhile product to sell and respects its customers and clients (Google's home page is a good example; it is very clean).

Next, take note of the first part of a Web address to determine where the site comes from: is it an educational institution, the government, another country (.de, .cz., .fr, etc.), an organization, or a business? In this case, the site is clearly from the Massachusetts Institute of Technology (MIT), visible both from the name on the page and the URL: ocw.mit.edu.

In order to learn about the organization, the first thing I did was to delete everything but the root address ocw.mit.edu and reload the page. This revealed a page similar to the one above, but with more information about the MIT's Open Courseware initiative. Both pages were a bit thin on information for what I was looking for at the time, so I started deleting parts of the address from the far end of the URL: ocw.mit.edu/OcwWeb/Global/AboutOCW, and then ocw.mit.edu/OcwWeb/Global, and then ocw.mit.edu/OcwWeb. Each truncation of the address revealed a directory of files rather than a new Web site, which is often the case (see Figure 8.7).

In general, discovering indexes like this is a good sign because it means the site is uncomplicated, and you can usually find what you are looking for with an index rather than having to search an unfamiliar Web page each time. Examining who the host (or owner) of a site is, and then back-tracking a few screens will often provide enough information for you to determine if the site owner is credible. If you still do not have enough information, you'll need to examine the site's background information.

Now to the real nuts and bolts of making a decision about a Web site's credibility: there are at least six questions a professional should ask of any information:

1. *Truthfulness.* Is the information accurate? If you are unfamiliar with the subject matter, you must examine several sources before you can decide this. Peer-reviewed (scholarly) sources make it easier to decide if a source is trustworthy.
2. *Agreement* of the information with other information (is the information supported by other credible sources?). Typically, if you are unfamiliar with an idea or a source, you cannot determine the general agreement of the ideas by other experts without reviewing some other scholarship.
3. *General Acceptance* of the information by experts (is this a radical or new idea or a well-established one?). New ideas are okay, as long as they come from credible sources and are compelling to the audience.
4. *Credibility* of the ideas and the source in the eyes of a potential audience (when constructing

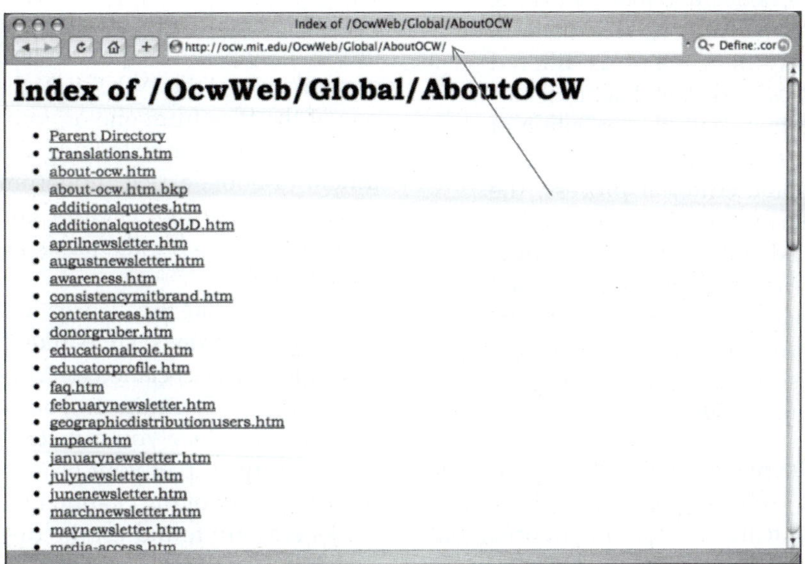

FIGURE 8.7 About OCW.
Source: MIT OpenCourseWare.

arguments). Remember, just because *you* trust a source does not mean the audience does. Although the Republican National Committee *might* be telling the truth, the fact that the information came from a Republican will not be compelling to a "Yellow Dog Democrat."

5. *Timeliness* of the information. The recency of information is vital in certain fields, such as computers, science, astronomy, and less so in others. Understanding how important new information is in particular areas is essential.
6. *Morality* of the information (is the source advancing ideas for the good of humanity or just using the audience as a means to an end, like selling products?).

What should be apparent from this list is that making an *informed* judgment is difficult. As Neil Postman put it, "Any fool can have an opinion; to know what one needs to know to have an opinion is wisdom" (1999, p. 96). The reason books and journal articles are considered more credible than most other sources is because of the "peer review" process. As Kent explains:

> What makes articles, books, government reports, etc., more valuable to professionals and academicians is the editorial process and "blind review" (also called "peer review" or "refereed"). More simply, the oversight of gatekeepers and experts improves the quality of research. For example, newspapers, books, and many journals, like *Public Relations Quarterly*, are edited. In edited journals, the content is filtered through experts who decide if submissions warrant publication. With the exception of news Web sites that (hopefully) filter content through some editorial process, the remainder of the information on the Web is essentially posted at the whim of site owners. Information on the Web is often posted for publicity, sales, marketing, and public relations purposes, and typically out of a desire to increase, not limit, what gets published. (2005c, pp. 38–39)

The Web is seductive. With very little practice, a child could create a Web site. Ease of publication is one of the wonderful features about the Internet, but also one of the burdens. How is the average person to know what can be trusted on a Web site? Even more insidious are the number of corporately authored Web sites trying to pass themselves off as "non-profit" sites (cf., Kent, 2001b; Kent, Harrison, & Taylor, 2006).

So, again, how can you decide if the content of Web pages can be trusted? The answer is, you often cannot. Research on the Internet suggests as much as half of all health information posted by individuals, corporations, insurance companies, and nonprofit organizations is incorrect. Other sources of information are inaccurate as well. As you become more knowledgeable in specialized areas as public relations professionals and use the Web more for substantive research, you will begin to notice the inaccuracies in Web content yourself. Since so much information on the Web is unreliable, since so much of the content on the Web is posted for promotion, since there are no filters for most content, very few gatekeepers and editors, and very little peer review, everything on the Web needs to be taken with a grain of salt.

Understanding Online Databases

A database (EBSCO, Elsevier, Science Direct, etc.) is a repository of documents *accessible* through the Web, but they are not "Web pages." A Web browser is just a program that reads HTML and other computer languages and is designed to create a "graphic user interface." The Internet is a GUI (pronounced goo-ee).

When you go to a URL for, say, Foster's beer, you are visiting a company "Web site" (.com). When you go through your library's Web site to access one of the dozens of databases you have access to, you are still using "the Web." But, the minute you access one of the files from one of your library's databases, you will no longer be looking at a Web site but a document (a book, article, government document, dissertation, theses, OED entry, conference paper, etc.) downloaded from a database, *not* downloaded from "the Web."

You will cite the "article" you downloaded using a proper citation system like the APA (American Psychological Association) or MLA (Modern Language Association). The minute you open an article via a database interface you can stop paying attention to what is at the top of your browser in the address bar (URL) box. All of the citation information for articles, books etc., are found on the documents themselves and have nothing to do with the database from which you obtained them.

The best way to be sure about whether a URL will actually bring you back to the document you just accessed online is to open another browser (open Firefox if you are in Safari, or Safari if you are in Firefox, etc.) and paste the URL into the search box. What you will discover is that 95 percent of the time, the URL will return an error. The "gibberish" found at the top of browser windows after a search for an article is often just instructions for finding *a specific* page, on *a specific* day, at *that* time, rather than an address to a permanent Web site anyone can access. In most cases, when you open or download an article from an online database, you cannot just cut and paste the information into a new browser window and return to the same place again. Database searches are time sensitive, and *your* search will not exist five minutes from now, or even two seconds from now if you accidentally close the search window.

Ultimately, what is important to understand when you obtain information through an interface you had to log into (or had access to while on campus) is that you are *not* using the "Internet," just a GUI that uses HTML on the Web. If you wind up at a Web site through a search engine like Google, you are on the Web. But, be aware that if Google Scholar (the Web) shunts you to EBSCO, Science Direct, or even a PDF of an article, you will be moving from "the Web" to a database, or a file accessed through the Web.

Always test the URLs you intend to use in citations to be sure they actually work. Also, be aware that Web addresses change all of the time; Web address often have a short shelf life—under a year in many cases. Thus, when citing items downloaded from any electronic source, the best approach is to cite the document itself (whenever possible), and if you need to cite a Web site, provide complete information about the site so someone else can track down your source if the site is moved or taken down.

Let me unpack the difference between a Web site and a database a little farther with one more example. Say you conduct a search for information on Google Scholar and are sent to your library's search page and EBSCO. As it turns out, your school does not subscribe to *Public Relations Review* and your school library cannot give you electronic access to the article. You wisely turn to Google Scholar's "Web Search" feature and discover "Professor Heath" has a copy of the article on his home page as a PDF, which you download to print and read later. Now, even though you obtained this "article" through the Internet and a Web page, you still would *not* cite a "Web page" in your research paper or white paper. The document you downloaded, an article, book chapter, government document, etc., is where you turn for citation information. Occasionally, citations include complete information to an article downloaded from the Web (not a database in this case), and *also* include the URL where others might obtain the article themselves. For example:

Lenhart, A. (2006). *Bloggers: A portrait of the Internet's new storytellers*. Pew Internet and American Life Project <www.pewinternet.org/PPF/r/186/report_display.asp>.

Lyons, C. (2009, July 24). Facebook can use your pictures for ads, no permission required. *Los Angeles Times*, Opinion, online. <opinion.latimes.com/opinionla/2009/07/facebook-can-use-your-pictures-for-ads-no-permission-required.html>.

Regan, T. (2007, Oct. 17). Maybe e-mail isn't such a great idea, after all. *Christian Science Monitor* <www.csmonitor.com/2007/1017/p16s01-stct.html>.

If you cut and past these URLs into a browser, they will take you to the actual documents. However, the URL below, taken from a search for an article in EBSCO, will take you nowhere, because the URL link only existed while I was on the page and logged into my account: <www.sciencedirect.com.ezproxy.lib.ou.edu/science?_ob=MImg&_imagekey=B6W5W-4TNTN25-1-1&_cdi=6581&_user=2967949&_pii=S0363811108001136&_orig=search&_coverDate=11%2F30%2F2008&_sk=999659995&view=c&wchp=dGLbV1W-zSkzV&md5=61640900be16a3f8be669707a84f6a78&ie=/sdarticle.pdf>.

As a rule, any time a URL is longer than about one line and contains incomprehensible strings of numbers and symbols, you are probably not looking at a permanent URL. Cut and past the URL into a new *browser* window (not just a new window, open a new *browser*—Firefox, Safari, Explorer—since, if you are logged into a database on one browser, it will probably open the link) to test if the link will actually work.

How you obtained a document is irrelevant. Citations are used to tell future readers where a document can be found, not from where *you* downloaded something. If you find a magazine in a doctor's waiting room and later want to cite one of the articles from the magazine, you would not mention that the magazine "was found in Dr. Miller's office" any more than you would mention you found an article using EBSCO, ScienceDirect, or Google. Who *published* an article matters so later, someone else—who does not see Dr. Miller—can obtain the same article.

COUNTERS, COOKIES, AND ANALYTICS

Web counters, cookies, and Web analytics are tools used to monitor Web site traffic. A ***counter,*** as the name implies, is simply a device (mechanical or electronic) that keeps track of something. A clock is a form of counter, as is an odometer, and the numerical "counters" you often see at the bottom of Web sites telling you how many times a page has been visited. Web counters can count up or down—counting down the days until the new year, counting up the national debt, or counting the number of times a Web page has been visited—and they can be visible or invisible (with data accessible only to the organization that controls a Web site).

Why are counters important? Because they allow you to monitor how your Web site is being used. For example, you have searched for information using a search engine like Google and then linked to the relevant page from the search engine's results page. In most cases, you do not enter a Web site through the front door, or the home page, but through one of the many pages on the site. If all an organization does is keep track of how many people came in through the "front door" by using a counter on the home page, the organization will miss out on valuable data about which pages are linked to from other sites, and which pages are of more interest to visitors to the organization's Web site. Thus, counters are often placed on every page (often invisibly), and allow more sophisticated data to be gathered.

A ***cookie*** refers to a small data file stored on the computer of a visitor to a Web site. Essentially, a cookie file contains information used by a Web site that someone visits to track that person's activities. As the Wisconsin Dental Association explains,[6] a cookie is:

> A unique string of letters and numbers that the web server stores in a file on your hard drive. This method is used by web designers to track visitors to a website so the visitors don't have to enter the same information every time they go to a new page or revisit a site. For example, web designers use cookies to keep track of purchases a visitor wants to make while shopping through a web catalog. Cookies may work through a single visit to a website, such as when tracking a shopping trip, or may be set to work through multiple sessions when a visitor returns to the site. (www.40260.com/help/glossary.aspx#c)

Another area related to cookies is "personally identifiable information," which is frequently stored in cookie files and can be accessed by other Web sites that are visited. As Eyetech Pharmaceuticals and Pfizer explain:

> Personally Identifiable Information (PII) [is information] that can be traced back to a specific individual user, e.g., name, postal address, e-mail address, telephone number, or Social Security number. Personal user preferences tracked by a Web site via a "Cookie" ... is also considered personally identifiable when linked to other Personally Identifiable Information provided by user[s] on line. (www.amdhelp.com/privacy_glossary.asp)

You may be asking, "Why do I need to care about this?" Because all Web sites are capable of using cookies, and cookies can be a rich source of data regarding how visitors interface with your organization, how they navigate your organization's Web site, and what areas/topics seem to be of the most interest to visitors.

Whether to use cookies, however, is something of an ethical issue. Many computer users do not trust organizations to use cookies and personal data ethically. Virtually all Web browsers allow users to opt out of using cookies and to control how they are used. However, many Web sites force users to activate cookies in order to enter the site. For this reason, many browsers—Firefox, for example—will automatically erase your cookies and personally identifiable information (PII) after you close the program.

The ethics of cookies is another one of those communication issues you will have to consider. The most democratic choice is to allow *all* visitors to use your site regardless of whether they are willing to let you set cookies. Cookies can be used to collect and track visitor information, but should not be used to exclude users or try to force them to provide information that individuals do not want to share. A more sophisticated form of Web tracking is called Web analytics.

Web analytics refer to the use of tracking software like Google Analytics (www.google.com/analytics/home) or StatCounter (www.StatCounter.com). Web site analysis is much more of an art than a science and involves drawing upon statistical (usability) data and patterns of visitor interaction to improve both the performance of a Web site and the experience of users.

The Internet is a dynamic system, and visitors to Web sites can come from virtually anywhere in the world. The mistake many people make is being fooled by the "Web" metaphor (Kent, 2001). The Internet is really not a "web" in the sense of community and connectivity—the Internet is more like an index or a big GPS system. The Web takes people to places rather than bringing people together (Kent, 1998, 2001, 2008). What the technical constraints of the Internet mean for organizational professionals is that if you want your organization's Web site to be seen and used, your sites need to be effectively indexed by databases like Google. You also need to create effective content that fits the logic of how users interface with the content and technology.

Web analytical software like Google Analytics allows you to compile data on the usage patterns of your organization's Web site so that you can improve the experience of users on your site, increase sales, and reorganize pages and sections to maximize the user experience. Google Analytics takes about an hour to set up (depending upon how many pages are tracked) and starts reporting data in about a day.

WEB METRICS

Web metrics refer to data that comes from tracking visitors to Web sites and analyzing how they interact with the content on the site. Web site analysis is an excellent way to find out how visitors are interacting with your organization's Web site and to make changes to improve its usefulness.

Web tracking software allows an assortment of data to be gathered. Types of data include how many people visit a Web site each day (week, month, year), how many *unique* visitors a site receives each day, how many returning visitors come to a site, how long each visitor stays on a site, how visitors enter sites (i.e., what page), the country of origin of visitors, how much money each visitor spends, etc. There are dozens of metrics that can be analyzed and compared in order to learn about the preferences of Web site visitors (cf., www.google.com/analytics/home).

In practice, Web analytics or Web metrics tend to be used by for-profit organizations. However, anyone can use the data to improve the usefulness of his/her Web site, including government, nonprofit, educational, or health organizations. My own Web site, for example, receives about 1,500 visitors per month (see figure 8.8). About three-quarters of those visitors are "unique visitors," meaning they have never visited before, and about one in four visitors spends some time on my site, meaning I have a 75 percent "bounce rate," which is good. The bounce rate is the number of people who arrive and then leave immediately. There are billions of Web sites, and since most people do not find what they are looking for the first time, every site has a bounce

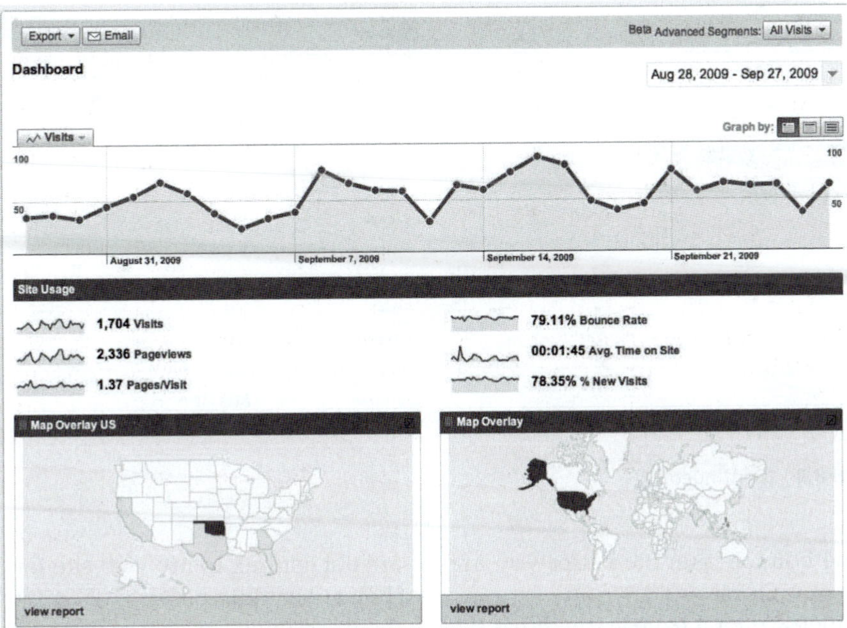

FIGURE 8.8 Graphic of Dashboard.
Source: © 2009 Google.

Browsers

Browser	Visits	% visits
Internet Explorer	873	51.23%
Firefox	432	25.35%
Safari	345	20.25%
Chrome	41	2.41%
Mozilla	4	0.23%
view report		

Operating Systems

Operating System	Visits	% visits
Windows	1,302	76.41%
Macintosh	384	22.54%
Linux	11	0.65%
(not set)	3	0.18%
iPhone	3	0.18%
view report		

Content Drilldown

Page	Pageviews	% visits
/~mkent/	1,557	66.65%
/K/	615	26.33%
/downloads/	160	6.85%
/cache.aspx?q="an+occasion+spee...	1	0.04%
/search?q=cache:Ydc9-qEhB8MJ:h...	1	0.04%
view report		

Keywords

Keyword	Visits	% visits
special occasion speeches	146	12.07%
special occasion speech	94	7.77%
occasion speeches	41	3.39%
occasion speech	27	2.23%
welcome occasion speech	24	1.98%
view report		

Top Exit Pages

Page	Exits	% visits
/~mkent/cm105sos.html	1,126	66.08%
/K/Michael.L.Kent-1/index.html	298	17.49%
/downloads/top100speeches	60	3.52%
/~mkent/Essays.html	52	3.05%
/K/Michael.L.Kent-1/documents.html	33	1.94%
view report		

Depth of Visit

Pageviews in the visit	Visits with this many pageviews
1 pageviews	79.11%
2 pageviews	13.85%
3 pageviews	3.99%
4 pageviews	1.17%
5 pageviews	0.88%
6 pageviews	0.47%
7 pageviews	0.18%
8 pageviews	0.12%
11 pageviews	0.12%
16 pageviews	0.06%
20+ pageviews	0.06%
view report	

Length of Visit

Duration of visit	Visits with this duration
0-10 seconds	80.46%
11-30 seconds	1.70%
31-60 seconds	3.35%
61-180 seconds	4.17%
181-600 seconds	5.28%
601-1,800 seconds	4.17%
1,801+ seconds	0.88%
view report	

Visitor Loyalty

Count of visits from this visitor including current	Visits that were the visitor's nth visit
1 times	78.46%
2 times	5.05%
3 times	1.06%
4 times	0.29%
5 times	0.29%
6 times	0.12%
7 times	0.06%
8 times	0.06%
9-14 times	0.41%
101-200 times	0.94%
201+ times	13.26%
view report	

Connection Speeds

Connection Speed	Visits	% visits
Unknown	542	31.81%
Cable	484	28.40%
DSL	328	19.25%
T1	319	18.72%
Dialup	27	1.58%
view report		

FIGURE 8.8 (Continued)

rate. The lower the bounce rate, the better you are meeting the needs of visitors.

By studying metric data, I have learned that the average visitor spends about three minutes on my site. Furthermore, most (90 percent) of my visitors are not coming to my Web site for "public relations," they are coming because of an interest in "entertainment speaking," a section of my Web site for my public speaking class. To help the majority of visitors to my site find what they need, I have provided links to a colleague's Web site that contains sample special occasion speeches. Linking to other sites increases my "bounce rate," but since I am a professor and not a businessperson, directing visitors to another site is okay. Organizations that are trying to sell products, services, or ideology to individuals and publics need to be aware of the importance of "stickiness" or keeping visitors on *their* site (cf., Kent & Taylor, 1998), and gathering metric data is probably the best means of monitoring usage.

The metric data can track which pages are visited and how often, which pages are the most popular, how long people spend on your site, how people enter and exit your site, which search engine people who come to your site use, what the key words are that people use to locate your site's content, etc. Google analytics can also be configured to help drive sales traffic on for-profit Web sites, as well as compile data about where users come from (continent, country, state, region, city, and even Internet host).

Many organizations do not realize that how their site is navigated is dictated by several factors: how the site is indexed, who is visiting the site (the type of individual), what the visitor is looking for (often not what you are offering), and how logically and effectively the site is organized. To address all of these issues, Web sites require "tweaking." Even the best, most professional Web sites do not get the site design perfect the first time. Organizations need to be willing and able to track how their sites are used by visitors and make changes to the site as needed.

The point to understand here is that how a page is designed (navigation cues, links, dialogic content), and how a page looks (professional design, legibility, readability, color, type style), has as much to do with the content of the page as anything else. In the simplest terms, both content and delivery matter. No design will ever be able to completely duplicate the experience of the "average user" until you know more about who the average user is and what s/he seeks. Simply having content on a Web site is no guarantee that anyone reads it or cares about what is there.

Thus, cookies, counters and Web analytic software are useful for tracking user data about an organization's Web site and also for making changes to the hierarchy and organization of the site to make it more useful, user friendly, and expedient for visitors. Well-organized Web sites (those requiring fewer clicks to find what you are looking for) also cut down on bandwidth demands making sites less expensive to run, and are generally more enjoyable for users.

CONCLUSION

As this chapter should have made clear, the number of secondary resources available for public relations professionals to access is impressive. More importantly, however, as this chapter and the previous chapter have explained, research is an essential part of public relations writing, just as understanding rhetorical and communication theories are. Effectively communicating with stakeholders, stakeseekers, and target publics requires that you understand your publics and their needs. You should learn how to use *all* of the databases mentioned in this chapter. Archival databases and search engines, such as Google Scholar and Lexis/Nexis are databases that might be accessed every few weeks. However, news resources and blogs that can be obtained through an RSS aggregator are something you will use on a daily basis. Technology has transformed the profession, and professionals who learn how to use technology well will be the most successful in years to come.

ACTIVITIES

1. Use a browser like Google or Yahoo to gather RSS feeds, or download one of the free aggregators like NewsGator (www.newsgator.com/Individuals/Default.aspx) or NewsLife (www.thinkmac.co.uk/newslife). Install it on your laptop or home computer. Add six different news feeds (RSS). Select three news sites from U.S. newspapers in diverse locations (California, Chicago, Texas, Boston, New York City, Maryland, etc.) and three from international sources (Australia, England, Germany, Scotland, etc.). Read the top headlines on each site for a week. How do the sources vary in terms of their coverage? Which sources seem most trustworthy and why?
2. Install an aggregator (see above) or use a browser interface like Google or Yahoo to collect your RSS feeds. Sign up for three to five RSS feeds in a specialized area of interest (automotive, fashion, music, sports, technology, woodworking, etc.). Monitor the news on each of the sites for a few days or a week—including reading the threaded dialogue. How are the

sources different? Which sources are better and why? What did you learn that you did not know before you started monitoring the sites?

3. Locate three blogs in an area of personal interest (skiing, skydiving, chess, videogames, etc.) by using one of the popular blog search engines like Blogger (www.blogger.com) or Technorati (Technorati.com) or by searching by topic on a regular search engine. Read a week's worth of entries on each blog. (Note: If the bloggers do not post daily, read several weeks' or months' worth of posts). Imagine that you work for an organization related to the area of interest you selected. Do the bloggers know anything that you do not already know or have access to information that is not readily available in the mainstream media? Would it be worth the time of a professional in your area to monitor any of the blogs you selected? Explain your answer.
4. Go to Appendix C and take my Web scavenger hunt. How quickly did you finish it? (15 minutes is pretty good, 30–40 minutes is typical). What search techniques were the most useful? Did you come up with any other search ideas of your own?
5. Visit Lexis/Nexis and locate everything you can about your state. What kind of information is available? Is the information mostly qualitative or quantitative? How timely and up-to-date is the information? Could you use any of it as a communication professional? What information did you find that you did not know was available before you started? Would your organization be willing to pay for a subscription to Lexis/Nexis, as thousands of organizations do, or do you think the information is not very useful?
6. Use SurveyMonkey or Zoomerang to create an online survey. Use at least one question from all of the question types that are offered. Send links to the survey to your fellow classmates and ask them to take it. Compile the data for the next class. How easy was the software to use? Which of your classmates' surveys were the best, and why? What should you keep in mind next time you use survey software?

NOTES

1. Many social networking sites like Facebook and MySpace allow members to conduct free surveys. These Web sites can also be a great way to learn about online surveys.
2. Many bloggers do not report their sources and pass off information as if they had gathered the information themselves (Barbaro, 2006). Dealing with bloggers who are not upfront about their sources raises ethical issues. The Public Relations Society of America's code of ethics, for example, calls for "accuracy and truth in communications" (article 4), forbids the use of "front groups" (article 8), and advises against "corrupting the channels of information" (article 6).
3. Most blogs are based on "threaded dialogue." Threads of dialogue (or conversation) are created when people post messages and then build on conversations.
4. There really is no official distinction between a true blog and a news blog. For our purposes, true blogs are the diary variety, where the blogger carps, rambles, rails, argues, praises, etc., about whatever injustice or situation strikes him/her on that particular day.

   A news blog, on the other hand, typically includes postings from online news and information sites, and then visitors or "subscribers" comment on the posting. The technology blog Slashdot.org is a good example of a news blog. Once a story is posted to the site, hundreds of readers immediately begin posting comments to the site, each typically building on a previous post or the original post. Each entry on the blog becomes a dialogue of comments, explanations, corrections, elaborations, retorts, and, frequently, insults.

   True blogs are much less widely read than many of the news blogs because they tend to have a very narrow audience (people who want to hear what one person has to say). By contrast, news blogs like the *Drudge Retort* draw in wider audiences because they report "news" items and report on stories that have an interest in particular areas, such as politics, science/technology, GLBTQ, space/astronomy, international news, etc. All blogs start out as little known and read; however, news blogs always have the potential to be of interest to more people.
5. Note: the link indicated here has been changed: <ocw.mit.edu/OcwWeb/web/about/about/index.htm>. However, the illustration below still works with the new URL.
6. Medical-related groups and organizations have very clear explanations about cookies and "personally identifiable information" because of changes to the U.S. privacy laws that require these organizations to inform clients/customers.

Chapter 9

Speeches and Professional Presentations

Although this is a writing book, speeches and presentations must also be written out before they are delivered. Effective speeches and presentations are not prepared on the back of a cocktail napkin five minutes before the presentation. Indeed, professionals spend a lot of their time preparing speeches and spoken content. At some point, you may be called upon to prepare an informative speech, an after dinner speech, an acceptance speech, a eulogy, a professional presentation, a pitch to stakeholders or clients, comments for a radio or television interview program, messages and notes for speakers in a speakers bureau, or conduct media training to prepare a supervisor or colleague to deliver an effective speech.

The art of speechwriting goes back about 2,500 years to the ancient Greeks, who first wrote speeches for others to deliver in law courts and politics. Since then, research on persuasion and human motivation has provided professional communicators with the knowledge needed to create very compelling messages.

Business professionals, politicians, and leaders of all kinds make public speeches every day. Most business professionals do not write their own speeches any more but have them prepared by communication professionals—that will be *you* someday. In general, the reason that professionals no longer write their own speeches is because the average business manager, CEO, or politician does not have the training. Thus, as public relations professionals, you will occasionally be called upon to write speeches for others.

The classic examples of speeches written by others are presidential speeches (inaugurals, State of the Union, holiday addresses, ceremonies, dedications), which are often written by a team of communication professionals. Professional speechwriters are already familiar with the audience for whom they are writing because the speechwriter often works in the same organization as the speaker. Occasionally, however, a speechwriter is asked to prepare a speech for an audience with whom the speechwriter is unfamiliar—an activist group, for example, or for a memorial service for an accident victim. In such cases, the speechwriter conducts audience and occasion analysis to learn how to structure the speech.

The first step in preparing a speech is to analyze the audience demographically, looking at age, gender, education, and income, and determine the audience's level of interest, knowledge, beliefs, and values about the topic (psychographics). Familiarity with a topic is helpful but not essential for writing an effective speech. Speeches are not lectures; most are brief, and a competent speechwriter can prepare a very compelling speech for someone else to deliver.

Once the audience, occasion, and speaker are understood, you can begin to prepare a speech that will appeal to the audience in question. Obviously a nonexpert cannot prepare a speech on a highly technical topic; however, very little of a speech actually involves reciting complicated facts, jargon, or statistics. The best speeches employ verbal forms of support and sound rhetorical techniques.

Public speeches tend to be of three types: persuasive, informative, and ceremonial. The secret to an effective speech is to understand the audience and its expectations rather than to memorize a lot of facts. The best speeches are extemporaneous, rather than memorized, and skilled speakers are capable of sensing the needs and temperament of the audience and changing and adapting speeches as necessary.

When you are writing a speech for someone else, you usually prepare a manuscript (word-for-word) of the speech, as well as accompanying note cards. The success of a manuscript style speech depends a lot on the skill and preparation of the speaker. Contrary to popular belief, manuscript speeches are not easier to deliver. Except for very skilled speakers, extemporaneous speeches (speeches delivered with notes only) are usually more compelling. When writing a speech for someone else, the speaker is encouraged to take the note cards and the manuscript and make the speech his/her own, so that it can be delivered extemporaneously.

Along with writing the speech, you may need to spend some time coaching the speaker how to *give* an effective speech. Ask the speaker to deliver the entire speech to you at least three times; take note of any verbal or nonverbal problems like **disfluencies** (um, ah, like, you know, and um), excessive or overly dramatic gesturing, too much or too little passion, physical ticks, pacing, swaying, or dancing around, etc. Videotaping the first or second delivery of the speech and then critiquing the video with the presenter is a good technique.

SPEECHWRITING

Ideally, you will have taken a public speaking course as part of your required plan of study in public relations. My own school, a large journalism and mass communication program, does not require public speaking for public relations majors; however, all of the other communication departments I have taught in do require public speaking. Since not every program requires public speaking, and since writing a speech is not exactly the same as delivering a speech, this section focuses on the basics of writing and content rather than delivery.

Rhetoric has been around for a long time. Going back to the ancient Greeks, we know that audience adaptation has always been seen as a prerequisite for success. Imagine, for example, that you were preparing a speech for a group of inner-city, mixed race, secondary school children about the importance of staying in school and going to college. The types of examples and support that you employ will need to be compelling to the age, ethnic, gender, and socioeconomic status of the audience. Just because *you* find former President Carter to be a positive role model does not mean they will—they won't. Similarly, when you are formulating examples, Sidney Poitier and Bill Cosby are probably not going to be as easily recognized and compelling as Snoop, Ice-T, or the latest hip-hop sensation. Similarly, if you were writing a speech for a supervisor to deliver at the local Rotary Club in Oklahoma City (a state in which not a single county voted Democratic in the last presidential election), invoking Democratic politicians, including President Obama, whose popularity rating nationwide might be very high, would be a mistake. Speeches need to take into account the age, demographics, and other features of the audience, as well as the occasion and context of the speech. *Compelling examples and sources need to be compelling to the audience, not to the speaker.*

That said, as mentioned in Chapters 1 and 2, public relations professionals do not lie, spin, or pander to audience to achieve our goals. Drawing upon compelling sources of examples and testimony to one's audience is not the same as using whatever it takes to achieve your communicative goal. Public relations professionals are always guided by sound ethical principles. If Barack Obama is not compelling to your audience and Rush Limbaugh is, but you personally find Limbaugh to be repugnant, you should not be using his words just to make your point. Never sacrifice your beliefs just to sway an audience. Remember the PRSA code of ethics.

The Canon of Rhetoric

The canon of rhetoric goes back thousands of years and refers to a list of the features that are considered part of all rhetoric: invention, disposition, elocution, delivery, and memory.

Invention is a process of discovery, the finding and gathering of materials. Invention is both a research technique of finding and gathering material, and a creative endeavor of deciding what information would be the most useful and what specific facts mean to your audience.

Disposition refers to organization and the arrangement of materials. Disposition also informs where, when, how, and if particular facts, statistics, and testimony will be used. For example, should you *start* with a startling statistic or *end* with it?

Elocution refers to artistic judgment: style, language use, and choice of words. Elocution, or style, also refers to rhetorical tactics, use of figures of speech, creating effective metaphors, using identification strategies, etc.

Delivery refers to a number of things including pronunciation, voice/diction, use of nonverbals (pauses, gestures, silence), composure, etc. Delivery has always been considered one of the most important aspects of all speeches; hundreds of philosophers and scholars have debated whether content or delivery is more important.

Memory, sarcastically called the forgotten canon, refers to a communicator's ability to draw on facts and adapt to one's audience while one speaks. Memory influences our ability to answer questions effectively, as well as contributing to a speaker's confidence and success.

The canon of rhetoric is the rhetorical equivalent of the RACE formula, describing the entire process of public speech with five concepts. Never overlook the importance of proper research, organization, and preparation (memory and practice).

Audience and Occasion Analysis

Audience analysis is a consideration of the traits, interests, and similarities of the audience, as well as an examination of the audience's attitudes toward your topic, you, and the occasion. A typical audience and occasion analysis addresses the following questions:

1. What is the nature of the speaking occasion?
2. What is the demographic composition of your audience (size, age, gender/sex, occupation, education, group memberships, and cultural and ethnic backgrounds)?
3. What is the audience's knowledge of the subject area?
4. What are the audience's general beliefs, attitudes, and values (economic, political, professional, religious, social)?
5. How interested will the audience be in the speech? Consider the "human interest story." Find a way to make your topic interesting to your audience.
6. How much knowledge of the subject does the audience have and what do they need to know? Do not tell the audience what they already know, but remember to include any background information they may need to properly appreciate and respond to the speech.
7. Does the audience have "a predisposition to evaluate an issue, action, object, symbol, person, or situation either favorably or unfavorably" (Tedford, 1991, p. 75)?
8. What is the audience's general attitude toward me as a speaker?
9. What is the audience's general attitude toward the subject, topic, and purpose?
10. Given your analysis, what do you need to know to prepare for this speech?

Based on your audience analysis, you make choices about content, organization, structure, examples, forms of support, and other features. The best audience and occasion analyses are more than just "thoughts in your head." Useful audience/occasion analyses are written down and the answers considered throughout the speechwriting process.

Occasion analysis is a consideration of the nature of the occasion (somber, celebratory, lighthearted), the date and hour, the location, the type of meeting (regular, special, ad hoc), and the overall program and where or why you fit in (mandatory, voluntary, invited, anticipated). Be sure you can answer the following questions: Should my audience care? Why should my audience care? How will you encourage the audience to care? Why should the audience listen? How will you encourage the audience to listen? Why should the audience listen to *you*?

Features of All Speeches

Once you have a thorough idea about who your audience is, how they are likely to respond, and what you need to be aware of about the audience and occasion as you prepare your speech, you are now ready to give some thought to outlining the speech.

There are 10 parts to a speech: (1) title, (2) subject, (3) general purpose, (4) specific purpose, (5) central idea, (6) introduction, (7) body, (8) conclusion, (9) transitions, and (10) support.

The title is important for a number of reasons. First, contrary to the adage about not being able to judge a book by its cover, people do it every day. The title of a speech or lecture will be used in marketing materials, in e-mail messages, in print materials, on Web sites, and is probably the primary reason that people who have a choice will choose to attend the speech. Second, and perhaps more importantly, in the age of the Internet, nothing ever goes away. Speeches wind up on YouTube, organizations post speeches for people to download, and search engines index information by key word. Having a carefully chosen title will make your documents and speeches easier for people to locate when using search engines. The actual title of a speech can be written at the beginning or end of the speechwriting process, but writing a compelling title is important. Titles should be interesting and exciting, and attract attention.

The **subject** of a speech refers to the "residual message." The subject is sort of like the bumper-sticker messages: "Drugs are bad," "Sales are looking up." The subject guides how you think about the speech as you prepare it. The subject should also function as a means of keeping you on track as you write the speech. If you stick to the subject throughout the speechwriting process you will be less likely to go off on tangents and more likely to write a well-organized, compelling speech.

Note that the subject is not the same as the title. A speech subject could be about how "new technology is important in public relations." However, the title, which should be designed to attract attention, might be "The Use and Abuse of New Technology in Public Relations: Learning How to Maximize Your Communication Plan." Titles raise interest and often only hint at a topic. However, the subject and the "specific purpose" (below) often match very closely.

The **general purpose** refers to a straightforward statement about the goal of the speech. There are only three choices: "to inform," "to persuade," or "to entertain." By having a general purpose firmly in mind while preparing a speech, you avoid the urge to be persuasive when your goal is to inform, or lecture (inform) when your job is to convince (persuade). Persuasion, information, and entertainment are very different kinds of speaking, and the best speeches are consistent with a single purpose. Note: Often, the goal of a speech is *both* to inform and persuade. Be sure to maintain balance when your general purpose includes both informing and persuading.

The **specific purpose** is a statement about what, exactly, the *audience* should come away from the speech with. Specific purposes are written as infinitive statements much like objectives (described earlier): "to convince the audience to … ." "to persuade all of the audience members from … to … ," "to make the audience aware of … ," etc. Specific purposes are not thesis statements. A specific purpose is a description of what the audience should know or believe after the speech. For example, a specific purpose for a technology speech might be, "For the audience to understand how to use blogs and threaded dialogue more effectively in their organizational activities." Always refer to what the audience gets when writing the speech purpose.

The **central idea** is essentially a thesis statement or claim. Central ideas usually include a "subject," a "position," and "support," and are often written as something that might actually be said in a speech. The purpose of a central idea is to force the speechwriter to actually articulate what his/her goal is early on in the speechwriting process. By referring back to the central idea throughout the speechwriting process, the writer is able to remain focused on the general and specific purposes and not stray from the main point of the speech. A central idea for our technology speech might be, "Blogs have received too much attention in the mainstream media but no research exists to back up the claims."

The **introduction** and conclusion are the most important parts of a speech. The introduction is important because it is the part of most speeches that everyone pays attention to. If you lose your audience with a weak introduction, you may not get them back until the end of the speech, when people listen again for the key points.

There are many techniques for creating a compelling introduction (see below). Perhaps the most important thing to keep in mind is that every introduction, whether for a 2-minute speech of introduction or a 25-minute after-dinner speech, does five things: gets attention and interest, reveals the topic, previews the body of the speech, transitions smoothly into the body of the speech, and establishes your credibility.

The length of an introduction and how each part of the introduction is executed varies widely. An introduction could be 15 seconds long or 15 minutes long. The length of the introduction depends upon the type of speech, the occasion, and the speaker's skills and background. In an outline, introductions are often written out word-for-word.

There are **transitions** between the introduction and the body, the body and the conclusion, and between all major points in an effective speech. Transitions are simply well-scripted phrases to get from one point to the next. Transitions are obvious, eloquent, often preceded by summaries or integrate summaries, and include previews: "Now that you understand the three features of organizational blogs, the next thing you need to know how to do is … ."

The **body** of your basic speech consists of about three to five main points fleshed out by a number of subpoints. The three-point structure is common across speech types (informative or persuasive) and length (whether you are talking for five minutes or an hour). Later in this chapter, I will describe several persuasive frameworks like Monroe's Motivated Sequence, which has five or more parts, but the body, or major content, of any speech tends to follow the 3–5 point rule.

Conclusions, like introductions, are important. People remember both. The conclusion is your last chance to make your message stick. Conclusions usually include some sort of summary of ideas, reinforce your specific purpose and central idea, include a last pitch (if giving a persuasive speech or presentation), signal the end of your presentation, and have a definite last or closing line that does not require the speaker to say "thank you" to let the audience know s/he is finished.

Creating Outlines

Skilled communicators usually create an outline before they actually write a speech. The outline includes each of the parts of speech identified above, and is guided by the following rules:

- Outlines include the 10 parts of a speech mentioned above as well as a thorough audience and occasion analysis. Going through the steps of creating a detailed outline ensures that the speechwriter stays focused on the general purpose and central ideas, and that the specific purpose is apparent in each section of the body.
- Introductions and conclusions are often written out word-for-word.
- Each section of a speech's body should be about the same length. You should not have a speech with three main points and devote three-quarters of your speech to one of them. If this happens, you need to restructure the speech to provide a balance to the information covered.
- Speech outlines, or the outline used to write a speech, are written in full sentences for every point and subpoint.
- Speaker outlines, for a speaker to use when delivering the speech, are often written as keyword outlines.
- Be sure that each major point has a clear relationship to your specific purpose and central idea.
- Be sure to include a variety of forms of support (see below) when you are creating arguments.
- Use hierarchy and symmetry when creating outlines. For example, to have an "A," you need a "B." To have a "1" requires a "2." Symmetry helps assure that the various parts of a speech's message are balanced.
- Create outlines using hanging indents and proper outline form so that you can clearly see relationships and ideas that are considered to be on the same level. Additionally, a quarter-inch indent is all that is needed between levels. If you use larger indents, by the time you get to a tertiary point you are halfway across the page and your outline will be five pages long. Note: Long outlines, because of poor formatting, make it more difficult to see the entire speech at once and make decisions about the content and structure of the speech.

OUTLINE HIERARCHY

- **I.** Major Point
    - **A.** Minor Point
        - **1.** Subpoint
            - **a.** Tertiary point
            - **b.** Tertiary point
            - **c.** Tertiary point
        - **2.** Subpoint
            - **a.** Tertiary point
            - **b.** Tertiary point
                - **i.** Quaternary point
                - **ii.** Quaternary point
                - **iii.** Quaternary point
    - **B.** Minor Point
        - **1.** Subpoint
            - **a.** Tertiary point
            - **b.** Tertiary point
        - **2.** Subpoint
            - **a.** Tertiary point
            - **b.** Tertiary point
- **II.** Major Point
    - **A.** Minor Point
        - **1.** Subpoint
            - **a.** Tertiary point
            - **b.** Tertiary point
        - **2.** Subpoint
            - **a.** Tertiary point
            - **b.** Tertiary point
        - **3.** Subpoint
            - **a.** Tertiary point
            - **b.** Tertiary point
    - **B.** Minor Point
        - **1.** Subpoint
            - **a.** Tertiary point
            - **b.** Tertiary point
        - **2.** Subpoint
            - **a.** Tertiary point
            - **b.** Tertiary point

C. Minor Point
  1. Subpoint
    a. Tertiary point
    b. Tertiary point
  2. Subpoint
    a. Tertiary point
    b. Tertiary point

Introductions and Conclusions

As mentioned earlier, introductions and conclusions are the most important parts of every speech. Introductions arouse audience interest and get their attention; conclusions serve to summarize key information and arguments and drives home the final point. There are a number of standard **introductory strategies:**

1. Use an appropriate quotation
2. Make a startling statement
3. Ask a challenging question
4. Tell a humorous story
5. Issue a challenge or call for immediate action
6. Make a personal reference or greeting
7. Refer to something relating specifically to the immediate audience
8. Use a visual aid
9. Initiate some activity or movement
10. Use suspense

Remember, you need to get an audience's attention right from the start. The first 15–30 seconds are crucial. Your opening and closing lines are what the audience will remember, so make the most of them. Always try to include a link to your audience in your introduction so that they feel that they are a part of what you are doing. Make them feel that this topic is important to them personally. Keep in mind the power of identification and the power of narrative. Speeches are especially conducive to telling stories and drawing upon narrative techniques. For inspiration, consider the speeches of Ronald Reagan, Mario Cuomo, Barbara Jordan, William Clinton, or Adlai Stevenson (www.americanrhetoric.com/top100speechesall.html).

The conclusion is equally important. Conclusions are your last chance to make your message stick, and neither you nor your audience should be left wanting. As with an introduction, there are a number of effective **conclusion strategies:**

1. Recite a memorable or relevant quotation
2. Make a dramatic statement
3. Refer back to the introduction (to reinforce your point and to repeat ideas and claims)
4. Challenge your audience
5. Use a series of repetitions ("I believe ... I believe ...")
6. Use an emotional appeal
7. Tell a personal story or anecdote

Introductions and conclusions should never be taken for granted. The most compelling speeches generate audience interest and make a connection to the audience (identification) right from the start, as well as draw listeners back in at the end of the speech, leaving them feeling good for having listened.

Forms of Support

When creating any written or spoken message, you need to consider how to best reach your audience. Different things move different people. For some, emotional appeals and anecdotes are compelling. Others prefer hard facts, data, statistics, and the word of experts. Still others are moved by the credibility and passion of the speaker. Thus, when Aristotle said to use "all of the available means of persuasion," he meant "multiple forms of support": emotion, logic, source credibility, etc.

There are two basic types of verbal support: clarification and proof. **Support for clarification** includes illustration, specific instance, analogy, restatement, and explanation:

Analogies involve comparison or contrast, usually involving that which is known to that which is unknown. *Literal analogies* are comparisons of like things—buildings to buildings, countries to countries—while *figurative analogies* are comparisons of unlike things—apples to oranges, men to women.

Explanation involves making things clearer, or providing additional, or multiple, examples to help your audience understand your point. Even obvious points can be made clearer by detailed and alternative explanations.

Illustrations are detailed stories (or anecdotes). Effective illustrations are related to the topic of the speech, representative or typical, and vivid in detail. *Factual illustrations* are detailed stories about things that actually happened. *Hypothetical illustrations* are detailed stories about things that may not have happened but could have happened.

Restatement involves rephrasing points, and saying something in a different way to help clarify your meaning. Restatement is often used with a quotation to clarify your intent. Restatement is also used as a figure of speech as repetition.

Anecdotes and specific instances involve short stories or examples. Specific instance are condensed factual illustrations. They are shorter than illustrations and lack imagery. Anecdotes often address issues of "who, what, when, where, why," and "how."

Support for proof includes testimony and statistics:

Testimony refers to statements made by someone else to support a point. "Experts" are often employed. Effective testimony consists of statements or quotations from a person who is qualified to speak on the subject (an expert on the subject) who has firsthand information, appears impartial, and is accepted by the audience as credible.

Statistics refer to numerical figures used to show the proportion of some event, activity, or behavior, or to show how many or few or how great or small. Statistics are numbers, but not all numbers are statistics. When using statistics, you want to be seen as unbiased, and the source of your statistics needs to be perceived as reliable and valid.

Remember, the best speeches draw upon multiple forms of support, not just a few. Since everyone is moved by different stimuli, using analogies, explanations, statistics, testimony, examples, etc., make for stronger, more compelling messages.

Organizational Patterns

Effective organization of a speech is essential for increasing your chances of success when speaking persuasively, or increasing the likelihood that your audience will retain your message when informing. "Logical," or coherent, organization is the most effective way to maximize your content or to say the most in a limited time and reduces the likelihood that you might forget to cover an important point.

For a speech to effectively communicate your ideas to an audience, it must satisfy these general criteria: (1) The speech must be adapted to the audience's needs and level of knowledge. You must make it interesting and compelling for them—based on *their* level of knowledge, *not* yours. (2) The organizational pattern must be appropriate and provide for full, balanced coverage of the speech content. (3) The speech must progress steadily toward a complete and satisfying finish. With the exception of television scripts and entertainment speeches, a speaker rarely employs the surprise ("whodunnit") conclusion. Professional presentations should be clear from the start. The audience must know the thesis, why they are listening, why they should care, and what you will tell them. Audience members in professional settings regularly ask, "Why are we here?" when they are being told something that is already well known or obvious.

There are several ways in which to structure a message for an audience: chronological, spatial, causal, topical, structure-function, problem–solution, and physical components.

Chronological: Using past or future events. Time, or when something happens, is the organizing framework. May be structured by hour/minute/second, date, epoch, events, births, deaths.

Spatial: Organization by space or physical proximity of objects, events, or people in relation to/with each other. Spatial organization may be by microns, inches, feet, yards, miles, light years, block/street, township, city, borough, district, state, country, continent, growth patterns (as in the rings of a tree, or a rhino's horn).

Causal: Cause–effect (present causes lead to future effects) or effect to cause (present conditions are the result of past causes).

Structure–Function: "This is how it is constructed and this is how/why it functions/operates the way that it does ..."

Topical: Organization by "topics" or points related to a central theme and linked to that theme, but not necessarily linked to each other; for example: dogs, cats, turtles, birds, and fish as "pets."

Problem–Solution: A persuasive pattern whereby a problem is identified/stated in the introduction or opening of the speech, and the rest of the speech is devoted to working through the steps necessary to solve the problem.

Physical Component: A pattern through which actual parts of an item are illustrated, demonstrated, described, etc., in order to draw on that insight to inform/persuade. Diagrams (and other visual aids) are essential for this sort of organizational structure.

The seven basic organizational forms described above barely scratch the surface. Almost anything could be used as the basis for an organization pattern: acronyms, words, extended metaphors. Consider the following possibilities:

Advantages/disadvantages
ABC, or 1, 2, 3
Acronyms (e.g., PETA, NEH, GOP)
Background, characteristics, accomplishments
Extended analogy/metaphor
Heredity/environment
Local, state, national, international
Need, desirability, practicality, alternative
Past, present, future, (other time sequence)
Physical, mental, emotional, spiritual
Political, economic, social
Resemblances/differences
Spell a word: "R-E-A-D-Y"
Stop, look, listen, (other catch phrase)
Symptom, prevention, cure
Theory/practice
Thinking, feeling, doing
Who, what, when, where, how, why

Your organizational strategy will depend upon the type of occasion and the message that you need to convey. Basic chronological and topical patterns are used in all kinds of speech situations and are often combined with other organizational patterns. Be flexible. Do not assume that one approach will work in every situation, and do not get locked into the same approach for every speech or presentation. Let the situation guide your choices.

Structural Recommendations

- Conduct a detailed audience analysis before you begin. Do not just conduct an audience analysis in your head; type up notes about the audience's demographics (size, age, sex, gender, SES, race, ethnicity, education, income), psychographics (beliefs, values, attitudes, heroes/villains), infographics (what the audience reads, listens to, watches, subscribes to), and gather details about the location where the speech will be delivered (be sure to visit the space to get a feel for the lighting, seating, acoustics).
- Prepare a manuscript for the speaker. Manuscripts should be double-spaced, have wide margins (at least 1.25"), printed at 16–18 points, and typed in an easily readable font (ask the speaker what *his/her* preference is). Include textual cues indicating when to pause for laughter or applause and phonetic pronunciations for *all names* unless patently un-screw-up-able (e.g., Smith, Lee, etc.). For example: "According to Bernays [Ber-NAYS] and Sproule [Sprule] ..." Be sure to manually break lines if necessary to keep text together, like names and pronunciation information. Encourage the speaker to review the manuscript a few times to make personal changes.
- Be prepared to work with the speaker to help him or her prepare for the speech. Be available to listen to the speech as many times as s/he is wiling to give it (typically two to three times is sufficient for everyday events). Advise the speaker on timing issues, pronunciation, posture, gestures, whether the speaker will be heckled and how to handle him/herself, etc. Indeed, if heckling is a possibility, bring in some practice hecklers to give the speaker some experience.
- Be sure that you have conducted a genre analysis of the speaking occasion: What has been done in the past? What are the expectations for this type of speech? Your goal in writing a memorable speech is not "to do what has always been done," nor to stray too far from what the audience expects. For example, after the Academy Awards, no one remembers the person who got up on stage and thanked his/her mother, agent, partner, God, etc. We remember the person who "deviated" slightly from the norm. In some cases the deviation is great (Michael Moore at the 2003 and 2004 Academy Awards, cf., www.alternet.org/election04/19385), in other cases the deviation is slight, such as not thanking *anyone*. The point is, if you stray too far from the norm the audience will get concerned and if all you do is give the audience the same thing as everyone else, the audience will not be moved. Striking this delicate balance is what separates a great speech from a banal one.

INFORMATIONAL SPEAKING

Tedford (1991) offered a brilliant description of informational speaking: "Spoken discourse that is limited in intent to the conveying of knowledge; its basic goal is to explain a subject to an audience so that those who listen achieve understanding" (p. 256). There are three parts to informational communication: motivation, clarification, and retention.

Motivation

One key to informational speaking is to establish speaker credibility early. Listeners learn more from speakers if they perceive them to have *ethos*: *competence*, (may be stated directly, but is also built by being well prepared); *integrity*, (honest, well prepared, well organized); and *good will* (smile, maintain eye contact, dress appropriately, be enthusiastic).

Effective informative strategies include employing positive incentives (e.g., "after this speech you too will be able to ..."), asking questions that arouse curiosity (e.g., "have you ever wondered why Google uses red, blue, and yellow for its logo?"), and promising rewards that are significant to the listeners.

Clarification

Clarification is essential to informational speaking: if your audience cannot readily grasp how what a speaker says relates to them, the message will usually be ignored. Clarification suggestions include:

1. Make your purpose and main points clear as you speak: Don't allow your audience an opportunity to become disinterested.
2. An early statement of purpose increases comprehension.
3. Previewing main points makes information easier to grasp.
4. Use sign-posting (spoken, visual, and written cues) after the statement of the central idea.
5. Repeat information before each point to build understanding through repetition. Well-organized speeches are more successful. Be sure to use voice and gestures to your advantage, holding up fingers to count points, etc.
6. Explain the unfamiliar in terms of the familiar: use metaphors and similes.
7. Use visual aids (a picture is worth a thousand words). However, always remember "KISS" (Keep It Simple, Stupid).

Retention

If your audience cannot remember what your points were after the speech, then the speaker might as well have stayed home. Retention suggestions include:

1. Use concrete language: Avoid abstract terms like "everyone knows," "a lot of people believe," "most people think." Tell your audience exactly how many people actually feel that way, or don't even mention it: "Three out of four Americans ..." or "Everyone in the office except Carl believes ..."
2. Summarize clearly: The conclusion is the place for this; however, for complicated subjects, internal summaries, or summaries after each section, are necessary.

The goal of informational speaking is to convey information (not to entertain or persuade), and to increase the knowledge and understanding of your audience. If you presuppose that there is only one "correct" position, you will fail. Informational speeches require balance, not one-sided claims.

All "information" has political and ideological implications. Just because you believe that you are right does not mean that there are not other valid possibilities. Although it may seem that information is politically neutral, it is not. Consider, for example, how the Bush administration placed a ban on federally funded clinics, preventing them from *providing information* concerning abortion to women, when school boards ban controversial books, and the prohibition on teaching religion in schools. Each of these issues involves the control of "information," and in each case, the consequences are substantial.

When attempting to "inform," be aware of what the information might mean (or be worth) to the audience. Be aware of the political value of the information to your audience. Just because *you* think that teaching sex education to grade-school children is important does not mean that everyone else will agree.

Like informational communication, persuasive speaking is quite common. Over the years, a number of models have been developed for creating persuasive messages, including Monroe's Motivated Sequence and McGuire's persuasion model.

MOTIVATIONAL STRUCTURE

Many scholars have studied persuasion and concluded that persuasion is often successful merely because the messages are structured effectively. Two such persuasive frameworks are Monroe's Motivated

Sequence (MMS) and McGuire's persuasion process (PACYRA).

Monroe's Motivated Sequence

Professor Alan Monroe of Purdue University developed Monroe's Motivated Sequence (MMS) as an organizing framework for speeches. The motivated sequence is intended to actuate (move to action), a more difficult goal than simply getting someone to agree with you on some issue. MMS has five parts: attention, need, satisfaction, visualization, and action **(ANSVA)**.

The ***attention* step** roughly corresponds to the introduction in a speech, except that, as part of the introduction, the persuader also introduces the "need" (or exigence) to be addressed. Never overlook the attention/introduction step nor take it lightly. The introduction is vitally important to creating desire in the mind of your audience to pay attention and continue listening/reading. Creating a compelling introduction is essential in MMS.

The ***need* step**, introduced in the introduction, involves explicitly telling the audience—and briefly explaining—what the problem is that "needs" to be solved. The need is not subtly implied, it is overtly stated: "In order to move forward with our war on terrorism, we need to ..." Or, "We need to make sure that the next presidential election is decided by the voters and not by the Supreme Court." The need is explicitly stated and typically followed by a few sentences elaborating on and supporting the claim.

The ***satisfaction* step** is essentially the body of the speech or text. Here, the persuader explains what the problem is and how his/her solution satisfies the need. In general, any organizational pattern may be used effectively: chronological, spatial, topical, problem–solution, etc. Additionally, counterarguments and claims are introduced and refuted in the satisfaction step, and the utility of the speaker or writer's solution is reinforced.

The ***visualization* step** is an extension of the body of the speech. The essence of the visualization step is that the speaker helps the audience "visualize" the future, depending upon whether the action that s/he is advocating is taken. There are three ways that visualization can be used: positive, negative, and a combination of both. **Positive visualization** involves vividly describing what might happen if the persuader's advice *is* followed: "Assuming that we make some changes to the voting procedures in the next election, we can look forward to a world where people's votes count. Imagine the visit to your precinct next year ..." **Negative visualization** is essentially just the opposite. The persuader helps the audience visualize what might happen if they do not act as you advocate: "History teaches us that change is slow and the powers that be have nothing to gain by enfranchising more voters. If you continue to say, 'My vote doesn't matter,' you can expect to see ..." The third form of visualization involves *combining both negative and positive visualization*. The order is unimportant, negative and then positive, or positive and then negative—both are effective.

The last step of MMS is the **action step**. This is essentially the conclusion. However, rather than merely offering some sort of summary that recounts the arguments, in a speech of actuation, the persuader provides the audience with the tools and knowledge to do what is asked. A speech of "action" must involve *action*. An issue advertisement or message on a Web site intended to move people to action must include specific steps for the audience to take.

The conclusion can never be, "Now that you understand the importance of voting, *hopefully* you will vote in the next election... ." An argument that seeks actuation does not seek mere agreement or thoughtful consideration from the audience but tangible, observable, quantifiable action. The audience must follow you to the polls, fill out a voter registration card *today*, volunteer to help a candidate, accompany you to a rally, sign a letter, open their wallet and make a donation, etc. Although obtaining signatures on a petition is an *action, giving money, helping to gather signatures* for a petition, or *participating* in a walkathon are more substantive actions and more likely to lead to long-term attitude change.

The whole point of the speech or message of actuation is the action step. Everything is designed to lead up to moving the audience to take some action. If the audience merely nods their heads and agrees with you, or promises to help at some point in the future, you have failed. The secret of an actuation speech, then, is to spend adequate time telling the audience how to actually take the action you are advocating, as well as providing the audience with the knowledge and skills to actually do what you want. Monroe's Motivated Sequence can be used to structure written messages as well as spoken messages, but in both cases the audience must be provided with the tools (knowledge, information, skills) to take the action that you advocate. Convince the audience that there is a pressing need, tell them what to do to solve the problem, and tell them what action to take to make it happen.

McGuire's Persuasion Model (PACYRA)

Like Monroe's Motivated Sequence, McGuire's persuasion model (PACYRA) relies on structure for creating persuasive messages. McGuire argues that during persuasion, individuals go through six steps from first awareness to final behavior: Presentation, Attention, Comprehension, Yielding, Retention, and Acting.

Presentation involves exposing your target public to your message at the optimum time and place for them. Presentation strategies use the relevant media or combinations of media to reach target publics (print for readers, radio for drivers, Internet for younger publics, signs for foot or automobile traffic).

Attention: Once you have determined the optimum means of delivering your message to your public (spoken or written), you need to get their attention. Strategies include ideographs (equality, freedom etc.), classic news strategies (timeliness, relevance, uniqueness, human interest), style/structure (graphic design, typography, compelling images, intriguing leads, metaphors, analogies), and relevant vocabularies ("props," "peeps" "professional grade," "home boys," "wicked," "extreme").

Hand-in-hand with attention is **comprehension** of your message by the audience. Messages must be tailored to the audience's vocabulary, interests, and behaviors. The message content must be at the appropriate comprehension level for the audience, and the message needs to be delivered by compelling/credible speakers.

Yielding: Once you have the audience's attention and you have crafted a message they find compelling, you must now convince them—through the strength of your logical appeals, emotional appeals, and the credibility and trustworthiness of your spokespeople—to take action. Persuasive appeals can be syllogistic, enthymematic, visual/graphic, subtle/complex, etc., depending upon the audience. Basically, all of the things you have learned about persuasion might apply here (identification, ideographs, etc.).

Retention: This refers to the audience's ability to remember your message. If the audience does not remember your message, they will not act on it. Strategies such as repetition, uniqueness, catchiness, ubiquity, and repeatability are essential here for success.

Action: Like MMS, *action* on the part of your audience is your final goal. For action to happen, messages may need to model desired behaviors or elaborate on them in more detail (cf., social learning theory, reasoned action, elaboration likelihood theory). Audiences must also be *capable* of taking the action you advocate (legally, emotionally, financially, etc.). As with MMS, you must also provide your audience with the tools to succeed. Be aware that behaviors do not change overnight. Behavioral change is a process and requires some adaptation and accommodation (cf., diffusion theory). McGuire does not really envision actually moving an audience to take action immediately. The PACYRA persuasion process is often used as part of marketing or advertising efforts rather than a speech guide like Monroe's Motivated Sequence.

One of the major issues that persuaders are confronted with is the problem of getting past the mental defenses of audience members. As I have mentioned, rhetorical theory tells us that people have differing ideological and psychological worldviews. One way to help create compelling messages is to understand how cognitive dissonance works.

COGNITIVE DISSONANCE (CD)

Cognitive dissonance is a "balance theory" that explains how people deal with conflicting information. Everyone experiences dissonance from time to time. For example, if you have two term papers due on the same day, which class gets priority? Or, if there is a party and a study session on Friday night—both offering rewards, both with consequences—which one will get your attention? When messages come into conflict, and organizations sometimes want to bring messages or behaviors into conflict, there are three possible responses: irrelevance, consonance, or dissonance.

Irrelevance refers to the fact that many messages that conflict with our personal views of the world are simply ignored. *Consonance* refers to messages that agree with our worldviews; we do not have to pay much attention to them because they already reinforce or acknowledge our beliefs, values, attitudes, and actions. *Dissonance*, which is what the theory is all about, refers to messages that conflict with our beliefs, values, and attitudes.

Public relations practitioners must understand cognitive dissonance for several important reasons. *First*, communicators must be aware that messages, if constructed improperly, can cause dissonance (where none is desired) or reduce dissonance (when dissonance is useful). And *second*, the desired result of a message is often to *cause* dissonance, as in an antismoking campaign. However, at other times, the intent of messages is to *reduce* dissonance, as when individuals or groups are being persuaded to try a new product or service as part of a informational campaign.

When behaviors or beliefs are challenged, messages that are often perceived as dissonant are ignored. In order to avoid audiences concluding that your messages is "irrelevant," dissonance needs to be reduced. Dissonance can be reduced in three ways: (1) by adopting a proposed behavior; (2) by avoiding new information; or (3) by seeking consonant information to bolster current beliefs. Knowing this, public relations professionals can create message that are difficult to ignore or avoid, or that refute consonant information, creating tension and forcing people to confront an issue.

Messages that are dissonant, or likely to be avoided, need to be designed in such a way as to avoid or reduce the potential for individuals to experience *irrelevance*. This can be done by focusing on creating attention-getting copy that avoids hot-button words, strengthening the credibility and logic of messages, and increasing the frequency of messages so that they are more ubiquitous, and difficult to avoid. Messages *designed* to create dissonance use similar tactics but *utilize* hot-button words and fear appeals, and draw more heavily on the enthymeme and symbolic persuasion rather than logic.

In order to get past the *irrelevance* response of people to messages that are considered unimportant, organizational communicators need to explain to people how messages are *relevant*. *Irrelevance* can often be avoided by creating provocative messages, using unexpected images and language in messages, and employing unexpected spokespeople (e.g., Bob Dole for Viagra, Paris Hilton for reading, etc.).

Consonant messages often offer rewards and reinforce preexisting beliefs and positive behaviors. Consonant messages are often ceremonial, praising individuals and members of groups for their support. Institutional advertising is one of the best examples of purely consonant messages.

In order to anticipate possible dissonant responses and to create messages intended to cut through dissonance, public relations professionals need to know what the competing messages are, how individuals and publics describe their experience, how they perceive your organization, etc. In other words, psychographic *research* into the beliefs, attitudes, and values of publics is required both to be able to anticipate dissonant responses and to craft messages that heighten or reduce dissonance.

RHETORICAL STRUCTURE: HOW TO CREATE COMPELLING MESSAGES

At the heart of all writing is an emphasis on form and structure. Without proper organization, virtually all writing would be ineffective. For example, consider how important it is to have something as seemingly unimportant as page numbers. Without them, we would not be able to have indexes or references, and studying texts would be much more difficult.

As you will learn later in this text, each type of public relations writing has its own unique constraints. Memos, for example, have very specific appearance characteristics and structure. Similarly, news releases have very rigid structural characteristics and a tone that differs from most other public relations documents. The rhetorical strategies described in this chapter can be used in hundreds of ways and are always contingent upon the situation and the audience involved. Structure is essential to effective messages.

Organization of Supporting Materials

Most types of documents have unique organizational characteristics. What virtually every document has in common, however, is a need for a compelling introduction and conclusion, and an internal structure (summaries, transitions, signposts). Introductions work to get an audience's attention and interest, reveal the topic, preview the message content, and provide a smooth transition into the document body.

Television provides a great example of the importance of organization and structure. How long does it take you to decide if you want to watch a particular television station when you are "channel surfing?" Most people do not devote even a full second to deciding if a program is worth watching. We are able to make such quick decisions because of the visual content of the message as well as our previous experience (structure) with the medium and the programming choices. A similar process occurs when people read newspapers and magazines. Readers scan pages looking for visual cues about the content—headlines, graphics, charts, diagrams, bolded text—and based on whether they find satisfying content, will begin to read the first paragraph of a story of interest. Typically, if the first few sentences do not get attention and interest, you will simply move on to the next item of interest. Thus, the importance of introductions cannot be overstated.

How introductions should be written varies widely. Obviously a news release is different than a speech; a speech of introduction is different than a persuasive speech; a persuasive speech is different than a pitch letter; a pitch letter is different than a cover letter. Understanding the differences among these rhetorical messages is important and will come with time.

For now, the key point to recognize is that every message (spoken, written, broadcast, electronic) needs a compelling introduction and conclusion. Messages are aided by structural cues like *transitions* (phrases used to move from one point to the next) and *signposts* (spoken, visual, and written cues identifying important information for a reader/listener). Messages are also aided by typographic cues, such as bold headings and subheadings, tables, bulleted lists, and boxes. On television, teasers, captions, sound, and informational graphics are used as structural cues; on radio, music, sound effects, narrative style, and dramatic copy are used to structure messages.

Typically, you never just jump straight to the key point, even in the case of an e-mail message or a news release. As an expert communicator, and a consumer of messages yourself, you should understand that audiences do not have an *obligation* to read or listen to what you say. You have to make people *want* to pay attention. Even if all you do is add a few sentences to the beginning of an e-mail message to include a proper greeting and some structure ("Dear Dr. Smith, ... How are you today? I am writing to ask about ... I have a question about two things from lecture, ..."), you can still get a reader's attention, reveal the topic, provide structural cues for the reader, and preview the content of the message in three sentences!

Like introductions, conclusions are also important. As you undoubtedly know as students, many written documents—especially books, reports, research papers—end with a summary/conclusion. The conclusion is your last chance to make your point, the conclusion is the only thing that some people read, and the conclusion provides one of the most powerful persuasive tools you have. Never ignore it. With the exception of news copy (news releases, feature stories), which is often written according to the inverted pyramid and does not include a proper conclusion, why would you *want* to ignore the power of the conclusion?

All documents also include identifying information, contact information, titles, dates, and authorship information. Never create documents of any kind (even writing done in class) that do not include the name and contact information for the organization or the creator. Identifying authorship and providing contact information is not an issue of vanity, just pragmatics. Not every document remains in its original context: Web pages are forwarded to people and linked to from other Web sites, brochures are left on tables and passed along to others, articles in newspapers and magazines are copied for colleagues, fact sheets are taken out of media kits. Students and researchers want to know sources of facts and information, and every organization wants interested individuals and publics to be able to get in touch with them. *Everything* should contain your name and contact information.

Timing

The Greek work for timing is ***kairos*** (HEAR-ohs). Timing, in the sense that I mean it here, is closer to arrangement. Timing has a place in both speeches and in writing. Timing generally refers to mentioning facts and information in a written document or speech when it will be received best, as well as *having kairos*, and knowing how to pause at the appropriate time, tell a joke, and sensing when an audience might be receptive to information or facts. Timing, then, is a strategic decision. Consider the persuasion research that tells us we should present good news first and then bad news when we have both good and bad news to report (see Table 5.1).

What the research can never tell us is where in a speech or document to actually *place* information. Should a speech or memo actually *begin* with the good news (placing it in a heading, in the title, using the information as part of an introduction)? Should good news be worked in to support a weaker point? Should the bad news be placed in a footnote or appendix so it is less prominent? Decisions about *when and how* to use information are rhetorical decisions.

A classic example of timing occurs when organizations have bad news to report. Organizations prefer bad news to be downplayed or ignored, so they will typically send out gloomy news releases late Friday afternoon—too late to be covered in prime time by television sources and often ignored over the weekend by business-oriented print publications. If an organization has good news, Monday morning is the best time to release it, since the organization will then have all week to talk about it. Timing is a strategic decision that influences both the structure of messages as well as their content, delivery, and reception.

Cadence

Cadence is another timing issue related to the way in which language and phrases are arranged. Messages with superior cadence are more compelling and interesting to read or listen to. Cadence is perhaps most pronounced in music and poetry, but can be used effectively in prose messages as well. As a basic illustration of how cadence works, consider the Marine Corp. marching chant (called "Jodies" or a "Jody") below:

> When My Granny was 91 … she did PT just for fun.
>
> When my Granny was 92 … she did PT better than you.
>
> When my Granny was 93 … she did PT better than me.
>
> When my Granny was 94 … she ran 2 miles, then ran 10 more.
>
> When my Granny was 95 … she did PT to stay alive.
>
> When my Granny was 96 … she did PT just for kicks.
>
> When my Granny was 97 … she up and died … and went to heaven.
>
> She met St. Peter at the pearly gates … said, "Hey, St. Peter, I hope I ain't late."
>
> St. Peter looked at her with a big ole grin … and said "Get down Granny and knock out 10."
>
> She knocked them out and did 10 more … dedicated them to the Marine Corps! (Knight, 1990)

The essence of cadence, then, is rhythm or tempo. In a speech, cadence can be manipulated by speeding up and slowing down—adding an air of necessity, or immanence—by using figures of speech and repetition, and by tone of voice or pitch. Manipulating cadence in written documents is more difficult. Cadence has obvious value when creating messages intended to be read aloud, or heard, but print-based messages require different techniques. Words are bolded and italicized to add emphasis; headings are used to emphasize words and phrases as readers move from section to section; and, more skillfully, many figures of speech (as mentioned in Table 2.1: alliteration, anaphora, assonance, asyndeton, consonance) can be used to generate cadence. Finally, sentence length can be varied. Short two or three-word sentences can be used with great impact. Words can also be repeated, eliminated, or changed.

Repetition

Repetition is a concept that is familiar to everyone. All of us have been subjected to repetition as we watch network television programs and see the same commercials over and over, when we hear radio commercials shouting the same phrase over and over, in print advertisements in magazines, and on billboards, buses, and buildings.

In spite of all of the negatives associated with repetition (mostly in advertising), repetition is an incredibly important rhetorical tool. In speeches, repetition of the same word or phrase is very compelling. Similarly, as with public speaking, repetition in the form of previews, signposts, and internal summaries helps an audience follow along with a speaker and better understand his/her message. In print, we use headers and footers, headlines, subheadings, and color, to draw attention to specific points.

Some repetition is desirable and necessary, especially when dealing with a difficult concept in writing, or when trying to help people memorize important information. The first thing to remember is that rarely is it possible to have too much repetition. Including headings, previews, summaries, and transitions in written documents is so commonplace and necessary that this sort of repetition is only noticed when it is absent.

The amount of repetition needed also depends upon the type of document or message being created. Some messages, such as informative and persuasive speeches and issue advertisements, require *more* repetition, while documents like news releases require very little repetition.

Shorter documents, like brochures, fact sheets, and news releases, often employ repetition in the form of bulleted lists:

- All packages include …
- All packages include …
- All packages include …

Additionally, some brief documents, like pitch letters, call for repetition in the form of previews and signposts, whereas a letter of thanks does not. Ultimately, you will develop a feel for how much repetition is needed as you learn more about different types of written documents.

Remember, repetition serves the audience. If an audience does not know something well (like your 800 number) then you will need to repeat the information several times. Begin to watch how others use repetition. When you find compelling and easy-to-follow messages, examine them for structural clues so that you can do the same thing, and save samples of effective messages to your "swipe file" for future inspiration.

Imagery

Imagery refers to language that is vivid, evocative, passionate, and compelling. Drawing upon compelling imagery can mean the difference between a banal message and a moving one, between a message that can bring tears to an audience's eyes and one that merely makes people smile or nod their heads. Compelling imagery has always played an important role in public communication. Take Nixon's famous "Checkers" speech, for example, where Nixon makes a passionate defense of his character in order to remain on the vice presidential ticket with Eisenhower:

> I should say this—that Pat doesn't have a mink coat. But she does have a respectable Republican cloth coat. And I always tell her that she'd look good in anything.
>
> One other thing I probably should tell you because if we don't they'll probably be saying this about me too, we did get something, a gift, after the election. A man down in Texas heard Pat on the radio mention the fact that our two youngsters would like to have a dog. And, believe it or not, the day before we left on this campaign trip we got a message from Union Station in Baltimore saying they had a package for us. We went down to get it. You know what it was?
>
> It was a little cocker spaniel dog in a crate that he'd sent all the way from Texas. Black and white spotted. And our little girl—Tricia, the 6-year old—named it Checkers. And you know, the kids, like all kids, love the dog and I just want to say this right now, that regardless of what they say about it, we're gonna keep it. (Nixon, "Checkers," September 23, 1952; www.Americanrhetoric.com/top100speechesall.html)

When Nixon makes the reference to Pat (his wife) not having a mink coat but having a "respectable Republican cloth coat," Nixon not only evokes the austere image of Pat Nixon that was well known to the audience at the time, but also evokes images of decadence among the mink coat crowd—namely his opposition. The story of Checkers *still* makes the hair stand up on the back of your neck and is one of those "awww" moments.

There are several things needed to use imagery effectively. Typically, imagery is first person, like Nixon's narrative. At the heart of imagery are realism, clarity, vividness, and detail. A speaker or writer can draw upon emotion to move an audience. As a persuasive tactic, imagery is very powerful. However, even when just informing an audience about everyday issues, detailed, realistic, illustrations that draw on vivid language and emotional themes can be employed to help cement ideas in an audience's mind. More importantly, imagery is memorable. For example, take Mario Cuomo's 1984 Democratic National Convention keynote address:

> But the hard truth is that not everyone is sharing in this city's splendor and glory. A shining city is perhaps all the President sees from the portico of the White House and the veranda of his ranch, where everyone seems to be doing well. But there's another city; there's another part to the shining the city; the part where some people can't pay their mortgages, and most young people can't afford one; where students can't afford the education they need, and middle-class parents watch the dreams they hold for their children evaporate.
>
> In this part of the city there are more poor than ever, more families in trouble, more and more people who need help but can't find it. Even worse: There are elderly people who tremble in the basements of the houses there. And there are people who sleep in the city streets, in the gutter, where the glitter doesn't show. There are ghettos where thousands of young people, without a job or an education, give their lives away to drug dealers every day. There is despair, Mr. President, in the faces that you don't see, in the places that you don't visit in your shining city... .
>
> It's an old story. It's as old as our history. The difference between Democrats and Republicans has always been measured in courage and confidence. The Republicans—The Republicans believe that the wagon train will not make it to the frontier unless some of the old, some of the young, some of the weak are left behind by

> the side of the trail. "The strong"—"The strong," they tell us, "will inherit the land."
>
> We Democrats believe in something else. We Democrats believe that we can make it all the way with the whole family intact, and we have, more than once... .

Whether you agree with Cuomo's sentiment, you cannot fail to find his imagery compelling: the shining city, the wagon train. Imagery, like many of the techniques outlined in this chapter, takes practice. Using imagery effectively and writing a compelling speech, organizational history, backgrounder, or research report takes great skill. Several skilled speechwriters often write speeches like Cuomo's (although Cuomo is considered a very skilled speechwriter and is believed to have written his own speech).

Lest you think that imagery is only used in speeches, many types of public relations documents use imagery and narrative (storytelling) effectively. Consider these historical backgrounders from the Ben & Jerry's Ice Cream Web site:

> Ben's first professional contact with ice cream came in his senior year of high school, when he worked as an "ice cream man," driving a truck, ringing bells, and selling ice cream pops to kids. He was promoted to the position of "boxman," meaning he worked in the freezer and distributed ice cream to other ice-cream truck drivers. (benandjerrys.com/our_company/about_us/our_history/benbio.cfm)
>
> At Oberlin, Jerry got his first taste of working in the ice cream industry when he took a job as a scooper in the college cafeteria. His favorite course, however, was "Carnival Techniques," where he picked up several useful skills, including fire-swallowing. (benandjerrys.com/our_company/about_us/our_history/jerrybio.cfm)

The narrative style used by Ben & Jerry's to portray the founders as "hard-working," "regular" people (Ben drove an ice cream truck and worked in the freezer while Jerry went to college but studied "Carnival Techniques") is fairly common. However, the imagery of "truck driver" and "ice cream scooper" is clearly intended to showcase Cohen and Greenfield as everyday people rather than elites. These analogies are similar to Nixon's reference to Pat's "cloth coat."

To develop skill in using imagery, you need to practice using imagery in your writing: keep a diary, write letters and holiday newsletters, and, in general, work to incorporate more imagery into all your writing.

SPECIAL OCCASION SPEECHES[1]

As explained in the beginning of this chapter, there are three basic types of speeches, deliberative (persuasive), forensic (informational), and epideictic (ceremonial/entertainment). This third category represents some of the most common types of speeches. Since many types of special occasion speeches are given everyday, I summarize several below.

Inspirational: One speaks to the converted. The pregame pep talk is a form of this speech. Party nomination speeches also have characteristics of inspiration. Emotional appeals are appropriate—no proof is necessary because of audience agreement. You are "preaching to the converted," or the congregation. What you want to make sure to do is provide "reasons" or links for the audience to grasp. That is, tell them why this event should be important to them and about why they should be excited. Drawing upon personal experiences here is often quite useful. Keep your point simple; be sure to make your point clear and identify specific behaviors the audience can engage in. Use of narrative is essential.

Commemoration or Celebration: Commemoration deals with past events, such as patriotic and historical occasions and celebrations of past events (cf., the speeches on Martin Luther King, George Washington, or Susan B. Anthony's birthday). Celebrations are often more focused on current events: graduations, celebrations of "specialness," bicentennials, sesquicentennials, and individual or group accomplishments. Be sure to have a coherent point. Narrative, personal and family experiences, and the retelling of important stories, are strategies that are often employed here. Memorable quotations are common but do not make them the body of your speech.

Nomination: Nomination speeches are persuasive and enthusiastic speeches to actuate—like a speech of tribute. Business-like and energetic, your goal is to stress the qualifications of the person involved. Begin with statement of intent—"I rise to place a name in nomination"; state the requirements needed for the job; name the candidate and state his/her qualifications for the position—your job is to show why the nominee is an excellent choice; finally, urge the audience to endorse the candidate as you formally place their name in nomination. Alternatively, you might start with the person's name if s/he is already well known and understood to be a potential candidate.

- Stress dominant traits.
- Mention only outstanding achievements.
- Give special emphasis to the skills of the person.
- Narration and anecdotes are appropriate here, as are metaphors.
- Try to "whip up the crowd"—especially supporters.

Goodwill: Create or strengthen favorable attitudes: Establish ethos. Goodwill speeches are based on creation or cultivation of modesty, tolerance, and good humor. Sometimes your goal will be to change uninformed beliefs and hostile attitudes. You must know and represent the facts clearly and show a tolerant, patient, attitude. Do not deride or attack opposing views or competitors; instead, be good-natured and good-humored. Keep in mind three things: (1) present interesting and novel information and facts about your subject; (2) show a relationship between the subject and the lives of your audience; (3) offer a definite service or information to the audience. Humility is often the key here. Do not so much attack oppositional views as offer to help the audience understand yours better. Introduction (of self) speeches, where a speaker identifies or explains his/her accomplishments and goals, are examples of this speech.

Tribute: Creates in those who hear it a sense of appreciation for the traits or accomplishments of the particular person or group. If you make the audience realize his/her/their essential worth you have succeeded; however, you should go beyond this. By honoring the person, you may arouse deeper devotion to the cause or vales the person or group represented. Avoid pedantic speech and overostentatious speaking—no "purple prose."

- Stress dominant traits.
- Mention only outstanding achievements.
- Give special emphasis to the influence of the group or person.

Toasts: Many cultures, including our own, employ a sophisticated tradition of toasting. Russian *tomadas*, for example, entertain, as well as serve as toast master/mistress. "Toastmasters" (the group), in a sense, practices a form of toasting; as does the Rotary club. Russians may toast all around the table, and Georgians (the former U.S.S.R, not the U.S. state) are considered great speakers and often give very beautiful and elaborate toasts.

- The purpose of the toast is to honor and call attention to someone or something.
- Toasts can be humorous or serious depending on the situation or speaker.
- In Western culture, keep it short and have a point (one to two minutes is about right; 30 seconds is too short).
- Panache, *kairos* (timing), polish, and poise are most important here. You want to give the most memorable toast at the table.
- Do not read from notecards.
- At the end, raise your glass high and actually *drink*. In many cultures, not drinking is an insult, as is toasting with water in some cultures.

Introduction: Make the audience receptive for the speaker and want to hear him/her: Talk with the speaker, perhaps consult his/her résumé or curriculum vitae. The speech of introduction is intended to highlight the accomplishments, credentials, activities, and characteristics of the speaker. There are several conventions to be observed when conducting an effective speech of introduction. Do this well and the audience will feel excited and rewarded to hear the speaker; do this poorly and the audience will just want you to shut up.

- Make the audience want to hear the speaker. You might relate an anecdote or (short) story, arouse curiosity, etc. Make an effort to get the audience to like/respect the person—use information that the audience would find interesting, significant, or appealing.
- Cover the aspects of the speaker's background that the audience would find pertinent: education, special honors, work, etc. (This

information can be gained by interviewing the speaker or getting an information sheet from him/her).

- Reveal the title or topic of the speech and make a connection between the speech and the audience—do not talk about the topic yourself.
- Never talk about yourself or your own ideas or theories on the subject. Although, you might relate some anecdote about how the person to speak was especially helpful, etc.
- Do not praise the speaker too highly.
- The more famous the speaker, the less you need to say.
- Some humor is okay, if it is in keeping with the occasion and tasteful.
- Ask the speaker how to pronounce his/her name, even if you are sure that you know how to pronounce it.
- As my public speaking teacher used to say: "Be brief—get up, speak up, shut up."

Farewell: When someone is bidding farewell to others, they often comment on the situation under which they are leaving—it may be bitter, as in Nixon's case, or fond, as when a respected school teacher or colleague retires. Farewell speeches are given by both the retiree, and by those who are remaining behind.

When expressing gratitude for another, note the experiences, kindness, support, helpfulness, opportunities, consideration, and warmth that the individual extended.

- Honor them—create a desire for the audience to emulate him/her.
- Do not try to tell everything about the person—pick out the dominant personal traits, outstanding achievements, and influences on others. Keep your lists short but keen.
- Although you may express regret at his/her departure, be positive about the future—tell where the person is going ... that you will miss him/her, but that s/he will go on to greater or better things.
- Do not depress the audience.
- Sometimes a gift is connected with the speech (the cliché gold watch). Present it at the end of the speech.

When you are *bidding farewell,* you should also note the experiences, kindness, support, helpfulness, opportunities, consideration, and warmth that your colleagues extended. The principles above also apply here. Avoid the temptation to say what you "really think" about those who have wronged you, impeded your progress or success, or were downright mean. Such speeches often follow people and lead to regret for giving them.

Entertainment: This is usually brief (three to five minutes). However, some may be longer, 5 to 10 minutes, or even 30 to 45 minutes. The speech to entertain requires more imagination, creativity, discretion, versatility, and judgment than perhaps any other type of speech.

> The purpose of the speech to entertain is, according to Robert G. King, "to interest, please and amuse your listeners." J. K. Horner writes that the primary purpose of the after-dinner [or entertainment] speech is "entertainment and good fellowship." Enjoyment is the desired response from the audience in a speech to entertain. Its function is to contribute favorably to the climate of fellowship among the listeners. In a successful speech to entertain, observes William Allen Wood, "we expect our intellect, our taste, and our affections to be pleased" (Hank Scheele, Purdue University, Course packet, Advanced Public Speaking, 1995).

Suggestions for composition and delivery of after-dinner speeches include:

A. Carefully select an interesting, timely, and appropriate topic. Having something familiar in the talk that the audience can relate to will enhance listener interest. Having a novel or surprise feature in the talk will enhance attention.
B. Build your speech around a central theme, moral, or one-point idea.
C. Support your main point or central theme with colorful stories, narrative, and examples.
D. Be imaginative and creative when delivering your talk. Few speeches demand more imagination and creativity than the speech to entertain.
E. Be genial and good-natured when delivering your talk—irony is acceptable but not bitterness.

F. Be optimistic and modest when speaking and create an appropriate mood for your listeners.
G. Use plenty of humor.
H. Humor is the key ingredient in speeches to entertain. Humor can be accomplished through satire, irony, banter, ridicule, and wit. Some of the recognized constituents of humor are:
   - *Exaggeration:* the process of taking an idea or statement beyond the limits of reality.
   - *Incongruity:* the process of provoking an unexpected response from one's speech material.
   - *Anticlimax:* arranges a series of items in a growing order of significance only to end suddenly in the absurd.
   - *Puns:* involve the humorous use of a word that can be interpreted multiple ways.
   - *Play on words:* deals with the imaginative and creative use of language designed to produce a humorous response.

Dedication: Dedication speeches are given for the person or people who were instrumental in the construction, fundraising, or placement of buildings, objects, monuments, artworks, ships (or any monumental vessel), and places (parks, play grounds, exhibits, etc.).

- State the purpose of the occasion or the meaning to the group or organization—yes, they know, but you do it anyway for any guests or media who might attend.
- Give brief, pertinent facts—the history of a building, object, or the persons involved with it, life facts about the person for a statue, etc.
- Express thanks for any person particularly instrumental in building, creating, and/or fundraising.
- What inspiration for the future can the assembled group (and those not assembled) draw from the occasion/event?
- Narration and anecdote is appropriate here, as are brief metaphorical stories or aphorisms.
- Eloquence, originality, and profundity are the key here. Do not rely on stereotypes, do not use puns, avoid dead metaphors, and try to say something lasting and something that will sound good on the five o'clock news.

NB: The champagne bottle is scored so that it will crack when it is struck on the ship or building (score it well so it only takes one shot). Bring safety glasses. If an elderly person is doing the breaking, be sure a couple of younger people are nearby to assist if s/he loses his/her balance.

PROFESSIONAL PRESENTATIONS

Professional presentations are given to pitch ideas to customers and clients, to report the results of studies to fellow organizational members, to provide information to stakeholders, etc. In general, the key to an effective professional presentation involves three things: practice, preparation, and an effective audience analysis. McElreath (1997, pp. 365–375) offered several suggestions for preparing effective presentations. I extend his suggestions below.

Presentation Suggestions

1. *Put your objectives into writing.* Be clear about your purpose before you begin. Be able to answer the following questions about your audience:
   - "What do they already know?"
   - "What do they need or want to know?"
   - "Why should they care?"
   - "How can I make them care?"
2. *Behave ethically.* Even when you do not work for an organization (such as independent practitioners) you should be accurate, honest, truthful, and fair—avoid hyperbole and unsupported claims. Know where your facts come from. Do not assume that because other professionals or the media are saying something that it must be true. Conduct the research and find out for yourself. Never plagiarize content from the Internet, newspapers, newsmagazines, or fellow professionals, and never try to pass off the research or work of others as your own. You will eventually get caught, and plagiarism violates the PRSA code of ethics and sometimes the law (in the case of copyright violations)! Being honest and upfront about your sources will bolster your credibility.
3. *Structure your presentation appropriately.* The written word is not the same as the spoken word—do not read, deliver! Do not follow a written script word-for-word. Decide which organizational pattern is most appropriate: chronological, spatial, topical, historical, cause and effect, problem to solution, and have a coherent thesis. Presentations are not just a bunch of random facts and claims all strung together. Be sure that everything in the presentation follows from a single premise.
4. *Support your claims.* Support includes case studies, testimonials, illustrations, analogies,

narratives, anecdotes, statistics, and research. Although support usually includes "numbers," support does not consist solely of reports of percentages or standard deviations. Support involves "words!" Explain *why* something is significant or insignificant and, more importantly, what the implications are for the client or public. Use the numbers to tell a story.

5. ***Practice (many times) and be prepared for the worst.*** Often, when speaking at professional conferences or meetings, prior speakers take longer than their allotted time (thereby reducing *your* time); equipment malfunctions or is sometimes not available (bulbs burn out, faulty cords do not function properly, an overhead projector is available rather than a *data projector*, etc.); attendees, and sometimes presenters, have trouble finding the room for the event. With practice and advance preparation, a 15-minute presentation can be effectively shortened to 5 minutes, paper copies can be substituted for overheads, etc. Like the Marines, be prepared to improvise.
6. ***Use an "on-target" style and format.*** Make your documents resemble the organizational documents of clients and publics. When doing a presentation in class, create handouts that resemble your professor's, when pitching an idea to a potential client, create documents and slides that resemble the client's. Remember, just because *you* love 10-point Times New Roman does not mean that everyone else does! I assure you that the 50-year-old CEO with bifocals does not. Making your documents resemble organizational documents makes them appear more familiar, and more compelling.
7. ***Properly format your documents and proofread carefully!*** Formatting suggestions:
   - Do not "double-space." You are not writing a class paper. However, be sure to incorporate some white space in handouts, materials, etc.
   - Use easy-to-read fonts. Serif fonts are best at 10–12 points (Bookman, Caslon, Galliard, Garamond, Palatino) while san serif fonts (Ariel, Gill Sans, Helvetica) are easier to read at large type sizes (18–36 point) and are appropriate for headings.
   - Use headings and subheadings, indent block quotes, include pull-quotes, etc.
   - Create *simple* charts and figures for visual aids. Do not create complex tables or charts; avoid "chart junk" (cartoons, dingbats or symbols rather than regular bullets, colors for the sake of color, lines and shading, etc.) (Tufte, 2006, pp. 140–185).
   - Use bulleted and numbered lists to separate related items.
8. ***Choose an appropriate media mix.*** PowerPoint, slides, transparencies, flipcharts, posters, chalk, white boards, etc., all have unique characteristics. Do not assume that PowerPoint is the "best" method simply because it is the latest—no one is impressed with Slideware presentations anymore, even when they are good! All media and delivery styles have pros and cons. Use what you are most comfortable with and what is most appropriate for the target audience. Sometimes, just talking with people and using handouts is the best approach.
9. ***Know what makes your audience laugh.*** But use humor *only* if you can! If you are not funny, do not tell jokes. Never mock a racial, cultural, social, or corporate stakeholder (even if your client does). Never engage in stereotyping.
10. ***Learn who the heroes, villains, and the corporate icons are.*** The most effective presentations are targeted to specific individuals and publics, use familiar vocabulary, avoid acronyms, and draw upon cultural images and ideas that are familiar and compelling to the audience. Be sure to explain the unfamiliar in terms of the familiar by using metaphors, analogies, etc.
11. ***Learn who the members of the dominant coalition are,*** and never forget that you are really giving your presentation to *them*. Although you should address the entire audience when giving a presentation, be sure to direct your attention to organizational leaders as well.
12. ***Prepare a worksheet or list*** to verify that you have completed all tasks when preparing a professional presentation.
13. ***Be prepared for questions.***
    - All answers should be short and focused—about 15–30 seconds.
    - Generate a list of possible questions and answers ahead of time.
    - Anticipate difficult questions and prepare concise and compelling answers.
    - Use visual and nonverbal heuristics when answering questions. For example, "There are three relevant issues here ... first ... second ... third ..."; or, "To answer your question requires that we consider two issues ... number one ... two ... three ..." Be sure to

support your verbal messages with nonverbals (hold up fingers to count out points).

14. *Remember the KISS rule.* Keep your answers brief.

AGENDA-SETTING THEORY (AST)

Given the rhetorical and strategic nature of public relations communication, public relations professionals always have a reason for communicating. News conferences, speeches given at special events, media pitches, and speeches posted on Web sites and blogs are given in hopes of attracting media attention and raising awareness about key organizational issues. Understanding agenda-setting theory is essential to understanding how to have success with the media and place organizational issues before the public. The idea behind **agenda-setting theory** is that the media provide individuals and publics with messages about the world around them essentially "setting the agenda" or telling people what to think *about* (Baran & Davis, 2000; Cohen, 1963; Iyengar and Kinder, 1987; McCombs & Shaw, 1976). Additionally, the research on agenda-setting theory suggest that the media do not have a lot of success telling people what to *believe*, but the media *do* influence what people think *about*.

On the surface, the idea that the media set the public agenda seems obvious. How would the average citizen learn about spousal abuse in Burundi, about President Bush's involvement in the leaking of CIA agent Valerie Plame's name, or about the latest iPad innovation from Apple if the media did not tell us? Before you can even conduct research on an issue, you have to know that an issue exists.

Having the ability to set the agenda is powerful. One of the problems with agenda-setting theory is that the theory is often naïvely seen as "neutral," with the media portrayed as unbiased guardians of the truth who objectively present the facts to the public on issue of public concern. The truth is that the "objective media" are a myth (Bagdikian, 2004; Kent, Harrison, & Taylor, 2006). Many people claim: "We'll use agenda-setting theory to get our idea out to the media and the public." That would be great if all you had to do was to send out a news release to be successful. In reality, however, how will you gain access to representatives from the media interested in doing what *your* organization wants, and why is talking about *your* cause in a media outlet's best interest when every major media outlet has hundreds of choices about what to cover?

Complicating the agenda-setting function of the media further is the phenomenon of the **information subsidy** (Gandy, 1982). The information subsidy refers to the relationship between media content and public relations content (nonnews content). In a typical newspaper, for example, the amount of actual "news" content is quite small—a few pages in the first section of the newspaper. The rest of the content consists of syndicated columns, op-ed (opinion and editorial) content, and, the vast majority of the remaining content, public relations. Consider the Sunday newspaper which, in some locations, is three inches thick and weighs five pounds. If newspapers actually had to generate that much original news content every week, they would require staffs of hundreds of full-time reporters.

Because of the information subsidy, what actually happens is that professionals in every area—automotive, health, education, entertainment, sports, professional associations for gardeners, school boards, travel agencies, real estate agents, and a host of other organizations—provide news content for free. The news release is just one manifestation of free news content. The remainder of a newspaper is advertising, which makes far more money than do newspapers sales—which barley cover the cost of printing. Newspapers are not published to provide citizens news, but to provide customers for advertisers. Indeed, to call newspapers *news*-papers is a misnomer. *Ad*-papers would be more accurate (Bagdikian, 2000; Schiller, 1989).

As Roy Megary, former publisher of the *Toronto Globe and Mail*, suggested more than twenty years ago: "By 1990, publishers of mass circulation daily newspapers will finally stop kidding themselves that they are in the newspaper [or news] business and admit that they are primarily in the business of carrying advertising messages" (Bagdikian, 2000, p. 195).

In many newspapers, the relationship between advertising and story coverage is ambiguous. Newspapers frequently include story support for advertising sections. "If you buy an advertisement in this special section on technology, we will allow you to include a story about your organization." The amount of space you receive is of course related to how big an advertisement you want to purchase. If you look in your Sunday paper, you will probably see a "special section" or "special report" at least once a month. Special sections are pure profit. They cost newspapers very little to produce, the content is free (provided by others), and a newspaper can sell advertisements in the special section that are related to the stories that the newspaper was paid to place.

The flow of agenda setting works as follows: messages flow from public relations specialists, nonprofit organizations, governmental leaders, etc., to the media. Messages then flow from the media to the public. The fact that the media do not have a lot of influence over what people *think* actually misses the point. Having control over *what* people think *about* is even better. Because of how the enthymeme works, when a person concludes that "immigration must be important" (because the media keep taking about it), that person has essentially convinced him or herself. Because of the myth of objectivity or "balance"—the media actually have a tremendous conservative bias because of corporate ownership and consolidation (Bagdikian, 2000; Kent, Harrison, & Taylor, 2006)—and the media's tendency to seek mainstream sources for facts and confirmation (Middleberg & Ross, 1999a, 2000a), the idea that the media are neutral presenters of the public agenda is actually a myth.

You need to understand several things about agenda-setting theory: First, public relations professionals have been taking advantage of the opportunity to influence *what* people think about for many years through issue advertising, letters to the editor, direct mail campaigns, editorials, interpersonal influence, etc. Agenda setting involves a lot more than sending out news releases. Organizations *do* influence the substance of debates in the media through "spokespeople," content on Web sites, and content in news releases and other organizational documents. Organizations probably have more control over *what* stakeholders think about issues than they get credit for.

Second, getting an issue on the public agenda in the first place is a lot harder than influencing an issue after it has reached critical mass. Once an issue is placed before the public by the media and begins to build momentum, the media begin searching for people to comment. But getting an issue front and center in the first place is more difficult. Important issues can receive attention through celebrity spokespeople, grassroots activist efforts, issue advertisements, politicians, pseudoevents (publicity stunts), etc., but there is no guarantee that any of these techniques will achieve success; usually, a combination of several tactics is needed.

The media are a cantankerous lot who do not like being told their business. Never lecture a reporter or editor in order to tell him or her why an issue is important. You must always pitch stories as having clearly identifiable news angles: human interest, public outreach, community development, public health, awards/recognition, historical, news services. Never try to use the media just to garner free publicity—they get that every day from everyone and have little patience for professionals who cannot tell "news" from "advertising." Once an issue lands on the public agenda, organizations that have a stake in the issue automatically benefit from the free publicity and public dialogue about the issue. Although landing an issue on the public agenda takes more work than sending out a few news releases, the payoff can be priceless. Public relations professionals need to work to cultivate relationships with the media in order to obtain success with agenda setting, and facilitate getting their client's issues before the public.

PITCHING AND PITCH LETTERS

As suggested of agenda-setting theory, public relations professionals try to garner media attention by bringing our issues before them. Verbal pitches and pitch letters are used to attract attention to an event or activity. Pitch letters are a form of business letter. Unlike news releases, which are typically about "hard news" (like what is found in the first section of the newspaper), pitch letters are about "soft news" (like what is found in the community, cooking, gardening, home, religion, sports, travel) sections.

As the name suggests, the goal of a pitch letter is to pitch some organizational goal, event, or activity to someone else, typically the media. Pitch letters and verbal pitches are also made to clients, potential customers, and other organizations. Typically, a pitch involves trying to push one of *several* (two or three) "story ideas." To be effective, pitch letters (or pitch calls) must offer suggestions for stories that would interest the source's readers, listeners, or viewers, be easy to do, involve pictures or video appropriate for newspaper, television, or magazine, and involve support on your part. Convincing the target of the pitch that what you are proposing will benefit their audiences is really the key to pitching.

What does not work in a pitch letter is to argue that "our event will really be improved by your coverage." The response you will get to such arguments is, "So what?" Media outlets serve *their* publics and your pitch must make the connection between covering your event and serving their publics.

Perhaps one of the best examples of what a pitch is all about is the two-minute "elevator pitch" held by Wake Forest University:

> Entrepreneurs will take their business ideas from the ground floor to the top—literally—in two minutes flat. ... Every

> second counts as MBA students from across the nation board elevators and try to persuade venture capitalists to invest in their business plans ... For the winner, the two-minute journey could become the ride of a lifetime. The winner will receive cash and professional services, including legal and marketing services, totaling $45,000. More importantly, the winner gets the undivided attention of potential investors. Venture capitalists from three firms representing more than $500 million in early stage funds will serve as judges. The winning team will enter discussions with one or more venture capital firms, with the possibility of getting its business plan funded. (www.mba.wfu.edu/newsDetail.aspx?id=37)

In the case of the elevator pitching competition, as you might expect, participants must convince the venture capitalists and potential investors that their product or service has the potential to be both successful and profitable. Venture capitalists will not give you the money just because you really need it. Everyone needs money, and everyone who pitches an idea to the media needs coverage, that is the idea behind the information subsidy.

A pitch letter involves some minor development of each "story" idea. Pitches are creative as well as strategic. The best pitch letters will point out that the source has "published stories like this in the past" and give an exact date (tailor and localize) in order to show that you are familiar with their publication and their audience's interests. See Table 9.1 for a pitch letter checklist.

Pitch Letter Structure

1. Begin with an *introduction*, designed to get attention and interest. Never use suspense in a pitch letter. Be upfront about what organization you represent from the beginning. This is not an Amway meeting. Reveal the client or interest whom you represent in your opening sentence and why you are writing. Create interest in the topic and in your client. Preview your ideas. Do all these things in a few carefully worded sentences.
2. *Present several story angles* in the body of the letter. Paragraphs two, three, and four should begin with something like, "My first story idea ... My second story idea ... My third story idea ... ." allowing the recipient to quickly scan through the letter, picking and choosing to read what interests him/her most or fits best with the format of the media outlet, or interests of the audience.
3. Be sure that all of your statements are accurate, and realistic. Avoid hyperbole and puffery. Few things are more annoying to a journalist than having someone tell them how to do their job, including what their readers' level of interest might be, or the level of importance of the topic. Never say, "Your readers would love to hear about... ." or "Our event will be the most exciting event of the summer." or "I know you will agree that... ." The last phrase might be the worst of the lot. Any time someone pitching something to a journalist begins with "Don't you agree," the journalist will be thinking, "No, I do not agree." The technique of asking the leading question is called the "foot in the door" (FID) technique. You are trying to get the person to agree so that s/he begins to convince him/herself. The research on FID suggests that the tactic really does not work very well. Research on persuasion suggests that educated audiences are harder to convince and unlikely to accept lopsided arguments or leading questions. Thus, give journalists more credit and stay away from exaggeration and puffery. The FID works best with uneducated or less educated audiences, and will irritate well-educated audiences who know that issues and publics are more sophisticated.
4. After you have pitched your three story ideas, offer yourself or another appropriate organizational member as a resource. The pitch letter draws upon the power of the information subsidy. If you can pitch an idea of interest to a journalist, and provide him/her with pictures, supporting materials, research, access to organizational leaders for interviews, etc., the journalist will likely jump at the opportunity. The key to a successful pitch is to be sure that you are pitching something that is clearly of interest to the journalist's readers/listeners. Pitch letters should never be framed as being about *your needs*. Of course you would like them to write a story featuring *your* organization. Journalist and editors *know that*. Trying to tell journalists or editors that you want them to

TABLE 9.1 Suggestions for Creating Pitch Letters (do what is in bold)

Opening

1. **Address the letter** to a person, not to a "business editor."
2. **Identify yourself** or your agency by name.
3. More adequately **explain why you are writing**.
4. **Allude to story ideas** in the first few sentences.
5. **Don't spend too much space on you** or your organization and not the story.
6. Do not make it too long—**cut to the chase**.
7. Present a smooth **transition** to the body.

Body

8. Use **concrete examples** of what you can do for the client.
9. Allude to **specific story ideas**—e.g., "the first story angle might discuss X ..."
10. **Elaborate** on story ideas.
11. **Avoid all jargon** if possible—be sure to explain any that is included.
12. **One thought per paragraph**.
13. **Letter is too long**—say it quickly, busy people do not read long letters.

Overall

14. Create **letterhead** to identify your organization.
15. Explain the **benefits** of the story for the readers of the news source.
16. **Personalize/localize** the letter and story ideas.
17. **Transitions are needed** between paragraphs.
18. **Offer yourself as a resource** for information, photos, interviews etc.
19. **Vague** explanation, point, or suggestion.
20. **Sentences/paragraphs** are long, rambling, pedantic, or difficult to follow.
21. **Lecture editor** about what readers "should do/know" or the newsworthiness of the story.
22. **Careful word choice**: think more carefully about the implicit and explicit meaning of words.
23. **Avoid** "we, them, they, their, its, the company," etc. Be specific with references.
24. **Avoid extra words**: just, in order to, is planning to, will be able to, etc.
25. **Hackneyed** phrase—avoid clichés.
26. **Check possessives**.
27. Awkward/Unclear.
28. **Verb/tense** agreement problems.
29. **Proofread more carefully**—especially spelling, spacing, grammar, run-ons/fragments.

Closing

30. **No wrapup** (make final appeal)—look back at your opening for suggestions to close.
31. **Explain the resources you bring to a story**: pictures, fact sheets, interview(s), etc.
32. **State the day and time that you will call** to discuss the story ideas.

Opening sentence creates interest in the topic and your client: ______________________

Statements are accurate and realistic: ______________________

Several story angles are presented: ______________________

Grammar, syntax, spelling, and punctuation are correct: ______________________

You offer yourself as a resource and/or other organizational members: ______________________

Final sentence anchors your claim that your ideas are newsworthy: ______________________

Total: Comments:

cover *your* organization or client shows both that you do not understand what *they* do for a living, and you do not know how to do your job very well.

5. In the final paragraph, make your last appeal and link back to the needs of journalists' publics. Be sure to anchor your claim as being newsworthy and show that you really understand their readers/listeners. Also, in the last paragraph, tell the recipient when you will contact him/her to discuss your story ideas. Be specific. Not "sometime next week," but "Monday morning." Indicating when you will call forces the reader to give at least a few seconds of thought to your proposed ideas (either to say no, or to ask for more information). Conclude the letter or call by thanking the recipient for his/her time.
6. Grammar, syntax, spelling, and punctuation are always essential. Grammatical, spelling, or other proofing mistakes serve to make you look lazy or incompetent. Why would a potential journalist (who makes his/her living by writing) want to work with someone who doesn't know the difference between to, two, and too?

Pitching Ideas by Telephone or Face-to-Face

Cold calling, or pitching ideas to journalists, potential donors, or professionals from related organizations takes practice. On the one hand, no one likes to be bothered by strangers, as you probably know from telemarketers and spammers, and all professionals are wary of having their time and resources wasted by other people pursuing their own agendas. However, on the other hand, all communication professionals understand that from time to time they will be contacted by other professionals (stakeseekers) who will pitch ideas to them, and they in turn will call to pitch ideas themselves.

Pitching ideas is quite common. Journalists pitch ideas to editors, public relations professionals pitch story ideas to journalists, and professionals in other organizations will occasionally pitch collaborative ideas to public relations professionals encouraging organizations to buy tables at professional events or luncheon, attend a charity golf tournament, donate money to high school athletics, etc.

Pitching Suggestions

- *Know your audience and be prepared.* Before you attempt to pitch anything, make sure you know what the needs are of the individual or organization that you will pitch, and how what you are pitching will be mutually beneficial to the organization and its stakeholders.
- *Practice your pitch and rehearse your key messages.* In class exercises, I actually bring a telephone to class and have students practice talking on the telephone. Learning how to properly ask for the person you want to speak with, how to identify yourself when asked why you are calling, etc., is as important as what you have to pitch. Additionally, you need to have a flexible message and excellent notes in order to sound articulate, spontaneous, and persuasive. Never read from a script! Cold calling is not telemarketing. The minute that you sound like I am just one of a hundred people that you are calling, I will tell you I am not interested. What you pitch must be framed as something that will be mutually beneficial.
- *Anticipate answers to possible questions.* Be sure that you have done adequate research before you make the call. Be sure to know something about the individual you are calling and his/her organization, know exactly how much money or time you are asking for, know the answers to questions about the timeline or logistics, and know about similar situations in which the person or organization you call participated. In short, be sure you have done your homework.
- *Know the lingo.* If you are talking to a stock photo provider, be sure to know the details of stock photography. If you are calling a journalist, be sure to ask if s/he is "on deadline," and know something about his/her blog, network, publication, or beat.
- *Know the details.* Do not make the call until you know what you want, what you want from the person you call, and are prepared to make what you are proposing happen. You do not pitch ideas for events until you have permission from your supervisor to hold the event; you do not ask a journalist to write a story about an upcoming campaign until the goals and objectives of the campaign have been firmly worked out.
- *If calling on the telephone:* Find out who the decision maker is before you call. Make sure to use proper telephone etiquette: speak slowly and articulate clearly, repeat information like names and telephone numbers several times, indicate when you will call back when leaving messages,

and leave *concise* messages. No one likes having to listen to a five-minute telephone message *twice* because of a missed telephone number. Speak slowly and give your name and telephone number, at both the beginning and end of the message.

Learning to effectively pitch ideas takes some practice. Do not get discouraged when you fail: most pitches fail. Use what you learn to create a more compelling pitch message in the future. As suggested, above, brevity is key—cut to the chase. A pitch is not the whole story. Effective pitches need to be short and compelling. Ellison (1996) explains how *Outland* was pitched to movie executives in the late '70s: seven words: "*Outland* is *High Noon* in Outer Space" (p. 92). Even the most skilled professionals do not have success with every pitch. The best pitches, however, are clearly of value to the recipient and have been carefully pitched to the best person. Thus, with research you can increase you chances of success.

CONCLUSION

As this chapter illustrates, there is a great deal to know in regard to effective public speaking. In order to maximize your success, you need to understand several theories and persuasion models—MMS and PACYRA, cognitive dissonance, and agenda-setting. You can increase your chances of becoming an effective public speaker by exposing yourself to opportunities for speaking. We learn by doing. If you have not already, take a public speaking class, or a B&P (business and professional communication) class. If you have *already* taken a public speaking class, get involved in some groups and get some more practice with public communication.

ACTIVITIES

1. Your CEO has been invited to speak at "JMC Week" (journalism and mass communication) at the state's flagship university (use your school for this). Prepare a two-page, single-spaced, audience analysis about your student body that includes demographics, psychographics, infographics, a list of the school's key "heroes" and "villains," and a list of key university symbols.
2. Create three pitch ideas for new academic holidays (like spring break, MLK Day, Celine Deon Day, etc.). Assume that you will be pitching the ideas face-to-face to the school president at an academic event. Spell out the details on what you will say and why (justify the idea), and be sure to identify the possible counterarguments to your idea and how you will respond. Develop responses to the potential questions you might expect.
3. You have been invited to give an address at your school's convocation ceremony. Read a few graduation speeches online, such as Alan Alda's famous speeches, then write the first 60 seconds of your address five times, each time using a different introductory strategy.
4. Victory Speech: Visit the "American Rhetoric" Web site at www.americanrhetoric.com/top100speechesall.html and listen to several acceptance addresses and nomination speeches. Read some "celebration"/"victory" speeches in some books of great speeches. Then, visit a local politician's Web site and create a one-page memo describing his/her key messages, themes, and positions. Listen to him/her speak (go to YouTube and listen to any speeches that you can find, listen to him/her on the radio or television, etc.) so that you can capture his/her style. Finally, write a 7- to 10-minute acceptance address that touches on key messages and themes; prepare a manuscript for the speech in 18-point, double-spaced type; and be prepared to deliver the speech on, or about, the day it is due.

NOTE

1. My public speaking teachers Professor Marcia Stratton of the University of Alaska Anchorage and Professor Hank Scheele of Purdue University are to be thanked for much of the information in this section.

Chapter 10

Dialogic Communication: An Ethical and Moral Approach to Public Relations

DIALOGUE AS A FRAMEWORK FOR ETHICAL PUBLIC RELATIONS

Online journalism has transformed the print world: hundreds of newspapers are closing nationwide and a near continuous debate is now taking place among journalism schools about how to teach journalism in the Internet age. In the publication world, Amazon's Kindle book reader allows you to download books to a handheld device. Google is set to launch its own competing reader any day now. Google has already digitized millions of books: a key word search with an author's name will bring up sections of those scanned books. If Google has its way, they will soon allow users to download every book ever written. RSS readers allow every user to personalize their own news content and receive only what interests them. In advertising and marketing, new technologies like RSS have also forced agencies to narrowcast and look for more compelling ways to sell things to "individuals" rather than groups. Thus, there is huge interest in social networking technologies among professional communicators.

Whether we like it or not, the new communication technologies have changed the way that all communication-oriented professions are practiced. Public relations has been no different. Technology experts like McLuhan (1999/1964) Negroponte (1995) predicted more than 40 years ago that this day would come. Professionals in the communication fields need to learn to take advantage of new technologies and incorporate new ways of ethical communication.

At the 2002 National Communication Association convention in New Orleans, Carl Botan, one of the leaders of the field, lamented that there are very few theories developed by public relations professionals, aside from the excellence model (Grunig, 1992) and some research in crisis and dialogue. More recently, at the International Communication Association Convention in Chicago, a group of leading scholars in public relations came together to talk about the state of the field and what they thought public relations should focus on. Although there was little agreement on many issues, most public relations and communication professionals already concur that rhetorical and communication theory is where the profession is going. Given the obvious changes that technology has brought to the communication professions, the dialogic approach has a lot to offer professionals in terms of a framework for making sense of their relationships with multiple stakeholders and informing the profession.

Dialogue, as the word implies, refers to conversation or talk. Dialogic public relations refers to a kind of interpersonal interaction that acknowledges individual self-worth and the value of others and tries to create long-lasting and stable relationships with other people. As a professional practice, dialogue includes the ability to listen (with an open mind), empathize with others, admit when you are wrong, and be changed or altered by the experience of communicating with others. Ultimately, dialogue is a collection of interpersonal communication skills and an orientation toward other people rather than a set of rules. Dialogic communicators do not ignore people because they can, or "try to get them off the line as fast as possible"; dialogic communicators try to understand the needs of others and *actually* value their opinions.

Many of our Web-based communication tools are founded on dialogic principles and an assumption that what other people have to say is important. As mentioned previously, when people feel valued, and validated, their trust, sympathy, and support increases. For example, the threaded dialogue present in blogging, instant messaging, chatting, and other real-time Web interaction involve features of face-to-face communication and conversation. The Web itself is a giant communication tool and represents the greatest medium in the history of the world to reach and interact with people. But mediated communication technologies also pose problems. As all of you probably know, communicating with others via e-mail or in chats can be difficult. Misunderstandings often occur and what we "meant," is often *not* what people understand.

As Reddy (1979) suggested many years ago, communication helps prove the second law of thermodynamics regarding the conservation of energy: *all communication takes work.* "Communication is an 'energy must be expended' system" (p. 186). Reddy's observation is one of the hurdles of mediated (online) communication. It takes work. In the popular press, all mediated communication is considered "dialogue." Every tweet represents someone letting his/her voice be heard. Unfortunately, "tweets" are not dialogue as public relations professionals mean it, and effective communication requires more than snippets of talk.

One area of online communication where technology has tried to fit into the dialogic model of communication has been social networking. Readers of this book are probably familiar with the many mainstream social networking Web sites, such as Facebook, MySpace, Second Life, and Twitter. Additionally there are thousands of other less well-known social networking Web sites, like Bebo, Cyworld, Flickr, Friendster, Couchsurfing, LinkedIn, LiveJournal, and Xanga. There are also thousands of specialized social networking sites: Christian (HolyPal.com; MyChurch.com); Jewish (MyJworld.com, Shmooze.com); Irish (www.IrishAbroad.com); Muslim (MuslimWorld.Ning.com; Muxlim.com); and LDS (Mormon) (www.LDSLinkup.com). The list of unique, special interest groups is almost limitless. What all of these sites have in common is a system of open communication through which people can communicate, or talk, directly with other people.[1] The abundance of social networking sites proves is that people have a desire to be heard, to rise above the din of everyday existence, and to feel like they are making connections with other human beings who share similar views.

Unfortunately, few organizations provide opportunities for stakeholders and stakeseekers to interact with organizational members and leaders, especially senior members of organizations. By contrast, dialogic organizations are open and honest with publics, and provide opportunities for stakeholders and stakeseekers to interact with organizational members. Some organizations create spaces for dialogue, like organizational blogs, while other organizations hold communication events where people can meet with and talk to organizational leaders (public meetings, online chats, etc.)

Rhetorical, dialogic, relational communication has become a central approach in public relations. Dialogue has been examined by dozens of scholars over the last 10 years and applied to advocacy organizations (Edgett, 2002), pharmaceutical organizations (Rennie & Mackey, 2002), South African NGOs (Naudéa, Froneman, Atwood, 2004), community colleges (McAllister, 2006), and several for-profit and nonprofit organizations (Avidar, 2007; Kent, Taylor, & White 2003; Taylor, Kent, & White, 2001).

This chapter deals with perhaps the most difficult concepts in the book. Most writing skills can be explained by reference to guidelines about how documents should look, how to be persuasive, rhetorical theory, and other communication theories, but dialogue is an *orientation* toward other people, an approach to creating relationships. Rather than a set of rules, dialogue is based on building relationships of trust and compassion with others over time.

Throughout this book, I have talked about rhetoric, or the use of language to create compelling messages. Dialogue is rhetorical. The rhetorical features of dialogue lie in understanding that how we treat others will have an influence on how they think about us. Rhetoric shapes perception, and dialogue is a rhetorical tool. Effective communicators select the most appropriate vocabulary, examples, and explanations to appeal to others. Effective dialogue involves making similar choices about how to communicate with others in a mutually beneficial fashion: avoiding accusations, soliciting comments and feedback from others, being open to new information, and being approachable. More importantly, building strong relationships with colleagues and stakeholders makes for stronger relationships and trust.

DEFINITIONS AND CLARIFICATIONS OF DIALOGUE

Dialogue can be defined in a number of ways. A dictionary would suggest that dialogue refers to talk or conversation, especially in interpersonal and political settings, often for purposes of negotiation. If you are a politician, dialogue means "talk" rather than interaction: "We need to open a dialogue with the voters on this issue" really means, "Let's ask people what they think and try to do that." If you are a philosopher, dialogue is a method for finding the truth that dates back to ancient Greece: "Let's turn to the text and open a dialogue with the author." For a family counselor, dialogue is something that dysfunctional families need to do to improve their relationship: "You need to have a dialogue with each other without being judgmental." For public relations professionals, dialogue refers to a process of interpersonal, group, and organization to public interaction focusing on honesty, truth, and positive regard for the other (Kent & Taylor, 1998, 2002).

Genuine dialogue is what happens when two or more close friends, colleagues, or even strangers get together in a safe and honest environment (whether at home, on the telephone, in a bar, on a bus or train, at church, temple, synagogue, mosque, or at work) and talk about important issues. Not all conversation is dialogic. Dialogue, as an orientation to others, involves *listening* to others, trying to understand others, and not assuming you are always correct. Dialogic communicators are willing to admit when they are wrong, and do not assume that their organization already knows everything. As Kent and Taylor (2002) explain, dialogue includes five features: *mutuality*, or the recognition of relationships; *propinquity*, or the temporality and spontaneity of interactions with publics; *empathy*, or the supportiveness and confirmation of shared goals and interests; *risk*, or the willingness to interact with individuals and publics on their own terms; and finally, *commitment*, or giving one's self over to dialogue, interpretation, and understanding with publics (pp. 24–25).

Dialogue is an orientation toward relationships that tries to treat other people with respect and value rather than merely seeing people instrumentally. When your goal in communicating with stakeholders is just to keep them smoking, drinking, eating, or using your product, or to vote for *you* rather than the other person, you are not being dialogic. In such cases, your communication focuses on the behavior sought rather than the good of the other. The relationships are asymmetrical rather than dialogic (see Table 10.1 below).

Some communication professionals argue, "profit-making organizations are not in the relationship business and their customers don't desire one" (Smith, 2005). As Dejan Vercic wryly noted in Korea a few years back at the International Communication Association Conference, "When I buy a Coke I do not want a relationship, I just want a Coke." On this point, no one really disagrees. But sales and marketing are not what public relations professionals are primarily responsible for. Public relations professionals' responsibility lies more fully

TABLE 10.1 Models of Public Relations

One-Way Models of Public Relations (Grunig and Hunt, 1984)	
Press Agentry	The press agentry/publicity model is largely a propagandist model. Like a promoter or an agent, publicists typically produce one-way messages promoting their employer's interests (news releases, advertisements, pseudo events, Web sites, etc.), for use in the mass media. Press agents (for celebrities, in the fashion and sports industries, politics, etc.) rarely conduct any research and usually are unconcerned with the truth of their claims. Examples: P. T. Barnum's "The greatest show on earth," "Must-see event," etc.
Public Information	The public information model is best exemplified by the many activist and social cause groups, such as Mothers Against Drunk Drivers (MADD), People for the Ethical Treatment of Animals (PETA), American Association of Retired People (AARP), public health organizations (cancer, AIDS, torticollis). Since public information groups are partisans who believe in the truth and accuracy of their cause, research is rarely conducted except to create more compelling messages (legibility, readability, etc.). The public Information model also uses one-way, mediated strategies for communicating with target publics but generally tries to present factual information. Examples: "Get a prostrate screening today!" "For free tax assistance call 1–800....""

(Continued)

TABLE 10.1 *Continued*

Two-Way Models of Public Relations (Grunig and Hunt, 1984)	
Two-Way Asymmetrical	The two-way asymmetrical model of public relations is a strategic model that uses research, scientific persuasion, psychology, etc., to persuade individuals and public to take the course of action advocated by the organization. Organizations that employ two-way asymmetrical communication typically advocate on behalf of organizational goals and initiatives. Although research and theory are used to understand the beliefs, values, and attitudes of publics, communication is still sender to receiver and utilizes whatever channel or persuasive method is likely to be the most useful for reaching target publics. In practice, asymmetrical organizations are partisan and tend to act on a predetermined set of beliefs, and are uninterested in opening themselves to other positions. Examples: Corporations and for-profit organizations, some politicians (congresspeople, governors, the president, congressional spokespeople, party leaders), military leaders.
Two-Way Symmetrical	The two-way asymmetrical model is the most ethical of the four Grunig and Hunt models of communication but is not appropriate in every situation. The goal of symmetrical communication is mutual understanding; it is guided by information and research into the attitudes, opinions, and level of knowledge (and understanding) of fellow participants. Symmetrical communication seeks balance and does not assume that all of the facts in a given situation are already known. Symmetrical communicators are in search of the truth and function as mediators on behalf of their organization and its publics. Examples: Educational institutions, organizations in highly competitive environments, organizations in highly regulated industries (nuclear power, chemical plants, etc.), public agencies and cooperatives.
Additional Models	
Personal Influence (Sriramesh, 2003)	The personal influence model of public relations is more common in countries and organizations that are hierarchical, tightly controlled by the government, or subject to cronyism. Personal influence is often exercised by local business professionals, organizational and government leaders, and by local politicians or party members. Power or influence is usually exercised behind the scenes. In low-context nations (see Chapter 10) like the U.S., having access to, or exercising, personal influence is not a requirement for organizational or personal success, but often helps. Some types of occupations and institutions rely more heavily on personal influence for success. In high-context cultures however, personal influence is crucial and members of in groups and those with "connections" are often more successful at achieving organizational and personal goals. Examples: Party members in communist or socialist states, members of in groups, royalty, individuals with higher social status, people from the upper castes, business people and individuals with more resources.
Dialogue (Pearson, 1989)	The dialogic model of public relations is the newest model and strives to maintain equality and equity among stakeholders. The goal of dialogic organizations is not simply to achieve organizational goals but also to serve the needs of stakeholders and stakeseekers. Dialogic communicators mediate between the interests of the organization and its key publics and seek mutual understanding rather than influence or adherence. Examples: A classroom, organizations with a small market share or that make specialty products designed to meet the needs of professionals, city councils and school boards (when run according to the needs of the community—as many school boards are stacked by religious partisans), etc.

in the symbolic or rhetorical realm, in the realm of relationships and communication with multiple stakeholders, rather than just customers (Broom, Casey, & Richey, 2000; Cheney & Dionisopoulos, 1989; Grunig & Huang, 2000; Heath & Coombs, 2006; Ledingham, 2006). Of course, advertisers and marketers also recognize the value of relationships. Coca-Cola and thousands of other major global brands *are* looking to foster brand identification and loyalty with customers through rhetorical and dialogic communication structures. *You* might just want a Coke, but Coca-Cola wants you to want *only* Coke, and to believe that Coke represents your true personality.

Dialogue is about understanding and respect rather than adherence and manipulation. Using dialogue is difficult and requires a commitment to effective communication, respect, and trust in others. As explained by Kent and Taylor (2002):

> For any approach to dialogue to be effective requires an organizational commitment and an acceptance of the value of relationship building … . Skills that are necessary include: listening, empathy, being able to contextualize issues within local, national and international frameworks, being able to identify common ground between parties, thinking about long-term rather than short-term objectives, seeking out groups/individuals with opposing viewpoints, and soliciting a variety of internal and external opinions on policy issues. (pp. 30–31)

Kent and Taylor go on to suggest that dialogue is possible through mediated channels but they do not mention anything about using dialogue *within* organizations. The remainder of this chapter will explain how public relations practitioners can use dialogue on an everyday basis, and how the principles of dialogue transcend instrumental uses.

DIALOGUE GUIDES ETHICAL PUBLIC RELATIONS

Many public relations students and professionals have learned about the "models of public relations" that describe the progression of the profession from a one-way press agentry and publicity model of public relations to a two-way practice with emphasis on persuasion and relationship management (Grunig & Hunt, 1984). See Table 10.1 for a summary of Grunig and Hunt and other models.

What the Grunig and Hunt model illustrates well is that there are very diverse ways in which public relations is practiced and different kinds of public relations contexts call for different techniques. Public information (and political public relations) for example, is guided by the assumption that the organization (or politician) knows what is best for the public. Thus, public information is often paternalistic, partisan, and unidirectional (sender to receiver). Consider presidential debates, where each candidate does his or her best *not* to "debate" anything. Each candidate focuses on giving a series of mini-speeches outlining individual policy positions, occasionally rebutting claims made by the opposition, and making promises of future action. The idea that a candidate might actually admit s/he was wrong is unheard of.

Some public relations professionals have argued that the two-way models of public relations are the best. But this argument ignores the fact that public relations is practiced differently in every organization, because organizations and their needs are different. If we extend "the two-way model is best" argument, we end up drawing the absurd conclusion that an organization like Mothers Against Drunk Drivers (which takes a public information approach) should be open to arguments (a two-way symmetrical approach) to lower the drinking age, or entertain arguments to weaken DUI laws. No single model of public relations, even dialogue, is appropriate in every situation. But, as a model for how to interact with others and treat external and internal publics, dialogue is the most ethical.

Objections to Dialogue

Individuals and organizations practicing dialogic public relations make a commitment to truth, honesty, and *trust* in their publics. Trust is frightening for many professionals: "How do we know they won't use this information against us?" is often the first question asked. An organization never knows for sure if an individual can be trusted, or whether an activist group might call for radical action or leak information to the media after meeting with you. Information sharing and self-disclosure are where risk comes in. The rewards of trust and candor, however, usually exceed the risk. The dialogic public relations model comes from interpersonal communication, where trust and risk are accepted as part of all relationships.

When a person first notices someone to whom s/he is attracted, she or he engages in varying levels of self-disclosure in order to determine if the person can be trusted with more sensitive and personal information—the classic "What's your major?" conversation. Trust cannot be built without risk. Trust, mutuality, and commitment are powerful forces. When we trust a person or an institution we are usually willing to accept that s/he or they will make a mistake from time to time. As long as the individual or institution admits the error and works to rectify it, people will usually forgive him/her/it (Benoit, 1995; Hearit, 2001). The dialogic approach involves acknowledging individuals and publics as partners and colleagues who have legitimate interests in an organization's well-being.

Dialogue is also criticized because of its difficulty, time-consuming quality, potential for abuse, risk to organizations, and potential to force organizations to expend resources fighting lawsuits if they admit wrongdoing or inappropriate behavior (Smith, 2005, passim). The risks are real. Dialogue is not a panacea for bad organizations. Organizations wanting to become dialogic actually have to spend some time getting their house in order, and actually acting more responsibly. However, the value of having well-established, dialogic, relationships, based on mutual trust, with stakeholders and stakeseekers, should be obvious (cf., Granovetter, 1973). Organizations that have dialogic relationships with a variety of publics can call upon those relational ties in times of crisis.[2]

Dialogic organizations and practitioners treat employees, stakeholders, and stakeseekers as valuable partners. Dialogic organizations have flatter organizational hierarchies, create fewer interactional barriers, and engage in humane communication at all levels of the organization.

Microsoft is one of the best examples of an asymmetrical organization that tends to be interested only in its bottom line. Microsoft currently has hundreds of lawsuits pending against it and has been criminally penalized in both the U.S. and the European Union *on several occasions* for behaving in ways that violate antitrust and fair competition laws. To what end? Microsoft already had a corner on the market for operating systems, and had one of the most used Internet browsers. What Microsoft spent on lawyers in several states and nations probably negates the profits it might have reaped by engaging in *legal* competition, innovation, and fair trade (for a related point, consider LeBow, July 30, 1997, *Talk of the Nation*, 26:50, <www.npr.org/templates/story/story.php?storyId=1010758>).

Organizations such as Apple and Google prove that respectable profits can be obtained by actually following the law, and yet Microsoft has continued to break it. There is no storehouse of public trust and support for Microsoft, nor are customers able to identify with an organization uninterested in producing a reliable product (as the scandals surrounding the Vista operating system show).[3]

Dialogue, as a public relations tool, is both a more ethical approach and a more humane approach. The dialogic approach to public relations can be applied in virtually every type of organization, from organizations relying upon one-way press agentry models to organizations using interactive two-way models of public relations. One of the key features of dialogue is that it leads to better decision making. Additionally, people are more willing to forgive others when they make a mistake if they have a relationship with the person or organization involved. Two examples come to mind to illustrate these points.

The first example has to do with how former presidents William Clinton and George W. Bush dealt with problems during their administrations. In a Doonesbury cartoon by Gary Trudeau, a college professor poses the following question to his class:

> The first president initiates a bloody, costly, unending war under false pretences and approves covert policies of illegal detention, kangaroo courts, extraordinary renditions, torture, and warrantless wiretapping of thousands [millions, as recent research suggests] of Americans. The second president lies about hooking up with an intern. Question: which one should be impeached? (Sunday, March 19, 2006, <Doonesbury.com>)

The Doonesbury cartoon highlights a real issue and alludes to something probably well known to any communication professional: people place a great value on apologies (see apologia, Chapter 11) and are willing to forgive people for mistakes when they admit them or accept responsibility (cf., Benoit, 1995, Hearit, 2001).

President Clinton is well known for his apologies. When something bad happened, Clinton usually admitted it and apologized. In some cases, Clinton's apologies seemed self-serving and disingenuous, like the famous "I did not have sexual relations with that woman ... " claim. However, Clinton's apologies are probably the reason he is so well liked today.

Bush, on the other hand, is well known for denying he *ever* made *any* mistakes, and never apologizing for anything. Bush also insulated himself from criticism, with his senior staff acting as "mindguards," a concept from "groupthink" (cf., Janis, 1982) where members of a group self censor themselves and ignore input from outsiders.

Abundant research on groupthink has demonstrated time and time again that effective leaders *must* seek the advice of individuals who are outside of their inner circles (Janis, 1982). The best leaders are not afraid to have their ideas challenged because the clash of ideas leads to better decisions. A leader should ultimately still act as his/her conscience

I FEEL LIKE I'M COMING DOWN FROM A WILD SUGAR HIGH.
HOW'S THAT, MAN?

FOR ABOUT TWO WEEKS, PEOPLE CONFUSED ME WITH APOLO OHNO.
I THOUGHT YOUR SOCIAL LIFE PICKED UP.

GRESS
S RIGHTS.
EDOM
ARMS
ON THIS POINT, SECTION 4 OF ARTICLE TWO OF THE CONSTITUTION GIVES LAWMAKERS LATITUDE.

HOW MUCH LATITUDE? WELL, CONSIDER THIS CASE OF TWO PRESIDENTS...

THE FIRST PRESIDENT INITIATES A BLOODY, COSTLY, UNENDING WAR ON FALSE PREMISES...
UNIVERSAL PRESS SYNDICATE © 2006 G.B. Trudeau

...AND APPROVES COVERT POLICIES OF ILLEGAL DETENTIONS, KANGAROO COURTS, EXTRAORDINARY RENDITIONS, TORTURE, AND WARRANTLESS WIRETAPPINGS OF THOUSANDS OF AMERICANS.

THE SECOND PRESIDENT LIES ABOUT HOOKING UP WITH AN INTERN.
3-19
www.doonesbury.com

QUESTION: WHICH ONE SHOULD BE IMPEACHED?
THE BABE HOUND, RIGHT?
THIS SOUNDS VERY FAMILIAR...

dictates; however, by cutting oneself off from competing ideas and information, the likelihood that a groupthink-related mistake will occur is great. Dialogic communication is one of the primary means of avoiding groupthink and faulty decision making because it forces decision makers to consider all of the options and actually weigh *alternative* solutions to problems as carefully as *preferred* options.

The second example comes from Microsoft again. While writing Chapter 12, I ran across several discussions in the news about typography. In the course of my reading, I began wondering whether I should talk about why Times was Microsoft Word's default font. What seemed obvious was to ask Microsoft why Times was selected. I already knew the answer from a dozen books on typography, but as a scholar, I wanted confirmation.

I visited Microsoft's Web site to find a contact person.[4] Since e-mail addresses for all employees are not posted on the company's Web site, I decided to ask one of the public relations managers. I composed a careful message introducing myself to the manager, explaining the book project, credentialing myself and listing some of my articles, and then posing my question. The next day I received a dismissive response from Ms. Jessica Crozier of Waggener Edstrom Worldwide (a firm representing Microsoft) stating:

Thanks for your email [sic]. I connected with my colleagues and learned, unfortunately, we are unable to provide you with any information at this time. I apologize for any inconvenience this may cause.

Please feel free to contact me with any future inquiries you may have.

Best of luck with your textbook.

Kind regards,

Jessica

Since Crozier was uncooperative, I tried to e-mail someone lower on the food chain on the off chance that s/he might "accidentally" give me an answer. Microsoft's online help representative was kind enough to give the following answer, a far cry from "we are unable to provide you with any information at this time," but still essentially useless:

> Hello Dr. Kent, Thank you for contacting Microsoft Customer Service.I [sic] understand that you would like to know why Microsoft Office Word uses "Times New Roman" as its default font, which will be included in the "Typography" section of your textbook. Although [sic] I cannot provide direct answers to the question that you have, I can give you some online resources that may be helpful to you in your research. Understand that some corporate information cannot be made publicly available.Typography [sic] news, where researchers discover that setting text in Times New Roman makes authors appear more impressive, is located at...." (<msconus@microsoft.com>, no name was provided.)

Four Web links were also included in the body of the message but only one of them worked. The hyperlink that did work connected to a Microsoft Web site that essentially told me "you can create professional-looking documents using Microsoft Word because Microsoft Word uses fabulous fonts like Times New Roman."

Had Crozier simply provided an answer, I would have used it, instead of using Crozier's response as an example of stonewalling. A dialogic approach to communication involves *trust* and *risk*. Crozier could easily have visited my Web site and in five minutes established that I meant the company no harm—come on, I was asking about a font. Instead, Crozier assumed the worse and acted on assumptions of suspicion.

Every professional communicator knows that "No comment" (or in this case, "We are unable to provide you with any information") should be avoided because the phrase is interpreted as if "they have something to hide." In this case, I suspect Ms. Crozier just did not want to bother to get an answer to the question. The Microsoft Word default font could not be a corporate secret. More than likely, Crozier did not know the answer; why would she know the answer to an esoteric decision about typography made 20 years ago when she was in high school?[5]

The connection between both of these examples (presidential decision making and Microsoft's public relations practices) may not be readily apparent, but it lies in the areas of openness and trust. Dialogue assumes all stakeholders and stakeseekers are important. Instead of treating people instrumentally, dialogic communicators listen to people and try to understand individual positions rather than ignoring someone simply because it is convenient. As an educator who teaches writing and publication courses, who has written a textbook on public relations writing, who sits on the Technology Committee at a large journalism and mass communication program and makes decisions about hardware and software purchases, I have had a lot of influence over what thousands of past (and future) professionals learn about. Why would a company like Microsoft *not* consider me an important stakeholder? A dialogic organization would recognize the importance of the educator–student relationship and how much of an influence over technology decisions professors and schools have. If we teach our students to use Macintosh computers, as many communication and journalism schools in the U.S., do, our students will use them after they graduate and push for them in the workplace.

Not every individual or organization can take the time to dialogically communicate with every person who might have something important to say. However, because an organization does not have the time or resources to hear everyone's *individual* story does not mean organizations should ignore smaller stakeholders. Although Crozier was undoubtedly quite busy with other problems,[6] Microsoft is an organization with thousands of employees and hundreds of managers, and all Crozier had to do was to forward my question to the right person.

THE ROLE OF DIALOGUE IN PUBLIC RELATIONS

As outlined above, the tenants of dialogue involve seeing the world in a different way. Dialogue involves risk and trust. Organizations of course have a vested interest in maintaining certain corporate secrets (manufacturing processes, unique technologies). However, in terms of how planning decisions are made, and crisis management, issues forecasting, and relationship building with key publics are orchestrated, the instrumental relationships, secrecy, self-centeredness, and circling-the-wagons mentality that are an outgrowth of the one-way models of communication and two-way asymmetrical communication are relics of authoritarian management. American workers, customers, and publics expect to be treated with respect.

As discussed above, our view of the world is shaped by the metaphors we use to think about the world as well as our individual, local, and national cultures (cf., Bitzer & Black, 1971; Held, 1987; Kent, 2001b; Lasch, 1979; Reddy, 1979; Sennett, 1976). Oftentimes we do things a certain way because that is how they have always been done. We will sometimes step around an object sitting in the middle of the floor for weeks, sometimes months, before it occurs to us to move the object to the side or put it away. So it is with how public relations professionals have practiced public relations for the last 50 years: we have simply done what was always been done. A dialogic approach to public relations is a step beyond the status quo.

Not every public relations professional acts as an organizational advisor, and many organizations that should seek public relations counsel do not avail themselves of it. The lack of understanding the public relations professional's advising role is unfortunate because as we move through this century, a number of significant issues (political, environmental, economic, social) have become central. Public relations professionals, as liberally trained, well-informed, and skilled communicators, need to take an active role in guiding organizations along the path of social responsibility.

Two case studies are offered to help show the importance of organizational professionals operating in open and dialogic environments. I treat both case studies in some detail as a means of establishing their importance in a variety of business and professional contexts and emphasizing how the role of dialogic public relations counselors needs to be enacted more fully. Before I continue, let me first point out that for some, these scenarios might seem like they are part of a "liberal" agenda. Indeed, criticizing oil use and supporting climate change research in many places—Oklahoma, Texas, Russia, and a number of other locations—labels you as a wacko.

As communication professionals, we have a responsibility to move beyond partisan debates. The state of the global energy supply and climate change issues are accepted in almost every nation as issues that represent a global crisis. Thus, in the spirit of dialogic communication and this chapter, I ask you, if you are unable to be open-minded about the issues, to do some research. I do not believe that you will be able to find *any credible source* that can refute the obvious effects of human-caused climate change or the scarcity of global supplies of oil.[7]

Dialogic Case Study I: The Oil Supply

Most Americans are unaware of the current scarcity of oil. Although the recent record high prices made U.S. leaders concerned about "securing sufficient oil reserves" for the nation, more recent low oil prices have allowed people to slip back into complacency, and sales of gas-guzzling trucks and SUVs have rebounded. Estimates by professionals in the oil business suggest we have already used up more than half of all of the oil that *exists* on Earth in liquid form, and within about 30 years, we will have used up 90 percent of what remains (Deffeyes, 2005, p. xii), leaving oil only for the production of globally important items like plastics and fertilizer.

What the oil situation means is that the world supply of petroleum (fuel oil, gasoline, lubricants, etc.) is almost gone. "Almost gone" does not even do justice to the situation when you consider that there will never be more oil for millions of years, and we will not be able to import it from any nation once the oil runs out. *No one will have any!* The meager supply of untapped oil that remains in places like the Arctic National Wildlife Refuge will satisfy the world demand for oil for a few days or the U.S.'s needs for a few months—hardly enough to delay the inevitable (Deffeyes, p. 182).

Estimates are dire. Interestingly, however, oil companies and geologists have known that this day was coming for 50 years, and have been quietly pulling out of the oil business for at least 10 years. Recently, Chevron began making light of the situation in its television commercials that features two men in the desert next to what looks like a manhole cover. The two men play Rochambeau (also known as "Rock, Paper, Scissors"); the loser climbs into the hole while the other sits in a lawn chair reading a magazine. After some time, the man in the hole reemerges with a dipstick, as the announcer says, "It took us 125 years to use the first trillion barrels of oil. We'll use the next trillion in 30."[8] What Chevron never mentions, however, is the "first trillion barrels of oil" were more than half of all the liquid oil in existence, and as countries like India, China, Russia, and someday North Korea, modernize, the rate of oil consumption increases exponentially.

Although the fact that we are rapidly running out of oil has been known for more than 50 years, politicians and world leaders have taken little interest in conservation and alternative energy development. In 2003, President Bush symbolically:

> announced a $1.2 billion program called the Freedom Fuel Initiative. This program, designed to speed the development of hydrogen-powered vehicles, received a pledge from the President to invest $720 million in new funding over the next five years to come up with the infrastructure needed to produce, store and distribute hydrogen." (www.energyvortex.com/pages/headlinedetails.cfm?id=616&archive=1).

Sadly, $720 million is a drop in the bucket in terms of developing an alternative energy infrastructure capable of being deployed nationwide. "Less money than was spent developing the Chevy Nova nearly fifty years ago," one scientist sardonically quipped. Indeed, most scientists agree that hydrogen fuel cell technology will be an environmental nightmare; is not likely to be more economical than other sources of energy for a long time, if ever; and is not really a long-term solution, since the spent fuel cells would likely be an environmental waste nightmare.

Considering former President Bush's background in the oil business, Bush clearly knew about "Hubbert's peak" (the date calculated more than half a century ago when half of all the oil in existence would be used up). So, the real question is, "Why didn't Bush make oil conservation and alternative energy a cornerstone of his energy policy," instead of just the opposite (Alterman & Green, 2004)?

What does U.S. energy policy have to do with dialogic public relations? As the controversy surrounding the state of California's fight to raise automobile emission standards has recently shown, progress often requires hard work on the part of change agents willing to take risks and working toward long-term benefits rather than short-term rewards. Public relations professionals, who work in industries with local, state, national, and international implications like petroleum, farming, plastics, or energy production, need to open a public dialogue about solving the problem. Only recently, as politicians and celebrities like former Vice President and Nobel Prize–winner Al Gore, Governor of California Arnold Schwarzenegger, and billionaire T. Boone Pickens of Oklahoma started talking about energy and environmental issues, have politicians and CEOs started paying attention. Had corporations, politicians, celebrities, and business leaders raised environmental issues sooner, the U.S. would be a lot further along in its combating of global warming and development of alternative energy.

Although conserving energy and saving the environment is not the job of most public relations professionals, cutting costs and implementing cost-effective, socially responsible activities are. The cost of a large wind turbine, the kind that are common across Europe and parts of the United States, is about $500,000 to 1,000,000. Each windmill produces enough energy for about 5,000 homes; or most of the energy consumed by one of the thousands of factories located across the U.S. in favorable wind zones. The cost of the windmill can be recovered in only a few years and after that provides essentially free, clean, energy worth millions for decades.

Dialogic organizations are open to innovation, actively seek out professionals in other areas, and engage in environmental scanning surrounding *all* aspects of organizational performance. Dialogic organizations are willing to hear what others have to say before they make decisions and are willing to admit when they are wrong. Dialogue, as a communication orientation, involves developing relationships with many stakeholders and maintaining open channels of communication with all publics.

As boundary spanner and environmental scanners, public relations professionals need to act in the best interest of their organizations, as organizational consciences. Although dialogue is an ethical orientation, it also makes economic sense. Had more U.S. organizations taken a long-term perspective in terms of their energy needs by installing solar panels on the roofs of factories, and utilizing wind energy, the U.S. would import much less energy from abroad and the cost of doing business across the nation would be lower.

Dialogic Case Study II: Global Warming

Anyone who has been living on Earth for the past 20 years knows that global warming is real. Setting aside anecdotal experiences about "last winter being one of the coldest on record" (which is related to global warming, by the way), we discover that virtually all scientists believe there will be serious repercussions from global warming. Predictions include increased hurricane and cyclone activity (something we have seen for a decade), detrimental tidal changes (including more red tides and dead zones in the ocean where nothing can live), a collapse of essential marine species, and a rise in global sea levels that will have devastating effects on every continent. Indeed, lower salinity in the oceans is already wreaking havoc on a number of ocean species and ecosystems, and some island nations are already faced with disappearing entirely beneath the ocean within a decade.

The debate is not really over *whether* global warming is occurring—it is—but how severe the impact will be. Recent research studies have suggested that global warming is accelerating faster than experts originally predicted. The polar ice caps are melting at alarming rates, well ahead of predictions. The worst-case scenarios involve putting a lot of real estate under water with a rise in sea levels by more than 50 feet in some places. (Above average, 2006; *New Scientist*, Oct. 18–24, 2008; Water world, 2006; What to do, 2006).[9] As PBS posits:

> What would happen to the world's coastlines if the West Antarctic Ice Sheet melted, raising global sea levels by as much as 20 feet? Some scientists say a collapse is inevitable, possibly even imminent.... No one believes this monstrous dome [the East Antarctic Ice Sheet] will disintegrate anytime soon. But if it did, it would raise seas around the world by as much as 200 feet. (Water world, 2000)

As a recent, internationally regarded study out of England makes clear, however, problems associated with global warming have already reached alarming proportions (Schellnhuber, et al., 2006). As Dennis Tirpak, head of the steering committee for the report on global climate change, notes in his executive summary:

> A number of critical temperature levels and rates of change relative to pre-industrial times were noted ... For example, a regional increase above present levels of 2.7°C [4.8°F] ... may be a threshold that triggers melting of the Greenland ice-cap, while an increase in global temperatures of about 1°C is likely to lead to extensive coral bleaching. In general, surveys of the literature suggest increasing damage if the globe warms about 1 to 3°C above current levels. Serious risk of large scale, irreversible system disruption, such as reversal of the land carbon sink and possible destabilisation of the Antarctic ice sheets is more likely above 3°C. Such levels are well within the range of climate change projections for the century. (Tirpak, et al, 2006, p. 2)

A minority of scientists still argue, without much evidence, that global warming will not really become a problem for many years. Additionally, some politicians, notably Senator Jim Imhoff of Oklahoma and vice presidential candidate and former Governor of

Alaska Sarah Palin have openly suggested (in speeches and advertisements) that global warming is not man-made and is just "God hugging us tighter"—as Tina Fey put it in a skit about Governor Palin on *Saturday Night Live*.

However, nearly every scientist in every branch of science believes that serious consequences caused by global warming are very near. The issue is not really about when it will happen, whose fault it is, or whether something should be done. The more important question is, "What will be done *now*?"

Again, what does this have to do with public relations dialogue? Like the energy situation, public relations professionals have a role to play in counseling their organizations in all areas, including green issues. The environment is just one area. Because of the oil situation, corn has been diverted for biofuels, resulting in higher food prices (think cornmeal, and "high-fructose corn syrup," used in everything sweet). Corn is used to make thousands of food products.

Often links among events are not obvious to the average citizen. However, professionals who work in specific industries—farming, oil, construction—are more aware of the issues than other people.

Oil and global warming are related. Farming and global warming are related (methane from cows, clear cutting). And oil and farming are related because fertilizer is made from petroleum. Public relations professionals in these and hundreds of other industries need to counsel their organizations regarding long-term, sustainable business models. Not because of some tree-hugging green agenda, but because threats like these and others are real, and public relations professionals as environmental scanners, issues managers, and boundary spanners have the greatest likelihood of recognizing the trends first and being trained to articulate the threats to organizational leaders.

WHY IS DIALOGUE IMPORTANT?

The days of the former-journalist-as-hired-gun public-relations professional are gone. Public relations professionals increasingly come from communication backgrounds, and are expected to understand business and be able to act as managers rather than just press agents (Stacks, Botan, Turk, 1999).

The most important reason for incorporating dialogue into everyday organizational practices is because dialogic communication practices are more ethical and moral. But, for many professionals, the ethical argument is not compelling enough. Many organizational professionals take exception to organizations spending money or taking action that does not serve a direct, tangible, benefit to shareholders or investors. As Smith argues of corporate social responsibility (CSR) (the idea that corporations should give something back to their communities):

> If everybody is responsible to everyone, we simply observe the Tragedy of the Commons. There is a value in civilization—and that has led to the creation of specialized institutions that do some things very well. The modern firm solves one (but only one) of the major problems of mankind—the creation of wealth. (2005, p.18)

Smith's declaration of corporate imperatives might sound compelling to many people who have been raised under U.S. capitalism, but there are tens of millions of unemployed people, and people who have been forced out of retirement, in the U.S. and abroad who would disagree with him. The stock market crash and financial crisis, which began in 2008, proves Smith wrong. There *are* other ways of seeing the world. How organizations behave and treat their employees varies from organization to organization, state to state, region to region, and country to country. Indeed, the fact that the U.S. is the only first-world nation without a national healthcare program for its citizens illustrates this point beautifully. Either Europe's 700 million people are wrong, or the U.S.'s 300 million people are wrong. I suspect that tens of millions of uninsured Americans would say that we are.

Virginia Held, a political scientist, has written about how the metaphor of corporate thinking guides the way Americans think about business:

> When subjected to examination, the assumptions and conceptions of contractual thinking seem highly questionable. As descriptions of reality they can be seriously misleading. Actual societies are the results of war, exploitation, racism, and patriarchy far more than of social contracts. Economic and political realities are the outcomes of economic strength triumphing over economic weakness more

> than of a free market. And rather than a free market of ideas, we have a culture in which the loudspeakers that are the mass media drown out the soft voices of free expression. (1987, p. 113)

Anyone who has traveled outside of the United States probably knows that Europeans, South Koreans, Argentineans, Indians, Russians, Chinese, and others see the world very differently than Americans do. Similarly, Americans see the world very differently now than we did 25 years ago when we were in the grip of the cold war. And no one in the United States probably sees the world in the same way since September 11, 2001, or the recession of 2008. Our perspectives on the world are shaped both by experience and events.

What public relations professionals need to be careful of is being seduced by the easy path of thinking that how we do things now is the only way, or the best way, of doing things. Kaufmann, writing in the prologue to Martin Buber's well-known book on dialogue *I and Thou,* put the difficulty of dialogue into perspective nicely when he wrote:

> *Mundus vult decipi*: the world wants to be deceived. The truth is too complex and frightening; the taste for the truth is an acquired taste that few acquire ... . The good way must be clearly good but not wholly clear. If it is quite clear, it is too easy to reject. (Buber, 1970, pp. 9 & 10, Kaufmann's emphasis)

What Kaufmann meant was that it is hard to behave ethically and do the right thing. Many organizations simply rely on cost–benefits analysis and reach the conclusion that being sued is cheaper than paying more to make a product or service safer. In the end, such felicity calculations (cf., Warnock, 1974), made to maximize shareholders' returns on their investments do not take into account the social costs of corporate misbehavior eventually passed off on consumers and citizens (the economic meltdown in late 2008 illustrates this point well). All communication professionals in business, journalism, the media, public relations, and a host of other fields must work to align business to serve the public good *now*, not because the environment, the oppressed, the underprivileged, the poor, or any other group demands it, but because doing the right thing is actually good for business and good for the nation.

DIALOGUE AS A SOCIAL FRAMEWORK

Returning to the earlier discussion of the models of public relations, there is a tendency to think of each model as mutually exclusive. However, what is forgotten is that public relations is characterized by multiple publics and multiple relationships. Yes, expecting members of huge corporations like Microsoft or AIG to engage in dialogue at *every level* of the organizational hierarchy or with *every stakeholder* or *stakeseeker* is silly. However, especially as is the case with large organizations and influential leaders cut off from the real world, the need to engage in dialogue with internal publics is essential, as is the necessity of regularly bringing in experts, opinion leaders, and advisors.

A dialogic approach calls for a revaluing of organizational members and stakeholders at all levels of an organization. Dialogic principles of mutuality, empathy, risk, propinquity, and commitment should guide interactions at all levels of the organization. Dialogue also requires a commitment of organizational resources and a willingness on the part of organizations to implement it.

As public relations pioneer Ivy Ledbetter Lee argued almost a century ago: (1) Business and industry should align themselves with the public interest, and not vice versa. (2) No program should be carried out without the active support and personal contributions of top management and executives. (3) Organizations should maintain open communication with the media and all stakeholders. (4) Public relations should humanize business, and encourage organizations to help the community, customers, and neighbors (Wilcox, Ault, & Agee, 1998, p. 35). What Lee argued was that public relations professionals should be dialogic, and they should model effective communication. Social learning theory informs this concept.

SOCIAL LEARNING THEORY (SLT): MODELING DIALOGIC COMMUNICATION

Bandura (1977, 1986, 1997) argues that people learn by modeling the behavior of others. People learn by observing how their parents, friends, teachers, peers, television actors, movie stars, athletes, models, and scout leaders, behave, by reading about fictional and nonfictional characters in books, and by observing how people are treated by others because of their behaviors and actions. People model the behaviors and vocabulary that they observe from other people and from print and broadcast sources.

According to Bandura, **social learning theory** (SLT) assumes the following sequence of events: A person notices the behavior of another; s/he admires the behavior and decides to emulate it so s/he mimics the behavior; if other people respond favorably to the new behavior the person may integrate the new behavior into his or her way of thinking and behaving. New behaviors lead people to act in new ways.

Bandura suggests that people model behaviors that they believe to be rewarding, valuable, and desirable (politeness, temperance, abstinence, fidelity), as well as undesirable/unhealthy (drinking, smoking, swearing, promiscuity, drug use). Importantly, all behaviors can be seen both positively and negatively depending upon how others we admire enact them.

People also model the communication patterns of their family, friends, colleagues, and mentors. People model behaviors because they like the way that the person they are mimicking behaves or is treated. When professionals are trying to change the behavior of other people, positive, desirable behaviors, must be modeled in order to instill confidence in a person's ability to succeed. Because of the importance of modeling positive behaviors to facilitate behavioral modification, many prosocial (socially positive) television commercials model appropriate behaviors to show that success is possible and that "anyone can do it." Prosocial messages are message such as advertisements encouraging people to stop smoking, advertisements encouraging parents to talk to their children about drugs, and advertisements designed to discourage spouse and child abuse.

Any time that a public relations professional is dealing with behaviors involving something that frequently happens (voting, buying, calling, e-mailing, speaking), SLT should play a prominent role. Imagine that you were working for a consulting firm that had been hired to assist a school district in developing a campaign to reduce tobacco use by school children. Behavioral modeling should be a staple of posters, signs, speeches, dramatizations, skits, advertisements on Web sites, etc.

In another example, imagine an organization trying to encourage employees to use an organizational Intranet (a private Internet) to find answers to benefits questions and cut down on time spent by human resources on "frequently asked questions." A basic strategy would be to have a member of the organization model the use of the Internet at organizational meetings and departmental events, to demonstrate to others that the technology is easy to use and effective. Similarly, public relations professionals should act as models for stakeholders and employees within the organization as well for external stakeholders and publics.

Bandura's research suggests that modeling behaviors works better when both words and images are employed and the person who might adopt the behavior spends some time mentally practicing the behavior before it is actually attempted (tip.psychology.org/bandura.html). Additionally, behaviors that have strategic or functional value, and behaviors that are portrayed by people who the audience respects or admires (celebrities, athletes, CEOs, politicians, billionaires) work better (tip.psychology.org/bandura.html). Depending upon the target audience, however, "Joe Six-Pack" or "Sarah Soccer Mom" may be the best choice to model behaviors. Social learning theory informs both how to construct effective public relations message for campaigns and programs, as well as how to behave as a communication professional. In essence, social learning theory is a "Do what I do and say what I say" approach to communication.

Many simple online techniques can be used to model effective organization-to-public communication and have been proposed for making organizational interaction with publics more productive. Kent and Taylor (1998; Taylor & Kent, 2007b) have pointed out that publishing the e-mail addresses and telephone numbers of organizational leaders; providing speeches, videos, and other organizational materials online; and encouraging organizational leaders to participate in online discussion groups and forums is a step in the right direction. Additionally, opening departmental, organizational and leadership meetings to the public (or interested publics) is also an effective means of facilitating dialogue.

Part of the problem with many organizations is the bunker mentality that exists. Obviously a technology company cannot simply open up its research and development meetings to the public; however, bringing in experts from outside of an organization with expertise in areas like ergonomics, green energy, safety, recycling, and repetitive stress injuries, only makes sense.

PUBLIC RELATIONS PROFESSIONALS AS ORGANIZATIONAL COUNSELORS

The first order of business for public relations professionals needs to be to become knowledgeable in facilitating dialogue, issues and crisis management, and apologia. Dialogue is of course important because it encourages organizations to develop networks of individuals, organizations, customers, citizens, activists, and others who have a vested interest in making organizations *better*, as well as making them better social entities.

Issues and crisis management should also be understood both because organizations will have crises, and socially responsible organizations need to be prepared. But, more importantly, understanding issues and crisis management and creating organizational mechanisms through which issues can be managed is essential.

Dialogue is something you can incorporate into almost any type of organization. On a modest level, when organizational leaders are helped to understand the value of seeking counsel from others in their decision making, better decisions are likely to result. Several points are worth repeating: research on trust (Kent, Taylor, & Turcilo, 2006) and the related concept of social capital (Ihlen, 2002, 2005), research on crisis communication and apologia (Benoit, 1995; Coombs, 1999; Hearit 2001), and an assortment of interpersonal, psychological, political, and ethics research (cf., Kent & Taylor, 2002) all support the utility of relationship building and dialogic communication.

Small group, interpersonal, leadership, and health communication research indicates that when individuals are involved in making decisions, they have greater commitment and believe they are acting properly. Conversely, when information is withheld, as in the familiar "No comment," people grow suspicious and lose trust in individuals, organizations, and institutions. On these facts alone, dialogue should be appealing. However, I will explore one final real-life example: open source software.

The idea behind open-source software is to make the source code (or programming data) of software available to everyone (Linux is entirely open source and Apple also shares its source code). As the Open Source Imitative (OSI) explains:

> The **basic idea behind open source** is very simple: When programmers can read, redistribute, and modify the source code for a piece of software, the software evolves. People improve it, people adapt it, people fix bugs. And this can happen at a speed that, if one is used to the slow pace of conventional software development, seems astonishing. (<opensource.linux-mirror.org>, OSI's emphasis)

The U.S. government adopted a dialogic or open source model of document translation with the millions of documents seized from Saddam Hussein. Because of a lack of qualified Arabic translators, millions of documents have been uploaded to the Internet and anyone interested is allowed to provide translations of the documents. Since posting the documents, the pace of translations has accelerated dramatically.

Another famous "dialogic" organizational model is MIT's Media Lab, formed in 1980 by Nicholas Negroponte, which allows participating members to have access to any of the research conducted by the Lab. As the Lab's Web site explains:

> Many sponsors find the Laboratory to be a uniquely valuable resource for conducting research that is too costly or too "far out" to be accommodated within a corporate environment. The *"multiplier" effect* of joining a community of sponsors to support advanced research has impressive results. For less than the cost of one senior scientist's salary plus benefits, a sponsor can gain access to the work of a 300-person research laboratory. (<www.media.mit.edu/sponsors/index.html>, MIT's emphasis)

Opens source software, the Media Lab, and dialogue are all manifestations of the same trend: trust, and an interest in improving the world we live in. To establish organizational trust, individual public relations professionals must make efforts to convince opinion leaders, stakeholders, and the dominant coalition of the value of dialogue to organizations.

CONCLUSION

What I advocate here is to expand the purview of organizational dialogue to include more than just dialogic structures (such as threaded dialogue), dialogic relationships, and dialogic counsel, and to see dialogue as a way of professional conduct. As new articles in the PRSA code of ethics:

- Use dialogue in your relations with all *internal* publics—even the cleaning and maintenance staff.
- Use dialogue with all *external* publics including professional colleagues, the media, educational professionals, and, whenever possible, individual customers/clients.
- Do not treat dialogue as merely another organizational hurdle or as a persuasion tactic but rather as a tool for organizational progress and success.
- Do not employ dialogue as a "strategy" but as a guiding model for good business.

As the various examples and cases discussed throughout this chapter illustrate, the U.S. (and the world) are faced with a number of dire environmental, economic, social, and political problems. Public relations has a role to play in issue management, nation building, crisis management, strategic planning, creating and maintaining a positive organizational climate, and creating and maintaining relationships between the organization and its publics. We have a global counseling responsibility that should not be ignored.

ACTIVITIES

1. Select an organization in which you have an interest. Examine the environmental or social issues relevant to your industry (for example, eating disorders and the fashion industry, illegal doping and sports, illegal logging in the rain forests, recycling and new technology). Write a three to five-page essay reporting how the organization could work to improve the issue. Structure the essay as follows: introduction and thesis, review of literature supporting the problem, and recommendations for improvements to the organization/industry you selected.
2. Using the Grunig and Hunt model, identify which model of public relations best describes how the following organizations likely practice public relations: the American Heart Association, the Fraternal Order of the Police, Marilyn Manson, Monsanto, the American Civil Liberties Union, the History Club, a Christian Rock Band, the Bahá'ís, a college classroom, the Cooperative Extension, Wal-Mart. Note: Be sure to look up any organizations you are unfamiliar with.
3. Visit three related social networking Web sites you have never visited before and prepare a two-page report about how each site differs in terms of types of members, topics of discussion, depth of content, friendliness or members, etc. Note: Using a search engine, you can type in almost anything and "social networking" and find a site: "Indian social networking," "Scottish social networking," "gay social networking," "kitten social networking," "pug social networking," "skydiving social networking," etc.
4. As explained above, dialogue is a way of interacting with other people that acknowledges the inherent value and worth of all people. Many organizations actually have "rules of dialogue" designed to ensure that everyone in a group setting has an equal opportunity to express him/herself and participate (cf., Pearson, 1989). Write three to five rules that could be employed in a group setting to ensure that everyone is able and encouraged to equally participate, and that everyone's opinion is valued and validated.
5. Assume you are a senator in your university or college's student government association. Your school decides, as a number of other schools across the U.S. have done, to bring a resolution before the faculty senate to reduce the amount of greenhouse gas emission that your school produces. How could you bring the proposal before the faculty senate in a dialogic manner, so that the members of the faculty senate want to discuss the motion?

NOTES

1. In practice, postings on social networking sites are terse and not intended to generate serious debate or conversation. Debate and discussion are more common on blogs, where individuals communicate using threaded dialogue. What *does* exist, however, is *the potential* for dialogue or discussion, which is largely absent from most organizational Web sites.

2. As they say in Jersey, "Friends will help you move. Real friends will help you move bodies." Ultimately, the best dialogic relationships are genuine *"relationships."* Individuals and public will not rally behind organizations that do not behave ethically or are deceptive, but they will support organizations that make mistakes and admit them. Luckily, organizations that have *strong* dialogic relationships are less likely to make mistakes. As discussed earlier in the text, individuals and organizations with a broader network of professional ties will have more success and make fewer mistakes and less subject to groupthink errors.
3. I could go on about Microsoft's flaws, but as we know from Burke (Identification by Unawareness) Microsoft users would have trouble not seeing this as an attack. The point here is not whether Microsoft makes quality products, but whether Microsoft behaves ethically. Microsoft often does not act in the best interest of its customers (not patching security flaws in a timely fashion, attempting to gather user data without permission, etc.). Apple has also made its share of mistakes (the release of the iPhone was followed by a price drop and rebate after the telephone did not sell as well as expected). Underestimating the market for a product, however, is a business mistake, not a legal one, and is not the same as breaking the law in several nations (antitrust) and then fighting legitimate penalties and fines in court rather than admitting the error.
4. Note: The best way to do this would have been by telephone or in person. However, since I was in Latvia at the time and had poor telephone access, I decided, unwisely, to use e-mail.
5. As suggested above, I already knew the answer to my question about Times; however, as a scholar, I was looking for confirmation (a citation). Once I reconsidered my question, I realized that Adobe Systems Inc., the company that worked with the early digital type customers, probably would be more than happy to answer my question.

   For those interested, the answer that David Lemon, senior manager, Type Development, Adobe Systems, Inc. gave was:

   In the 1970s and '80s, Times was offered by several (maybe all) of the leading printer manufacturers. I suspect this is because it was fairly widely used for scientific papers, and the printer companies were staffed with computer scientists who were more focused on such uses than the general market might warrant. Times was also (and remains) popular in court documents (another niche), for the same general reasons: It's pretty legible, while using significantly less space than other text faces of the day (thus saving space and paper).

   Over time, Times became widely used for general office documents, even though it's not particularly appropriate in that context. Part of the reason may have been a desire to pick up on the "official" look of legal and scientific documents, but I suspect a major factor was that it was simply one of the few decent proportional fonts available on common printers.

   When Adobe defined the set of fonts for the first PostScript printers in 1984, Times' broad popularity made it an obvious choice. (The first LaserWriter had thirteen fonts: four of Times, Four of Helvetica, four of Courier, and Symbol. The inclusion of Symbol suggests the same bias toward scientific usage that I imagine in printer companies; I know it was a factor in computer companies).

   In the early 1990s, I was told that Times was the most-used typeface in the world. I don't know how reliable this statement was (nor is), nor what kind of research it was based on—but I found it quite credible. Frankly, I suspect that if Adobe had picked a different serif text face for the basic set, Times would have faded back to only niche uses. But with the explosion of PostScript printers, everybody had easy access to Times (and often little else), and boy, did it get used.

   Nowadays, people have broad font choices, even if they're restricted to the fonts that come free with Windows. As you noted, most desktop-publishing and word-processing applications use Times as their default font. This wouldn't make a lot of sense if the practice had started in the 21st century (there are many fonts that are clearly better suited now), but it reflects a legacy of customer expectations based on earlier applications and common font sets. The irony is that, if modern applications were to stop offering Times as the default, I believe its usage would plummet. This is a good example of the way that habit and infrastructure tend to reinforce each other.

6. Crozier was a member of the "Worldwide Emergency Response Team" that was dealing with several of Microsoft's lawsuits and problems related to the delay in the release of an operating system upgrade.
7. For many Americans, climate change is a moral issue. However, there are millions of Americans who refuse to believe the evidence and instead insist that God is causing climate change, or that climate change is just part of a natural climate cycle. This is an unfortunate position. Mainstream churches have been 15 to 20 years behind science for more than 200 years and this is one of these issues. The Christian

church once argued that the world was flat, even in the face of overwhelming evidence, and actually put heretical scientists to death who disagreed. Climate change is not an issue of science versus religion. There is no fight here. God is not causing the planet to warm any more than God "intended" for the world to be flat. The world is round. The planet is warming. As professionals, we should not create battles where there are none. Hundreds of religious sects including the Bahá'ís, the Catholic Church, and many fundamentalist Christian sects, have acknowledged the influence of humans on the Earth's surface. As public relations professionals, we have an obligation to become informed about consequential issues like these, and use our communication skills and training to counsel organizations, politicians, stakeholders, and others about how to act. I could have picked other less controversial issues but difficult issues like these are at the heart of our counseling role.

8. This Chevron Web link is now defunct. The site is still up, however (www.willyoujoinus.com). See www.youtube.com/watch?v=6Xdn1GzcfoQ for a similar advertisement.
9. Sea level varies around the globe because of tidal influences, gravitational forces from the moon, and rebound from continental areas in Greenland and Antarctica that have been covered by thousands of feet of ice but that are beginning to rise as massive amounts of ice melt.

Chapter 11

Writing for International and Intercultural Audiences

International, and intercultural, public relations has become increasingly common. Few public relations professionals will spend their careers dealing only with the "dominant culture."[1] As the United States becomes more diverse, and as organizations increasingly participate in a global economy, professionals need to be prepared to communicate with diverse publics and create message that are compelling across town, and across the globe.

In general, writing for any public is the same. At the heart of all effective communication are thorough audience analysis and sound rhetoric. Effective writing is effective writing, no matter what the public. That said, writing for diverse publics requires knowledge that writing for the dominant culture does not. Cultural issues like face, power, an understanding of time, and tolerance for uncertainty all influence what you might say to inform or persuade various publics. Becoming familiar with different cultural heroes and villains is essential. In many cases, you also need to understand that the heroes and villains for the dominant cultures are often not the same as those of other ethnic and social groups.

Robin Hood stole from the rich and gave to the poor. To the rich, Hood was a criminal, a villain; to the poor, Hood was a man of the people, a hero. Although this characterization is oversimplified, it is not far from the mark. Different cultural and ethic groups see the world in very different ways. To create compelling messages for unfamiliar or diverse publics requires an understanding of intercultural and international communication.

Central to understanding how to create effective messages targeted to diverse publics is an understanding of a number of basic intercultural concepts. By understanding how culture influences people's perceptions and beliefs about the world, you will be better prepared to build valuable interpersonal relationships with stakeholders, to create effective persuasive messages, to negotiate with people from other cultures, and to make more ethical decisions.

Understanding other cultures is difficult, just as understanding your own culture is difficult. For example, in the U.S., people on the East and West Coasts have different conceptions about time and punctuality. In California, if you invite some friends over to a party that will "start at seven," do not expect anyone to arrive much before eight or even nine. Conversely, a party that is supposed to start at seven o'clock in Massachusetts, or New Jersey, will start around 7:15–7:30, while that same seven o'clock party held in Michigan, Oklahoma, or Texas, may have people waiting in the driveway or down the street at ten of seven. Time is not a trivial issue. Many cultures, such as the Germans and the Japanese, are very punctual. Keeping a colleague waiting is a great insult in some cultures, while arriving early is seen as a lack of "patience" to others.

Time is of course not the only issue you need to understand, other important issues include nonverbal communication, perceptions of power, and the concepts of individualism and collectivism. Some issues are trivial, like holding up your index finger to order a beer in Germany will get you two beers, since they start counting from one with their thumbs. Other issues are more significant. In Spain, for example, the "okay" gesture (making a circle with your thumb and index finger) means "You're a zero," or refers to a part of the body that one usually does not talk about in polite company. Learning about international business communication issues like nonverbal communication and punctuality can be easily achieved by buying a book on international business (cf., Morrison & Conway, 2006), or by taking a course in Intercultural Communication. However, in order to create compelling interethnic/ intercultural message, communicators need a broader array of knowledge than a few pages in a reference book.

For example, in many cultures, the timing of a message often means more than what is said. Countries with high uncertainty avoidance (discussed below) expect organizations to respond more quickly than countries that tolerate uncertainty better. Similarly, the person making an announcement is more important in high-power distance cultures. Lower level employees will not be seen as credible spokespeople in times of crisis. Thus, many intercultural issues inform your communication more than dictate what you should do.

KEY INTERCULTURAL CONCEPTS

Being able to communicate with individuals and publics from other regions, states, and nations, is not just a matter of speaking the language (although that helps). A great deal of international business takes place in English. However, when planning messages for individuals and publics with different cultural backgrounds than your own, you need to understand how people from other cultures see the world. Having messages "translated" into another language is easy; creating a compelling message that will appeal cross-culturally is an entirely different matter. There are a number of key concepts that are useful for understanding how to communicate cross-culturally including face, context, and time (Hall, 2000a, 2000b).

Other issues that are often taken for granted include how cultures view and solve environmental and cosmological problems. Kluckhohn and Strodtbeck (1961) argue that cultures need to find solutions to common human problems (p. 4). Kluckhohn and Strodtbeck posit five problems for which all cultures must find solutions:

(1) What is the character of innate human nature?: Good, evil, a combination of good and evil, or neutral. The human nature orientation also assumes that human nature is either changeable (mutable), or unchangeable (immutable). Thus, a culture that believes that the people are basically evil and cannot change are not likely to support social service initiatives. Similarly, a group or country like India or Thailand might see people as neither good nor bad, but, because of beliefs in destiny or reincarnation, might not believe that they should interfere in the well being of other groups.

(2) What is the relation of humanity to nature and the supernatural? The human–nature [or environment] orientation hints at the relation between humans and nature and is subcategorized into: *mastery over nature* (all natural forces can and should be overcome and/or put to use by humans), *harmony with nature* (human life, nature, and the supernatural are all extensions of each other), and *subjugation to nature* (nothing can be done to control nature—fate must be accepted). Cultures that believe in mastery over nature, like the U.S., would build sea walls to keep out rising tides, while cultural groups that believe in harmony with nature would simply build houses on stilts to let rising tides flow past.

(3) What is the temporal focus of human life (time orientation)? The temporal feature of human life concerns: the *past* (cultures that value traditions and their ancestors), *present* (cultures that have no traditions or believe in fate), and *future* (where change is valued highly: new is better than old) (see also Hall's polychronic/monochronic time below).

(4) What is the modality of human activity? The primary characteristic of the activity orientation is its emphasis on modes of self-expression in activity:

- ***Being:*** Self-gratification. Spontaneous expressions of human personality.
- ***Being in becoming:*** Concerned with who we are in society and not whether our accomplishments measure up to external standards. People are not valued for their accomplishments so much as for who they are status wise.
- ***Doing:*** A demand for the kind of activity that results in accomplishments that are measurable by external standards.

(5) What is the modality of humanities relationship to other humans? The relational orientation: hierarchical (status matters, people know their place in society), individualistic (people look out for themselves and their families), coequal (relationships should be constructed democratically; people are equal) (Gudykunst & Ting-Toomey, 1988, p. 50; cf., also, <nw08.american.edu/~zaharna/kluckhohn.htm>; <www.ac.wwu.edu/~culture/Hills.htm>).

Intercultural communication, like rhetoric, is an interpretative activity. There are no cheat sheets telling you where a country or individual falls on some continuum (with rare exceptions like Hofstede, below). However, with a little knowledge of a culture and experience interacting with members of a culture, you come to understand where they might fall in categories like Kluckhohn and Strodtbeck. Indeed, the effort to "figure out" or identify where a culture falls along each continuum is a valuable activity and will provide you will deeper insight into each culture you explore and allow you to create more compelling messages.

Ethnocentrism

One important issue to understand about "intercultural" communication, or communication *across* cultures, is that every city, state, region, and nation contains multiple cultures. Even the most seemingly harmonious regions contain individuals and groups who share different cultural values in relation to the dominant culture.

Many people mistakenly think that all cultures are like our own. The word for this is **"ethnocentrism,"** which is a tendency to judge other cultures in comparison to our own, and to believe that our own culture is superior to other cultures. Every culture is ethnocentric. Indeed, one of the best examples of this is to look at maps of the world when you travel abroad. Almost every nation places itself at the center of the world on its maps.

Avoiding ethnocentrism is essential to being able to create compelling cross-cultural messages. Until you are able to see the members of the culture whom you want to reach as inherently valuable in spite of (or because of) their differences, your messages will fall on deaf ears and may be perceived as offensive or provocative.

Consider, for example, U.S. culture, where approximately half of all residents are pro-life and half pro-choice, and about half of all Americans support gun legislation and half do not. Or, that younger people (in most cultures) tend to be more "being" oriented than older people. Some nations, however, are collectively more "doing" oriented, in spite of how young people may behave (dominant culture versus co-cultures).

Although value issues are highly charged and often bipolar, both sides are sure that they are right and there is very little side-switching. Avoiding ethnocentrism requires that public relations professionals suspend their judgment and try to make sense of the world from the perspective of their intended audience. To illustrate the dynamic nature of intercultural values within a culture, consider Steele and Redding's "American Value Premises."

American Values: Premises for Persuasion

More than 40 years ago, Steele and Redding (1962) wrote a revolutionary essay outlining a body of relatively stable value premises that functioned in American rhetoric. A **premise** is a proposition upon which an argument is based or from which a conclusion is drawn. For example, in a speech about the importance of a "liberal arts education," the arguments might be based upon the idea of "patriotism" (educated Americans are better citizens), "ethical equality" (everyone has a right to a quality education), or "the value of the individual" (a proper education levels the playing field). Such propositions are the "premises" of arguments. Premises are integrated into the arguments that you make and the documents that you write. In particular, speeches require sound rhetorical premises in order for your messages to be clear to your audiences. Similarly, organizational materials designed for the media or educated stakeholders (fact sheets, white papers, Web content) are more compelling when they are grounded in clear and compelling premises.

Steel and Redding identified 17 American value premises that they argued were common and enduring. An examination of their list of premises indicates that many of them, indeed most, are still used in public messages today, and are still valuable as persuasive premises (see Table 11.1).

You may have observed that many of Steele and Redding's value premises conflict. Having conflicting values or premises is natural: there are two sides to every issue. Although children are taught in school to conform and do what they are told (value premise 14), children are also taught that they should reject authority if it is tyrannical or oppressive (value premise 9). Ultimately what you should understand from the 17 value premises is that there *are* a number of commonalities of thought that characterize our

TABLE 11.1 American Value Premises

Puritan and Pioneer Morality: The idea that virtues, such as abstinence, honesty, simplicity, cooperation, self-discipline, courage, orderliness, personal-responsibility, and humility should be celebrated and encouraged (p. 85).

The Value of the Individual: The idea that individual happiness and welfare are to be honored, including comfort, privacy, labor, physical integrity, personal property, and health (p. 86).

Achievement and Success: The idea that the ideal American is a "self-made-man who rose from rags to riches" (p. 86).

Change and Progress: The idea that the present is better than the past and the future will be better than the present. Change and progress includes optimism for the future, and denigration of the "old fashioned" and "backwards" (pp. 86–87).

Ethical Equality: The idea that individuals are spiritually and ethically equal; education should be free; everyone should have the right to vote; everyone should have equal rights before the law, etc. (p. 87).

Equality of Opportunity: The idea that each individual, regardless of circumstances of birth shall have the opportunity to rise in the economic and social system. Equality of opportunity does not mean people are all economically and socially equal, just that everyone should have the potential to succeed (p. 87).

Effort and Optimism: The idea that hard work leads to success; that "idle hands are the Devils tools"; that people should work hard (p. 87).

Efficiency, Practicality, and Pragmatism: The idea that hard work is not enough, people should also use their resources wisely (efficiently, practically); that problems are to be "solved." "Dreamers" and "thinkers" do not give as much back as hardworking, practical people (pp. 87–88).

Rejection of Authority: The idea that while people should respect the rights of others and the law, they should be free to choose their own occupation, marriage partner, political party, religion, place of residence, etc. (p. 88).

Science and Secular Rationality: The idea of faith in human reason, clarity, and order; the universe is a rational place that we can, with time, control; science has an answer for everything—often easy answers (p. 88).

Sociality: The idea that people need friends to get by. Also, the acknowledgement that "connections" can lead to greater wealth and power; however, the fear of being taken in by false friends and people who would use us also runs through this premise (pp. 88–89).

Material Comfort: The idea that the good life consists of having the most stuff, of consuming. "Whoever dies with the most toys wins" (p. 89).

Quantification: The idea that more and bigger are necessarily better. Americans quantify everything—I.Q., grades, attractiveness, processor speed. Bigger is always better even if it does not mean quality—big cars, big houses, big parties (p. 89).

External Conformity: The idea that being like others and pleasing others is a good thing. The ceaseless need to "keep up with the Joneses"; that success necessitates conformity, etc. (p. 89–90).

Humor: The idea that humor is okay. Americans make fun of themselves, their bosses, their political system, etc. Humor levels the playing field (p. 90).

Generosity and Considerateness: The idea of the Golden Rule; that we should "do unto others as we would have them do unto us." Americans are known for their spontaneous giving, often in a missionary sense, to bring others closer to "God's benevolence" (p. 90).

Patriotism: The idea that a nation's people come together in times of strife; the idea of complete loyalty and obedience. Throughout U.S. history, people who disagree with the nation's leaders during times of war are accused of being disloyal (communists, traitors, etc.) (p. 90).

nation. The American value premises represent U.S. values, and every nation has premises of its own that everyone from that nation, or region, implicitly understands. When constructing arguments, the value premises are natural starting places. The many conflicting premises also provide professional communicators with natural starting places for creating counterarguments and rationales for taking different courses of action.

Understanding and Maintaining Face

The concept of face is a metaphor that refers to politeness, respect, pride, dignity, honor, shame, etc. When we speak of "face," we often talk about someone "losing face" (being embarrassed, insulted) or "maintaining face" (not being criticized publicly, not being shamed, not being put on the spot). Everyone has a sense of face (pride, dignity) although in many cultures, like the U.S., face is not something that people consciously think about in public situations. For example, imagine when a teacher asks a student a question in class and the student is not prepared. If the teacher, once s/he recognizes that the student is unprepared, shifts the question to the entire class, or someone else who raises his or her hand, the teacher is attempting to help the student maintain face. By not embarrassing the student, each one saves face. The student is not embarrassed in front of his/her peers, and the professor does not appear mean-spirited.

Preventing another person from being embarrassed or ridiculed both allows the person being put on the spot to maintain face, as well as helps the person who challenged the other's face to maintain her/her own face by not appearing mean, spiteful, or unkind. Thus, face functions in three dimensions: maintaining one's own face, helping others to maintain their face, and avoiding challenging someone else's face. Indeed, helping another to maintain face is more valued than retaining one's own face in many cultures.

"Face management" and face needs vary in different cultures. Thus, in some cultures (like the U.S.), being perceived as clever for making a witty comment in a public situation, thereby embarrassing someone else or making him/her look foolish, is sometimes seen as socially desirable. In high face cultures, however, embarrassing someone else with a snide comment makes both the recipient of the comment look bad, and the person who made the comment look worse.

Being aware of the value placed on face is also essential when communicating with people from high-context cultures. In particular, be cautious when creating e-mail messages and Web content. We all know how easy it is for someone to misunderstand what we meant when they speak our own language. When responding to e-mail message from colleagues in high context, high face, cultures, be cautious about being overly direct and about correcting others when they misunderstand what you mean. Remember, helping others to maintain their face is more important than preserving your own face.

Understanding High and Low Context

Context may be best understood as "situation." Context provides meaning and behavioral cues that guide people in how to act and react in intercultural encounters (Taylor, 2000). Hall's (2000a) work suggests that the "context" in which a conversation takes place will significantly influence the interpersonal/intercultural interaction. Hall identified two types of context: high and low. High-context cultures are characterized by communication that is influenced by both the situation and the relationship of the parties involved. In high-context situations, much of what the participants communicate is unspoken or relationally based: Employees *know* exactly what their supervisors want, partners and friends try to guess the needs of the other rather than asking them—and when they guess wrong, politeness or (face) prevents a guest from telling the host. Relationships in high-context societies are very structured. In low-context cultures, communication is driven by what is actually spoken or written. Participants from low-context cultures "say what they mean," and rely on written documents and formal agreements. When a person from a low-context culture is uncertain about what someone wants, they ask. From a public relations standpoint, professionals need to understand that in high-context communication settings (e.g., Asia, South America, the Middle East), indirectness and subtlety are highly regarded, while in low-context communication settings (the U.S., Australia, Canada, France, Germany), directness and candor are preferred (cf., Robinson, 2003).

Another minor issue where context matters is in the rules for forms of address. In the U.S., many people take names and titles for granted, especially when using e-mail (see Chapter 13 for details). Because Americans tend to be low context, and because of ethnocentrism, Americans often mistakenly assume that being less formal will make someone feel closer. By calling someone by his/her first name, "Bob," rather than "Dr. Heath" or Robert Heath, you are showing them that you are friendly and likable. In high-context cultures, not only is such a move considered disrespectful, but referring to someone informally implies that you think that you are of the same or higher status as the other person (which may or may not be true), and that you have little awareness of cultural norms.

Understanding Monochronic and Polychronic Time

Hall (2000b), in his intercultural research, also identified different cultural orientations toward time. Not all cultures place the same value on time or see it in the same way. For example, in the U.S., you were raised hearing the expression "time is money." However, in other nations, such as Italy, Mexico, and Spain, practically the entire nation shuts down on weekdays between noon and 2 p.m. for the siesta; in many nations, no one works on Sundays with the exception of a few restaurant owners. In the U.S., we have 24-hour shopping, banking, and gas stations, but in many nations, weekends are for families and people cannot conduct business (even if they want to) during the siesta or on weekends. In many European nations, such as Estonia, Finland, Latvia, Russia, and Sweden, urban residents leave the cities on the weekends to go to the mountains, the beach, or "the country." In some nations, half of the population takes a month off for "holiday" (vacation) in the summer. During these downtimes, people do not conduct business, check their e-mail, use their PDAs or laptop computers, or talk to colleagues or clients on their cellular telephones. In Finland, for example, many country homes have no electricity or running water and people take the weekends off to read, sit in their family sauna, hike, or ride bicycles. No business is conducted, and a U.S. public relations professional looking to contact his/her foreign colleagues over the weekend will have no success.

Hall identified two orientations toward time that can help explain the behaviors and actions of other cultures: monochronic and polychronic time—also called "M time" and "P time." Monochronic time involves the North European system of doing things sequentially, one thing at a time; polychronic time, on the other hand, "stresses involvement of people and completion of transactions rather than adherence to preset schedules" (2000b, p. 280). Hall offers a wonderful illustration that helps clarify both M- and P-time as well as cultural orientations toward time.

> Once, ... when I was in Petras, Greece, which is in the middle of the P-time belt, my own time system was thrown in my face ... [as] an impatient Greek hotel clerk, anxious to get me and my ménage settled in some quarters ... was pushing me to make a commitment so he could continue with his siesta.... Out of the blue, the clerk blurted, "Make up your mind. After all, time is money!" How could you reply to that at a time of day when literally nothing was happening? ... If there ever was a case of time not being money, it was in Patras during siesta in the summer. (p. 281)

Polychronic time places an emphasis on "doing" rather than "accomplishing." We often hear of people from the U.S. "multitasking" or doing more than one thing at a time. Multitasking is similar to polychronic except that polychronic cultures do not do several things at the same time as a way to be more productive. Rather, as Hall explains,

> P-time stresses involvement of people and completion of transactions rather than adherence to preset schedules. Appointments are not taken as seriously and, as a consequence, are frequently broken. P-time is treated as less tangible than M-time. For polychronic people, time is seldom experienced as "wasted," and is apt to be considered a point rather than a ribbon or a road, but that point is often sacred. (pp. 280–281)

Public relations professionals, who are working with colleagues and stakeholders from other nations and geographic regions within the same nation, need to understand how time influences interactions, and how to frame messages so that they are effective. In many European and Latin American cultures, people are reluctant to do business with a person whom they do not know well and trust. Thus, in order to be successful at conducting business in such cultures, professionals need to spend some time getting to know each other before any business can be conducted.

Once, while visiting South Korea for a conference, a colleague and I had arranged for a Korean student to help us secure a ride from the airport to our lodging (a Korean apartment). The student actually picked us up at the airport herself and presented us with a bag of gifts (food, drinks, candy, fruit, homemade baked goods, etc.). The student also insisted on picking us up herself each day and driving us to our destinations (conference hotel, tourist sites, shopping, restaurants, etc.). Later, we learned that teachers are valued so highly in Korean culture that taking us around was considered a great honor. Another student (a graduate student), told us that when his mother found out that he was going to dinner with his professors she told him if he did not pay for the dinner "she would beat him."

Because of such cultural dynamics, many foreigners are insulted when they come to the U.S. to meet with clients and are picked up by an assistant (or a driver with a sign) at the airport, dropped at their hotel *alone* to "rest," or told that they will be picked up by a limo driver after they have had breakfast *alone*, and brought to a meeting, rather than being joined by the host for breakfast, or picked up by a high-ranking organizational member and taken to breakfast. Relationships and time spent with others are inextricably bound in many cultures. One does not end a meeting that is running long with one person so that s/he can begin a new meeting with someone else. Such behavior would be seen as a tremendous insult. Similarly, "impatience," or a desire to "get started" before spending time in polite conversation over some tea or a drink would be seen by many foreigners as uncivil and "rude."

APOLOGIA, OR HOW TO SAY YOU ARE SORRY

Besides the many interpersonal communication interactions where you might offend other people, another important issue is what to do when an organization makes a mistake and to say it is sorry. An issue that has become important in public relations is the area of "apologia," or how to apologize. Formal apologies, however, are not the same as when your mother told you to "tell your sister you're sorry!" When an organization, or even a nation, does something inappropriate on the international stage, the repercussions can be staggering. More importantly, organizations that want to succeed cannot simply go around apologizing for everything that makes someone else unhappy. Admitting fault involves potential legal liabilities, and, more importantly, no one can really know who is to blame when an industrial accident, natural disaster, or other mishaps occurs. Thus, formal apologies consist of everything from shifting the blame or scapegoating others to admitting wrongdoing and trying to move on (cf., Coombs, 2007; Hearit, 2005).

The study of apologia goes back decades to the work of Ware and Linkugel (1973) and includes important work by Benoit (1995), Coombs (2007), Hearit (2001, 2005), Heath (1998), and others. Although the world "apologia" sounds like it refers simply to an apology, the formal process of apologia such as practiced by celebrities, politicians, organizations, or nations involves more than just saying you are sorry. The best organizations take steps to move on after a crisis (Ulmer & Sellnow, 2002). And *how* to respond depends a lot upon the cultural beliefs and traditions of the nation and its people, as well as the relationships with stakeholders and the reputation of the organization apologizing. For example, Taylor in her (2000) study of a tainting scare of Coca-Cola in Belgium, France, and Spain, suggests that the proper response of Coke should have been guided by cultural issues like those raised by Hofstede (below), rather than responding paternalistically, as if Coke knew best, and that the counties that were concerned should just trust Coke.

The best apologia is informed by cultural issues as well as by rhetorical issues. To cover all of the important features of apologia could easily take up the remainder of this chapter. However, a number of stable approaches to apologia can be found in Coombs' (2007b) recent crisis work:

Primary crisis response strategies

Deny crisis response strategies

Attack the accuser: Crisis manager confronts the person or group claiming something is wrong with the organization.

Denial: Crisis manager asserts that there is no crisis.

Scapegoat: Crisis manager blames some person or group outside of the organization for the crisis.

Diminish crisis response strategies

Excuse: Crisis manager minimizes organizational responsibility by denying intent to do harm and/or claiming inability to control the events that triggered the crisis.

Justification: Crisis manager minimizes the perceived damage caused by the crisis.

Rebuild crisis response strategies

Compensation: Crisis manager offers money or other gifts to victims.

Apology: Crisis manager indicates the organization takes full responsibility for the crisis and asks stakeholders for forgiveness.

Secondary crisis response strategies

Bolstering crisis response strategies

Reminder: Tell stakeholders about the past good works of the organization.

Ingratiation: Crisis manager praises stakeholders and/or reminds them of past good works by the organization.

Victimage: Crisis managers remind stakeholders that the organization is a victim of the crisis too. (p. 170, Coombs' emphasis)

Situational and organizational features always inform crisis responses. As with rhetorical strategies, there is no single correct apologia response to an organizational issue or crisis, although in certain situations, some responses are considered better than others. As has been true throughout this text, as professional communicators, you need to learn as much as possible about a situation before you can formulate a proper response, and in intercultural and cross-cultural contexts, understanding Hofstede is an important first step toward knowing how to respond.

Crisis responses take a variety of forms: holding news conferences to respond to questions from the media, writing letters to the editor to express organizational sadness and remorse, writing Web content responding to crisis issues. Writing news releases outlining organizational actions, and creating fact sheets and backgrounders to distribute to the media.

HOFSTEDE'S CULTURAL RESEARCH

The work of Geert Hofstede (1984, 1997, 2001, 2005) has been used as a foundation in business, communication, intercultural, interpersonal, and public relations research. Both Hofstede and Hall understood that culture and context-bound issues like power, uncertainty, and individualism, have a profound impact on communication. Hofstede identified five cultural variables that have a big impact in intercultural settings: power distance, uncertainty avoidance, masculinity/femininity, individualism/collectivism and Confucianism, or "long-term orientation."

Power Distance

Hofstede's first dimension, power distance, refers to the extent to which the less powerful members of institutions and organizations within a country expect and accept that power is distributed unequally. Power distance is the perceived difference between a superior and a subordinate in society as experienced by the less powerful in society (child–parent, employee–supervisor, student–teacher). In high-power distance cultures like Malaysia, Hong Kong, and Panama, subordinates are reluctant (or unwilling) to express opinions to "superiors" and "class" differences are taken for granted. For example, the curtain between the first or business class cabin and the coach cabin on a British Airway flight is called the "class divider," a clear acknowledgement of power distance and class differences. In low-power distance cultures like Israel and Australia, parents treat children as equals, and decentralization and collectivist decision making are preferred.

Uncertainty Avoidance

Hofstede's second dimension, uncertainty avoidance, refers to the extent to which the members of a culture feel threatened by uncertain or unknown situations. Uncertainty avoidance measures the ability of humans to cope with uncertainty. In high uncertainty avoidance cultures, those with lower scores, like Greece and Portugal, stress is higher, and a fear of the unknown, a tendency to conform, more written rules and regulations, and a preference for consensus is common. Low uncertainty avoidance cultures like Hong Kong and Sweden are more comfortable with uncertainty and do not feel the need to have rules for everything or agree on everything.

Masculinity Femininity

Hofstede's third dimension, masculinity, looks at the value placed on things, power and assertiveness, as well as the distribution of tasks across a culture. In feminine cultures, like Finland and Sweden, there tends to be less gender segregation with both men and women participating equally in work and family roles; emphasis is placed on family and relationships over acquiring things and power. In masculine cultures, such as Japan and Italy, there exists greater gender segregation in work and family occupations. Women tend to perform tasks associated with caregiving and raising the family; occupations for women include nurses and secretaries, while men engage in occupations associated with assertiveness: working outside of the home as managers, engineers, hourly laborers, etc.

Individualism/Collectivism

Hofstede's fourth dimension, individualism, refers to how collectivistic the members of a culture are. In cultures with high individualism, such as the U.S. and Australia, people tend to care more about themselves, their professional success, and holding positions of power. In low individualism or "collectivist" cultures, such as Panama and Venezuela, people tend to value family and group membership and harmony above their own interests.

Confucian Dynamism or "Long-Term Orientation" (LTO)

Hofstede's fifth dimension, Confucian dynamism, or "long-term orientation," refers to issues of thrift, perseverance, and the desire for orderly relationships with others. Confucianism dynamism is new and has only been measured in a few cultures. In cultures with high Confucian values, such as China, individuals who are extravagant and unpredictable are seen as suspicious and threatening to the social order; thrift and perseverance are valued. In low Confucian cultures, such as Pakistan and the U.S., people tend to value individualism and try to accept people as individuals rather than expecting conformity.

By understanding Hofstede's categories, a person traveling in another country or interacting with people from another culture can have a better idea how people from that culture view the world. From a professional standpoint, the actual scores on Hofstede's categories do not mean as much as understanding how big the differences might be in relation to other nations.

Knowing that the Philippines has one of the highest scores on power distance of all the nations in Hofstede's study will not mean as much as the practical consequences: many cultures do not believe that "all people are created equal." Because of the high-power distance score, in the Philippines you can expect a strict hierarchy. A professional should spend most of his or her time talking to the oldest (or most senior) person. During negotiations, you would want to send someone of higher status or seniority to avoid being ignored by high-ranking organizational members. Similarly, as suggested earlier, in many collectivist societies, outsiders are not trusted and local people are not comfortable doing business with someone whom they do not know well. Relationships need to be built and trust established before business or collaborative partnership can succeed.

Be sure to devote time to building relationship through informal channels like e-mail. Sharing personal information—marital status, information about children, upcoming holiday activities—can allow people from collectivist cultures to identify with you. Be subtle, be sincere.

TRANSLATION AND LANGUAGE ISSUES

There are two types of translation issues that are important in public relations. The first issue has to do with literal translations from one language to another. The classic means of illustrating this is to look at one of the many lists of marketing blunders where messages were poorly translated. For example, when Parker Pen marketed a ballpoint pen in Mexico, its ads were supposed to say "It won't leak in your pocket and embarrass you." However, the Spanish word *embarazar* was mistakenly used to mean "embarrass." The ad actually said: "It won't leak in your pocket and make you pregnant." In Taiwan, the translation of the Pepsi slogan "Come alive with the Pepsi Generation" came out as "Pepsi will bring your ancestors back from the dead." Hunt-Wesson introduced its Big John products in French Canada as "Gros Jos" before finding out that the phrase, in slang, means "big breasts." (The mistake did not have a noticeable effect on sales) (www.i18nguy.com/translations.html).

Mistakes like these are easily avoided by hiring professional translators—rather than relying on the intern in the office who is in his/her second year of college Spanish—or by having potential marketing/advertising messages vetted by local professionals in the target nation before creating print materials or messages. In general, words cannot be translated literally into other languages and slang (or connotative) expressions need to be carefully adapted to local culture. In the U.S. for example, we might say someone who was killed would be "pushing up the daisies," while in Thailand, the expression might be "reading the newspaper in the street." In the U.S. we might see a television advertisement of an angry motorist honking the horn and shouting at a slow motorist, "Come on!" or "Move it!" while in Thailand, the cry would be, "It's not your backyard!"

The second, perhaps more important, translation issue has to do with effectively translating messages when conducting research. As you know, research is at the heart of effective public relations and primary research (surveys, interviews, etc.) is often necessary to gauge public opinion or understand the complexity of issues. As suggested above,

TABLE 11.2 Hofstede Table

	PDI Rank	PDI Score	IDV Rank	IDV Score	MAS Rank	MAS Score	UAI Rank	UAI Score	LTO Rank	LTO Score
Arab countries	7	80	26/27	38	23	53	27	68	.	.
Argentina	35/36	49	22/23	46	20/21	56	10/15	86	.	.
Australia	41	36	2	90	16	61	37	51	15	31
Austria	**53**	**11**	18	55	2	79	24/25	70		
Belgium	20	65	8	75	22	54	5/6	94		
Brazil	14	69	26/27	38	27	49	21/22	76	6	65
Canada	39	39	4/5	80	24	52	41/42	48	20	23
China	.	.	.	.	.	.	.	.	**1**	**118**
Chile	24/25	63	38	23	46	28	10/15	86	.	.
Colombia	17	67	49	13	11/12	64	20	80	.	.
Costa Rica	42/44	35	46	15	48/49	21	10/15	86	.	.
Denmark	51	18	9	74	50	16	51	23	.	.
East Africa	21/23	64	33/35	27	39	41	36	52	.	.
Ecuador	8/9	78	52	8	13/14	63	28	67	.	.
Finland	46	33	17	63	47	26	31/32	59	.	.
France	15/16	68	10/11	71	35/36	43	10/15	86	.	.
Germany FR	42/44	35	15	67	9/10	66	29	65	14	31
Great Britain	42/44	35	3	89	9/10	66	47/48	35	18	25
Greece	27/28	60	30	35	18/19	57	**1**	**112**	.	.
Guatemala	2/3	95	**53**	**6**	43	37	3	101		
Hong Kong	15/16	68	37	25	18/19	57	49/50	29	2	96
India	10/11	77	21	48	20/21	56	45	40	7	61
Indonesia	8/9	78	47/48	14	30/31	46	41/42	48	.	.
Iran	29/30	58	24	41	35/36	43	31/32	59	.	.
Ireland (Republic of)	49	28	12	70	7/8	68	47/48	35	.	.
Israel	52	13	19	54	29	47	19	81	.	.
Italy	34	50	7	76	4/5	70	23	75	.	.
Jamaica	37	45	25	39	7/8	68	52	13	.	.

Japan	33	54	22/23	46	**1**	**95**	7	92	4	80
Malaysia	**1**	**104**	36	26	25/26	50	46	36		.
Mexico	5/6	81	32	30	6	69	18	82	.	.
Netherlands	40	38	4/5	80	51	14	35	53	10	44
New Zealand	50	22	6	79	17	58	39/40	49	16	30
Norway	47/48	31	13	69	52	8	38	50	.	.
Pakistan	32	55	47/48	14	25/26	50	24/25	70	**23**	**00**
Panama	2/3	95	51	11	34	44	10/15	86	.	.
Peru	21/23	64	45	16	37/38	42	9	87	.	.
Philippines	4	94	31	32	11/12	64	44	44	21	19
Portugal	24/25	63	33/35	27	45	31	2	104	.	.
Salvador	18/19	66	42	19	40	40	5/6	94	.	.
Singapore	13	74	39/41	20	28	48	**53**	**8**	9	48.
South Africa	35/36	49	16	65	13/14	63	39/40	49	.	.
South Korea	27/28	60	43	18	41	39	16/17	85	5	75
Spain	31	57	20	51	37/38	42	10/15	86	.	.
Sweden	47/48	31	10/11	71	**53**	**5**	49/50	29	12	33
Switzerland	45	34	14	68	4/5	70	33	58	.	.
Taiwan	29/30	58	44	17	32/33	45	26	69	3	87
Thailand	21/23	64	39/41	20	44	34	30	64	8	56
Turkey	18/19	66	28	37	32/33	45	16/17	85	.	.
Uruguay	26	61	29	36	42	38	4	100	.	.
USA	38	40	**1**	**91**	15	62	43	46	17	29
Venezuela	5/6	81	50	12	3	73	21/22	76	.	.
West Africa	10/11	77	39/41	20	30/31	46	34	54	.	.
Yugoslavia	12	76	33/35	27	48/49	21	8	88	.	.

language is as complicated in other nations as it is in the United States. Expressions do not translate exactly. Cultures do not have the same connotations about public officials and institutions. In the U.S., for example, we regularly mock our elected officials in cartoons and newspaper editorials, but in many nations, making fun of important elected officials (like a prime minister or king), or religious figures (like Mohammed or Christ), could land you in prison for a very long time. Additionally, in many countries a **courtesy bias** exists. A courtesy bias is associated with face and essentially involves telling the other person what you *think* they want to hear, or nonverbally agreeing (smiling, head nodding, etc.) with what someone is saying as a means of being polite, when in fact you actually disagree with that the person is suggesting. Conducting reliable research and engaging in effective decision making and planning requires an understanding of translation and language issues.

Only professionals who have spent time learning about other cultures (especially high-context cultures) can hope to communicate effectively with professionals within that culture. Seemingly minor nonverbal behaviors can have great meaning to people within a culture but will often be almost invisible to someone unfamiliar with the culture. Koreans, for example, often act on a principle called *Nunch'i*, which refers to "figuring out" what the other person wants without actually asking the other person (Robinson, 2003). People who are able to quickly and accurately anticipate the needs of others are considered both clever and socially desirable. People who are poor at figuring out what other people want are considered slack-witted and impolite. Effective communication, then, involves more than just translating words or questions into another language but of also *understanding* what the words might mean to the other person.

In order to avoid creating surveys or developing interview questions that might be culturally offensive or incorrect, a technique called **back translation** is used. In back translation, messages are translated by one translator into another language, and then back into the native tongue of the researcher by another translator. For example, a survey to be conducted in Sweden would require translation of the survey by a bilingual Swede from English to Swedish, and then back from Swedish to English by another translator. Once messages are translated accurately, there is an assumption of greater validity and trust in the research and survey questions.

Translation is not only an issue when communicating with people from different countries or who speak different languages but also with individuals and publics who are from the same culture but are in different age groups or have different knowledge. As professional communicators, you should consult experts in the area you are researching. Thus, surfers should be involved in obtaining data from surfers; videogame players should inform research about videogames. In ethnographic research, this person is known as a "confidant" and helps with translation of metaphors, jargon, and slang.

Like translation, understanding the subtleties of another language is important to crafting effective messages. In the U.S., for example, the Midwestern, accent-free dialect spoken by all of the major network television news anchors and most state anchors is seen as a "generic" choice designed to offend no one. Research does suggest that in the U.S., people who talk more slowly or with a Southern accent are perceived as less intelligent than someone with no accent (Cargile, 2003, pp. 216 ff). The same is true in other nations: people raised in specific cultures have stereotypes about others based on their accent or dialect. For example, one of my Russian colleagues once told me about how former Prime Minister Mikhail Gorbachev sounded like a "Kolkhoznik" or a "collective farmer." In the U.S., people from the Midwest, North, or either coast might say that a Southern politician sounded like a "good ol' boy." Indeed, President George W. Bush was criticized for sounding like a "Texan," when his other family members have East Coast accents. And President James Earl Carter was ridiculed for his Georgian accent. Organizational spokespeople need to be selected with care in order to ensure that they sound like the target audience and do not have an accent that might be looked down upon or found offensive.

DOING BUSINESS IN OTHER COUNTRIES: GESTURES, NONVERBALS, AND ACCULTURATION

Nonverbal communication is an important part of all face-to-face communication. As you may have learned in a "Fundamentals of Communication" class or a "Nonverbal Communication" class, when the spoken and nonverbal channel are in conflict (i.e., you look nervous, unsure, or evasive) people tend to believe the nonverbal channel. In cross-cultural situations, different cultures have different expectations of professional behavior. Thus, understanding nonverbal rules, gestures, and symbols is an important aspect of achieving success in cross-cultural or intercultural contexts.

Given the focus of this textbook on public relations writing, I cannot teach you everything that you need to know to communicate effectively in every culture. However, here are some of the basic skills needed to help prepare for international settings:

1. **Learn the language of the culture you will be interacting with.** If you are not able to learn the language, study the basics of interpersonal interaction and politeness. Learn the exchange rate of the currency and how to count or use numbers. Learn how to say "please" and "thank you" and proper greetings. Learn how to ask for directions. Essentially, if you can learn the basics of politeness and "survival" (outlined in most travel books), you will be on your way to "not offending" anyone.
2. **Spend some time in the culture in which you will be working before you conduct any business or interact with professionals from the country.** Ideally, you should spend at least four to six weeks in the region learning about its food, customs, cultural mannerisms, and proper greetings.
3. **Learn as much as you can about the cultural icons, artwork, religion, heroes and villains, and politics.** However, you probably should not engage a foreigner in any critical discussions about his/her form of government or religion until you thoroughly understand these institutions and you have a very solid relationship with your colleagues. You *should* understand whether a country has five major political parties or two, how many ethnic groups there are, whether there are any points of contention among social groups, and , learn about the natural resources and economy of the region.
4. **Learn the essentials of formal interactions.** Should you *shake hands* (how hard, with both sexes, with children?), *kiss* (one cheek, two cheeks, or three times? Are they "air kisses" or do you make contact?), *bow* (how low, for whom?), or *wai* (an age-based greeting of respect where both hands are placed palm-to-palm and raised to the chest)? Also, learn if it is polite to initiate contact with people yourself or whether you will need formal introductions.
5. **Learn whether it is appropriate for men and women, or supervisors and employees, to interact.** Be aware that in many countries, status is based on age, and a proper address for someone, especially a married or single woman, depends upon his or her marital status. Do not be concerned if a professional colleague asks you how old you are, when your birthday is, or whether you have children. Such inquiries are made as a means of understanding your status and how to interact with you. Many people, even the well educated, are openly superstitious about dates, numbers, astrological signs, directionality, and animals.
6. **Many cultures also take social conventions much more seriously than we do in the U.S.** A Thai colleague of mine, for example, would send out almost a thousand holiday cards each New Year to professional colleagues, influential acquaintances, and of course, friends and family.
7. **Learn something about the media system in the country that you visit,** how people obtain their information, what news sources are considered to be the most trustworthy and credible, and which sources are considered to be trivial or unreliable? Also, learn how public relations professionals interact with the media (directly, through clubs or organizations, or via governmental officials).
8. **Examine the archetypal or symbolic features of the culture and language in the nation or region you will visit.** Find out what motivates people to act/react, how citizens perceive people from the U.S., and if a preexisting cultural narrative (the cowboy, greedy, invaders) exists.
9. **Examine the symbolic issues that communicators need to be aware of when creating messages** (i.e., respect for elders, the role of the government, religious and social features, trust, level of uncertainty, power distance, perception of time etc.) (cf., Kent, 1997, pp. 158–159; Kent & Taylor, 2007).

If this list of cultural features seems long, it should. To be successful at communicating with individuals or publics from another culture, region, or nation, you should have a thorough understanding of the nation's culture. That said, most of this knowledge can be found in books on international business and travel, in historical texts, in online sources like national Web sites, the *CIA World Factbook* (www.cia.gov/library/publications/the-world-factbook/index.html), via international colleagues and contacts in professional associations, and by visiting the nation or region. Learning about other cultures is usually something people enjoy.

TABOOS: COLORS, IMAGES, HEROES AND VILLAINS

The town of Pristine, Kosovo, in the former Yugoslavian province of Serbia, has two main streets named after people whom everyone reveres: Mother Theresa Boulevard and William J. Clinton Boulevard. On Clinton's birthday, the city is covered with posters of the former president, announcing the event. In Thailand, mocking the king is a crime punishable by imprisonment. In Malaysia, yellow is the color of mourning (rather than black, in the U.S.). Orange cats are believed to bring good luck in Latvia, while black cats bring bad luck in the United States.

Every country has its share of heroes and villains, superstitions, topics that are taboo, or best avoided in mixed company, and symbols and icons that everyone from that country or region instantly recognizes. In the U.S., the American flag has so much meaning for some people, and so little meaning for others, that they put it everywhere: on their houses, their automobiles, their clothing, even their pajamas and undergarments. Such expressions of "patriotism" are much less common in other nations (for example, Northern Europe) and even seen in bad taste. Many nations consider their flags to be formal symbols of government rather than something someone might choose to put on the seat of their pants or on the bumper of their SUV.

Other kinds of symbols have nothing to do with specific icons but have just as much meaning. For example, in France, wine, bread, and cheese are closely tied to the national identity, just as beer and sauerkraut are associated with Germany, bagpipes and Scotch with Scotland, and poetry and Guinness with Ireland. Although we may see some of these cultural icons as simple stereotypes, the U.S. has its own share of baggage that influences how others see us. When traveling abroad, Americans are known for being impolite and loud and wearing baseball caps and university clothing (sweat shirts or t-shirts), and, of course, America is home to cowboys and the Big Mac. Lest we think that our cultural icons are harmless, McDonald's restaurants can be found outside some of the world's greatest national treasures: next to the Pantheon (Rome), at the entrance to old town Riga (Latvia), and in Venice (Italy). How would Americans feel about having a Russian fast food restaurant on the Mall in Washington D.C., or an Indian vegetarian chain restaurant at the foot of Mount Rushmore? Understanding cultural icons, images, and heroes and villains is part of intercultural research.

As you develop an appreciation for cultural heroes and villains as well as moving symbols, you can begin to integrate these messages into organizational documents and into your interpersonal conversations with people from other cultures. Understanding cultural issues takes time, but professionals who truly grasp how another culture thinks about the world are able to create compelling intercultural messages.

CONSTRAINTS: MESSAGE DESIGN, TECHNOLOGICAL ACCESS, LIFESTYLES, WAGES

Many Americans mistakenly think that because the U.S. leads the world in media and entertainment, we also lead the world in everything else. This is simply not the case. Many nations have more advanced telecommunications (Italy, Japan, South Korea, Finland), and many nations, because of geographic and economic constraints, have put their technology to more sophisticated uses. For example, in Africa, where there is limited infrastructure for banking and commerce, a system of economic exchange using cellular telephones has sprung up. Essentially, the cellular telephone is used like an Internet bank account, allowing people to conduct bank transfers from any location in the nation via their telephone. Moreover, since the average citizen in many nations cannot afford to purchase a PC or laptop computer, or pay for Internet access, many everyday Internet tasks like searching the Web for information and news are conducted via cellular telephones. Additionally, in most nations, incoming calls on a cellular telephone are free. Thus, everyone has a cellular telephone regardless of whether they can afford to make outgoing calls.

Imagine the difference that technology makes in the conduct of public relations. For example, when I ask my U.S. students how to reach college students with a message, their first response is "use the Internet or a cellular telephone." Many students have difficulty thinking of communication strategies and tactics beyond broadcast, print, and the Internet. What is often overlooked, and crucial in many parts of the world, are interpersonal relationships, group memberships, political and cultural affiliations, and professional ties. Moreover, the humble sign (posters, billboards, transit signs) is used extensively in every nation to share information with key publics.

Communication professionals working outside of the U.S. need to be aware of political and economic constraints. In many nations, the key public for any organization is often the government and political leaders. For example, in Thailand and Malaysia, the first telephone call that an organization might make after a crisis is to a governmental official. In Korea, before the media publish negative stories about organizational activities, politicians, or political figures, the organization or individual involved is given the opportunity to respond to the story (Berkowitz & Lee, 2004). And in China, the government monitors all Internet traffic and blocks access to tens of thousands of Christian, anti-Chinese, and other "heretical" Web sites, as well as sites critical of the Chinese government. The notion of a free press and trusted media is a myth in many nations (cf., Taylor & Kent, 1999). Throughout Europe, Russia, the Baltic region, and Asia, messages in the media are taken with a grain of salt. Although polls of Americans often suggest that people do not trust the media, the media are even less trusted in many other nations. Indeed, in some nations, the government *controls* the media.

WEB SITES: TRANSLATIONS AND ACCESSIBILITY

There are several issues to consider when creating Web content that regional or international publics will use. The first is whether to create different versions of Web sites in each language (English, Spanish, French, German), or whether to create one Web site. On the one hand, English is widely used in business throughout the world, so having an English language–only Web site may not be a problem for some types of organizations. Indeed, China will soon become the nation with the most English-speaking people on the planet. However, on the other hand, by providing Web content that has been translated into other languages, organizations show a higher level of respect for their publics, and have a greater chance of creating compelling messages. McDonald's corporate Web site (www.aboutmcdonalds.com/mcd/select_your_country_market.html), for example, offers access to dozens of country specific Web sites. Each site is tailored to the local culture and uses local symbols, imagery, language, music, and advertising jingles. Other organizations, like Microsoft (www.microsoft.com/worldwide), offer access to Web sites that have been translated into local languages and alphabets, but every site more or less resembles the parent company's home page. More modestly, even small Web-based companies like the Netherlands–based Lemkesoft (www.lemkesoft.com), offer versions of their Web site in multiple languages (Dutch and English). Professional associations that have international clientele, like the International Communication Association, make their Web page available in seven languages (Chinese, English, French, German, Korean, and Spanish). Many nonprofit organizations like the Rotary Club (www.rotary.org) offer *versions* of their home page in different languages (Dutch, Spanish, French, Japanese, Korean, Swedish). Other organizations with international ties create sites that are tailored by language (English, French, Dutch, Netherlands) or region (for example, India, where sites are in English but the content is focused on the Indian nation).[2]

If the decision *is* made to provide translated Web content, you will need to consider whether to include culturally relevant symbols, colors, and imagery, or just to translate everything into another language. Obviously, creating Web sites that are tailored to each nation can be expensive, and requires the input of professional communicators from each nation to be targeted. However, local Web sites will probably be seen as more credible and more closely linked to local values.

ETHICS, GOVERNMENT AND MEDIA RELATIONS, BRIBERY

When working in international contexts, one of the first things that you should be aware of is that each country has its own set of laws that are often very different than in the United States. Additionally, how the media and the system of governance work also dramatically influences what kind of communication strategies are used, what channel to use to get one's message out (print, broadcast, face-to-face, Internet), and what media are likely to be the most effective. In nations where the print and broadcast media are still owned or closely monitored by the government, the chance of an antigovernment story being published, or any story that the government does not deem important, is remote.

A number of other legal and governmental issues also need to be considered. For example, the PRSA code of ethics forbids paying for news coverage, but in many newly democratic nations where news readership and sales are low, pass-on of print media to others is high, and the only way that many organizations can get a story or a news release printed about them in a newspaper is for an organization to buy an advertisement (cf., Kruckeberg & Tsetsura, 2003; www.business-anti-corruption.com/country-profiles/).

In many postcommunist nations (like Eastern Europe), citizens are distrustful of all media for good reason. Thus, even when organizations are willing to place advertisements or pay for story placement in order to obtain coverage, their messages do not have the impact that they might have in nations with more prosperous and privately owned media.

The U.S. ranks near the top of a 66-nation survey of nations least likely to require pay-for-placement (Kruckeberg & Tsetsura), but we still fall behind a dozen European nations and Canada. Pay for placement still happens in the U.S. every day. Moreover, many newspapers publish special sections about technology, automotive, pharmaceuticals, gardening, and education that are essentially "pay for coverage models," and provide the advertisers with fixed space based on the size of the advertisement that is purchased. Since special sections are not "news," the newspapers are technically not requiring organizations to pay to have newsworthy stories printed, but the principle is the same. Organizations with fewer resources are not able to afford coverage and are left out. Television has been offering pay-for-placement opportunities for years with product placement, and providing favored clients or potential advertisers advance opportunities to buy advertisements before stories that they might like to be associated with air. Not to be left out of the game, radio stations have been fined by the FCC on many occasions for pay-for-play schemes where record companies provided bribes to stations and deejays to play songs from their labels. Given all of the pay-for-placement opportunities, you might think that paying for placement is just part of the profession, unethical but legal.

The fact is that bribery is illegal and is a much more serious offense in many nations than in the U.S. More importantly, professionals who violate communication laws, or engage in bribery or corruption in other countries, are subject to the laws of the country they are in when they are caught. Given the harshness of the punishments in some nations, no communication professional should ever consider engaging in bribery or corrupting the channels of information (a violation of the PRSA Code and the law), nor should you simply look the other way if his/her organization wants to do business that way. Given the ubiquity of the Internet, the tens of thousands of blogs that spring up every month, and the need of the broadcast and Internet news media to fill every second of every day with content, the likelihood that an organization will be caught engaging in illegal or unethical activities is high.

To illustrate the seriousness of breaking the law in another nation, consider the recent case of a British schoolteacher in Sudan. Gillian Gibbons innocently named the class teddy bear "Mohamed" at the prompting of one of her primary school students named Mohamed (November, 2007, <Http://news.bbc.co.uk/2/hi/africa/7115400.stm>, <news.bbc.co.uk/2/hi/africa/7112929.stm>). The penalty for Gibbons' crime, "insulting religion and inciting hatred," was up to six months in jail and 40 lashes.[3] Of course, Gibbons' crime was not bribery, but it illustrates the seriousness of breaking laws that might seem to be trivial. China, Malaysia, and Vietnam have a death penalty in serious bribery cases; even Sweden, considered one of the most liberal and fair nations in Europe, has a penalty of from two to six years in prison for bribery, depending upon whether the offense involves private citizens or government employees.

U.S. and international law prohibits bribery. Thus, although bribery might be accepted in some nations, and in some cases is seen as expected and compulsory, public relations professionals are not allowed to engage in bribery. This holds true even in nations like Thailand that has published lists of recommended bribes for public officials in the newspaper.

Many public relations professionals naively assume that what works in one nation will work in another, without regard for the differences in media, politics, individual freedom, activism, economic conditions, race, religion, gender, or ethnicity. As this chapter should make clear, the idea that one way of communicating with publics might work in every nation is simply naive. Conducting international public relations requires knowledge and experience in other nations, particularly those with whom one wants to work, as well as an understanding of intercultural communication issues, language, culture, media, politics, and religion.

One model that has been advanced as a means of understanding international public relations activities is a genre (or generic) approach. Kent and Taylor (2007) argued that there are several issues that should be considered when conducting international public relations research or preparing international campaigns:

(1) Identify features of the situation/strategies used. In the case of international public relations, for example, cultural issues like gender roles, status, age, and other variables might need to be examined.
(2) Identify the intended audience effects. Are the goals of organizations' communication efforts persuasion, propaganda, or marketing? And what do local practitioners see as their role?
(3) Clarify the motivational intent of the organization and publics (to placate, to entertain, to inspire, to build the nation, to monitor an organization, to learn about products/services, to meet social emotional needs).
(4) Examine the archetypal or symbolic nature of language in order to understand cultural and historical issues, who the heroes and villains are, and to understand what motivates citizens to act/react.
(5) Examine the strategic considerations that communicators are aware of when creating messages (i.e., respect for elders, the role of the government, religious and social features, trust, perception of time, etc.). And, most importantly,
(6) Use communication principles and theory to understand the culture being examined and how cultures influences organizations and communication. (pp. 11–12)

Issues like those suggested by Kent and Taylor, coupled with an understanding of cultural issues, Hofstede and Hall's cultural categories, nonverbal communication, language, message constraints, and technology, would make for a highly skilled communication professional who has much to offer an organization. Such knowledge, understanding, and skills do not come overnight from a single book, or even from one class; however, with a continuous and concerted effort, any public relations professional can obtain international communication skills.

CONCLUSION

The skills involved in effective intercultural communication have value in all aspects of professional communication. Understanding face, time, power distance, cultural values, ethnocentrism, and other cultural factors give professionals insight and rhetorical skills not understood by others. Additionally, understanding issues like apologia, having an understanding of media relations, and Web design allow public relations professionals to construct more effective messages in international contexts.

ACTIVITIES

1. Using Hofstede's numbers for the U.S. as a baseline, select one of the nations from the list in Table 11.2 and explain how someone from that nation might see the world in light of their score. Comparing the scores of the nation that you selected and the U.S. scores, what should a professional thinking about conducting business in that nation consider?
2. Visit PRNewswire.com and find a local (from your state) news release that interests you. Using Steele and Redding's list of American value premises, write three new headlines and corresponding leads, each using a different value premise. Stick to the basic facts of the story, and do not make anything up.
3. Go to McDonald's Web site (www.aboutmcdonalds.com/mcd/select_your_country_market.html) and visit four countries of your choice. How are cultural values displayed on each site? Be sure to consider the following: typography, color, music, images, products offered, interactivity of the site, and any other apparent "cultural issues." How does each differ from the U.S. site? Be specific. Summarize your answers in a 1.5- to 2-page (single-spaced) memo.
4. A client is interested in reaching out to a large ethnic group in his her city. Select one of the following: An Alaskan Native, Arabic, Korean, or Indian (India) group. Answer the following questions: What cultural issues are likely to be most important when developing messages? What media (local, state, national, other—name them) and medium (print, broadcast, etc.) would be the most effective for reaching members of the cultural group that you selected, and why? Be specific. Conduct some research to answer this question that goes beyond the Internet. Summarize your answers in a 1.5- to 2-page (single-spaced) memo. Include a list of sources consulted at the end (and do not count this in the page total).
5. Assume the following chain of unfortunate events occurred: One of your fellow students, an English major, tells you that he is having trouble in one of his classes because he cannot understand what the

professor wants. He shows you an assignment and you, unwisely, agree to help him with the paper by writing a first draft for him. After the professor grades the paper, he calls the student into his office to talk about the paper. He tells the student that he is going to try and have him expelled for cheating, and wants the name of the student who helped write the paper. Before your friend goes to the professor's office, he asks you if you will come along with him and admit what you did in hopes of saving both of your academic careers. Using the apologia categories, describe how you might use each of Coombs' 10 strategies (denial, bolstering, etc.) in your conversation with the professor. Briefly describe how you would use each strategy in a paragraph. Based on your analysis of the potential strategies, the situation that you are faced with, and your knowledge of the audience (an English professor), what do you believe the best strategy might be, and why?

6. First: Make a list of 10 of the biggest ideological heroes and 10 of the biggest villains from the United States (or your own nation if you are an international student). Note: These are ideological heroes and villains, not social or religious ones. Do not include Jesus, Mary, Mohammed, Krishna, the Devil, Judas, Lassie, Count Dracula, celebrities, or your parents. Make a list of people who have clear social importance. Heroes may include Lincoln, Thomas Edison; villains could be Bernie Madoff, Sam Walton. Second: If any of your selections are not self-evident, like my inclusion of Sam Walton (Wal-Mart) as a villain, be able to justify your choice. Third: Choose from among Hungary, Israel, Kosovo, Russia, and Venezuela and explain which of the people on your list might still be seen as a heroes or villains in that nation, and why. Fourth: In light of your analysis, what historical, mythic, or contemporary figures have rhetorical value if you were constructing a speech to give in that country?

NOTES

1. The "dominant culture" is an intercultural communication term referring to those who are in power. In the U.S., this is mostly older, white men.
2. Some countries, such as India, have so many languages (India has hundreds), that business and everyday affairs are often conducted in a more "universal" language like English or French. The U.K. colonized India for almost two centuries, which is why English is essentially the national language there. As Wikipedia notes: "According to Census of India of 2001, 29 languages are spoken by more than a million native speakers, 122 by more than 10,000" (http://en.wikipedia.org/wiki/Languages_of_India).
3. After this international incident, Gibbons was eventually sentenced to 14 days in jail and deported from the country.

Chapter 12

Important Public Relations Software

Before the invention of affordable computers and software that allowed anyone to become a publisher, public relations professionals' lives were a lot easier. Now, knowing how to use an assortment of software has become a *requirement* for public relations professionals. As suggested in an earlier chapter, because more than half of all public relations professionals will work for small and medium-sized nonprofit, governmental, health, and educational organizations rather than agencies, they are often responsible for developing organizational materials and publications.

Although PCs are more common in the business world—especially abroad, where Macintosh computers are neatly unheard of—design professionals and graphic artists still prefer "Macs," and many communication and journalism programs in the U.S. teach classes on Macs. Since you never know what platform your employer might be using, you should learn to use both Macintosh and Windows.

Macintosh Computers offer the best interface for graphic software, and many organizations allow design professionals to use Mac computers for graphics work. However, since so many businesses and clients are PC based, communication professionals need to be comfortable opening and saving files on any platform and know how to search for files and update virus software on both platforms.

Public relations professionals should know how to use Adobe Acrobat, Illustrator, InDesign, and Photoshop; HTML principles; and word processing programs, and spreadsheet programs like Word and Excel. Learning to use desktop publishing (DTP) software like InDesign, or graphics and photographic software like Illustrator and Photoshop, is not something you can do in a weekend, or something I can teach you in one chapter. Hundreds of books have been written on how to use the major DTP and graphics software. Ultimately, if your school does not require you to take a publication or design course where you learn how to use Adobe products, you must take this course on your own at a community college or neighboring school.

Understanding how to use graphics and publishing software has become one of the skills sought in new professionals. Although you will likely not be hired just for your graphics skills, understanding how to use the programs and how to talk to and work with graphic artists and design professionals is valuable.

Many years ago, one of my colleagues told me about a student assistant he had hired to help with a newsletter. He interviewed several students and asked them all if they knew how to use PageMaker. The student he hired said he did. A day before the project was due to the publisher, my colleague called the student and asked him how the work was progressing, and if he had all of the stories laid out in the newsletter. The student hesitated and replied that he was having some trouble. My colleague asked what was wrong. "You told me that you knew how to use PageMaker." The student replied, "I *do* know how to use it. I opened the folder on the disk you gave me and double clicked on the program. Now what do I do?" That was PageMaker 10 years ago! InDesign and QuarkXPress have replaced PageMaker and are considerably more complex. Although it was theoretically possible to read a short instruction manual on PageMaker and use the program, the same is not true for today's desktop publishing programs.

Many students' knowledge of software applications is not much more sophisticated than the student described above. Thus, I will begin this discussion by covering the basics of word processing. Microsoft Word has become the industry standard. Although Word has many faults, it is still a powerful program once you understand how to use it effectively.

WORD PROCESSING SOFTWARE

Over the last 20 years, several world-processing packages have gained and lost popularity: MacWrite, Nisus, WordPerfect, etc. Microsoft is by no means the best program and will probably be replaced someday by a new program, like the many Web-based word-processors that have been developed. For now, Microsoft Word is probably the most ubiquitous program in the world and the one that you should know how to use.

Microsoft Word does nearly everything a typical public relations practitioner might need to do to produce professional-looking word-processed documents. Word can create mail merges; automatically generate envelopes, labels, bulleted and numbered lists; create templates and simple graphics; designate style sheets; sort lists; and do dozens of other simple desktop publishing functions.

MICROSOFT WORD

Given the prominence of writing in public relations, you will undoubtedly do more writing than other work on your computer. If you use another program like WordPerfect, be sure that you save your files intended for clients in the RTF format or PDF formats (discussed below).

Word has many useful features. However, before I go into any details, the first thing you should learn how to do is customize your toolbar so it has all of the commands you use on a regular basis (or would use if you knew where to find them). Figure 12.1 presents my own toolbars. I will briefly explain how to customize the toolbars and then move on to briefly discussing several of the features found in Word that you should know how to use.

Microsoft Word has a number of toolbars and menus that when open take up more than 60% of the screen area (see Figure 12.2). Turning off the Formatting Pallet and Navigation Pane—as I have done for the examples that follow—frees up about 30% more space. Most of the items on the formatting pallet are rarely used and the formatting pallet only allows for limited customization—you cannot remove or add specific items from individual menus.

If you go to View/Toolbars, you will see a pull-down menu with about 16 possible menus to choose from. Most people typically have two or three toolbars open. If you do not already have "standard" and "formatting" open, do so now. Place your menus where they serve you best. On my laptop, I prefer my menus stacked at the top of the page; however, you can also place them along the sides, or at the bottom if you have a large monitor. Next, point your mouse at each of the items in the menus that you do not recognize and pause for a few seconds. An explanation of what it does will appear. If you do not understand what the feature does (see for example, Figure 12.3, the Format Painter, which most people have never used) then make a note of the toolbar item and check what it does later when you open the "Customize" window.

Make note of the toolbar commands you are sure you would never use. You will be removing them and replacing them. For example, I never use "cut," "copy," or "paste" from the toolbars because I execute these commands from the keyboard with keystroke shortcuts.

Once you have identified what each of the icons in the stock toolbars do, and which commands you probably will not use, go to the "View/Toolbars" menu again, scroll to the bottom, and open "Customize ..." (Figure 12.4): "View/Toolbars/Customize. ..." Select the "Commands" tab (Figure 12.5). Once this window is open, *be very careful with your toolbars and menu bar at the top of the*

FIGURE 12.1 My MSW Toolbar.
Source: Used with permission from Microsoft.

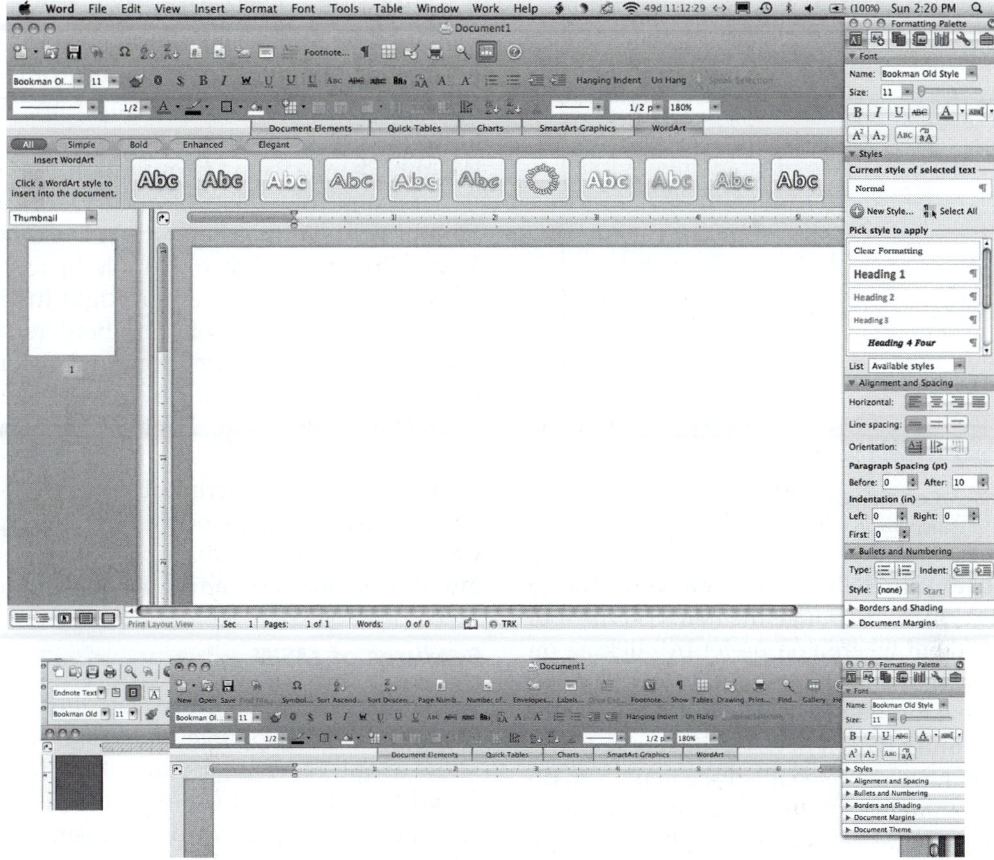

FIGURE 12.2 New Microsoft Word interface and old/new interfaces compared.
Source: Used with permission from Microsoft.

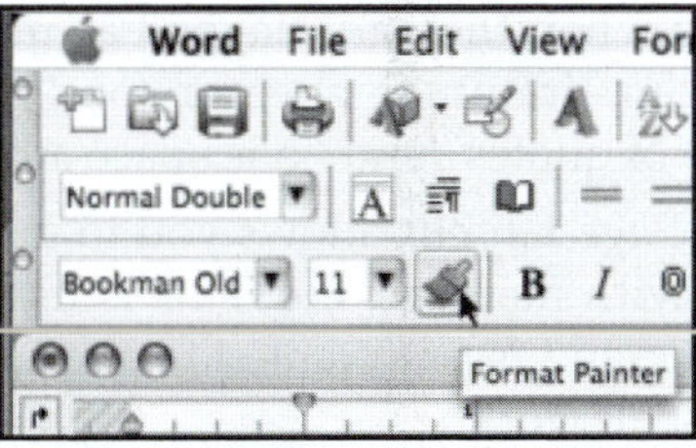

FIGURE 12.3 Picture of Style Painter.
Source: Used with permission from Microsoft.

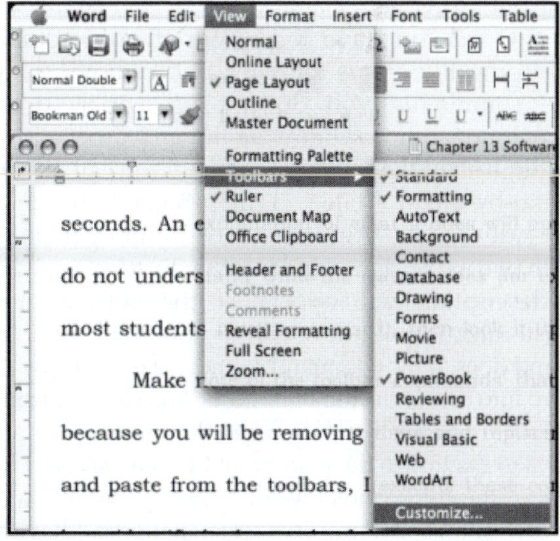

FIGURE 12.4 "Customize" window.
Source: Used with permission from Microsoft.

screen. If you wanted to (do not experiment, trust me), you could remove the "View" menu simply by dragging it off to the side or down out of its location. Once gone, accessing the "reset" button (located in the commands tab) will be very difficult. Here you can browse the various commands and add in any feature you might find useful: there are hundreds of them that you have probably never knew existed.[1]

Begin by dragging all of the commands out of the toolbars you determined earlier you would not use. Simply click on an item and drag it out of its toolbar onto your desktop somewhere. Once pulled out of the menu, let go of the mouse button and the item will disappear. To restore an item if you make a mistake, drag the item from the commands window

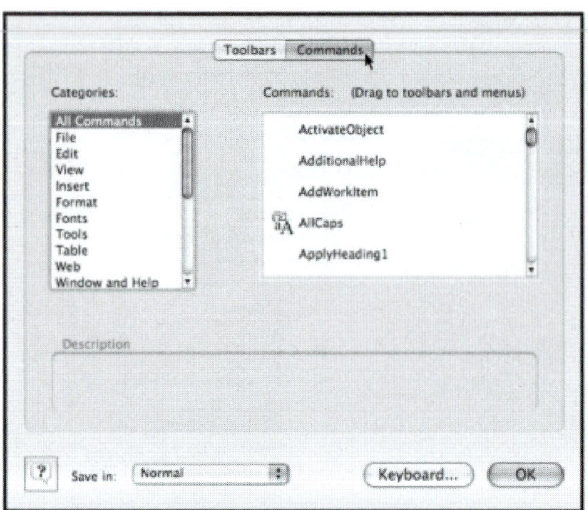

FIGURE 12.5 "Commands" Tab.
Source: Used with permission from Microsoft.

and drop it back into the toolbar where you want to place it. You can also rearrange the items on the tool bar and place them where you prefer by clicking on each one (holding the mouse button down), moving the item to a new location (or a different toolbar), and releasing the mouse button once the item is in place.

After you have removed all of the items you do not want, I recommend closing the "Customize" window and restarting Microsoft Word (MSW) to save the changes. As many of you know, Word can be unstable, so as you proceed with the remainder of the toolbar editing, quit from time to time and restart to prevent losing your changes.

Once you have reconfigured your toolbars, grouping like items together, and removing all of the commands you do not use, open up the "Customization" window again, and proceed to go through *all* of the MSW commands. You can either go menu-by-menu ("File," "Edit," "View," etc., on the left side) or use "All Commands," and then click on each one in the right window. As you select each item, a description will appear at the bottom of the Customization window telling you what each command does. If the command sounds useful, simply drag it up into one of the toolbars. Note: You can "rearrange" the features after you have used the program for a few days to maximize the placement of each feature. I have placed the commands I use regularly in my menu bars to correspond with my own usage patterns. I have also grouped like items together like underlining or changing case to make them easier to locate and use.

Here is a summary of the commands from my own toolbar I have found useful, starting at the top row (Figure 12.1): New Blank Document, Open, Save, Print, Find, Find File, Web Page Preview, Insert a Symbol, List Sort Ascending, List Sort Descending, Insert Page Number, Insert Number of Pages, Create Envelopes, Create Labels, Drop Cap, Insert Note, Show/Hide Formatting, Drawing, Line Style, Line Weight, Change Page Magnification, and Help.

Second row: Style, Normal View, Page Layout, Format Font, Format Paragraph, Document Layout, Single Space, 1.5 Space, Double Space, Align Left Justified, Align Center, Align Right Justified, Align Both Margins, Create Columns, Borders and Shading Menu, Outside Border, Background Color, Highlight Color, Font Color, Fill Effects, More Colors.

Third row: Font, Font Size, Format Painter, Outline, Shadow, Bold, Italic, Word Underline, Dotted Underline, Single Underline, Double Underline, Small Caps, Strikethrough, Double Strikethrough, Change Case, All Capitals, Subscript, Superscript, Bullets, Numbering, Increase Indent, Decrease Indent.[2]

Features of MSW

As mentioned above, MSW has hundreds of commands that most people never use or do not even know about. Here are several of the features I have found to be the most useful. Most of these features are available on any word processing program and will improve your work efficiency.

Preferences/Spelling and Grammar allows you to create a custom dictionary and begin adding words when they are flagged as misspellings. Set your grammar checker for "punctuation inside of quotes" and "one space after periods."

View/Page Layout allows you to see the actual page with margins, etc. This is useful for formatting and is preferable to "normal" view for almost all work.

Insert/Picture/From File allows you to place a graphic into your document. Once a graphic has been placed, you can double click the graphic to open the "Format Picture" menu allowing you to scale the picture to fit, add a border, adjust the text wrap, etc.

Format/Font/Character Spacing allows you to adjust the spacing between characters to reduce or increase the spacing (called kerning). Kerning is very useful when you are one or two words long on a document and want to run the word back. Simply reduce the line spacing of the last line (or last paragraph) by .1–.3 pts, and no one but a graphic artist or typesetter will notice the difference. Note: reducing spacing by whole points will be obvious. A point is 1/72 of an inch. A tenth of a point is 1/720 of an inch.

Format/Paragraph allows you to adjust the spacing before and after paragraphs, set absolute spacing (12.5 pts., 18 pts., 24 pts.) rather than relative spacing (single, double), create hanging indents, force lines to stay together, and set widow and orphan control.

Widow/Orphan control prevents words or lines from being left at the bottom or the top of pages. "Widows" occur when a new paragraph starts at the bottom of a page and only one line of the paragraph will fit on the page. An orphan occurs when a paragraph breaks to the top of another page, with only one line or a few words.

Format/Document allows you to adjust the margins and control the placement of headers and footers.

Format/Bullets and Numbering allows you to designate any of several different types of bullets, or several types of numbered lists. Using automatic bullets and numbering is preferable to creating them manually. Be sure not to use hyphens, periods, o's, and dashes in place of bullets. Learn to make proper bullets and numbered lists.

Format/Borders and Shading allows you to place borders around entire pages, paragraphs or sections, or individual words.

Format/Columns allows you to designate the number of columns you want, alter the width between columns, place lines between columns, or create columns of differing widths.

Format/Drop Caps allows you to create drop or margin caps and to designate how many lines they will span (explained in more detail later).

Format/Style allows you to create style sheets (Figure 12.6). The best way to create style sheets is to close all open documents, open the "Normal" template and set all of the file defaults you want (widow/orphan control, font, spacing, etc.). Designate everything in your template you might want for each style, including header and footer preferences, margins, and tabs. There are dozens of style sheets commands that can be designated. If changes are made to the "Normal" template, then all future documents created will have those parameters and your style sheets will be the same for every new document.

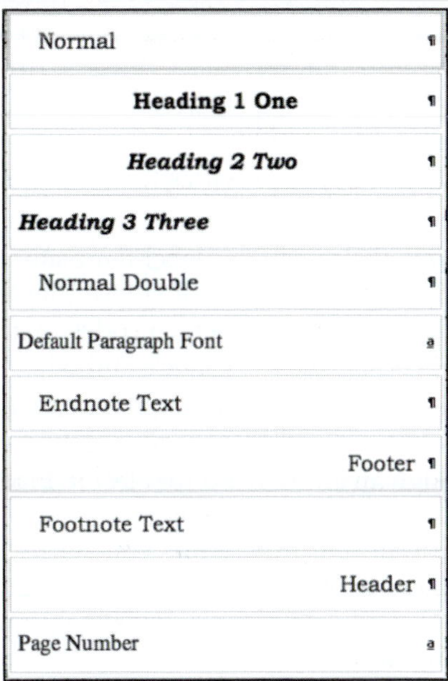

FIGURE 12.6 Format/Style.
Source: Used with permission from Microsoft.

Change the size of a font from the keyboard by highlighting the words, holding the Shift and Command keys, and then hitting the angle bracket (< >) to increase or decrease the font size to the next default size (8, 9, 10, 11, 12, 14, 16, 18, etc.).

Quickly adjust the amount of indentation in a paragraph by using the increase or decrease indent keys. Be sure to install increase or decrease indentation in one of your tool bars. Adjusting the indentation is very common. Changes are made at ½″ increments.

Open the Tools/AutoCorrect ... /AutoCorrect menu and add the following AP style changes: replace "website" with "Web site," webpage with "Web page," "world wide web" with "World Wide Web," "pubic" with "public," and add any other frequently misspelled words. Add to this list anytime you identify mistakes you regularly make or the auto correct function does not already recognize. Over time, you'll have dozens of personalized corrections that relate specifically to your particular typing habits or profession.

Use Tools/Hyphenation ... /Auto hyphenate whenever you are justifying *both* the left and right margins. Note: hyphenation is not used in AP style. However, when creating final draft documents that have both margins justified, you must hyphenate to avoid erratic paragraph spacing.

Tools/Word Count does exactly that, and also counts letters and lines.

Tools/Envelopes provides template for printing envelopes.

Tools/Labels provides label templates for all of the hundreds of types of labels. The templates are based on the numerical codes that come on label packages (Avery labels and others).

Words can be selected by double clicking anywhere in a word. You do not have to drag through an entire word to select it. Placing your cursor anywhere in a word and dragging left or right will select the word you started with, as well as adjacent words or lines. Dragging up, or down, will select entire lines, beginning with the word where you started.

Triple clicking anywhere in a line of text selects the entire paragraph.

Multiple words or blocks of text from different locations in a document may be selected all at once by first selecting a word, paragraph, section, etc., and then holding down the command key while you make additional selections of text from different locations in the document. MSW assembles these selections in the order you highlight them so this feature can be very useful for quickly rearranging sentences, paragraphs, or sections of text (Figure 12.7). Simply highlight the sentences or paragraphs in the order you want, and then cut (or copy) and paste them into a new document or to a new location.

Drag-and-Drop editing is possible (if you have it turned on in the "Preferences/Edit" menu) if you highlight a series of words or paragraphs and then release the mouse button. Then, click anywhere on the highlighted text again (one time) while holding the mouse button down, drag the text to where you want to drop it and then let go of the mouse button. Drag-and-drop editing takes a bit of practice but is worth learning how to do. Text can be dragged to anywhere in the document, up or down, for several pages, and then dropped. On a Macintosh computer, selections dragged off of the page to the desktop and then dropped remain in the document but are copied to the desktop as clippings.

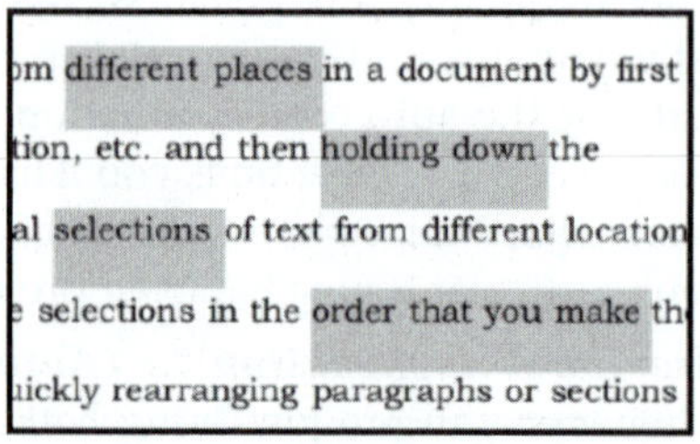

Characters, words, and paragraphs can be duplicated and pasted elsewhere by holding down the command key while moving the highlighted text. For example, say you want to use the same phrase to start several sentences (alliteration). Just highlight the words in question, let go of the mouse button, depress the option key, and "drag-and-drop" the words to the new location. As you begin to move the selected text, a green plus sign will appear indicating the text is being copied rather than moved.

Edit/Find and Change can be used for dozens of purposes if you think through what you want to do. For example, when you are finished with a document, search for all extra spaces (literally, search for two spaces, press the space bar twice), and replace both spaces with one space to eliminate all double spaces after periods, etc. Be sure to run this a few times to be sure triple or quadruple spaces are removed as well (continue "replace all" until you get "zero replacements"). You can also use "Find/Replace" to edit text downloaded from the Internet, as well as dozens of other uses. Be creative, think through what you want to do first, and then do it in several steps. I have often edited a text file (an e-book, for example, from "Gutenberg Project") and stripped out all of the manual line breaks while maintaining the paragraph breaks to make the text easier to read and quote.[3]

Paste Special: When you have text in another format or copied from another document, the Internet, or even a different section of your document, you can use paste (Command/V) to copy the text and formatting features of the typeface. However, by using Edit/Paste Special instead, you can paste the text in a variety of formats, including "unformatted text," which will match the typeface where the text is being inserted.

Insert/Footnote: Microsoft Word automatically changes your footnotes to a default font style

om different places in a document by first
tion, etc. and then holding down the
al selections of text from different location
e selections in the order that you make th
uickly rearranging paragraphs or sections

FIGURE 12.7 Multiple Text Selections in MSW.
Source: © 2010 Michael L. Kent.

different than your "normal" font (unless you have designated a footnote style in your style sheets). Be sure your footnote formatting matches the rest of the document if you are writing in APA style.

Format Painter: the blue paintbrush-looking icon on your toolbar, is very useful. With it you can copy the formatting in one place (a heading or bulleted list) to another. Simply place your cursor in the paragraph where you want to copy the formatting, then click on the style painter. A plus sign will appear next to your cursor, and when you highlight a new word, paragraph, or section (you must drag over the text, not double click), the style will be copied and applied. If you change your mind before you apply the style, simply click the paintbrush again and the plus sign will disappear, or use the "undo" command after the change has been made.

ACCESSIBILITY SOFTWARE: ACROBAT (PDF) & RICH TEXT FORMAT (RTF)

Often you will want to share documents electronically with a colleague at another location or make documents available on your Web site. The four standard document formats that can be read by virtually everyone, everywhere, are Adobe Acrobat (PDF), HTML, text (txt), and Rich Text Format (RTF).

Rich Text Format (RTF)

Rich text format, or RTF, is a universal word processing format that can be read by virtually *every* computer and word processing program (with few exceptions). However, RTF is not a universal data format like PDF. Rich text files are best used when you have to exchange word processing files with colleagues or clients and you are not sure if you both are using the same software. Similarly, rather than posting Microsoft Word documents to the Web (".doc," especially ".docx," which is new), which not everyone can read, you should post RTF files or Acrobat files. RTF has been around for more than 20 years and is one of the most compatible file formats. To create RTF files in MSW, you simply select "File/Save As/Format/Rich Text Format." RTF files will have a ".rtf" suffix rather than ".doc" or ".docx."

Adobe Acrobat, Portable Document Format (PDF)

Adobe Acrobat creates what are called "portable document format" or PDF files. PDF files are saved in a universal format much like data sent to a printer. As Adobe explains:

> Invented by Adobe Systems and perfected over 15 years, Adobe Portable Document Format (PDF) lets you capture and view robust information—from any application, on any computer system—and share it with anyone around the world. Individuals, businesses, and government agencies everywhere trust and rely on Adobe® PDF to communicate their ideas and vision. (www.adobe.com/products/acrobat/adobepdf.html)

Adobe offers a free download of Acrobat, the "Acrobat Reader," so that PDF files can be accessed by anyone. Organizations using Acrobat files often provide a link to Adobe's download site on Web pages that contain PDF files. The latest versions of MSW has an "Adobe Acrobat PDF Maker" toolbar (Mac: View/Toolbars/Adobe Acrobat PDF Maker) that allows you to easily convert Word files into PDF files. Additionally, all Macintosh printing software drivers provide a PDF option in the print window. Thus, virtually anything that can be saved or printed can be turned into a PDF with little effort.

For example, on a Mac, Web pages, and almost any document sent to a printer (graphics, spreadsheets, text files, PowerPoint documents, DTP files), can be converted to a PDF file before the actual print command is selected in the print dialog box. Instead of hitting "print," simply choose to save the document as a PDF file.[4] The PDF option opens a new window asking you where to save the file, what to call it—just like a save command. The PDF document that is created will exactly resemble the file that would have been printed, and still will have limited editing potential.

PDF files are also preferable when you want to control exactly how something looks. Since PDF files just consist of printer data and embedded font data, the recipient does not need to have the same fonts, or even the same program used to create the document, for the file to open and print exactly the same on every computer. PDF files are also used when you want to have strict control over how something will print on other printers. Thus, documents like brochures, fact sheets, forms, and instruction booklets (anything with very precise formatting) that are not saved in the PDF format will look and print differently on different computers unless all of the same

Acrobat Features	
Attach Files to PDFs (like in e-mail) **Attaching PDF files** (to e-mail messages) **Check Spelling** (in comments, boxes, etc.) **Combine Files** (merge multiple files into single PDF, combine pages into one document, etc.). **Copy** (screen capture) **areas of the Page** **Create PDFs** (from other programs, scanner, Web pages, clipboard images, etc.) **Crop Pages** **Create Forms** (from PDF or scanned pages, form field recognition, edit forms, etc.) **Create Check Boxes and List Boxes** **Create Form Fields** **Create Interactive Buttons** **Create Text Fields** **Edit Text in PDF Files** (text can be edited and corrected/changed on completed files) **Export Files** (as EPS, HTML, JPG, RTF, TIFF, Word, etc. Formatted Word files can also be exported). **Free Reader Mac or PC** (allows for editing and markup, forms, etc.) **Full Screen, "Slideshow" mode** (also, automatic page scrolling)	**Grid & Rulers** (including snap-to grid) **Guides** (create layout guides) **Highlight, Underline, or ~~Strikethrough~~ Text** **Insert** (Include) Movies **Interactive Meetings** (Acrobat Connect: Host interactive meetings with others in remote locations) **Optical Character Recognition** (OCR) (OCR will also recognize hand written notes in the margins, if your handwriting is good, and convert to searchable text) **Optimize PDFs** (reduce size, control version of Acrobat, etc.) **Rearrange Pages** (within documents) **Read Out Loud** **Redact** (text or images) **Review & Comment** (sticky notes, markup tools) **Rotate Pages** **Secure** (password encrypt, restrict printing or copying, restrict print resolution to 150 dpi) **Sign** (create legally binding, digital signatures, for contracts, etc.) **Watermark & Backgrounds** (add, remove, update)

FIGURE 12.8 Acrobat Features List.
Source: © 2000 Adobe Systems Incorporated.

fonts are on the recipient computer, and the printers are similar. PDF solves that problem.

As professionals, you should learn how to use Acrobat. Occasionally, you will need to edit PDF files rather than create new files. With Acrobat, you can crop pages; make minor changes to letters, words, and dates; rearrange the order of pages or insert/delete individual pages from files; and create files that require passwords or authentication to alter or change them—which can be very useful for copyrighted documents. See Figure 12.8 for a list of major acrobat features.

GRAPHIC DESIGN SOFTWARE: ILLUSTRATOR, PHOTOSHOP

Adobe illustrator and Photoshop are two of the most powerful programs available for creating graphics, signs, and posters or editing digital photographs. A book on public relations writing is not the place to try to teach you how to use each program. Instead, I will highlight some of the more interesting/useful software features that a professional should learn how to use.

There are currently dozens of books available on each program. If you are willing to spend a few weeks or a month going through some of the tutorials, you can achieve a solid base of knowledge and skills. I recommend purchasing a book or two on both Illustrator and Photoshop and studying them on your own (if you learn well that way), taking a course at your local university, college, or community college on how to use Adobe software, or taking advantage of the many online tutorials like www.Lynda.com, KelbyTrainingLive.com, *Photoshop User* magazine's archives, or the thousands of free podcasts.

Every public relations professional should, at the very least, be acquainted with what is possible with these two programs. Photoshop and Illustrator are standards in the printing and graphic design industries for creating everything from magazine covers and cereal boxes to infographics and special effects on Web sites.

Adobe Illustrator CS5

Illustrator has some powerful features (Figure 12.9). One of the most useful is the ability to edit and alter fonts. For example, fonts can be stretched horizontally or vertically to create interesting/unique logos and

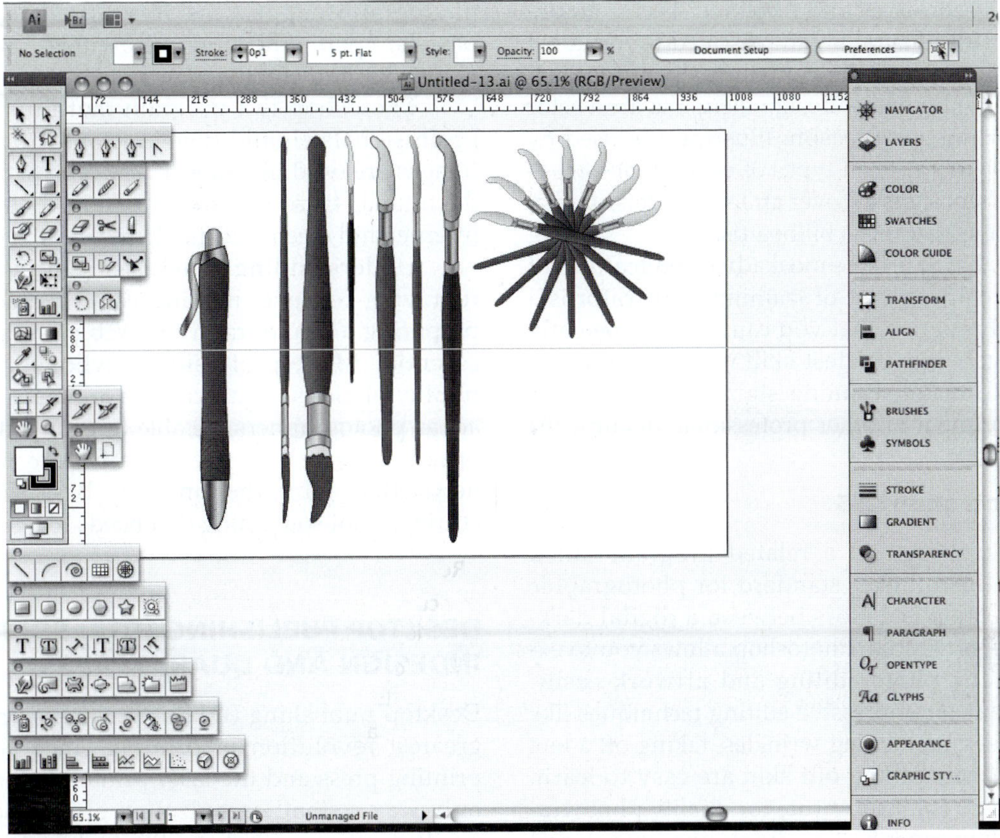

FIGURE 12.9 Illustrator Interface and Menus.
Source: © 2010 Michael L. Kent.

type effects. Additionally, an assortment of special effects can be applied to text or other graphics, including drop shadows, adding color or texture to fonts, intertwining characters or words, and "Distorting & Transforming" fonts (Figures 12.9 and 12.10).

The one thing Illustrator is probably most famous for is its ability to create "vector graphics." Vector graphics are like scalable fonts that look good at any size. For example, the paintbrushes in Figure 12.10 all came from the same brush, drawn once, and then

Bookman Old Style

FIGURE 12.10 Bookman Type face. Stylized in Illustrator.
Source: © 2010 Michael L. Kent.

stretched taller or wider and recolored. Vector graphics created with Illustrator can be scaled up or down without losing any of their quality. Most organizational logos and creative design elements are vector graphics for this very reason. Illustrator is used by professionals to create all types of creative designs—from simple tent signs to cover art for booklets, annual reports, posters, and even billboards.

Being able to use the most advanced features of Illustrator requires a lot of training. Illustrator is a professional program that you cannot just open and use. However, only modest skill is required to use Illustrator to make stunning signs, creative logos, and an assortment of other professional documents.

Adobe Photoshop CS5

Adobe Photoshop, and a related program called Bridge, are the industry standard for photographic work. Photoshop is a cross between a digital darkroom and an art studio. Photoshop allows you to execute dramatic photo editing and artwork easily. Many of the most impressive editing techniques like whitening teeth, removing wrinkles, taking off a few pounds, and smoothing out skin are easy to learn. Although there is no substitute for quality photography, Photoshop can take a mediocre photograph and make it much better.

Photo 12.1 shows a severely underexposed photograph (on the left) of the inside of a church taken near Paderno del Grappa, Italy, taken without a flash (none was allowed in the church). Two friends from a different photograph taken in Greece several years earlier have been extracted from their backgrounds and added to the first image. The exposure of both images was also adjusted, and some noise added so that the image of the two people from Greece would have the same grainy look as the church. Total time for the entire procedure: 15 minutes.

Photoshop also allows you to remove unwanted objects or people from photographs (which is desirable if someone in a group photograph resigns), or extract people from their backgrounds and move them elsewhere, as illustrated in Photo 12.2.

Besides being useful for a variety of special photographic effects, Photoshop also allows you to correct colors (hair, clothing, eyes, objects), eliminate "red eye," and repair damaged photographs (scratched, torn, water damaged, etc.). Photographs can also be easily scaled, cropped, rotated, and montaged. Additionally, Photoshop offers an assortment of filters, and special effects can be applied to make photographs appear as frescos, chalk drawings, pastels, pen and ink drawings, watercolors, woodcuts, and embossed images.

Photoshop is a program that public relations professionals should develop some aptitude with. Images are used in almost every type of professional document, from newsletters and brochures to the Internet and electronic media kits.

Understanding some basic editing skills like removing red eye, making color corrections, and preparing a photograph for Web posting are really essential. Many professionals who work for small public relations organizations are also expected to act as photographers, be able to post pictures to the organization's Web site, and include images in a newsletter—all in the same day. Basic digital photo editing is not something that needs to be outsourced.

DESKTOP PUBLISHING (DTP) SOFTWARE: INDESIGN AND QUARKXPRESS

Desktop publishing (DTP) software is probably the greatest revolution in printing since Gutenberg's printing press and the laser printer. Before DTP, the only way a small organization or individual could produce professional quality publications was to consult a professional printer. Although life was easier when all you had to know was how to use was a typewriter or a word processing program, the freedom to produce professional quality content has opened up tremendous communication possibilities for professionals.

DTP software is not very complicated. What really matters is having some publishing and graphic design skills. If you compared the tools and commands of Illustrator or Photoshop to InDesign or QuarkXPress, for example, you would discover you needed to know a lot more to be able to use most graphics programs than you would to use DTP software. Indeed, if you compared any of the DTP programs to Microsoft Word's interface with a half-dozen to a dozen toolbars, you might get the impression that Word is the hardest program to use.

The average DTP program is not difficult: text, images, objects, and shapes/lines are arranged and manipulated to create print and electronic documents. Indeed, nearly any type of printed document—comic books, telephone books, billboards, textbooks, brochures, and newspapers—can be produced using QuarkXPress or InDesign. In the professional world,

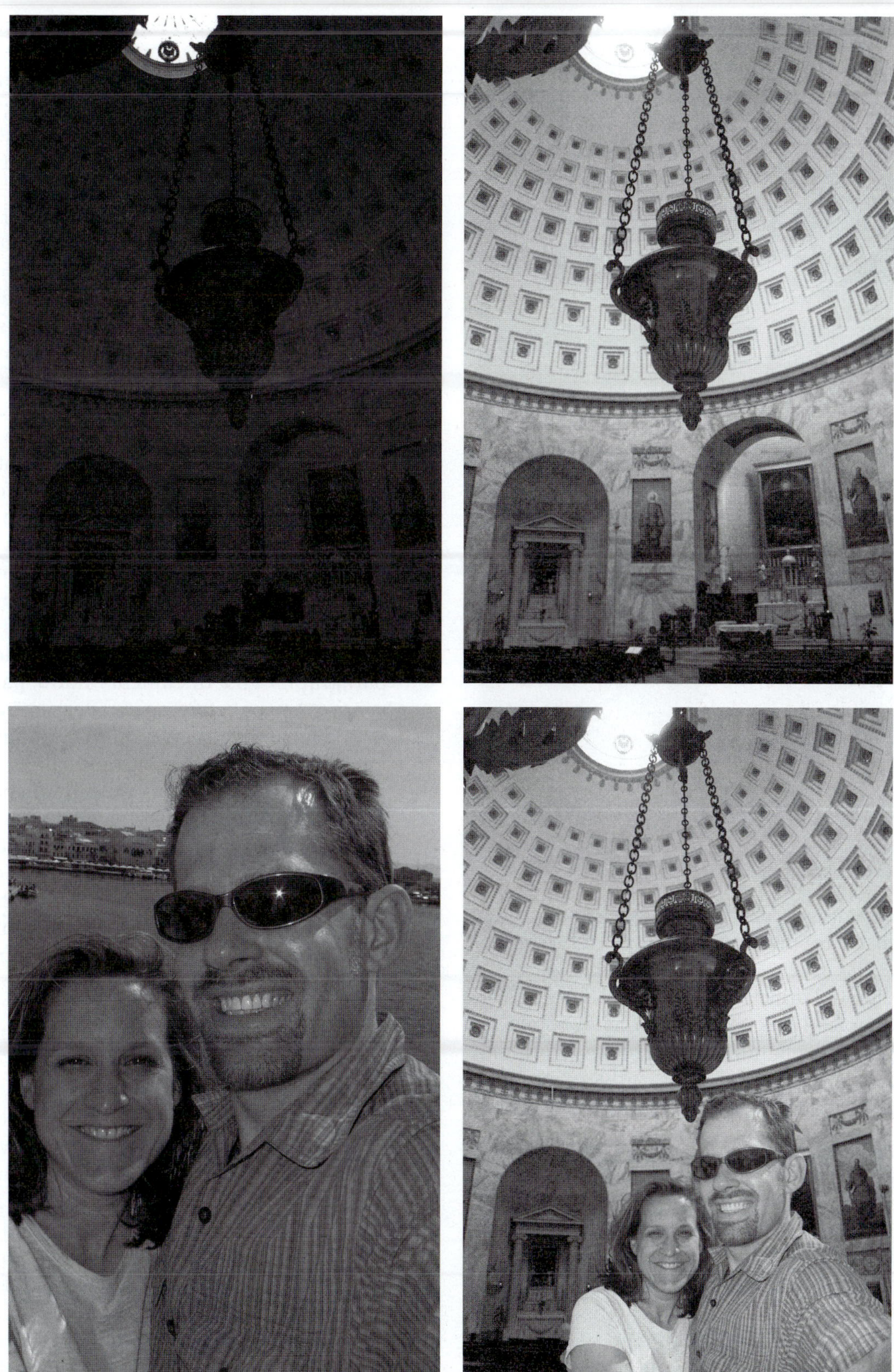

PHOTO 12.1 Color Corrected Photos
Photos Courtesy of Michael L. Kent, © 2010.

PHOTO 12.2 Slovenia, Lake Bled, edited photographs.
Source: Photo Courtesy of Michael L. Kent, © 2010.

99 percent of all print publications in the world (tens of thousands of newspapers, magazines, and annual reports) are produced with one of these two programs.[5]

Knowing the principles of effective design (discussed in Chapter 11) is important when it comes to producing professional documents. The additional skills needed to be able use DTP software are few, and are summarized in the following list:

- ***Style sheets.*** Style sheets allow you to adjust every word, paragraph, or block of text that shares the same style characteristics. All major headings, minor headings, and body text located on any page of a multipage document can be simultaneously changed to something new just by editing the style sheet. By changing the style instructions, the headings on 10 pages or 1,000 pages will all be updated at the same time.
- ***Color management.*** Pantone, and the difference between spot and process color. Understanding color is important to creating consistent organizational documents.
- ***Principles of effective design and layout.*** Learning how to balance elements on a page, create symmetrical and asymmetrical layouts, place photographs and graphics effectively, as well as using typography well is important.
- ***Cropping and scaling photographs.*** Effective cropping and scaling is necessary to create professional-looking layouts.
- ***Using text wrap.*** Professional documents integrate photographs and typography. Using text wrap improves the appearance of final draft documents.
- ***Grids, rules, and rulers.*** These ensure perfect alignment. All DTP programs have several types of rule options. Perfect alignment is difficult without taking advantage of the layout tools. Some programs like InDesign have automatic "Smart Guides" that allow for very precise alignment without the need for grid lines.
- ***Leading*** (spacing between lines), **kerning** (spacing between letters), **tracking** (adjusting the space between all of the words and letters in paragraphs and documents), **and paragraph spacing** (space before, space after) are important to understanding type and important in design.
- ***Hyphenation.*** All programs allow manual hyphenation as well as auto-hyphenation in order to achieve a professional appearance.
- ***Text flow.*** Use this to flow text from section to section.
- ***Most Importantly: Develop attention to detail.*** This will ensure that everything in a multipage document layout is exactly the same from section to section and page to page.

USING TYPE EFFECTIVELY

Everyone knows that when you create a document using a word processor you use Times New Roman as your font, right? Wrong. The more important question is, Why do so many people use Times for everything? Times was originally created for the *New York Times* in 1931 to accommodate more words on the page (Potlatch Papers, 1999). The font was designed to be denser and more readable at small sizes than the font that the *Times* was using at the time. Since most writing is not about putting more words on a page but having a clear message, why is Times still so widely used today? Times was never intended to become a universal font. If you look at the publisher information in the front of books or journals, you will find that many sources list the font(s) in which the document has been typeset. Times is used occasionally, but is more common when space is at a premium—the purpose for which it was designed. More commonly, fonts like Bodoni, Caslon, Galliard, Garamond, or Palatino are used because they are better suited for book text (see, <www.adobe.com/type/fontfinder>, "Body Text"). The reason Times is so widely used as a default font by Microsoft and Apple is probably because Times was popular with computer scientists when word processing programs were first created, not because it has any unique typographic features or aesthetic beauty, apart from its intended use as a dense and legible font at small sizes.

In order to use type effectively, you need to understand the role that type plays in designing effective documents. As Boag explains:

> Typography is designing with type in order to communicate a message ... You might easily be tempted to "jazz up" your documents with all the special effects you can muster—if you do this, you may end up having more fun than your readers. Restraint is essential so that the content of documents is clearly understood. (1992, p. 5)

Typography and design is as much about the audience, as rhetoric and persuasion are about audiences.

The font you select can have a dramatic impact on the feeling of professionalism, playfulness, or excitement engendered by a document. Many organizations have specific organizational fonts or "house styles" that they use for everything, so that all their messages resemble each other. In order to create harmonious documents, you need to understand typography and some of its basic rules. Understanding typefaces (or fonts) is one of the best places to begin.

Understanding Type

As Kent (2005a) explains in the *Encyclopedia of Public Relations*, fonts are grouped into categories like modern (Helvetica, Bernhard Modern, Times Roman), old style (Baskerville, Bookman Old Style, Palatino), heading/titling (**Benguiat Gothic Heavy**, **Caslon Black**, Officiana Sans), display/decorative (**Cooper Black**, **JUNIPER**, OXFORD, **VAG Rounded Black**), script (*Zapf Chancery*, *Zapfino*), and blackletter (Old English). Fonts are also grouped into **serif fonts**, or those fonts with serifs (curls or flourishes on the end of characters), and **sans serif fonts**. Arial is a sans serif font and Bookman is a serif font. Fonts are selected for readability as well as for the "feel" they impart. Fonts like "Wild Thing," "Van Rose," and "**STENCIL**" are called titling fonts and are used at larger sizes in titles and headings to create a particular mood. Titling fonts are not appropriate for use as body text or for extended textual content.

Fonts that share the same basic shape/style/proportion characteristics but vary in weight, width, or size are called **font families**. An example of a font family is Helvetica, which includes dozens of different versions, including Helvetica Roman, **Helvetica Black**, **Helvetica Compressed**, Helvetica Neue, Helvetica Neue Light, Helvetica Neue Ultra Light, **Helvetica bold**, Helvetica Narrow, and more than 70 other weights, widths, and styles.

Many graphic artists and designers fall back on only a few great fonts for most purposes. Many of you already have some of the best fonts on your computer, such as Akzidenz-Grotesk, Baskerville, Benguiat, **Bodoni**, Bookman, Caslon, **Cooper Black**, Didot, Franklin Gothic, Frutiger, Galliard, Garamond, Gill Sans, Goudy, Helvetica, Janson, Optima, Palatino, Sabon, and *Zapf*, and others (Biegeleisen, 1995; Meggs & Carter, 1993). Indeed, using only *one* large type family such as Helvetica, a professional designer can create entire books, annual reports, newsletters, advertisements, posters, signs, or any other document.

Examine some of your books, magazines, newspapers, or even the labels on products in the supermarket. Almost all professional documents use variations and weights of the same font, rather than different fonts, so that everything in the document has the same look and feel (consistency/harmony).

Therefore, one of the rules of effective typography is to use only a couple of fonts (or a single font family) per document. By using a font *family* like Helvetica, an individual has the ability to create headings (using **Helvetica Black**, **Helvetica Compressed**, or 70 other typeface variations), or to change the aesthetic feel of a document by using a narrow typeface, or reducing the character weight. A designer will often use a sans serif font like Helvetica for headings and a serif font like Caslon or Sabon for body text. As a rule, stay away from combining two serif or two sans serif fonts in documents. With the possible exception of display or titling fonts, which might be in any typeface useful for attracting attention, body text is usually presented in a serif font and headings in san serif fonts.

Another thing to keep in mind is that fonts are not free. Although you have many fonts on your computer, you probably have very few of the "best," most professional fonts used in publishing. A single typeface of a particular font may cost $25–$100, and a whole font *family* may cost $500–1,000.[6] Several of the most respected type companies are Adobe (www.adobe.com/type), Monotype (www.fonts.com), ITC (www.itcfonts.com), and Linotype (www.linotype.com).

Determine Proper Type Size

One of the hallmarks of professional design is conservativeness of the font size. Examine several professional business cards. The font on most business cards is *very* small, on the order of 6–8 points. Even the person's name on the business card is unlikely to be any larger than about 9–10 points. Conservativeness in font size applies equally to most other kinds of printed documents (books, magazines, product packaging). One of the best places to see typography used well is to go to the supermarket and look at product packaging. Labels are designed to be distinctive, to make products stand out, and to be read from about 3–5 feet. The brand of product and the name of products are usually the only things on a package that can be read from a distance. The other textual elements on the package will be in much smaller type sizes that can only be read if the item is picked up. The same holds true for almost all printed materials, such as books and magazines, posters, and other informational documents. Start paying attention to type as you look at professional documents so you can develop an eye for typography and learn how to use type well.

Type Mechanics

Understanding the mechanics of type is important. Fonts are measured in **points**. There are 72 points per inch (see appendix D for details). Here is Bookman Old Style in five different type sizes:

6 point: ABCDEFGHIJKLMNOPQRSTUVWXYZabcdefghijklmnopqrstu vwxyz1234567890¥¶ (1/12")

9 point: ABCDEFGHIJKLMNOPQRSTUVWXYZ abcdefghijklmnopqrstuvwxyz123456 (1/8")

12 point: ABCDEFGHIJKLMNOP QRSTUVWXYZabcdefghijkl (1/6")

18 point: ABCDEFGHI JKLMNOPQRST (1/4")

24 point: ABCD EFGHIJKL (1/3")

A 12-point font will typically yield six lines per inch of text at single spacing. We say "typically," because as Bruno explains: "Corresponding letters in the same size type may vary in height. We say that the face is either small on body ... or large on body" (2000, p. 37). For example, below are 24-point lower case Xs, all in different fonts. Notice the **x-height** (the height of the lower case letter x) varies a great deal, even though each letter is typeset at 24-points.[7]

x x x x x x x x x

Ultimately, what matters is how the font looks on the printed page rather than what size the font is set at. Another type concept to understand is leading.

Leading (pronounced LED-ing, from hot lead type) refers to the spacing between lines of text (Lupton, 2004, p. 83). There is no absolute rule for how much leading to use. Leading is visual. Leading is reduced or increased to facilitate readability and to achieve typographic effects. Some typefaces look better with a bit more space added between lines of type, and some typefaces look better with a less space. Consider the examples in Figure 12.3. Notice that the 8/8, 8/9, and 9/9 passages are more difficult to read, while the 8/10 and 9/10 and 9/11 are easier.[8] Decisions about leading are made by the eye. As Figure 12.3 illustrates, you cannot just assume every 10-point font is equally legible. Over time, you will develop a better understanding of what spacing works best with particular typefaces and sizes and what can be done to achieve particular aesthetic effects.

Line Lengths also influence readability. In general, the rule of thumb is to create lines about 9–10 words long or about 55–60 characters in length (White, 2002; <www.adobe.com/education/pdf/type_primer.pdf>, p. 5). Begin looking at how type

TABLE 12.1 Paragraph Leading Examples, Chart for Calculating Leading

Bookman Old Style 8/8

Had Grant been a Congressman one would have been on one's guard, for one knew the type. One never expected from a Congressman more than good intentions and public spirit. Newspaper-men as a rule had no great respect for the lover house; Senators had less; and Cabinet officers had none at all. Indeed, one day when Adams was pleading with a Cabinet officer for patience and tact in dealing with Representatives, the Secretary impatiently broke out: "You can't use tack with Congressman! A Congressman is a hog! You must take a stick and hit him on the snout!"—Henry Adams, *The Education of Henry Adams*

Bookman Old Style 8/9

Had Grant been a Congressman one would have been on one's guard, for one knew the type. One never expected from a Congressman more than good intentions and public spirit. Newspaper-men as a rule had no great respect for the lover house; Senators had less; and Cabinet officers had none at all. Indeed, one day when Adams was pleading with a Cabinet officer for patience and tact in dealing with Representatives, the Secretary impatiently broke out: "You can't use tack with Congressman! A Congressman is a hog! You must take a stick and hit him on the snout!"—Henry Adams, *The Education of Henry Adams*

Bookman Old Style 8/10

Had Grant been a Congressman one would have been on one's guard, for one knew the type. One never expected from a Congressman more than good intentions and public spirit. Newspaper-men as a rule had no great respect for the lover house; Senators had less; and Cabinet officers had none at all. Indeed, one day when Adams was pleading with a Cabinet officer for patience and tact in dealing with Representatives, the Secretary impatiently broke out: "You can't use tack with Congressman! A Congressman is a hog! You must take a stick and hit him on the snout!"—Henry Adams, *The Education of Henry Adams*

Bookman Old Style 9/9

Had Grant been a Congressman one would have been on one's guard, for one knew the type. One never expected from a Congressman more than good intentions and public spirit. Newspaper-men as a rule had no great respect for the lover house; Senators had less; and Cabinet officers had none at all. Indeed, one day when Adams was pleading with a Cabinet officer for patience and tact in dealing with Representatives, the Secretary impatiently broke out: "You can't use tack with Congressman! A Congressman is a hog! You must take a stick and hit him on the snout!"—Henry Adams, *The Education of Henry Adams*

Bookman Old Style 9/10

Had Grant been a Congressman one would have been on one's guard, for one knew the type. One never expected from a Congressman more than good intentions and public spirit. Newspaper-men as a rule had no great respect for the lover house; Senators had less; and Cabinet officers had none at all. Indeed, one day when Adams was pleading with a Cabinet officer for patience and tact in dealing with Representatives, the Secretary impatiently broke out: "You can't use tack with Congressman! A Congressman is a hog! You must take a stick and hit him on the snout!"—Henry Adams, *The Education of Henry Adams*

Bookman Old Style 9/11

Had Grant been a Congressman one would have been on one's guard, for one knew the type. One never expected from a Congressman more than good intentions and public spirit. Newspaper-men as a rule had no great respect for the lover house; Senators had less; and Cabinet officers had none at all. Indeed, one day when Adams was pleading with a Cabinet officer for patience and tact in dealing with Representatives, the Secretary impatiently broke out: "You can't use tack with Congressman! A Congressman is a hog! You must take a stick and hit him on the snout!"—Henry Adams, *The Education of Henry Adams*

is used in advertisements, brochures, books, and other documents, and acquire copies of appealing design choices for your swipe file. You can gather design ideas from professional graphics arts magazines, such as *How* (www.howdesign.com), *InDesign* (www.indesignmag.com), or *Photoshop User* (www.photoshopuser.com).

THE IMPORTANCE OF HYPHENATION

As with leading, hyphenation and alignment choices are not made by accident but to create specific formatting effects (cf., Lupton, 2004, pp. 84–85). As a rule, when you create a final draft document or a document where both margins are justified, you must use hyphenation. **Hyphenation** involves breaking long words between syllables so that lines of type appear more uniform. Hyphenating documents will give them a more professional appearance. Consider the examples of the same passage in Tables 12.2 and 12.3.

Simply turning on the "auto hyphenate" command will make the passage look tighter and more professional, eliminating the gaps that appear between words and letters. When using professional Desktop Publishing DTP software like InDesign or QuarkXPress, tighter control over spacing is possible, and professional-looking paragraph layouts may be achieved. Lines of type with inconsistent word spacing are more difficult to read and should be corrected with hyphenation and "tracking" (a feature that adjusts the spacing between letters and words).

KERNING AND TRACKING

Adjusting the space between characters is called **kerning;** this is measured in points and fractions of points. Kerning can be increased or decreased to achieve specific typographic effects. Learn to adjust character spacing using the commands of the word processing or design program you use, rather than trying to add spaces after each letter. Kerning is most important when dealing with fonts at large type sizes like in headlines and titles. Additionally, a small amount of kerning between words and letters (called tracking) over a lengthy document could reduce the overall size of the printed document by several pages. More often, when a document runs over to another page by a line or two, tightening the tracking of the document will bring the line back to the previous page, saving an entire page and making the document appear more professional (see Figure 12.4 for a tracking example).

When we look at a word typed at 12-points, small differences in spacing between letters are less apparent. Most typefaces will automatically adjust the kerning between common letter pairs, like the lowercase F and I (fi), F and L (fl), and T and I (ti) that are used in words like "time," "fire," and "flat." (See Table 12.4). Notice how the I is actually slid under the F and looks like it is part of a single letter. Combined letters are called "ligatures" (and you probably never noticed them at body text size). When we look at the same word at a bigger type size, 36, 48, or 72 points, letters sometimes appear too far apart, and ligatures sometimes appear misshapen. Ligatures rely on an optical illusion to make words more legible. The effect only works at smaller type sizes. Letter pairs that

TABLE 12.2 Sample Hyphenated Paragraphs

Clifford Stoll (1999, p. xiv).

I believe that good schools need no computers. And a bad school won't be much improved by even the fastest Internet links. That a good teacher can handle her subject without any multimedia support. That the enjoyment of scholarship has nothing to do with making learning fun. That it's unnecessary—and misleading—to push children's work onto the Internet. That students, justifiably, recognize computer assignments primarily as entertainment, rather than education.

Left justified, no hyphenation

I believe that good schools need no computers. And a bad school won't be much improved by even the fastest Internet links. That a good teacher can handle her subject without any multimedia support. That the enjoyment of scholarship has nothing to do with making learning fun. That it's unnecessary—and misleading—to push children's work onto the Internet. That students, justifiably, recognize computer assignments primarily as entertainment, rather than education.

Left justified, hyphenation

I believe that good schools need no computers. And a bad school won't be much improved by even the fastest Internet links. That a good teacher can handle her subject without any multimedia support. That the enjoyment of scholarship has nothing to do with making learning fun. That it's unnecessary—and misleading—to push children's work onto the Internet. That students, justifiably, recognize computer assignments primarily as entertainment, rather than education.

Both margins justified, no hyphenation

I believe that good schools need no computers. And a bad school won't be much improved by even the fastest Internet links. That a good teacher can handle her subject without any multimedia support. That the enjoyment of scholarship has nothing to do with making learning fun. That it's unnecessary—and misleading—to push children's work onto the Internet. That students, justifiably, recognize computer assignments primarily as entertainment, rather than education.

Both margins justified, hyphenation

I believe that good schools need no computers. And a bad school won't be much improved by even the fastest Internet links. That a good teacher can handle her subject without any multimedia support. That the enjoyment of scholarship has nothing to do with making learning fun. That it's unnecessary—and misleading—to push children's work onto the Internet. That students, justifiably, recognize computer assignments primarily as entertainment, rather than education.

Both margins justified, hyphenation, tracking

TABLE 12.3 Differently Justified Paragraphs

Justified type is very common on all final draft documents. Justifying both margins creates a nice, clean line of text and achieves a professional look. For justified text to work best, you must use hyphenation (which I have not done here); otherwise, lines of type may have very different spacing. When you hyphenate, you also need to avoid ladders (rows of stacked hyphens), which spoil the clean line of text blocks. Sometimes you need to manually hyphenate your text to force words to break properly. What you want to achieve with text blocks is for paragraphs to have a grayish look (called the "color" of the paragraph), with no inconsistent gaps between words. Squint your eyes and look at this paragraph and the next and you will notice that the left justified paragraph has more consistent color because of the left justification and hyphenation.

Left justification (called "ragged right") is used to avoid the uneven text that can occur with justified text, especially at larger type sizes. When you use ragged left or ragged right, you want to try to avoid uneven lines, with some lines very long and others shorter. Most formal professional documents like business letters are typed with a ragged right margin. Justifying both margins is usually reserved only for final draft documents, such as newsletters, annual reports, etc. When hyphenation is not used with left or right justification, the lines may look overly jagged, as they do here, where there is no hyphenation.

Right justification (called "ragged left") is often used stylistically to break up monotony, in headings, and to create margin notes, and sidebars. Right justification can be an effective way of showing hierarchy as well as drawing a reader's eyes to a specific page location. As with left justification and justifying both margins, use hyphenation. Watch what happens when this paragraph is repeated with hyphenation:

Right justification (called
"ragged left") is often used sty-
listically to break up monotony,
in headings, and to create margin
notes and sidebars. Right justifi-
cation can be an effective technique.

Centered text is used to show formality and to create hierarchy.
Very often, titles and headings are centered.
Do not center *everything* on a page
unless you have a compelling reason to do so.
Centered text is often used in pull quotes and for subheadings.
When creating headings, subheadings, and pull quotes,
do not hyphenate!
Instead, break your lines for readability and clarity.
Hyphenate only when absolutely necessary.

TABLE 12.4 Kerning & Ligatures

final final, final final, final final, final final

flat flat, flat, flat, flat, flat flat, flat, flat, flat

Michael Michael, Mich Mich, Mich Mich, Mich Mich, Mich

look fine at 9–12 points often appear too wide at headline or titling sizes.

START COLUMNS AT THE SAME HEIGHT

When creating blocks of text, as you might with columns in a newsletter or an annual report, starting columns at the same level or height is more important than where each column ends. For example, headings and titles in magazines and newspapers typically span the entire story so that the text columns that relate to a particular headline all begin at the same level, underneath the headline. That the individual columns may not be as long as each other because of advertisements or graphics is not really a problem because readers know that when a column ends, they skip back to the top. If the columns at the top are placed at different levels, however, readers may face a moment of confusion as they try to determine where to go next.

Group Copy Blocks

Blocks of text, like stories in a newsletter, need to be organized so that readers know where to go. When you design text content, do not break up three-column layouts with a picture or graphic in the middle of a column because it may not be self-evident where readers should go next: should they go back to the top of the next column, or skip past the graphic and continue down the column (see Figure 12.11)? More importantly, never position a graphic in the center of a wide column of text and require the reader to skip back and forth to either other side of the graphic to read the content. Instead, pull the graphic off to the side, or move it to the top or bottom corner of the layout.

Readers get confused when they are not clear about whether to jump over a graphic to continue reading a story or move to the top of an accompanying column. If a document layout allows for it, pull graphics partially out to the side of the column and allow the text to wrap around them so the reading flow is not disrupted; or place graphics at the bottom or top of columns so readers know how to read the document. When a graphic spans several columns, the best design solution is often to move the graphic to the bottom or top of the page and add a clear identifying caption.

USE STYLE SHEETS

In publishing, a style sheet is a sample page listing all of the designated styles for a document (brochure, newsletter, book, etc.). A style sheet helps typesetters and proofreaders make sure that all of the design elements in a document are consistent. The modern technology of word processing and desktop publishing allows you to create electronic style sheets that can be applied to sections of text with the click of the

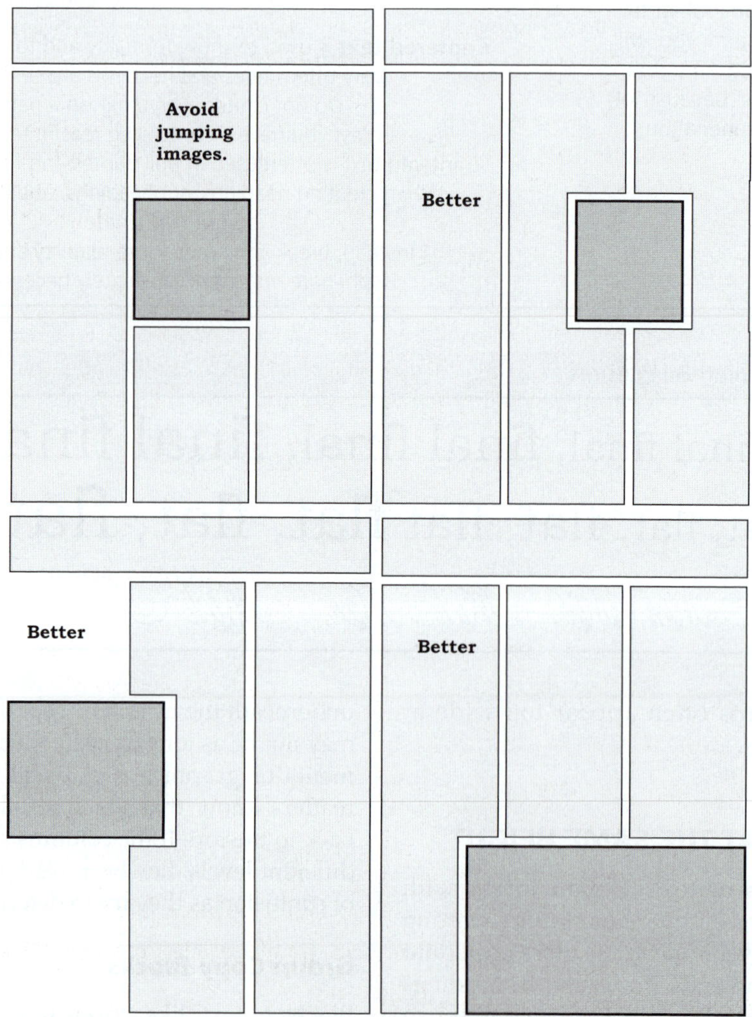

FIGURE 12.11 Grouped Copy Blocks.

mouse. The significance of a style sheet is that it allows you to globally update all of the instances of specific graphic or textual styles (font, size, leading, kerning, color, alignment, drop shadows).

A **style sheet** is essentially a set of instructions for how to format paragraphs and text (font, color, spacing, border, indenting, etc.). Style sheets are one of the most powerful and useful tools that you can use to create lengthy or sophisticated documents or projects (see Figure 12.12).

For example, imagine you created a 32-page newsletter for a client using different typographic styles (two font families in different weights and sizes) for headings and subheadings, body text, pull quotes, and tables of contents. Once the client sees the newsletter, s/he decides the headlines should be in a different typeface, and informs you that s/he does not like the style on the block quotes. If you used style sheets to create the newsletter, all you have to do is edit the style instructions on the style sheet for these items. Once saved, every font/paragraph in the entire document that is assigned that style will be automatically updated.

Similarly, imagine that after this book was nearly completed, we make a decision to change all of the major headings from Gill Sans to Akzidenz-Grotesk, and then to base the lower order headings on the new font. As you can imagine, just making one such change could easily take hours (or days) for a project of this length. And then, after the change was made, the book would have to be examined very carefully—in changing hundreds of headings by hand, some mistakes would inevitably occur. Now, imagine another realistic possibility. We make a decision to change the body text. Obviously, a global "change all" would also change all of the headings. Thus, were it not for style sheets, each section of body text would need to be manually selected and changed by hand to the new font.

In professional practice, decisions to change fonts really do happen all the time. Occasionally, a client will decide s/he does not like a particular font or some design element that runs through an entire project. Making design changes can slow down productivity for days if style sheets have not been used.

Using style sheets involves setting up a few typographic instructions at the beginning of a job—or as you work—and then just clicking on the appropriate style buttons as you progress through the document. Style sheets can be found in word processing programs as well as in DTP programs like InDesign and QuarkXPress. Once style sheets have been created and paragraph formatting assigned to specific "styles," all

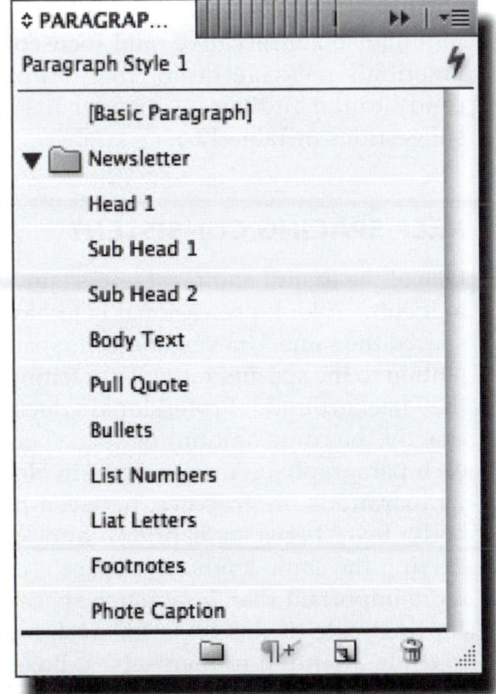

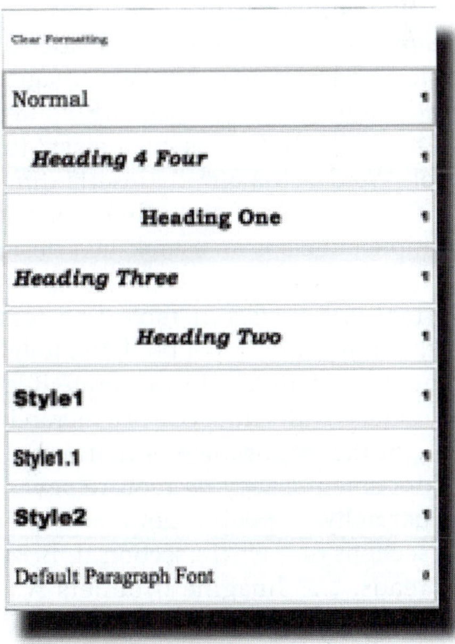

FIGURE 12.12 Grouped Copy Blocks & Graphic.

someone has to do to change all of the paragraphs that share a style is to change the instructions in the style sheet and, *voilà*, everything updates automatically. Moreover, by using style sheets, you can easily experiment with different looks by altering headings, colors, bullets, body text, and other textual features in seconds. Style sheets are tremendously useful, and worth experimenting with and learning how to use. Style sheets allow for increased productivity, clarity, and hierarchy.

STRIVE FOR SIMPLICITY, CLARITY, AND HIERARCHY

The KISS rule ("Keep it simple, Stupid") always applies to graphic design. You need to ask yourself, honestly, whether a new design element helps to clarify the layout or if it is only being used because it is "cool." Just because you can make a "whirling, flaming, spinning logo" for your organization's Web site does not mean you should. Just because you *have* "cat bullets" (dingbats that resemble cats) does not mean your newsletter needs them.

Will novel or creative design elements improve the overall clarity and persuasiveness of your message? Many novice design professionals allow their word processing programs to automatically add different kinds of bullets as they indent sections. Unfortunately, clearer messages are not obtained simply by using different bullets. The important question is whether different bullets make the next level of hierarchy clearer or easier to follow. Consider the examples in Table 12.5: Do diamond bullets or square bullets really add anything or make the content clearer? Does a hierarchy of bullets even exist? Just because Microsoft Word automatically inserts different bullets at different levels of an outline does not mean using multiple bullets is an established design technique.

The important visual cues in Table 12.5 come from the *indents*, not the bullets, the bold, the italics, or the numbering. Bullets are used to separate items on a list, not to designate different levels of a hierarchy. A good example of the importance of hierarchy is found in legal documents; they *do* require several clear levels of hierarchy so people can make reference to specific sections of law: "In section II, B, 3, i, a, the contract reads. …" Imagine if bullets were used instead of letters and numbers: "In section black bullet, open bullet, square bullet, diamond bullet, and about five star bullets down. …" Different bullets do not facilitate *discussion* of complicated documents, nor are multiple bullet styles needed to clarify messages.

If bullets are not being used to clarify your message, then all that is needed is visual clarity. Geometric bullets, fish bullets, and star bullets are not necessary to clarify a message. The same content is just as clear without any bullets at all, or with only one type of bullet, since the clarity of the content comes, most effectively, from indenting and typography (including bold, italics, and capitals) and not the bullets.

MINIMIZE THE NUMBER OF ELEMENTS ON A PAGE

Whenever possible, group photos together as part of a design block rather than spreading them around the page, or interspersing them throughout the text. Too many design elements on a page—whether symbols, pictures, fonts, or headings—will result in a less professional-looking layout. Examine some professional publications. Magazines such as *People* or *Soap Opera Digest* might fill a page with overlapping photographs of celebrities, text, color swatches, and other design features, but such layouts are very uncommon in more reserved, professional publications like the *Economist*, annual reports, newsletters, brochures, and training manuals. Professional documents tend to be much more minimalist, conservative, and focused on the organization's message rather than on providing eye candy to the audience. Consider the list of design suggestions in Table 12.6.

KEEP SPACING CONSISTENT

One of the easiest and most important ways to make a document look professional is to have everything spaced the same. Uneven or erratic spacing draws attention to the spacing rather than letting it blend into the background. Professional documents have exactly the same amount of space before and after each paragraph, on inset spacing in block quotes, on wraparounds on graphics, between headlines and body text, between captions and graphics, etc. Having the same amount of space *everywhere* is far more important than how much space you use. The cardinal rule of design is for design elements not to draw attention to themselves. Boxes should not appear out of alignment, text should not have 7-points of leading in one place and 8.5-points in another, etc.

TABLE 12.5 Visual Hierarchy Illustrations

HIERARCHY
- Numbering
  - Roman
  - Capitalized
  - Lower case
- Indenting
  - Hanging
  - Tabbed
  - Spaced
- Wording
  - Symmetrical
  - Consistent
  - Equivalent

HIERARCHY
- *Numbering*
  - Roman
  - Capitalized
  - Lower case
- *Indenting*
  - Hanging
  - Tabbed
  - Spaced
- *Wording*
  - Symmetrical
  - Consistent
  - Equivalent

HIERARCHY
- **Numbering**
  - Roman
  - Capitalized
  - Lower case
- **Indenting**
  - Hanging
  - Tabbed
  - Spaced
- **Wording**
  - Symmetrical
  - Consistent
  - Equivalent

HIERARCHY
1. Numbering
   a. Roman
   b. Capitalized
   c. Lower case
2. Indenting
   a. Hanging
   b. Tabbed
   c. Spaced
3. Wording
   a. Symmetrical
   b. Consistent
   c. Equivalent

HIERARCHY
- • Numbering
  - ◦ Roman
  - ◦ Capitalized
  - ◦ Lower case
- • Indenting
  - ◦ Hanging
  - ◦ Tabbed
  - ◦ Spaced
- • Wording
  - ◦ Symmetrical
  - ◦ Consistent
  - ◦ Equivalent

HIERARCHY
- • Item 1 A
- • Item 1 B
  - ◦ Item II A
  - ◦ Item II B
    - o Item III A
    - o Item III B
      - ✶ Item IV A
      - ✶ Item IV B

HIERARCHY
- Item 1A
- Item 1B
  - Item IIA
  - Item IIB
    - Item IIIA
    - Item IIIB
      - Item IVA
      - Item IVB

HIERARCHY
- • Item 1A
- • Item 1B
  - • Item IIA
  - • Item IIB
    - • Item IIIA
    - • Item IIIB
      - • Item IVA
      - • Item IVB

Be sure to carefully align *everything* the *same* in all documents. The best spacing is "invisible."

USING PULL QUOTES AND DROP CAPS FOR EMPHASIS

Pull quotes can be found in magazines, books, annual reports, newspapers, brochures, fact sheets, and newsletters. A **pull quote** refers to a few sentences or a paragraph of quoted text pulled out of a document to attract attention. Pull quotes are placed in boxes, pulled to the side, inserted between lines, placed in a different typeface, or otherwise emphasized to make the message stand out from the surrounding text. Pull quotes work like headlines, captions, and graphics. Indeed, pull quotes often serve as a form of inexpensive graphic intended to draw attention to a specific point, just

TABLE 12.6 Top Ten Design Suggestions

1. **Do not double-space.** Double-spacing is for draft documents. Double-spacing is a special design effect, use it sparingly.
2. **Most fonts should be smaller.** Most professional documents use a smaller font size than what you are familiar with. Look at books, newspapers, magazines, brochures, business cards, etc., for examples.
3. **Design everything with no more than two fonts.** Nearly all professionals' documents use only one font at different sizes and weights. Use no more than one serif and one san serif, or one display and one body font in any document.
4. **Avoid putting boxes around everything.** A "block of text" is called that because it resembles a box already. Learn to use white space and balance to designate spaces rather than boxes and rules.
5. **Avoid overused fonts like Times and Arial.** Consider using some of the great fonts instead: Akzidenz-Grotesk, Baskerville, Benguiat, Benton, Bodoni, Bookman, Caslon, Didot, Frutiger, Galliard, Garamond, Gill, Goudy, Helvetica, Janson, Optima, Palatino, Sabon, Zapf, and others.
6. **Avoid clip art.** All clip art always looks like "clip art." That is why it is free. Instead of clip art, purchase appropriate images from a stock photo agency or take a picture yourself.
7. **Do not center everything.** Asymmetrical layouts almost always look more interesting and more professional. Avoid creating posters, signs, or other documents that are centered down the middle.
8. **Every page does not need a border.** Just because you created a sweet border design or have a vector graphic of a logo does not mean you should use it on every page.
9. **Do not put watermarks or background images on every page.** See rule 8.
10. **Space text blocks, images, rules, etc., carefully.** Having the same space among elements on your page is more important than how much space you have. Having a professional design is not about much space is used, but that everything is the same on every page. Use style sheets to help achieve perfect alignment.

like pictures do (Table 12.7). Pull quotes are easy to create and may be incorporated into almost any type of document.

Drop caps are another typographic technique designed to emphasize a paragraph of text. All word processing and DTP programs have automatic drop cap features. Drop caps can take many forms, including dropped into text, placed at the beginning of a sentence in a larger font, placed in the margin, boxed, or reversed text. See the examples in Table 12.8. Drop caps work to draw attention to the beginning of stories and sections.

STATIONERY AND BUSINESS CARDS

Stationery and business cards are used to demonstrate credibility and professionalism. Who would trust a professional organization that just printed everything on copy paper? Clients and stakeholders like to see organizational trademarks and logos on business documents and appreciate the feel of quality letterhead and business cards. Most established organizations already have stationery and business cards. Stationery and business cards are printed in bulk by professional printers rather than produced in house on an *a la carte* basis.

Occasionally, professionals are asked to design stationery or other creative documents for special projects, mergers, acquisitions, etc. Creative documents are best designed by publication professionals. However, when no budget exists for creative professionals, here are some of the issues to consider:

For stationery, select a paper color that copies, scans, and faxes well. Select paper and cardstock based on its look and feel. Touch several paper samples so that you know how the stationery will feel when it lands in a client's hands.

Try to design stationery so that the left and right margins are as close to standard as possible. If you

TABLE 12.7 Pull Quotations

Media critic Marshall McLuhan is famous for saying "the medium is the message." What McLuhan meant was that the media (broadcast, print, etc.) have specific features and create expectations that audiences expect to have met, otherwise messages are ignored or misunderstood. For example, the 70s television show *Quincy M.E.,* which aired from 1976–1983, was about a medical examiner/crime investigator who "let the body tell the story." *Quincy* had many similarities to contemporary forensic dramas like *CSI* and *Crossing Jordan,* but few younger viewers would probably watch it today. Television dramas of today feature ensemble casts, graphic special effects, faster cuts, etc. For *Quincy* to air today (other than in reruns) the show would need substantial reworking. Jack Klugman (who played Quincy) would probably not appeal to the 18- to 35-year-old crowd, and the plots would need to be more dramatic and faster moving than they once were.

This is an example of a pull quote. utilizing a box. Avoid breaking words and break lines for readability.

What McLuhan said was true of all media. The medium is the message. For a public relations professional to create an effective feature story, he or she must understand the source for the story. The story needs to fit the source. You need to answer questions such as, "What do readers expect?" and "What have previous stories been like?" before you start writing. You always need to conform to the expectations of your audience if you want your audience to attend to your message.

Often, as in this example, pull quote text is placed in another font. Text can be centered, or left/right justified as appropriate.

What is also important to understand is that not all print messages are the same. As Lupton (2004) points out, readers of Web content have different expectations than other types of print readers do (p. 74). And, just as each kind of media (print, electronic, or broadcast) have content and stylistic features, print messages also have aesthetic features.

Aesthetics refers to the study of beauty or features that make something pleasant or appealing. As mentioned earlier, one of the things that a public relations professional is responsible for is making aesthetic decisions about written work that s/he produces, or deciding how to make organizational materials look good. The kinds of documents that professionals are responsible for producing vary from electronic content placed on an organization's Web site, to print materials produced for everything from an organizational picnic to a research paper. People naturally respond more favorably to messages that "appear" more credible, or have "ethos," to things that are attractive. My goal in this chapter is to help you to understand some of the basic design skills that will make your work more professional-looking and more compelling.

Understanding how to create more professional documents requires an understanding of everything from typography and paper to basic graphic design principles. Until relatively recently (about the last 20 years), producing attractive-looking documents without the aid of a professional publisher was virtually impossible. About the best tools that organizations had at their disposal were "memory typewriters" and "daisywheel" printers. Most organizations did not have more than two fonts available to them, and those fonts only came in one size (on the typewriter or daisywheel printer). Because most people could not produce their own high-quality, professional documents, the expectations of "professional" quality and aesthetic excellence were lower. Organizations that could not afford to pay for professional printing services were at a distinct disadvantage when it came to producing compelling materials; however, since most people were not used to seeing perfect documents from organizations anyway, a few mistakes did not matter.

Text can be pulled to the side, boxed, run in between columns of text, surrounded by horizontal/ vertical rules, etc.

In the mid-80s, the laser printer revolutionized desktop publishing when it became an affordable tool for small organizations and individuals. Coupled with the introduction of personal computers and early desktop publishing software like PageMaker, producing

place design information down the left or right side of the page, everyone who uses the stationery will need to measure the stationery with a ruler and adjust their margins, or you will need to create templates in your word processing programs for use with the letterhead. Although templates are easy to create, using a standard format when designing letterhead eliminates the need for templates.

Watch the type size. Except for logotypes and names, the contact information on a piece of stationery is typically small (6-9 points). Be sure that the typeface and type size that are selected fax and scan well

TABLE 12.8 Drop Caps

The media critic Marshall McLuhan is famous for saying "the medium is the message." What McLuhan meant was that the media (broadcast, print, etc.) have specific features and create expectations that audiences expect to have met, otherwise messages are ignored or misunderstood. For example, the 70s television show *Quincy M.E.,* which aired from 1976–1983, was about a medical examiner/crime investigator who "let the body tell the story." *Quincy* had many similarities to contemporary forensic dramas like *CSI* and *Crossing Jordan,* but few younger viewers would probably watch it today. Television dramas of today feature ensemble casts, graphic special effects, faster cuts, etc. For *Quincy* to air today (other than in reruns), the show would need substantial reworking. Jack Klugman (who played Quincy)

The media critic Marshall McLuhan is famous for saying "the medium is the message." What McLuhan meant was that the media (broadcast, print, etc.) have specific features and create expectations that audiences expect to have met, otherwise messages are ignored or misunderstood. For example, the 70s television show *Quincy M.E.,* which aired from 1976–1983, was about a medical examiner/crime investigator who "let the body tell the story." *Quincy* had many similarities to contemporary forensic dramas like *CSI* and *Crossing Jordan*, but few younger viewers would probably watch it today. Television dramas of today feature ensemble casts, graphic special effects, faster cuts, etc. For *Quincy* to air today (other than in reruns), the show would need substantial reworking. Jack Klugman (who played Quincy)

The Media critic Marshall McLuhan is famous for saying "the medium is the message." What McLuhan meant was that the media (broadcast, print, etc.) have specific features and create expectations that audiences expect to have met, otherwise messages are ignored or misunderstood. For example, the 70s television show *Quincy M.E.,* which aired from 1976–1983, was about a medical examiner/crime investigator who "let the body tell the story." *Quincy* had many similarities to contemporary forensic dramas like *CSI* and *Crossing Jordan,* but few younger viewers would probably watch it today. Television dramas of today feature ensemble casts, graphic special effects, faster cuts, etc. For *Quincy* to air today (other than in reruns) the show would need substantial reworking. Jack Klugman (who played Quincy)

The media critic Marshall McLuhan is famous for saying "the medium is the message." What McLuhan meant was that the media (broadcast, print, etc.) have specific features and create expectations that audiences expect to have met, otherwise messages are ignored or misunderstood. For example, the 70s television show *Quincy M.E.,* which aired from 1976–1983, was about a medical examiner/crime investigator who "let the body tell the story." *Quincy* had many similarities to contemporary forensic dramas like *CSI* and *Crossing Jordan,* but few younger viewers would probably watch it today. Television dramas of today feature ensemble casts, graphic special effects, faster cuts, etc. For *Quincy* to air today (other than in reruns) the show would need substantial reworking. Jack Klugman (who played Quincy)

The media critic Marshall McLuhan is famous for saying "the medium is the message." What McLuhan meant was that the media (broadcast, print, etc.) have specific features and create expectations that audiences expect to have met, otherwise messages are ignored or misunderstood. For example, the 70s television show *Quincy M.E.,* which aired from 1976–1983, was about a medical examiner/crime investigator who "let the body tell the story." Quincy had many similarities to contemporary forensic dramas like *CSI* and *Crossing Jordan,* but few younger viewers would probably watch it today. Television dramas of today feature ensemble casts, graphic special effects, faster cuts, etc. For *Quincy* to air today (other than in reruns) the show would need substantial reworking. Jack Klugman (who played Quincy)

The Media critic Marshall McLuhan is famous for saying "the medium is the message." What McLuhan meant was that the media (broadcast, print, etc.) have specific features and create expectations that audiences expect to have met, otherwise messages are ignored or misunderstood. For example, the 70s television show *Quincy M.E.,* which aired from 1976–1983, was about a medical examiner/crime investigator who "let the body tell the story." Quincy had many similarities to contemporary forensic dramas like *CSI* and *Crossing Jordan,* but few younger viewers would probably watch it today. Television dramas of today feature ensemble casts, graphic special effects, faster cuts, etc. For *Quincy* to air today (other than in reruns) the show would need substantial reworking. Jack Klugman (who played Quincy) so that contact information will not be lost when documents are sent.

Unless your organization has a manual of "house style" (and if it did, it would probably have letterhead already), use Associated Press style when writing telephone numbers, fax numbers, and other contact information. Additionally, this might be the time to give serious thought to developing a manual of style for your organization and selecting a couple of house fonts to use in all organizational documents.

Subtly bolding key words like "Telephone" "E-mail" etc., make such information easier for clients to pick out when they are using the documents.

Obtain at least a dozen samples of professional stationery from other organizations and consider "imitating" the basic design of one or several of the documents (this is where a swipe file comes in).

Stationery templates usually incorporate vector graphics or scaleable artwork (from Illustrator) for logotypes. Be sure not to distort organizational logos, trademarks, or service marks, change color schemes, add borders, etc.

Once you have stationery and business card designs, you will need to create template files to make using the documents easier. Most word processing programs have built-in templates for things like business cards, tent cards, CD labels, nametags, etc. All you need to do to use the templates is to pick from a cafeteria list of document types (or use the label number like Avery labels), and the word processor will set up an automatic template to match. As noted above, if your stationery has nonstandard margins on the left or right, set these margins in a template, and set the top and bottom margins to the minimum distance that will work given the design of the template.

HYPERTEXT MARKUP LANGUAGE (HTML)

The beauty of HTML is that it is a universal platform. A visitor to your Web site on a high speed, wireless Dell laptop computer in Paris, France, will see exactly the same thing (more or less, depending upon his or her system preferences), as someone from Paris, Texas, on a five-year-old Mac with a dial-up connection. Many changes have been introduced to basic HTML coding that have not really improved the experience of using the World Wide Web but allow programmers to exert more control over the way users experience Web pages. As will be explained below, some of these improvements are useful and some are not. Ultimately, the best Web sites will load quickly on every computer and within every browser platform.

Basic HTML Design Issues

Design horizontally. The computer screen is a wide, not a tall space. Many Web designers still have not embraced the wider page and try to mimic a standard "tall" (8.5 × 11") page. The technique of creating tall pages with blank voids on either side of the page is a poor choice for many reasons. "White space" is important. Pages like this one (Photo 12.3) from the International Communication Association are actually harder to read, even though the designer was trying to create the appearance of a newsletter page and has balanced the "white space." Additionally, the tall layout forces the viewer to scroll down to read content that, if the space were used more carefully, could have been placed on the home page.

Create intuitive navigation. The best Web sites do not try to position their site as a *tour de force* of Internet design. If your organization is a design firm, then it may be desirable to have cutting-edge design. However, most Internet users (especially the media) do not like Web sites that are difficult to navigate, slow, or require a lot of thought to figure out (cf., Kent, 2001; Kent & Taylor, 1998). A very nice resource for learning about Web design is Vincent Flanders' Web site, "Web Pages That Suck" (www.WebSitesThatSuck.com). Web Pages That Suck has been around since 1996 and has some excellent discussions (and examples) of what *bad* Web sites look like, as well as good ones. As Flanders asks rhetorically:

> Does Your Web Site Use Bad Web Design Techniques? Learn from the mistakes of FedEx, Brown University, The Pope, Microsoft, Qualcomm, Adobe, Apple, Harvard Business Review, Tom Peters, Saturn Auto, Memorex, Minolta, Saab, Intel, Chevrolet, Swatch, Canon, and thousands of other sites featured here for using bad web design techniques (ibid).

Avoid Cascading Style Sheets (CSS). As much as I have touted style sheets for other applications, they are absolutely dreadful for creating effective Web pages. Web pages should open quickly, be usable by anyone, and be easy to use. The sin of the cascading style sheet is it assumes everyone is like the designer (has good eyes, likes the same fonts and colors, enjoys reading san serif fonts on computer screens—this is currently a popular design choice. Unfortunately, san serif fonts are more difficult to read at small type sizes).

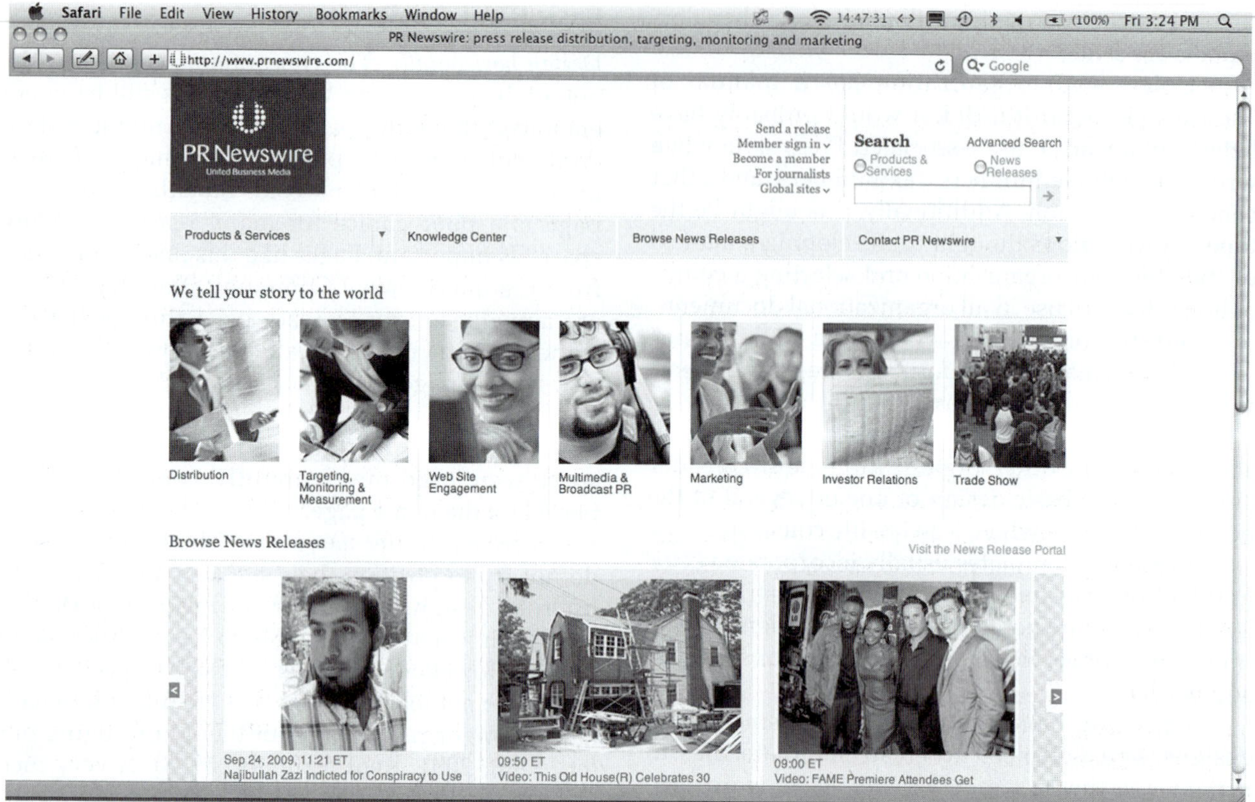

PHOTO 12.3 PRNewswire Home Page
Source: © 2009 PR Newswire Association LLC. All Right Reserved.

The CSS fallacy is part of a class of computer-related fallacies that include, "But I don't have any trouble using the Web site ...," or, "The site loads fine on Internet Explorer. ..." Many Web designers seem to have had limited graphic arts training and regularly ignore issues of readability and legibility when designing Web content. Millions of Web sites are designed like the ICA Web site above, ignoring 30 percent or more of the real estate of the computer screen in order to be able to control the exact dimensions of the page on *every* computer and force the page to resemble a printed document.

If you want to judge the effectiveness of a Web site, invite your grandmother to lunch and ask her to visit your organization's Web site and (objectively) tell you how to make it more user-friendly. Never let an expert "Web designer" make the decision. Technology professionals are not the "average" users. Relying on a Web master or designer's judgment about his/her own designs is a bit like asking a chef to criticize his/her own food. "It tastes great to me!"

The cascading style sheet robs Web site visitors (your guests, your publics, and the people whose happiness should be important to you), of the ability to make their own decisions about how they want to obtain information. With the exception of graphic design and creative Web sites (whose sole purpose *is* to demonstrate their craft), style sheets are a bad idea. Additionally, efforts by organizations to try to enforce "house style" rules are equally misguided since most users only have a few dozen fonts available to them on their computers.[9]

Never create pages (or allow your Web master to create pages) that only work properly on the Microsoft platform. My admonition is not so much an endorsement of Linux or Macintosh, but a caution, because Microsoft has created a number of platform-specific HTML codes that do not work on all systems. Like public relations, the Internet is supposed to be about access to information. Do not subvert that purpose by allowing your site designer to corrupt your electronic communication channels. Rather than manually testing your Web pages on a variety of computers and software platforms, you can use a number of free tools to test your sites (cf., www.FixingYourWebSite.com/drhtml.html). Be sure to design Web pages for all browser platforms rather than a select few.

Optimize graphics for quick loading. You can do this by reducing their size (as much as possible) and creating tiny thumbnail versions that can be expanded. One of the reasons Web pages are slow to load is because of an abundance of graphics and special effects (flash, Java, etc.). Minimize the use of graphics and special effects on home pages so the initial experience of visitors to your site is positive.

Additionally, avoid creating bitmaps for navigation. Bit-mapped areas, background images, and sounds only slow down the speed at which a page loads. Users are not really coming to your Web site to be entertained; they are coming for some purpose of their own (usually information). One way to get around the problem of a slow interface for organizations that feel they simply must have the latest supercharged Web site is to give users with fast connections the choice on a splash page between a "basic" (or RSS) interface and a "supercharged" interface (Kent & Taylor, 1998). Users with slow connections or who are only interested in your "information" will appreciate your forethought. Remember, 10 percent of Americans (30,000,000) still use dial-up connections (www.eschoolnews.com/news/top-news/news-by-subject/research/index.cfm?i=54428).

Opening pages in frames versus opening new pages: When a link takes a Web visitor to a new site (not your own), the link should open in a new tab or window so the visitor will not have difficulty getting back to the originating site (your site). For internal links, let utility be the guide. Opening links to documents (PDFs, text files, videos, sound files) in new window is often best. Links to other content pages within your organization's Web site can be usefully opened within the current frame or in new pages. Be consistent with what you do so visitors know how to navigate your Web site.

LISTSERVS AND ELECTRONIC MAILING LISTS

An electronic mailing list is a common tool used by organizations to reach employees, customers, members, and the media. Activist groups in particular have taken to using e-mail lists as a means of marshalling support for protests, causes, and other public events for many years (Kent & Alex, 2002; Sommerfeldt, 2007). Many activist groups send out "action alerts" advising members about important legislation, providing background information, and encouraging them to e-mail or write lawmakers.

Most e-mail systems allow individuals to easily prepare bulk mailing lists for internal audiences. For external audiences (customers, shareholders, the media), a better solution, especially for a very large organization, might be an electronic mailing list or a LISTSERV.[10] Other organization–public electronic communication options include creating subscriber lists based on selections made on Web sites, and creating "media advisory lists."

Electronic mailing lists and Listservs enable organizations to send their messages directly to interested parties without intermediaries. Before the Internet and electronic mail, about the only way organizations could reach individuals and publics directly was by calling people on the telephone (a poor choice when you need to reach thousands of people), direct-mailing interested parties (expensive and slow), and faxing messages using "broadcast fax" and "fax on demand." Having control over the message is obviously important, as is being able to distribute messages quickly to interested parties. Organizations in almost every industry should give considerable thought to how on use electronic communication to its fullest.

CONCLUSION

Teaching you how to use software packages that require hundreds of hours to master is of course impossible in only a few chapters. There is no substitute for having a basic understanding of public relations software. You will need to spend some of your free time understanding software and keeping up on technology. One of the key things that organizations now look for in students who want to secure internships is the ability to use publication and graphics software. Take a course, buy some books, or complete some online tutorials. The University of Oklahoma's Gaylord College of Journalism and Mass Communication has a series of online tutorials called Pacesetter (pacesetter. ou.edu), that offers free video training in the basics of InDesign, Photoshop, Illustrator, Flash, and other programs. As a professional, you probably will not be able to ignore learning how to use these programs.

That said, do not make the mistake of thinking that the most important part of this chapter is an understanding of what the software can do. Software changes quickly. When I was in college, drawing programs like Illustrator did not exist, and PageMaker, the first desktop publishing program, was in its infancy. Now, what you can do in Photoshop, InDesign, and the other graphics programs is amazing. However, what have not changed are basic design skills (space, balance, harmony, hierarchy). You will not create compelling print and electronic publications by having the latest software, but by understanding the rhetorical and situational features that shape your messages. The software is just a tool that needs to be informed by research, audience analysis, and a thorough understanding of your audience and the situation.

ACTIVITIES

1. Customize the toolbar on Microsoft Word. Take a screenshot of your customized toolbar (shift/command/3 [or 4] on a Mac) and bring it to class. What features of MSW did you discover that you did not know existed? Why did you organize your toolbar the way you did?
2. Type the following words on a page using a font that most closely matches the feeling/mood evoked by the word: angry, bored, confused, drowsy, heartbroken, jealous, overjoyed, sad, suspicious, and timid. Which words seem to call for serif fonts and which words evoke san serifs, and why? Which words are best emphasized by big typefaces and which by smaller typefaces? Explain your choices?
3. Spend some time with Adobe Acrobat. Take the last several papers you wrote for class and combine them into a single PDF document (you can do this by sending each of the documents to the printer and selecting "PDF" rather than print. Then, in Acrobat, go to "Create PDF/From Multiple Files"). Reorganize the pages, remove some pages, and edit some of the pages to get a feel for what you can do with Acrobat.
4. Conduct an analysis of your department's Web site. Does the site take advantage of the screen real estate? Is the site easy to navigate? Are there a lot of graphics on the page? How quickly does the page load? How are links handled—were you sent to new pages, new frames, new windows? What might be changed to improve the Web site?
5. Visit the Flanders' Web Pages That Suck (www.WebPagesThatSuck.com) site and review some of the Web sites for next class. Be prepared to explain the answers to these questions: What makes a Web site suck? What makes a Web site more effective? How is it possible that so many "experts" might still create such poor Web sites?
6. Visit the L-Soft search page for LISTSERV (www.lsoft.com/lists/list_q.html) and sign up for three lists. Send a copy of the list names to your instructor. Be prepared to discuss your lists in class in a week.

NOTES

1. The Menu bars used here are from the previous version of Word, which is still widely used. The latest edition of Microsoft Word is still customized as described here. However, many people do not know how to shut off the default toolbars that open when the program is launched and use the program as it opens by default. See Figure 12.1 and 12.2, which compares the new and old toolbars and also shows the Formatting Pallet.
2. The "Formatting Pallet" (View/Formatting Pallet) allows access to many of the formatting commands that I have explained how to add to toolbars. Unfortunately, the Formatting Pallet takes up a lot of screen real estate. On a laptop, the formatting pallet covers a lot of the page window and makes it difficult to use the scroll bar when the pallet obscures it. Finally, placement of the menu items on the Formatting Pallet (Font, Style, Alignment, etc.) do not correspond to your personalized menu edits and include default commands only, many of which you may never use.
3. Here is the procedure: In the find box, search for two paragraph breaks: ¶¶ (toggle the window bigger for "special" commands); in the replace box, replace the two paragraph breaks with a symbol that is not in the text itself. I usually use a bullet: • (option/8) or a dagger † (option/t). Select "replace all" and change all of the paragraph breaks to bullets. Next, replace all of the single paragraph breaks with a space: search for ¶ and replace with a "single space"—one tap of the space bar. Select "replace all" to eliminate all of the unnecessary paragraph breaks. You should now have a continuous paragraph of text that has bullets wherever proper paragraph breaks would be located. Finally, convert the bullets back to proper paragraph breaks: search for • (or whatever symbol you used) and replace with a paragraph break and a tab break (toggle the arrow in edit/replace for the special menu). *Voilà*, you will have eliminated all manual returns at the ends of lines and created proper paragraph breaks.

   Once you get good at using "find/change," you can use the feature to make a lot more subtle changes in documents. I have used find/change for textual analysis by searching for specific words and changing their color or to make the words easier to locate and to highlight their relations to other words, etc.

4. Adobe has offered software organizations the opportunity to incorporate Acrobat free of charge. Not all companies have embraced it. Microsoft, for example, allows users to create PDFs in word via a PDF Toolbar but does not incorporate the PDF link into its print commands window the way Apple does. Similarly, when using Adobe Illustrator, Photoshop, or InDesign on a Macintosh, the procedure for creating PDFs varies. In InDesign, the "Export" command is used (Command/E), In Photoshop, documents can be saved as PDFs using File/"Save As."
5. Twenty years ago, the industry standard was a DTP program called PageMaker, by a company called Aldus. Adobe, a major typography company, then wisely bought Aldus. In the late 90s–early 2000s, a program called QuarkXPress had supplanted PageMaker and was giving Adobe a run for its money. Adobe responded by offering its "Create Suite" (now, version CS5) which included five major workflow programs described in this chapter: Acrobat, Illustrator, InDesign, Photoshop, and Bridge (not described). Quark has had trouble competing with Adobe over the last five years since Adobe now also offers more than a dozen programs, including graphics, print, Web, video and special effects programs. Indeed, probably because Adobe offers the Creative Suite, in which the software programs are all integrated, Quark has been slowly dying. Photoshop and Illustrator are the industry standard for illustration and photo correction so to use these programs with a "foreign" program invites some problems. Thus, again, although Quark is a great program, many professionals believe it is essentially dead. No one not already committed to QuarkXPress in his/her workflow would buy it rather than InDesign and the Adobe Creative Suite.
6. If you already own a typeface yourself, you can send a publisher a PDF or Adobe InDesign "package" (which contains typefaces, graphics, etc.). However, if you want a document printed using a typeface that you do not own, unless the printer you select has the typeface that you need, you will need to buy it.
7. Typefaces: Garamond, Times, Impact, Chicago, Carroll, Onyx, Matrix Wide, Arial Black, Cheapskate, Oxford, Wide Latin.
8. Most readers are familiar with single, double, and one-and-a-half–spacing their documents using programs like Microsoft Word. When a line of type is single-spaced, the spacing between lines, measured in "points" (72 points per inch) matches the font size that you are typing in. Thus, when you select single-spaced in Microsoft Word, while typing in a 12-point font, you are setting the type to about 12/12 (a 12 point font with 12-points of leading). If you were typing in an 18 point font, and wanted your lines to be single spaced, you would have 18/18 or an 18-point font with 18-points of leading. To double space, you would use twice the font size you are using in leading. Thus, a 12-point font, double-spaced, would be 12/24, a 12-point font at one-and-a-half–spaced would be 12/18, etc.
9. In case you are not aware, every Web browser allows the user to set his or her font and page style preferences (within limits). I happen not to see very well so I have set my preferences to open pages in a slightly bigger than average font. Many designers go out of their way to impose the currently fashionable preference for 10-point Arial on the rest of the world. Unfortunately, what such designers do not understand is that their Web site's visitors do not think their Web site is so "cool" when they cannot read the labels in the links or navigate the site. Visitors will instead find the site to be frustrating and irritating.

   For many years, the International Communication Association's Web site used a font so small for the navigation menu that it could not be read on most computers (and pages would not even load properly on Macintosh computers). Recently, after years of complaints, the ICA relented and fixed the site. As a life member of the organization I had little choice but to suffer with their poor design. However, if I had been a media representative, I would not have hesitated for a minute to go elsewhere for my facts or information. When professionals are conducting Web research and run into Web sites that are so badly designed they cannot read the pages, they ignore the site and move on (as you know, there are a million other Web sites to choose from).
10. A LISTSERV is a type of automated mailing list. "LISTSERV" is a brand name for an electronic mailing list and not a generic name for all automated mailing lists. As L-Soft explains:

> LISTSERV is a powerful email [sic] list management software solution that sets the industry standard. It allows you to easily manage opt-in email lists, like e-mail newsletters, announcement lists and discussion groups. LISTSERV was originally developed in 1986 and was the first email list management software available. It has since been continuously developed and is a highly robust, scalable and easy-to-use software solution. (www.lsoft.com/products/listserv.asp)

Listservs are a lot harder to run than to use. Lists can be moderated, or open to any member to post, and lists can be open to anyone or limited to specific members. Running a listserv can be a time-consuming activity so careful thought should be given before creating a moderated list. One caution however: unmoderated lists often attract spammers and messages from unrelated, or tangentially related sources. Few groups or organizations opt for completely open Listservs.

Chapter 13

Ethics and Regulatory Issues

HOW ETHICS SHOULD DRIVE YOUR WRITING

One of the public relations concepts that you might have learned about in your introduction to public relations course is "reputation." Organizations have reputations and "brand" value. As a representative of an organization, you are responsible for assuring that the organization's reputation and relationship with their environment (its social capital) remain high (Ihlen, 2005).

As I have mentioned several times, part of the job of protecting your organization's reputation involves acting as an organizational counselor and telling the organization when a particular course of action has the potential to cause harm. Managers, executives, CEOs, and other leaders do not like to be told that they are making a mistake, so acting as an organizational counselor (and sometimes conscience) is difficult. Beyond your professional responsibilities as an organizational counselor, however, you also need to understand a variety of legal issues associated with all communication-oriented professions. This chapter will review some of the key legal issues in public relations as well as reviewing several of the government agencies that public relations professionals should understand.

TELLING THE TRUTH

Although most professional codes of ethics, such as the Public Relations Society of America's "Code of Ethics," have injunctions against lying, corrupting the channels of communication, and obstructing the free flow of information, admonitions to tell the truth go back centuries. Plato (1999) said of rhetoric that it should be speech worthy of the gods and as such should be honest and productive for society. Cicero (1976) said that rhetoric linked wisdom and eloquence for the enhancement of the state (pp. 1 ff.). Quintilian, a contemporary of Cicero, said that effective communication consisted of "A good man skilled in speaking" (Quintilian, 1989, I.i.9 ff). And, more recently, Richard Weaver (1985) claimed that rhetoric was "The truth, plus its artful presentation" (p. 15).

What all of this boils down to is that public relations professionals are part of a long tradition of public communicators that goes back thousands of years. Although you have an obligation to act in the best interest of your organization whenever possible, you also have an obligation to various external groups and publics, and an obligation to help ensure that your organization behaves ethically. In order to fulfill the obligations to your organization, and to your clients and publics, you need to understand a variety of legal and regulatory issues.

MAKING ETHICAL DECISIONS

One of the issues that should be clear at this point is that the difficulty of acting ethically and using rhetorical principles is great. Ethical messages do not write themselves. Public relations professionals have to be vigilant about conducting adequate research, taking into account multiple stakeholders, and balancing the desires of organizational superiors with decisions about right and wrong. Ethical decision making is a complicated process because it involves taking into account different priorities and balancing the needs of many individuals and groups.

Earlier, I discussed the ethical orientations that might guide your decision making. Here I would like to offer a well-known model for ethical decision making called the "Potter Box" (cf., en.wikipedia.org/wiki/Potter_Box).

The Potter Box

The Potter Box was developed many years ago by Ralph B. Potter Jr., a professor at the Harvard Divinity School. Potter believed that ethical decisions were influenced by four interrelated variables: loyalties, principles, situation, and values.

> ***Loyalties***—What individuals or groups are important in this situation? Do not just arbitrarily identify "all publics" or your supervisor. In public relations, stakeholders are always relevant publics; however, not every stakeholder needs to be considered in every situation. A personnel issue is unlikely to involve shareholders, while a management crisis will. Where do your loyalties lie: with your key publics, your boss, a past employer, your colleagues, your family?
>
> ***Principles***—Identify principles (the collectivity of moral or ethical standards or judgments; a decision based on principle rather than expediency; a fixed or predetermined policy or mode of action). Identify relevant ethical principles that should guide your action: looking out for number one, survival of the fittest, silence is golden, the golden mean, a categorical imperative, dialogue, situational, absolutist, utilitarian, Judeo–Christian, utilitarian, economic, political, organizational, etc.
>
> ***Situation***—What are the problems/opportunities inherent in this situation? Identify both without judging or elaborating. Although you might be facing a crisis, what are the opportunities? Similarly, what good might come out of the ethical situation that you are facing? Are you under time constraints, are there legal issues, are there alternative explanations for events?
>
> ***Values***—Identify values (a principle, standard, or quality considered worthwhile or desirable). What are the values that should be taken in account (friendship, trust, loyalty, compassion, success, etc.)? Be sure to be consistent with your ethical beliefs and the PRSA code.

Potter created a four-quadrant "box," or grid, where a decision maker might identify each of the categories and be better able to make a decision. The categories of the box can be considered in any order and the heuristic of the box can lead to very different decisions when different people use the box, or when the same person uses the box at a different time. The Potter box is a tool for ethical decision making and can help professionals identify relevant issues that they might not have considered.

PLAGIARISM AND RECYCLING ORGANIZATIONAL CONTENT

Plagiarism is the unauthorized or inappropriate use of the words or ideas of others. Plagiarism occurs when written or spoken material is borrowed, in whole or in part, and passed off as original by a writer or speaker. Plagiarism includes, but is not limited to, presenting someone else's ideas, speech, presentation,

Situation	Values
Principles	Loyalties

research, poetry, prose, and music as original works. Plagiarism also includes failing to document or cite the source of word-for-word or paraphrased material in oral presentations or written documents.[1]

Plagiarism is an important issue in public relations and is relatively easy to understand. First, you do not have to worry about plagiarizing from yourself or citing yourself unless your organization happens to be a publisher. Organizations reuse content in a hundred different ways. Boilerplate organizational statements are used, word for word, in news releases, annual reports, on organizational Web sites, in brochures and fact sheets, and no acknowledgement of who wrote the text or where it originally appeared is ever made. Indeed, unlike in college, where each assignment is expected to consist of the individual ideas, expression, research, and prose of one student, public relations professionals create corporate documents and reuse as much of their own content as they can. You simply do not have the time to reinvent the wheel every time you have a document to write. More importantly, repeating portions of text from various organizational documents in different messages provides a consistent tone to organizational messages.

Although you are free to reuse your organization's own messages, you have no right to use other people's or organizations' content or borrow from the Internet, newspapers, magazines, research articles and reports, PowerPoint presentations, or any other source (copyrighted or not). The same rules that apply to citing sources in class apply in the real world: If you use the work of others you have to cite it. For-profit organizations have very limited legal rights to quote the work of others without their permission under the fair-use clause.[2]

In the professional world, you cannot use more than very small excerpts of someone else's work without permission. You are never allowed to incorporate the copyrighted work of others into your organization's own work without obtaining a signed consent form from the copyright holder and paying royalty fees.

In the professional world, the consequences of plagiarism are more serious. In college, you might receive an F for cheating—the worst thing that could happen is expulsion. Although this may sound bad, expulsion is nothing compared to being fired after a reporter writes a story about how your organization plagiarized content from a magazine article or book, or created false testimonials attributed to fictitious people. In the case of a journalist or public relations professional, plagiarism is likely to ruin your career as word spreads through local, national, and international professional associations. Legal sanctions are also possible, and include being assessed legal costs and civil penalties depending upon whether the content used was sold for profit or produced in great numbers.

A related issue to understand is copyright. You need to understand both how to avoid violating copyright law and how to obtain copyright protection for organizational documents and symbols.

UNDERSTANDING COPYRIGHT, TRADEMARK, AND SERVICE MARK PROTECTION

Copyright protection, as well as trademark and service mark protection, is designed to protect individuals and organizations from having their creative works used by others without their permission. According to the U.S. copyright office:

> Copyright protects original works of authorship, while a patent protects inventions or discoveries. Ideas and discoveries are not protected by the copyright law, although the way in which they are expressed may be. A trademark protects words, phrases, symbols, or designs identifying the source of the goods or services of one party and distinguishing them from those of others. (www.copyright.gov/help/faq/faq-general.html#protect)

The U.S. copyright office Web site also notes:

> Copyright is a form of protection grounded in the U.S. Constitution and granted by law for original works of authorship fixed in a tangible medium of expression. Copyright covers both published and unpublished works … . Copyright, a form of intellectual property law, protects original works of authorship including literary, dramatic, musical, and artistic works, such as poetry, novels, movies, songs, computer software, and architecture. Copyright does not protect facts, ideas, systems, or methods of operation, although it may protect the way these things are expressed … . Copyrightable works include the following categories: (1) literary works; (2) musical works, including any accompanying words; … (5) pictorial, graphic, and sculptural works. (www.copyright.gov/help/faq)

Be aware that whenever a professional writes or creates documents while in the employment of another person or organization, the work created legally belongs to the employer unless a prior agreement between the employer and the employee exists. The same is true of creative work done on your own time and based loosely on work done for an employer. In other words, you cannot profit by work you have done for someone else or that is made possible because of your professional responsibilities or access.

Must I File for Copyright Protection to Be Protected?

Many people are unsure about whether a copyright has to be registered in order to receive legal protection. The answer is no; however, copyright filing does have legal benefits. Spend an hour perusing the U.S. copyright Web site (www.copyright.gov). In general, a work is under copyright protection the second it is "created and fixed in a tangible form that it is perceptible either directly or with the aid of a machine or device" (<www.copyright.gov/circs/circ1.pdf>, p. 2) However, if copyright protection for work is *not* registered, it is more difficult to obtain protection if an organization's work is used without permission.

How to File for Copyright Protection

Currently the cost of filing for copyright protection is $45 per work, and it takes about four months for the process to be completed. Copyright forms may be obtained online (www.copyright.gov/fls/sl35.pdf). The copyright office also encourages online filing for a $35 fee (www.copyright.gov/register). When you file for protection, you must also submit paper copies of documents that will not be returned and become the property of the U.S. Copyright and Patent Office.

How Long Does Copyright Protection Last?

For works created by individuals after January 1, 1978, copyright protection lasts for the life of the author plus 70 years. For work made for hire, the copyright endures for a term of 95 years from the year of its first publication or for a term of 120 years from the year of its creation, whichever expires first (www.copyright.gov/help/faq/faq-duration.html#duration).

DEFAMATION

As a public relations professionals, you are the mouthpiece of the organization and therefore open yourself, and your organization, up to litigation—an issue of some concern in our increasingly litigious society. Indeed, 35 percent of all laws touch on communication issues.

In general, few public relations practitioners should be concerned about writing or saying anything defamatory. The majority of the documents that you will produce will be informational rather than critical or editorial. However, understanding defamation and how to avoid it is still important.

Defamation refers to false or misleading statements that cause a person or organization to be held up for hate, ridicule, or contempt. Printed or broadcast defamation is called **libel**; spoken defamation is called **slander**. Although proving defamation is difficult and the vast majority of cases are thrown out, defamation suits are often brought as nuisance lawsuits and are costly and time-consuming.

Forms of Defamation

Mistaken Identification—this is not an excuse if it damages the reputation of another.

Odious Labels—calling someone a "drunk," a "deadbeat," "dishonest," a "bum," etc.

Professional Injury—damaging an individual's means of making a living by suggesting that s/he is untrustworthy, corrupt, or incompetent (intentionally causing professional injury is also a violation of the PRSA Code of Ethics).

Trade Libel—suggesting in an interview, organizational literature, or an advertisement that *your* product is safer than the competitor's, that their product might causes harm, etc.

"Per Quod" libel—suggesting that someone had a few too many drinks at an office party is not necessarily libelous. However, if that individual happens to be a lay minister, on antidepressant or pain medication, or physically impaired in some other way, a jury might be convinced that s/he was injured. Suppress the urge to write funny captions under pictures of organizational members even in internal-only documents, Web sites, newsletters, or blogs, or to provide narrative accounts of individual actions or behaviors when creating messages that will be read by others.

Although the opportunities for writing or saying something defamatory are few in most fields, the Internet has created a number of places where public relations professionals can get into trouble. Be vigilant about only discussing professional issues when blogging, posting to social networking or news sites,

Listservs, or communicating with others in online interactive venues, like Second Life (an online world where interactants create avatars to interact). Defamation is as much about the intention of the communicator as the facts of the situation. If your intent in writing or saying something is to cause another individual or organizational harm, then you are guilty of defamation, whether or not what you wrote or said is actually true. Since the PRSA code of ethics states that professionals should "never damage the professional reputation of another practitioner" Defamation should never occur.

In general, truth is not considered a defense against a libel charge because defamation involves trying to intentionally harm another person or organization. That a person or organization happens to be "bad" (in your eyes), does not give you the legal right to cause harm. Unless you are a journalist reporting newsworthy events, you have no legal right to speak ill of another individual or organization. As a public relations professional, you should never consider making statements that have the potential to damage the professional reputation or livelihood of another individual or organization.

ELECTRONIC MAIL (E-MAIL)

Many students take e-mail for granted because "it has been around forever." Indeed, the things in life that seem trivial are sometimes the most important, so let me put things into perspective: One in six information technology professionals watch what employees are doing on their computer while they are at work. More importantly,

> A 2005 survey by the American Management Association found that three-fourths of employers monitor their employees' web site visits in order to prevent inappropriate surfing. And 65% use software to block connections to Web sites deemed off limits for employees. About a third track keystrokes and time spent at the keyboard. Just over half of employers review and retain electronic mail messages. (www.privacyrights.org/fs/fs7-work.htm)[3]

Public relations professionals need to understand two things: *First,* as suggested above, e-mail is *not* a private medium; most employers read employee e-mail from time to time and the practice is perfectly legal. Never assume that e-mail, the telephone, or the Internet are private. They are not. Aside from employers watching and reading what you do at work, the USA Patriot Act also gives the government the right to read your e-mail and listen to your telephone conversations without informing you. *Second,* precisely because e-mail is not private, it should be treated as a formal, professional means of communication at all times. Always include proper header and contact information on all your e-mail messages. Communicate with colleagues and supervisors formally, even when you have a very informal relationship with them. Always assume that *someone* is reading your e-mail—even if it is "only the government."[4]

Additional E-mail Suggestions

As a professional writing medium, e-mail should not be treated casually. As noted, employee e-mail is *legally read* by *most* (three-fourths) U.S. employers and is archived by many organizations for future reference (especially in legal cases). Never use organizational e-mail for casual messages and correspondence that are not fully professional. In general, the following rules of e-mail etiquette apply:

- *Put your name on every message sent.* Additionally, set up your e-mail program to *automatically* include a **signature file** with complete contact information for you on all e-mail messages with your full name, telephone (work/home, fax, cell), postal or physical address, e-mail addresses, and company or home URL.
- Never write in all uppercase letters. Typing in all uppercase is difficult to read, and considered SHOUTING in electronic communication. Use all caps for emphasis only.
- Set up your e-mail server to send out messages in standard-size fonts (11- or 12-point). Do not use special effects (bolding, color) or reduce/increase the size of the font. If your organization has a particular house style, you may need to use that in your e-mail messages. Avoid creating messages that *require* HTML or rich text format (RTF) to be read. Not all users view e-mail messages using rich text format, and these messages may cause problems for some.
- *Always spell-check every message before you send it.* You are a professional now.
- *Do not use emoticons* (;-o, :-), ☺). They are considered unprofessional in most business and

professional settings and many people find them childish.

- *Begin every message professionally,* with a proper greeting and an acknowledgement of your respect for the recipient. For example:

> Dr. Cypher (or "Professor Cypher),
>
> I hope your day is going well. I know the traffic was brutal today coming from Highland Park—I live near there. (Be creative; do not type the same thing every time and spend a few lines doing more than just asking for something).
>
> I have a question about our recent class assignment. Although you suggested in class that we should … I am having trouble … (Be clear about what you want and use complete sentences. E-mail is professional correspondence).
>
> Could you please … (note the use of politeness). If not, I will come by tomorrow at 5 P.M. during your office hours. (Again, notice the politeness—"if not. … " No one is required to do what you ask. We do things for people because we are professionals. Be sure to treat others, as you would like to be treated yourself).
>
> Thank you for your help. (Always end by thanking the recipient of the e-mail for their time, help, or courtesy).
>
> Include your name and *complete* contact information here. (Do not assume that your professor, customer, or client knows who you are from your e-mail address or the context of your message).

- Be careful not to begin relationships too informally, i.e., by using a client's first name. Only in the U.S. is courtesy taken for granted. Many international clients/colleagues *always* use full names and even titles at work. Opt for more rather than less formality. Do not assume that using someone's first name will show friendliness. Just as often, being casual with names and titles shows a lack of respect. Take the cue from your colleague and wait until you have been given permission to become less formal, or until *s/he* addresses *you* less formally.
- *Create an e-mail address that contains your name or name and initials.* For example, "SLake@BigCorp.com" "EEC@BigCorp.com," "IngridaGrauze@GMail.com," etc. As a student or a professional looking for work, do not use meaningless names like "SexPistols@GMail.Com," "HotChick@HotMail.com," or "VelvetBlue@ … . " Many spammers and viruses use fake names, and a lot of e-mail spam servers will filter messages out with key words that might be associated with spam messages. Because of the number of viruses and Trojan Horses in the computer world, many professionals will not read e-mail messages from unfamiliar senders. Having an e-mail address with an unidentifiable name, increases the chance that your messages will be ignored or deleted without being read.
- Few e-mail systems are case sensitive. Thus, it does not matter if you use uppercase or lowercase letters. Since reading words/names that are run together using both upper and lowercase letters is easier, use title case style when you print e-mail addresses in documents or type e-mail address on messages. Rather than <yournamehere@mail.com>, use <YourNameHere@Mail.com>.
- Many people do not know that periods and commas cannot appear at the end of e-mail addresses. Thus, whenever an e-mail address will be followed by a period, like the examples in the paragraph above, be sure to enclose the address in brackets or parenthesis so that the period is not mistakenly added to the e-mail address.
- Use uppercase letters when letters and numbers might be confused (e.g., a lowercase el (l) and a one (1)—bhl1@mail.com. Instead, use BHL1@ … .
- Never lapse into informality. Your employer, potential employer, or professor is *not* your friend (although s/he might like you). Do not assume that speaking (or writing) to professionals informally (as with your friends or parents) is okay. Take your cues from the people you send messages to.

Ultimately, you need to appreciate that when you use e-mail (or any other electronic device), you might as well be standing in front of a camera on the steps of the state house. E-mail is regularly forwarded to other people. Many e-mail messages are sent with a BCC (blind carbon copy, which CCs someone else without the primary recipient knowing). Most people keep copies of potentially incriminating e-mail messages. E-mail is not private, and e-mail is not like an instant message to your friend in class. E-mail is a professional medium and should be treated just like any other professional correspondences—such as a business letter.

PROFESSIONAL ISSUES AND THE WORLD WIDE WEB

In terms of the World Wide Web, there are three important things to understand:

(1) Organizational Web sites *will* be visited by the media for informational purposes, especially in times of crisis, and therefore must be kept up to date with complete and accurate contact information of key organizational members (Kent & Taylor, 1998, 2002).

(2) Never store private information on the Internet. The Internet is *not* secure. Thousands of people spend their every waking moment trying to break into organizational databases and obtain private or sensitive information, or just plain snooping. Consider setting up an *intra*net (an internal network, not connected to the Internet) if you want to use a network interface for employees to store or access private information.

(3) *Never, under any circumstances,* post graphic, audio, video, or textual content that you obtained from the Internet on an organizational Web site. Using an image that was downloaded from the Internet (as students routinely do for class reports) is a violation of copyright law. Indeed, as a communication professional, you must assume that even when using content that is not clearly labeled with a copyright mark (a picture on someone's blog, for example), you must obtain a photo or art release before using the content. Moreover, images, sound, or textual content used on an organization's Web site with permission (but not licensed) must be properly cited. A law called "fair use" protects students and professors from getting into trouble for using copyrighted content for educational purposes; however, no other organization is allowed to use another person's or organization's intellectual or artistic property for business or professional purposes without the owner's permission.

Obtaining permission to use copyrighted content extends even to documents used internally. For example, if you just read a great article in the *Economist* that you want all of your colleagues to read before your next meeting, you need to buy each of them a separate copy of the magazine or arrange for them to pass the magazine from person to person (Casarez, 1997). Making copies of books, magazines, newspapers, and broadcast copy without first obtaining copyright permission or paying a licensing fee is a violation of copyright law. All major publishers sell "reprints" of stories for professional purposes and organizations regularly order hundreds of reprints of favorable articles for use in media, investor, or informational kits.

As a public relations professional, you are also a "communication professional" and expected to understand laws and regulations that pertain to communication issues. Moreover, you should have a firm grasp of governmental regulations and laws that touch on organizational communication. As suggested, spend some time visiting the many regulatory and governmental agencies mentioned above. In the long run, your understanding of communication laws and regulations will make you a more competent and skilled professional.

CRAFTING AND OBTAINING PHOTO RELEASES

Obtaining photo releases, consent forms, and copyright permissions is just part of doing business. To be on the safe side, you should maintain current photographs and photo release forms for all employees. A generic photo release form should either be kept in each employee's personal file, or obtained before photographs are published. Always maintain up-to-date photos and signed release forms for all employees.

Group photos are especially problematic because individuals move on to new positions, move to different departments, and, in some cases, pass away. You clearly cannot use a group photograph of senior management from 18 months ago if one of the people in the picture now works for a competitor. Thus, keeping up-to-data photographs goes hand in hand with keeping copies of signed photo release forms. See Appendix B for how to write a sample release form.

REGULATORY AND GOVERNMENT AGENCIES

The U.S. government has a number of regulatory agencies devoted to ensuring that organizations behave ethically, legally, and safely. Public relations professionals need to be concerned with a number of regulatory agencies—in particular, all publicly owned organizations need to be aware of SEC regulations. Organizations that deal with food, drugs, cosmetics, and other products need to be concerned with the FDA. Communication organizations need to be concerned with the FCC. The remainder of this chapter describes many of the relevant regulatory agencies.

The Food and Drug Administration (FDA)

The FDA is responsible for the safety and regulation of products and services related to biologics (blood, product research, etc.), cosmetics, drugs (OTC and prescription), foods, medical devices, radiation emitting electronic products, and veterinary products (www.fda.gov/comments/regs.html). The FDA also monitors and regulates product labeling, marketing, and advertising (related to prescription drugs and medical devices) claims for products, as well as overseeing manufacturing and licensing procedures and product standards and testing. What the FDA *is not* responsible for is advertising, alcohol, consumer products, drug abuse, health insurance, meat and poultry, pesticides, inspecting restaurants and grocery stores, and water (www.fda.gov/comments/noregs.html).

Rather than enumerating *all* the types of products and organizations that may be regulated by the FDA here (which include egg products, drugs, mammography, milk, paint, product packaging, poultry, etc.) (www.fda.gov/opacom/ laws), you should visit the FDA Web site and familiarize yourself with what the FDA regulates (www.FDA.gov). As a public relations professional, you need to be cautious about any medical or health claims that are made on product labels, in news releases and brochures, in blogs, in advertisements, and on organizational Web sites.

Federal Communication Commission (FCC)

The Federal Communication Commission was "established by the Communications Act of 1934 and is charged with regulating interstate and international communications by radio, television, wire, satellite and cable. The FCC's jurisdiction covers the 50 states, the District of Columbia, and U.S. possessions" (www.fcc.gov/aboutus.html). The formal charge of the FCC can be summed up in twenty-eight words: to "ensure that the American people have available, at reasonable costs and without discrimination, rapid, efficient, Nation- and world-wide communication services; whether by radio, television, wire, satellite, or cable" (www.fcc.gov/omd/history).

As mentioned earlier, communication law experts suggest that 35 percent of *all* laws touch on communication issues in some way. The U.S. Committee on Energy and Commerce has an 844-page summary of communications law available through its Web site (<energycommerce.house.gov/images/stories/Documents/PDF/publications/108-D.pdf>, cf., also, <www.fcc.gov/omd/history>) that attests to the quantity of communication law. Moreover, with the increasing complexity of communication laws (advertising, copyright, marketing, patents, privacy, sales), and because of the many new communication technologies (cellular, GPS, networking, Internet, Radio Frequency Identification Tags—RFID), legal issues associated with communication must be a prominent concern for all public relations and communication professionals.

The FCC not only regulates all forms of electronics that produce radio waves (cellular telephones, radios, televisions, wireless routers, cordless telephones, radio-controlled toys, microwave ovens, electronic cash registers, garage door openers, keyless entry systems, E-ZPass and similar toll devices), but also regulates access to the airwaves for politicians and nonprofit organizations. The FCC's control over the airwaves also extends to monitoring and responding to complaints made by consumers against broadcasters, cable television, telephone providers, and Internet service providers. The FCC polices everything from obscenity complaints to slamming.

Public relations professionals should understand the provisions for public service that can allow nonprofit organization to take advantage of free, "public service" advertising as well as provisions for equal time (in the case of a politician seeking access to the airwaves). However, "equal time" does not mean "free time." When one candidate is allowed to purchase airtime for advertisements or campaign messages, other candidates are also allowed to *purchase* airtime.[v] However, if a candidate for political office cannot afford to buy airtime, networks are not obliged to give it away for free.

Federal Trade Commission (FTC)

The Federal Trade Commission is perhaps the most important organization to the average public relations professional. The FTC regulates interstate commerce and works to protect consumers from unfair business practices, including advertising claims; Internet commerce; unethical marketing; identity theft; truth-in-lending practices; telemarketing; pyramid schemes; food, drug and dietary supplement claims; weight loss product claims; children's advertising; claims about product performance made in national or regional newspapers, magazines, radio and television commercials; claims made in infomercials, through direct mail, and through the Internet. The FTC also oversees an assortment of consumer education campaigns (www.ftc.gov/ftc/about.shtm).

At first glance, the activities of the FTC might seem unfamiliar; however, as the FTC explains:

> As a consumer or business person, you may be more familiar with the work of the Federal Trade Commission than you think.
>
> The FTC deals with issues that touch the economic life of every American. It is the only federal agency with both consumer protection and competition jurisdiction in broad sectors of the economy. The FTC pursues vigorous and effective law enforcement; advances consumers' interests by sharing its expertise with federal and state legislatures and U.S. and international government agencies; develops policy and research tools through hearings, workshops, and conferences; and creates practical and plain-language educational programs for consumers and businesses in a global marketplace with constantly changing technologies. (www.ftc.gov/ftc/about.shtm)

As a public relations professional, you must be careful not to run afoul of the FTC. In general, large professional agencies and corporations have legal departments that approve news release and organizational documents before publication so FTC problems can be avoided. However, public relations professionals are often responsible (or should become increasingly responsible) for policing other aspects of an organization's performance and advising or counseling the organization when proposed activities or objectives might cause regulatory concerns.

Public relations professionals are advised to visit the FTC Web site and examine the content for both "consumers" and "businesses" (www.ftc.gov/index.html). Understanding the types of issues likely to get an organization in trouble is as important as understanding what consumers expect from businesses and communication professionals.

Securities and Exchange Commission (SEC)

The Securities and Exchange Commission works to protect the financial health of the United States. According to the SEC's Web site:

> The mission of the U.S. Securities and Exchange Commission is to protect investors, maintain fair, orderly, and efficient markets, and facilitate capital formation.
>
> As more and more first-time investors turn to the markets to help secure their futures, pay for homes, and send children to college, our investor protection mission is more compelling than ever.
>
> As our nation's securities exchanges mature into global for-profit competitors, there is even greater need for sound market regulation.
>
> The laws and rules that govern the securities industry in the United States derive from a simple and straightforward concept: all investors, whether large institutions or private individuals, should have access to certain basic facts about an investment prior to buying it, and so long as they hold it. To achieve this, the SEC requires public companies to disclose meaningful financial and other information to the public. This provides a common pool of knowledge for all investors to use to judge for themselves whether to buy, sell, or hold a particular security. Only through the steady flow of timely, comprehensive, and accurate information can people make sound investment decisions.
>
> Crucial to the SEC's effectiveness in each of these areas is its enforcement authority. Each year the SEC brings hundreds of civil enforcement actions against individuals and companies for violation of the securities laws. Typical infractions include insider trading, accounting fraud, and providing false or misleading information about securities and the companies that issue them. (www.sec.gov/about/whatwedo.shtml)

Public relations practitioners who work for publicly traded organizations need to understand the importance of federally mandated financial reporting and the legal implications for misrepresentation. For example, a news release overestimating or misrepresenting an organization's stock, financial status, or involvement in an upcoming merger or acquisition might inflate the organization's stock price, and represents a violation of federal law. Additionally, public relations practitioners need to understand the implications of insider trading, fair disclosure, and other SEC mandated activities—violations of which can lead to large fines and jail time.

INSIDER TRADING

As the SEC explains, "Insider trading refers generally to buying or selling a security, in breach of a fiduciary duty or other relationship of trust and confidence, while in possession of material, nonpublic information about the security" (www.sec.gov/answers/insider.htm). In essence, if an "insider," who has access to information that is not public, or has not yet been made publicly available, uses the information to make investments, or advise others to invest on his/her behalf, s/he is guilty of insider trading. Although at this point in your professional career "insider trading" may seem like something that only happens on television and to big corporate CEOs or celebrities like Martha Stewart, the potential for insider trading exists when you are working for any publicly traded company.

According to the SEC's 2005, *Performance and Accountability Report*, about 7 to 8 percent of all cases brought by the SEC are for insider trading issues (<www.sec.gov/about/secpar/secpar2005.pdf>, p. 8). Indeed, in many cases, insider trading occurs by lower level employees (traders, communication professionals, etc.) and often leads to very large fines for the organization itself and potential jail time for the person(s) involved. In the case of intentional deception or fraud, insider trading can lead to jail time, as Martha Stewart's 2004–2005 stint in federal prison demonstrates. As with copyright and trademarks, students are advised to visit the SEC Web site and spend some time learning about SEC-related issues (www.sec.gov/index.htm).

UNITED STATES POSTAL SERVICE (USPS)

"What do I need to know about the post office?" you might ask. Well, a great deal, actually. Understanding the regulations for bulk mailings, media mail, customs declarations, direct mailing and other rules is essential. At some point, you very likely will want to ship a box of annual reports or brochures, send direct-mail messages, obtain bulk mailing permits, etc.

Additionally, for documents that are designed to be mailed (newsletters, brochures, fundraising letters), the cost of postage can be a big factor in budgeting and needs to be considered *before* final design decisions are made. Furthermore, many organizations choose to include return envelopes with their correspondences, and there are very specific rules for how envelopes and documents must be packaged or sealed (which will also affect the overall design costs of the document). The USPS Web site provides a wealth of information about postal options, including "tips for preparing packages," and is worth visiting before making budgeting decisions on projects that include mailing fees (www.usps.com/business/customersupport/welcome.htm).

DIRECT MAIL

Direct mail is almost always conducted through the U.S. Postal Service. Direct mail refers to those annoying letters that marketing, credit, nonprofit, and other organizations constantly send out to raise money, and convince people to subscribe to magazines, apply for credit cards, etc. I could spend the rest of this chapter explaining the principles of direct mail. If your organization is considering employing direct mailing/marketing, familiarize yourself with one of the hundreds of books on the subject or hire a direct mail firm.

If you choose to go the route of hiring a "professional" mail/marketing agency, understand that marketers tend to have little in the way of ethical boundaries. Many nonprofit organizations use fundraising/marketing professionals to raise money and receive only 10¢ on the dollar after the fundraiser's cut. Additionally, many marketing organizations use deceptive pitches, subtle fear appeals, and other unethical persuasive tactics to achieve their goals. Deceptive marketers often try to make call recipients believe that there is an actual fireperson or police officer on the other end of the telephone. Finally, many organizations (especially nonprofit social cause organizations) continuously pester members for financial support, and the names of friends and relatives, for help with "emergencies," etc.

If you intend to hire a professional agency, be sure that you are vigilant and maintain control over the fund-raising" tactics used, and the message content. Better to raise less money but consistently maintain the trust and support of your members than have to continuously rely on costly membership campaigns because you drive so many people away with your fundraising.

There are three important things to understand about direct mail (or calling):

(1) Direct mail is expensive and requires up-to-date, accurate, and targeted mailing lists and professional print materials.

(2) As a rule, people do not like to receive direct mail (also called junk mail). Be sure your targeted mailings have intrinsic value to recipients (newsletters, reports, calendars of upcoming events, catalogues). Be sure that if your organization is going to use direct mail (or direct calling) as part of a campaign or to keep individuals and publics informed, that the recipients actually want to receive your mailings. Be aware that a national "do-not-call" registry (www.DoNotCall.Gov) exists and calling individuals who have registered is illegal unless your organization is a nonprofit, religious, or political organization. A similar list exists for direct postal mail.

(3) A more personal medium (face-to-face, personal telephone calls, letters) is always preferable to direct mail, which is almost always readily identifiable as "junk mail" and thrown out, unopened, by many people.

In political contexts, canvassing by volunteers and the candidate is an infinitely more powerful persuasive tool and much more likely to yield results than direct mail. Similarly, with fundraising efforts, actual, personal correspondence is much more powerful than form letters with "Dear Mr. Snizzle" mail merged at the top of the page.

You should also remember the paradox of "the live one" in fundraising. Most sales and marketing professionals know that people who give money can be persuaded to give *more* money. However, many donors feel that once they have given some money, they should not be contacted for more money again until a reasonable period of time has elapsed (typically about a year). Unfortunately, many organizations routinely follow-up on donations and subscriptions with requests for *more* money, extended subscriptions, etc. Public relations professionals need always to keep the organization–public relationship in mind. Never employ "sleazy" fundraising tactics just because they might yield short-term success or were recommended by a direct mail or fundraising firm. Always place your relationships with stakeholders first.

CONCLUSION

Making ethical decisions is driven by a number of forces, including sound rhetorical strategies from the start. The ethical organization has to spend less time and devote fewer resources to dealing with ethical problems. Nevertheless, ethical issues will arise from time to time (for example, a client who asks for a male account representative rather than a female account rep., or a local newspaper who demands that you "buy some advertising space" if you want your news releases published). Indeed, in an international study commissioned by the Institute for Public Relations (USA) and the International Public Relations Association, and conducted by Kruckeberg and Tsetsura (2003) (www.instituteforpr.org/files/uploads/Bribery_Index_2003.pdf), the U.S. falls fifth on the list behind nine more ethical countries (some of which are tied).[6] Asking for cash for coverage or various quid-pro-quo coverage schemes is quite common, and every public relations professional will be faced with ethical and legal decisions. By understanding how to evaluate ethical situations, and understanding how various regulatory agencies influence our ethical practices, public relations professionals have a greater chance of avoiding ethical dilemmas and resolving ethical problems.

ACTIVITIES

1. Using one of the scenarios below identified by your teacher, evaluate the situation in light of the features of the Potter box. Be able to justify your decisions in class.
   - **A.** You take a news release to the real estate editor of the daily newspaper in your town. The release is a newsworthy announcement on a new complex that your agency is building nearby. The editor suggests that "the story needs some advertising support." In other words, he wants your agency to buy an ad before he will run the news story. What do you do?
   - **B.** You are promoting a boat show. You have sent out ads and news releases about the participants, etc.

Three weeks before the show, two major boat makers decide not to come to the show or donate their door prizes. Do you contact the media and tell them about the pull out or do you keep quiet and scramble to make the best of the situation?

C. You are a partner in a medium-size public relations agency. You have two excellent young female associates who are great account executives. You just landed a new client and you have sent one of the young female associates over to manage the account. Two hours later, the client (a hospital manager) calls and says that he wants "someone more mature and authoritative" to work with. What do you do?

D. You work for an organization that makes computers. The production and technical staff are "way behind schedule" and the shareholders are getting anxious. The end of the financial quarter has arrived and the president has promised that the stock price will remain stable. To make it look like everything is on schedule, you are asked to write a news release announcing the unveiling of the new computer next week. There is no way that the computer will be ready. What do you do?

2. Visit the U.S. copyright office, download Form TX, (www.copyright.gov/forms/formtxi.pdf) or Short Form TX (www.copyright.gov/forms/formtxs.pdf), and prepare the correct document needed to copyright one of your literary works. Use the short form for sole authored work or the long form for co-authored works. Bring the completed forms and documents to the next class in an (unsealed) envelope as if you were really going to file the documents. What kind of organizations should copyright their documents and why? Why do you think the U.S. government does not copyright governmental reports or other documents?
3. Create a photo release form suitable for professional purposes based on the sample in Appendix B and obtain releases for three different photographs that you have previously taken, or that you have taken for this assignment. Attach copies of the images for which the releases apply. Create the form so that you might have "unlimited rights" to use the image as part of "educational materials while in college." What are some of the ethical issues associated with release forms?
4. Imagine that you work for a publicly traded, *Fortune* 500 company and you own 5,000 shares of stock. You are writing a news release announcing a merger between your company and a competitor that is expected to cause the stock price to increase dramatically. Visit the SEC Web site and find out how long you must wait until you can sell some (or all) of your stock (www.sec.gov). Hint: Review the insider trading rules.
5. Visit the United States Postal Service Web site and locate the information about obtaining a bulk mailing permit and sending bulk mail. What are the costs associated with bulk mailings? Why would an organization want to use bulk mail to send out its messages? What rules apply to bulk mailing in terms of weight, size, quantity, etc.?
6. Go into your e-mail application and set up a signature file (contact information that automatically appears on every message sent) and an address card (a file that allows people to easily add your contact information to their address book). Once you have created your signature file and address card, send a polite message to your professor. Note: You can create multiple signature files for use in different situations. If you do not want to share your address or telephone with someone, create an address file that just has name, title, and e-mail. Be sure that you include complete contact information (name, title, organization, cell and land telephone numbers, fax, e-mail, Web site URL, etc.). For example:

    Michael L. Kent
    Public Relations Student
    Your University
    Cell: 111-222–3333
    Telephone: 111-222–3333 [note, spell out the word telephone and use AP style when writing the telephone number itself]
    E-mail: Your_E-Mail_Here.com [be sure to use upper and lower case letters to make the e-mail address easier to read and be sure to create a professional name for your account if you do not have one already].
    Address [write as two or three lines]: 1111 College Ave.
    City State Zip (punctuate the address properly)
    Country (if relevant)
    URL (if you have a URL use it here)

NOTES

1. In terms of full disclosure, this definition of plagiarism has been adopted and shaped by me over the last 10 years for use in my classroom materials. It originally came from policies at several universities, including the University of Oregon, Purdue University, and Montclair State University. The statements that I have used are generic statements from teaching seminars, student handbooks, and academic dishonesty seminars.
2. According to the U.S. Copyright Office, fair use depends upon several factors, including:

    a. "the purpose and character of the use, including whether such use is of commercial nature or is for nonprofit educational purposes;

b. the nature of the copyrighted work;
c. amount and substantiality of the portion used in relation to the copyrighted work as a whole; and
d. the effect of the use upon the potential market for or value of the copyrighted work.

The distinction between "fair use" and infringement may be unclear and not easily defined. There is no specific number of words, lines, or notes that may safely be taken without permission. Acknowledging the source of the copyrighted material does not substitute for obtaining permission." (www.copyright.gov/fls/fl102.html)

3. As an interesting aside, when you search Google for "how many employers read employee e-mail?" (without quotation marks), the first link that comes up is for the Privacy Rights Clearinghouse, a perfectly legitimate social cause organization that is designed to provide citizens with information about their rights. The second link in the list is for an organization called Nolo: "Our mission—provide do-it-yourself legal solutions for consumers and small businesses" (www.nolo.com/about.cfm). Nolo is essentially the evil twin of Privacy Rights Clearinghouse. According to Nolo:

> Technology now makes it possible for employers to keep track of virtually all workplace communications by any employee—on the phone and in cyberspace. And many employers take advantage of these tracking devices: A survey of more than 700 companies by the Society for Human Resource Management (SHRM) found that almost three-quarters of the companies monitor their workers' use of the Internet and check employee email, [sic] and more than half review employee phone calls. According to a study by the American Management Association, businesses offering financial services—such as banks, brokerage houses, insurance firms, and real estate companies—are most likely to monitor their workers' communications.
>
> Employers have a legitimate interest in keeping track of how their employees spend their work hours. After all, no one wants workers surfing X-rated websites, [sic] sending offensive email, [sic] or calling in bets on the ponies on the company's dime. And employers may want to take steps to make sure employees are not giving trade secrets to competitors, engaging in illegal conduct at work, or using company communications equipment to harass their coworkers. (www.nolo.com/legal-encyclopedia/article-29853.html)

4. E-mail messages are one of the first things that the government grabs when there is an investigation. The last thing you or anyone else in your organization would want to be made public are messages with inappropriate language, racial or sexual content, links to unprofessional Web sites, etc. Assume every e-mail message written *will* be taken out of context—that is the nature of "incriminating e-mails." You do not want to be the one who makes the five o'clock news for misogynist, racist, sexual, or off-color jokes in your e-mail messages.
5. Provisions for equal time and broadcast services for the public good (public service announcements, etc.) only extend to *broadcast* television; *pay* television (cable, satellite, etc.) providers are free to chose whether or not to air political advertisements, and for whom, with no legal requirement to provide "equal time."
6. Note: Several countries tie for third, fourth, fifth, etc.

APPENDIX A

SAMPLE WRITING TESTS

Below are a number of sample writing tests that were submitted to me by members of the International Association of Business Communicators. I have changed the scenarios to protect the integrity of the original tests but these exercise are essentially real.

SAMPLE 1

There are two parts to this test.

PART I,

Edit the attached news release directly on the page using proofreader marks.

[The organization will usually provide one of their own news releases where various subtle and obvious errors have been inserted.]

PART II,

Write a 300-word story for our online newsletter based on the news release you edited.

SAMPLE 2

Test of professional and creative writing ability (15 minutes)

Please read the following narrative and write a letter of response to the customer.

We have been clients of yours for over five years. In that time you have performed very well. However, since the Y2K has arrived we have experienced nothing but problems with our monthly statements. We have had to constantly telephone to verify "missing" information or to request client statements. Frankly, we are getting tired of this and considering switching to a new service provider when our contract ends in November.

SAMPLE 3

Correct the following AP style errors in the sentence below. If a sentence is correct, leave it alone. If the sentence is incorrect, circle the error(s) and write corrections for the error(s) in the space provided.

1. Sponsorship for the event is $3,000.00. ____________________
2. To who do we direct the invoice? ____________________
3. The media analysis will be based on the MOM. ____________________
4. Jamal was there to except the award. ____________________
5. The meeting was scheduled for 10:00 A.M. ____________________
6. The buick open will be held next week. ____________________
7. Kuac FM has agreed to cover the event ____________________
8. The music will include Dust in the Wind. ____________________
9. Protests were staged over inclusion of the "Bible" and the "Koran" in the materials and not other important texts like the "Bhagavad-Gita." ____________________
10. The meeting was attended by Mr. Carl Botan. ____________________

11. The meeting is scheduled for Wed. morning. ____________
12. The convention site is 4 miles from the hotel. ____________
13. Neither Paco or Juan could attend the ceremony. ____________
14. We invited grandmother Larissa to come to the meeting. ____________
15. Most of the members attended, however ¼ were out sick. ____________
16. The department of state rep. was unable to come. ____________
17. Employee holidays include easter, christmas, and mlk day. ____________
18. Professor M.L.Kent was at the meeting. ____________
19. Twenty five people attended the meeting last week. ____________
20. A plurality of voters (2,300/4,500) approved the measure. ____________
21. Mankind is on the brink of a new era. ____________
22. According to reports, the day of the event is January 5. ____________
23. Mr. Morgan and Mr. Doerfel will attend. ____________
24. Barrett, Ph.D., and Fafard, Ph.D., will give lectures. ____________
25. The article was written by Arthos's brother Earl. ____________
26. The principle investigator on the project will be Tyler. ____________
27. The busiest months at the firm are spring and fall. ____________
28. Contact us at 333.444.5555, or by e-mail at ... ____________
29. The organizational website has seen controversy. ____________
30. The 1980s were difficult for the organization. ____________

The Items below contain a number of grammatical, style and other errors. Where a sentence has an error, line it out and insert a correction (use proper proofreader marks if you know how to)

1. The contract is for a 50-year mortgage.
2. ... agreed with the decision but 19 said no.
3. The items are all priced under $200.00.
4. I told you we should of been at the meeting.
5. The judgement was against the plantiff.
6. Noxos's church is in the center of town.
7. We tried, but its' plan was not fathomable.
8. The club had no vacancys for Sunday's match.
9. Contact us after next Febuary about the job.
10. The Meeting starts at 7 P.M.
11. The team could of won if we had the support.
12. It's the client's fault not our's

A typical section like this has 30-40 questions.

APPENDIX B

ADULT MODEL RELEASE

In consideration of my engagement as a model, upon the terms herewith stated, I hereby give to ______________________________ his/her heirs, legal representatives and assigns, those for whom ______________________________ is acting, and those acting with his/her authority and permission:

a. the unrestricted right and permission to copyright and use, re-use, publish, and republish photographic portraits or pictures of me or in which I may be included intact or in part, composite or distorted in character or form, without restriction as to changes or transformations in conjunction with my own or a fictitious name, or reproduction hereof in color or otherwise, made through any and all media now or hereafter known for illustration, art, promotion, advertising, trade, or any other purpose whatsoever.

b. I also permit the use of any printed material in connection therewith.

c. I hereby relinquish any right that I may have to examine or approve the completed product or products or the advertising copy or printed matter that may be used in conjunction therewith or the use to which it may be applied.

d. I hereby release, discharge and agree to save harmless ______________________________, his/her heirs, legal representatives or assigns, and all persons functioning under his/her permission or authority, or those for whom he/she is functioning, from any liability by virtue of any blurring, distortion, alteration, optical illusion, or use in composite form whether intentional or otherwise, that may occur or be produced in the taking of said picture or in any subsequent processing thereof, as well as any publication thereof, including without limitation any claims for libel or invasion of privacy.

e. I hereby affirm that I am over the age of majority and have the right to contract in my own name. I have read the above authorization, release and agreement, prior to its execution; I fully understand the contents thereof. This agreement shall be binding upon me and my heirs, legal representatives and assigns.

Dated: ______________________________

Signed: ______________________________

Address: ______________________________

City: ______________________________

State/Zip: ______________________________

Telephone: ______________________________

Witness: ______________________________

Name/description of image: ______________________________

Attach a copy of image(s): ______________________________

MINOR MODEL RELEASE

For valuable consideration, I hereby confer on ______________________________ the absolute and irrevocable right and permission with respect to the photographs that he/she has taken of my minor child in which he/she may be included with others:

- **a.** To copyright the same in ______________________________ name or any other name that he/she may select;
- **b.** To use, re-use, publish and re-publish the same in whole or in part, separately or in conjunction with other photographs, in any medium now or hereafter known, and for any purpose whatsoever, including (but not by way of limitation) illustration, promotion, advertising and trade, and;
- **c.** To use my name or my child's name in connection therewith if he/she so decides. I hereby release and discharge ______________________________ from all and any claims and demands ensuing from or in connection with the use of the photographs, including any and all claims for libel and invasion of privacy.

This authorization and release shall inure to the benefit of the legal representatives, licensees and assigns of photographer photographer's name goes here as well as the person(s) for whom he/she took the photographs. I have read the foregoing and fully understand the contents hereof. I represent that I am the [parent/guardian] of the above named model. For value received, I hereby consent to the foregoing on his/her behalf.

Dated: ______________________________

Minor's Name: ______________________________

Parent or Guardian: ______________________________

Address: ______________________________

City: ______________________________

State/Zip: ______________________________

Telephone: ______________________________

Witness: ______________________________

Name/description of image: ______________________________

Attach a copy of image(s): ______________________________

SAMPLE RELEASE

The University of Oklahoma

GAYLORD COLLEGE OF JOURNALISM AND MASS COMMUNICATION

Friday, May 14, 2010

Name
Address
City State, Zip

I am writing a book tentatively titled *A Rhetorical Approach to Public Relations Writing,* which is scheduled for publication by Allyn & Bacon, a Pearson Education imprint, in 2010. I would like to include the following:

> *Description of the item requested here including page numbers, dates, etc. and attach a copy or scan of the item/page(s).*

May I have your permission to include this material in my forthcoming book and in all future editions, versions, and revisions of it, as well as in derivative works and all ancillaries, as needed? This includes non-exclusive world rights in all languages, and in all formats and media. These rights will in no way restrict republication of your material in any other form by you or others authorized by you. Should you not control these rights in their entirely, would you please tell me who does?

A release form is included below and a copy of this letter is enclosed for your files. Your prompt consideration of this request is appreciated.

Cordially,

Michael L. Kent, Ph.D.
Associate Professor
Telephone: (405) 325–7346
E-mail: MKent@OU.edu

I (we) grant the permission requested on the terms stated in this letter.

The undersigned hereby represents that they have the right to grant the permission requested above, and that the material does not infringe upon the copyright or other rights of third parties. The undersigned is the owner/author of such materials.

CREDIT LINE TO BE USED:

By: ______________________________ Date: ______________________________

Fee: ______________________________

Social Security Number or Federal Identification Number (FID):

APPENDIX C

WEB SCAVENGER HUNT

Instructions: The purpose of this exercise is to teach you how to effectively use the Web for conducting research. Below is a list of facts/information for you to locate. In order for you to be successful at this exercise you will need to employ some of the principles outlined on the "How to Use the Web More Effectively" handout. Spend no more than an hour on this activity and be prepared to report your results to the class. *Write down answers and Web sites in the space provided (or print and attach).*

Web-Hunt Questions

1. In Farmington, New Mexico there is a bed and breakfast built into a cave in the wall of a cliff. What is the name of the bed and breakfast and where can I learn more about this place? ________________
   http:// ________________

2. Which University in Ohio was the site of the famous 1993 "Sexual Offense Policy," and what was the first clause of the policy? ________________
   http:// ________________

3. What is Naproxen Sodium, how/where is it used, and where can I learn more about it? ________________
   http:// ________________

4. When was the role-playing game "Dungeons and Dragons" invented, where, and by whom? ________________
   http:// ________________

5. Here are the names of three reported viruses: Red Alert, Walker, and Death69. Two of them are hoaxes and one of them is real. Which one is real and what can it do?
   ____
   http:// ________________

6. The University of Alaska holds a yearly festival called "Starvation Gulch." When is it held? ________________
   http:// ________________

7. How many rows of whiskers does a cat have (don't peek!)? ________________
   http:// ________________

8. How are funeral eulogies structured? ________________
   http:// ________________

APPENDIX D

UNDERSTANDING POINTS AND PICA

In U.S. publishing, we use a measurement system called Pica that consists of "Points and Pica," just like we have "Inches and Feet." Pica is a measuring system used in graphic arts, publishing, and typography, that allows for more precise measurements.

Many people do not realize that there are many systems of measurement. Americans are of course most familiar with inches and feet, while Europeans are more comfortable with the Metric system. In some cases, like engineering and publishing, very precise measurement is crucial. Indeed, NASA once lost a multimillion dollar spacecraft because of a mix-up in measurement systems between the U.S. system of inches and feet and the British system of inches and feet called "Imperial units" (based on a decimal system). Not to be outdone, the French also have a 230 year old typographic measurement system called Cicero, which is slightly larger than Pica.

Like space science, creating compelling graphic documents also requires great precision—less than sending a spaceship to Mars, of course. Although a 32nd of an inch might not sound like a lot of space, the eye readily notices even very small alignment variations and print documents look unprofessional when they are misaligned or out of proportion. As explained below, there are 72 points per inch, allowing for more discrete division of space.

Pica: 6 per inch.

Points: 72 per Inch.

One Pica: 12 points.

How to Write: When you are writing inches and feet, you use inch and feet symbols (e.g., 6'2"). When writing points and pica you write pica first and then points with a "p" in the middle (e.g., 6p3 or six pica, three points, which is an inch and a 24th).

How to Measure Type: When indicating how many points a block of text is written in and how many points of spacing the lines have, we write points over points. For example, 12/12 means that you have a 12-point font set with 12 points of spacing (or "single spaced"), 9/12 would be a nine-point font with about 1.25 spacing. This paragraph is written in 10 points with 12 point spacing between paragraphs.

Whenever you have *about* the same following space as the size of the font (6/6, 9.5/9.5, 12/12, 18/18, etc.), you are essentially "single spacing." Thus, if you are typing in a 9-point font, and want "double spaced" lines, you would use 9/18 (a 9-point font with 18 points of space after each line break).

Desktop publishing programs like InDesign and QuarkXpress have an "Auto" leading setting that adds just a bit more than absolute single spacing: 10/12, 11/13.2, 12/14.4, 18/21.6, etc.

How to Write points and Pica

$\frac{1}{8}$" = 9 points, or 0p9

$\frac{1}{4}$" = 18 points, or 1p6 (12 pts. or 1 pica, plus 6 pts.)

$\frac{3}{8}$" = 27 pts. or 2p3 (2 pica = 24 pts., plus 3 more pts.)

$\frac{1}{2}$" = 36 pts. or 3p0

$\frac{5}{8}$" = 45 pts. or 3p9

$\frac{3}{4}$" = 54 pts. or 4p6

$\frac{7}{8}$" = 63 pts. or 5p3

1" = 72 pts. or 6p0

1.25" = 90 pts., or 7p6

1.5" = 108 pts. or 9p0

5" = 360 pts. or 30p0

10" = 720 pts. or 60p0

How to Calculate Points and Pica *(do not look above for answers)*

$\frac{1}{2}$" = ___ points or ___ p0

$\frac{1}{4}$" = ___ points or 1p ___

$\frac{1}{6}$" = ___ points or ___ p0

A 9 point font, "single spaced" = ___/___

A 12 point font, "double-spaced" = ___/___

A 13 point font, "1.5 spaced" = ___/___

A 7 point font "triple-spaced" = ___/___ .

If you want an extra half space after each paragraph of that 7 pt. font, you would add how much "space after?": ___.

BIBLIOGRAPHY

"Above average" hurricane season expected: National Hurricane Center director doesn't expect it to top 2005 record (2006, March 31). Washington: The Associated Press. <www.msnbc.msn.com/id/12094155>

Alterman, E., & Green, M. J. (2004). *The book on Bush: How George W. (mis)leads America.* New York: Viking Press.

Anderson, R., Cissna, K. N., & Arnett, R. C. (Eds.) (1994). *The reach of dialogue: Confirmation, voice, and community.* Cresskill, NJ: Hampton Press Inc.

Aristotle (Kennedy, G. A., trans.) (1991). *Aristotle on rhetoric: A theory of civic discourse.* New York: Oxford University Press.

Azjen, I., & Fishbein, M. (1980). *Understanding attitudes and predicting social behavior.* Englewood Cliffs, NJ: Prentice Hall.

Bagdikian, B. H. (2000). *The media monopoly.* Boston: Beacon Press.

Bagdikian, B. H. (2004). *The new media monopoly.* Boston: Beacon Press.

Bandura, A. (1977). *Social learning theory.* New York: General Learning Press.

Bandura, A. (1986). *Social foundations of thought and action.* Englewood Cliffs, NJ: Prentice-Hall.

Bandura, A. (1997). *Self-efficacy: The exercise of control.* New York: W.H. Freeman.

Barbaro, M. (2006, March 7). Wal-Mart enlists bloggers in its public relations campaign. *New York Times,* Business/Financial Desk, Late Edition—Final, Section C, p. 1, col. 2. <reclaimdemocracy.org/walmart/2006/enlists_blogs.php>.

Baran, S. J., & Davis, D. K. (2000). *Mass communication theory: Foundations, ferment, and future.* Belmont, CA: Wadsworth Publishing.

Benoit, W. L. (1995). *Accounts, excuses, and apologies: A theory of image restoration strategies.* Albany NY: State University of New York Press.

Berkowitz, D. & Lee, J. (2004). Media relations in Korea: Cheong between journalist and public relations practitioner. *Public Relations Review 30,* 431–437.

Biegeleisen, J. I. (1995). *Classic type faces and how to use them: Including 91 complete fonts.* New York: Dover Publications.

Bitzer, L. F. (1968). The rhetorical situation. *Philosophy & Rhetoric 1*(1), 1–14.

Bitzer, L. F., & Black, E. (Eds.). (1971). *The prospect of rhetoric: Report of the National Development Project.* Englewood Cliffs, NJ: Prentice Hall.

Black, E. (1970). The second persona. *The Quarterly Journal of Speech LVI,* 109–118.

Black, E. (1978). *Rhetorical criticism: A study in method.* Madison WI: University of Wisconsin Press.

Blumer, H. (1946). Elementary collective groupings, in A. M. Lee (ed), *New Outlines of the Principles of Sociology* (pp. 178–198). New York: Barnes & Noble.

Boag, A. (1992). Designing business documents. Chicago IL: Monotype Typography Inc. Note: this manual originally accompanied a type package sold by Apple Computers.

Bormann, E. G. (1972). Fantasy and rhetorical vision: The rhetorical criticism of social reality. *Quarterly Journal of Speech, 58*(4), 396–407.

Bormann, E. G. (1977). Fetching good out of evil: A rhetorical use of calamity. *Quarterly Journal of Speech, 63*(2), 130–139.

Bormann, E. G., Cragan, J. F., Shields, D. C., (1994). In defense of Symbolic Convergence Theory: A look at the theory and its criticisms after two decades. *Communication Theory 4*(4), 259–294.

Bostdorff, D. M. (1992). "The decision is yours" campaign: Planned Parenthood's characteristic argument of moral virtue. In E. L. Toth, & R. L. Heath (Eds.), *Rhetorical and critical approaches to public relations* (pp. 301–313). Hillsdale NJ: Lawrence Erlbaum Associates.

Botan, C. H. & Hazleton, V. (Eds.), (2006). *Public relations theory II.* Hillsdale NJ: Lawrence Erlbaum Associates.

Botan, C. H. & Taylor, M. (2005). The role of trust in channels of strategic communication in building civil society. *Journal of Communication, 55,* 687–702

Boulding, K. D. (1977). *The image: Knowledge in life and society.* Ann Arbor, MI: The University of Michigan Press.

Bowen, S. A. (2004). Expansion of ethics as the tenth generic principle of public relations excellence: A Kantian theory and model for managing ethical issues. *Journal of Public Relations Research, 16*(1), 65–92.

Broom, G. M. (1977). Coorientational measurement of public issues. *Public Relations Review 3*, 110–119.

Brummett, B. (1984). Pre-millennial Apocalyptic as a rhetorical genre. *Central States Speech Journal 35*(Summer), 84–93.

Brummett, B. (1991) *Contemporary apocalyptic rhetoric.* New York: Praeger.

Bruno, M. H. (2000). *Pocket pal: A graphic arts production handbook.* Memphis, TN: International Paper.

Bryant, D. C. (1953). Rhetoric its function and scope. *Quarterly Journal of Speech, 39*, 401–424.

Buber, M. (W. Kaufmann, trans.) (1970). *I and thou.* New York: Charles Scribner's Sons.

Buber, M. (R. G. Smith trans.) (1985). *Between man and man.* New York: Collier Books.

Burke, K. (1961). *Attitudes toward history.* Berkeley, CA: University of California Press.

Burke, K. (1966). *Language as symbolic action: Essays in life, literature, and method.* Berkeley, CA: University of California Press.

Burke, K. (1968/1931). *Counter-statement.* Berkeley, CA: University of California Press.

Burke, K. (1969a). *A grammar of motives.* Berkeley, CA: University of California Press.

Burke, K. (1969b). *A rhetoric of motives.* Berkeley, CA: University of California Press.

Burke, K. (1973a). The rhetorical situation. In, L. Thayer (ed.), *Communication: Ethical and moral issues* (pp. 263–275). London: Gordon & Breach.

Burke, K. (1973b). *The philosophy of literary forms.* Berkeley, CA: University of California Press.

Burke, K. (1984). *Permanence and change: An anatomy of purpose (third edition).* Berkeley, CA: University of California Press.

Caldiero, C., Taylor, M., & Ungureanu, L. (2009). Image repair tactics and information subsidies during fraud crises. *Journal of Public Relations Research 21*(2), 218–228.

Cargile, A. C. (2003). Discriminating attitudes toward speech. In L. A. Samovar, & R. E. Porter (Eds.), *Intercultural communication: A reader (10th edition)* (pp. 216–222). Belmont, CA: Wadsworth.

Casarez, N. B. (1997). Penny-wise, pound-foolish: What public relations professionals must know about photocopying and fair use. *Public Relations Quarterly 42*(3), 43–47.

Chaffee, S. H., & McLeod, J. M. (1968). Sensitization in panel design: A coorientational experiment. *Journalism Quarterly 45*, 661–669.

Cheney, G., & Dionisopoulos, G. N. (1989). Public relations? No, relations with publics: A rhetorical–organizational approach to contemporary corporate communications. In C. H. Botan, & V. Hazleton, Jr. (Eds.), *Public relations theory* (pp. 111–131). Hillsdale NJ: Lawrence Erlbaum Associates.

Cicero (1976) [H. H. Hubbell, trans.]. *Cicero in twenty-eight volumes: II: De inventione: De optimo genere: Oratorum: Topica.* Cambridge MA: Loeb Classical Library: Harvard University Press.

Cohen, B. (1963). *The press and foreign policy.* Princeton, NJ: Princeton University Press.

Condit, C. M., & Condit, D. M. (1992). Smoking or health: Incremental erosion as a public interest group strategy. In E. L. Toth, & R. L. Heath (Eds.), *Rhetorical and critical approaches to public relations,* (pp. 241–256). Hillsdale NJ: Lawrence Erlbaum Associates.

Coombs, W. T. (1999). *Ongoing crisis communication: Planning managing and responding.* Thousand Oaks, CA: Sage.

Coombs, W. T. (2007). *Ongoing crisis communication: planning, managing, and responding (2nd Edition).* Thousand Oaks, CA: Sage.

Coombs, W. T. (2007b). Protecting organization reputations during a crisis: The development and application of situational crisis communication theory. *Corporate Reputation Review, 10*(3), 163–177.

Courtright, J. L. & Smudde, P. M. (Eds.) (2007). *Power and public relations.* Cresskill, NJ: Hampton Press.

Crable, R. E., & Vibbert, S. L. (1985). Managing issues and influencing public policy. *Public Relations Review XI*(2), 3–16.

Cragan, J. F., Shields, D. C. (1981). *Applied communication research: A dramatistic approach.* Prospect Heights IL: Waveland.

Cutlip, S. M., Center, A. H., & Broom, G. M. (1994). Effective public relations. Englewood Cliffs, NJ: Prentice-Hall Inc.

Daft, R. L., & Lengel, R. H. (1986). Organizational information requirements, media richness and structural design. *Management Science, 32*(5), 554–571.

Daft, R. L., Lengel, R. H., & Trevino, L. K. (1987). Organizational information requirements, media richness and structural design. *MIS Quarterly, 11*(3), 355–366.

Deffeyes, K. S. (2005). *Beyond oil: The view from Hubbert's Peak*. New York: Hill & Wang.

Dewey, J. (1927). *The public and its problems*. Chicago: Swallow.

Dionisopoulos, G. N, & Goldzwig, S. R. (1992). The atomic power industry and the new woman. In E. L. Toth, & R. L. Heath (Eds.), *Rhetorical and critical approaches to public relations* (pp. 205–224). Hillsdale NJ: Lawrence Erlbaum Associates.

Ellison, H. (1996). *Edgeworks: Volume one: The collected Ellison: Over the edge*. Clarkston GA: White Wolf Publishing.

Emerson, R. M. (1962). Power-dependence relations. *American Sociological Review, 27*, 31–41.

Entman, R. M. (1989). How the media effect what people think: An information processing approach. *Journal of Politics, 51*, 347–370.

Etzioni, A. (1993). *The spirit of community: The reinvention of American society*. New York: Simon and Schuster.

Fallows, D. (2004). *The Internet and daily life: Many Americans use the Internet in everyday activities, but traditional offline habits still dominate*. Washington, DC: Pew Internet and American Life Project. <www.pewinternet.org/Reports/2004/The-Internet-and-Daily-Life.aspx?r=1>

Fenno, R. F. Jr. (1978). *Home style: House members in their districts*. Boston: Little Brown and Company.

Finneran, K. (2006, winter). Editor's journal: To blog, or not to blog? *Issues in Science and Technology, 22*(2), 23–24. <www.issues.org/22.2/editorsjournal.html>

Fishbein, M., & I. Azjen. (1975). *Belief, attitude, intention, and behavior: An introduction to theory and research*. Reading, MA: Addison-Wesley.

Fisher, Walter R. (1978). Toward a logic of good reasons. *The Quarterly Journal of Speech, 64*, 376–384.

Fisher, W. R. (1984). Narration as a human communication paradigm: The case for public moral argument. *Communication Monographs, 51*, 1–21.

Fisher, W. R. (1985). The narrative paradigm: An elaboration. *Communication Monographs, 52*, 347–367.

Flanders, V., & Peters, D. (2002). *Son of web pages that suck: Learn good design by looking at bad design*. Alameda, CA: SYBEX Inc. <www.webpagesthatsuck.com/sonof>

Frank, M. (2004, August 30). Notebook/campaign '04, Kerry in combat: Setting the record straight. *Time Magazine*, p. 16.

Franke, R. H., & Kaul, J. D. (1978). The Hawthorne experiments: First statistical interpretation. *American Sociological Review, 43*, 623–643.

Franken, A. (2004). *Lies, and the lying liars who tell them: A fair and balanced look at the right*. New York: Plume.

Frey, L. R., Botan, C. H., Friedman, P. G., Kreps, G. L. (1992). *Interpreting communication research: A case study approach*. Englewood Cliffs, NJ: Prentice Hall.

Gandy, O. H. Jr. (1982). *Beyond agenda setting: Information subsidies and public policies*. Norwood, NJ: Ablex.

Goffman, E. (1959). *The presentation of self in everyday life*. New York: Doubleday.

Granovetter, M. S. (1973). The strength of weak ties. *American Journal of Sociology 78*(6), 1360–1380.

Grunig, J. E., & Hunt, T. (1984). *Managing public relations*. New York: Holt, Rinehart, and Winston.

Grunig, J. E. (1989). Sierra Club study shows who becomes activists. *Public Relations Review 15(3), 3–24*.

Grunig, L. A. (1992). Activism: How it limits the effectiveness of organizations and how excellent public relations departments respond. In J. E. Grunig (Ed.), *Excellence in public relations and communication management* (pp. 503–530). Hillsdale, NJ: Erlbaum.

Grunig, J. E., & Huang, Y. (2000). From organizational effectiveness to relationship indicators: Antecedents of relationships, public relations strategies, and relationship outcomes. In J. A. Ledingham & S. D. Bruning (Eds.), *Public relations as relationship management: A relational approach to the study and practice of public relations* (pp. 23–53). Mahwah, NJ: Lawrence Erlbaum Associates.

Gudykunst, W. B., & Ting-Toomey, S. (1988). *Culture and interpersonal communication*. Newbury Park, CA: Sage Publications.

Gunson, D., & Collins, C. (1997). From the *I* to the *we*: Discourse ethics, identify, and the pragmatics of partnership in the West of Scotland. *Communication Theory 7*(4), 278–300.

Haley, J. (1969). *The power tactics of Jesus Christ and other essays*. New York: Grossman Publishers.

Hall, E. T. (2000a). Context and meaning. In L. A. Samovar, & R. E. Porter (Eds.), *Intercultural communication: A reader (9th edition)* (pp. 34–42). Belmont, CA: Wadsworth.

Hall, E. T. (2000b). Monochronic and polychronic time. In L. A. Samovar, & R. E. Porter (Eds.), *Intercultural communication: A reader (9th edition)* (pp. 380–386). Belmont, CA: Wadsworth.

Hallahan, K. (1999). Seven models of framing: Implications for public relations. *Journal of Public Relations Research, 11*(3), 205–242.

Hearit, K. M. (2001). Corporate apologia: When an organization speaks in defense of itself. In R. L. Heath, & G. Vasquez (Eds.), *Handbook of public relations* (pp. 501–511). Thousand Oaks CA: Sage.

Hearit, K. M. (2005). *Crisis management by apology*. Mahwah New Jersey: Lawrence Erlbaum.

Heath, R. L. (1990). Chapter 2: Corporate issues management: Theoretical underpinnings and research foundations. In L. A. Grunig, & J. E. Grunig, *Public Relations Research Annual: Volume 2* (pp. 29–65). Hillsdale, NJ: Lawrence Erlbaum.

Heath, R. L. (1992). Critical perspectives on public relations. In E. L. Toth, & R. L. Heath (Eds.), *Rhetorical and critical approaches to public relations* (pp. 37–61). Hillsdale NJ: Lawrence Erlbaum Associates.

Heath, R. L. (1997). *Strategic issues management: Organizations and public policy challenges*. Thousand Oaks CA: Sage.

Heath, R. L. (1998). *Crisis management for managers and executives*. Upper Saddle River, NJ: Pitman Publications.

Heath, R. L. (2005). *Encyclopedia of public relations: Vol. I.* Thousand Oaks California: Sage.

Heath, R. L. (2006). Chapter 3: A rhetorical theory approach to issues management. In C. H. Botan & V. Hazleton (Eds.), *Public Relations Theory II* (pp. 63–99). Mahwah New Jersey: Lawrence Erlbaum.

Heath, R., L., & Coombs, W. T. (2006). *Today's public relations: An introduction*. Thousand Oaks, CA: Sage.

Held, V. (1987). Non-contractual society: A feminist view. *Canadian Journal of Philosophy, 13*, 111–137.

Hofstede, G. (1997). *Cultures and organizations: Software of the mind*. New York: McGraw-Hill.

Hofstede, G. (1984). *Culture's consequences: International differences in work-related values*. Newbury Park, CA: Sage.

Hofstede, G. (2001). *Culture's consequences: Comparing values, behaviors, institutions, and organizations across nations (second edition)*. Thousand Oaks CA: Sage.

Hofstede, G. & Hofstede, G. J. (2005). *Cultures and organizations: Software of the mind. (revised and expanded 2nd edition)*. New York: McGraw-Hill.

Hopkins, N. & Reicher, S. (1997). Social movement rhetoric and the social psychology of collective action: A case study of anti-abortion mobilization. *Human Relations, 50*(3), 261–286.

Hunt, T., & Grunig, J. E. (1994). *Public relations techniques*. Fort Worth, TX: Harcourt Brace College Publishers.

Ihlen, Ø. (2002). Rhetoric and resources: Notes for a new approach to public relations and issues management. *Journal of Public Affairs, 2*(4), 259–269.

Ihlen, Ø. (2005). The power of social capital: Adapting Bourdieu to the study of public relations. *Public Relations Review 31*, 492–496.

Iyengar, S., & Kinder, D. R. (1987). *News that matters: Television and American opinion*. Chicago: University of Chicago Press.

Janis, I. L. (1982). *Groupthink: Psychological studies of policy decisions and fiascoes*. Boston: Houghton Mifflin.

Jaques, T. (2007). Issue management and crisis management: An integrated, non-linear, relational construct. *Public Relations Review 33*, 147–157.

Jones, B. L., & Chase, W. H. (1979). Managing public policy issues. *Public Relations Review 2*, 3–23.

Kahneman, D. & Tversky, A. (1982). The psychology of preferences. *Scientific American, 246*, 160–173.

Kellner, D. (1990). *Television and the crisis of democracy*. Boulder CO: Westview Press.

Kent, M. L., (1995). *Academic community development: Feminist communitarianism and rhetorical critique*. Competitive paper delivered to Temple University's Sixteenth Discourse Analysis Conference, Literacy in and Across the Discipline, Philadelphia, PA.

Kent, M. L. (1997). *The rhetoric of eulogies: A generic critique of classic and contemporary funeral oratory*. Unpublished doctoral dissertation, Purdue University, West Lafayette Indiana. Advisor: Ralph Webb.

Kent, M. L. (1999). How to evaluate Web site validity and reliability. *The Communication Teacher 13*(4), 4–7.

Kent, M. L. (2000). Getting the most from your search engine. *Communication Teacher 15*(1), 4–7.

Kent, M. L. (2001a). Essential tips for searching the Web. *Public Relations Quarterly 46*(1), 26–30.

Kent, M. L. (2001b). Managerial rhetoric and the metaphor of the World Wide Web. *Critical Studies in Media Communication 18*(3), 359–375.

Kent, M. L., (2005a). Font (encyclopedia entry). In R. L. Heath [Ed.], *Encyclopedia of public relations: Volume I* (pp. 334–335). Thousand Oaks, CA: Sage.

Kent, M. L., (2005b). Stylebook (encyclopedia entry). In R. L. Heath [Ed.], *Encyclopedia of public relations: Volume II* (pp. 826–827). Thousand Oaks, CA: Sage.

Kent, M. L. (2005c). Conducing better research: Google Scholar and the future of search technology. *Public Relations Quarterly 50*(4), 35–40.

Kent, M. L. (2008). Critical analysis of blogging in public relations. *Public Relations review 34*(1), 32–40.

Kent, M. L., & Alex, L. (2002). *Dialogic theory as a framework for extending relationships in public relations*. Public Relations division, Enlarging the Public Relations Theoretical Canon, delivered to the 2002 meeting of the National Communication Association, New Orleans, LA.

Kent, M. L., Harrison, T. R., & Taylor, M. (2006). A critique of Internet polls as symbolic representation and pseudo-events. *Communication Studies 57*(3), 299–315.

Kent, M. L., & Taylor, M. (1998). Building dialogic relationships through the World Wide Web. *Public Relations Review 24*(3), 321–334.

Kent, M. L. & Taylor, M. (2002). Toward a dialogic theory of public relations. *Public Relations Review 28*(1), 21–37.

Kent, M. L., & Taylor, M. (2007). Beyond "excellence" in international public relations research: An examination of generic theory in Bosnian public relations. *Public Relations Review 33*(1), 10–20.

Kent, M. L., Taylor, M., & Turcilo, L. (2006). Public relations by newly privatized businesses in Bosnia-Herzegovina. *Public Relations Review 32*(1), 10–17.

Kluckhohn, F. R. & Strodtbeck, F. L. (1961). Variations in value orientations. Evanston, Illinois: Row, Peterson.

Knight, J. P. (1990). Literature as equipment for killing: Performance as rhetoric in military training camps. *Text and Performance Quarterly, 10*(2), 157–168.

Kotler, P., & Zaltman, G. (1971). Social marketing: An approach to planned social change. *Journal of Marketing 35*, 3–12.

Kruckeberg, D., & Tsetsura, K. (2003). Research report: A composite index by country of variables related to the likelihood of the existence of "cash for news coverage." Commissioned by the Institute for Public Relations (USA), The International Public Relations Association (UK), and sponsored by Hürriyet, a member of Dogan Media Group (Turkey). <banners.noticiasdot.com/termometro/boletines/docs/marcom/comunicacion/ipr/2003/index-cash-for-news-2003-final.pdf>

Laing, R. D. (1969). *Self and others (2nd Edition)*. New York: Pantheon Books.

Lakoff, G. & Johnson, M. (1980). Metaphors we live by. Chicago Illinois: Chicago University Press.

Lasch, C. (1979). *The culture of narcissism: American life in an age of diminishing expectations*. New York: W.W. Norton and Company.

Lenhart, A. (2006). *Bloggers: A portrait of the Internet's new storytellers*. Pew Internet and American Life Project. <www.pewinternet.org/Reports/2006/Bloggers.aspx>

Lenhart, A., Horrigan, J., Rainie, L., Allen, K., Boyce, A., Madden, M., & O'Grady, E. (2003). *The ever-shifting Internet population: A new look at Internet access and the digital divide*. Washington, DC: The Pew Internet & American Life Project. <www.pewinternet.org>

Lenhart, A., Rainie, L., & Lewis, O. (2001). *Teenage life online: The rise of the instant-message generation and the Internet's impact on friendships and family relationships*. Washington, DC: The Pew Internet & American Life Project. <www.pewinternet.org/Reports/2001/Teenage-Life-Online.aspx>

Levinson, P. (1997). *The soft edge: A natural history and future of the information revolution*. New York: Rutledge.

Lupton, E. (2004). *Thinking with type: A critical guide for designers, writers, editors, & students*. New York: Princeton Architectural Press.

Mackey, A. G. (1882). The symbolism of freemasonry: Illustrating and explaining its science and philosophy, its legends, myths and symbols. Project Guttenberg EBook. <www.gutenberg.org/etext/11937>

Madden, M. (2006). Internet penetration and impact. PEW Internet and American life peoject.

<www.pewinternet.org/~/media//Files/Reports/2006/PIP_Internet_Impact.pdf.pdf>

Mandrik, C. A., Fern, E. F., & Bao, Y. (2005). Intergenerational influence: Roles of conformity to peers and communication effectiveness. *Psychology & Marketing* 22(10), 813–832.

McAllister-Greve, S. (2006). Forming dialogic relationships via community college Web sites. Unpublished doctorial dissertation, Rutgers University.

McAllister, S., & Kent, M. L. (2009). Dialogic public relations and resource dependency: New Jersey community colleges as models for web site effectiveness. *Atlantic Journal of Communication, 17*(4), 220–239

McCaffrey, D., & Keys, J. (2000). Competitive framing processes in the abortion debate: Polarization-vilification, frame saving, and frame debunking. *The Sociological Quarterly, 41*(1), 41–61.

McCombs, M. E., & Shaw, D. L. (1976). Structuring the "unseen environment." *Journal of Communication* 26(2), 18–22.

McElreath, M. P. (1997). *Managing systematic and ethical public relations campaigns (second edition).* New York: McGraw-Hill.

McGee, M. C. (1980). The "Ideograph": A link between rhetoric and ideology. *The Quarterly Journal of Speech, 66*, 1–16.

McGee, M. C., & Martin, M. A. (1983). Public knowledge and ideological argumentation. *Communication Monographs, 50*, 47–65.

McLuhan, M. (1999/1964). *Understanding media: The extensions of man*. Cambridge, MA: The MIT Press.

Meggs, P., & Carter, R. (1993). *Typographic specimens: The great typefaces*. New York: John Wiley & Sons Inc.

Metzler, K. (1989). *Creative Interviewing: The writer's guide to gathering information by asking questions.* New Jersey: Prentice-Hall.

Middleberg, D., & Ross, S. S. (1999a). *Media in cyberspace study 1998 (fifth annual national survey).* New York: Middleberg and Associates.

Middleberg, D., & Ross, S. S. (1999b, October). *The first annual broadcast media in cyberspace study*. New York: Middleberg and Associates.

Middleberg, D., & Ross, S. S. (2000a). *Sixth annual print media in cyberspace study*. New York: Middleberg and Associates.

Middleberg, D., & Ross, S. S. (2000b). *Survey of media in the wired world*. New York: Middleberg Euro RSGC.

Middleberg, D., & Ross, S. S. (2002). *The MiddlebergRoss media survey: Change and its impact on communication*. New York: Middleberg Euro RSGC.

Milgrim, S. (1970). *Obedience to authority*. New York. Harper and Row.

Morrison, T., & Conway, W. A. (2006). *Kiss, bow, or shake hands (second edition): The best selling guide to doing business in more than 60 countries.* Adams MA: Adams Media.

Multhauf, A. P., Willower, D. J., & Licata, J. W. (1978). Teacher pupil-control ideology and behavior and classroom environmental robustness. *Elementary School Journal* 79(1), 40–46.

Negroponte, N. (1995). *Being digital*. New York: Alfred A. Knopf.

Nelson, J. S., Megill, A., & McCloskey, D. N. (1987). *The rhetoric of the human sciences: Language and argument in scholarship and public affairs*. Madison Wisconsin: University of Wisconsin Press.

Ortony, A. (1979). *Metaphor and Thought*. Cambridge MA: Cambridge University Press.

Osborn, M. (1967). Archetypal metaphor in rhetoric: The light-dark family. *Quarterly Journal of Speech LIII*(2), 115–126.

Osborn, M. (1977). Evolution of the archetypal sea in rhetoric and poetic. *Quarterly Journal of Speech* 63(4), 347–363.

Pagels, E. (1988). *Adam, Eve, and the serpent*. New York: Random House.

Pagels, E. (1989). *The Gnostic gospels*. New York: Random House.

Pagels, E. (1995). *The origin of Satan*. New York: Random House.

Perelman, C., & Olbrechts-Tyteca, L. [Wilkinson J, & Weaver, P, trans.] (1968). *The new rhetoric: A treatise on argumentation*. Notre Dame, IN, University of Notre Dame Press.

Pearson, R. (1989). A theory of public relations ethics. Unpublished doctoral dissertation, Ohio University.

Pearson, R. (1992). Perspectives on public relations history. In E. L. Toth, & R. L. Heath (Eds.), *Rhetorical and critical approaches to public relations* (pp. 111–130). Hillsdale NJ: Lawrence Erlbaum Associates.

Petty, R. E., & Cacioppo, J. T. (1981). *Attitudes and persuasion: Classic and contemporary approaches.* Dubuque, IA: William C. Brown.

Petty, R. E., & Cacioppo, J. T. (1984). The effects of involvement on responses to argument quantity and quality: Central and peripheral routes to persuasion. *Journal of Personality and Social Psychology 46*, 69–81.

Petty, R. E., & Cacioppo, J. T. (1986a). *Communication and persuasion: Central and peripheral routes to attitude change.* New York: Springer-Verlag.

Petty, R. E., & Cacioppo, J. T. (1986b). The elaboration likelihood model of persuasion. In L. Berkowitz (Ed.), *Advances in experimental social psychology (vol. 19)*, (pp. 123-205). San Diego, CA: Academic Press.

Pfeffer, J., & Salancik, G. (1978). *The external control of organizations: A resource dependency perspective.* New York: Harper & Row

Plato (Benjamin Jowett, trans.) (1999a). *Gorgias.* Project Guttenberg, E-text. <www.gutenberg.org/etext/1672>

Plato (Benjamin Jowett, trans.) (1999b). *Phaedrus.* Project Guttenberg, E-Text. <www.gutenberg.org/etext/1636>

Postman, N. (1984). *Amusing ourselves to death: Public discourse in the age of show business.* New York: Penguin Books.

Postman, N. (1999). *Building a bridge to the 18th century.* New York: Vintage Books.

Postman, N. & Paglia, C. (1991, March). Dinner conversation: She wants her tv! He wants his book!. *Harper's Magazine*, 44–56.

Postman, N. & Weingartner, C. (1969). *Teaching as a subversive activity.* New York, N.Y.: Dell Publishing.

Potlatch Papers (1999). *Potlatch design series: Volume 1: Vintage: typography.* Cloquet, Minnesota: Potlatch Corporation.

Quintilian (1979). *The institutio oratoria (Volume I: Loeb classical library, four volumes)* (H. E. Butler, trans.). Cambridge MA: Harvard University Press.

Quintilian (1989). *The institutio oratoria (Volume I: Loeb classical library, four volumes)* (H. E. Butler, trans.). Cambridge MA: Harvard University Press.

Reddy, M. (1979). The conduit metaphor: A case of frame conflict in our language about language. In A. Ortony (Ed.), *Metaphor and Thought (Second Edition)*, pages 164–201. Cambridge MA: Cambridge University Press.

Robinson, J. H. (2003). Communication in Korea: Playing things by the eye. In L. A. Samovar, & R. E. Porter (Eds.), *Intercultural communication: A reader (10th edition)* (pp. 57–64). Belmont, CA: Thompson/Wadsworth.

Rogers, C. (1994). The necessary and sufficient conditions of therapeutic personality change. In, R. Anderson, K. N. Cissna, & R. C. Arnett (Eds.), *The reach of dialogue: Confirmation, voice, and community*, (pp. 126–140). Cresskill, NJ: Hampton Press Inc.

Rogers, E. M. (1995). *Diffusion of innovations (fourth edition).* New York: The Free Press.

Rosenfield, L. W. (1971). An autopsy of the rhetorical tradition. In, L. F. Bitzer, & E. Black (Eds), *The prospect of rhetoric: Report of the national development project*, (pp. 64–77). Englewood Cliffs, New Jersey: Prentice Hall.

Schellnhuber, H. J. (Ed.), Cramer, W., Nakicenovic, N., Wigley, T., Yohe, G., (co-Eds.) (2006). *Avoiding dangerous climate change.* Cambridge England: Cambridge University Press.

Schiller, H. I. (1989). *Culture inc.: The corporate takeover of public expression.* New York: Oxford University Press.

Schlosser, E. (2002). *Fast food nation: The dark side of the all-American meal.* New York: Harper Perennial.

Sennett, R. (1976). *The fall of public man.* New York: W. W. Norton and Co.

Simon, H. W. (1990). *The rhetorical turn: Invention and persuasion in the conduct of inquiry.* Chicago: University of Chicago Press.

Smith, F. L. Jr. (2005, Dec. 6). Big Issues: Corporate social concerns: Are they good citizenship, or a rip-off for investors? *The Wall Street Journal*, R6.

Smith, R. D. (2002). *Strategic planning for public relations.* Mahwah NJ: Lawrence Erlbaum Associates.

Sommerfeldt, E. (2007). *Activism, public relations, and the Internet: A case study of moveon.org.* Unpublished Master's Thesis, Western Michigan University.

Springston J. K. & Keyton, J. (2001). Public relations field dynamics. In R. L. Heath, & G. Vasquez, *Handbook of public relations* (pp. 115–126). Thousand Oaks CA: Sage.

Springston J. K., Keyton, J., Leichty, G. B., & Metzher, J. (1992). Field dynamics and public relations theory: Toward the management of multiple publics. *Journal of Public Relations Research* 4(2), 81–100.

Sproule, M. J. (1987). Propaganda studies in American social science: The rise and fall of the critical paradigm. *Quarterly Journal of Speech 73*, 60–78.

Sproule, J. M. (1988). The new managerial rhetoric and the old criticism. *Quarterly Journal of Speech, 74*, 468–486.

Sproule, J. M. (1989). Progressive propaganda critics and the magic bullet myth. *Critical Studies in Mass Communication* 6(3), 225–246.

Sriramesh, K. (2003). *The global public relations handbook.* Hillsdale, NJ: Lawrence Erlbaum Associates, Inc.

Stacks, D. W., Botan, C., Turk, J. V. (1999). Perceptions of public relations education. *Public Relations Review* 25(1), 9–28.

Steele, E. D., & Redding, W. C. (1962). The American value system: Premises for persuasion. *Western Speech 26*, 83–91.

Stephenson, M. T, Benoit, W. L, & Tschida, D. A. (2001, Winter). Testing the mediating role of cognitive responses in the Elaboration Likelihood Mode. *Communication Studies*, (no pagination, electronic version). <findarticles.com/p/articles/mi_qa3669/is_200101/ai_n8946419/print>.

Stewart, C., & Cash, W. B. (1994). *Interviewing: Principles and practices.* Dubuque, Iowa: William. C. Brown Co.

Stoll, C. (1999). High-tech heretic: Why computers don't belong in the classroom and other reflections by a computer contrarian. New York, NY: Doubleday.

Tan, A. S. (1985). *Mass communication theories and research.* New York: John Wiley.

Taylor, M. (2000). Cultural variance as a challenge to global public relations: A case study of the Coca-Cola scare. *Public Relations Review* 26(3), 277–293.

Taylor, M. (2004). Media richness theory as a foundation for public relations in Croatia. *Public Relations Review, 30*(1), 145–160.

Taylor, M., & Kent, M. L. (2000). Media transition in Bosnia: From propagandistic past to uncertain future. *Gazette 62*(5), 355–378.

Taylor, M., & Kent, M. L. (2006). Nation building: Public relations theory and practice. In V. Hazelton & C. Botan (Eds.), *Public relations theory II*, (pp. 341–359). Hillsdale, NJ: Lawrence Erlbaum Associates, Publishers.

Taylor, M., & Kent, M. L. (2007). Issue management and policy justification in Malaysia. In J. L. Courtright & P. M. Smudde (Eds.), *Power and public relations*, (pp. 125–147). Cresskill, NJ: Hampton Press.

Taylor, M., Kent, M., & White, W. (2001). How activist organizations are using the Internet to build relationships. *Public Relations Review* 27(3), 263–284.

Taylor, M., & Kent, M. L. (1999). Challenging assumptions of international public relations: When government is the most important public. *Public Relations Review* 25(2), 131–144.

Tedford, T. L. (1991). *Public Speaking in a Free Society.* New York: McGraw-Hill.

Tirpak, D., (chair), et al., (2006). *Avoiding dangerous climate change: Scientific symposium on stabilisation [sic] of greenhouse gases: February 1st to 3rd, 2005: Executive summary of the conference report.* London: Department for Environment, Food and Rural Affairs. <www.defra.gov.uk/environment/climatechange/research/dangerous-cc/pdf/avoid-dangercc-execsumm.pdf>

Toth, E. L., & Heath, R. L. (Eds.). (1992). *Rhetorical and critical approaches to public relations.* Hillsdale, NJ: Lawrence Erlbaum Associates.

Treadwell D. F., & Treadwell, J. B., (2000). *Public relations writing: Principles in practice.* Boston: Allyn & Bacon Publishing.

Tufte, E. R. (1990). *Envisioning information.* Cheshire Connecticut: Graphics Press LLC.

Tufte, E. R. (1997). *Visual explanations: Images and quantities, evidence and narrative.* Cheshire Connecticut: Graphics Press LLC.

Tufte, E. R. (2001). *The visual display of quantitative information (Second Edition).* Cheshire Connecticut: Graphics Press LLC.

Tufte, E. R. (2003). *The cognitive style of PowerPoint.* Cheshire, Connecticut: Graphics Press, LLC.

Tufte, E. R. (2006). *Beautiful evidence.* Cheshire Connecticut: Graphics Press LLC.

Ulmer, R. S., Sellnow, T. L. (2002). Crisis management and the discourse of renewal: understanding the potential for positive outcomes of crisis. *Public Relations Review, 28*, 361–365.

Vasquez, G. M. (1993). A Homo Narrens paradigm for public relations: Combining Bormann's

Symbolic Convergence Theory and Grunig's Situational Theory of Publics. *Journal of Public Relations Research 5*, 201–216.

Wander, P. (1984). The third persona: An ideological turn in rhetorical theory. *The Central States Speech Journal, 35*, 197–216.

Wander, P. & Jenkins, S. (1972). Rhetoric society and the critical response. *Quarterly Journal of Speech, 58*, 441–450.

Ware, B. L., & Linkugel, W. A. (1973). They spoke in defense of themselves: On the generic criticism of apologia. *Quarterly Journal of Speech, 59*, 273–283.

Wartella, E. (1984). Cognitive and affective factors of TV advertising's influence on children. *Western Journal of Speech Communication 48*, 171–183.

Water world (2006). PBS Online and WGBH/NOVA/FRONTLINE. <www.pbs.org/wgbh/warming/waterworld>

Watzlawick, P., Beavin, J. H. & Jackson, D. D. (1967). *Pragmatics of human communication: A study of interactional patterns, pathologies, and paradoxes*. New York: W.W. Norton.

Weaver, R. (1985). *The ethics of rhetoric*. Hillsdale NJ: Lawrence Erlbaum

Weiss, P. (1993). Feminism and Communitarianism: Exploring the relationship. In, P. Weiss, *Gendered community: Rousseau, sex, and politics*. New York: New York University Press.

What to do about warming? Experts weigh in whether individuals can even make a difference at his point is debatable (2006, April 3). Washington: The Associated Press. <www.msnbc.msn.com/id/12052708>

White, A. W. (2002). *The elements of graphic design: Space, unity, page architecture, and type*. New York: Allworth Press.

White, H. (1973). *Metahistory: The historical imagination in nineteenth-century Europe*. Baltimore MD: The Johns Hopkins University Press.

Wichelns, H. A. (1925). The literary criticism of oratory. In, *Studies in Rhetoric and Public Speaking in Honor of James Albert Winans, by Pupils and Colleagues* (pp. 40–73). New York: The Century Company.

Wichelns, H. (1958). The literary criticism of oratory. In, Bryant, D. C., [Ed.], *The rhetorical idiom: Essays in rhetoric, oratory, language, and drama*. Ithaca, NY: Cornell University Press.

Wilcox, D. L., Ault, P. H., & Agee, W. K. (1998). *Public relations: Strategies and tactics*. New York: Longman.

Wittig, M. (1976). Client control and organizational dominance: The school, its students, and their parents. *Social Problems* (24)2, 192–203.

Warnock, M. (1974). *John Stewart Mill: Utilitarianism, on liberty, essay on Bentham*. New York: Penguin Books.

Wright, D. K. (2001). *The magic communication machine: Examining the internet's impact on public relations, journalism, and the public. Gainesville FL: Institute for Public Relations Research*. <www.InstituteForPR.com>

INDEX

Q

R